TRIUMPH GT6
Mk 1 and Mk 2 / GT6+
Spare Parts Catalogue

MK 1 CARS:- COMMISSION No. KC1 UP TO KC50000
MK 2 CARS:- COMMISSION No. KC50001 AND FUTURE

GENUINE STANPART REGD TRADE MARK
PARTS & ACCESSORIES

Part No. 515754 Second Edition

STANDARD-TRIUMPH SALES LIMITED
SPARES DIVISION
COVENTRY   ENGLAND

FOREWORD

This catalogue has been compiled to assist all purchasers requiring Spare Parts for the Triumph G.T.6 models.

You are requested to note carefully the method and procedure for ordering parts which is contained in the introductory notes.

The Sale of Spare Parts is always made in accordance with the Company's current conditions of sale.

STANDARD-TRIUMPH SALES LTD.

SPARES DIVISION:
FLETCHAMSTEAD HIGHWAY, COVENTRY
Telegrams: STANPART, COVENTRY
Telephone: 75511 (16 lines)

SERVICE DIVISION:
BIRMINGHAM ROAD, ALLESLEY, COVENTRY
Telegrams: STANSER, COVENTRY
Telephone: 22115 (5 lines)

CONTENTS

	Page
Foreword	2
How to Order Parts	4
Unit Serial Numbers	8
Alphabetical Index	10
Numerical Index	15
Engine - Mk 1	86
Engine - Mk 2	136
Clutch	172
Gearbox	174
Gear Shift Mechanism	182
Engine Mounting	186
Chassis Frame	188
Front Suspension	192
Anti-Roll Bar	198
Rear Axle	200
Rear Suspension	206
Propellor Shaft and Road Wheels	212
Steering	214
Acceleration Control	218
Clutch and Brake Pedals	222
Master Cylinder	224
Hydraulic Pipes	228
Handbrake	232
Brakes	236
Radiator	240
Exhaust System	242
Petrol System	246
Service Kits and Tools	250
Electrical Equipment	252
Body and Fittings	296
Miscellaneous Body Details	460
Overdrive	462
Accessories	472

HOW TO ORDER PARTS

<u>VERY IMPORTANT</u>

Read this section on how to order, even if you are in the habit of dealing with auto spares.

DESCRIPTION

The part required should be referred to in the catalogue and the part number quoted with the technical description. If any doubt exists as to the name and number of the part, a sketch or the old part should be sent to assist in correct interpretation. When trim material is ordered, a specimen of the material required should be sent whenever possible.

INTERPRETATION OF CATALOGUE

Details forming part of an assembly are indicated by insetting the alignment of the description, as shown in the following example.

EXHAUST MANIFOLD ASSEMBLY

    Stud, inlet manifold attachment,
    Stud, exhaust pipe attachment,
    Pin, spring anchor,
    Peg, spring stop,
Spring (bi-metal), flap valve spindle,
Stop, spring,
Pin, split, retaining spring and stop,
Weight, balance,
Pin, Mills, balance weight attachment.

Thus, the four items immediately following the assembly form part of the assembly, whilst the remaining five are individual items and are subject to separate order.

PATTERNS

When parts are sent as patterns it is important that they should be carefully and individually labelled indicating the address of the sender together with advice by separate post giving any reference or order number to which they refer. All patterns must be sent Carriage Paid to the Spares Division, Fletchamstead Highway, Coventry, and unless special instructions are given on the order they will not be returned.

RIGHT- AND LEFT-HAND PARTS

Where Right-hand and Left-hand Parts are required it is essential that this is clearly stated on the order.

QUANTITIES

Do not designate the quantities by sets but state specifically the number of parts that are required.

ORDERS

Orders for replacement parts should be submitted to the nearest Standard-Triumph Distributor or Dealer.

SPECIAL NOTE FOR DISTRIBUTORS

It is helpful to ensure that:—

(a) The address is clearly stated and the order submitted on the approved Order Form.

(b) Parts required are in numerical sequence.

(c) Where possible, the order should be typed or written in ink.

NOTICE OF MODIFICATION

When modifications relevant to these models are introduced Bulletins will be issued to Standard-Triumph Distributors and Dealers to ensure that the catalogue may be amended in accordance with the latest information.

CHASSIS NUMBERS

Where there is doubt about the correct description for a spare part, always quote the chassis number with prefix or suffix letters (if any) of the car concerned. This will save delay and ensure speedier despatch. The Chassis number may be found stamped on a brass plate, on the scuttle under the bonnet.

CAR REPAIRS. Note to Customers

A Service School is established where the representatives from our Distributors and Dealers are trained in the upkeep and maintenance of Standard-Triumph Cars. Customers should therefore avail themselves of the service which our agents are able to give in all matters relative to service and maintenance.

CODING PROCEDURE — EXTERIOR PAINT, INTERIOR TRIM

In order to assist all purchasers of Spare Parts in which paint or trim details are involved, the following coding system has been devised to cover the basic colours and their varying shades.

(a) BASIC COLOURS

There are **Nine Basic Colours** which have been allocated the following numbers:—

1. Black	4. Yellow	7. Purple
2. Red	5. Green	8. Grey
3. Brown	6. Blue	9. White

(b) SHADES OF COLOUR

To cover **Shades of the above Colours,** a second figure commencing at '1' is used as a prefix to the above numbers, each shade having a different prefix number.

The current range of codes is as follows:—

Basic Colour	1st Shade	2nd Shade	3rd Shade	4th Shade	5th Shade
Black	11 Black				
Red	02 Red	32 Signal Red			
Brown	13 Light Tan				
Yellow	34 Jasmine				
Green	25 Conifer				
Blue	16 Midnight	26 Wedgwood	36 Dark Blue	56 Royal Blue	66 Valencia
Purple	27 Shadow Blue				
Grey	18				
White	19 White				

(c) DUAL COLOURS

Dual colours are shown as two codes divided by a stroke, the first code being the predominant or main colour, e.g., 26/11 denotes Wedgwood Blue and Black, Wedgwood Blue being the main colour.

(d) **TRIM MATERIALS**

The following Prefix Letters are added to the colour code to indicate the main trim material used

    Leathercloth   No Prefix Letter
    Leather   Prefix Letter 'H'
    Cloth   Prefix Letter 'C'

(e) **RECORDING**

The paint and trim colours and materials used are recorded in the spaces provided on the Commission No. Plate as shown below.

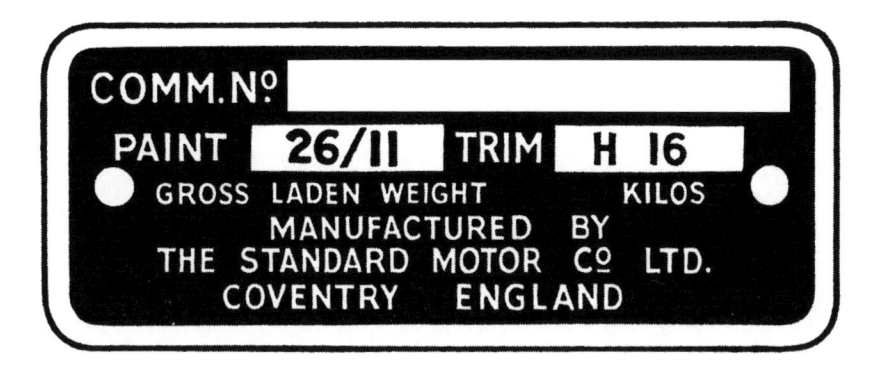

```
COMM. No. [            ]
PAINT  [ 26/11 ]  TRIM  [ H 16 ]
   GROSS LADEN WEIGHT       KILOS
         MANUFACTURED  BY
      THE STANDARD MOTOR Co LTD.
           COVENTRY   ENGLAND
```

(f) **ACRYLIC PAINT**

To denote vehicles which are finished with Acrylic paint a prefix letter 'A' is added to the colour code figures, i.e. "A25" denotes that the vehicle is painted with Conifer Green Acrylic Paint.

CAUTION

WHEN REPLACEMENTS ARE MADE IT IS OF THE UTMOST IMPORTANCE THAT PARTS OF GENUINE STANDARD MOTOR CO. LTD. MANUFACTURE SHOULD BE USED. THIS ENSURES THAT THE SERVICE GIVEN BY THE ORIGINAL PART WILL BE MAINTAINED BY THE REPLACEMENT. REMEMBER THE GENUINE PART CARRIES WITH IT A GUARANTEE.

THE EXPERIENCE GAINED BY THE MANUFACTURERS ENSURES THAT THE HIGHEST QUALITY MATERIAL IS USED AND THE STRICTEST ACCURACY MAINTAINED IN MANUFACTURE.

UNIT SERIAL NUMBERS

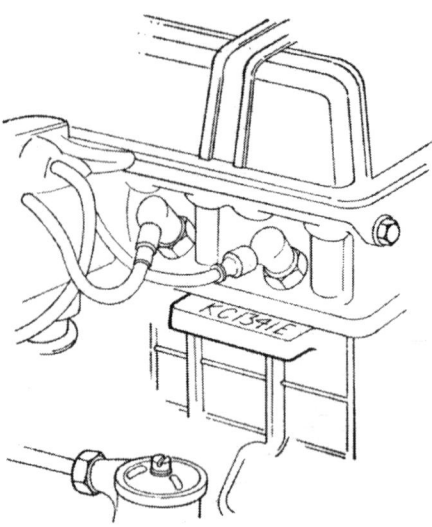

ENGINE SERIAL NUMBER

Commencing at KC1E for normal engines and KD5001E for USA anti-air pollution engines, this number is stamped on the left-hand side of the cylinder block.

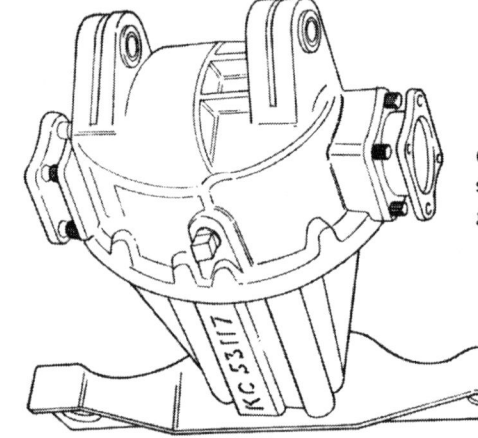

GEARBOX SERIAL NUMBER

Commencing at KC1 GB, this number is stamped on the right-hand side of the gearbox casing.

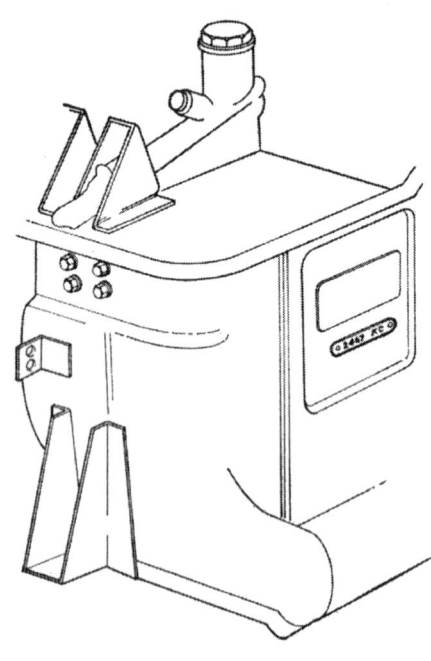

REAR AXLE SERIAL NUMBER

Commencing at KC1 for normal axles and FD1 or KD50001 for overdrive axles, this number is stamped on the bottom flange of the axle casing.

BODY SERIAL NUMBER

Commencing at 1 KC, this number is stamped on a plate which is riveted to the left-hand bulkhead panel.

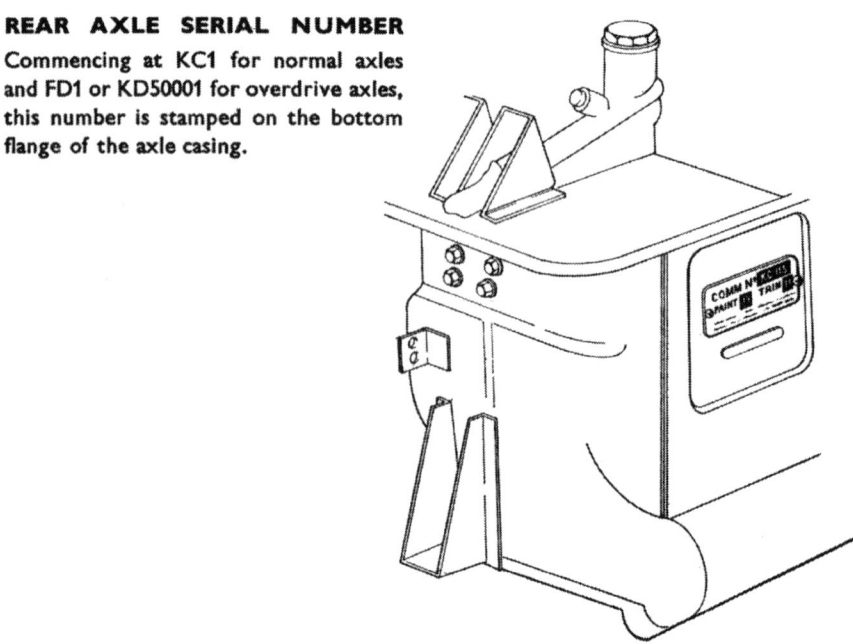

COMMISSION NUMBER

This number is stamped on a plate which is riveted to the left-hand bulkhead panel. Commission number details are listed on the following page.

RIGHT-HAND SIDE OR OFF SIDE

RIGHT-HAND STEERING

FRONT

REAR

LEFT-HAND SIDE OR NEAR SIDE

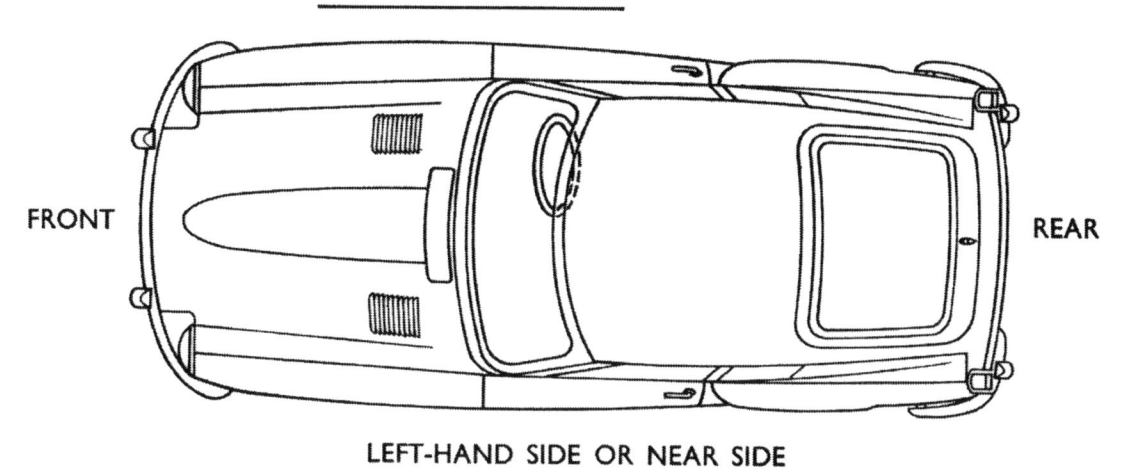

COMMISSION NUMBERS AND SUFFIX

| Right-Hand Steering | … | … | … | … | KC | … | |
| Left-Hand Steering | … | … | … | … | KC | … | L |

RIGHT-HAND SIDE OR NEAR SIDE

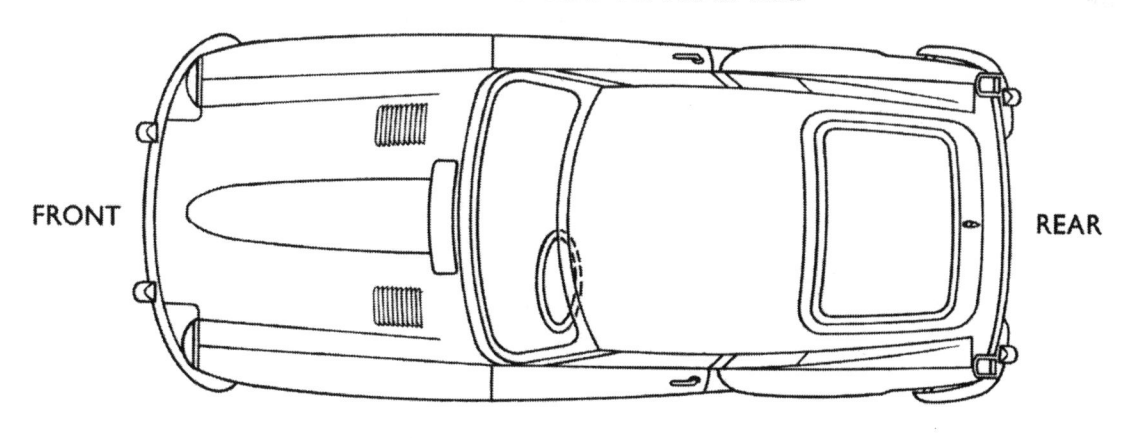

FRONT

REAR

LEFT-HAND STEERING

LEFT-HAND SIDE OR OFF SIDE

9

ALPHABETICAL INDEX

Description	Page	Plate
ENGINE — MK I	1 - 25	
Air Cleaner	23	N
Alternator Attachment	25	Q
Breather Details	11	F
Camshaft	7	C
Camshaft Chainwheel	7	C
Carburettor	15, 21	K, L
Carburettor Jets	16, 20	K, L
Carburettor Linkage	16, 20	K, L
Carburettor Needle	16, 19	K, L
Carburettor Pipes	17, 22	K, M
Connecting Rod	7	C
Connecting Rod Bearing	7	C
Connecting Rod Bush	7	C
Constant Pinion Bush	6	C
Crankshaft	6	C
Crankshaft Bearing	6	C
Crankshaft Chainwheel	6	C
Crankshaft Pulley and Damper	6	C
Crankshaft Thrust Washer	6	C
Cylinder Block	1	A
Cylinder Head	4	B
Cylinder Head Gasket	4	B
Cylinder Liner	2	
Decarbonising Gasket Set	1	
Dipstick	3	A
Distributor Driving Gear	8	C
Distributor Pedestal	8	C
Dynamo Bracket	24	P
Dynamo Link	24	P
Dynamo Pulley	24	P
Engine Gasket Set	1	
Engine Lifting Eyes	3	A
Exhaust Manifold	10	E
Fan	6	C
Fan Belt	6	C
Fan Pulley and Damper	6	C
Flywheel	6	C
Flywheel Gear Ring	6	C
Front Engine Plate	3	A
Gasket Sets	1	
Ignition Leads	24	
Inlet Manifold	10	E
Inlet Manifold Adaptor	10	E
Inlet Manifold Heater Pipes	10	E
Oil Filler Cap	5	B
Oil Filter Assembly	12	G
Oil Pressure Adjustment Details	2	A
Oil Pressure Switch	3	A
Oil Pump	2	A
Oil Sump	3	A
Petrol Pipes	17	
Petrol Pump	13, 14	H, J
Piston	8	C
Piston Rings	8	C

Description	Page	Plate
ENGINE—continued		
Push Rod	5	B
Push Rod Tappets	5	B
Rear Engine Plate	3	A
Rockers	5	B
Rocker Cover	5	B
Rocker Shaft	5	B
Rocker Shaft Pedestal	5	B
Rocker Spring	5	B
Sparking Plug	24	
Temperature Transmitter	9	D
Timing Chain	7	C
Timing Chain Tensioner	7	C
Timing Cover	7	C
Timing Cover Oil Seal	7	C
Valve	5	B
Valve Collar	5	B
Valve Rocker	5	B
Valve Spring	5	B
Water Delivery Tube	4	B
Water Drain Tap	2	A
Water Pump	9	D
Water Thermostat	9	D
ENGINE — MK II	26 - 45	
Air Cleaner	44	AC
Alternator Mounting	45	AD
Breather Details	34	W
Camshaft	30	T
Camshaft Chainwheel	30	T
Carburettor	40, 42	AA
Carburettor Linkage	41	AA
Carburettor Needle	40	AA
Carburettor Pipes	40, 43	AB
Connecting Rod	31	T
Connecting Rod Bearing	31	T
Connecting Rod Bush	31	T
Constant Pinion Bush	30	T
Crankshaft	30	T
Crankshaft Bearing	30	T
Crankshaft Chainwheel	30	T
Crankshaft Pulley and Damper	30	T
Crankshaft Thrust Washer	30	T
Cylinder Block	26	R
Cylinder Head	28	S
Cylinder Head Gasket	28	S
Cylinder Liner	26	
Decarbonising Gasket Set	26	
Dipstick	27	R
Distributor Driving Gear	31	T
Distributor Pedestal	31	T
Engine Gasket Set	26	
Engine Lifting Eyes	27	R
Exhaust Manifold	33	V
Fan	30	T

Description	Page	Plate
ENGINE—continued		
Fan Belt	30	T
Fan Pulley and Damper	30	T
Flywheel	30	T
Flywheel Gear Ring	30	T
Front Engine Plate	27	R
Gasket Sets	26	
Ignition Leads	45	
Inlet Manifold	33	V
Inlet Manifold Adaptor	33	V
Inlet Manifold Heater Pipes	33	V
Oil Filler Cap	29	S
Oil Filter Assembly	35	X
Oil Pressure Adjustment Details	27	R
Oil Pressure Switch	27	R
Oil Pump	27	R
Oil Sump	27	R
Petrol Pipes	42	
Petrol Pump	36	Y
Piston	31	T
Piston Rings	31	T
Push Rod	28	S
Push Rod Tappets	28	S
Rear Engine Plate	27	R
Rockers	29	S
Rocker Cover	29	S
Rocker Shaft	29	S
Rocker Shaft Pedestal	29	S
Rocker Spring	29	S
Sparking Plug	45	
Timing Chain	30	T
Timing Chain Tensioner	31	T
Timing Cover	31	T
Timing Cover Oil Seal	31	T
Valve	28	S
Valve Collar	28	S
Valve Rocker	28	S
Valve Spring	28	S
Water Drain Tap	26	R
Water Pump	32	U
Water Thermostat	32	U
CLUTCH	46	
Cover Assembly	46	AE
Driven Plate Assembly	46	AE
Operating Lever	46	AE
Slave Cylinder	46	AE
Throw-out Bearing	46	AE
GEARBOX	47 - 50	
Attachment Details	48	
Casing	47	AF
Clutch Housing and Front End Cover	47	AF
Constant Pinion Bearing	49	AG
Constant Pinion Shaft	49	AG

10

ALPHABETICAL INDEX

Description	Page	Plate
GEARBOX—*continued*		
Countershaft	50	AG
Countershaft Bearing	50	AG
Countershaft Gears	50	AG
Extension	47	AF
Extension Oil Seal	47	AF
Front End Cover	47	AF
Front End Cover Oil Seal	47	AF
Mainshaft	49	AG
Mainshaft Bearing	49	AG
Mainshaft Flange	49	AG
Mainshaft Gears	49	AG
Operating Sleeve	49	AG
Reverse Idler Gear	50	AG
Reverse Idler Spindle	50	AG
Reverse Light Switch Bracket	48	AF
Reverse Operating Lever	50	AG
Selector Fork	48	AF
Selector Shaft	48	AF
Selector Shaft Plunger	48	AF
Speedometer Driven Gear	47	AF
Speedometer Driven Gear Bearing	47	AF
Synchronising Sleeve	49	AG
Top Cover	48	AF
GEAR SHIFT MECHANISM	**51 - 52**	
Gear Lever (External)	51	AH
Gear Lever Grommet	52	AH
Gear Lever (Internal)	51	AH
Gear Lever Knob	52	AH
Gear Lever Shaft	51	AH
Gear Lever Shaft Coupling	51	AH
Operating Shaft	51	AH
Reverse Light Switch Operating Arm	51	AH
Top Cover Extension	51	AH
ENGINE MOUNTING	**53**	
Front Engine Mounting	53	AJ
Rear Engine Mounting	53	AJ
Rear Engine Mounting Platform	53	AJ
Rebound Stop	53	AJ
CHASSIS FRAME	**54 - 55**	AK
Front Suspension and Engine Mounting Bracket	55	AK
Outrigger Assembly	54	AK
Rear Damper Mounting Bracket	54	AK
Skid Plate	55	

Description	Page	Plate
FRONT SUSPENSION	**56 - 58**	
Bottom Trunnion	58	AL
Bottom Trunnion Oil Seal	58	AL
Caliper Mounting Plate	57	AL
Front Damper	58	AL
Front Damper and Road Spring Attachment Details	58	AL
Front Road Spring	58	AL
Hub	57	AL
Hub Bearing	57	AL
Lower Wishbone	57	AL
Lower Wishbone Fulcrum Bracket	57	AL
Steering Tie Rod Lever	57	AL
Stub Axle	57	AL
Stub Axle Oil Seal	57	AL
Upper Wishbone Assembly	56	AL
Upper Wishbone Ball Joint	56	AL
Vertical Link	56	AL
ANTI-ROLL BAR	**59**	AM
REAR AXLE	**60 - 62**	
Axle Casing	60	AN
Axle Shaft Assembly	62	AN
Crown Wheel and Pinion	60	AN
Differential Bearing	60	AN
Differential Casing	60	AN
Differential Gears	60	AN
Hub Bearing	62	AN
Inner Axle Shaft	62	AN
Inner Axle Shaft Oil Seal	62	AN
Oil Filler Plug	60	AN
Outer Axle Shaft	62	AN
Pinion Bearing	61	AN
Pinion Flange	61	AN
Rear Hub and Stud Assembly	62	AN
REAR SUSPENSION — MK I	**63**	
Pivot Bracket	63	AP
Radius Arm Assembly	63	AP
Rear Damper	63	AP
Road Spring	63	AP
Vertical Link	63	AP
REAR SUSPENSION — MK II	**64 - 65**	
Bump Rubber	65	AQ
Damper	65	AQ
Driven Flange	65	AQ
Hub	65	AQ
Intermediate Drive Shaft	65	AQ
Lower Wishbone	64	AQ
Outer Drive Shaft	65	AQ
Outer Drive Shaft Bearings	65	AQ

Description	Page	Plate
REAR SUSPENSION — MK II *continued*		
Radius Arm	64	AQ
Radius Arm Adjuster	64	AQ
Radius Arm Bracket	64	AQ
Road Spring	64	AQ
Rotoflex Coupling	65	AQ
Vertical Link	64	AQ
PROPELLOR SHAFT	**66**	AR
ROAD WHEELS	**66**	AR
Nave Plate	66	AR
Wheel Trim	66	AR
Wire Wheel Kit	66	AR
STEERING	**67 - 68**	
Ball Joint	68	AS
Column, Upper and Lower	67	AS
Flexible Joint	67	AS
Mounting Block, Rack and Pinion	68	AS
Rack and Pinion Assy.	67, 68	AS
Steering Wheel	67	AS
ACCELERATION CONTROL	**69 - 70**	
Control Rods	70	AU
Fulcrum Bracket	69	AT
Link Rod	69	AT
Operating Lever	69, 70	AT, AU
Pedal	69, 70	AT, AU
Return Spring	69, 70	AT, AU
CLUTCH AND BRAKE PEDALS	**71**	
Brake Pedal	71	AV
Clutch Pedal	71	AV
Pedal Mounting Bracket	71	AV
Pedal Pad	71	AV
Pedal Return Spring	71	AV
MASTER CYLINDER	**72 - 73**	
Brake Master Cylinder	72	AV
Brake Master Cylinder Support Bracket	72	AV
Clutch Master Cylinder	72	AV
Clutch Master Cylinder Support Bracket	72	AV
Master Cylinder Service Kits	72, 73	AV, AW
Tandem Brake Master Cylinder	73	AW

ALPHABETICAL INDEX

Description	Page	Plate
HYDRAULIC PIPES	74 - 75	
Brake Pipes	74, 75	AX
Clutch Pipes	75	AX
Pipe Clips	74, 75	AX
HANDBRAKE	76 - 77	
Compensating Sector	77	AY
Handbrake Assembly	76	AY
Handbrake Cable	76	AY
Pawl Release Rod	76	AY
Relay Lever	77	AY
Relay Lever Bearing	77	AY
Seal	77	AY
BRAKES	78 - 79	
Front Brake Caliper Assy.	78	AZ
Front Brake Caliper Repair Kit	78	AZ
Front Brake Lining Pad	78	AZ
Rear Brake Back Plate	78	AZ
Rear Brake Drum	79	AZ
Rear Brake Shoe Assembly	79	AZ
Rear Brake Wheel Cylinder	79	AZ
Rear Wheel Cylinder Repair Kit	79	AZ
RADIATOR	80	
Block	80	BA
Cowl	80	BA
Filler Cap	80	BA
Hose	80	BA
Overflow Bottle	80	BA
Overflow Bottle Mounting Bracket	80	BA
EXHAUST SYSTEM — MK I	81	
Attachment Details	81	BB
Front Pipe	81	BB
Intermediate Pipe and Front Silencer	81	BB
Rear Silencer and Tail Pipe	81	BB
EXHAUST SYSTEM — MK II	82	
Attachment Details	82	BC
Front Pipe	82	BC
Silencer and Tail Pipe	82	BC
PETROL SYSTEM — MK I	83	
Filler Cap	83	BD
Fuel Pipes	83	BD
Gauge—Tank Unit	83	BD
Tank	83	BD
Tank Attachment Details	83	BD
Vent Pipe	83	BD

Description	Page	Plate
PETROL SYSTEM — MK II	84	
Filler Cap	84	BE
Fuel Pipes	84	BE
Gauge—Tank Unit	84	BE
Tank	84	BE
Tank Attachment Details	84	BE
SERVICE KITS AND TOOLS	85	
Instruction Book	85	
Jack	85	
Service Kits	85	
Tools	85	
ELECTRICAL EQUIPMENT	86 - 107	
Alternator	90, 91	
Alternator Brush	90, 91	BJ, BK
Alternator Brush Box	90, 91	BJ, BK
Alternator Fan	90, 91	BJ, BK
Alternator Heatsink Diodes	90	BJ
Alternator Pulley	90, 91	BJ, BK
Alternator Rectifier	91	BK
Alternator Regulator	91	BK
Alternator Rotor	90	BJ
Alternator Slip Ring	91	BK
Alternator Stator	90	BJ
Alternator Sundry Parts Set	90, 91	
Battery	102	
Body Harness	102	
Choke Control Cable	105, 107	BR, BS
Choke Control Cable Knob	105, 107	BR, BS
Control Box	102	BQ
Courtesy Light Switch	103	BQ
Distributor	86, 87	BF, BG
Distributor Cap	86, 87	BF, BG
Distributor Condenser	86, 87	BF, BG
Distributor Contact Set	86, 87	BF, BG
Distributor Rotor	86, 87	BF, BG
Distributor Spring Set	86, 87	BF, BG
Distributor Vacuum Control Unit	86, 87	BF, BG
Dual Brake Warning Light	105, 107	
Dynamo	88	BH
Dynamo Armature	88	BH
Dynamo Brush Set	88	BH
Dynamo Field Coils	88	BH
Engine Leads	103	
Flasher Switch	93	BL
Flasher Unit	93	BL
Front Flasher Lamp	97, 98	BO
Front Side Flasher Lamp	98	BO
Front Side Marker Lamp	98	

Description	Page	Plate
ELECTRICAL EQUIPMENT—continued		
Front Side Lamp	97	BO
Fuel Gauge	104, 106	BR, BS
Fuse Box	102	
Headlamp	96, 97	BO
Heater Switch	105, 107	BR, BS
Hazard Flasher Unit	93	BL
Hazard Warning Light	107	BS
Horn	92	BL
Horn Push	92	BL
Horn Relay	92	BL
Ignition Coil	86	BF
Ignition and Starter Switch	106, 107	BR, BS
Lighting and Instrument Illumination Master Switch	105, 106	BR, BS
Main Harness	102, 103	
Rear Flasher Lamp	99, 100	BP
Rear Number Plate Lamp	101	BP
Rear Side Marker Lamp	100	
Reverse Lamp	100	BP
Reverse Light Switch	103	BQ
Revolution Counter	104, 106	BR, BS
Revolution Counter Cable	104, 106	BR, BS
Roof Lamp	101	BP
Roof Lamp Switch	105	BR
Side, Head and Dip Switch	93	BL
Speedometer	104, 106	BR, BS
Speedometer Cable	104, 106	BR, BS
Starter Motor	88	BH
Starter Motor Armature	88	BH
Starter Motor Brush Set	88	BH
Starter Soleniod Switch	89	BH
Stop Lamp Switch	102	BQ
Stop/Tail Lamp	99	BP
Temperature Gauge	104, 106	BR, BS
Temperature Transmitter	104, 106	BR, BS
Voltage Regulator	102	BQ
Windscreen Wiper Arm	94, 95	BM, BN
Windscreen Wiper Blade	94, 95	BM, BN
Windscreen Wiper Crosshead and Rack	94, 95	BM, BN
Windscreen Wiper Motor	94, 95	BM, BN
Windscreen Wiper Switch	105, 107	BR, BS
Windscreen Wiper Wheelbox	94, 95	BM, BN
BODY AND FITTINGS	108 - 190	
'A' Post Panels	112, 113	BV
Air Box	113	BV
Air Box Drain Flap	137	CC
Air Extractor Grille	146	CK

ALPHABETICAL INDEX

Description	Page	Plate
BODY AND FITTINGS—continued		
'B' Post Panels	113, 114	BV
Back Door Assembly	141	CF
Back Door Glass	142	CF
Back Door Glazing Rubber	142	CF
Back Door Handle	142	CF
Back Door Handle Locking Device	142	CF
Back Door Hinge	141	CF
Back Door Lock	141	CF
Back Door Lock Striker	141	CF
Back Door Sealing Rubber	142	CF
Back Door Torsion Bar Clamp	141	CF
Battery Box	113	BV
Battery Fixing Rod	113	
Body Complete	108	
Body Mouldings	145, 146	CJ, CK
Body Mounting Details	109	BT
Body Shell	108	
Body Side Panels	112, 114	BV
Bonnet Assembly	115, 118	BW, BX
Bonnet Badge	116, 119	BW, BX
Bonnet Catch Assembly	116, 119	BW, BX
Bonnet Catch Plate	116, 119	BW, BX
Bonnet Hinge Tube	115, 118	BW, BX
Bonnet Letters	116	BW
Bonnet Mouldings	145, 146	CK
Bonnet Sealing Rubber	116, 119	BW, BX
Bonnet Stay Link	116, 119	BW, BX
Cantrail	114	BV
Carpets	151	CM
Dash Panel Assembly	112	BV
Dash Shelf Panel	112	BV
Dash Side Panel	112	BV
Demister Outlet Capping	137, 139	CC, CD
Drip Mouldings	113	BV
Engine Bay Valance	117, 120	BW, BX
Facia Ash Tray	129, 132	CA, CB
Facia Panel	129, 130, 132, 133	CA, CB
Facia Panel Attachment Details	130, 133	CA, CB
Floor Panel Details	110, 111	BU
Front Bumpers	143, 144	CG, CH
Front Bumper Overrider	143, 144	CG, CH
Front Bumper Overrider Attachment Details	143, 144	CG, CH
Front Bumper Overrider Mounting	143, 144	CG, CH
Front Door Assembly	121	BY
Front Door Check Arm	125	BY
Front Door Glass	122	BY
Front Door Glass Channel	122	BY
Front Door Hinges	121	BY
Front Door Inner Waist Sealing Strip	121	BY

Description	Page	Plate
BODY AND FITTINGS—continued		
Front Door Lock	123, 124	BY
Front Door Lock Striker	123	BY
Front Door Outer Waist Sealing Strip	121	BY
Front Door Private Lock	125	BY
Front Door Remote Control Handle	124	BY
Front Door Remote Control Mechanism	124	BY
Front Door Sealing Details	126	BY
Front Door Trim Pad	125, 126	BY
Front Door Ventilator	121	BY
Front Door Ventilator Glass	121	BY
Front Door Ventilator Locking Handle	121	BY
Front Door Window Regulator	123	BY
Front Door Window Regulator Channel	122	BY
Front Door Window Regulator Handle	123	BY
Front Floor Assembly	110	BH
Front Seat Assembly	155, 187 CN, CP, CQ	
Front Seat Cushion Assembly	161, 170, 178, 185 CN, CP, CQ	
Front Seat Cushion Cover	162, 171, 179, 186 CN, CP, CQ	
Front Seat Frame	157, 166, 175, 182 CN, CP, CQ	
Front Seat Frame and Squab Assembly	156, 165, 174, 181 CN, CP, CQ	
Front Seat Slide	163, 172, 187 CN, CP, CQ	
Front Seat Squab Cover	158, 167, 175, 182 CN, CP, CQ	
Front Valance Assembly	117, 120	BW, BX
Front Wheelarch Panel	115	BW
Front Wing	115	BW
Gearbox Cover	111	BU
Handbrake Cover and Centre Armrest	152, 153	CM
Headlining	149	CM
Headlining Listing Rods	149	CM
Heater Airbox Panel	113	BV
Heater Control	136, 137	CC, CD
Heater Demister Hose	136, 139	CC, CD
Heater Demister Nozzle	136, 139	CC, CD
Heater Switch	136, 138	CC, CD
Heater Unit	136, 138	CC, CD

Description	Page	Plate
BODY AND FITTINGS—continued		
Heater Water Pipes	136, 138	CC, CD
Heater Water Valve	136, 138	CC, CD
Interior Driving Mirror	127	BZ
Luggage Floor Assembly	147	CL
Occasional Seat	188, 190	CR
Radiator Grille	117, 120	BW, BX
Rear Body Badge	145, 146	CJ, CK
Rear Body Letters	145	CJ
Rear Bumper	143, 144	CG, CH
Rear Bumper Overrider	143	CG
Rear Bumper Overrider Moulding	143	CG
Rear Floor Assembly	110	BU
Rear Header Panel	114	BV
Rear Quarter Vent	141	CF
Rear Quarter Vent Frame	141	CF
Rear Quarter Vent Glass	141	CF
Rear Quarter Vent Toggle	141	CF
Rear Seat Pan	110	BU
Rear Spring Access Cover	110	BU
Rear Valance Panel	111	BU
Rear Wing Outer Panel	113	BV
Roof Panel Assembly	114	BV
Safety Harness	154	
Sill Panel, inner	110	BU
Sill Panel, outer	113	BV
Sound Insulation Pads	149	CM
Spare Wheel Cover	148	CL
Spare Wheel Mounting	148	CL
Steering Column Cowl	130, 134, 135	CA, CB
Steering Column Support	131, 134	CA, CB
Sun Visor	128	BZ
Trim Pads	149, 150	CM
Trunk Floor	111	BU
Tunnel Cover	153, 154	CM
Valance Panel, Engine Bay	117, 120	BW, BX
Wheelarch Inner Panel	110	BU
Wheelarch Outer Panel	110	BU
Windscreen Frame	127	BZ
Windscreen Glass	127	BZ
Windscreen Washer	140	CE
Windscreen Weatherstrip	127	BZ
MISCELLANEOUS BODY DETAILS	191	
Blanking Plugs	191	
Grommets	191	
Wing Mirror	191	
OVERDRIVE	192 - 196	
Adaptor	192	CS
Annulus	195	CT
Cam	194	CT

13

ALPHABETICAL INDEX

Description	Page	Plate
OVERDRIVE—*continued*		
Cam Lever	194	CT
Clutch Brake Ring	195	CT
Clutch Sliding Member	195	CT
Clutch Spring	195	CT
Coupling Flange	196	CT
Cover Plate	192	CS
Drain Plug	194	CT
Flexible Mounting	192	CS
Front Casing	194	CT
Harness	192	CS
Inhibitor Switch	193	CS
Mainshaft	192	CS
Mounting Platform	192	CS
Oil Filter	194	CT
Oil Filter Magnet	194	CT
Oil Pump Plunger	194	CT
Operating Arm	192	CS
Operating Valve	194	CT
Operating Valve Lever	194	CT
Overdrive Unit	192, 194	CS
Planet Carrier	195	CT
Propellor Shaft	143	CS
Rear Casing	196	CT

Description	Page	Plate
OVERDRIVE—*continued*		
Rear Oil Seal	196	CT
Relay	192	CS
Relief Valve Kit	194	CT
Side Cover Plate	194	CT
Solenoid	195	CT
Speedometer Angle Drive	193	CS
Speedometer Cable	193	CS
Speedometer Driven Gear	196	CT
Speedometer Driving Gear	196	CT
Sun Wheel	195	CT
Switch	192	CS
Switch Escutcheon	192	CS
ACCESSORIES	197 - 200	
Anti Frost Shield	197	
Bonnet Lock Kit	197	
Brake Fluid	197	
Cigarette Lighter	197	
Continental Touring Kit	198	
Defroster	199	
Emergency Windscreen	199	
Fire Extinguisher	197	

Description	Page	Plate
ACCESSORIES—*continued*		
Fog Lamp	199	
Fuel Line Filter	197	
Headrest	200	
Heater Kit	197	
Instrument Mounting Panel	200	
Mud Flap	198	
Nave Plate Medallion	198	
Oil Cooler Kit	199	
Roof Rack	199	
Safety Belt	198	
Safety Warning Triangle	200	
Sill Protector	198	
Sparking Plug	199	
Sparking Plug Spanner	200	
Spot Lamp	199	
Steering Column Lock Kit	200	
Steering Wheel Glove	200	
Towing Attachment	199	
Tow Rope and Luggage Strap	199	
Touch-In-Paint	200	
Wing Mirrors	197, 198	

NUMERICAL INDEX

KEY TO MODELS MENTIONED IN NUMERICAL INDEX

A	Triumph Herald	L	Triumph TR.4 and 4A
B	Atlas Commercial Vehicle	M	Leyland 2 Tonner
C	Vanguard VI	O	Triumph 2000
D	Leyland 15 cwt. Van	P	Standard 8, 10, Pennant and 7 cwt. Van
E	Vitesse	R	Triumph TR.2, 3 and 3A
E	2-Litre Vitesse	T	Vanguard III and Sportsman
F	Spitfire 4	V	Leyland 20
G	Triumph TR.250 and TR.5 P.I.	Y	Ensign and Ensign De-Luxe
J	Vanguard I and II	Z	Triumph 1300

Part No.	Description	Plate No.	Page	Also Used on Models
27378	Plug, Core	B6	4	A, B, E, E — 2 Litre, F, J, O, P, R, T, V, Y, Z
30123	Wire, Lead		4, 28	A, B, E, E — 2 Litre, F, J, L, O, P, R, T, V, Y, Z
32307	Washer, Felt	R55	2, 27	A, B, E, E — 2 Litre, F, G, J, O, P, R, T, V, Y, Z,
33214	Pin, Anchor	C39	7, 31	A, B, E, E — 2 Litre, F, G, O, P, Z
35960	Chain Wheel	C30	7, 30	A, B, E, E — 2 Litre, F, G, O, P, Z
36234	Piece, Filler	A25	2, 26	A, B, E, E — 2 Litre, F, G, O, P, Z
36411	Plate	C32	7, 30	A, B, E, E — 2 Litre, F, G, O, P, Z
37948	Shim	AG12	49	A, B, E, E — 2 Litre, F, J, P, R, T, V, Y
42243	Grommet	BB21	81, 82	A, F, O, P, R, Y, Z
42244	Grommet	BB20	81, 82	A, F, L, O, R, Y, Z
42425	Trunnion	C38	7, 31	A, B, E, E — 2 Litre, F, G, O, P, Z
43752	Plate	C36	7, 31	A, B, C, E, E — 2 Litre, F, G, P, Z
44473	Plug, Core	A5	1	A, B, E — 2 Litre, F, J, O, P, R, T, V, Y
46172	Plug, Core	A8	1, 10, 33	A, E, E — 2 Litre, F, G, L, M, O, P, Y, Z
46549	Plug	A6	1	A, B, E, E — 2 Litre, L, O, P, Z
52413	Pin, Mills	AH28	51, 192	A, E — 2 Litre, F, J, T, V, Y
52479	Link	J18	13, 14, 36	E, E — 2 Litre, G, J, L, O, R, T, Y
52483	Pin	J19	13, 14, 36	A, B, E — 2 Litre, G, J, L, O, P, R, T, V, Y
52484	Clip, Securing Pin	J20	13, 14, 36	A, B, E, E — 2 Litre, G, J, L, O, P, R, T, V, Y
52486	Washer	J21	13, 14, 36	E, E — 2 Litre, G, J, L, O, R, T, Y
52490	Screw	H23	13	A, B, E, E — 2 Litre, F, J, L, O, P, R, T, V, Y, Z
52492	Spring, Diaphragm	J10	14, 36	G, J, L, R, T, V, Y
52494	Spring	J16	13, 14, 36	A, E, E — 2 Litre, G, J, L, O, R, T, Y
52498	Spring	J15	13, 14, 36	E, E — 2 Litre, G, J, L, O, R, T, Y
55800	Clip	BC6	82	D, J, V, Y
56305	Screw		47	A, E, E — 2 Litre, F, J, L, R, T, V, Y
56712	Plug, Core	A7	1	A, B, E, E — 2 Litre, F, M, O, P
56934	Nipple		56	A, F, G, J, L, M, P, R, T, V, Y
57103	Gasket	D28	9, 32	A, B, E, E — 2 Litre, F, G, J, O, P, R, T, V, Y, Z
57110	Nut	B42	5, 29	A, B, E, E — 2 Litre, F, G, J, M, O, P, R, T, V, Y
57361	Washer	H24	13	A, B, E, E — 2 Litre, F, J, M, O, P, R, V, Y, Z
57458	Cover Band Assembly	BH33	88	A, B, C, E, F, G, O, P,
57492	Spring	BM4	94	A, B, E, G, L, O, P, R, T, V, Y
57591	Bulb	BO16	97, 98	F, J, L, M
58258	Clamp	V13	33	
58261	Gaiter		56	A, E, F, P
58465	Fuse, 35 amp		102	A, E, F, G, L, M, O, R, V, Y, Z
58923	Guide, Valve, Inlet	S2	28	
59015	Pedestal	P16	24	E, E — 2 Litre, J, O, R, T, V, Y

15

NUMERICAL INDEX

Part No.	Description	Plate No.	Page	Also Used on Models
59115	Bolt	P18	24	
59191	Clip	AX34	75, 83, 84, 74, 75	A, B, E, F, G, J, L, O, P, R, T, Y
59380	Clip		74, 75	
59426	Spanner		85	A, E — 2 Litre, F, P, T, Y, Z
59427	Combination Tool		85	A, B, E, F, P, T, V, Y
59445	Washer, Knob	BS29	106, 136	
59467	Side Bulb	BP47	101	A, B, E, F, G, J, L, O, R, T, V, Y, Z
59474	Nut	BQ9	103, 193	A, E — 2 Litre, J, O, T, Y
59492	Bulb	BR8	104, 106	A, E — 2 Litre, F, L, M, O, P, Y, Z
59650	Cover, Filter	J5	14, 36	E — 2 Litre, G
59660	Screw	H9	13	A, B, E, E — 2 Litre, F, J, L, M, O, P, R, T, V, Y, Z
59813	Screw, s/t		102	
59844	Defroster, Electric		199	A, E, F, G, J, O, P, R, T, Y
59897	Bulb	BF75	101	A, E — 2 Litre, J, O, P, T, Y, Z
60070	Bush, Bearing Cap	AN18	60	A, E, E — 2 Litre, F, P, V, Y
60142	Nut, Tubing	BE22	84	G, L, R, T, V, Y,
60176	Nut, Tubing	K86	17, 42, 83	G
60313	Bearing Seal	D8	9, 32	A, B, E, E — 2 Litre, F, G, J, L, M, O, R, V, Y, Z
61478	Water Tap	A27	2, 26	A, B, E, E — 2 Litre, F, G, L, O, R, T, V, Y, Z
61917	Grommet	BF56	101, 105, 107, 136, 140, 191	A, B, E, E—2 Litre, F, G, L, O, R, T, V, Y, Z
70391	Sundry Parts Set		88	
100148	Clip, Speedo Gear	AB5	22, 43, 103, 104	A, E, F, L, M, R, Y, Z
100433	Stud	A20	2, 26	A, B, E, E — 2 Litre, F, M, O, P, V, Z
100455	Nut	BB3	81	A, B, E, E — 2 Litre, O, P
100498	Nut	E16	10, 33	A, B, E, E — 2 Litre, F, G, O, P, Z
100500	Screw, Set	C31	7, 30	A, B, E, E — 2 Litre, F, G, O, P, Z
100501	Screw	A26	2, 26	A, B, E, E — 2 Litre, F, G, O, P, Z
100764	Bearing	D11	9, 32	A, B, E, E — 2 Litre, F, G, O, P, V, Z
100851	Circlip	D13	9, 32	
100962	Stud	D2	9	
101022	Screw, Set	B7	4, 28	A, B, E — 2 Litre, F, G, O, P, Z
101089	Spanner, Tube		85	
101092	Washer	D9	9, 32	A, B, E, E — 2 Litre, F, G, J, L, M, O, P, T, V, Y, Z
101302	Nut, Tubing	E31	10, 33	
101343	Adaptor	E29	10, 33	
101962	Stud	A21	2, 4, 9, 10, 26, 28, 32	A, B, E, E — 2 Litre, F, G, O, P, Z
102564	Valve, Spring	B24	5, 28	A, B, E, E — 2 Litre, F, G, L, O, V, Y
102729	Sleeve, Tubing	K87	17, 42, 83	A, E, E — 2 Litre, F, G, L, M, O, Z
103810	Nut	S19	28	G, V, Y
104420	Bush	AG46	50	A, B, E, E — 2 Litre, F, P
104433	Bearing Ball	AG4	49	A, B, E, E — 2 Litre, F, P
104445	Spring	AG26	49	A, B, E, E — 2 Litre, F, P
104552	Ball Joint Assembly, Upper Wishbone		56	A, F, P
104554	Bolt	AN19	60	A, E, E — 2 Litre, F, P
104581	Key	AN74	62	A, E, E — 2 Litre, F, P
104582	Catcher, Oil	AN69	62	A, E, E — 2 Litre, F, P
104585	Bearing	AN65	62	A, E, E — 2 Litre, F, P
104737	Pawl		76	A, E, G, O, P, Z
104738	Pin	AY3	76	A, E, F, G, L, P
104740	Spring	AY5	76	A, E, F, G, L, O, P, Z
104742	Ratchet	AY7	76	A, E, F, L, P
104743	Pin	AY8	76	A, E, F, P

NUMERICAL INDEX

Part No.	Description	Plate No.	Page	Also Used on Models
104749	Fork-end	AY13	76, 77, 89	
104750	Pin	AY16	76	A, E, F, G, L, O, P, Z
104773	Housing	AN67	62	A, E, E — 2 Litre, F, P
104775	Seal, Oil		68	A, B, F, P
104819	Bearing, Main	C2	6	A, B, E, E — 2 Litre, O, P
104820	Washer	C4	6	A, B, E, E — 2 Litre, F, O, P
104826	Tube, Sealing	B2	4	A, B, E — 2 Litre, F, O, P
104831	Pedestal	B35	5	A, B, E — 2 Litre, F, O, P
104832	Pedestal, Rocker	B33	5	A, B, E — 2 Litre, F, O, P, Z
104838	Collar	B45	5	A, B, E — 2 Litre, F, O, P
104839	Spindle	D5	9, 32	A, B, E — 2 Litre, F, O, P
104840	Impellor	D7	9, 32	A, B, E, E — 2 Litre, F, G, O, P, Z
104841	Piece, Distance	D12	9, 32	A, B, E, E — 2 Litre, F, G, O, P, Z
104859	Screw	B34	5, 29	A, B, E, E — 2 Litre, F, G, O, P, V, Z
104863	Block, Sealing	A24	2	A, B, E, E — 2 Litre, F, G, O, P, Z
104897	Pulley, Dynamo	P4	24	A, B, E — 2 Litre, O, P, Z
104903	Hose	BA6	80	A, B, C, F, P
104939	Washer, Joint	C63	8, 31	A, B, E, E — 2 Litre, F, G, O, P, Z
104963	Plug, Core		2, 27	A, B, E, E — 2 Litre, F, G, O, P
105114	Plate	C29	7, 30	A, B, E, E — 2 Litre, F, G, O, P, Z
105123	Stud	B10	4, 28	A, B, E, E — 2 Litre, F, G, O, P, Z
105124	Stud	B15	4, 28	A, B, E, E — 2 Litre, F, G, L, O, P, Z
105125	Stud	S18	28	A, B, F, G, P, Z
105131	Chain, Timing	C33	7, 30	A, B, E, E — 2 Litre, F, G, O, P, Z
105143	Bush	C15	6, 30	A, B, E, E — 2 Litre, F, P
105290	Plate, Clamp	BB37	81, 82	G
105292	Strip	BB35	81, 82	G
105321	Washer, Joint	R34	2, 27	A, B, E, E — 2 Litre, F, G, O, P, Z
105322	Spring, Rocker	B43	5, 29	A, B, E, E — 2 Litre, F, G, O, P, Z
105438	Nut, Steering Wheel	AS2	67	
105605	Bush	AV2	71	A, B, E, E — 2 Litre, F, P, T, Y
105676	Cap, Bleed Screw	AE33	46, 78, 79	G
105689	Spring	AZ39	79	
105690	Spring	AZ40	79	
106036	Clip	AY19	76	A, B, E, F, P,
106084	Spring	AE27	46	A, B, F, L, M, P, R
106088	Retainer, Spring	AV29	72	A, B, E, E — 2 Litre, F, G, L, P, R, V, Y, Z
106090	Washer, Spring	AV27	72	A, B, E, E — 2 Litre, F, G, L, P, R, V, Y, Z
106092	Circlip	AV34	72	A, B, E, E — 2 Litre, F, G, L, P, R, V, Z
106093	Cover	AV49	72	A, E, E — 2 Litre, G, L, P, R, Z
106094	Lid, Reservoir	AV36	72	A, E, E — 2 Litre, G, L, P, Z
106095	Gasket	AV37	72	A, E, E — 2 Litre, F, G, L, P, Z
106155	Plunger	AV30	72	A, E, E — 2 Litre, F, P
106156	Spring	AV28	72	A, E, E — 2 Litre, F, L, M, P, R, V, Z
106157	Stem Valve	AV25	72	A, B, E, E — 2 Litre, F, G, L, P, R, V, Y, Z
106158	Seal, Valve	AV24	72	A, B, E, E — 2 Litre, F, G, L, P, R, V, Y, Z
106254	Reverse Operating Lever Assembly	AG51	50	A, B, E, E — 2 Litre, F, P
106262	Washer	AG16	49	A, E, E — 2 Litre, F, P
106268	Fork, Selector	AF34	48	A, B, E, E — 2 Litre, F, P
106269	Washer, Joint	AF42	48	A, B, E, E — 2 Litre, F, P
106270	Washer, Thrust	AG44	50	A, B, E, E — 2 Litre, F, P
106365	Thrower	AG34	49	A, B, E, E — 2 Litre, F, P
106388	Spring, Plunger	AG13	49	A, B, E, E — 2 Litre, F, P, R
106437	Gasket	AF21	47, 192	A, B, E, E — 2 Litre, F, P
106448	Fulcrum	AG52	50	A, B, E, E — 2 Litre, F, G, L, O, P
106477	Screw	AG49	50	A, B, E, E — 2 Litre, F, P
106478	Pin	AF37	48	A, B, E, E — 2 Litre, F, P
106481	Plunger	AF39	48	A, B, E, E — 2 Litre, F, G, L, O, P, V
106489	Spring	AF41	48	A, B, E, E — 2 Litre, F, G, L, O, P, V

NUMERICAL INDEX

Part No.	Description	Plate No.	Page	Also Used on Models
106663	Cone, Split	B29	5, 28	A, B, E, E — 2 Litre, F, G, L, M, O, P, R, V, Z
106664	Washer	AN68	62	A, E, E — 2 Litre, F, P,
106957	Stud	AF25	48	A, E, E — 2 Litre, F, P, R
106958	Washer, Joint	BC2	82	G, L, R
107072	Gasket, Hose	AX31	75	
107099	Plug	AF27	48	A, B, E, E — 2 Litre, F, P
107176	Seal	AZ27	79	
107193	Seal	AN66	62	A, E, E — 2 Litre, F, P
107246	Plug	R40	2, 27	A, B, E, E — 2 Litre, F, G, O, P, Z
107401	Dowel	C50	7, 31	A, B, E, E — 2 Litre, F, G, O, P, Z
107857	Washer, Tab	C22	6, 30	E, E — 2 Litre, G, L, O, R
107858	Piece, Balance	C20	6, 30	E, E — 2 Litre, L, O, R
107948	Nut	AR13	66	A, E, F, L, R
107949	Nut		66	A, E, F, G, L, R
108021	Shaft, Selector, 3rd/top	AF31	48	A, E, E — 2 Litre, F, P
108446	Clip	BC24	82	G, L
108450	Mallet		66	A, E, F, G, L, R
108495	Washer	C19	6, 30	E, E — 2 Litre, G, L, O, R
108496	Bush	C17	6, 30	E, E — 2 Litre, G, L, O, R
108499	Sleeve	C18	6, 30	E, E — 2 Litre, G, L, O, R
108657	Brush	BL2	92	G
108756	Screw, Bleed	AE32	46, 78, 79,	A, B, E, E — 2 Litre, F, G, L, P, R, V, Y, Z
108757	Seal, Oil	AF19	47	A, B, E, E — 2 Litre, F, G, O, P
108860	Casing	BM18	94, 95	A, B, E, F, G, L, O, P, R, T, V, Y
108943	Clamp	CC26	136, 138	F
108951	Nut	BC4	82	D, G, L, R, T, V, Y
108976	Bolt	AS17	67	A, E, F, P, T, Y, Z
108977	Bush, Rubber	AS15	67	A, E, F, P, T, Y, Z
109023	Rocker, No. 1	B38	5, 29	A, F, G
109024	Rocker, No. 2	B39	5, 29	A, B, E, F, G, O, P, Z
109190	Seal	AV31	72	A, E, E — 2 Litre, F, P
109495	Ball Pin	B41	5, 29	E — 2 Litre, G, L, M, O, R, T, V, Y
110376	Pin	AN31	61	A, E — 2 Litre, F, P, Z
110461	Strip, Conductor	AS19	67	A, E, F, P, Z
110748	Nut	B19	4	
110960	Plate	AS14	67	A, E, F, P, Z
111054	Tappet	AZ23	78	A, D, E — 2 Litre, F, G, L, P, Y
111163	Spacer, Valve	AV26	72	A, B, E, E — 2 Litre, F, G, L, M, P, R, V, Y, Z
111422	Washer, Thrust	AG19	49	A, B, E, E — 2 Litre, F, P
111869	Valve Guide	S3	28	A, B, F, G, P
111870	Collar, Valve	B26	5, 28	A, E, E — 2 Litre, F, G, O, Z
111871	Collar, Spring, Lower	B23	5	
111979	Seal Taper, on Plunger	AV32	72	A, E, E — 2 Litre, F, P
112394	Circlip	AG23	49	A, B, E, E — 2 Litre, F, P
112429	Stud	AL21	57, 62, 65	A, E, E — 2 Litre, F, P, Z
112626	Gasket	CS8	192	E, E — 2 Litre, F, P
112635	Nut	AN40	61	B, C, E — 2 Litre, G, L, O, R, T, Y
112654	Ring, Snap	AG7	49	A, B, E — 2 Litre, F, P
113071	Spindle	AG48	50	A, B, E, E — 2 Litre, F, P
113087	Nut, Wheel	AR8	66	A, E, F, Z
113150	Bolt	AZ15	78	A, E, E — 2 Litre, F, G, L, R
113229	Washer, Thrust	AG43	50	A, B, E, E — 2 Litre, F, P
113256	Medallion Assembly		198	A, E, F, G, L, O, R
113797	Cup, Synchro, 3rd/top Gears	AG28	49	A, B, E, E — 2 Litre, F, P
113868	Fork, Selector, 1st/2nd	AF33	48	A, B, E, E — 2 Litre, F, P
114006	Button, Thrust	AP3	63, 64	A, E, F, T, Y
114178	Grommet	K89	17, 42	A, E — 2 Litre, F, G, O

NUMERICAL INDEX

Part No.	Description	Plate No.	Page	Also Used on Models
114210	Bracket, Four-way		54	F, G, L
114438	Spring, Pedal Return	AV7	71	
114749	Washer	AN42	61	A, E, E — 2 Litre, F, P
114774	Plug, Taper	B12	3, 4, 27, 28, 47, 60	A, B, E, E — 2 Litre, F, G, L, M, O, P, R, T, V, Y, Z
115459	Hose Assembly, Rear	AX30	75	A, F, L, R
115696	Stud	V2	33	G
115706	Boot		103	G
115783	Connector, Flexible	BD25	83	
115784	Connector, Flexible	BE24	84	G, L, M, R, T, V, Y
115990	Washer	AN39	61	B, C, E — 2 Litre, G, L, O, T, Y
116201	Gasket	AV53	72	F, L, M
116459	Rear Flasher Lamp (Red Glass)		99	
116460	Front Flasher Lamp (Amber Glass)		99	B, F, L, P, R, T, V, Y
116511	Plug, Taper	A12	1, 4, 26	E, E — 2 Litre, G, M, O, V
117509	Washer	AG2	49	
117510	Seal, Oil	AF16	47	A, B, E, E — 2 Litre, F, P
117511	Bearing, Mainshaft	AF15	47	
117575	Bush, Rubber	AP2	63, 64	A, E, F
117853	Bearing	AN58	62	A, E, E — 2 Litre, F
117952	Seal, Oil	AN49	62	A, E, E — 2 Litre, F
118040	Lever, Gear, Internal	AH25	51	A, E, F, P
118041	Shaft, Gear Lever		51	A, E, F, P
118053	Seal, Oil Shaft to Cover	AH29	51	A, E, F, P
118054	Screw	AH17	51	A, E, F, P
118599	Pin, Fulcrum	AP27	63	A, E, F
118632	Plug	A9	1, 26	A, B, E, E — 2 Litre, F, G, M, O, P, T, V, Y, Z
118686	Plug	A11	1, 26	E — 2 Litre, G, L
118826	Plug, Core		60	A, E — 2 Litre, F, G, L, O, Z
118977	Washer	AK30	55, 61	A, E — 2 Litre, F, G, L, O, P, R, T, Y, Z
119072	Snap on Rim	BO1	96, 97	G
119096	Bearing, End Thrust		47	A, E, E — 2 Litre, F
119099	Seal, Oil	AF20	47	A, E, E — 2 Litre, F
119100	Gear, Speedo Driven	AF17	47	A, E, E — 2 Litre, F
119131	Gear, Speedo Driving	AG3	49	A, E, E — 2 Litre, F
119142	Bolt	AL53	58	E, E — 2 Litre, F
119251	Spring	AH7	51	
119252	Spring	AH5	51	A, E, F, P
119262	Bush, Operating Shaft	AH12	51	A, E, F, P
119263	Circlip	AH6	51	A, E, F, P
119272	Top Wishbone Arm and Bush	AL1	56	A, E, E — 2 Litre, F
119313	Spring	B44	5, 29	E, E — 2 Litre, G, O, T
119322	Washer	B49	5, 29	E, E — 2 Litre, O, T
119324	Washer, Spherical	E22	10	C, E, E — 2 Litre, O
119389	Wheel	C5	6, 30	C, E, E — 2 Litre, G, O
119390	Oil Deflector	C9	6, 30	E, E — 2 Litre, G, O, T
119450	Bush, Rubber	AL59	58, 64	A, E, E — 2 Litre, F, G, L, Z
119451	Bush, Rubber	AL2	56, 63	A, E, E — 2 Litre, F
119573	Washer, Dished Outer	AH9	51	
119575	Shaft, Pedal	AV14	71	A, E, E — 2 Litre, F
119583	Bracket, Master Cylinder	AV59	72	A, E, E — 2 Litre, F
119622	Guide	B3	4	E, E — 2 Litre, O, T
119758	Stud, Long	A17	2	
119759	Washer	B40	5	E, E — 2 Litre, O, T
119811	Push Rod		5	E — 2 Litre, O, T
119813	Bush, Small End	C49	7, 31	A, E, E — 2 Litre, F, G, O, P
119891	Ring, Retaining	AG41	50	
119893	Needle Rollers	AG42	50	B, E, E — 2 Litre

19

NUMERICAL INDEX

Part No.	Description	Plate No.	Page	Also Used on Models
120124	Pin	AZ19	78	A, B, E, E — 2 Litre, F, P, R
120134	Cover, Dust	AZ29	79	A, B, E, E — 2 Litre, F, P
120135	Retainer	AZ30	79	
120137	Spring, Plate	AZ34	79	A, B, E, E — 2 Litre, F, P, Z
120138	Plate, Retaining	AZ33	79	A, B, E, E — 2 Litre, F, P, Z
120139	Cover, Dust	AZ37	79	A, B, E, E — 2 Litre, F, P
120142	Adjuster Unit Assembly		78	
120305	Washer	AH30	52	A, E, F, P
120307	Plate, Reverse Baulk	AH2	51	A, E, F, P
120308	Master Cylinder Assembly (Clutch)		72	A, E, E — 2 Litre, F
120331	Connection	K91	17	A, E — 2 Litre, F, L, O, R, Z
120694	Angle, Drive	CS49	193	E, E — 2 Litre, F, G, L, O
120843	Stud		2	C, E, E — 2 Litre, O
120941	Shim		68	A, E, F, G, L, O
120946	Plunger	AS32	68	A, E, F, G, L, O
120948	Bellows	AS45	68	A, E, F, G, L, O, Z
120949	Shim	AS34	68	A, E, F, G, L, O, Z
120953	Spring	AS42	68	A, E, F, G, L, O, Z
120955	Socket, Ball	AS39	68	A, E, F, G, L, O, Z
120957	Washer, Tab	AS40	68	A, E, F, G, L, O, Z
120959	Shim	AS34	68	A, E, F, G, L, O, Z
121174	Rear Wheel Cylinder Assembly		79	
121251	Valve, Spring	B25	5	A, B, E, E — 2 Litre, F, O, P, Z
121269	Starter Solenoid Switch	BH39	89	G
121295	Nut, Wheel	AR14	66	A, E, F, G, L
121296	Nut, Wheel		66	A, E, F, G, L
121297	Spanner		66	A, E, F, G, L
121355	Side Lamp, Front (White Lens)		97	C, E, J
121356	Flasher Lamp, Front (Amber Lens)		97	F, J, L
121398	Oil Pressure Indicator Switch	R73	3, 27	A, B, E, E — 2 Litre, F, G, M, O, P, V, Z
121699	Compensating Sector	AY30	77	A, E, F, O
121755	Seal, Dust (Rubber)	AY27	77	A, E, F
121757	Bearing	AY25	77	A, E, F
121758	Washer, Tab	AY29	77	A, E, F
121759	Pin, Shouldered	AY28	77	A, E, F
121760	Seal, Felt	AY26	77	A, E, F
121765	Bracket, Fulcrum	BU2	110	A, E, F, G, L
121766	Handbrake Cable Assembly	AY11	76	A, E, F
121782	Connector	AX21	74	A, B, E, F, G, L, V, Z
121860	Washer, Tab	AN71	62	A, E, E — 2 Litre, F
121862	Bolt	AN70	62	A, E, E — 2 Litre, F
122022	Shim	AL46	57	A, E, E — 2 Litre, F
122115	Water Pump Plug	D4	9, 32, 62	A, B, E — 2 Litre, F, G, O, P, Z
122126	Seal, Oil	AL56	58	A, E, E — 2 Litre, F, L
122137	Plate, Spring	AL62	58	A, E, E — 2 Litre, F
122257	Valve	B21	5	C, E, E — 2 Litre, O
122289	Pad, Rubber	AV3	71	A, E — 2 Litre, F, G, L, R, Z
122296	Rod, Push	AV33	72	A, E, E — 2 Litre, F
122534	Seal, Dirt	AL51	58	A, E, E — 2 Litre, F
122569	Washer, Joint	AF9	47	A, B, E, E — 2 Litre, F, P
122653	Screw, Set	AH26	48, 51	A, B, E, E — 2 Litre, F, G, L, M, O, P, V, Y
122669	Clamp, Steering Column	AS8	67	A, E, F, G, L
122689	Rear Engine Mounting	AJ10	53	A, E, F
122718	Cap, End	AS6	67	A, E, F, G, L
122719	Washer, Bearing	AS7	67	A, E, F, G, L
122745	Spanner		85	A, E, F, Z
122746	Pouch, Tool		85	A, E, F, O
122747	Clip	AK26	55	F, L

NUMERICAL INDEX

Part No.	Description	Plate No.	Page	Also Used on Models
122806	Plate, Nave	AR9	66	A, E, F
123135	Operating Lever Assembly	AZ35	79	A, E, E — 2 Litre, F P
123203	Plate, Stiffening		55	A, F
123231	Cap, Spring	AL63	58	A, E, E — 2 Litre, F, Z
123312	Bolt	AL32	57	A, E, E — 2 Litre, F
123415	Gasket, Exhaust Flange	BB2	81	A, E, E — 2 Litre, F, O, P
123502	Bracket	AM3	59	A, F, Y
123715	Eye, Lifting, Rear	R70	3, 27	E, E — 2 Litre, O
123716	Eye, Lifting, Front	R69	3, 27	C, E, E — 2 Litre, F, G, O
123760	Clamp	E21	10	C, E, E — 2 Litre, O
123761	Plate, Clamp	E20	10	C, E, E — 2 Litre, O
123803	Screw	AN50	62	A, E, E — 2 Litre, F
123813	Shim, ·009″	AN23	60	A, E, E — 2 Litre, F
123814	Shim, ·013″	AN23	60	A, E, E — 2 Litre, F
123815	Shim, ·014″	AN23	60	A, E, E — 2 Litre, F
123817	Shim, ·020″	AN23	60	A, E, E — 2 Litre, F
123998	Bush	AM2	59	A, E, F
124594	Gasket	A31	2	
125054	Bolt	AH15	51	A, E, F, P, V
125074	Stud	AM9	59	A, E, F
125217	Cover, Dust	AV11	71	A, E, E — 2 Litre, F, G
125441	Packing, Front Road Spring		58	A, E, E — 2 Litre, F
125481	Link Assembly—R.H.	AM7	59	A, E, F
125482	Link Assembly—L.H.	AM8	59	A, E, F
125505	Feeler Gauge Assembly		85	A, E, F, G, P, Y, Z
125531	Ring, Sealing	G8	12, 35	C, E — 2 Litre, G, O, T
125631	Seal, Oil	C35	7, 31	C, E, E — 2 Litre, G, O
125713	Element	G18	12, 35	C
125714	Element	G7	12, 35	
125715	Oil Filter Assembly		12, 35	C
125733	Strut	AL38	57	A, E, E — 2 Litre, F
125781	Screw, Locating	AS10	67	A, E, F, G, L
125782	Plate, Locating	AS9	67	A, E, F, G, L
126607	Cap, Top Cover Extension	AH10	51	
126746	Bracket	AF46	48	A, E, E — 2 Litre, F
126750	Arm Assembly	AH27	51	A, E, E — 2 Litre,
126754	Dowel, Gear Control		51	A, F
126765	Spring	AS33	68	A, F, G, L, O
126784	Pedestal	C62	8, 31	E — 2 Litre, G, O
126785	Gear	C60	8, 31	E — 2 Litre, G, O
126786	Drive Shaft Assembly	C59	8, 31	E — 2 Litre, G, O
126792	Relay, Overdrive	CS39	192	E — 2 Litre, F, G, L, O, R, Y
126938	Bearing	C3	6	E — 2 Litre, O
127262	Ring, Compression	C54	8, 31	E — 2 Litre, O, T
127264	Ring, Scraper	C56	8, 31	C, E — 2 Litre, O
127265	Pin, Gudgeon	T56	31	
127380	Reverse Lamp Switch	BQ8	103, 193	G
127398	Dowel, Special	B14	4	E, E — 2 Litre, O
127651	Ignition Starter Switch	BR16	104, 107	G
127652	Tube, Dipstick	R56	3, 27	E — 2 Litre, G, O
127653	Dipstick Assembly	R54	3, 27	E — 2 Litre, O
127732	Body Assembly	R42	2, 27	C, E — 2 Litre, G, O
127740	Shaft	AH24	51, 193	A, E — 2 Litre, F
127741	Coupling	AH19	51	A, F
127883	Dowel	T25	6, 30	A, E — 2 Litre, F, G, L, O, P, V, Y, Z
127916	Rear No. Plate Lamp		101	A, F, L
127997	Bush, Lower Pinion	AS24	68	A, F, G, L, O
127998	Bush, Upper Pinion	AS28	68	A, E, F, G, L, O
127999	Washer	AS27	68	A, E, F, G, L, O

21

NUMERICAL INDEX

Part No.	Description	Plate No.	Page	Also Used on Models
128000	Washer	AS25	68	A, E, F, G, L, O
128001	Plug, End	AS30	68	A, E, F, G, L, O
128002	Bush, Rack Tube		67	A, E, F, G, L, O, Z
128004	Bellows, Pinion End	AS44	68	A, E, F, G, L, O, Z
128008	Pin		68	A, E, F, G, L, O
128020	Cover, End		67	G
128021	'O' Ring	AS29	68	A, E, F, G, L, O, Z
128022	Nut, Lock	AS51	68	A, E, E — 2 Litre, F, G, L, O, Z
128023	Pin, Ball	AS38	68	A, E, F, L
128024	Housing, Ball	AS37	68	A, E, F, G, L, O, Z
128133	Unit Package	AN53	62, 65	
128135	Shaft, Yoke, Assembly		62, 65	
128262	Sleeve	M8	17, 22, 43	
128334	Valve, Inner Collar	B28	5, 28	A, B, C, E, E — 2 Litre, F, G, L, O, P
128335	Valve, Outer Collar	B27	5, 28	A, B, C, E, E — 2 Litre, F, G, L, O, P
128348	Bolt		198	A, E, F
128352	Plate, Spring	AP4	63, 64	A, F
128356	Shim	AK34	55	A, E, F
128373	Washer, Dished, Inner	AH8	51	
128391	Bearing, Big End	C52	7	C, E, E — 2 Litre, O
128397	Rear Number Plate Lamp	BR45	101	A, F, G, L
128404	Plug, Sparking		24, 45	A, E, E — 2 Litre, F, G, O, Z
128424	Pedestal	B35	5	A, E, E — 2 Litre, F, O, P, T
128425	Pedestal	B33	5	A, E, E — 2 Litre, F, O, P, T
128469	Flinger		62	A, E — 2 Litre, F
128484	Voltage Stabiliser	BR2	104, 106	
128572	Bearing, Ball	AN46	62	A, E — 2 Litre,
128978	Seal, Oil	AN59	62	A, E, E — 2 Litre, F
129058	Rod, Push	B30	5	E, E — 2 Litre, O
129119	Sleeve	AH14	51	A, B, E, F, V
129242	Plug	AL11	56	A, E, E — 2 Litre, F, Z
129383	Stud	E11	10	E — 2 Litre, L, O
129619	Stud	E12	10	C, E, O
129650	Plate, Tapping	AK31	55	A, F
129781	Bolt		61	
129795	Gauze	A51	3	E — 2 Litre, O
129839	Circlip	AG37	49	
129889	Adaptor	A26	2	E, M, O
129897	Bearing, Hub, Outer	AL22	57	D, E, E — 2 Litre, O
129914	Bracket Assembly—L.H.	BL12	92	A, E
129915	Bracket Assembly—R.H.	BL11	92	A, E
129952	Shaft, Operating Assembly	AH11	51	A, E, F
129961	Inner Ball Joint Assembly		68	A, E, F, L
129963	Sleeve, Adaptor	AS41	68	A, E, F, G, L, O, Z
130031	Shim, ·002"	AS40	68	A, E, F, G, L, O, Z
130032	Shim, ·010"	AS40	68	A, E, F, G, L, O, Z
130355	Differential Bearing	AN22	60	A, E, E — 2 Litre, F, P
130757	Bracket, Front	AL40	57	A, E, E — 2 Litre, F
130758	Bracket, Rear	AL41	57	A, E, E — 2 Litre, F
130813	Insert, Exhaust Valve Seat	B5	4	C, E, E — 2 Litre, O
130814	Insert, Valve Seat	B4	4	
131008	Stud, Rear Road Spring	AN4	62	A, E, E — 2 Litre
131155	Grommet	BD17	83, 94, 95, 191	F, G, L, O
131169	Screw, s/t		102	C, E, F, Y, Z
131211	Connector	M7	22	A, L, P
131251	Flasher Unit	BL18	93	E, F, L, M, O
131312	Grip, Handbrake Lever	AY6	76	A, E, F, G, L, M, O, Z
131535	Spring, Piston	R39	2, 27	A, E, E — 2 Litre, F, G, O, P, Z
131567	Rear Hub and Stud	AN72	62	A, E, E — 2 Litre, F

NUMERICAL INDEX

Part No.	Description	Plate No.	Page	Also Used on Models
131570	Packing, Starter Motor		89	A, E, F, O, P
131608	Reverse Lamp		100	
131796	Rubber, Lower	AN12	62	A, E, E — 2 Litre, F, O
131806	Spring	AY41	77	A, D, E, F, V
131807	Plate	AY42	77	A, E, F, Z
131843	Thrust Washer		49	A, E
131995	Front Flasher Lamp (White Lens)		97	A, F, L
132023	Bolt	AN54	62, 65	
132053	Cap, Screwed	AS35	68	A, E, F, G, L, O
132055	Shim, ·010″	AS34	68	A, E, F, G, L, O, Z
132065	Stub Axle	AL15	57	D, E, E — 2 Litre,
132066	Bearing, Hub, Inner	AL19	57	D, E, E — 2 Litre, G, L, O
132068	Nut, Wing		113	E, F, O, V, Y, Z
132077	Clutch Housing and Front End Cover Assembly	AF4	47	E, E — 2 Litre
132078	Cover, Front End	AF5	47	E, E — 2 Litre
132079	Pin, Fulcrum	AF7	47	E, E — 2 Litre
132080	Clutch Operating Lever Assembly	AE25	46	E, E — 2 Litre
132097	Gear, 3rd Speed	AG21	49	E, E — 2 Litre
132104	Bracket, Suspension Inner Support Assembly R.H.		54	A, E, F
132105	Bracket, Suspension Inner Support Assembly L.H.	AK4	54	A, E, F
132107	Piston, Oil Relief	R38	2, 27	A, E, E — 2 Litre, F, G, O, P, Z
132115	Stud	CS1	192	E, E — 2 Litre, F
132135	Ignition/Starter Switch		200	A, E, F, L, O
132239	Rod, Push	AE34	46	E
132292	Seal, Oil	AF8	47	E, E — 2 Litre
132300	Outer Axle Shaft and Flinger Assembly (B.R.D.)	AN52	62	E, E — 2 Litre
132328	Flange, Yoke	AQ47	62, 65	
132419	Washer	AN14	62	E — 2 Litre, F
132435	Bracket, Mounting	AK20	54	A, E, F
132439	Bolt	AZ12	78	A, E, E — 2 Litre, F, Z
132495	Stud, Rocker Pedestal	B9	4, 28	A, C, E, E — 2 Litre, F, G, L, O, P, Z
132565	Tap, Water Drain	BA3	80	A, F, G, L, Z
132586	Lever, Handbrake	AY1	76	A, E, F
132588	Rod Assembly		76	
132589	Handbrake Assembly		76	A, E
132664	Seal, Oil	AT18	57	A, D, E, E — 2 Litre, F, P
132665	Cover, Hub End	AL26	57	E, E — 2 Litre
132666	Washer	AL23	57	D, E, E — 2 Litre, O
132668	Seal, Felt		57	
132669	Mounting, Engine, Front	AJ5	53	
132754	Bracket Assembly—R.H.	AK25	55	F
132763	Rear Vertical Link Assembly—R.H.		63	A, E, F
132764	Rear Vertical Link Assembly—L.H.	AP21	63	A, E, F
132819	Bracket Assembly—L.H.	AK24	55	F
132856	Bolt	AN10	60	A, E — 2 Litre, F, G, L
132872	Bolt		48	A, E — 2 Litre, F, O
133070	Shim	AP12	63	F
133071	Bracket		92	E, O
133103	Plug, Grease	AS36	68	A, E, F, L, O, Z
133122	Bracket		54	F
133234	Key	C8	6, 30	E — 2 Litre, G, O
133235	Sleeve	C10	6, 30	E — 2 Litre, G, O
133238	Adaptor, Fan	C12	6, 30	E — 2 Litre
133239	Pulley	D14	9, 32	E — 2 Litre, G, O
133244	Pulley and Damper	C11	6, 30	E, E — 2 Litre, O
133258	Housing, Bearing, Assembly		9, 32	E, E — 2 Litre, G, O
133284	Front Engine Mounting Bracket Assembly—R.H.	AJ1	53	
133285	Front Engine Mounting Bracket Assembly—L.H.		53	
133524	Bush, Rubber	AP27	63	

NUMERICAL INDEX

Part No.	Description	Plate No.	Page	Also Used on Models
133568	Mounting Rubber, Upper	AN11	62	A, E — 2 Litre, D, F
133579	Reservoir	AV55	72	
133580	Adaptor	AV52	72	
133581	Cap, Filler	AV58	72	
133582	Seal, Adaptor	AV54	72	F
133770	Bracket Assembly	CS46	193	E — 2 Litre, F
133771	Arm Assembly	CS11	51, 192	E — 2 Litre, F
133803	Stud, Short	A18	2	E — 2 Litre, O
133868	Support, Pivot Bracket—R.H.	AK9	54	F
133869	Support, Pivot Bracket—L.H.	AK10	54	F
133875	Plate	AS54	68	A, E — 2 Litre, F, G, O
133913	Grommet	AY12	76	F
133915	Cable Assembly	AY34	77	F
133919	Mounting Bracket Assembly		110	F
134001	Rod Assembly	AY4	77	F
134065	Bearing	AN32	61	E — 2 Litre
134070	Bearing	AN35	61	E — 2 Litre
134072	Pin, Cross	AN30	61	A, E — 2 Litre
134073	Gear, Differential, 16 Teeth	AN26	61	A, E — 2 Litre
134074	Pinion, Differential, 10 Teeth	AN28	61	A, E — 2 Litre
134075	Washer, Thrust	AN27	61	A, E — 2 Litre
134076	Washer, Thrust	AN29	61	A, E — 2 Litre
134143	Pawl	AY2	76	F, L
134229	Mounting, Flexible	CS15	192	E, E — 2 Litre, F
134253	Handbrake Assembly		76	F
134295	Link Pivot Assembly, Bonnet	AK8	54	F
134301	Lead, Earth		103	E, G, L, O
134330	Harness, Gearbox	CS37	192	E, E — 2 Litre
134336	Tool, Nave, Plate		85	A, E, F, O
134399	Outrigger Assembly R.H.—Intermediate	AK15	54	F
134400	Outrigger Assembly L.H.—Intermediate	AK16	54	F
134503	Brake Pedal	AV12	71	F
134504	Clutch Pedal—L.H.S.	AV1	71	F
134529	Stop Lamp Switch	BQ1	102	A, E — 2 Litre, F, G, L, M, O, Z
134532	Bracket	AV17	71	A, E — 2 Litre, F
134540	Bearing	AT11	69, 70	E, F, M
134545	Throttle Operating Link Rod Assembly		69	
134574	Washer	BD12	83, 84	
134575	Ring, Locking	BD13	83, 84	
134580	Bracket, Mounting	AK12	54	F
134589	Bearing, Outer	AQ16	65	
134746	Wheelbox	BM12	94	F
134747	Bush	BM13	94, 95	F
134748	Bush	BM15	94, 95	F
134751	Seal, Rubber	BM14	94, 95	F
134757	Trip, Flex, Speedo	BR3	104, 106	F
134761	Cover, Top, Sub-assembly	AF24	48	A, E, E — 2 Litre
134862	Relay Lever Assembly	AY24	77	A, F
134887	Engine Lead Complete, No. 4		24	E, E — 2 Litre, F, G, O, Z
134953	Washer, Felt	AT12	69, 70	E, F, O
136482	Bolt, Shouldered	AU16	70	G, L, O
136581	Rear Flasher Lamp		99	F, L
136600	Ball Joint Assembly	AS48	68	A, E — 2 Litre, F
136604	Ball Joint Assembly	AL5	56	A, E — 2 Litre, F
136868	Piece, Distance		54	F
136869	Bolt	AN5	62	
136885	Clamp Assembly	AS53	68	E — 2 Litre, F, G, L, O
136890	Bracket Assembly	AJ16	53	A, F
136908	Connection, 3-way, Rear	AX23	74, 75	

NUMERICAL INDEX

Part No.	Description	Plate No.	Page	Also Used on Models
136939	Connection, 4-way	AX2	74	A, E, F, L, Z
136990	Plunger	AF40	48	A, E, E — 2 Litre, F, G
137015	Bracket	AT4	69	F
137048	Clip	AX8	74	A, F, G, L, O
137308	Spring, Ring	CT22	194, 195	E, E — 2 Litre, F
137482	Spring, Throttle Return	AT28	69	
137531	Weight, Balance, ½ oz.		199	F, G, L, O, Z
137532	Spring		50	E — 2 Litre
137615	Gear, 2nd Speed	AG17	49	E — 2 Litre
137624	Strap	BA16	80	O
137632	Overflow Bottle	BA12	80	G
137687	Piece, Distance	AG47	50	E — 2 Litre
137691	Cap, Filler	BA2	80	G
137705	Temperature Transmitter	BR6	9, 32, 104, 106	A, E — 2 Litre, F, G, O
137743	Cap	BA13	80	G
137747/1	Horn Relay		92	F, L, O
137747/2	Horn Relay	BL6	92	F, L, O
137775	Washer	AG8	49	E — 2 Litre
137801	Stop	AJ14	53	A, E
137811	Plug, Rocker Shaft	S46	29	
137834	Collar, Split	AG10	49	E, E — 2 Litre, Z
137841	Valve	B22	5	E, E — 2 Litre, O
137842	Bracket Assembly	AV6	71	A, E — 2 Litre, F
137876	Hose	E27	10, 33	E — 2 Litre, F, O
137881	Washer, Joint	Z82	17	A, E — 2 Litre, O, Z
137882	Washer, Insulating	Z81	17	A, E — 2 Litre, O, Z
137978	Bush	A13	1, 26	E — 2 Litre, G, O
138051	Ring, Sealing	AL29	57	A, E, E — 2 Litre, F
138077	Support, Bracket	AV60	72	F
138126	Plate	A30	2	E, E — 2 Litre, O
138311	Strip	N3	23, 44	E — 2 Litre, O
138316/I	Cable, Inner—L.H.S.		104, 106	E, F
138316/O	Cable, Outer—L.H.S.		104, 106	E, F
138322	Extension		192	F
138323	Extension	CS36	192	F
138386	Petrol Pipe Assembly	Z90	17, 42	E — 2 Litre, G, O
138440	Washer, Thrust	AN29	61	A, E — 2 Litre
138441	Washer, Thrust	AN29	61	
138442	Washer, Thrust	AN29	61	A, E — 2 Litre
138478	Wiper Blade	BM21	94	F
138479	Wiper Arm—R.H.S.	BM20	94	F
138480	Wiper Arm—L.H.S.		94	F
138516	Bracket	Z88	17, 42	E — 2 Litre, G, O
138526	Bolt, Place		6	
138529	Bolt, Place	C51	7, 31	A, C, E, E — 2 Litre, F, G, O, Z
138530	Adaptor	E25	10, 11, 33, 34	
138548	Connecting Rod Assembly	C48	7	C, E, E — 2 Litre, O
138559	Water Shield	AL14	56	A, E, E — 2 Litre, F
138608	Grommet		22, 43	F
138685	Bush, Spherical	AH4	51	A, E, F
138686	Bush	AH13	51	A, E, F
138701	Gasket	D18	9, 32	A, C, E, E — 2 Litre, F, G, O, Z
138737	Cigarette Lighter (Pull-out Type)		197	
138791	Gasket	H25	13, 36	C, E, E — 2 Litre, G, O
138792	Gasket	D21	9, 32	C, E, E — 2 Litre, G, O
138807	Clip	BB12	81	E — 2 Litre, F, G, L, O
138810	Adaptor	E5	10, 33	E — 2 Litre, G, O
138822	Elbow	E10	10, 33	E — 2 Litre, O
138887	Suction Pipe	M11	17, 22	E — 2 Litre, G, O

NUMERICAL INDEX

Part No.	Description	Plate No.	Page	Also Used on Models
138892	Clip	M16	17, 22	
138926	Operating Valve	CT14	194	E, E — 2 Litre, F
139126	Bracket, Stowage	AM4	59	F
139288	Cover Assembly, Oil Pump Body		2	E, E — 2 Litre, G
139289	Oil Pump Assembly		2	E, E — 2 Litre, G
139500	Engine Lead Complete No. 2		24	E, E — 2 Litre, G, O
139521	Bracket—R.H.		55	A, E, F
139522	Bracket—L.H.		55	A, E, F
139523	Pipe Assembly—L.H.	AX29	75	A, E, F
139530	Cap, Bearing	AN48	62	A, E, E — 2 Litre
139531	Inner Axle Shaft Assembly	AN45	62	E — 2 Litre
139532	Circlip	AN47	62	E — 2 Litre
139538	Engine Lead Complete, No. 1		24	E, E — 2 Litre, G, O
139539	Engine Lead Complete, No. 3		24	E, E — 2 Litre, G, O
139540	Engine Lead Complete, No. 5 & 6		24	E, E — 2 Litre, G, O
139809	Piston Assembly	C53	8, 31	E — 2 Litre, O
139819	Ring, Compression	C55	8, 31	E — 2 Litre, O
139827	Bracket	BB17	81	F
139836	Stud	A19	2, 26	E, E — 2 Litre, G, O
140073	Weight, Balance, 1 oz.		199	F, G, L, O, Z
140074	Weight, Balance, 1½ oz.		199	F, G, L, O, Z
140075	Weight, Balance, 2 oz.		199	F, G, L, O, Z
140549	Clip	AS5	67, 200	A, E, F, G, L, Z
140690	Front Flasher Lamp and Cable Assembly (White Lens)		98	F, L
140727	Washer	AG22	49	E — 2 Litre
140755	Steering Column Upper Assembly	AS4	67	A, E, F
140790	Shim, ·030″	AN36	61	E — 2 Litre
140791	Shim, ·010″	AN36	61	E — 2 Litre
140792	Shim, ·005″	AN36	61	E — 2 Litre
140793	Shim, ·003″	AN36	61	E — 2 Litre
140892	Bearing	AL49	58	A, E, E — 2 Litre, F
140893	Piece, Distance	AL50	58	A, E, E — 2 Litre, F
140894	Water Shield	AL48	58	A, E, E — 2 Litre, F
140895	Water Shield	AL52	58	A, E, E — 2 Litre, F
140913	Flange	AN38	61	E — 2 Litre
140919	Bottom Trunnion Assembly—R.H.		58	A, E, E — 2 Litre, F
140920	Bottom Trunnion Assembly—L.H.	AL47	58	A, E, E — 2 Litre, F
140970	Thermostat Unit (82° opening)	D26	9, 32	A, E, E — 2 Litre, F, G, L, O, Z
140986	Hose	E33	10, 33	E, E — 2 Litre
141185	Seal, Dirt	AN63	62	A, E — 2 Litre, F, L
141218	Bearing	AN62	62	A, E, E — 2 Litre, F
141221	Piece, Distance	AN60	62	A, E, E — 2 Litre, F
141242	Seal, Oil	AN37	61	E — 2 Litre
141244	Clutch Spring Diaphragm	AE10	46	O
141357	Clutch Throwout Bearing	AE23	46	E — 2 Litre, O
141443	Shim	AN64	62	A, E, E — 2 Litre, F
141444	Shim	AN61	62	A, E, E — 2 Litre, F
141850	Bolt, Outer	AQ58	65	
142123	Pipe, Overflow	BA15	80	E
142139	Adaptor, Flexible Joint	AS16	67	A, F, Z
142140	Flexible Joint Assembly		67	A, F, Z
142224	Bracket Assembly	AK11	54	
142281	Clip	BB6	81	
142301/1	Horn, Low Note		92	O
142301/2	Horn, Low Note	BL5	92	
142333	Washer	AN75	62, 65	
142337	Seal, Oil, Outer	AQ62	65	

NUMERICAL INDEX

Part No.	Description	Plate No.	Page	Also Used on Models
142340	Shim	AQ66	65	
142462	Lever Assembly	AT14	69	
142519	Throttle Operating Link Rod Assembly	AT25	69	
142597	Hub Adaptor—R.H.	AR11	66	A, E, F
142598	Hub Adaptor—L.H.		66	A, E, F
142795	Nut, Lock	AS43	68	E, E — 2 Litre, G, L
142919	Bearing, Inner	AQ60	65	
143136	Knob	BR24	105	A, Z
143289	Washer, ·093"/·091" th.	AG5	49	E — 2 Litre
143290	Washer, ·096"/·094" th.	AG5	49	E — 2 Litre
143291	Washer, ·099"/·097" th.	AG5	49	E — 2 Litre
143292	Washer, ·102"/·100" th.	AG5	49	E — 2 Litre
143313	Bracket	F6	11, 34	E — 2 Litre, L
143320	Hose	AX14	74	E — 2 Litre, G, L
143323	Hose	F9	11, 34	E — 2 Litre, L, O
143393	Cap, Oil Filler	B48	5, 29	A, E — 2 Litre, F, G, L, O, Z
143407	Valve, Emission Control	F5	11	E — 2 Litre, F, L, O
143437	Bracket	P6	11, 24	E — 2 Litre
143456	Seal, Oil	R33	2, 27	A, E, E — 2 Litre, F, G, O, Z
143552	Valve, Tappet	B31	5, 28	A, E, E — 2 Litre, F, G, O, Z
143577	Fuel Gauge	BR7	104	
143650	Link, Dynamo Adjusting	P20	24	E — 2 Litre
143689	Flywheel Assembly	C24	6	E — 2 Litre
143706	Hose, Inlet Manifold	F3	11, 34	E — 2 Litre, O
143707	Sleeve, Clutch Throw-out	AE24	46	E — 2 Litre
143747	Link, Throttle Return Spring	AT29	69	
143775	Fan	BJ23	90	
143794/1	Horn, High Note	BL4	92	
143794/2	Horn, High Note		92	
143796	Body, Harness		102	
143802	Nut, Clevloc	Q8	25, 45	
143826	Seal, Oil, Inner	AQ59	65	
143841	Windscreen Wiper Switch	BR35	105	
143843	Roof Lamp Switch	BR38	105	
143923	Piece, Distance	AQ65	65	
143924	Piece, Distance	AQ65	65	
143925	Piece, Distance	AQ65	65	
143952	Washer		68	
144095	Knob	AH38	52	E — 2 Litre, Z
144193	Bearing, Big End		7	E — 2 Litre
144194	Bearing		6	E — 2 Litre
144195	Washer, Thrust	T3	6, 30	E — 2 Litre, G
144233	Key	AQ50	65	
144278	Rear Damper	AP25	63	
144326	Bracket		55	F, G
144351	Horn, High Note		92	G
144353	Lead, Interior Light		102	
144354	Lead		103	
144370/O	Cable, Outer—R.H.S.	BR14	104, 106	
144370/I	Cable, Inner—R.H.S.	BR13	104, 106	
144504	Nut	AR12	66	A, F
144509	Hose, Bleed	BA8	80	
144510	Ring, Sealing	BE2	83, 84	O
144530	Switch, Heater	BR32	105, 136	
144542	Petrol Pipe Assembly		83	A, F
144580	Reverse Idler Gear Assembly	AG45	50	E — 2 Litre
144595	Countershaft	AG38	50	E — 2 Litre
144621	Bearing, Speedo Assembly	AF18	47	E — 2 Litre
144627	Gear, 1st Speed	AG9	49	E — 2 Litre

27

NUMERICAL INDEX

Part No.	Description	Plate No.	Page	Also Used on Models
144648	Plug, Core		4, 28	A, E — 2 Litre, F, G, L, Z
144656	Cable	BP57	101	F
144668	Bolt	AN25	61	
144686	Plug, Core	R7	1, 26, 28	A, E — 2 Litre, F, G, O, Z
144687	Plug, Core	R8	1, 26	A, E — 2 Litre, F, G, O, Z
144688	Plug, Core	R6	1, 26	A, E — 2 Litre, F, G, O, Z
144690	Flange and Stoneguard—Mainshaft	AG29	49	E — 2 Litre
144782	Bearing	AG33	49	E — 2 Litre
144795	Hose	BD20	83, 84	
144817	Vent Pipe	BD14	83	
144826	Pipe, Outlet	BD15	83	
144866	Bracket Assembly	CS13	192	E — 2 Litre
144868	Platform Assembly	CS14	192	E — 2 Litre
144961	Bolt	AR3	66	
145002	Temperature Gauge	BR5	104	
145007	Hub and Stud Assembly	AL20	57	E — 2 Litre
145021	Cylinder Liner	A34	2, 26	G, O
145106	Plate—R.H.		57	E — 2 Litre
145107	Plate—L.H.	AL28	57	E — 2 Litre
145108	Plug, Nylon		67	A, F, G, L, O
145155	Bolt, Banjo	E7	10	E — 2 Litre, O
145199	Piece, Distance	AJ7	53	
145203	Lighting and Instrument Illumination Master Switch Assembly	BR29	105	
145232	Brake Master Cylinder Assembly		72	E — 2 Litre
145275	Shim, ·004"	C7	6, 30	E — 2 Litre, G, O
145276	Shim, ·006"	C7	6, 30	E — 2 Litre, G, O
145308	Extension		116	
145418	Bracket Assembly—L.H.	AX19	74	E — 2 Litre
145419	Bracket Assembly—R.H.	AX18	74	E — 2 Litre
145452	Bracket	AX15	74	
145454	Bracket—L.H.	AX11	74	E — 2 Litre
145455	Bracket—R.H.	AX10	74	E — 2 Litre
145671	Bracket	BA20	80	
145793	Flasher Indicator Switch	BL25	93	E — 2 Litre
145794	Lighting Switch—R.H.S.	BL28	93	E — 2 Litre
145795	Lighting Switch—L.H.S.		93	E — 2 Litre
145867	Pedestal, No. 1	S33	29	
145868	Pedestal, Intermediate	S34	29	
145869	Pedestal, No. 6	S35	29	
145890	Clip	BQ12	103	A, E — 2 Litre, F, G, Z
145908	Harness, Overdrive	CS35	192	F
145909	Switch, Overdrive—R.H.S.	CS32	192	E — 2 Litre
145910	Switch, Overdrive—L.H.S.		192	E — 2 Litre
145918	Shim, ·075"	AN33	61	E — 2 Litre
145919	Shim, ·0765"	AN33	61	E — 2 Litre
145920	Shim, ·078"	AN33	61	E — 2 Litre
145921	Shim, ·0795"	AN33	61	E — 2 Litre
145922	Shim, ·081"	AN33	61	E — 2 Litre
145923	Shim, ·0825"	AN33	61	E — 2 Litre
145924	Shim, ·084"	AN33	61	E — 2 Litre
145925	Shim, ·0855"	AN33	61	E — 2 Litre
145926	Shim, ·087"	AN33	61	E — 2 Litre
145927	Shim, ·0885"	AN33	61	E — 2 Litre
145928	Shim, ·090"	AN33	61	E — 2 Litre
145929	Shim, ·0915"	AN33	61	E — 2 Litre
145930	Shim, ·093"	AN33	61	E — 2 Litre
145931	Shim, ·0945"	AN33	61	E — 2 Litre
145932	Shim, ·096"	AN33	61	E — 2 Litre

NUMERICAL INDEX

Part No.	Description	Plate No.	Page	Also Used on Models
145933	Spacer	AN34	61	E — 2 Litre
145938	Adaptor Assembly	E6	10, 33	E — 2 Litre
145968	Driven Plate Assembly	AE8	46	E — 2 Litre
146027	Pad, Lining	AZ6	78	E — 2 Litre
146028	Rear Wheel Cylinder Assembly		79	E — 2 Litre
146086	Felt	BD2	83, 84, 147	
146087	Felt, Strip	CL29	147	
146088	Felt, Strip	BD3	83, 84	
146102	Coupling, Flange	CT101	196	E — 2 Litre
146112	Coil, Ignition	BF33	86	E — 2 Litre, F, G, O
146113	Engine Lead		24, 45	E — 2 Litre, G, O
146128	Valve, Inlet	S21	28	
146163	Bracket	BB5	81	
146186	Lever, Throttle	K13	15	E — 2 Litre
146199	Pipe Assembly—R.H.S.	AX35	75	
146200	Stud	R17	26	G
146240	Shaft, Selector 1st/2nd	AF29	48	E — 2 Litre
146241	Sleeve, 1st/2nd, Selector Shaft	AF30	48	E — 2 Litre
146250	Horn, Super Post		92	O
146258	Lead, Reverse Light Switch	BQ10	103	E — 2 Litre
146273	Plate		199	G
146275	Seal		199	G
146285	Adaptor		199	G
146297	Lever Assembly	AT23	69	
146303	Washer, Plain		51	A
146305	Lead		103	F
146315	Bracket, Pivot—R.H.		63	
146316	Bracket, Pivot—L.H.	AP10	63	
146317	Radius Arm Assembly	AP14	63	
146321	Bush, Rubber	AP16	63	
146366	Pouch, Tool		85	F, G, O
146413	Brake Master Cylinder Support Bracket		72	F, G
146431	Thermostat Unit (88° opening)		9, 32	A, E — 2 Litre, F, G, O
146454	Connecting Rod Assembly	T47	31	E — 2 Litre, G
146496	Insert, Valve Seat, Inlet Valve	S5	28	
146497	Insert, Valve Seat, Exhaust Valve	S4	28	
146711	Horn, Post		92	
146728	Ball Joint Assembly		68	A, F, Z
146906	Lever, Hand Assembly	AH3	51	
147249	Washer, Thrust	AN29	61	A, E — 2 Litre
147250	Washer, Thrust	AN29	61	A, E — 2 Litre
147251	Washer, Thrust	AN29	61	A, E — 2 Litre
147252	Washer, Thrust	AN29	61	A, E — 2 Litre
147299	Bolt, Flywheel	T26	6, 30	
147333	Fan, Dynamo Pulley	P5	24	A, E — 2 Litre, O
147354	Bush	AG18	49	E — 2 Litre
147374	Rivet		48, 193	E — 2 Litre
147394	Actuator, Reverse Gear	AF35	48	E — 2 Litre
147395	Shaft, Selector, Reverse Actuator	AF32	48	E — 2 Litre
147471	Reverse Light Switch		103	F
147474	Washer, Alum.	AH21	51	A, E — 2 Litre
147496	Lever, Throttle	Z13	15	E — 2 Litre
147530	Pulley	BJ24	90, 91	G
147547	Side and Flasher Lamp		98	F
147548	Side and Flasher Lamp		98	F
147549	Gasket, Lens Seating	BO52	98	F
147550	Rear Flasher Lamp, Red Lens		100	F
147551	Rear Flasher Lamp, Amber Lens		100	F
147552	Gasket, Lamp Seating	BP32	100	F

NUMERICAL INDEX

Part No.	Description	Plate No.	Page	Also Used on Models
147553	Bezel, Flasher Lamp	BP33	100	F
147592	Plinth, Flasher Lamp	BP34	100	F
147621	Lead Set, Extension		200	F
147629	Platform, Overdrive Mounting		192	
147630	Plate, Support, Overdrive		192	
147632	Mounting, Rear Engine		192	
147659	Washer, Joint	L83	20, 41	
147660	Washer, Insulating	L82	20, 41	
147668	Harness, Overdrive		192	F
147706	Link, Alternator Adjusting	Q9	25	
147747	Pipe Assembly, Rear, L.H.S. only		74	
147748	Pipe Assembly, Front, L.H.S. only		74	
147775	Cover, Top Sub-assembly		48	E — 2 Litre, F
147777	Extension		103	G
147788	Support Assembly—R.H.		54	F
147789	Support Assembly—L.H.		54	F
147852	Mounting Rubber, Rack and Pinion Assembly	AS52	68	
147906	Pulley, Dynamo		24	A, E — 2 Litre
147951	Bolt		200	F
147990	Fan, Alternator	BK15	91	
147993	Bush, Mounting	AN3	60	A, F
148006	Gasket	N5	23, 44	
148042	Flywheel Assembly	T23	6, 30	E — 2 Litre
148083	Segment, Ratchet		76	A, G
148099	Shim, ·077"	AN33	61	
148100	Shim, ·079"	AN33	61	
148101	Shim, ·080"	AN33	61	
148102	Shim, ·082"	AN33	61	
148103	Shim, ·083"	AN33	61	
148104	Shim, ·085"	AN33	61	
148105	Shim, ·086"	AN33	61	
148124	Bracket, Mounting—R.H.		199	
148125	Bracket, Mounting—L.H.		199	
148156	Tandem Brake Master Cylinder Bracket	AW29	73	
148322	Seal	D6	9, 32	
148353	Plug	R5	1, 26	A, G
148387	Valve, Exhaust		5	
148400	Valve, Vacuum Control	M1	22	G
148409	Cup, Synchro, 1st/2nd Gears	AG15	49	
148461	Strap, Anti-torque		131, 200	
148504	Hose Assembly, Oil Cooler to Filter		199	
148505	Hose Assembly, Oil Cooler to Cylinder Block		199	
148513	Clip, Hoses to Bracket		199	
148514	Bracket, Hoses to Front Engine Mounting Bolts		199	
148533	Steering Column Locking Device and Ignition Switch Kit		200	
148576	Hazard Flasher Unit	BL24	93	G
148644	Flasher Unit	BL23	93	G
148646	Lead, Loop		93	
148647	Lighting Switch, Headlamp Dip and Flash, L.H.S.	BL29	93	
148805	Washer, Thrust	AN29	61	A
148830	Hazard Warning Light	BS33	105, 107	
148850	Spacer		65	
148874	Bush, Lower Wishbone	AQ25	64	
148926	Bush, Outer	AQ26	64	
148939	Water Shield	AQ28	64	
148940	Water Shield	AQ30	64	
148948	Tube, Distance	AQ27	64	
148950	Seal, Dust	AQ29	64	

NUMERICAL INDEX

Part No.	Description	Plate No.	Page	Also Used on Models
148957	Plug, Sparking		24, 54, 199	G
148963	Bracket Assembly	AQ20	64	
148969	Bolt	AQ40	64	
148972	Stop, Throttle, Adjustable	AU21	70	G
148975	Bracket Assembly, Mounting		64	
148976	Bracket Assembly	AQ11	64	
149003	Bolt	AQ32	64	
149025	Spring, Throttle Return	AU25	70	
149027	Lever Assembly	AU8	70	
149028	Connecting Link and Socket Assembly	AU24	70	
149030	Lever, Bell Crank	AU15	70	
149051	Rear Hub and Stud Assembly	AQ63	65	
149081	Bearing, Big End	T51	7, 31	
149082	Bearing, Main	T2	6, 30	G
149137	Tube, P.V.C.		105, 107	
149185	Rear Damper	AQ36	65	
149309	Pipe Assembly	M9	22	
149310	Pipe Assembly	M6	22	
149353	Plate Assembly		77	
149361	Bolt, Banjo	M18	22	
149362	Banjo, Connector	M17	22	G
149380	Sleeve	M14	22	G
149381	Connector	M10	22	G
149386	Pipe Suction, P.V.C.	M13	22	
149426	Washer, Tab		79	
149435	Throttle Operating Link Rod Assembly		69	
149621	Filter, Oil Pump	R45	27	
149633	Spring, Valve, Outer	S25	28	
149634	Oil Pump Assembly		27	
149636	Filter, Petrol		83, 84	
149649	Bracket Assembly—L.H.		55	
149650	Bracket Assembly—R.H.		55	
149658	Valve, Exhaust	S22	28	
149698	Tube, Distance—L.H.S.		67, 130	
149717	Collar, Spring, Lower	S23	28	
149753	Wiper Arm—L.H.S.		94	
149759	Wiper Blade—L.H.S.		94	
149769	Lower Wishbone Assembly—R.H.		64	
149770	Lower Wishbone Assembly—L.H.	AQ24	64	
149776	Bush, Oil Pump Drive Shaft	A13	1, 26	G
149777	Adjustable Control Rod Assembly	AU10	70	
149842	Clip, Filter		83, 84	
149843	Connector, Top		83	
149844	Connector, Bottom		83	
149865	Stoneguard		65	
149878	Special Oil		85	E — 2 Litre
149945	Bracket—R.H.		55	
149963	Washer, Thrust		49	
149967	Lead, Extension		103	G
149971	Switch, Warning Light		74	G
149973	Hose, Flexible Rear—R.H.		75	
149974	Pipe Assembly		75	
149975	Pipe Assembly		75	
149976	Piston Assembly (Graded F, G & H)		8, 31	
149977	Hose, Flexible, Rear—L.H.		75	
149991	Bracket Assembly, Rear Axle Mounting		54	
150030	Engine Lead Assembly, No. 2		24, 45	
150031	Engine Lead Assembly, No. 3		24, 45	
150032	Engine Lead Assembly, No. 6		24, 45	

NUMERICAL INDEX

Part No.	Description	Plate No.	Page	Also Used on Models
150038	Engine Lead Assembly, No. 1		24, 45	
150039	Engine Lead Assembly, No. 4 & 5		24, 45	
150052	Engine Lead		24, 45	
150064	Steering Lock Upper Assembly		67	
150162	Fuel Gauge	BS15	106	
150163	Temperature Gauge	BS13	106	
150277	Horn Push Assembly	BL1	92	
150340	Link, Adjusting, Alternator	AD8	45	
150377	Heated Back Door Glass Switch	BS17	106	
150378	Windscreen Wiper and Washer Switch (2 Speed)	BS35	107	
150379	Interior Lamp Switch	BS16	106	
150380	Lighting and Instrument Illumination Master Switch Assembly	BS18	106	
150381	Hazard Warning Light Switch	BS34	107	
150383	Knob, Gear Lever		52	
150461	Body Harness		102	
150516	Interior Light and Heated Backlight Harness		102	
150531	Gasket	R23	26	
150550	Engine Lead Assembly, No. 1		24, 45	
150551	Engine Lead Assembly, No. 2		24, 45	
150552	Engine Lead Assembly, No. 3		24, 45	
150553	Engine Lead Assembly, No. 4		24, 45	
150554	Engine Lead Assembly, No. 5		24, 45	
150555	Engine Lead Assembly, No. 6		24, 45	
150583	Rubber, Bump	AQ44	65	
150592	Pipe Assembly	BE37	84	
150593	Pipe Assembly	BE27	84	
150698	Connector, Flexible	BE36	84	
150786	Screw, 'Taptite'	AQ45	65	
150804	Lead, Extension		102	
150844	Pad, Fixing, Rubber	BN7	95	
150845	Sleeve, Rubber		95	
150846	Strap and Sleeve Assembly	BN6	95	
150987	Driven Plate Assembly (Laycock)	AE16	46	
151073	Push Rod	S30	28	
151092	Radius Arm Assembly		64	
151093	Eye, Front	AQ14	64	
151094	Eye, Rear	AQ13	64	
151099	Adjuster	AQ15	64	
151100	Pipe, Suction		22	
151101	Pipe, Suction, Nylon	AB1	22, 43	
151102	Pipe, Suction	AB3	43	
151110	Nut, Lock	AQ16	64	
151134	Block, Sealing	R22	26	
151141	Plate, Stiffener		135	
151190	Strap, Anti-torque		135, 200	
151219	Wheelbox Assembly		95	
151343	Bracket, Support	BC5	82	
151493	Shroud Assembly, Steering Column		134	
151496	Steering Column Upper Assembly		67, 200	
151658	Valve, Emission Control	W5	35	
151824	Stud, Rear Road Spring		62	
151872	Side Marker Assembly—Front—Amber		98	
151873	Side Marker Assembly—Rear—Red		100	
151956	Wiper Arm—L.H.		95	
151957	Wiper Arm—R.H.	BN16	95	
151958	Wiper Blade	BN17	95	
152273	Rotoflex Coupling	AQ56	65	
152330	Steering Column Locking Kit		200	

NUMERICAL INDEX

Part No.	Description	Plate No.	Page	Also Used on Models
200535	Starter Motor		86	A, B, E, F, G, O, P
201316	Housing, Bearing	D3	9, 32	
201350	Ring, Gear	C25	6	
203077	Brake Drum	AZ41	79	A, E, E — 2 Litre, P
204226	Rear Hub Inner Assembly	AN56	62	A, E, E — 2 Litre, F
204736	Rocker Shaft	B32	5	E, E — 2 Litre, O, P, T
204741	Clip	BL3	92	G
205456	Front Engine Plate	A58	3	A, B, E, E — 2 Litre, P
205504	Tie Rod Lever—R.H.		57	A, E, E — 2 Litre, F
205505	Tie Rod Lever—L.H.	AL27	57	A, E, E — 2 Litre, F
206623	Petrol Pump Assembly		13	E — 2 Litre, O
206685	Lower Wishbone—R.H.		57	A, E, E — 2 Litre, F
206686	Lower Wishbone—L.H.	AL36	57	A, E, E — 2 Litre, F
207093	Anti-roll Bar		59	A, E, F
207102	Gasket	B13	4	E — 2 Litre, O, T
207492	Timing Cover Assembly	C34	7	B, E, E — 2 Litre, O
208022	Front Damper	AL58	58	A, E, E — 2 Litre
208058	Rack, Steering	AS23	67	A, E, F
208532	Stop Tail Lamp		99	F
208934	Bracket, Damper Support—L.H.		54	E
208935	Bracket—R.H.	AK21	54	A, E, F
208943	Crossmember Assembly	AK23	55	A, E, F
208952	Control Box	BQ4	102	E, E — 2 Litre, M, O
209000	Dynamo		86	F, M, O
209018	Platform, Rear Engine Mounting	AJ19	53	E, F
209072	Vertical Link—R.H.		56	E, E — 2 Litre
209073	Vertical Link—L.H.	AL10	56	E, E — 2 Litre
209259	Back Plate—L.H.	AZ18	78	E, E — 2 Litre
209260	Back Plate—R.H.		78	E, E — 2 Litre
209331	Bracket, Support Assembly	AK22	54	A, E, F
209398	Outrigger Assembly, Front—R.H.	AK13	54	F
209399	Outrigger Assembly, Front—L.H.	AK14	54	F
209423	Bearing Assembly	CA41	130, 134	A, E, F, G, L, P
209438	Crossmember	AK5	54	F
209439	Gusset Assembly—R.H.	AK6	54	F
209440	Gusset Assembly—L.H.	AK7	54	F
209465	Bracket Assembly—L.H.	AK18	54	F
209466	Bracket Assembly—R.H.	AK17	54	F
209590	Gearbox Extension	AF14	47	A, E, E — 2 Litre, F
209688	Steering Column, Lower	AS3	67	F
209754	Pipe—L.H.S.		74	F
209755	Pipe—R.H.S.	AX1	74	F
209836	Bracket and Clutch Pedal—L.H.S.		71	F
209837	Brake Pedal Mounting Assembly		71	F
210601	Rear Crossmember and Axle Mounting Bracket Assembly		54	F
210829	Tube	B18	4	E, E — 2 Litre, O
210834	Pipe	E30	10, 33	E — 2 Litre, O
210908	Rocker Cover Assembly	S48	29	E, E — 2 Litre, O
210926/M	Scissor Jack Assembly		85	A, E, F, Z
210926/MH	Handle		85	A, E, F, Z
210926/P	Scissor Jack Assembly		85	A, E, F, Z
210926/PH	Handle		85	A, E, F, Z
210943	Cover	N1	23	E — 2 Litre, O
210953	Towing Attachment Kit, Rear		199	F
211125	Washer	R51	3, 27	C, E, E — 2 Litre, G, O
211126	Gasket	C42	7, 31	A, C, E, E — 2 Litre, F, G, O, Z
211146	Clutch Cover Assembly (Laycock)	AE9	46	O
211399	Pipe Assembly	AX28	75	A, E, F

NUMERICAL INDEX

Part No.	Description	Plate No.	Page	Also Used on Models
211514	Rear Engine Plate	R66	3, 27	E, E — 2 Litre
211555	Washer	E15	10	C, E, E — 2 Litre, O
211819	Plate, Mounting	AN8	60	E — 2 Litre
211962	Alternator, 11AC—Positive Earth		90	O
211986	Fan Assembly	C16	6	E, E — 2 Litre, G, L, O
212067	Flange, Driven	AQ49	65	
212310	Accelerator Pedal Assembly—R.H.S.	AT1	69	
212344	Road Wheel, Wire	AR10	66	A, F
212425	Spring, Road, Front		58	
212622	Oil Seal Housing, Rear	R32	2, 27	
212667	Accelerator Pedal Assembly—L.H.S.	AT16	69	
212683	Belt, Fan	C23	6	
212766	Washer	A59	3	A, E — 2 Litre, F, O, Z
212770	Manifold, Exhaust	E3	10	E — 2 Litre
212811	Pipe Assembly	BD26	83	
212938	Front Damper and Road Spring Complete Assembly		58	
212971	Elbow, Water	D27	9, 32	
212993	Gear Cluster	AG40	50	E — 2 Litre
213018	Mainshaft	AG1	49	E — 2 Litre
213113	Constant Pinion Shaft	AG32	49	E — 2 Litre
213121	Alternator, 11AC—Negative Earth		90	
213150	Propellor Shaft, B.R.D.	AR1	66	
213151	Propellor Shaft	CS51	66, 193	
213186	Distributor Assembly		86	E — 2 Litre
213190	Revolution Counter	BR4	104	
213227	Friction Disc, Front Brake Caliper	AZ14	78	E — 2 Litre
213232	Cover, Dust—R.H.		78	E — 2 Litre
213233	Cover, Dust—L.H.	AZ17	78	E — 2 Litre
213249	Hose, Bottom	BA10	80	
213330	Pipe Assembly	AX9	74	E — 2 Litre
213469	Axle Housing	AN1	60	E — 2 Litre
213496	Rocker Cover Assembly		5	G
213501	Clutch Cover Assembly (Borg and Beck)		46	E — 2 Litre
213502	Carburettor Assembly, Front		15	E — 2 Litre
213514	Speedometer—Mile	BR1	104	
213515	Speedometer—Kilo		104	
213516	Speedometer—Mile		104	
213517	Speedometer—Kilo		104	
213540	Rear Brake Assembly—R.H.		78	E — 2 Litre
213541	Rear Brake Assembly—L.H.		78	E — 2 Litre
213561	Mainshaft	CS2	49, 192	E — 2 Litre
213577	Petrol Pump Assembly		14, 36	G
213627	Brake Master Cylinder Assembly		72	
213635	Pinion—L.H.S.		68	E — 2 Litre
213636	Pinion—R.H.S.	AS26	68	E — 2 Litre
213658	Washer, Joint		3	G
213690	Brake Master Cylinder Assembly		73	
213776	Gasket, Cylinder Head	S15	28	
213777	Front Engine Plate		3	E — 2 Litre, G
214176	Pipe Assembly, Front		74	
214246	Fan Belt	Q15	25	
214268	Bracket, Alternator Mounting	AD1	25, 45	
214314	Fan Belt		6	E — 2 Litre
214413	Plate, Back	N2	23, 44	
214414	Air Cleaner and Silencer Assembly		23, 44	
214415	Element, Filter	N4	23	
214521	Towing Attachment Kit—Rear		199	
214559	Rocker Shaft	S32	29	

NUMERICAL INDEX

Part No.	Description	Plate No.	Page	Also Used on Models
214562	Rocker Shaft		5	
214572	Oil Cooler		199	
214614	Drive Shaft Assembly, Outer	AQ57	65	
214622	Washer, Joint	V12	33	
214623	Intermediate Drive Shaft Assembly	AQ46	65	
214638	Rear Brake Assembly—R.H.		78	
214639	Rear Brake Assembly—L.H.		78	
214645	Bracket, Mounting—R.H.		54	
214646	Bracket, Mounting—L.H.		54	
214665	Bracket, Support	AU14	70	
214666	Accelerator Pedal Assembly—L.H.S.	AU1	70	
214787	Cable Assembly, Choke Control		105	
214817	Back Plate Assembly—R.H.		78	
214818	Back Plate Assembly—L.H.		78	
214824	Rear Brake Assembly—R.H.		78	
214825	Rear Brake Assembly—L.H.		78	
214830	Fan Belt	T22	30	
214842	Cover, Oil Pump Assembly	R44	27	
214973	Pipe Assembly—R.H.		75	
215038	Speedometer—Mile	BS1	106	
215039	Speedometer—Kilo		106	
215042	Speedometer—Mile		106	
215043	Speedometer—Kilo		106	
215044	Revolution Counter	BS9	106	
215104	Valve Assembly		74	
215166	Pipe Assembly	BE21	84	
215346	Alternator, 15ACR—Negative Earth		91	
215349	Front Engine Plate	R57	27	
215350	Washer, Joint	R58	27	
215398	Front Damper		58	
215418	Front Damper and Road Spring Complete Assembly		58	
215496	Air Cleaner and Silencer Assembly		44	
215497	Cover, Front	AC1	44	
215502	Choke Control Complete Assembly—L.H.S.	BS27	107	
215511	Distributor Assembly		86	
215537	Plate, Mounting		60	
305137	Adaptor, Gearbox	CS3	192	E, E — 2 Litre, F
305592	Bracket Assembly—R.H.	AK27	55	A, E
305593	Bracket Assembly—L.H.	AK28	55	A, E
305764	Pipe Assembly	AX20	74	A, E, F
305778	Casing, Differential		60	A, E — 2 Litre
305911	Pipe Assembly	AX22	74	F
306152	Extension, Top Cover	AK1	51	F
306468	Gearbox Case	AF1	47	E — 2 Litre
306483	Manifold, Exhaust	E1	10	E — 2 Litre, O
306785	Camshaft	C28	7	E — 2 Litre, O
307039	Oil Sump Assembly	A49	3	E, E — 2 Litre
307095	Body, Water Pump	D1	9, 32	E — 2 Litre, G, O
307155	Front Exhaust Pipe Assembly	BB1	81	
307324	Rear Transverse Road Spring Assembly	AP1	63	
307324/M	Leaf, Main		63	
307325	Petrol Tank Assembly	BD1	83	
307405	Road Wheel	AR7	66	A, E — 2 Litre
307471	Petrol Pipe Assembly	K85	17, 42	E — 2 Litre
307474	Gauge, Fuel	BE12	83, 84	
307518	Main Harness—R.H.S.		102	
307519	Main Harness—L.H.S.		102	
307537	Pipe Assembly	BD22	83	

35

NUMERICAL INDEX

Part No.	Description	Plate No.	Page	Also Used on Models
307566	Pipe Assembly—L.H.S.		75	
307619	Steering Wheel		67	E — 2 Litre
307621	Camshaft (U.S.A. only)		7, 30	
307624	Radiator Block Assembly	BA1	80	
307642	Differential Casing	AN21	60	
307718	Crankshaft	C1	6	E — 2 Litre
307755	Pipe Assembly	AX7	74	E — 2 Litre
307811	Rear Silencer and Tail Pipe Assembly	BB29	81	
307830	Rack and Pinion Assembly—R.H.S.		67	E — 2 Litre
307831	Rack and Pinion Assembly—L.H.S.		67	E — 2 Litre
307843	Front Brake Caliper Assembly—L.H.	AZ1	78	E — 2 Litre
307844	Front Brake Caliper Assembly—R.H.		78	E — 2 Litre
307862	Overdrive Unit		192, 194	E — 2 Litre
307869	Intermediate Silencer and Exhaust Pipe Assembly	BB11	81	F
308034	Crankshaft		6	E — 2 Litre
308158	Pipe Assembly—L.H.S.		75	
308159	Pipe Assembly		74	
308170	Rack and Pinion Assembly R.H.S.		67	
308171	Rack and Pinion Assembly—L.H.S.		67	
308263	Skid Plate Assembly		55	
308290	Manifold, Exhaust		33	
308353	Fan Assembly		6	G
308372/2	Distributor Assembly		87	
308411	Main Harness—L.H.S.		102	
308437	Rear Vertical Link—R.H.		64	
308438	Rear Vertical Link—L.H.	AQ10	64	
308487	Carburettor Assembly, Front		18	
308488	Carburettor Assembly, Rear		18	
308499	Rear Transverse Road Spring	AQ1	64	
308499/M	Leaf, Main		64	
308542	Pipe Assembly		74	
308571	Oil Sump Assembly	R49	27	
308601	Main Harness and Fuse Box Assembly—L.H.S.		103	
308607	Steering Wheel (Dull Finish Spokes)	AS1	67	
308671	Manifold, Inlet		33	
308678	Petrol Tank Assembly	BE1	84	
308682	Main Harness and Fuse Box Assembly—R.H.S.		103	
308778	Camshaft	T27	30	
308802	Front Exhaust Pipe Assembly	BC1	82	
308804	Silencer and Tail Pipe	BC23	82	
308864	Front Carburettor Assembly		40	
308865	Rear Carburettor Assembly		40	
402396	Cable, Outer	BR23	105	
402397	Cable, Inner	BR22	105	
402572	Chassis Frame Complete		54	
402644	Chassis Frame Assembly		54	
402759	Pipe, Intermediate	BE25	84	
500047	Circlip, on Spindle	D10	9, 32	A, E — 2 Litre, F, G, L, M, O, R, T, V, Y
500172	Washer	CA25	129, 133	F, G, L
500186	Circlip	AY10	76	A, E, F, J, L, P, T, Y
500309	Washer, Plain	CA20	129, 133	A, E, T
500381	Washer		188	A
500412	Pin, Mills	CT10	194, 195	E, E — 2 Litre, F, P, Y
500463	Washer, on Setscrew	A27	2	E, J, L, M, O, R, T, V, Y
500464	Bolt	AF11	47	
500469	Washer	B8	4, 27, 28	A, B, E, E — 2 Litre, G, M, O, P, V, Z
500492	Glass, Rear Number Plate Lamp	BP62	101	A, E, F, G, L,
500524	Service Kit, Petrol Pump		14, 36, 85	G, J, L, R, T, V
500568	Washer	CT17	194	E, E — 2 Litre, F, G, L, O, P, R, T, Y

NUMERICAL INDEX

Part No.	Description	Plate No.	Page	Also Used on Models
500591	Plunger	CT19	194	E, E — 2 Litre, F, G, J, L, O, P, R, T, Y
500594	Seal	CT13	194	E, E — 2 Litre, F, G, J, L, O, P, R, T, Y
500613	Washer	CT71	195	E, E — 2 Litre, F, G, J, L, O, P, R, T, Y
500633	Spring	CT24	194	E, E — 2 Litre, F, G, J, L, O, P, R, T, Y
500642	Washer	CT55	195	E, E — 2 Litre, F, G, J, L, O, P, R, T, Y
500872	Circlip	AG6	49	
500892	Pinion and Sleeve	BH35	88	A, B, E, F, G, O, P
500926	Bush	BH25	88	A, B, E, F, G, O, P
500927	Bush	BH21	88	A, C, E, F, G, O, P
500974	Pin, Mills	C61	8, 31	A, E, E — 2 Litre, F, G, O, P
500975	Pin, Mills	B46	5	A, B, E, E — 2 Litre, F, G, O, P
501005	Diaphragm Assembly	J9	13, 14, 36	E, E — 2 Litre, G, J, L, O, R, T, Y, Z
501258	Washer	R41	2, 27	A, B, E, F, G, L, O, P, Z
501362	Window	BP48	101	F, L, P
501436	Bulb	BP61	101	A, E, E — 2 Litre, F, L, P, V, Y, Z
501478	Connector	BO6	96, 97	G
501606	Pin, Mills		196	E, E — 2 Litre, F
501704	Cap	BH34	88	A, B, E, F, G, O, P
501705	Brush Set	BH31	88	G
501706	Bracket Assembly	BH24	88	A, B, E, F, G, O, P
501708	Spring Set	BH26	88	A, B, E, F, G, O, P
501709	Nut	BH38	88	A, B, E, F, G, O, P
501710	Spring	BH37	88	G
501711	Spring, Main	BH36	88	A, B, E, F, G, O, P
501712	Bracket Assembly	BH20	88	A, B, E, F, G, O, P
501714	Armature Assembly	BH16	88	A, B, E, F, G, O, P
501715	Coil	BH15	88	A, B, E, F, G, O, P
501794	Washer, Plain		113	A, E, L, O, P, V, Z
501795	Washer, Plain		147	
501823	Bulbholder		100	
502136	Washer, Plain	AS18	67	A, E, F, O, P, Z
502146	Washer	CS44	103, 193	G
502148	Wire		67	A, E, F, P, T, Y, Z
502210	Bolt	BH32	88	A, B, E, F, G, O, P
502264	Cover	BP49	101	A, F, G, L
502287	Bulb	BP5	99	A, E, F, G, L, M, O, P, V, Y, Z
502379	Bulb	BO25	97, 98, 99, 100	G
502450	Nut		147	
502459	Wing Mirror		198	A, E, F, O, P, R, T, Y
502476	Screw		154	A, E, L, O, P
502544	Screw, Capping		129	B, T, Y
502550	Roller Set, Steel	CT69	195	E — 2 Litre, G, J, L, O, P, R, T, Y
502559	Cage, Free Wheel	CT68	195	E, E — 2 Litre, F, G, J, L, O, P, R, T, Y
502560	Breather	CT105	196	E — 2 Litre, F, G, L, P, R, T, Y
502650	Nipple, Spoke		66	A, F, G, L, R
503213	Sleeve, P.V.C.		75, 102	G
503479	Screw, Set		147	
503604	Crosshead and Rack	BN8	95	B, C, T, V, Y, Z
503661	Washer, Plain		187	A, B, E, G, Y
503847	Tool, Combination		85	P, T
503923	Washer, Plain		170, 178, 185	G, P
504603/O	Cable, Outer—L.H.S.		193	A, P, T, Y
504603/I	Cable, Inner—L.H.S.		193	A, P, T, Y
504621/O	Cable, Outer—R.H.S.	CS48	193	E, F, O, P
504621/I	Cable, Inner—R.H.S.	CS47	193	E, F, O, P
504806	Tube, P.V.C.		96, 97	G
504826	Ring, Piston Sealing	AZ3	78	E — 2 Litre, L, R, Y
504827	Boot, Rubber	AZ4	78	E — 2 Litre, G, L, R, Y
504848	Piston	AE29	46	E — 2 Litre, L, R

NUMERICAL INDEX

Part No.	Description	Plate No.	Page	Also Used on Models
504850	Circlip	AE30	46	E — 2 Litre, L, R
504877	Shoe, Hold Down Spring	AZ20	78	A, B, E, E — 2 Litre, F, P, R, Z
504878	Cup, Washer	AZ21	78	A, B, E, E — 2 Litre, F, P, R, Z
504948/O	Cable		104, 106	L, P, Y
504948/I	Cable		104, 106	L, P, Y
505155	Clip		199	G, L, P, R, Z
505239	Valve Assembly	H6	13	A, B, E, E — 2 Litre, F, L, M, O, P, T, V, Y, Z
505240	Retainer	H9	13	A, B, E, E — 2 Litre, M, O, P, T, V, Y, Z
505241	Gasket	H8	13	A, B, E, E — 2 Litre, F, M, O, P, T, V, Y, Z
505307	Washer	CC28	136, 138, 147, 172, 187, 189, 190	G
505704	Service Kit		46, 85	E — 2 Litre, L, R
505771	Nut		189, 190	F, G
505825	Wing Mirror Bezel		198	A, E, F, O, P, R, T, Y
505869	Sundry Parts Set		94	G, L, O, P
505883	Body, Rubber	BO27	97, 99, 100	F, G, L, M, P, R, V, Y
505884	Rim	BO14	97, 100	F, G, L, M, P, R, V, Y
505886	Lens (White)	BO24	97, 100	F, L, M, P, R, V, Y
505887	Lens (Amber)	BO24	97	F, L
506044	Sunwheel Assembly	CT61	195	E, E — 2 Litre, F, P
506066	Bearing	CT90	196	E, E — 2 Litre, F, P
506067	Speedometer Driving Gear Assembly	CT89	196	E — 2 Litre, F, P
506070	Spring	CT18	194	E, E — 2 Litre, F, G, L, O, P
506071	Screw	CT95	196	E, E — 2 Litre, F, G, L, O, P
506076	Screw	CT26	194	E, E — 2 Litre, F, P
506081	Bearing, Housing	CT51	195	E, E — 2 Litre, F, P
506082	Stud	CT2	194	E, E — 2 Litre, F, P
506083	Stud	CT3	194	E, E — 2 Litre, F, P
506084	Piece	CT57	195	E, E — 2 Litre, F, P
506091	Ring	CT62	195	E, E — 2 Litre, F, P
506097	Plate	CT41	194	E, E — 2 Litre, F, P
506098	Washer	CT45	194	E, E — 2 Litre, F, P
506099	Speedometer Driving Gear	CT97	196	E, E — 2 Litre, F, P
506101	Joint Washer		194	E, E — 2 Litre, F
506103	Stud	CT5	194	E, E — 2 Litre, F, P
506104	Plate	CT52	195	E, E — 2 Litre, F, P
506105	Stud	CT4	194	E, E — 2 Litre, F, P
506108	Washer	CT96	196	E, E — 2 Litre, F, G, O, P
506109	Plate	CT82	195	E, E — 2 Litre, F, P
506111	Bearing	CT76	195	E, E — 2 Litre, F, P
506112	Bearing	CT50	195	E, E — 2 Litre, F, P
506113	Bearing	CT74	195	E, E — 2 Litre, F, P
506114	Plug	CT42	194	E, E — 2 Litre, F, P
506115	'O' Ring	CT92	196	E, E — 2 Litre, F, P
506117	Plug	CT16	194	E, E — 2 Litre, F, G, L, O, P
506118	Washer	CT38	194	E, E — 2 Litre, F, P
506119	Gear	CT91	196	E, E — 2 Litre, F, P
506129	'O' Ring	CT35	194	E, E — 2 Litre, F, P
506130	'O' Ring	CT60	195	E, E — 2 Litre, F, P
506157	Nut	AH39	32	A, E — 2 Litre, G, O
506542	Circlip	AV5	71	A, C, E, E — 2 Litre, F, G, O
506559	Seal		79	A, L, R
506667	Service Kit	AZ5	78, 85	E — 2 Litre, G, L
506731	Screw, Set		172, 187	A, E — 2 Litre, G
507086	Screw	BO4	96, 97	G

NUMERICAL INDEX

Part No.	Description	Plate No.	Page	Also Used on Models
507223/O	Cable, Outer	BR10	104, 106	A, F, L
507223/1	Cable, Inner	BR9	104, 106	A, F, L
507261	Washer	CF13	141	A, B, E, V
507298	Lead, Flasher	BO28	97, 98	
507299	Lead, Side Lamp	BO19	97	J, L, Y
507300	Lead, Earth	BO20	97, 98	F, K, Y
507865	Wheel Cylinder Kit		79	A, B, F, P, V
508162	Body, Rubber	BO18	97	
508163	Rim	BO23	97, 99	G
508164	Glass, Amber	BP11	99	B, F, G, M, P, V
508165	Bulbholder	BO26	97, 99, 100	G
508169	Gear, Brush	BM2	94	A, E, F, G, L, M, O, V, Y
508170	Brush Set	BM3	94	A, E, F, G, L, M, O, V, Y
508182	Crosshead and Rack	BM11	94	A, E, F, G, L
508186	Pin, Mills	BO17	97	F, T, Y
508194	Screw, Set	CR23	190	A, O,
508271	Screw		147	
508289	Washer, Plain		28	
508433	Service Kit		79, 85	
508445	Service Kit, Master Cylinder		72, 85	A, E, E — 2 Litre, F
508566	Screw, s/t		126, 141	O, Z
508726	Clip, Cable		103	A, E, G, L, Y
508790	Screw		189	Y
508822	Glass, Red	BP11	99	F, L, P
508875	Washer, Plain	BL8	85, 92, 147, 172, 187, 189, 190, 192	E — 2 Litre, F, G
508955	Repair Kit, Water Pump		85	
508975	Rotor and Spindle Assembly	R43	2, 27	E — 2 Litre, G, O
508978	Circlip	C58	8, 31	A, C, E, E — 2 Litre, F, G, O, P
508980	Retainer	J13	13, 14, 36	E, E — 2 Litre, G, O
508981	Washer, Oil Seal	J12	13, 14, 36	E, E — 2 Litre, G, O, T
508983	Rocker Arm	H18	13	E, E — 2 Litre, O, T
509058	Pin	AZ8	78	E — 2 Litre, G, L, Y
509059	Clip	AZ9	78	E — 2 Litre, G, L, Y
509140	Screw, Set		170, 178, 185	B
509260	Bush	AL64	58	A, E, E — 2 Litre, F, Y, Z
509304	Bush	BH13	88	
509305	Oil Assembly	BH14	88	
509306	Spring Set	BH15	88	
509307	Bearing	BH4	88, 90	G
509309	Nut, Shaft	BH18	88, 90	
509310	Washer, Spring	BH19	88, 90	
509312	Retainer	BH7	88	E, M, O
509313	Collar	BH6	88	E, M, O
509314	Washer, Thrust	BH9	88	E, M, O
509315	Terminal Set (Lucar)	BH11	88	E, M, O
509317	Sundry Parts Set		88	
509356	Screw		130, 133	A, E, F
509361	Spanner		85	A, E, F
509537	Circlip	AS31	68	A, E, F, G, L, O, Z
509539	Plug, Screwed	AN57	62	A, E, E — 2 Litre, F, L
509556	Screw		128, 132	A, G, Y
509560	Screw, s/t	CK22	146	B, L, O
509651	Synchro Operating Sleeve Assembly	AG24	49	A, E — 2 Litre, F, L, P
509736	Nut, Dome	BP50	101	A, F, L
509809	Lead		103	B, V
509817	Bracket Assembly	BH27	88	A, C, E, F, G, O, P
509818	Bush	BH28	88	A, C, E, F, G, O, P

NUMERICAL INDEX

Part No.	Description	Plate No.	Page	Also Used on Models
509819	Spring Set	BH30	88	G
509820	Sleeve	BH29	88	A, C, E, F, G, O, P
509860	Bolt, Wedglok	AF10	47	E — 2 Litre, F
509878	Shell Assembly	G1	12, 35	T
509879	Bolt, Centre	G2	12, 35	T
509880	Gasket	G3	12, 35	T
509881	Spring	G4	12, 35	T
509882	Valve Assembly	G5	12, 35	T
509883	Centraliser, element	G6	12, 35	E — 2 Litre, G, O
509923	Glass, Bowl	H3	13	E, E — 2 Litre, O, T
509924	Screen Assembly	H2	13	E, E — 2 Litre, O, T
509925	Spring Diaphragm	H11	13	E, E — 2 Litre, O, T
509926	Body and Primer Assembly	J11	13, 14, 36	E, E — 2 Litre, G, O, T
509927	Primer Parts Set	J14	13, 14, 36	E, E — 2 Litre, G, O
509928	Casting, Upper	H1	13	E, E — 2 Litre, O, T
509929	Bail Assembly	H5	13	E, E — 2 Litre, O, T
509930	Gasket	H4	13	E, E — 2 Litre, O, T
510125	Screw, s/t	BZ35	128	A, E — 2 Litre
510127	Washer, Plain		98, 100	A, E, M, O
510218	Bulb		96	G
510219	Bulb, 12 Volt		97	A, E, F, G, L, M, O, R, Y, Z
510273	Screw, s/t	CA43	130, 134	
510293	Screw, Set		116, 119	A, E, F
510369	Nut	BR18	104, 107	G
510498	Gasket	J8	14, 36	A, E, G, M, V, Y
510503	Screw, Set	BL7	92	E, F, L
510506	Washer, Lock		147	
510618	Nut, Nyloc	AN76	62, 65	A, E, E — 2 Litre, F, P, Z
510792	Piston	AZ2	78	G, Y
510809	Shim	AZ7	78	E — 2 Litre, G, L, Y
510844	Cap, Filler	AV50	72	E — 2 Litre, L
510845	Gasket, Filler	AV51	72	E — 2 Litre, L
510857	Screw, s/t	BZ25	127, 154	A, F, G, L
510892	Light Unit	BO2	96	F, G, L, V
510893	Spring		96, 97	G
510907	Interior		97, 98, 99	A, E, F, G, L, M, O, Z
510940	Cover, Dust	AV35	72	E, E — 2 Litre, F
510969	Clip	BR11	104, 106, 193	D, L, V
510996	Screw, Set		190	E
511001	Bolt, Fixing	BM8	94	A, C, E, F, G, L, M, O, V, Y
511003	Armature	BM6	94	A, C, E, F, G, L, M, V, Y
511005	Stud		94	A, C, E, F, G, L, M, V, Y
511006	Switch, Parking	BM10	94	C, E, F, G, L, M, O, Y
511094	Cover, End	BM1	94	G, L
511095	Coil, Field	BM5	94	G, L
511096	Rod, Connecting	BM9	94	A, E, F, G, L, Y
511137	Plunger	AV45	72	E — 2 Litre, L, Z
511138	Seal	AV46	72	E — 2 Litre, L, Z
511290	Pinion and Barrel		88	A, F, G, O
511345	Clip	BQ11	103, 192	E, E — 2 Litre, F
511384	Screw	BZ47	128	G
511475	Spacer	CG18	143	F
511506	Nut, Nyloc	AN55	62, 65	
511541	Sleeve		102	F
511551	Sleeve		102	F
511585	Cover	BQ13	102	
511586	Resistance, Swamp	BQ4	102	
511587	Resistance, Point	BQ5	102	
511589	Bracket Assembly	BH12	88	E, M, O

40

NUMERICAL INDEX

Part No.	Description	Plate No.	Page	Also Used on Models
511593	Armature Assembly	BH8	88	E, M, O
511594	Coils	BH10	88	E, M, O
511596	Bolt	BH17	88	G, M
511664	Screw	BY127	126	F
511765	Screw, Set	CC27	136, 138	F
511800	Lens	BP1	99	F
511801	Screw	BP2	99	F, O
511802	Gasket	BP3	99	F
511803	Gasket	BP6	99	F
511813	Housing, Bearing		9, 32	E — 2 Litre, G, O
511837	Rotor	BF2	86, 87	E, E — 2 Litre, F
511838	Contact Set	BF3	86	E, E — 2 Litre, F
511839	Stud	BF4	86	E, E — 2 Litre, F
511841	Nut	BF6	86	E, E — 2 Litre, F
511842	Screw	BF7	86, 87	E, E — 2 Litre, F
511843	Condenser	BF8	86	E, E — 2 Litre, F
511844	Screw	BF9	86, 87	E, E — 2 Litre, F
511846	Lead, Earth	BF11	86	E, E — 2 Litre, F
511847	Plate	BF13	86	E, E — 2 Litre, F
511851	Wick	BF15	86, 87	E, E — 2 Litre, F
511856	Washer	BF18	86, 87	E, E — 2 Litre, F
511857	Clip	BF21	86	E, E — 2 Litre, F
511859	Gear	BF23	86, 87	E, E — 2 Litre, F
511860	Washer	BF24	86, 87	E, E — 2 Litre, F
511861	Plug	BF25	86, 87	E, E — 2 Litre, F
511862	Clamp	BF26	86, 87	E, E — 2 Litre, F
511863	Ring	BF29	86, 87	E, E — 2 Litre, F
511864	Washer	BF30	86, 87	E, E — 2 Litre, F
511865	Pin, Coupling	BF32	86, 87	E, E — 2 Litre, F
511866	Coupling	BF31	86, 87	E, E — 2 Litre, F
511930	Screw	CA23	129, 133	F
512106	Washer	CA24	129, 133	F
512114	Solenoid	CT79	195	E, E — 2 Litre, F
512156	Screw, s/t		128	G, O, Z
512222	Gasket	BO10	96, 97	G
512223	Headlamp Assembly		96	G
512224	Headlamp Assembly		96	G
512231	Light Unit	BO2	96	
512241	Light Unit	BO2	97	G
512244	Headlamp Assembly		97	A, F, G, L
512274	Screw and Spring Washer	K47	16, 18, 40	A, E — 2 Litre, L, O, Z
512276	Screw	K44	16	A, E — 2 Litre, L, O, Z
512280	Screw	K50	16, 18, 40	E — 2 Litre, G, L, O
512281	Screw		40	G, L
512282	Spring	K17	15, 19, 40	A, E — 2 Litre, G, L, O, Z
512284	Screw	K22	15, 19	E — 2 Litre, G, L
512287	Nut	K19	15, 19, 40	A, E — 2 Litre, G, L, O, Z
512288	Screw	K18	15	A, E — 2 Litre, L, O, Z
512296	Spring	K35	15	A, E — 2 Litre, L, O, Z
512298	Ring	K37	15	A, E — 2 Litre, L, O, Z
512301	Washer, Needle Seating	K64	16	A, E — 2 Litre, L, O, Z
512303	Float Chamber		20	L
512304	Washer	K69	16, 41	E — 2 Litre, G, L, O, Z
512307	Screw	K59	16	A, E — 2 Litre, L, O, Z
512308	'O' Ring	K60	16	A, E — 2 Litre, L, O, Z
512311	'O' Ring	K58	16, 20, 21, 41, 42	E — 2 Litre, G, L, O, Z
512312	Screw	K57	16, 20	A, E — 2 Litre, L, O, Z
512315	Spring	K55	16	A, E — 2 Litre, L, O, Z

NUMERICAL INDEX

Part No.	Description	Plate No.	Page	Also Used on Models
512316	Washer	K54	16	A, E — 2 Litre, L, O, Z
512317	'O' Ring	K53	16, 20	A, E — 2 Litre, L, O, Z
512318	Bushing	K51	16, 20	A, E — 2 Litre, L, O, Z
512319	Washer	K52	16, 20	A, E — 2 Litre, L, O, Z
512324	Clip	K40	15	A, E — 2 Litre, L, O, Z
512334	Nut	K74	16, 20, 41	E — 2 Litre, L, O
512335	Coupling Assembly		16, 20, 41	G, L
512339	Washer	K75	16, 20, 41	E — 2 Litre, G, L, O
512340	Screw	K73	16, 20, 41	E — 2 Litre, G, L, O
512343	Ring	AE11	46	G, O
512344	Clip	AE12	46	G, O
512419	Gaiter Assembly	AL6	56	A, E, E — 2 Litre, F
512420	Gaiter Assembly	AS49	68	A, E — 2 Litre, F
512461	Screw	BZ27	127	G, O, Z
512462	Screw, Set		117, 120	F, G, L
512541	Pad, Lining Assembly		78	E — 2 Litre, G, L
512554	Screw, s/t		161, 170, 178, 185	O
512781	Wire	AS47	68	F, G, L
512802	Seal, Valve		73	A, F, G, M
512803	Washer, Spring		73	A, F, G, M
512827	Cylinder Head Assembly (7 to 1 Compression Ratio)		4	E — 2 Litre, O
512829	Engine Gasket Set		1, 85	E — 2 Litre, O
512830	Decarbonising Gasket Set		1, 85	E — 2 Litre, O
512944	Owners Handbook—English		85	
512945	Owners Handbook—French		85	
512946	Owners Handbook—German		85	
512947	Workshop Manual—English		85	
512948	Workshop Manual—French		85	
512949	Workshop Manual—German		85	
512987	Plate	BO3	96, 97	G
512955	Rubber, Wiper Blade		94	A, F
513195	Annulus Assembly	CT73	195	E, E — 2 Litre, F
513196	Oil Pump Plunger Assembly	CT23	194	E, E — 2 Litre, F
513198	Rear Casing Assembly	CT99	196	E, E — 2 Litre, F
513199	Spring	CT56	193	E, E — 2 Litre, F
513200	Clutch Sliding Member Assembly	CT48	195	E, E — 2 Litre, F
513201	Washer	CT86	195	E, E — 2 Litre, F, O
513202	Oil Filter	CT39	194	E, E — 2 Litre, F
513203	Bolt	CT53	195	E, E — 2 Litre, F
513204	Washer	CT83	195	E, E — 2 Litre, F
513205	Magnet Set	CT40	194	E, E — 2 Litre, F, G, L, O
513206	Plug	CT31	194	E, E — 2 Litre, F
513207	Spring	CT29	194	E, E — 2 Litre, F
513208	Spring	CT70	195	E, E — 2 Litre, F, O
513209	Freewheel Inner Member	CT66	195	E, E — 2 Litre, F
513210	Spring	CT67	195	E, E — 2 Litre, F
513211	Tube	CT98	196	E, E — 2 Litre, F
513214/1	Washer, Adjustment	CT78	195	E, E — 2 Litre, F
513214/2	Washer, Adjustment	CT78	195	E, E — 2 Litre, F
513214/3	Washer, Adjustment	CT78	195	E, E — 2 Litre, F
513214/4	Washer, Adjustment	CT78	195	E, E — 2 Litre, F
513215	Plate	CT72	195	E, E — 2 Litre, F
513216	Cam	CT20	194	E, F
513219	Spring	CT59	195	E, E — 2 Litre, F
513220	Piston	CT58	195	E, E — 2 Litre, F
513222	Body	CT25	194	E, E — 2 Litre, F
513223	Spring	CT63	195	E, E — 2 Litre, F

NUMERICAL INDEX

Part No.	Description	Plate No.	Page	Also Used on Models
513224	Bearing, Needle Roller		195	E, E — 2 Litre, F, G, L
513225	Screw, Set	CT87	195	E, E — 2 Litre, F, G, L, O
513226	Screw, Set	CT84	195	E, E — 2 Litre, F, G, O
513227	Nut	CT54	195	E, E — 2 Litre, F
513228	Ring	CT49	195	E, E — 2 Litre, F
513229	Bearing	CT77	195	E, E — 2 Litre, F
513231	Seal, Oil	CT100	196	E, E — 2 Litre, F
513265	Rim	BO5	96, 97	G
513266	Spring	BO7	96, 97	G
513267	Screw	BO9	96, 97	A, E — 2 Litre, F, G, L, M, Z
513400	Clip, Cap	BG18	87	
513683	Main Body Assembly	K1	15	E — 2 Litre, O
513684	Spindle, Throttle	K3	15	E — 2 Litre, O
513685	Stop Throttle	K5	15	E — 2 Litre, O
513687	Nut	K7	15, 19, 40, 41	
513688	Washer, Shakeproof	K8	15, 19, 40, 41	
513689	Throttle	K21	15, 19	A, E — 2 Litre, O, Z
513691	Spring	K20	15	A, E — 2 Litre, O, Z
513692	Bar, Starter	K23	15	E — 2 Litre, O
513693	Lever, Choke	K25	15	A, E — 2 Litre, O, Z
513694	Diaphragm	K42	16	A, E — 2 Litre, O, Z
513696	Bush	K28	15	E — 2 Litre, O
513697	Screw	K16	15	A, E — 2 Litre, O, Z
513700	Jet, Orifice	K56	16, 20	A, E — 2 Litre, O, Z
513702	Needle	K63	16	A, E — 2 Litre, O, Z
513705	Gasket	K66	16	A, E — 2 Litre, O, Z
513706	Float Chamber	K65	16	A, E — 2 Litre, O, Z
513710	Spring	K45	16	A, E — 2 Litre, O
513713	Roll Pin	K72	16	E — 2 Litre, O
513714	Coupling	K71	16	E — 2 Litre, O
513715	Coupling	K76	16	E — 2 Litre, O
513716	Main Body Assembly	K2	15	E — 2 Litre, O
513718	Lever	K9	15	A, E — 2 Litre, O, Z
513719	Nut	K10	15	E — 2 Litre, O
513720	Washer, Tap	K11	15, 19, 40	E — 2 Litre, O
513721	Bar, Starter	K24	15	E — 2 Litre, O
513723	Screw	K30	15, 19, 41	A, E — 2 Litre, O, Z
513724	Nut	K32	15	E — 2 Litre, O, Z
513726	Spring, Return	K34	15	A, E — 2 Litre, O, Z
513730	Grommet	BO42	98	F, L, O
513800	Package Unit	AR2	66	A, E — 2 Litre, F, O
513888	Dowel	CT12	194	E — 2 Litre, G, O
513962	Shaft and Gear Assembly	BM7	94	F
513992	Cap, Distributor	BF1	86	E, E — 2 Litre
513993	Lead, Earth	BG9	87	E
513994	Lead, L.T.	BG8	87	E
513999	Screw	BG19	87	
514023	Sleeve		88	A, F, G, O
514024	Cup, Shaft		88	A, F, G, O
514025	Bushing		88	G
514026	Armature Assembly		88	G
514048	Clip		103	G, O, Z
514062	Lens	BP17	99	F, L
514063	Screw, Lens Fixing	BP18	99	F, L
514064	Washer	BO49	98, 99	A, E — 2 Litre, O, Z
514065	Gasket	BO39	98, 100	F, G, L
514066	Interior, Bulbholder		99, 100	F, L
514067	Grommet	BP23	99, 100	F, L
514106	Pop-out Unit		197	F, O

43

NUMERICAL INDEX

Part No.	Description	Plate No.	Page	Also Used on Models
514200	Adjusting Screw and Locknut Assembly	CT81	195	E, E — 2 Litre, F
514201	Crown Wheel and Pinion Assembly		60	E — 2 Litre,
514397	Water Pump Assembly		9, 32	E — 2 Litre, E, G, O
514421	Lens (White)	BO38	98	F, L
514422	Screw, Lens Fixing	BO37	98	F, G, L
514438	Washer, Plain		117, 120	F, Z
514517	Wire Wheel Kit		66	A, E, F
514518	Wire Wheel Kit		66	A, E, F
514578	Light Unit	BO2	96	A, F, G, L
514579	Headlamp Assembly		96	F, G, L
514600	"Powerstop" Vacuum Servo Kit		197	
514639	Special Grease		85	E — 2 Litre, F, O
514735	Rivet	AE7	46	E — 2 Litre, G, L
514791	Lead, Battery to Earth—Negative		103	
514792	Lead		103	
514793	Lead—R.H.S.		103	
514889	Pin, Spring Support	CT30	194	E — 2 Litre
514926	Screw	CA12	129	Z
514930	Spoke, Short		66	A, F
514931	Spoke, Long		66	A, F
514940	Bracket		197	F
514964	Spindle, Throttle	K4	15	A, E — 2 Litre, Z
514965	Stop, Throttle	K12	15	A, E — 2 Litre
514968	Lever, Loose	K29	15	E — 2 Litre, O
514969	Pin	K38	15	A, E — 2 Litre, O, Z
514970	Spring	K39	15	A, E — 2 Litre, O, Z
514971	Pin	K62	16	A, E — 2 Litre, O, Z
514972	Screw, Long	K67	16, 20, 41	A, E — 2 Litre, G, O, Z
514973	Screw	K68	16, 18, 20, 40, 41	A, E — 2 Litre, G, O, Z
514977	Washer	K6	15, 40	A, E — 2 Litre, Z
514980	Washer	K70	16, 18, 20, 40, 41	A, E — 2 Litre, G, O, Z
515036	Valve	J2	14, 36	G, M, V
515037	Gasket	J3	14, 36	G, M, V
515060	Grommet	BO56	98	F, Z
515061	Grommet	BO57	98	F, G, Z
515111	Cover	K46	16	A, E — 2 Litre, O, Z
515112	Damper Assembly	K48	16	A, E — 2 Litre, O, Z
515129	Crown Wheel and Pinion Assembly	AN24	60	
515170	Screw, Set		188	
515186	Battery, Dry		102	
515279	Screw, Set	CA19	129, 133	
515328	Screw, Set		117, 120	F, Z
515329	Front Suspension Unit—R.H.		56	E — 2 Litre
515330	Front Suspension Unit—L.H.		56	E — 2 Litre
515377	Sleeve Assembly	AG11	49	
515379	Top Cover Extension and Hand Lever Assembly		51	
515382	Hypoid Housing Assembly	AN16	60	E — 2 Litre
515396	Switch		200	A, E, E — 2 Litre, O, Z
515448	Fuel Pipe Link Filter		197	A, E, E — 2 Litre, O, Z
515450	Gearbox Assembly		47	E — 2 Litre
515452	Gearbox Assembly		47	E — 2 Litre
515479	Engine Unit (9·5 to 1 Compression Ratio)		1	
515479/R	Engine Unit (9·5 to 1 Compression Ratio) (Reconditioned Unit)		1	
515482	Cylinder Head Assembly		4	E — 2 Litre
515483	Cylinder Head Assembly	B1	4	E — 2 Litre
515492	Rear Axle Centre Assembly		60	

NUMERICAL INDEX

Part No.	Description	Plate No.	Page	Also Used on Models
515495	Brake Shoe Assembly	AZ38	79	E — 2 Litre
515507	Rear Axle Centre Assembly		60	E — 2 Litre
515517	Top Cover Extension and Hand Lever Assembly (Overdrive Condition)		51	
515553	Cylinder Head Assembly (Less Valves, Spring and Studs)		4	
515562	Screw		150	
515589	Brush Set	BH16	88	
515590	Bracket Assembly	BH1	88	
515591	Plate	BH2	88, 90	
515592	Circlip	BH3	88, 90	G
515593	'O' Ring	BH5	88, 90	G
515610	Cylinder Block Assembly	A1	1	E — 2 Litre, O
515616	Overdrive Kit—R.H.S.		192	
515617	Overdrive Kit—L.H.S.		192	
515633	Spring, Diaphragm	AE2	46	E — 2 Litre
515634	Rivet	AE4	46	E — 2 Litre, G
515635	Cover and Straps, Sub-assembly	AE1	46	E — 2 Litre, G
515636	Plate, Pressure	AE5	46	E — 2 Litre
515637	Clip, Retaining	AE6	46	E — 2 Litre
515638	Ring	AE3	46	E — 2 Litre, G
515640	Facing Package		46	
515658	Motor and Gearbox		94	
515710	Washer, Lock	BF5	86	E — 2 Litre, F
515711	Lead, L.T	BF10	86	E — 2 Litre, F
515712	Mainshaft and Cam Assembly	BF16	86	E — 2 Litre
515713	Spring Set	BF17	86	E — 2 Litre
515714	Vacuum Control Assembly	BF19	86	E — 2 Litre
515721	Float, Nylon	K61	16	A, E — 2 Litre, O, Z
515722	Washer	K43	16	E — 2 Litre, O
515723	Air Valve, Shaft and Diaphragm Assembly	K41	16	E — 2 Litre
515724	Needle, Metering	K49	16	E — 2 Litre, O
515740	Oil Pump Assembly		2	E — 2 Litre
515741	Gearbox Assembly (Reconditioned Unit)		47	E — 2 Litre
515742	Gearbox Assembly (Reconditioned Unit)		47	E — 2 Litre
515743	Rear Axle Centre Assembly		60	
515744	Rear Axle Centre Assembly		60	E — 2 Litre
515786	Service Kit		72, 85	E — 2 Litre
515810	Non-return Valve Body	CT27	194	E — 2 Litre
515811	Valve Operating Shaft	CT9	194	E — 2 Litre
515812	Cam Lever	CT11	194	E — 2 Litre
515813	Valve Operating Lever	CT8	194	E — 2 Litre
515814	Main Casing Assembly	CT1	194	E — 2 Litre
515815	Planet Carrier Assembly	CT65	195	E — 2 Litre
515816	Relief Valve Sub-Assembly		194	E — 2 Litre
515817	Locknut	CT103	196	E — 2 Litre
515818	Washer	CT102	196	E — 2 Litre
515825	Rotor, Heater Unit		136, 138	
515827	Resistor		136, 138	
515828	Motor and Shell		136, 138	
515852	Continental Touring Kit		198	
515873	Lead, Battery Positive to Solenoid—L.H.S.		103	F
515930	Cylinder Block Assembly		1	E — 2 Litre
515932	Engine Unit (9·5 to 1 Compression Ratio)		1	
515932/R	Engine Unit (9·5 to 1 Compression Ratio) (Reconditioned Unit)		1	
515953	Front Suspension Unit—R.H.		56	
515954	Front Suspension Unit—L.H.		56	
515979	Top Cover Assembly		48	E — 2 Litre

45

NUMERICAL INDEX

Part No.	Description	Plate No.	Page	Also Used on Models
516005	Washer	AA61	20, 21, 41, 42	G
516042	Bolt, through Frame	BJ20	90	
516043	Bracket, Frame	BJ1	90	
516044	Washer	BJ2	90	
516045	Rotor	BJ7	90	
516046	Bracket	BJ11	90	
516047	Bearing	BJ12	90	
516048	Seal, Bearing	BJ13	90	
516049	Heatsink, with Cathode Base Diodes	BJ10	90	
516050	Heatsink, with Anode Base Diodes	BJ9	90	
516051	Brush Complete with Spring and Lucar Blade	BJ17	90	
516052	Brush Box	BJ16	90	
516053	Connector	BJ18	90	
516054	Screw, Heatsink Fixing	BJ14	90	
516055	Washer, Insulating	BJ15	90	
516056	Stator	BJ8	90	
516057	Sundry Parts Set	BJ19	90	
516059	Heatsink, with Cathode Base Diodes		90	
516060	Heatsink, with Anode Base Diodes		90	
516062	Carburettor Assembly, Rear		15	E — 2 Litre
516099	Top Cover Assembly		48	E — 2 Litre
516100	Top Cover Extension and Hand Lever Assembly		51	
516110	Gearbox Assembly		47	E — 2 Litre
516111	Gearbox Assembly		47	E — 2 Litre
516112	Gearbox Assembly (Reconditioned Unit)		47	E — 2 Litre
516113	Gearbox Assembly (Reconditioned Unit)		47	E — 2 Litre
516134	Bolt	S52	5, 29	E — 2 Litre
516224	Circlip		73	A, F
516237	Condenser	BG6	87	F
516274	Crown Wheel and Pinion Assembly		60	
516275	Crown Wheel and Pinion Assembly		60	
516278	Spot Lamp		199	A, E — 2 Litre
516279	Fog Lamp		199	A, E — 2 Litre
516288	Screw, Set, Front		129, 133	
516301	Lens, Amber	BP27	100	F
516302	Lens, Red	BP27	100	F
516303	Screw	BP28	100	F
516304	Rim	BO47	98	F
516305	Screw, Rim Fixing	BO48	98	F
516306	Lens, Flasher, Amber	BO51	98	F
516307	Lens, Flasher, White	BO51	98	F
516308	Lens, Side Lamp	BO50	98	F
516309	Lens, Side Lamp	BO50	98	F
516375	Oil Cooler Kit		199	
516392	Engine Unit (7 to 1 Compression Ratio)		1	
516392/R	Engine Unit (7 to 1 Compression Ratio) (Reconditioned Unit)		1	
516394	Engine Unit (7 to 1 Compression Ratio)		1	
516394/R	Engine Unit (7 to 1 Compression Ratio) (Reconditioned Unit)		1	
516506	Cover, Fuse Box		102	
516536	Rocker Arm	J17	14, 36	E — 2 Litre, G
516537	Bolt	J7	14, 36	E — 2 Litre, G
516538	Casting	J1	14, 36	E — 2 Litre, G
516539	Filter	J4	14, 36	E — 2 Litre
516540	Gasket	J6	14, 36	E — 2 Litre, G
516541	Screw	J22	14, 36	E — 2 Litre, G
516542	Repair Kit, Complete		14, 36, 85	E — 2 Litre, G
516543	Tow Rope and Luggage Rack Strap		199	E — 2 Litre

NUMERICAL INDEX

Part No.	Description	Plate No.	Page	Also Used on Models
516614	Hose	AX12	74, 75	G
516657	Shell, Oil Filter		199	
516665	Emission Control Valve Kit		11	G, Z
516675	"Plugmaster" Sparking Plug Spanner		200	
516676	"Levermaster" Wheel Brace		200	
516762	Woodscrew	CB29	133	
516770	Glove, Steering Wheel, Brown Leather		200	
516771	Glove, Steering Wheel, Simulated Brown Leather		200	
516788	Clutch Slave Cylinder Assembly (Less Push Rod)		46	E — 2 Litre
516789	Seal, Piston		46	E — 2 Litre
516790	Boot, Rubber		46	E — 2 Litre
516823	Cylinder Head Assembly		4	
516824	Cylinder Head Assembly		4	
516834	Washer, Plain		170, 178	
516945	Spring	AA21	18, 40	
516948	Spindle, Throttle		19, 40	
516949	Lever	AA32	19, 40	
516950	Nut, Extension	AA36	19, 40	
516951	Spring	AA31	19, 40	G
516952	Screw	AA28	19, 40	
516953	Cover, Starter Box	AA45	41	
516954	Spindle	AA42	19, 41	G
516955	Spring	AA44	19, 41	G
516956	'C' Washer	AA43	19, 41	G
516957	Spring	AA50	19, 41	G
516958	Cam Lever Assembly	L46	19	
516959	Lever, Starter	AA51	19, 41	
516960	Screw	AA55	19, 41	G
516961	Washer, Shakeproof	AA56	19, 41	G
516962	Clip, for Bracket	AA58	19, 41	G
516963	Screw	AA59	19, 41	G
516964	Bracket	AA57	19, 41	
516965	Screw	AA33	19, 40	G
516966	Valve, By-pass	L3	18	
516967	Gasket	L2	18, 21, 42	G
516968	Cover	L10	18, 40	G
516969	Screw	L11	18, 40	G
516971	Washer	AA14	18, 21, 40	G
516972	Washer	AA15	18, 21, 40, 42	G
516973	Screw	AA11	18, 40	G
516974	Washer	AA12	18, 40	G
516975	Screw	AA3	40	G
516976	Spring	AA2	40	G
516977	Float and Arm	AA62	19, 41	G
516979	Plug	AA70	41	G
516980	Gasket	AA65	20, 21, 41, 42	G
516981	Float Chamber	AA64	20, 41, 42	G
516983	Seal, Throttle Spindle	AA29	40, 42	
516984	Diaphragm	AA18	40, 42	
516985	Spindle, Throttle		19, 40	
516986	Coupling Spindle Assembly	AA72	20, 41	
516987	Sleeve, Split	AA77	16, 20, 41	
516988	'O' Ring, Damper		40, 42	G
516989	Lubrication Pack		21, 42	G
516990	Repair Kit, Complete		21, 42	G
516991	Repair Kit, Complete		42	
517016	Plunger Assembly		73	
517017	Seal, Gland		73	

NUMERICAL INDEX

Part No.	Description	Plate No.	Page	Also Used on Models
517018	Plunger, Secondary		73	
517019	Seal, Ring, Two-way		73	
517020	Cover, Dust		73	
517028	Spring		73	G
517029	Stem, Valve		73	G
517030	Retainer, Spring		73	G
517031	Spring		73	G
517032	Spacer		73	G
517033	Tipping Valve Assembly		73	G
517034	Valve Seat		73	G
517035	Spring, Valve		73	G
517036	Circlip		73	G
517037	Nut, Valve		73	G
517038	Seal		73	G
517039	Reservoir, Fluid, Assembly		73	G
517040	Cap, Filler		73	G
517041	Baffle		73	G
517042	Gasket		73	G
517043	Seal		73	G
517044	Screw, Set		73	G
517045	Washer, Spring		73	G
517046	Push Rod Assembly	AW27	73	
517050	Insulator	BG4	87	
517119	Screw	AA20	18, 40	G
517134	Pin, Float Pivot	AA63	20, 41	
517145	Screw		124	G
517148	Screw		124	G
517150	Screw		124	G
517189	Bolt, through Frame	BK12	91	
517236	Stator	BK6	91	
517237	Sundry Parts Set	BK13	91	
517294	Spring, Valve		194	
517300	Bush, Gude	L69	20	
517301	Spring	L70	20	
517333	Service Kit, Reservoir		73	
517342	Engine Lead Kit		24, 45	
517388	Coupling, Spindle		16	
517427	Ring, Sump Sealing	G19	12, 35	
517428	Collar	G15	12, 35	
517429	'O' Ring	G16	12, 35	
517430	Valve, Relief	G14	12, 35	
517431	Seal, Bolt	G12	12, 35	
517432	Spring, Element	G13	12, 35	
517433	Bolt, Centre	G10	12, 35	
517434	Plate, Element Locating	G17	12, 35	
517435	Sump	G9	12, 35	
517436	Contact Set	BG3	86, 87	
517437	Plate, Breaker	BG10	12, 87	
517438	Mainshaft and Cam Assembly	BG13	12, 87	
517439	Spring Set	BG14	12, 87	
517440	Vacuum Control Assembly	BG16	12, 87	
517442	Cover, Starter Box	L41	19	
517443	Screw	L6	18	
517444	Temperature Compensator Assembly	L7	18	
517447	Screw and 'O' Ring Assembly	L47	20	
517448	Diaphragm	L16	18, 21	
517449	Damper Assembly	AA16	18, 40	
517450	Clip, Locking		20	
517451	Wire, Sealing		20	

NUMERICAL INDEX

Part No.	Description	Plate No.	Page	Also Used on Models
517452	Needle, Metering	L22	18	
517453	Valve, Needle	AA60	20, 21, 41, 42	
517478	Screw, Set		188	
517486	Washer	G11	12, 35	
517599	Choke Control Cable Outer Assembly—R.H.S.	BS25	107	
517600	Choke Control Cable Inner Assembly—R.H.S.	BS26	107	
517601	Choke Control Cable Outer Assembly—L.H.S.		107	
517602	Choke Control Cable Inner Assembly—L.H.S.		107	
517607	Engine Unit (9·25 to 1 Compression Ratio)		26	
517607/R	Engine Unit (9·25 to 1 Compression Ratio) (Reconditioned Unit)		26	
517609	Cylinder Head Assembly (9·25 to 1 Compression Ratio)		28	
517610	Cylinder Head Assembly (9·25 to 1 Compression Ratio)	S1	28	
517611	Cylinder Block Assembly	R1	26	
517612	Decarbonising Gasket Set		26	
517613	Engine Gasket Set		26	
517620	Blade, Rubber		94	
517621	Windscreen Wiper Motor (2 Speed)		95	
517622	Gear Assembly—L.H.S.		95	
517632	Fluid, Clutch and Brake		75, 85, 197	
517633	Fluid, Clutch and Brake		75, 85, 197	
517634	Fluid, Clutch and Brake		75, 86, 197	
517643	Armature	BN2	95	
517644	Brush Assembly	BN3	95	
517645	Switch, Parking	BN4	95	
517646	Gear Assembly—R.H.S.	BN5	95	
517647	Cover	BK11	91	
517648	Regulator	BK10	91	
517649	Rectifier	BK7	91	
517650	Brush Box Assembly (Complete with Brushes)	BK9	91	
517651	Brush Set		91	
517652	Rotor	BK3	91	
517653	Slip Ring	BK4	91	
517654	Bracket, Frame	BK1	91	
517655	Service Kit	BK2	91	
517656	Bracket	BK8	91	
517657	Bearing Kit	BK5	91	
517662	Service Kit		73	
517666	Rubber Bush	AQ37	65	
517667	Sleeve	AQ37a	65	
517764	Cam Lever Assembly	AA50	41	
517765	Screw, Cover to By-pass Body	AA8	40	
517766	Valve, By-pass	AA5	40	
517767	Gasket, By-pass Valve	AA4	40	
517768	Temperature Compensator Assembly	AA9	40	
517769	Screw	AA24	40	
517770	Needle, Metering	AA25	40	
545029	Owners Handbook—Flemish		85	
545057	Owners Handbook—English		85	
545058	Owners Handbook—French		85	
545059	Owners Handbook—German		85	
545060	Owners Handbook—Flemish		85	
550924	Washer, Waved	BY100	124	A, E, F, G, L, O, Z
552218	Moulding, P.V.C.	CH2	144	F, G, L, R
553121	Clip	BY120	125	C, F, L, T, Y
553252	Button	CM48	151	A, C, E, F, G, P, T, Y, Z
554021	Stud	CM50	151	F, O, T, Y, Z

NUMERICAL INDEX

Part No.	Description	Plate No.	Page	Also Used on Models
554264	Touch-in paint—Signal Red		200	A, E — 2 Litre, F
554449	Fire Extinguisher		197	A, E, E — 2 Litre, F, G, O, P, T, Y
554517	Socket	CM35	151	A, C, E, F, G, L, O, P, T, Y, Z
554700	Bolt	CG7	143	C, T, Y
556141	Rivet		112	A, B, D, E, F, G, L, V, Z
557493	Wing Mirror, Desmo 169		198	
557922	Rivet, Imex	CL7	147	A, E, F, L, O
559702	Stud	CL25	147, 148	A, E, L
559980	Screw	CC17	136, 138	A, E, F, G, L, O, P, Y, Z
560026	Rivet, Imex	CF2	141	Z
560632	Exterior Driving Mirror—'D' Type		198	F, O, R
561210	Rivet, Imex	CM38	151, 157, 166, 175, 182	A, E, F, G, L, O, Z
562116	Bonnet Lock Kit		197	A, E, F,
563032	Plate, Back		130, 133	F, L
563769	Rivet, Imex	CL26	147, 148, 151	A, E, F, G, L, O, Z
565747	Button	CN36	163, 172, 179, 187, 188	F, G, L
565748	Socket, Dot		188	F, G, L
565756	Cap, Tubular		130, 133	E, F, L
565760	Eyelet		147	F, L
567642	Socket	CN37	163, 172, 179, 187	F
568496	Safety Harness Kit, 3 Point Fixing		198	F, G, L
568511	Safety Harness Kit, 2 Point Fixing		198	F, G, L
569116	Cigarette Lighter		197	A, E — 2 Litre, F
569254	Button	CM33	151	F, L, O
569286	Touch-in Paint—Conifer Green		200	A, E — 2 Litre, F, G, L, O, Z
569521	Touch-in Paint—New White		200	A, F, G, L, O, Z
569527	Touch-in Paint—Wedgwood Blue		200	A, E — 2 Litre, F, G, L, O, Z
569945	Rivet, Imex	CL57	148	
570145	Nut, Spire		128	G, O
570220	Washer	BY27	121	O
570409	Wing Mirror (Wingard)		198	F, O
571201	Spring	BY109	124	F, L
571228	Touch-in Paint—Royal Blue		200	A, F, G, O, Z
571276	Touch-in Paint—Conifer Green/Acrylic		200	F, O, Z
571283	Push Button	BY108	124	F, L
571287	Screw, Set		124	F, L
571288	Washer, Shakeproof		124	F, L
571289	Screw, Set		124	F, L
571450	Body Shell, Prime Finish—L.H.S.		108	
571451	Body Shell, Prime Finish—R.H.S.		108	
572534	Heater Kit		136	
572540	Barrel	BR21	104, 107	A, F, L
572759	Anti-frost Shield (Windscreen)		197	
573081	Pins	BY28	121	Z
573096	Mud Flap Kit		198	F
573349	Wing Mirror, Desmo 166		197	
573461	Wing Mirror		197	Z
573673	Body Complete, Painted and Trimmed (Including Seats)—R.H.S.		108	
573674	Body Complete, Painted and Trimmed (Less Seats)—R.H.S.		108	
573675	Body Complete, Painted and Trimmed (Including Seats)—L.H.S.		108	
573676	Body Complete, Painted and Trimmed (Less Seats)—L.H.S.		108	
573677	Wing Mirror—Racing Type		197	F

NUMERICAL INDEX

Part No.	Description	Plate No.	Page	Also Used on Models
573843	Glass, Toughened	CF9	141	
573900	Diaphragm	CN5	157, 166, 175, 182	
573948	Nut		117, 120	
574061	Clamp, Hinge	CF28	141	
574062	Clamp and Bolt Assembly	CF27	141	
574063	Glass, Ventilator—L.H.	BY22	121	
574064	Glass, Ventilator—R.H.		121	
574090	Surround and Guide Rail Assembly—L.H.	BY14	121	
574091	Surround and Guide Rail Assembly—R.H.		121	
574092	Pivot, Top, Outer—L.H.	BY15	121	
574093	Pivot, Top, Outer—R.H.		121	
574094	Plate, Catch—L.H.	BY16	121	
574095	Plate, Catch—R.H.		121	
574096	Rivet		121	
574097	Screw, Chrome		121	
574098	Weatherseal—L.H.	BY17	121	
574099	Weatherseal—R.H.		121	
574100	Cover, Top Corner	BY18	121	
574101	Frame Assembly—L.H.		121	
574102	Frame Assembly—R.H.		121	
574103	Frame Assembly—L.H.	BY19	121	
574104	Frame Assembly—R.H.		121	
574105	Pivot, Top, Inner—L.H.	BY20	121	
574106	Pivot, Top, Inner—R.H.		121	
574107	Rivet,		121	
574109	Strip Glazing	BY23	121	
574110	Handle, Catch—L.H.	BY24	121	
574111	Handle, Catch—R.H.		121	
574112	Tube, Spacer	BY29	122	
574113	Washer	BY30	122	
574114	Spring, Friction		122	
574115	Washer, Tab	BY31	122	
574116	Bracket—L.H.	BY21	121	
574117	Bracket—R.H.		121	
574118	Rivet		121	
574119	Locking Device, Back Door	CF40	142	
574120	Frame Assembly—L.H.		141	
574121	Frame Assembly—R.H.		141	
574122	Frame, Front—L.H.	CF4	141	
574123	Frame, Front—R.H.		141	
574124	Bracket, Top, Joint	CF5	141	
574125	Bracket, Bottom, Joint	CF6	141	
574126	Screw	CF7	141	
574127	Frame, Rear—L.H.	CF8	141	
574128	Frame, Rear—R.H.		141	
574129	Strip, Glazing	CF10	141	
574130	Toggle Assembly—L.H.	CF11	141	
574131	Toggle Assembly—R.H.		141	
574132	Screw	CF12	141	
574133	Nut, Dome	CF14	141	
574134	Hinge Assembly—L.H.	CF1	141	
574135	Hinge Assembly—R.H.		141	
574245	Body Mounting Details Pack		109	
574579	Extension Kit		197	
574580	Replacement Flat Glass Lens for 573461 and 573349		197	
574581	Retainer		123	G
574586	Wing Mirror, Magnatex 09		198	
574592	Heated Backlight		200	

NUMERICAL INDEX

Part No.	Description	Plate No.	Page	Also Used on Models
574626	Touch-in Paint—Valencia Blue		200	
574704	Roof Rack		199	
574722	Emergency Windscreen		199	
574761	Single Gauge Instrument Mounting Panel		200	
574762	Double Gauge Instrument Mounting Panel		200	
574841	Fix, Multi-prong		172, 187	
574862	Wing Mirror, Desmo 166		197	
574863	Wing Mirror, Desmo 168		197	
574885	Touch-in Paint—Jasmine		200	
574890	Safety Warning Triangle		200	
574937	Head and Stem Assembly	BZ29	127	G
575144	Bolt, "Longlok"	BZ43	128	
575170	Body Assembly, Complete, Prime Finish—R.H.S.		108	
575171	Body Assembly, Complete, Prime Finish—L.H.S.		108	
575172	Body Complete, Painted and Trimmed (with Seats)—R.H.S.		108	
575173	Body Complete, Painted and Trimmed (with Seats)—L.H.S.		108	
575174	Body Complete, Painted and Trimmed (Less Seats)—R.H.S.		108	
575175	Body Complete, Painted and Trimmed (Less Seats)—L.H.S.		108	
575194	Touch-in-Paint—Damson		200	
575246	Headrest, Black (MK. I Cars only)		200	
575292	Occasional Seat Kit, Leathercloth—Black		188	
575293	Occasional Seat Kit, Leathercloth—Shadow Blue		188	
575294	Occasional Seat Kit, Leathercloth—Red		188	
575295	Occasional Seat Kit, Leathercloth—Light Tan		188	
575296	Occasional Seat Kit, Leather—Black		188	
575297	Occasional Seat Kit, Leather—Shadow Blue		188	
575298	Occasional Seat Kit, Leather—Red		188	
575299	Occasional Seat Kit, Leather—Light Tan		188	
575323	Body Shell, Prime Finish—L.H.S.		108	
575324	Body Shell, Prime Finish—R.H.S.		108	
575326	Body Complete, Painted and Trimmed (Including Seats)—L.H.S.		108	
575327	Body Complete, Painted and Trimmed (Less Seats)—L.H.S.		108	
600396	Grommet		102, 104, 106, 191	A, D, F, G, J, L, M, P, T, V, Y, Z
600398	Plug		191	B, D, F, J, M, O, P, R, T, V, Y, Z
600399	Plug		83, 191	F, G, J, L, O, P, R, T, Y, Z
600421	Plug, Blanking	BY67	122, 191	E, F, R
600832	Pin		123, 124	A, E, F, G, L, O, P, T
601597	Plate, Retaining	CA50	131, 134	A, E, F, P
602037	Grommet	CG28	143, 191	A, C, E, G, L, O, P, R, T, Y
602638	Hose—R.H.		136, 139	F, G
602821	Seal, Check Arm	BY119	125	A, E, F, Y
603344	Spring		112	A, E, F, G, L, Z
603382	Spring		123, 124	A, E, F, G, P, O
603559	Clip		110, 111, 112, 115, 118, 129, 132	G
603811	Clip		130, 133, 167, 176, 183	C, F, T, Y
604132	Tubing	CE13	140	
604146	Tubing	CE6	140	
605953	Sleeve, Terminal		96, 97, 98, 99, 103	G

52

NUMERICAL INDEX

Part No.	Description	Plate No.	Page	Also Used on Models
606239	Courtesy Light Switch	BQ7	103	O, T, Y
606240	Courtesy Light Switch	BQ6	103	O, T, Z
606698	Clip	AU11	70	A, D, E, G, O, V
607085	Piece, Packing	CG8	143	A, F, G, L
607621	Bracket, Mounting		112	F
607628	Bracket		115, 118	E
607637	Plate, Mounting Bracket		112	F
607663	Bonnet Catch Assembly	BW45	116, 119	A, E, F
607664	Catch Plate	BW46	116, 119	A, E, F
607711	Plate, Backing	BW29	115, 118	A, E, F
607788	Bush, Tube		115	E
607823	Pin, Door Hinge	BY3	121	A, E, F, Z
607824	Hinge, Door Assembly	BY2	121	A, E, F
607869	Bracket, Anchor	BW28	115, 118	A, E, F
607910	Spacer	BW32	116	A, E, F
608135	Support		130, 134	F
608136	Channel		130, 134	A, E, F, G, L
608139	Insulator	CA40	130, 134	F
608185	Support Bracket Clamp	CA65	131	A, E, F, G, L
608222	Felt Strip	CA66	131	A, E, F, G, L
608223	Felt Strip	CA67	131	A, E, F, G, L
608307	Clip, Locating	CM13	149	A, E, F, G, L
608356	Cable Slip Ring	CA39	130, 134	A, F, G, L
608380	Badge Assembly	BW37	116	A, E, F
608383	Plate, Retaining	BU35	111	A, E, F, L
608454	Front Door Remote Control Handle	BY103	124	A, E, F, L, O, P
608462	Slip Ring and Insulator Assembly	CA38	130, 134	
608467/M	Wing Mirror, Morgan		198	A, F, O
608467/W	Wing Mirror, Wingard		198	F, O
608491	Moulding	CG4	143	A, E
608511	Clip	BY122	126, 150	A, E, E — 2 Litre, F, G, L, O, Z
608516	Clip, Long	BY123	126, 150, 169, 178, 185	A, E, E — 2 Litre, F, G, O, Z
608520	Clip		116, 119	A, E, F, O
608540	Button, Push	BY25	121	A, E, O
608542	Spring	BY26	121	A, E, O
608563	Seal Rear	BU35	111	A, E, F
608604	Clip	BY13	121	A, E, F, G, L, O, Z
608643	Packing		115, 118	A, E, F, R
608703	Clip	BY102	124	A, E, F, G, L, O, Z
608817	Clip	CM19	150, 158, 159, 160, 168, 169, 176, 177, 184, 185	A, E, E — 2 Litre, F, L, M, O, Z
608854	Washer	CH32	144	A, F
608862	Clip, Trim	CN22	159, 160, 168, 169, 177, 184, 185	A, E, E — 2 Litre, L
609123	Trunnion	CC16	136, 138	A, E, F, G, L, Y, Z
609172	Container, Water	CE1	140	V
609173	Plunger	CE8	140	A, E, L, V, Y
609526	Spacer	CE9	140	C, E, F, L, Z
609629	Cup		131, 134	F
609639	Spring	CA57	131, 134	A, E, F, G, L
609649	Washer, Sealing Rubber	BY81	123	A, F, G, L
609792	Bezel	CS33	192	C, E, E — 2 Litre, F, G, L, O
609793	Bezel	BR20	104, 107	A, C, E, F, G, L
609795	Bezel	BR31	105, 136	A, E, F, G, L

NUMERICAL INDEX

Part No.	Description	Plate No.	Page	Also Used on Models
609919	Bezel	CE10	140	C, E, F, L
609931	Plate, Tapping	BW47	116, 119	A, F
609964	Spring, Catch Rod—L.H.	CN41	163	F
609965	Spring, Catch Rod—R.H.		163	F
609966	Knob	CN40	163	F
610042	Washer	BY9	121	A, E, F
610152	Washer, Rubber	CG49	143	A
610520	Clip, Trim	CN15	158, 159, 160, 168, 169, 177, 184, 185	A, E, E — 2 Litre, F, G, L, M, O, Z
610573	Clip		136	
610624	Stud	CL9	147, 151, 157, 166, 175, 182, 190	A, E, F, G, L, O
610657	Rubber, Sealing	CF50	142	
610675	Rubber, Sealing	BW36	116, 119	F, G, L
610676	Seal	BW50	117, 120	F
611011	Label, Instructions—L.H.S.		93	G, L
611012	Label, Instructions—R.H.S.		93	G, L
611177	Washer, Rubber	AH35	52	A, E, E — 2 Litre, F, O
611364	Steering Column Cowl Assembly	CA37	130, 134	A, E, F
611368	Clamp, Upper Half	CA56	131, 134	A, E, F
611369	Cover, Harness Assembly	CA45	131, 134	A, E, F, G, L
611399	Label, Instructions—L.H.S.		93	A
611400	Label, Instructions—R.H.S.		93	A
611437	Cover	BZ5	127, 142	A, E, F, G, L, Z
611665	Reinforcement		113	
611822	Pad, Rubber	BU38	111	F, L
611938	Plate, Cover		192	E, E — 2 Litre, F
611953	Plug, Blanking		191, 200	A, E, O
611957	Seal, Top	BU36	111	A, E
611974	Escutcheon		192	E — 2 Litre, F, G
612260	Door Seal, Glass Top		126	A, E
612261	Hook Diaphragm		175, 182	A, E, E — 2 Litre, G, L, M, O, Z
612297	Reinforcement Assembly		111	F
612301	Plug		191	F
612306	Wing Mirror		191, 198	A, C, F, O, P, Y
612527	Mounting Bracket—L.H.	BU5	110	F
612528	Mounting Bracket—R.H.		110	F
612531	Eyebolt	CM68	154	A, E — 2 Litre, G, L, O
612577	Angle		110	F
612601	'T' Piece	CE12	140	A, C, E, F, G, L, O, V, Y, Z
612616	Bracket, Bonnet Location	BV9	112	F
612617	Plate, Locating	BV8	112	F
612659	Support—L.H.	BW23	115, 118	F
612660	Support—R.H.		115, 118,	F
612829	Bracket—L.H.	BW51	117, 120	
612830	Bracket—R.H.		117, 120	
612838	Bracket, Pivot	BW30	115	F
612850	Plate, Support		112	
612873	Bracket—L.H.	BW18	115, 118	
612874	Bracket—R.H.		115, 118	
612900	Bracket	CA61	131	F
612938	Angle, Rear valance to Wheelarch	BU32	111	
612962	Bonnet Location Peg	BW9	115, 118	A, E, F
612963	Tube, Distance	BW31	116	F
612970	Tube	BV16	113	F
612981	Gusset, Pedals—L.H.	BV14	112	F
612982	Gusset, Pedals—R.H.		112	F

NUMERICAL INDEX

Part No.	Description	Plate No.	Page	Also Used on Models
613017	Handle	BY77	123	A, E, F, L, O
613024	Check Arm	BY118	125	F
613025	Grommet	BV17	113	F
613045	Link Assembly, Upper	BW34	116, 119	F
613076	Clamp Assembly		115, 118	F
613093	Plinth	BP66	101	E, F, L
613097	Cover Plate, Demister		137	F
613110	Seal	BP67	101	F, L
613155	Rubber Pad, Battery		113	A, E — 2 Litre, F
613169	Clip	BY11	121	F
613178	Block, Mounting	BT8	109	F
613186	Ashtray	CA17	129, 133	A, F, G
613239	Rivet		125	F
613303	Spring	CN48	163	L
613314	Bezel	CC14	136	A, E, F
613344	Bracket Assembly	BU10	110	F
613350	Bracket Assembly—L.H.		112	F
613351	Bracket Assembly—R.H.		112	F
613378	Glass, Stop	BY82	123	F
613466	Pad, Sealing	CA51	131, 134	F
613474	Washer		116, 119	F
613478	Bracket, Support		111	F
613488	Hose, Water	CC9	136, 138	
613506	Cap, Petrol	BD18	83, 84	F, G, L
613607	Ring	AH34	52	F
613627	Pad, Lamp Mounting	BP24	99	F, L
613648	Seal	CC3	136, 138	F
613650	Jet Mounting Assembly	CE14	140	F, V
613656	Tubing	BM17	94	F
613663	Shoot Bolt	CR5	188	A
613666	Seal, Rear	BW35	116, 119	F
613685	Gusset	BV13	112	F
613686	Gusset, Dash	BV12	112	F
613687	Gusset, Dash	BV11	112	F
613745	Washer, Cup	CN52	163	L
613746	Buffer, Rubber	CN50	165	L
613751	Link Assembly	BW33	116, 119	F
613766	Clip, Beading	CK2	146	A, F, G
613769	Clip, Trim	CN30	161, 169, 178, 185	L
613770	Clip, Trim		150, 161, 169, 178, 185	L
613812	Cover	BU16	110	F, L
613871	Interior Mirror Assembly	BZ24	127	F, L
613886	Clip	CK3	146	F
613941	'D' Washer	CC7	136, 138	F
613954	Moulding, Finisher	BZ4	127	F, G, L
613955	Finisher	CF48	142	A, F, L
613966	Hook, Diaphragm, Short	CN9	157, 166, 175, 182	L, M, O, Z
614006	Bush, Friction		116, 119, 145, 146	A, E, E — 2 Litre, F, G, L, O, Z
614081	Grommet		151	F
614107	Clip	CJ4	145	O, Z
614118	Hose	CC10	136, 138	F
614125	Seal	CC2	136, 138	F
614126	Clip	CE2	140	F
614337	Hose—R.H.		139	O

NUMERICAL INDEX

Part No.	Description	Plate No.	Page	Also Used on Models
614338	Hose—R.H.		139	O
614344	Hose, Heater Vent—L.H.S.		139	
614345	Hose, Heater Vent—L.H.S.		139	
614346	Hose, Heater Vent—R.H.S.	CD53	139	
614347	Hose, Heater Vent—R.H.S.		139	
614348	Hose, Heater Vent—R.H.S.	CD54	139	
615699	Washer, Plate		117, 120	F
615706	Bracket	BV4	112	F
615707	Clip		75, 83, 84	A, E, O, Z
615710	Spacer	CG45	143	F
615810	Reinforcement		111	F
615813	Bar—R.H.	CG26	143	
615814	Bar—L.H.	CG27	143	
615825	Bar	CG22	143	F
615829	Washer	CH12	144	O, Z
615924	Clip, Cable		103	A, Z
615980	Plate	BU3	110	E — 2 Litre, F
615981	Washer	BU4	110	F
616034	Trunnion	CD30	138	O
616046	Washer, P.V.C.	BR19	104, 107	A, E
616048	Washer, P.V.C.	BS37	107	A, E
616050	Bezel	BR30	105, 136	A, E
616196	Plasti-Rivets		198	
616206	Drain Flap	CC36	137	A, E, F
616415	Plinth	BO43	98	F
616416	Gasket, Lamp Seating	BO44	98	F, G, L
616627	Seal	CC4	136, 138	F
616861	Clip, Spring	BY117	125	Z
616925	Grommet	BA14	80, 105	G, L, O, Z
617078	Pad		121	F
617164	Strip, Glazing	BY55	122	
617286	Roof Lamp Assembly	BP74	101	O, Z
617321	Weatherstrip	BY12	121	
617402	Washer, Seating, Front	BY110	124	F, G
617403	Washer, Seating, Rear	BY113	124	F, G, Z
617884	Clip	CL34	148	Z
618091	Rivet	CL44	148	
618179	Panel Assembly	BV37	114	
618274	Retainer	BV25	113	F
618275	Retainer—R.H.		113	F
618277	Remote Control Mechanism and Link Assembly—L.H.	BY96	124	F
618278	Remote Control Mechanism and Link Assembly—R.H.		124	F
618282	Private Lock Assembly—L.H.	BY116	125	F
618283	Private Lock Assembly—R.H.		125	F
618290	Washer	BR17	104, 107	A, E — 2 Litre, F
618342	Striker Dovetail Assembly—L.H.	BY92	123	F
618343	Striker Dovetail Assembly—R.H.		123	F
618397	Bracket, Fixing	BU30	111	
618398	Bracket, Support	BU25	111	
618399	Bracket Assembly	BU14	110	
618401	Bracket, Mounting	BU23	111	
618403	Bracket Assembly	BU15	110	
618407	Bracket, Mounting	BU29	111	
618410	Stud Plate—L.H.	CG29	143	
618420	Bracket, Outer	BU24	111	
618430	Latch	CL6	147	

NUMERICAL INDEX

Part No.	Description	Plate No.	Page	Also Used on Models
618432	Stud	CL36	148	
618486	Plate, Attachment—L.H.	CA5	129, 132	
618487	Plate, Attachment—R.H.		129, 132	
618488	Angle, Attachment	CA6	129	
618493	Plate Assembly	BV28	113	
618505	Stud Plate Assembly	CA4	129, 132	
618515	Hook-Bolt Assembly	CL48	148	
618789	Rubber, Plinth Mounting	BP55	101	F
618944	Ferrule, Gear Lever	CM42	151	Z
618945	Insert		151	Z
618946	Bezel	BS30	107	A
618947	Washer	BR27	105	
618954	Demister Outlet Capping Assembly	CC32	137	
618960	Bracket, Fixing	BU31	111	
619011	Top Assembly, Bonnet	BW24	115	
619012	Body Shell, Prime Finish—R.H.S.		108	
619013	Body Shell, Prime Finish—L.H.S.		108	
619048	Bracket		114	
619076	Washer, Sealing	BY93	123	F
619099	Plate, Tapped	BV24	113	F
619100	Plate, Tapped Lock Striker—R.H.		113	F
619109	Plinth, Side and Flasher Lamps—L.H.		97	F
619110	Plinth, Side and Flasher Lamps—R.H.	BO32	97	F
619216	Retainer	CR9	188	O
619242	Bracket Assembly	BY35	122	L
619244	Bracket Assembly	BY34	122	
619249	Bracket Assembly—L.H.	BY24	122	
619250	Bracket Assembly—R.H.		122	
619266	Bracket—L.H.	BY86	123	
619267	Bracket—R.H.		123	
619383	Block, Striker	CF37	141	
619384	Sleeve	CF34	141	
619420	Grommet	BD19	83	
619437	Pad, Foam, Side	CM60	152	
619439	Pad, Foam, Top	CM61	152	
619440	Pad, Foam, Front	CM62	152	
619482	Reinforcement		113	
619496	Escutcheon	CF41	141	
619498	Strap Assembly, Squab	CN7	157, 166, 175, 182	O
619499	Strap Assembly, Squab	CN8	157, 166, 175, 182	
619500	Strap Assembly, Squab	CN9	157, 166, 175, 182	
619501	Strap Assembly, Squab	CN10	157, 166, 175, 182	
619558	Pad, Spare Wheel to Floor	CM59	151	
619607	Washer, Cup	CL38	148	
619618	Washer, Cup	CN32	161, 170, 178, 185	
619680	Door-pull Assembly	BY126	126	
619739	Bracket—L.H.	BW2	115, 118	F
619740	Bracket—R.H.		115, 118	F
619776	Felt Strip, Black	CL46	148	
619777	Felt Strip, Black	CL45	148	
619778	Felt Strip, Black	CL47	148	
619779	Felt Strip	CL30	147	
619780	Felt Strip	CL31	147	

NUMERICAL INDEX

Part No.	Description	Plate No.	Page	Also Used on Models
619812	Insert, Ferrule	CM43	151	
619822	Clip, Edge		117, 120	F
619844	Push/Pull Control Assembly	CC12	136	
619845	Push/Pull Control Assembly	CC18	136	
619848	Tie Bar—R.H.S.	CA54	131	
619849	Tie Bar—L.H.S.		131	
619850	Clamp, Lower Half	CA55	131, 134	
619854	Valve, Water	CC8	136, 138	
619860	Badge, G.T.6.	CJ13	145	
619864	Rod, Battery Fixing		113	
619882	Tube, Distance	BZ12	127	
619884	Plate	BZ13	127	
619946	Strap Assembly	CL55	148	
619949	Plate, Retaining	CL56	148	
619950	Bracket		111	
620121	Bracket	BV3	112	
620171	Finisher, Upper—L.H.	CM14	149	
620181	Finisher, Upper—R.H.		149	
620191	Cover, Trim, L.H.—Black	BZ9	127	
620201	Cover, Trim, R.H.—Black	BZ10	127	
620211	Finisher, Lower, L.H.—Black	CM16	149	
620212	Finisher, Lower, L.H.—Red	CM16	149	
620213	Finisher, Lower, L.H.—Light Tan		149	
620216	Finisher, Lower, L.H.—Midnight Blue		149	
620217	Finisher, Lower, L.H.—Shadow Blue		149	
620221	Finisher, Lower, R.H.—Black		149	
620222	Finisher, Lower, R.H.—Red		149	
620223	Finisher, Lower, R.H.—Light Tan		149	
620226	Finisher, Lower, R.H.—Midnight Blue		149	
620227	Finisher, Lower, R.H.—Shadow Blue		149	
620311	Cover, Trim	CM29	150	
620321	Cover, Trim	CM28	150	
620349	Finisher, Upper, L.H.	CM15	149	
620359	Finisher, Upper, R.H.		149	
620361	Trim, Back Door, L.H.—Black	CM25	150	
620362	Trim, Back Door, L.H.—Red	CM25	150	
620363	Trim, Back Door, L.H.—Light Tan	CM25	150	
620366	Trim, Back Door, L.H.—Midnight Blue	CM25	150	
620367	Trim, Back Door, L.H.—Shadow Blue	CM25	150	
620371	Trim, Back Door, R.H.—Black	CM24	150	
620372	Trim, Back Door, R.H.—Red	CM24	150	
620373	Trim, Back Door, R.H.—Light Tan	CM24	150	
620376	Trim, Back Door, R.H.—Midnight Blue	CM24	150	
620377	Trim, Back Door, R.H.—Shadow Blue	CM24	150	
620389	Cover, Trim	CM23	150	
620408	Ring, Clamping	CB4	132	G, O
620410	Clip	CL43	148	
620411	Cover Assembly, Sewn, Side Panel Outer, Leathercloth, L.H.—L.H. Seat (Black)	CN21	159	
620412	Cover Assembly, Sewn, Side Panel Outer, Leathercloth, L.H.—L.H. Seat (Red)	CN21	159	
620413	Cover Assembly, Sewn, Side Panel Outer, Leathercloth, L.H.—L.H. Seat (Light Tan)		159	
620416	Cover Assembly, Sewn, Side Panel Outer, Leathercloth, L.H.—L.H. Seat (Midnight Blue)	CN21	159	
620417	Cover Assembly, Sewn, Side Panel Outer, Leathercloth, L.H.—L.H. Seat (Shadow Blue)		159	
620421	Cover Assembly, Sewn, Side Panel Outer, Leathercloth, R.H.—R.H. Seat (Black)	CN21	159	

NUMERICAL INDEX

Part No.	Description	Plate No.	Page	Also Used on Models
620422	Cover Assembly, Sewn, Side Panel Outer, Leathercloth, R.H.—R.H. Seat (Red)	CN21	159	
620423	Cover Assembly, Sewn, Side Panel Outer, Leathercloth, R.H.—R.H. Seat (Light Tan)		159	
620426	Cover Assembly, Sewn, Side Panel Outer, Leathercloth, R.H.—R.H. Seat (Midnight Blue)	CN21	159	
620427	Cover Assembly, Sewn, Side Panel Outer, Leathercloth, R.H.—R.H. Seat (Shadow Blue)		159	
620431	Cover Assembly, Sewn, Side Panel Outer, Leather, L.H.—L.H. Seat (Black)	CN21	159	
620432	Cover Assembly, Sewn, Side Panel Outer, Leather, L.H.—L.H. Seat (Red)	CN21	159	
620433	Cover Assembly, Sewn, Side Panel Outer, Leather, L.H.—L.H. Seat (Light Tan)	CN21	159	
620436	Cover Assembly, Sewn, Side Panel Outer, Leather, L.H.—L.H. Seat (Midnight Blue)	CN21	159	
620437	Cover Assembly, Sewn, Side Panel Outer, Leather, L.H.—L.H. Seat (Shadow Blue)	CN21	159	
620441	Cover Assembly, Sewn, Side Panel Outer, Leather, R.H.—R.H. Seat (Black)		159	
620442	Cover Assembly, Sewn, Side Panel Outer, Leather, R.H.—R.H. Seat (Red)		159	
620443	Cover Assembly, Sewn, Side Panel Outer, Leather, R.H.—R.H. Seat (Light Tan)		159	
620446	Cover Assembly, Sewn, Side Panel Outer, Leather, R.H.—R.H. Seat (Midnight Blue)		159	
620447	Cover Assembly, Sewn, Side Panel Outer, Leather, R.H.—R.H. Seat (Shadow Blue)		159	
620451	Cover Assembly, Sewn, Side Panel Inner, Leathercloth, L.H.—R.H. Seat (Black)	CN27	160	
620452	Cover Assembly, Sewn, Side Panel Inner, Leathercloth, L.H.—R.H. Seat (Red)	CN27	160	
620453	Cover Assembly, Sewn, Side Panel Inner, Leathercloth, L.H.—R.H. Seat (Light Tan)	CN27	160	
620456	Cover Assembly, Sewn, Side Panel Inner, Leathercloth L.H.—R.H. Seat (Midnight Blue)	CN27	160	
620457	Cover Assembly, Sewn, Side Panel Inner, Leathercloth, L.H.—R.H. Seat (Shadow Blue)	CN27	160	
620461	Cover Assembly, Sewn, Side Panel Inner, Leathercloth, R.H.—L.H. Seat (Black)		160	
620462	Cover Assembly, Sewn, Side Panel Inner, Leathercloth, R.H.—L.H. Seat (Red)		160	
620463	Cover Assembly, Sewn, Side Panel Inner, Leathercloth, R.H.—L.H. Seat (Light Tan)		160	
620466	Cover Assembly, Sewn, Side Panel Inner, Leathercloth, R.H.—L.H. Seat (Midnight Blue)		160	
620467	Cover Assembly, Sewn, Side Panel Inner, Leathercloth, R.H.—L.H. Seat (Shadow Blue)		160	
620471	Cover Assembly, Sewn, Side Panel Inner Leather, L.H.—R.H. Seat (Black)	CN27	160	
620472	Cover Assembly, Sewn, Side Panel Inner, Leather, L.H.—R.H. Seat (Red)	CN27	160	
620473	Cover Assembly, Sewn, Side Panel Inner, Leather, L.H.—R.H. Seat (Light Tan)	CN27	160	
620476	Cover Assembly, Sewn, Side Panel Inner, Leather, L.H.—R.H. Seat (Midnight Blue)	CN27	160	
620477	Cover Assembly, Sewn, Side Panel Inner, Leather, L.H.—R.H. Seat (Shadow Blue)	CN27	160	

NUMERICAL INDEX

Part No.	Description	Plate No.	Page	Also Used on Models
620481	Cover Assembly, Sewn, Side Panel Inner, Leather, R.H.—L.H. Seat (Black)		160	
620482	Cover Assembly, Sewn, Side Panel Inner, Leather, R.H.—L.H. Seat (Red)		160	
620483	Cover Assembly, Sewn, Side Panel Inner, Leather, R.H.—L.H. Seat (Light Tan)		160	
620486	Cover Assembly, Sewn, Side Panel Inner, Leather, R.H.—L.H. Seat (Midnight Blue)		160	
620487	Cover Assembly, Sewn, Side Panel Inner, Leather, L.H.—R.H. Seat (Shadow Blue)	CN27	160	
620501	Grommet, Handbrake Assembly—Leathercloth, (Black)	CM64	153	
620502	Grommet, Handbrake Assembly—Leathercloth, (Red)	CM64	153	
620503	Grommet, Handbrake Assembly—Leathercloth, (Light Tan)	CM64	153	
620506	Grommet, Handbrake Assembly—Leathercloth, (Midnight Blue)	CM64	153	
620507	Grommet, Handbrake Assembly Leathercloth, (Shadow Blue)	CM64	153	
620511	Grommet, Handbrake Assembly—Leather, (Black)	CM64	153	
620512	Grommet, Handbrake Assembly—Leather, (Red)	CM64	153	
620513	Grommet, Handbrake Assembly—Leather, (Light Tan)	CM64	153	
620516	Grommet, Handbrake Assembly—Leather, (Midnight Blue)	CM64	153	
620517	Grommet, Handbrake Assembly—Leather, (Shadow Blue)	CM64	153	
620543	Knob	CE11	140	
620547	Plate, Tapped	CA60	131, 134	
620619	Clip, Trim		150	
620656	Rubber, Sealing	BY130	126	
620711	Carpet, Dash Side—R.H.	CM39	151	F
620721	Carpet, Dash Side—L.H.	CM40	151	F
620750	Screw	CD23	138	O
620761	Carpet, Formed, Heelboard	CM52	151	F
620771	Carpet, Sill—L.H.	CM45	151	F
620781	Carpet, Sill—R.H.	CM44	151	F
620821	Carpet, Rear Wheelarch Cover—L.H.	CM58	151	
620831	Carpet, Rear Wheelarch Cover—R.H.	CM57	151	
620847	Clamp	CB6	132	G, O
620848	Nut, Knurled	CB5	132	G, O
620871	Channel	CL2	147	
620889	Ring, Base		150	
620914	Strip, Sealing	BY129	126	
621101	Pad, Mounting	BT16	109	F, G,
621112	Plate Assembly		110	E — 2 Litre, F
621252	Extension	CH29	144	F
621266	Bracket Attachment, Safety Catch and Lever	CP49	172, 187	
621292	Washer, Plain		154	F, G
621308	Eyebolt		154	A, F, G, Z
621340	Hook, Strap		157	
621370	Bolt		154	A, E — 2 Litre, F, G
621371	Spacer		154	A, E — 2 Litre, F, G
621373	Washer, Seating		142	
621374	Washer, Waved		154	A, E — 2 Litre, F, G, O, Z
621408	Piece, Distance		130	

60

NUMERICAL INDEX

Part No.	Description	Plate No.	Page	Also Used on Models
621409	Tube, Spacer	CA28	130	
621418	Tube, Distance	BX31	119	F
621419	Spacer	BX32	119	F
621421	Finisher, Rear Tunnel		154, 199	
621458	Knob	CP47	172, 187	G
621510	Spacer	BS36	107	A
621515	Buffer	CP29	170, 178, 185	G
621535	Nut, Special	CR29	190	A
621671	Bracket Assembly—L.H.		123	
621672	Bracket Assembly—R.H.		123	
621704	Base	BZ28	127	G
621705	Retainer	BZ30	127	G
621706	Gusset, L.H.—L.H.S.		112	
621707	Gusset, R.H.—L.H.S.		112	
621714	Plate		124	G
621732	Washer, Seating		125	F
621733	Clip		125	F
621767	Interior Mirror Assembly		127	
621768	Knob		123	G
621770	Remote Control Handle		124	G
621771	Clip, Beading	CK8	145, 146	
621773	Private Lock Assembly—L.H.		125	F, G
621776	Clip	CP48	172, 187	G
621811	Window Regulator Handle Assembly		123	G
621834	Angle, Battery Retaining		113	
621867	Finisher, Rear Tunnel		154	
621876	Door Lock Striker Dovetail—L.H.		124	G
621877	Door Lock Striker Dovetail—R.H.		124	G
622031	Steering Column Cowl Assembly (Locking)		130	
622136	Ring, Clamp	CB13	132	
622138	Tube Assembly, Foot Level Vent—R.H.S.	CD48	139	G
622150	Clip, Heater Hose		113	
622153	Bezel	CK21	146	
622220	Bracket Assembly		132	
622222	Plate, Switch Retainer	CB22	132	
622223	Washer, Plate	CB23	132	
622224	Spacer	CD16	138	
622228	Knob Assembly, Heater Control	CD13	138	
622229	Knob Assembly, Ventilator Control	CD21	138	
622230	Plate, Retainer	CB19	132	
622235	Spacer	CD15	138	
622236	Lever, Control, Ventilator	CD20	138	
622237	Lever, Control, Water Valve	CD12	138	
622260	Nameplate, "Triumph"	CK14	146	
622275	Washer, Plain		67	
622276	Nut, "Dotloc"		67	
622350	Stem Assembly, Door Mirror		126	G
622351	Head Assembly, Door Mirror		126	G
622352	Door Mirror, Passenger Side		126	G
622431	Retainer, Sun Visor	BZ46	128	
622443	Bezel	BS39	107	
622496	Nameplate, "G.T.6 +"	CK9	119, 146	
622497	Nameplate, "G.T.6 +"	CK12	146	
622500	Bonnet Top Assembly	BX24	118	
622507	Bracket, Foot Level Vent—L.H.	CB8	132	
622508	Bracket, Foot Level Vent—R.H.		132	
622509	Clamp	CB76	135	
622510	Support Bracket Assembly, Steering Column (Lower)	CB72	135	

NUMERICAL INDEX

Part No.	Description	Plate No.	Page	Also Used on Models
622514	Tube Assembly, R.H.—L.H.S.		139	
622553	Bracket, Vent Tube Clip—R.H.S.	CD49	139	
622566	Clip, Vent Tube Retaining—R.H.S.	CD50	139	
622611	Grille, Inner	CK20	146	
622682	Nut, Spacer	BS38	107	
622683	Grommet	BE18	84	
622812	Demister Outlet Capping Assembly	CD39	137, 139	
623067	Hinge, Squab Board	CR2	188	
623070	Plate, Packing	CR6	188	
623312	Clip		75	
623314	Clip		75, 83, 84	
623341	Cover Assembly, Sewn, Side Panel Inner, Leathercloth, R.H.—L.H. Seat (Black)	CP22	169, 177, 184	
623342	Cover Assembly, Sewn, Side Panel Inner, Leathercloth, R.H.—L.H. Seat (Red)	CP22	168, 177, 184	
623343	Cover Assembly, Sewn, Side Panel Inner, Leathercloth, R.H.—L.H. Seat (Light Tan)	CP22	168, 177, 184	
623346	Cover Assembly, Sewn, Side Panel Inner, Leathercloth, R.H.—L.H. Seat (Midnight Blue)	CP22	168	
623347	Cover Assembly, Sewn, Side Panel Inner, Leathercloth, R.H.—L.H. Seat (Shadow Blue)	CP22	169, 177, 168	
623351	Cover Assembly, Sewn, Side Panel Inner, Leathercloth, L.H.—R.H. Seat (Black)		169, 177, 184	
623352	Cover Assembly, Sewn, Side Panel Inner, Leathercloth, L.H.—R.H. Seat (Red)		168, 177, 184	
623353	Cover Assembly, Sewn, Side Panel Inner, Leathercloth, L.H.—R.H. Seat (Light Tan)		168, 177, 184	
623356	Cover Assembly, Sewn, Side Panel Inner, Leathercloth, L.H.—R.H. Seat (Midnight Blue)		168	
623357	Cover Assembly, Sewn, Side Panel Inner, Leathercloth, L.H.—R.H. Seat (Shadow Blue)		168, 177, 184	
623361	Cover Assembly, Sewn, Side Panel Inner, Leather, R.H.—L.H. Seat (Black)	CP22	169, 177, 184	
623362	Cover Assembly, Sewn, Side Panel Inner, Leather, R.H.—L.H. Seat (Red)	CP22	169, 177, 184	
623363	Cover Assembly, Sewn, Side Panel Inner, Leather, R.H.—L.H. Seat (Light Tan)	CP22	169, 177, 184	
623366	Cover Assembly, Sewn, Side Panel Inner, Leather, R.H.—L.H. Seat (Midnight Blue)	CP22	169	
623367	Cover Assembly, Sewn, Side Panel Inner, Leather, R.H.—L.H. Seat (Shadow Blue)	CP22	169, 177, 184	
623371	Cover Assembly, Sewn, Side Panel Inner, Leather, L.H.—R.H. Seat (Black)		169, 177, 184	
623372	Cover Assembly, Sewn, Side Panel Inner, Leather, L.H.—R.H. Seat (Red)		169, 177, 184	
623373	Cover Assembly, Sewn, Side Panel Inner, Leather, L.H.—R.H. Seat (Light Tan)		169, 177, 184	
623376	Cover Assembly, Sewn, Side Panel Inner, Leather, L.H.—R.H. Seat (Midnight Blue)		169	
623377	Cover Assembly, Sewn, Side Panel Inner, Leather, L.H.—R.H. Seat (Shadow Blue)		169, 177, 184	
623381	Cover Assembly, Sewn, Side Panel Outer, Leathercloth, L.H.—L.H. Seat (Black)	CP17	168, 176, 183	
623382	Cover Assembly, Sewn, Side Panel Outer, Leathercloth, L.H.—L.H. Seat (Red)	CP17	167, 176, 183	
623383	Cover Assembly, Sewn, Side Panel Outer, Leathercloth, L.H.—L.H. Seat (Light Tan)	CP17	167, 176, 183	
623386	Cover Assembly, Sewn, Side Panel Outer, Leathercloth, L.H.—L.H. Seat (Midnight Blue)	CP17	167	

NUMERICAL INDEX

Part No.	Description	Plate No.	Page	Also Used on Models
623387	Cover Assembly, Sewn, Side Panel Outer, Leathercloth, L.H.—L.H. Seat (Shadow Blue)	CP17	167, 176, 183	
623391	Cover Assembly, Sewn, Side Panel Outer, Leathercloth, R.H.—R.H. Seat (Black)		169, 176, 183	
623392	Cover Assembly, Sewn, Side Panel Outer, Leathercloth, R.H.—R.H. Seat (Red)		167, 176, 183	
623393	Cover Assembly, Sewn, Side Panel Outer, Leathercloth, R.H.—R.H. Seat (Light Tan)		167, 176, 183	
623396	Cover Assembly, Sewn, Side Panel Outer, Leathercloth, R.H.—R.H. Seat (Midnight Blue)		167	
623397	Cover Assembly, Sewn, Side Panel Outer, Leathercloth, R.H.—R.H. Seat (Shadow Blue)		167, 176, 183	
623401	Cover Assembly, Sewn, Side Panel Outer, Leather, L.H.—L.H. Seat (Black)	CP17	168, 176, 184	
623402	Cover Assembly, Sewn, Side Panel Outer, Leather, L.H.—L.H. Seat (Red)	CP17	168, 176, 183	
623403	Cover Assembly, Sewn, Side Panel Outer, Leather, L.H.—L.H. Seat (Light Tan)	CP17	168, 176, 183	
623406	Cover Assembly, Sewn, Side Panel Outer, Leather, L.H.—L.H. Seat (Midnight Blue)	CP17	168	
623407	Cover Assembly, Sewn, Side Panel Outer, Leather, L.H.—L.H. Seat (Shadow Blue)	CP17	168, 176, 184	
623411	Cover Assembly, Sewn, Side Panel Outer, Leather, R.H.—R.H. Seat (Black)		168, 176, 184	
623412	Cover Assembly, Sewn, Side Panel Outer, Leather, R.H.—R.H. Seat (Red)		168, 176, 183	
623413	Cover Assembly, Sewn, Side Panel Outer, Leather, R.H.—R.H. Seat (Light Tan)		168, 176, 183	
623416	Cover Assembly, Sewn, Side Panel Outer, Leather, R.H.—R.H. Seat (Midnight Blue)		168	
623417	Cover Assembly, Sewn, Side Panel Outer, Leather, R.H.—R.H. Seat (Shadow Blue)		168, 176, 184	
623420	Piece, Filler		166, 175, 182	
623485	Spring, Tension—L.H.		172, 187	
623486	Spring, Tension—R.H.	CP52	172, 187	
623488	Tie Bar—R.H.S.	CB65	134	
623489	Tie Bar—L.H.S.		134	
623490	Felt Strip	CB77	135	
623491	Felt Strip	CB78	135	
623796	Bracket Assembly		110	
623803	Bracket, Attachment, Outer	CQ46	187	
623843	Escutcheon, Inside Handle—Black		123, 124	
623853	Bracket, Squab Support—L.H.	CR27	190	
623854	Bracket, Squab Support—R.H.		190	
623872	Nameplate (G.T.6 MK. II)—Rear Panel	CK13	146	
623873	Nameplate (G.T.6 MK. II)—Bonnet	CK10	119, 146	
623877	Clip, Diaphragm		175, 182	
623881	Strap Squab Retaining	CR8	188	
623911	Carpet Assembly, Squab Board	CR13	189	
624193	Cable Assembly, Heater Screen	CD28	138	
624194	Cable Assembly, Water Valve	CD29	138	
624276	Label, "Pull Boost"	CD22	138	
625491	Bracket Assembly, Trimmed, Squab Support—L.H.	CR22	189	
625501	Bracket Assembly, Trimmed, Squab Support—R.H.		189	
625511	Tensioner, Fly		183	
625549	Washer, Cup		132	
625580	Washer, Special, Rubber		98, 100	

63

NUMERICAL INDEX

Part No.	Description	Plate No.	Page	Also Used on Models
625608	Hinge Assembly, Back Door—L.H.		141	
625609	Hinge Assembly, Back Door—R.H.		141	
625616	Roof Lamp Assembly		101	
650016	Disc, Clamping	CL53	148	G, L
650017	Bolt, Hook	CL52	148	G, L
650019	Nut, Wing	CL54	148	G, L
650130	Rubber, Sealing	BZ7	127	F, G, L
650247	Grommet	BE16	84	F, G, L
650261	Escutcheon	BY79	123, 124	A, E, F, L, O
703862	Letter 'T'	BW38	116, 145	A, B, E, F, L, O, R, Z
703863	Letter 'R'	BW39	116, 145	A, B, E, F, L, O, R, Z
703864	Letter 'I'	BW40	116, 145	A, B, E, F, L, O, R, Z
703865	Letter 'U'	BW41	116, 145	A, B, E, F, L, O, R, Z
703866	Letter 'M'	BW42	116, 145	A, B, E, F, L, O, R, Z
703867	Letter 'P'	BW43	116, 145	A, B, E, F, L, O, R, Z
703868	Letter 'H'	BW44	116, 145	A, B, E, F, L, O, R, Z
704881	Knob, Heater Switch	CC19	136	A, B, E, F, L, V
704884	Knob, Water Valve	CC13	136	A, E, F, L, Z
705787	Panel, Inner—L.H.		110	A, E, F
705788	Panel, Inner—R.H.	BU18	110	A, E, F
706159	Reinforcement Assembly—L.H.	BU13	110	F
706160	Reinforcement Assembly—R.H.		110	F
706288	Panel, Lower—L.H.	BV33	113	F
706289	Panel, Lower—R.H.		113	F
706311	Panel, Filler—L.H.	BW20	115, 118	F
706312	Panel, Filler—R.H.	BW19	115, 118	F
706422	Panel, Front—L.H.	BV34	113	F
706423	Panel, Front—R.H.		113	F
706453	Reinforcement		115, 118	F
706512	Bracket—L.H.	BW52	117	F
706513	Bracket—R.H.		117	F
706539	Tube Assembly	BW25	115, 118	F
706548	Panel, Inner—L.H.	BW15	115, 118	F
706549	Panel, Inner—R.H.	BW14	115, 118	F
706550	Bracket	BV19	113	F
706556	Joint Finisher	CK1	146	F
706583	Overrider Assembly, Rear—L.H.	CG37	143	F
706584	Overrider Assembly, Rear—R.H.	CG36	143	F
706600	Finisher	BV29	113	F
706728	Nozzle, Demister	CC29	136	F
706768	Tubing	BM16	94	F
706975	Pad, Insulation—L.H.	CM2	149	
706976	Pad, Insulation—R.H.	CM1	149	
707315	Heelmat, L.H.—L.H.S.		151	F
707316	Heelmat, R.H.—R.H.S.	CM31	151	F
707319	Finisher	CK4	146	F
708479	Escutcheon	CA42	130, 134	A, E, F, L
708633	Handle	CA27	130	F
708759	Trim Cover, Windscreen, Bottom	BZ8	127	E, L
709281	Panel—L.H.	BV43	114	
709282	Panel—R.H.		114	
709283	Panel—L.H.	BV44	114	
709284	Panel—R.H.		114	
709285	Panel—L.H.	BV45	114	
709286	Panel—R.H.		114	
709300	Hinge Assembly—L.H.	CF19	141	
709301	Hinge Assembly—R.H.	CF18	141	
709386	Door Handle Assembly, Outside	BY107	124	F
709564	Bracket, Reinforcing	BU27	111	

NUMERICAL INDEX

Part No.	Description	Plate No.	Page	Also Used on Models
709567	Bracket Assembly	BU46	114	
709662	Support, Outer	BV30	113	
709663	Support, Outer	CL20	147	
709691	Bracket	CA2	129, 132	
709692	Support Assembly—L.H.	CA35	130, 133	F
709693	Support Assembly—R.H.	CA36	139, 133	F
709753	Buffer Assembly	CH5	144	F, O
709807	Panel	BU28	111	
709811	Listing Rail, Front	CM10	149	
709812	Listing Rail, Centre	CM11	149	
709813	Listing Rail, Rear	CM12	149	
709840	Cover Plate	CA26	129	
709841	Plate, Mounting		129	
709842	Cover Plate	CB43	129, 133	
709843	Plate, Adjusting		129, 133	
709845	Plinth, Number Plate Lamp	BP54	101	F
709862	Cover, Gearbox	BU33	111	
709863	Door Seal, "Neoprene"—L.H.	BY128	126	
709864	Door Seal, "Neoprene"—R.H.		126	
710061	Mounting, Centre	BZ34	128	
710086	Finisher	CJ1	145	
710194	Channel, Glass—L.H.	BY56	122	
710195	Channel, Glass—R.H.		122	
710290	Lock Assembly		141	
710291	Front Door Trim Pad Assembly, L.H.—Black	BY121	125	
710292	Front Door Trim Pad Assembly, L.H.—Red	BY121	125	
710293	Front Door Trim Pad Assembly, L.H.—Light Tan	BY121	125	
710296	Front Door Trim Pad Assembly, L.H.—Midnight Blue	BY121	125	
710297	Front Door Trim Pad Assembly, L.H.—Shadow Blue	BY121	125	
710301	Front Door Trim Pad Assembly, R.H.—Black		125	
710302	Front Door Trim Pad Assembly, R.H.—Red		125	
710303	Front Door Trim Pad Assembly, R.H.—Light Tan		125	
710306	Front Door Trim Pad Assembly, R.H.—Midnight Blue		125	
710307	Front Door Trim Pad Assembly, R.H.—Shadow Blue		125	
710449	Gusset—L.H.	BU22	111	
710450	Gusset—R.H.	BU21	111	
710497	Handle Assembly	CF39	142	
710498	Footrest, Gearbox Cover	BU37	111	
710573	Strip, Rubber—L.H.	BY10	121	
710574	Strip, Rubber—R.H.		121	
710587	Luggage Strap (Rear Floor)		197	
710619	Channel Assembly—L.H.	BY54	122	
710620	Channel Assembly—R.H.		122	
710650	Rubber, Glazing	BY68	122	
710651	Rubber, Glazing	BY69	122	
710679	Channel	BW1	115, 118	F
710680	Strut Centre	BW3	115, 118	F
710686	Finisher—L.H.	CJ3	145	
710687	Finisher—R.H.	CJ2	145	
710702	Luggage Floor Assembly	CL8	147	
710703	Luggage Floor Assembly	CL24	147	
710704	Luggage Floor Assembly	CL35	148	
710705	Bracket, Support—L.H.	CG3	143	
710706	Bracket, Support—R.H.	CG2	143	

NUMERICAL INDEX

Part No.	Description	Plate No.	Page	Also Used on Models
710714	Gusset—L.H.	BW4	115, 118	F
710715	Gusset—R.H.		115, 118	F
710716	Overrider Assembly, Front—L.H.	CG6	143	
710717	Overrider Assembly, Front—R.H.	CG5	143	
710820	Grommet	AH33	52	
710841	Carpet, Gearbox Cover Assembly—R.H.S.	CM41	151	
710851	Carpet, Gearbox Cover Assembly—L.H.S.		151	
710901	Headlining Assembly—Black		149	
710909	Headlining Assembly—White	CM9	149	
711021	Cover Assembly, Tunnel, Centre—Leathercloth (Black)	CM65	153	
711022	Cover Assembly, Tunnel, Centre—Leathercloth (Red)	CM65	153	
711023	Cover Assembly, Tunnel, Centre—Leathercloth (Light Tan)	CM65	153	
711026	Cover Assembly, Tunnel, Centre—Leathercloth (Midnight Blue)	CM65	153	
711027	Cover Assembly, Tunnel, Centre—Leathercloth (Shadow Blue)	CM65	153	
711031	Cover Assembly, Tunnel, Centre—Leather (Black)	CM65	153	
711032	Cover Assembly, Tunnel, Centre—Leather (Red)	CM65	153	
711033	Cover Assembly, Tunnel, Centre—Leather (Light Tan)	CM65	153	
711036	Cover Assembly, Tunnel, Centre—Leather (Midnight Blue)	CM65	153	
711037	Cover Assembly, Tunnel, Centre—Leather (Shadow Blue)	CM65	153	
711041	Cover Assembly, Tunnel, Rear—Leathercloth, L.H. (Black)	CM67	153	
711042	Cover Assembly, Tunnel, Rear—Leathercloth, L.H. (Red)	CM67	153	
711046	Cover Assembly, Tunnel, Rear—Leathercloth, L.H. (Midnight Blue)	CM67	153	
711051	Cover Assembly, Tunnel, Centre—Leathercloth, R.H. (Black)	CM66	153	
711052	Cover Assembly, Tunnel, Centre—Leathercloth, R.H. (Red)	CM66	153	
711056	Cover Assembly, Tunnel, Centre—Leathercloth, R.H. (Midnight Blue)	CM66	153	
711061	Cover Assembly, Tunnel, Rear—Leather, L.H. (Black)	CM67	153	
711062	Cover Assembly, Tunnel, Rear—Leather. L.H. (Red)	CM67	153	
711066	Cover Assembly, Tunnel, Rear—Leather, L.H. (Midnight Blue)	CM67	153	
711071	Cover Assembly, Tunnel, Centre—Leather, R.H. (Black)	CM66	153	
711072	Cover Assembly, Tunnel, Centre—Leather, R.H. (Red)	CM66	153	
711076	Cover Assembly, Tunnel, Centre—Leather, R.H. (Midnight Blue)	CM66	153	
711081	Handbrake Cover and Centre Armrest Assembly, Leathercloth (Black)		152	
711082	Handbrake Cover and Centre Armrest Assembly, Leathercloth (Red)		152	
711083	Handbrake Cover and Centre Armrest Assembly, Leathercloth (Light Tan)		152	

NUMERICAL INDEX

Part No.	Description	Plate No.	Page	Also Used on Models
711086	Handbrake Cover and Centre Armrest Assembly, Leathercloth (Midnight Blue)		152	
711087	Handbrake Cover and Centre Armrest Assembly, Leathercloth (Shadow Blue)		152	
711091	Handbrake Cover and Centre Armrest Assembly, Leather (Black)		152	
711092	Handbrake Cover and Centre Armrest Assembly, Leather (Red)		152	
711093	Handbrake Cover and Centre Armrest Assembly, Leather (Light Tan)		152	
711096	Handbrake Cover and Centre Armrest Assembly, Leather (Midnight Blue)		152	
711097	Handbrake Cover and Centre Armrest Assembly, Leather (Shadow Blue)		152	
711101	Cover Assembly, Handbrake, Leathercloth—(Black)	CM63	152	
711102	Cover Assembly, Handbrake, Leathercloth—(Red)	CM63	152	
711103	Cover Assembly, Handbrake—Leathercloth (Light Tan)	CM63	152	
711106	Cover Assembly, Handbrake—Leathercloth (Midnight Blue)	CM63	152	
711107	Cover Assembly, Handbrake—Leathercloth (Shadow Blue)	CM63	152	
711111	Cover Assembly, Handbrake—Leather (Black)	CM63	153	
711112	Cover Assembly, Handbrake—Leather (Red)	CM63	153	
711113	Cover Assembly, Handbrake—Leather (Light Tan)	CM63	153	
711116	Cover Assembly, Handbrake—Leather (Midnight Blue)	CM63	153	
711117	Cover Assembly, Handbrake—Leather (Shadow Blue)	CM63	153	
711131	Cover Assembly, Cushion—Leathercloth—L.H. Seat (Black)	CN35	162, 171, 179	
711132	Cover Assembly, Cushion—Leathercloth—L.H. Seat (Red)	CN35	162, 171, 179	
711133	Cover Assembly, Cushion—Leathercloth—L.H. Seat (Light Tan)	CN35	162, 171, 179	
711136	Cover Assembly, Cushion—Leathercloth—L.H. Seat (Midnight Blue)	CN35	162, 171	
711137	Cover Assembly, Cushion—Leathercloth—L.H. Seat (Shadow Blue)	CN35	162, 171, 179	
711141	Cover Assembly, Cushion—Leathercloth—R.H. Seat (Black)		162, 171, 179	
711142	Cover Assembly, Cushion—Leathercloth—R.H. Seat (Red)		162, 171, 179	
711143	Cover Assembly, Cushion—Leathercloth—R.H. Seat (Light Tan)		162, 171, 179	
711146	Cover Assembly, Cushion—Leathercloth—R.H. Seat (Midnight Blue)		162, 171	
711147	Cover Assembly, Cushion—Leathercloth—R.H. Seat (Shadow Blue)		162, 171, 179	
711151	Cover Assembly, Cushion—Leather—L.H. Seat (Black)	CN35	163, 172, 179	
711152	Cover Assembly, Cushion—Leather—L.H. Seat (Red)	CN35	162, 171, 179	
711153	Cover Assembly, Cushion—Leather—L.H. Seat (Light Tan)	CN35	163, 171, 179	

NUMERICAL INDEX

Part No.	Description	Plate No.	Page	Also Used on Models
711156	Cover Assembly, Cushion—Leather—L.H. Seat (Midnight Blue)	CN35	163, 171	
711157	Cover Assembly, Cushion—Leather—L.H. Seat (Shadow Blue)	CN35	163, 172, 179	
711161	Cover Assembly, Cushion—Leather—R.H. Seat (Black)		163, 172, 179	
711162	Cover Assembly, Cushion—Leather—R.H. Seat (Red)		162, 171, 179	
711163	Cover Assembly, Cushion—Leather—R.H. Seat (Light Tan)		163, 171, 179	
711166	Cover Assembly, Cushion—Leather—R.H. Seat (Midnight Blue)		163, 171	
711167	Cover Assembly, Cushion—Leather—R.H. Seat (Shadow Blue)		163, 171, 179	
711251	Cover Assembly, Squab—Sewn, Leathercloth—L.H. Seat (Black)	CN14	158	
711252	Cover Assembly, Squab—Sewn, Leathercloth—L.H. Seat (Red)	CN14	158	
711253	Cover Assembly, Squab—Sewn, Leathercloth—L.H. Seat (Light Tan)	CN14	158	
711256	Cover Assembly, Squab—Sewn, Leathercloth—L.H. Seat (Midnight Blue)	CN14	158	
711257	Cover Assembly, Squab—Sewn, Leathercloth—L.H. Seat (Shadow Blue)	CN14	158	
711261	Cover Assembly, Squab—Sewn, Leathercloth—R.H. Seat (Black)		158	
711262	Cover Assembly, Squab—Sewn, Leathercloth—R.H. Seat (Red)		158	
711263	Cover Assembly, Squab—Sewn, Leathercloth—R.H. Seat (Light Tan)		158	
711266	Cover Assembly, Squab—Sewn, Leathercloth—R.H. Seat (Midnight Blue)		158	
711267	Cover Assembly, Squab—Sewn, Leathercloth—R.H. Seat (Shadow Blue)		158	
711271	Cover Assembly, Squab—Sewn, Leather—L.H. Seat (Black)	CN14	158	
711272	Cover Assembly, Squab—Sewn, Leather—L.H. Seat (Red)	CN14	158	
711273	Cover Assembly, Squab—Sewn, Leather—L.H. Seat (Light Tan)	CN14	158	
711276	Cover Assembly, Squab—Sewn, Leather—L.H. Seat (Midnight Blue)	CN14	158	
711277	Cover Assembly, Squab—Sewn, Leather—L.H. Seat (Shadow Blue)	CN14	158	
711281	Cover Assembly, Squab—Sewn, Leather—R.H. Seat (Black)		158	
711282	Cover Assembly, Squab—Sewn, Leather—R.H. Seat (Red)		158	
711283	Cover Assembly, Squab—Sewn, Leather—R.H. Seat (Light Tan)		158	
711286	Cover Assembly, Squab—Sewn, Leather—R.H. Seat (Midnight Blue)		158	
711287	Cover Assembly, Squab—Sewn, Leather—R.H. Seat (Shadow Blue)		158	
711311	Trim Board Assembly, L.H. (Black)	CM22	150	
711312	Trim Board Assembly, L.H. (Red)	CM22	150	
711313	Trim Board Assembly, L.H. (Light Tan)	CM22	150	
711316	Trim Board Assembly, L.H. (Midnight Blue)	CM22	150	
711317	Trim Board Assembly, L.H. (Shadow Blue)	CM22	150	

NUMERICAL INDEX

Part No.	Description	Plate No.	Page	Also Used on Models
711321	Trim Board Assembly, R.H. (Black)	CM21	150	
711322	Trim Board Assembly, R.H. (Red)	CM21	150	
711323	Trim Board Assembly, R.H. (Light Tan)	CM21	150	
711326	Trim Board Assembly, R.H. (Midnight Blue)	CM21	150	
711327	Trim Board Assembly, R.H. (Shadow Blue)	CM21	150	
711351	Carpet Assembly, Rear Seat Pan	CM53	151	
711381	Carpet Assembly, Rear Door—L.H.	CM47	151	
711391	Carpet Assembly, Rear Door—R.H.	CM46	151	
711441	Carpet, Front Floor Assembly, R.H.—R.H.S.	CM32	151	
711461	Carpet, Front Floor and Heel Mat Assembly, R.H.—R.H.S.	CM30	151	
711481	Carpet, Front Floor, and Heel Mat Assembly, L.H.—L.H.S.		151	
711501	Carpet, Front Floor Assembly, L.H.—L.H.S.		151	
711537	Retainer—L.H.	BV32	113	
711538	Retainer—R.H.		113	
711621	Angle, Front	CL1	147	
711759	Sun Visor and Outer Mounting Assembly (with Mirror)—L.H.—L.H.S.	BZ33	128	
711769	Sun Visor and Outer Mounting Assembly (no mirror)—R.H.—R.H.S.	BZ32	128	
711779	Sun Visor and Outer Mounting Assembly (no mirror)—L.H.—L.H.S.		128	
711789	Sun Visor and Outer Mounting Assembly (with mirror)—R.H.—R.H.S.		128	
712390	Panel, Wheelarch Inner Assembly—L.H.		110	F
712391	Panel, Wheelarch Inner Assembly—R.H.		110	
712431	Cover Assembly, Tunnel, Rear—Leathercloth—L.H. (Black)	CM67	154	
712432	Cover Assembly, Tunnel, Rear—Leathercloth—L.H. (Red)	CM67	154	
712433	Cover Assembly, Tunnel, Rear—Leathercloth—L.H. (Light Tan)	CM67	154	
712436	Cover Assembly, Tunnel, Rear—Leathercloth—L.H. (Midnight Blue)	CM67	154	
712437	Cover Assembly, Tunnel, Rear—Leathercloth—L.H. (Shadow Blue)	CM67	154	
712441	Cover Assembly, Tunnel, Rear—Leathercloth—R.H. (Black)	CM66	154	
712442	Cover Assembly, Tunnel, Rear—Leathercloth—R.H. (Red)	CM66	154	
712443	Cover Assembly, Tunnel, Rear—Leathercloth—R.H. (Light Tan)	CM66	154	
712446	Cover Assembly, Tunnel, Rear—Leathercloth—R.H. (Midnight Blue)	CM66	154	
712447	Cover Assembly, Tunnel, Rear—Leathercloth—R.H. (Shadow Blue)	CM66	154	
712451	Cover Assembly, Tunnel, Rear—Leather—L.H. (Black)	CM67	154	
712452	Cover Assembly, Tunnel, Rear—Leather—L.H. (Red)	CM67	154	
712453	Cover Assembly, Tunnel, Rear—Leather—L.H. (Light Tan)	CM67	154	
712456	Cover Assembly, Tunnel, Rear—Leather—L.H. (Midnight Blue)	CM67	154	
712457	Cover Assembly, Tunnel, Rear—Leather—L.H. (Shadow Blue)	CM67	154	
712461	Cover Assembly, Tunnel, Rear—Leather—R.H. (Black)	CM66	154	

NUMERICAL INDEX

Part No.	Description	Plate No.	Page	Also Used on Models
712462	Cover Assembly, Tunnel, Rear—Leather—R.H. (Red)	CM66	154	
712463	Cover Assembly, Tunnel, Rear—Leather—R.H. (Light Tan)	CM66	154	
712466	Cover Assembly, Tunnel, Rear—Leather—R.H. (Midnight Blue)	CM66	154	
712467	Cover Assembly, Tunnel, Rear—Leather—R.H. (Shadow Blue)	CM66	154	
712563	Bar, Spring, Assembly—L.H.	CH19	144	
712564	Bar, Spring, Assembly—R.H.	CH18	144	
712565	Support, Rear Bumper—L.H.	CH24	144	
712566	Support, Rear Bumper—R.H.	CH23	144	
712567	Bracket Support, Front Valance—L.H.	BX45	120	F
712568	Bracket Support, Front Valance—R.H.		120	F
712571	Carpet Assembly, Rear Floor (Black)		151	
712600	Safety Harness		154, 198	A, F, G
712705	Overrider Assembly, Front—L.H.	CH4	144	F
712706	Overrider Assembly, Front—R.H.	CH3	144	F
712726	Bracket, Hinge	BX30	119	
712731	Seat Safety Catch and Control Lever Assembly—L.H.		172	
712732	Seat Safety Catch and Control Lever Assembly—R.H.	CP46	172	
712907	Knob	BS28	107	G
712913	Knob	BS40	107	A
712985	Moulding, Sill—L.H.		146	
712986	Moulding, Sill—R.H.	CK7	146	
713035	Channel Assembly, Bottom		122	
713040	Louvre, Foot Level, Facia	CB3	132	G
713790	Escutcheon, Heater Controls	CB18	132	
714115	Glass, Heated, Rear Door		142	
714199	Roof Assembly, Complete		114	
714421	Veneered Facing Assembly—L.H.S.		129	
714422	Veneered Facing Assembly—R.H.S.		129	
714432	Frame Assembly, Windscreen		127	
714434	Nozzle Assembly, Demister	CD43	136, 139	
714491	Front Door Trim Pad Assembly—L.H. (Black)		126	
714492	Front Door Trim Pad Assembly—L.H. (Red)		126	
714493	Front Door Trim Pad Assembly—L.H. (Light Tan)		126	
714496	Front Door Trim Pad Assembly—L.H. (Midnight Blue)		126	
714497	Front Door Trim Pad Assembly—L.H. (Shadow Blue)		126	
714501	Front Door Trim Pad Assembly—R.H. (Black)		126	
714502	Front Door Trim Pad Assembly—R.H. (Red)		126	
714503	Front Door Trim Pad Assembly—R.H. (Light Tan)		126	
714506	Front Door Trim Pad Assembly—R.H. (Midnight Blue)		126	
714507	Front Door Trim Pad Assembly—R.H. (Shadow Blue)		126	
714571	Glass, Heated, Rear Door		142	
714650	Remote Control Mechanism and Link Assembly—L.H.		124	
714651	Remote Control Mechanism and Link Assembly—R.H.		124	
714655	Bracket Assembly—L.H.		110	
714656	Bracket Assembly—R.H.		110	

NUMERICAL INDEX

Part No.	Description	Plate No.	Page	Also Used on Models
714671	Cover Assembly, Squab—Sewn, Leathercloth—L.H. Seat (Black)	CP14	167, 175	
714672	Cover Assembly, Squab—Sewn, Leathercloth—L.H. Seat (Red)	CP14	166, 175	
714673	Cover Assembly, Squab—Sewn, Leathercloth—L.H. Seat (Light Tan)	CP14	166, 175	
714676	Cover Assembly, Squab—Sewn, Leathercloth—L.H. Seat (Midnight Blue)	CP14	167	
714677	Cover Assembly, Squab—Sewn, Leathercloth—L.H. Seat (Shadow Blue)	CP14	167, 175	
714681	Cover Assembly, Squab—Sewn, Leathercloth—R.H. Seat (Black)		167, 175	
714682	Cover Assembly, Squab—Sewn, Leathercloth—R.H. Seat (Red)		166, 175	
714683	Cover Assembly, Squab—Sewn, Leathercloth—R.H. Seat (Light Tan)		166, 175	
714686	Cover Assembly, Squab—Sewn, Leathercloth—R.H. Seat (Midnight Blue)		167	
714687	Cover Assembly, Squab—Sewn, Leathercloth—R.H. Seat (Shadow Blue)		167, 175	
714691	Cover Assembly, Squab—Sewn, Leather—L.H. Seat (Black)	CP14	167, 176	
714692	Cover Assembly, Squab—Sewn, Leather—L.H. Seat (Red)	CP14	167, 176	
714693	Cover Assembly, Squab—Sewn, Leather—L.H. Seat (Light Tan)	CP14	167, 176	
714696	Cover Assembly, Squab—Sewn, Leather—L.H. Seat (Midnight Blue)	CP14	167	
714697	Cover Assembly, Squab—Sewn, Leather—L.H. Seat (Shadow Blue)	CP14	167, 176	
714701	Cover Assembly, Squab—Sewn, Leather—R.H. Seat (Black)		167, 176	
714702	Cover Assembly, Squab—Sewn, Leather—R.H. Seat (Red)		167, 175	
714703	Cover Assembly, Squab—Sewn, Leather—R.H. Seat (Light Tan)		167, 176	
714706	Cover Assembly, Squab—Sewn, Leather—R.H. Seat (Midnight Blue)		167	
714707	Cover Assembly, Squab—Sewn, Leather—R.H. Seat (Shadow Blue)		167, 176	
714774	Cap, Petrol Filler	BE17	84	
714780	Board Assembly, Squab, Hinged	CR1	188	
714783	Seat Safety Catch and Control Lever Assembly—L.H.	CQ42	187	
714784	Seat Safety Catch and Control Lever Assembly—R.H.		187	
715084	Bracket Assembly—L.H.		110	
715085	Bracket Assembly—R.H.		110	
715088	Panel Assembly, Inner—L.H.		110	
715089	Panel Assembly, Inner—R.H.		110	
715151	Pad, Foam—L.H.	CR14	189	
715152	Pad, Foam—R.H.	CR15	189	
715171	Cover Assembly, Squab—Sewn, Leathercloth (Black)	CR12	189	
715172	Cover Assembly, Squab—Sewn, Leathercloth (Red)	CR12	189	
715173	Cover Assembly, Squab—Sewn, Leathercloth (Light Tan)	CR12	189	
715177	Cover Assembly, Squab—Sewn, Leathercloth (Shadow Blue)	CR12	189	

NUMERICAL INDEX

Part No.	Description	Plate No.	Page	Also Used on Models
715181	Cover Assembly, Squab—Sewn, Leather (Black)	CR12	189	
715182	Cover Assembly, Squab—Sewn, Leather (Red)	CR12	189	
715183	Cover Assembly, Squab—Sewn, Leather (Light Tan)	CR12	189	
715187	Cover Assembly, Squab—Sewn, Leather (Shadow Blue)	CR12	189	
715211	Cover, Sewn, Assembly, Occasional Seat—Leathercloth (Black)	CR16	139	
715212	Cover, Sewn, Assembly, Occasional Seat—Leathercloth (Red)	CR16	189	
715213	Cover, Sewn, Assembly, Occasional Seat—Leathercloth (Light Tan)	CR16	189	
715217	Cover, Sewn, Assembly, Occasional Seat—Leathercloth (Shadow Blue)	CR16	189	
715221	Cover, Sewn, Assembly, Occasional Seat—Leather (Black)	CR16	189	
715222	Cover, Sewn, Assembly, Occasional Seat—Leather (Red)	CR16	189	
715223	Cover, Sewn, Assembly, Occasional Seat—Leather (Light Tan)	CR16	189	
715227	Cover, Sewn, Assembly, Occasional Seat—Leather (Shadow Blue)	CR16	189	
716633	Pad, Squab, Upper		182	
716703	Luggage Floor Assembly, Centre		147	
716803	Tubing, Wheelbox to Wheelbox	BN13	95	
716851	Cover Assembly, Squab and Headrest—Sewn, Leathercloth—L.H. Seat (Black)	CQ17	183	
716852	Cover Assembly, Squab and Headrest—Sewn, Leathercloth—L.H. Seat (Red)	CQ17	182	
716853	Cover Assembly, Squab and Headrest—Sewn, Leathercloth—L.H. Seat (Light Tan)	CQ17	182	
716857	Cover Assembly, Squab and Headrest—Sewn, Leathercloth—L.H. Seat (Shadow Blue)	CQ17	182	
716861	Cover Assembly, Squab and Headrest—Sewn, Leathercloth—R.H. Seat (Black)		182	
716862	Cover Assembly, Squab and Headrest—Sewn, Leathercloth—R.H. Seat (Red)		182	
716863	Cover Assembly, Squab and Headrest—Sewn, Leathercloth—R.H. Seat (Light Tan)		182	
716867	Cover Assembly, Squab and Headrest—Sewn, Leathercloth—R.H. Seat (Shadow Blue)		182	
716871	Cover Assembly, Squab and Headrest—Sewn, Leather (Black), L.H. Seat	CQ17	183	
716872	Cover Assembly, Squab and Headrest—Sewn, Leather (Red), L.H. Seat	CQ17	183	
716873	Cover Assembly, Squab and Headrest—Sewn, Leather (Light Tan), L.H. Seat	CQ17	183	
716877	Cover Assembly, Squab and Headrest—Sewn, Leather (Shadow Blue), L.H. Seat	CQ17	183	
716881	Cover Assembly, Squab and Headrest—Sewn, Leather (Black), R.H. Seat		183	
716882	Cover Assembly, Squab and Headrest—Sewn, Leather (Red), R.H. Seat		183	
716883	Cover Assembly, Squab and Headrest—Sewn, Leather (Light Tan), R.H. Seat		183	
716887	Cover Assembly, Squab and Headrest—Sewn, Leather (Shadow Blue), R.H. Seat		183	
716891	Cover Assembly, Cushion—Leathercloth (Black), L.H. Seat	CQ39	186	

NUMERICAL INDEX

Part No.	Description	Plate No.	Page	Also Used on Models
716892	Cover Assembly, Cushion—Leathercloth (Red), L.H. Seat	CQ39	186	
716893	Cover Assembly, Cushion—Leathercloth (Light Tan), L.H. Seat	CQ39	186	
716897	Cover Assembly, Cushion—Leathercloth (Shadow Blue), L.H. Seat	CQ39	186	
716901	Cover Assembly, Cushion—Leathercloth (Black), R.H. Seat		186	
716902	Cover Assembly, Cushion—Leathercloth (Red), R.H. Seat		186	
716903	Cover Assembly, Cushion—Leathercloth (Light Tan), R.H. Seat		186	
716907	Cover Assembly, Cushion—Leathercloth (Shadow Blue), R.H. Seat		186	
716911	Cover Assembly, Cushion—Leather (Black), L.H. Seat	CQ39	186	
716912	Cover Assembly, Cushion—Leather (Red), L.H. Seat	CQ39	186	
716913	Cover Assembly, Cushion—Leather (Light Tan), L.H. Seat	CQ39	186	
716917	Cover Assembly, Cushion—Leather (Shadow Blue), L.H. Seat	CQ39	186	
716921	Cover Assembly, Cushion—Leather (Black), R.H. Seat		186	
716922	Cover Assembly, Cushion—Leather (Red), R.H. Seat		186	
716923	Cover Assembly, Cushion—Leather (Light Tan), R.H. Seat		186	
716927	Cover Assembly, Cushion—Leather (Shadow Blue), R.H. Seat		186	
716966	Tie Bar, Outer Steering Column to Facia, R.H.S.		134	
716967	Tie Bar, Outer Steering Column to Facia, L.H.S.		134	
716971	Carpet Assembly, Rear Seat Pan		151	
717006	Panel, Rear Valance Assembly		111	
806144	Rubber, Sealing	BZ6	127	F, G, L
806357	Pad, Sound Insulation	BU34	111	E
806634	Panel—L.H.	BU11	110	F
806635	Panel—R.H.		110	F
806638	Sill Panel, Inner—L.H.	BU7	110	F
806639	Sill Panel, Inner—R.H.	BU6	110	F
806707	Battery Box Assembly—R.H.S.	BV15	113	F
806882	Tube Assembly, Bonnet Hinge—L.H.	BW27	115	F
806883	Tube Assembly, Bonnet Hinge—R.H.	BW26	115	F
806900	Rear Corner Bumper Assembly—L.H.	CG21	143	F
806901	Rear Corner Bumper Assembly—R.H.	CG20	143	F
806956	Front Bumper Bar	CG1	143	F
807004	Parcel Tray—L.H.—R.H.S.	CA33	130	F
807005	Parcel Tray—R.H.—L.H.S.		130	F
807030	Battery Box Assembly—L.H.S.		113	F
807102	Reinforcement Assembly, Side Front Wing, L.H.	BW8	115, 118	F
807103	Reinforcement Assembly, Side Front Wing, R.H.	BW7	115, 118	F
807104	Heelboard, Crossmember Assembly	BU9	110	F
807136	Front Valance	BW49	117	F
808270	Sill Protector—L.H. (Black Plastic)		198	F
808271	Sill Protector—R.H. (Black Plastic)		198	F
809402	Panel, Closing—L.H.	BV38	114	
809403	Panel, Closing—R.H.		114	
809405	Panel Assembly	CF17	141	
809409	Glass	CF46	142	O

NUMERICAL INDEX

Part No.	Description	Plate No.	Page	Also Used on Models
809509	Panel Assembly, Outer—L.H.	BV23	113	F
809510	Panel Assembly, Outer—R.H.		113	F
809516	Stiffener Assembly	BV36	114	
809675	Floor Assembly	BU26	111	
809677	Rail, Support	BU20	110	
809739	Panel Assembly—L.H.	BV2	112	
809740	Panel Assembly—L.H.		112	
809741	Panel Assembly—R.H.	BV1	112	
809742	Panel Assembly—R.H.		112	
809747	Air Box Assembly	BV20	113	
809785	Channel Assembly—R.H.S.	BV22	113	
809786	Channel Assembly—L.H.S.		113	
809799	Panel, Dash Shelf—R.H.S.	BV10	112	
809800	Panel, Dash Shelf—L.H.S.		112	
809803	Panel Assembly	BV21	113	
809915	Floor Assembly, Main	BU1	110	
809917	Parcel Tray—R.H.S.	CA34	130	
809918	Parcel Tray—L.H.S.		130	
809926	Panel Assembly—L.H.	BV7	112	
809927	Panel Assembly—R.H.	BV6	112	
809930	Heater Unit Assembly	CC1	136	
809946	Rail—L.H.	BV42	114	
809947	Rail—R.H.		114	
810017	Seal—L.H.	CF3	141	
810018	Seal—R.H.		141	
810037	Pad, Sound Insulation—L.H.	CM5	149	
810038	Pad, Sound Insulation—R.H.		149	
810041	Glass, Window—L.H.	BY53	122	
810042	Glass, Window—R.H.		122	
810100	Side Panel Assembly, Inner—L.H.—R.H. Seat (Foamed)	CN23	159	
810101	Side Panel Assembly, Inner—R.H.—L.H. Seat (Foamed)		159	
810240	Pad, Cushion, Front—L.H. Seat	CN33	162, 171, 179, 186	
810241	Pad, Cushion, Front—R.H. Seat		162, 171, 179, 186	
810242	Pad, Cushion, Rear—L.H. Seat	CN34	162, 171	
810243	Pad, Cushion, Rear—R.H. Seat		162, 171	
810252	Panel, Footrest—R.H.	BU5	112	
810253	Panel, Footrest—L.H.		112	
810254	Board, Trim—L.H.	CM17	149	
810255	Board, Trim—R.H.		149	
810260	Panel Assembly—L.H.	BW22	115, 118	
810261	Panel Assembly—R.H.	BW21	115, 118	
810291	Door Lock Assembly—L.H.	BY90	123	F
810292	Door Lock Assembly—R.H.		123	F
810312	Front Door Ventilator Assembly, Complete, L.H.		121	
810313	Front Door Ventilator Assembly, Complete, R.H.		121	
810334	Radiator Cowl Assembly	BA25	80	
810373	Seat Slide Assembly—L.H. Seat	CN39	163	
810374	Seat Slide Assembly—R.H. Seat	CN38	163	
810400	Window Regulator Assembly—L.H.	BY70	123	
810401	Window Regulator Assembly—R.H.		123	
810402	Radiator Grille Assembly	BW48	117, 120	F
810630	Pad, Squab, Upper	CN12	157, 166, 175	
810631	Pad, Squab, Lower—L.H. Seat	CN13	158, 166, 175, 182	
810632	Pad, Squab, Lower—R.H. Seat		157, 166, 175, 182	

NUMERICAL INDEX

Part No.	Description	Plate No.	Page	Also Used on Models
810641	Capping—L.H.		126	
810651	Capping—R.H.		126	
810681	Bracket Assembly	CA18	129, 133	
810699	Cover, Back Door Hinge	CM20	150	
810731	Back Panel Assembly, Trimmed—L.H. Seat (Black)	CN28	161	
810732	Back Panel Assembly, Trimmed—L.H. Seat (Red)	CN28	160	
810733	Back Panel Assembly, Trimmed—L.H. Seat (Light Tan)	CN28	160	
810736	Back Panel Assembly, Trimmed—L.H. Seat (Midnight Blue)	CN28	161	
810737	Back Panel Assembly, Trimmed—L.H. Seat (Shadow Blue)	CN28	161	
810741	Back Panel Assembly, Trimmed—R.H. Seat (Black)		161	
810742	Back Panel Assembly, Trimmed—R.H. Seat (Red)		160	
810743	Back Panel Assembly, Trimmed—R.H. Seat (Light Tan)		160	
810746	Back Panel Assembly, Trimmed—R.H. Seat (Midnight Blue)		160	
810747	Back Panel Assembly, Trimmed—R.H. Seat (Shadow Blue)		161	
810781	Trim Board Assembly—L.H. (Black)	CM27	150	
810782	Trim Board Assembly—L.H. (Red)	CM27	150	
810783	Trim Board Assembly—L.H. (Light Tan)	CM27	150	
810786	Trim Board Assembly—L.H. (Midnight Blue)	CM27	150	
810787	Trim Board Assembly—L.H. (Shadow Blue)	CM27	150	
810791	Trim Board Assembly—R.H. (Black)	CM26	150	
810792	Trim Board Assembly—R.H. (Red)	CM26	150	
810793	Trim Board Assembly—R.H. (Light Tan)	CM26	150	
810796	Trim Board Assembly—R.H. (Midnight Blue)	CM26	150	
810797	Trim Board Assembly—R.H. (Shadow Blue)	CM26	150	
810837	Pad, Insulation, Upper	CM4	149	
810841	Carpet Assembly, Luggage Floor	CM54	151	
811091	Crash Pad Assembly, Facia	CA13	129	
811419	Wheel Trim		66	E—2 Litre
811476	Rear Corner Bumper Assembly—L.H.	CH17	144	F
811477	Rear Corner Bumper Assembly—R.H.	CH16	144	F
811660	Front Bumper Bar Assembly	CH1	144	F
811676	Front Valance Assembly (Mk. II Cars only)	BX42	120	F
811679	Tube Assembly, Bonnet Hinge—L.H.	BX27	118	F
811680	Tube Assembly, Bonnet Hinge—R.H.	BX26	118	F
811741	Seat Back Assembly, Trimmed—L.H. Seat (Black)	CP23	169, 178, 185	
811742	Seat Back Assembly, Trimmed—L.H. Seat (Red)	CP23	169, 177, 185	
811743	Seat Back Assembly, Trimmed—L.H. Seat (Light Tan)	CP23	169, 177, 185	
811746	Seat Back Assembly, Trimmed—L.H. Seat (Midnight Blue)	CP23	169	
811747	Seat Back Assembly, Trimmed—L.H. Seat (Shadow Blue)	CP23	169, 178, 185	
811751	Seat Back Assembly, Trimmed—R.H. Seat (Black)		169, 178, 185	
811752	Seat Back Assembly, Trimmed—R.H. Seat (Red)		169, 177, 185	

NUMERICAL INDEX

Part No.	Description	Plate No.	Page	Also Used on Models
811753	Seat Back Assembly, Trimmed—R.H. Seat (Light Tan)		169, 177, 185	
811756	Seat Back Assembly, Trimmed—R.H. Seat (Midnight Blue)		169	
811757	Seat Back Assembly, Trimmed—R.H. Seat (Shadow Blue)		169, 177, 185	
811797	Trim Assembly, Road Wheel		66	
812651	Steering Wheel Assembly		67	
812652	Trim Assembly, Steering Wheel		67	
812682	Seat Slide Assembly—L.H. Seat	CP38	172	
812683	Seat Slide Assembly—R.H. Seat	CP39	172	
812684	Bracket—L.H.		128	G
812685	Bracket—R.H.	BZ42	128	G
812711	Sun Visor Assembly (Black)	BZ37	128	G
812741	Sun Visor Trimmed Assembly—R.H.S. (Passenger's)	BZ38	128	G
812751	Sun Visor Trimmed Assembly—L.H.S. (Passenger's)		128	G
812760	Bar	BZ39	128	G
812761	Bar—L.H.	BZ41	128	G
812762	Bar—R.H.	BZ40	128	G
812981	Padding Assembly, Facia, Lower—R.H.S.	CB27	132	
812991	Padding Assembly, Facia, Lower—L.H.S.		132	
813096	Panel—R.H.S.		112	
813097	Panel—L.H.S.		112	
813271	Padding Assembly—R.H.S.	CN28	132	
813281	Padding Assembly—L.H.S.		132	
813351	Crash Pad Assembly, Facia	CB30	129, 133	
813365	Panel Assembly, Outer—L.H.		113	
813366	Panel Assembly, Outer—R.H.		113	
813678	Seat Slide Assembly—L.H. Seat	CQ49	187	
813679	Seat Slide Assembly—R.H. Seat	CQ50	187	
813681	Carpet, Sill—L.H.		151	
813691	Carpet, Sill—R.H.		151	
813713	Heater Unit Assembly	CD1	138	
813735	Grille Assembly, Outer—L.H.		146	
813736	Grille Assembly, Outer—R.H.	CK16	146	
813741	Board Trim, Quarter Headlining—L.H.		149	
813742	Board Trim, Quarter Headlining—R.H.		149	
813745	Parcel Tray Assembly—R.H.S.	CB45	133	
813746	Parcel Tray Assembly—L.H.S.		133	
813753	Parcel Tray Assembly—R.H.S.	CB44	133	
813754	Parcel Tray Assembly—L.H.S.		133	
813936	Pad, Rear, Front Seat Cushion—L.H.	CP34	179, 186	
813937	Pad, Rear, Front Seat Cushion—R.H.		179, 186	
813942	Tubing Assembly, Motor to Wheelbox		95	
813944	Panel, Dash Shelf—L.H.S.		112	
813945	Panel, Dash Shelf—R.H.S.		112	
813946	Air Box Assembly		113	
814012	Rail, Support		110	
814046	Support Rail		147	
814089	Pad, Foam, Squab	CR11	188	
814661	Carpet Assembly, Luggage Floor		151	
815560	Pad Assembly, Headrest		182	
815601	Cushion Assembly, Complete, Occasional Seat —Leathercloth (Black)		189	
815602	Cushion Assembly, Complete, Occasional Seat —Leathercloth (Red)		189	
815603	Cushion Assembly, Complete, Occasional Seat —Leathercloth (Light Tan)		189	

NUMERICAL INDEX

Part No.	Description	Plate No.	Page	Also Used on Models
815607	Cushion Assembly, Complete, Occasional Seat —Leathercloth (Shadow Blue)		189	
815611	Cushion Assembly, Complete, Occasional Seat —Leather (Black)		189	
815612	Cushion Assembly, Complete, Occasional Seat —Leather (Red)		189	
815613	Cushion Assembly, Complete, Occasional Seat —Leather (Light Tan)		189	
815617	Cushion Assembly, Complete, Occasional Seat —Leather (Shadow Blue)		189	
902367	Glass	BZ2	127	F, L
902369	Rubber, Glazing	BZ3	127	F, G, L
903088	Side Front Wing—L.H.	BW6	115	F
903089	Side Front Wing—R.H.	BW5	115	F
903090	Panel, Nose—L.H.	BW17	115	F
903091	Panel, Nose—R.H.	BW16	115	F
903095	Rear Wing Outer Panel—L.H.	BV27	113	F
903096	Rear Wing Outer Panel—R.H.	BV26	113	F
903097	Outer Sill Panel—L.H.	BV31	113	F
903098	Outer Sill Panel—R.H.		113	F
903134	Heelboard Panel	BU8	110	F
903137	Panel, Front, Wheelarch Outer—L.H.	BW13	115, 118	F
903138	Panel, Front, Wheelarch Outer—R.H.	BW12	115, 118	F
903146	Panel, Wheelarch, Rear, Front Outer—L.H.		110	F
903147	Panel, Wheelarch, Rear, Front Outer—R.H.	BU17	110	F
903148	Panel, Wheelarch, Outer—L.H.		110	F
903149	Panel, Wheelarch, Outer—R.H.	BU19	110	F
903466	Windscreen Glass—L.H.S.	BZ2	127	F, G, L
903467	Windscreen Glass—R.H.S.	BZ2	127	F, G, L
904471	Roof Panel Assembly	BV35	114	
904478	Panel, Cantrail—L.H.	BV39	114	
904479	Panel, Cantrail—R.H.		114	
904480	Panel, Drip Moulding—L.H.	BV40	114	
904481	Panel, Drip Moulding—R.H.		114	
904482	Panel—L.H.	BV41	114	
904483	Panel—R.H.		114	
904487	Rubber, Glazing	CF47	142	
904600	Frame Assembly—L.H. Seat	CN2	157	
904601	Frame Assembly—R.H. Seat		157	
904621	Facia Panel Assembly—R.H.S.	CA1	129	
904623	Facia Panel Assembly—L.H.S.		129	
904713	Seat Panel Assembly—Rear	BU12	110	
904719	Frame Assembly	BZ1	127	
904990	Moulding—R.H.S.	CA8	129	
904991	Moulding—L.H.S.		129	
904992	Moulding	CA9	129	
904993	Moulding	CA10	129	
904994	Moulding—R.H.S.	CA11	129	
904995	Moulding—L.H.S.		129	
905060	Side Panel Assembly, Outer (Foamed) L.H.—L.H. Seat	CN17	158	
905061	Side Panel Assembly, Outer (Foamed) R.H.—R.H. Seat		158	
905207	Veneered Facing Assembly—R.H.S. (with Heater)		129	
905208	Veneered Facing Assembly—L.H.S. (with Heater)		129	
905209	Veneered Facing Assembly—R.H.S. (no Heater)	CA3	129	
905210	Veneered Facing Assembly—L.H.S. (no Heater)		129	
905221	Front Bay Valance Assembly—L.H.	BW54	117	
905222	Front Bay Valance Assembly—R.H.	BW53	117, 120	

NUMERICAL INDEX

Part No.	Description	Plate No.	Page	Also Used on Models
905230	Front Door Assembly—L.H.	BY1	121	
905231	Front Door Assembly—R.H.		121	
905302	Bonnet Assembly		115	
905324	Pad, Sound Insulation, Roof	CM7	149	
905325	Pad, Sound Insulation, Rear	CM8	149	
905471	Front Seat Complete Assembly, Trimmed —Leathercloth—L.H. (Black)		155	
905472	Front Seat Complete Assembly, Trimmed —Leathercloth—L.H. (Red)		155	
905473	Front Seat Complete Assembly, Trimmed —Leathercloth—L.H. (Light Tan)		155	
905476	Front Seat Complete Assembly, Trimmed —Leathercloth—L.H. (Midnight Blue)		155	
905477	Front Seat Complete Assembly, Trimmed —Leathercloth—L.H. (Shadow Blue)		155	
905481	Front Seat Complete Assembly, Trimmed —Leathercloth—R.H. (Black)	CN1	155	
905482	Front Seat Complete Assembly, Trimmed —Leathercloth—R.H. (Red)	CN1	155	
905483	Front Seat Complete Assembly, Trimmed —Leathercloth—R.H. (Light Tan)	CN1	155	
905486	Front Seat Complete Assembly, Trimmed —Leathercloth—R.H. (Midnight Blue)	CN1	155	
905487	Front Seat Complete Assembly, Trimmed —Leathercloth—R.H. (Shadow Blue)	CN1	155	
905491	Front Seat Complete Assembly, Trimmed —Leather—L.H. (Black)		156	
905492	Front Seat Complete Assembly, Trimmed —Leather—L.H. (Red)		155	
905493	Front Seat Complete Assembly, Trimmed —Leather—L.H. (Light Tan)		155	
905496	Front Seat Complete Assembly, Trimmed —Leather—L.H. (Midnight Blue)		156	
905497	Front Seat Complete Assembly, Trimmed —Leather—L.H. (Shadow Blue)		156	
905501	Front Seat Complete Assembly, Trimmed —Leather—R.H. (Black)	CN1	156	
905502	Front Seat Complete Assembly, Trimmed —Leather—R.H. (Red)	CN1	155	
905503	Front Seat Complete Assembly, Trimmed —Leather—R.H. (Light Tan)	CN1	155	
905506	Front Seat Complete Assembly, Trimmed —Leather—R.H. (Midnight Blue)	CN1	156	
905507	Front Seat Complete Assembly, Trimmed —Leather—R.H. (Shadow Blue)	CN1	156	
905511	Front Seat Frame and Squab Assembly, Trimmed —Leathercloth—L.H. (Black)		157	
905512	Front Seat Frame and Squab Assembly, Trimmed —Leathercloth—L.H. (Red)		156	
905513	Front Seat Frame and Squab Assembly, Trimmed —Leathercloth—L.H. (Light Tan)		156	
905516	Front Seat Frame and Squab Assembly, Trimmed —Leathercloth—L.H. (Midnight Blue)		156	
905517	Front Seat Frame and Squab Assembly, Trimmed —Leathercloth—L.H. (Shadow Blue)		156	
905521	Front Seat Frame and Squab Assembly, Trimmed —Leathercloth—R.H. (Black)		157	
905522	Front Seat Frame and Squab Assembly, Trimmed —Leathercloth—R.H. (Red)		156	

NUMERICAL INDEX

Part No.	Description	Plate No.	Page	Also Used on Models
905523	Front Seat Frame and Squab Assembly, Trimmed —Leathercloth—R.H. (Light Tan)		156	
905526	Front Seat Frame and Squab Assembly, Trimmed —Leathercloth—L.H. (Midnight Blue)		156	
905527	Front Seat Frame and Squab Assembly, Trimmed —Leathercloth—L.H. (Shadow Blue)		156	
905531	Front Seat Frame and Squab Assembly, Trimmed —Leather—L.H. (Black)		157	
905532	Front Seat Frame and Squab Assembly, Trimmed —Leather—L.H. (Red)		157	
905533	Front Seat Frame and Squab Assembly, Trimmed —Leather—L.H. (Light Tan)		157	
905536	Front Seat Frame and Squab Assembly, Trimmed —Leather—L.H. (Midnight Blue)		157	
905537	Front Seat Frame and Squab Assembly, Trimmed —Leather—L.H. (Shadow Blue)		157	
905541	Front Seat Frame and Squab Assembly, Trimmed —Leather—R.H. (Black)		157	
905542	Front Seat Frame and Squab Assembly, Trimmed —Leather—R.H. (Red)		157	
905543	Front Seat Frame and Squab Assembly, Trimmed —Leather—R.H. (Light Tan)		157	
905546	Front Seat Frame and Squab Assembly, Trimmed —Leather—R.H. (Midnight Blue)		157	
905547	Front Seat Frame and Squab Assembly, Trimmed —Leather—R.H. (Shadow Blue)		157	
905551	Cushion Assembly, Trimmed, Complete —Leathercloth—L.H. Seat (Black)		161, 170	
905552	Cushion Assembly, Trimmed, Complete —Leathercloth—L.H. Seat (Red)		161, 170	
905553	Cushion Assembly, Trimmed, Complete —Leathercloth—L.H. Seat (Light Tan)		161, 170	
905556	Cushion Assembly, Trimmed, Complete —Leathercloth—L.H. Seat (Midnight Blue)		161, 170	
905557	Cushion Assembly, Trimmed, Complete —Leathercloth—L.H. Seat (Shadow Blue)		161, 170	
905561	Cushion Assembly, Trimmed, Complete —Leathercloth—R.H. Seat (Black)		161, 170	
905562	Cushion Assembly, Trimmed, Complete —Leathercloth—R.H. Seat (Red)		161, 170	
905563	Cushion Assembly, Trimmed, Complete —Leathercloth—R.H. Seat (Light Tan)		161, 170	
905566	Cushion Assembly, Trimmed, Complete —Leathercloth—R.H. Seat (Midnight Blue)		161, 170	
905567	Cushion Assembly, Trimmed, Complete —Leathercloth—R.H. Seat (Shadow Blue)		161, 170	
905571	Cushion Assembly, Trimmed, Complete —Leather—L.H. Seat (Black)		162, 171	
905572	Cushion Assembly, Trimmed, Complete —Leather—L.H. Seat (Red)		161, 170	
905573	Cushion Assembly, Trimmed, Complete —Leather—L.H. Seat (Light Tan)		162, 170	
905576	Cushion Assembly, Trimmed, Complete —Leather—L.H. Seat (Midnight Blue)		162, 171	
905577	Cushion Assembly, Trimmed, Complete —Leather—L.H. Seat (Shadow Blue)		162, 171	
905581	Cushion Assembly, Trimmed, Complete —Leather—R.H. Seat (Black)		162, 171	
905582	Cushion Assembly, Trimmed, Complete —Leather—R.H. Seat (Red)		161, 170	

NUMERICAL INDEX

Part No.	Description	Plate No.	Page	Also Used on Models
905583	Cushion Assembly, Trimmed, Complete —Leather—R.H. Seat (Light Tan)		162, 170	
905586	Cushion Assembly, Trimmed, Complete —Leather—R.H. Seat (Midnight Blue)		162, 171	
905587	Cushion Assembly, Trimmed, Complete —Leather—R.H. Seat (Shadow Blue)		162, 171	
905654	Pad, Insulation, Lower	CM3	149	
906707	Glass, Windscreen		127	F
907077	Panel, Outer Rear Wing—L.H.		113	F
907078	Panel, Outer Rear Wing—R.H.		113	F
907157	Panel Nose—L.H.	BX17	118	F
907158	Panel Nose—R.H.	BX16	118	F
907177	Door Lock Assembly—L.H.		124	G
907178	Door Lock Assembly—R.H.		124	G
907241	Padding, Seat Side Outer L.H.—L.H. Seat	CP16	167, 176, 183	
907242	Padding, Seat Side Outer R.H.—R.H. Seat		167, 176, 183	
907243	Padding, Seat Side Inner R.H.—L.H. Seat	CP21	168, 177, 184	
907244	Padding, Seat Side Inner L.H.—R.H. Seat		168, 177, 184	
907317	Frame Assembly—L.H. Seat	CP2	166	
907318	Frame Assembly—R.H. Seat		166	
907941	Front Seat Complete Assembly, Trimmed, —Leathercloth—L.H. (Black)		164	
907942	Front Seat Complete Assembly, Trimmed, —Leathercloth—L.H. (Red)		164	
907943	Front Seat Complete Assembly, Trimmed, —Leathercloth—L.H. (Light Tan)		164	
907946	Front Seat Complete Assembly, Trimmed, —Leathercloth—L.H. (Midnight Blue)		164	
907947	Front Seat Complete Assembly, Trimmed, —Leathercloth—L.H. (Shadow Blue)		164	
907951	Front Seat Complete Assembly, Trimmed, —Leathercloth—R.H. (Black)	CP1	164	
907952	Front Seat Complete Assembly, Trimmed, —Leathercloth—R.H. (Red)	CP1	164	
907953	Front Seat Complete Assembly, Trimmed, —Leathercloth—R.H. (Light Tan)	CP1	164	
907956	Front Seat Complete Assembly, Trimmed, —Leathercloth—R.H. (Midnight Blue)	CP1	164	
907957	Front Seat Complete Assembly, Trimmed, —Leathercloth—R.H. (Shadow Blue)	CP1	164	
907961	Front Seat Complete Assembly, Trimmed, —Leather—L.H. (Black)		165	
907962	Front Seat Complete Assembly, Trimmed, —Leather—L.H. (Red)		164	
907963	Front Seat Complete Assembly, Trimmed, —Leather—L.H. (Light Tan)		165	
907966	Front Seat Complete Assembly, Trimmed, —Leather—L.H. (Midnight Blue)		165	
907967	Front Seat Complete Assembly, Trimmed, —Leather—L.H. (Shadow Blue)		165	
907971	Front Seat Complete Assembly, Trimmed, —Leather—R.H. (Black)	CP1	165	
907972	Front Seat Complete Assembly, Trimmed, —Leather—R.H. (Red)	CP1	164	
907973	Front Seat Complete Assembly, Trimmed, —Leather—R.H. (Light Tan)	CP1	164	
907976	Front Seat Complete Assembly, Trimmed, —Leather—R.H. (Midnight Blue)	CP1	165	
907977	Front Seat Complete Assembly, Trimmed, —Leather—R.H. (Shadow Blue)	CP1	165	

NUMERICAL INDEX

Part No.	Description	Plate No.	Page	Also Used on Models
907981	Front Seat Frame and Squab Assembly, Trimmed, —Leathercloth—L.H. (Black)		166	
907982	Front Seat Frame and Squab Assembly, Trimmed, —Leathercloth—L.H. (Red)		165	
907983	Front Seat Frame and Squab Assembly, Trimmed, —Leathercloth—L.H. (Light Tan)		165	
907986	Front Seat Frame and Squab Assembly, Trimmed, —Leathercloth—L.H. (Midnight Blue)		165	
907987	Front Seat Frame and Squab Assembly, Trimmed, —Leathercloth—L.H. (Shadow Blue)		165	
907991	Front Seat Frame and Squab Assembly, Trimmed, —Leathercloth—R.H. (Black)		166	
907992	Front Seat Frame and Squab Assembly, Trimmed, —Leathercloth—R.H. (Red)		165	
907993	Front Seat Frame and Squab Assembly, Trimmed, —Leathercloth—R.H. (Light Tan)		165	
907996	Front Seat Frame and Squab Assembly, Trimmed, —Leathercloth—R.H. (Midnight Blue)		165	
907997	Front Seat Frame and Squab Assembly, Trimmed, —Leathercloth—R.H. (Shadow Blue)		165	
908001	Front Seat Frame and Squab Assembly, Trimmed, —Leather—L.H. (Black)		166	
908002	Front Seat Frame and Squab Assembly, Trimmed, —Leather—L.H. (Red)		166	
908003	Front Seat Frame and Squab Assembly, Trimmed, —Leather—L.H. (Light Tan)		166	
908006	Front Seat Frame and Squab Assembly, Trimmed, —Leather—L.H. (Midnight Blue)		166	
908007	Front Seat Frame and Squab Assembly, Trimmed, —Leather—L.H. (Shadow Blue)		166	
908011	Front Seat Frame and Squab Assembly, Trimmed, —Leather—R.H. (Black)		166	
908012	Front Seat Frame and Squab Assembly, Trimmed, —Leather—R.H. (Red)		166	
908013	Front Seat Frame and Squab Assembly, Trimmed, —Leather—R.H. (Light Tan)		166	
908016	Front Seat Frame and Squab Assembly, Trimmed, —Leather—R.H. (Midnight Blue)		166	
908017	Front Seat Frame and Squab Assembly, Trimmed, —Leather—R.H. (Shadow Blue)		166	
908021	Front Door Assembly—L.H.		121	
908022	Front Door Assembly—R.H.		121	
908113	Side, Front Wing—L.H.	BX5	118	
908114	Side, Front Wing—R.H.	BX5	118	
908116	Bonnet Assembly		118	
908121	Veneered Facing Assembly—R.H.S.	CB17	132	
908122	Veneered Facing Assembly—L.H.S.		132	
908123	Facia Panel Assembly—R.H.S.	CB1	132	
908124	Facia Panel Assembly—L.H.S.		132	
908161	Duct—L.H.		146	
908162	Duct—R.H.	CK17	146	
908393	Frame Assembly—L.H. Seat	CQ2	182	
908394	Frame Assembly—R.H. Seat		182	
908395	Frame Assembly—L.H. Seat	CP2	175	
908396	Frame Assembly—R.H. Seat		175	
908721	Squab Assembly, Complete, Occasional Seat, —Leathercloth (Black)		188	
908722	Squab Assembly, Complete, Occasional Seat, —Leathercloth (Red)		188	

NUMERICAL INDEX

Part No.	Description	Plate No.	Page	Also Used on Models
908723	Squab Assembly, Complete, Occasional Seat, —Leathercloth (Light Tan)		188	
908727	Squab Assembly, Complete, Occasional Seat, —Leathercloth (Shadow Blue)		188	
908731	Squab Assembly, Complete, Occasional Seat, —Leather (Black)		188	
908732	Squab Assembly, Complete, Occasional Seat, —Leather (Red)		188	
908733	Squab Assembly, Complete, Occasional Seat, —Leather (Light Tan)		188	
908737	Squab Assembly, Complete, Occasional Seat, —Leather (Shadow Blue)		188	
909820	Seat Pan Assembly, Rear		110	
909841	Front Seat Complete Assembly, Trimmed, —Leathercloth—L.H. (Black)		173	
909842	Front Seat Complete Assembly, Trimmed, —Leathercloth—L.H. (Red)		173	
909843	Front Seat Complete Assembly, Trimmed, —Leathercloth—L.H. (Light Tan)		173	
909847	Front Seat Complete Assembly, Trimmed, —Leathercloth—L.H. (Shadow Blue)		173	
909851	Front Seat Complete Assembly, Trimmed, —Leathercloth—R.H. (Black)	CP1	173	
909852	Front Seat Complete Assembly, Trimmed, —Leathercloth—R.H. (Red)	CP1	173	
909853	Front Seat Complete Assembly, Trimmed, —Leathercloth—R.H. (Light Tan)	CP1	173	
909857	Front Seat Complete Assembly, Trimmed, —Leathercloth—R.H. (Shadow Blue)	CP1	173	
909861	Front Seat Complete Assembly, Trimmed, —Leather—L.H. (Black)		174	
909862	Front Seat Complete Assembly, Trimmed, —Leather—L.H. (Red)		173	
909863	Front Seat Complete Assembly, Trimmed, —Leather—L.H. (Light Tan)		173	
909867	Front Seat Complete Assembly, Trimmed, —Leather—L.H. (Shadow Blue)		174	
909871	Front Seat Complete Assembly, Trimmed, —Leather—R.H. (Black)	CP1	174	
909872	Front Seat Complete Assembly, Trimmed, —Leather—R.H. (Red)	CP1	173	
909873	Front Seat Complete Assembly, Trimmed, —Leather—R.H. (Light Tan)	CP1	173	
909877	Front Seat Complete Assembly, Trimmed, —Leather—R.H. (Shadow Blue)	CP1	173	
909881	Front Seat Frame and Squab Assembly, Trimmed, —Leathercloth—L.H. (Black)		174	
909882	Front Seat Frame and Squab Assembly, Trimmed, —Leathercloth—L.H. (Red)		174	
909883	Front Seat Frame and Squab Assembly, Trimmed, —Leathercloth—L.H. (Light Tan)		174	
909887	Front Seat Frame and Squab Assembly, Trimmed, —Leathercloth—L.H. (Shadow Blue)		174	
909891	Front Seat Frame and Squab Assembly, Trimmed, —Leathercloth—R.H. (Black)		174	
909892	Front Seat Frame and Squab Assembly, Trimmed, —Leathercloth—R.H. (Red)		174	
909893	Front Seat Frame and Squab Assembly, Trimmed, —Leathercloth—R.H. (Light Tan)		174	

NUMERICAL INDEX

Part No.	Description	Plate No.	Page	Also Used on Models
909897	Front Seat Frame and Squab Assembly, Trimmed,—Leathercloth—R.H. (Shadow Blue)		174	
909901	Front Seat Frame and Squab Assembly, Trimmed,—Leather—L.H. (Black)		175	
909902	Front Seat Frame and Squab Assembly, Trimmed,—Leather—L.H. (Red)		174	
909903	Front Seat Frame and Squab Assembly, Trimmed,—Leather—L.H. (Light Tan)		174	
909907	Front Seat Frame and Squab Assembly, Trimmed,—Leather—L.H. (Shadow Blue)		175	
909911	Front Seat Frame and Squab Assembly, Trimmed,—Leather—R.H. (Black)		175	
909912	Front Seat Frame and Squab Assembly, Trimmed,—Leather—R.H. (Red)		175	
909913	Front Seat Frame and Squab Assembly, Trimmed,—Leather—R.H. (Light Tan)		175	
909917	Front Seat Frame and Squab Assembly, Trimmed,—Leather—R.H. (Shadow Blue)		175	
909921	Cushion Assembly, Trimmed—L.H. Seat—Leathercloth (Black)		178	
909922	Cushion Assembly Trimmed,—L.H. Seat—Leathercloth (Red)		178	
909923	Cushion Assembly, Trimmed—L.H. Seat—Leathercloth (Light Tan)		178	
909927	Cushion Assembly, Trimmed—L.H. Seat—Leathercloth (Shadow Blue)		178	
909931	Cushion Assembly, Trimmed—R.H. Seat—Leathercloth (Black)		178	
909932	Cushion Assembly, Trimmed—R.H. Seat—Leathercloth (Red)		178	
909933	Cushion Assembly, Trimmed—R.H. Seat—Leathercloth (Light Tan)		178	
909937	Cushion Assembly, Trimmed—R.H. Seat—Leathercloth (Shadow Blue)		178	
909941	Cushion Assembly, Trimmed—L.H. Seat—Leather (Black)		179	
909942	Cushion Assembly, Trimmed—L.H. Seat—Leather (Red)		178	
909943	Cushion Assembly, Trimmed—L.H. Seat—Leather (Light Tan)		178	
909947	Cushion Assembly, Trimmed—L.H. Seat—Leather (Shadow Blue)		179	
909951	Cushion Assembly, Trimmed—R.H. Seat—Leather (Black)		179	
909952	Cushion Assembly, Trimmed—R.H. Seat—Leather (Red)		178	
909953	Cushion Assembly, Trimmed—R.H. Seat—Leather (Light Tan)		178	
909957	Cushion Assembly, Trimmed—R.H. Seat—Leather (Shadow Blue)		179	
910045	Engine Bay Valance Assembly—L.H. (MK. II Cars only)	BX47	120	
910171	Front Seat Assembly, Complete, Trimmed, (with Headrest)—L.H.—Leathercloth (Black)		180	
910172	Front Seat Assembly, Complete, Trimmed, (with Headrest)—L.H.—Leathercloth (Red)		180	
910173	Front Seat Assembly, Complete, Trimmed, (with Headrest)—L.H.—Leathercloth (Light Tan)		180	

NUMERICAL INDEX

Part No.	Description	Plate No.	Page	Also Used on Models
910177	Front Seat Assembly, Complete, Trimmed, (with Headrest)—L.H.—Leathercloth (Shadow Blue)		180	
910181	Front Seat Assembly, Complete, Trimmed, (with Headrest)—R.H.—Leathercloth (Black)	CQ1	180	
910182	Front Seat Assembly, Complete, Trimmed, (with Headrest)—R.H.—Leathercloth (Red)	CQ1	180	
910183	Front Seat Assembly, Complete, Trimmed, (with Headrest)—R.H.—Leathercloth (Light Tan)	CQ1	180	
910187	Front Seat Assembly, Complete, Trimmed, (with Headrest)—R.H.—Leathercloth (Shadow Blue)	CQ1	180	
910191	Front Seat Assembly, Complete, Trimmed, (with Headrest)—L.H.—Leather (Black)		181	
910192	Front Seat Assembly, Complete, Trimmed, (with Headrest)—L.H.—Leather (Red)		180	
910193	Front Seat Assembly, Complete, Trimmed, (with Headrest)—L.H.—Leather (Light Tan)		180	
910197	Front Seat Assembly, Complete, Trimmed, (with Headrest)—L.H.—Leather (Shadow Blue)		181	
910201	Front Seat Assembly, Complete, Trimmed, (with Headrest)—R.H.—Leather (Black)	CQ1	181	
910202	Front Seat Assembly, Complete, Trimmed, (with Headrest)—R.H.—Leather (Red)	CQ1	180	
910203	Front Seat Assembly, Complete, Trimmed, (with Headrest)—R.H.—Leather (Light Tan)	CQ1	180	
910207	Front Seat Assembly, Complete, Trimmed, (with Headrest)—R.H.—Leather (Shadow Blue)	CQ1	180	
910211	Front Seat Frame, Squab and Headrest Assembly, Trimmed—L.H.—Leathercloth (Black)		181	
910212	Front Seat Frame, Squab and Headrest Assembly, Trimmed—L.H.—Leathercloth (Red)		181	
910213	Front Seat Frame, Squab and Headrest Assembly, Trimmed—L.H.—Leathercloth (Light Tan)		181	
910217	Front Seat Frame, Squab and Headrest Assembly, Trimmed—L.H.—Leathercloth (Shadow Blue)		181	
910221	Front Seat Frame, Squab and Headrest Assembly, Trimmed—R.H.—Leathercloth (Black)		181	
910222	Front Seat Frame, Squab and Headrest Assembly, Trimmed—R.H.—Leathercloth (Red)		181	
910223	Front Seat Frame, Squab and Headrest Assembly, Trimmed—R.H.—Leathercloth (Light Tan)		181	
910227	Front Seat Frame, Squab and Headrest Assembly, Trimmed—R.H.—Leathercloth (Shadow Blue)		181	
910231	Front Seat Frame, Squab and Headrest Assembly, Trimmed—L.H.—Leather (Black)		182	
910232	Front Seat Frame, Squab and Headrest Assembly, Trimmed—L.H.—Leather (Red)		181	
910233	Front Seat Frame, Squab and Headrest Assembly, Trimmed—L.H.—Leather (Light Tan)		182	
910237	Front Seat Frame, Squab and Headrest Assembly, Trimmed—L.H.—Leathercloth (Shadow Blue)		182	
910241	Front Seat Frame, Squab and Headrest Assembly, Trimmed—R.H.—Leather (Black)		182	
910242	Front Seat Frame, Squab and Headrest Assembly, Trimmed—R.H.—Leather (Red)		181	
910243	Front Seat Frame, Squab and Headrest Assembly, Trimmed—R.H.—Leather (Light Tan)		181	

NUMERICAL INDEX

Part No.	Description	Plate No.	Page	Also Used on Models
910247	Front Seat Frame, Squab and Headrest Assembly, Trimmed—R.H.—Leather (Shadow Blue)		182	
910251	Cushion Assembly, Trimmed—L.H. Seat—Leathercloth (Black)		185	
910252	Cushion Assembly, Trimmed—L.H. Seat—Leathercloth (Red)		185	
910253	Cushion Assembly, Trimmed—L.H. Seat—Leathercloth (Light Tan)		185	
910257	Cushion Assembly, Trimmed—L.H. Seat—Leathercloth (Shadow Blue)		185	
910261	Cushion Assembly, Trimmed—R.H. Seat—Leathercloth (Black)		185	
910262	Cushion Assembly, Trimmed—R.H. Seat—Leathercloth (Red)		185	
910263	Cushion Assembly, Trimmed—R.H. Seat—Leathercloth (Light Tan)		185	
910267	Cushion Assembly, Trimmed—R.H. Seat—Leathercloth (Shadow Blue)		185	
910271	Cushion Assembly, Trimmed—L.H. Seat—Leather (Black)		186	
910272	Cushion Assembly, Trimmed—L.H. Seat—Leather (Red)		186	
910273	Cushion Assembly, Trimmed—L.H. Seat—Leather (Light Tan)		186	
910277	Cushion Assembly, Trimmed—L.H. Seat—Leather (Shadow Blue)		186	
910281	Cushion Assembly, Trimmed—R.H. Seat—Leather (Black)		186	
910282	Cushion Assembly, Trimmed—R.H. Seat—Leather (Red)		185	
910283	Cushion Assembly, Trimmed—R.H. Seat—Leather (Light Tan)		186	
910287	Cushion Assembly, Trimmed—R.H. Seat—Leather (Shadow Blue)		186	
CD23802	Ring, Pronged	CM56	151	C, G, L, O, P, T, Y
CD23803	Socket	CM55	151	C, G, L, O, P, T, Y
CD24152	Washer, Cup		126	A, E, F, G, L, O, Z
CD24153	Washer, Cup		129	G, L, O
CD24256	Washer, Cup		129, 154	O, R
CD25672	Plug, Rubber		191	B, F, L, M, P, R, V
CD27769	Plug		191	B, D, F, L, P, R, V, Y
CS4009	Clip, Bellows	AS46	68	A, E, F, G, L, M, O, Z
CS4011	Clip, Supergrip	BV18	113	A, E, F, O
CS4012	Clip	BV18	10, 11, 33, 34, 113, 136, 138	A, B, E, E—2 Litre, F, G, L, O, P, R, V, Y, Z
CS4013	Clip		10, 33, 34	A, B, C, E—2 Litre, O, P, R
CS4015	Clip	BA9	80	
CS4020	Clip		68	A, E, F, G, L, O, Z
CS4024	Clip	BA7	80	F, G, L, M, O, Z
CS4025	Clip	BA7	80	G
CS4027	Clip, Hose	CC31	139, 136	F
CS4029	Clip	CD57	139	B, L, R, T, V, Y
CS4030	Clip		139	G

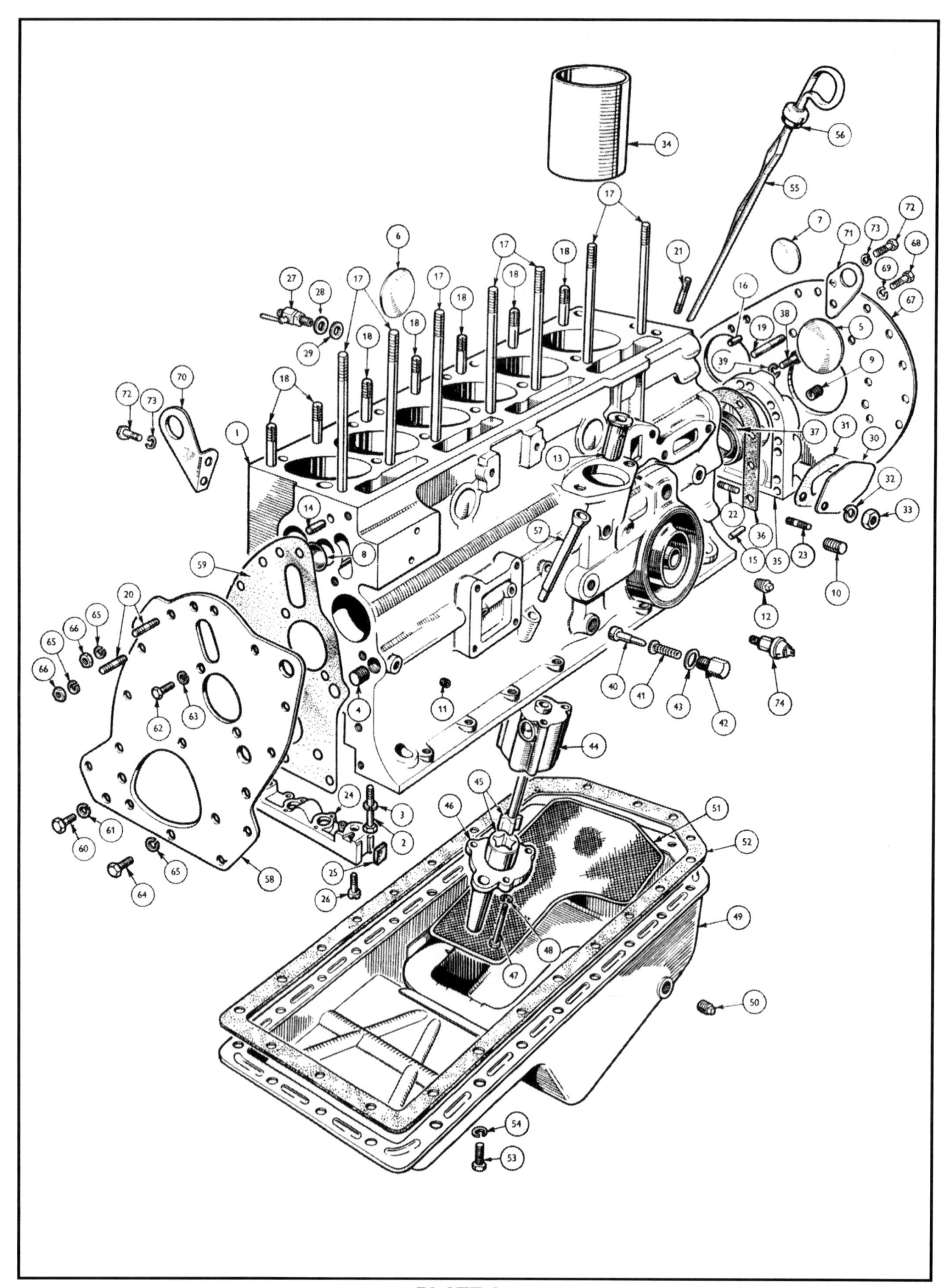

PLATE A

ENGINE
MARK I CARS FITTED UP TO ENGINE No. KC/KD50000E ONLY

Plate No.	Part No.	Description	No. per Unit	Remarks
	515479	†ENGINE UNIT (9.5 to 1 Compression Ratio)	1	Fitted up to Engine No. KC5000E only
	515479/R	†ENGINE UNIT (9.5 to 1 Compression Ratio) (RECONDITIONED UNIT)	1	
	516392	†ENGINE UNIT (7.0 to 1 Compression Ratio)	1	
	516392/R	†ENGINE UNIT (7.0 to 1 Compression Ratio) (RECONDITIONED UNIT)	1	
	515932	†ENGINE UNIT (9.5 to 1 Compression Ratio)	1	Fitted from Engine No. KC/KD5001E and future
	515932/R	†ENGINE UNIT (9.5 to 1 Compression Ratio) (RECONDITIONED UNIT)	1	
	516394	†ENGINE UNIT (7.0 to 1 Compression Ratio)	1	
	516394/R	†ENGINE UNIT (7.0 to 1 Compression Ratio) (RECONDITIONED UNIT)	1	

Note:- The above Units are supplied less water pump, distributor, dynamo, petrol pump, oil filter, thermostat, exhaust and inlet manifolds, carburettors, and sparking plugs.

Plate No.	Part No.	Description	No. per Unit	Remarks
	512829	**ENGINE GASKET SET** (includes Decarbonising Set)	1	
	512830	**DECARBONISING GASKET SET**	1	
A1	515610	**CYLINDER BLOCK ASSEMBLY**	1	Fitted up to Engine No. KC5000E only
	515930	**CYLINDER BLOCK ASSEMBLY**	1	Fitted from Engine No. KC/KD5001E and future
A2	HB1024	**Bolt** ⎫ Caps to	8	
A3	WL0210	**Washer,** lock ⎭ block	8	
A4	PS1103	**Plug,** core, screwed—Oil gallery, front	1	
A5	44473	**Plug,** core, rear of camshaft	1	Alternative fitment to 148353
	148353	**Plug,** core, bucket type—Rear of camshaft	1	Alternative fitment to 44473
A6	46549	**Plug,** core, welch—Front face R.H. side block	5	Alternative fitment to 144688
	144688	**Plug,** core, bucket type—Front face R.H. side block	5	Alternative fitment to 46549
A7	56712	**Plug,** core, welch—Rear face L.H. side block	3	Alternative fitment to 144686
	144686	**Plug,** core, bucket type—Rear face L.H. side block	3	Alternative fitment to 56712
A8	46172	**Plug,** core, welch—Front face of block	1	Alternative fitment to 144687
	144687	**Plug,** core, bucket type—Front face of block	1	Alternative fitment to 46172
A9	118632	**Plug,** dry seal—oil gallery, rear	1	
A10	PU1404	**Plug,** ¾", oil gallery	1	
A11	118686	**Plug,** ⅛", oil gallery	6	
A12	116511	**Plug,** oil gallery	1	
A13	137978	**Bush,** oil pump drive shaft	1	Fitted up to Engine No. only
	149776	**Bush,** oil pump drive shaft	1	Fitted from Engine No. and future
A14	DP0514	**Dowel,** timing cover attachment	2	

Note:—Items marked thus † are available on our Factory Exchange Unit Scheme

1

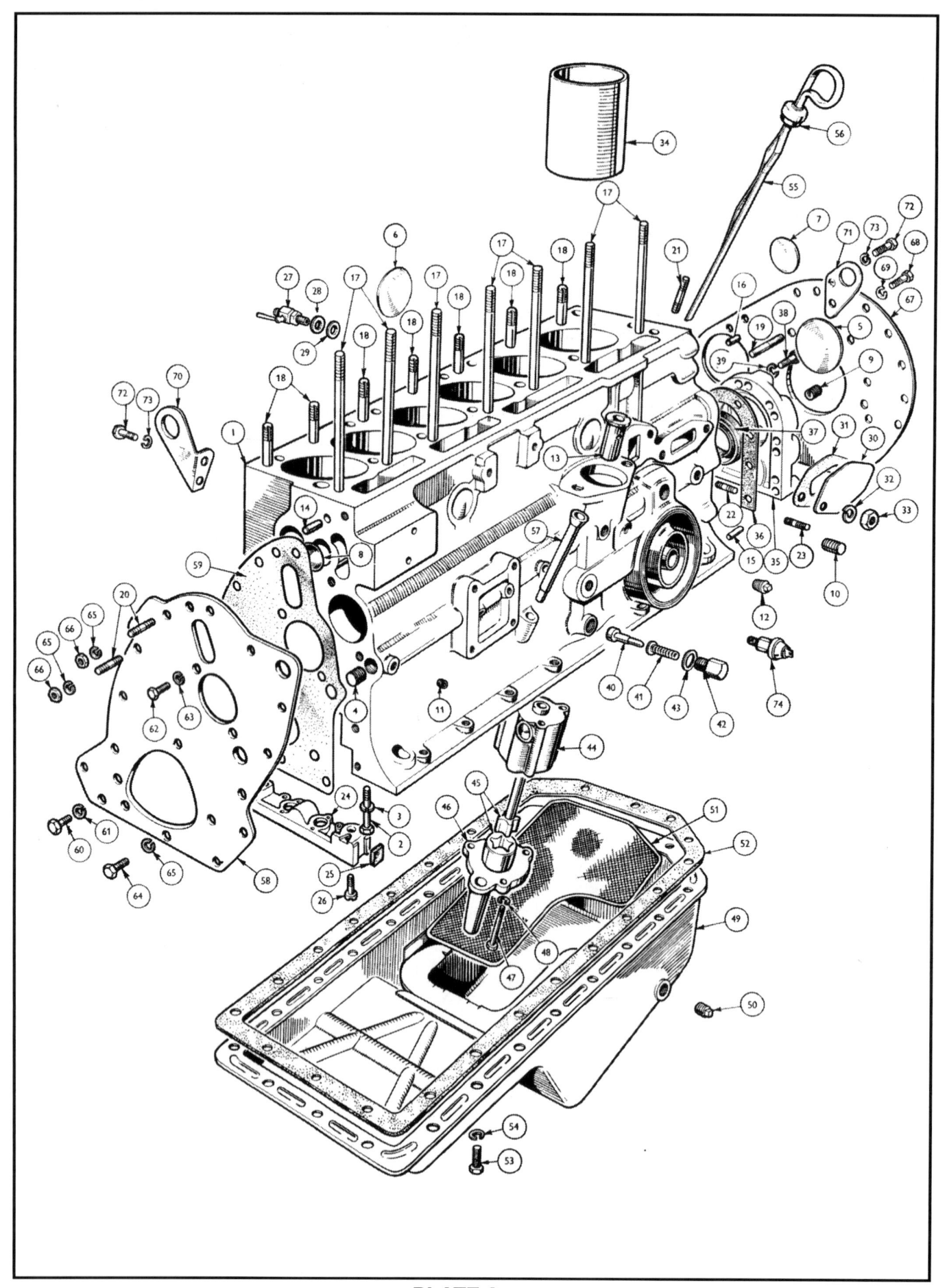

PLATE A

ENGINE

MARK I CARS FITTED UP TO ENGINE No. KC/KD50000E ONLY

Plate No.	Part No.	Description	No. per Unit	Remarks
		CYLINDER BLOCK—continued		
A15	DP0612	**Dowel,** rear engine plate attachment	1	
A16	DP0616	**Dowel,** rear engine plate attachment	1	
		Note:— Welch washer and bucket type core plugs used as alternative fitment are not interchangeable.		
A17	119758	**Stud,** long, cylinder head attachment	7	
A18	133803	**Stud,** short, cylinder head attachment (High compression)	7	
	120843	**Stud,** short, cylinder head attachment (Low compression)	7	
A19	139836	**Stud,** gearbox and rear engine plate attachment	3	
A20	100433	**Stud,** timing cover and engine plate	2	
A21	101962	**Stud,** distributor pedestal attachment	2	
A22	100433	**Stud,** breather pipe outlet blanking plate attachment	2	
A23	100433	**Stud,** petrol pump attachment	2	
A24	104863	**Block,** sealing, front	1	
A25	36234	**Piece,** filling ⎫ Sealing block to	2	
A26	100501	**Screw** ⎭ cylinder block	2	
	129889	**Adaptor,** oil pressure switch	1	⎫ Fitted up to Engine No.
	500463	**Washer,** copper, for adaptor	1	⎭ KC5000E only
A27	61478	**Tap,** drain	1	
A28	WF0511	**Washer,** fibre	A/R	
A29	WF0525	**Washer,** fibre	A/R	
A30	138126	**Plate,** blanking ⎫	1	
A31	124594	**Gasket** ⎬ Blanking breather	1	
A32	WL0208	**Washer,** lock ⎪ pipe outlet	2	
A33	HN2008	**Nut** ⎭	2	
A34	145021	**CYLINDER LINER**	6	
A35	212622	**OIL SEAL HOUSING—REAR**	1	
A36	105321	**Washer,** joint, between oil seal housing and cylinder block	1	
A37	143456	**Seal,** oil, crankshaft	1	
A38	HB0809	**Bolt** ⎫	7	
A39	WL0208	**Washer,** lock ⎬ Oil seal housing to cylinder block	6	
	500469	**Washer,** copper ⎭	1	Fitted under head of top bolt
		OIL PRESSURE ADJUSTMENT DETAILS		
A40	132107	**Piston,** relief valve	1	
A41	131535	**Spring**	1	
A42	107246	**Plug,** relief valve	1	
A43	501258	**Washer**	1	
	139289	†**OIL PUMP ASSEMBLY**	1	
	515740	†**OIL PUMP ASSEMBLY (RECONDITIONED UNIT)**	1	
A44	127732	**Body** assembly, oil pump	1	
	104963	**Plug,** core, oil pump body	1	
A45	508975	**Rotor and spindle** assembly	1	
A46	139288	**Cover,** oil pump body	1	
A47	HB0724	**Bolt** ⎫ Oil pump to	3	
A48	WL0207	**Washer,** lock ⎭ cylinder block	3	

Note:—Items marked thus † are available on our Factory Exchange Unit Scheme

2

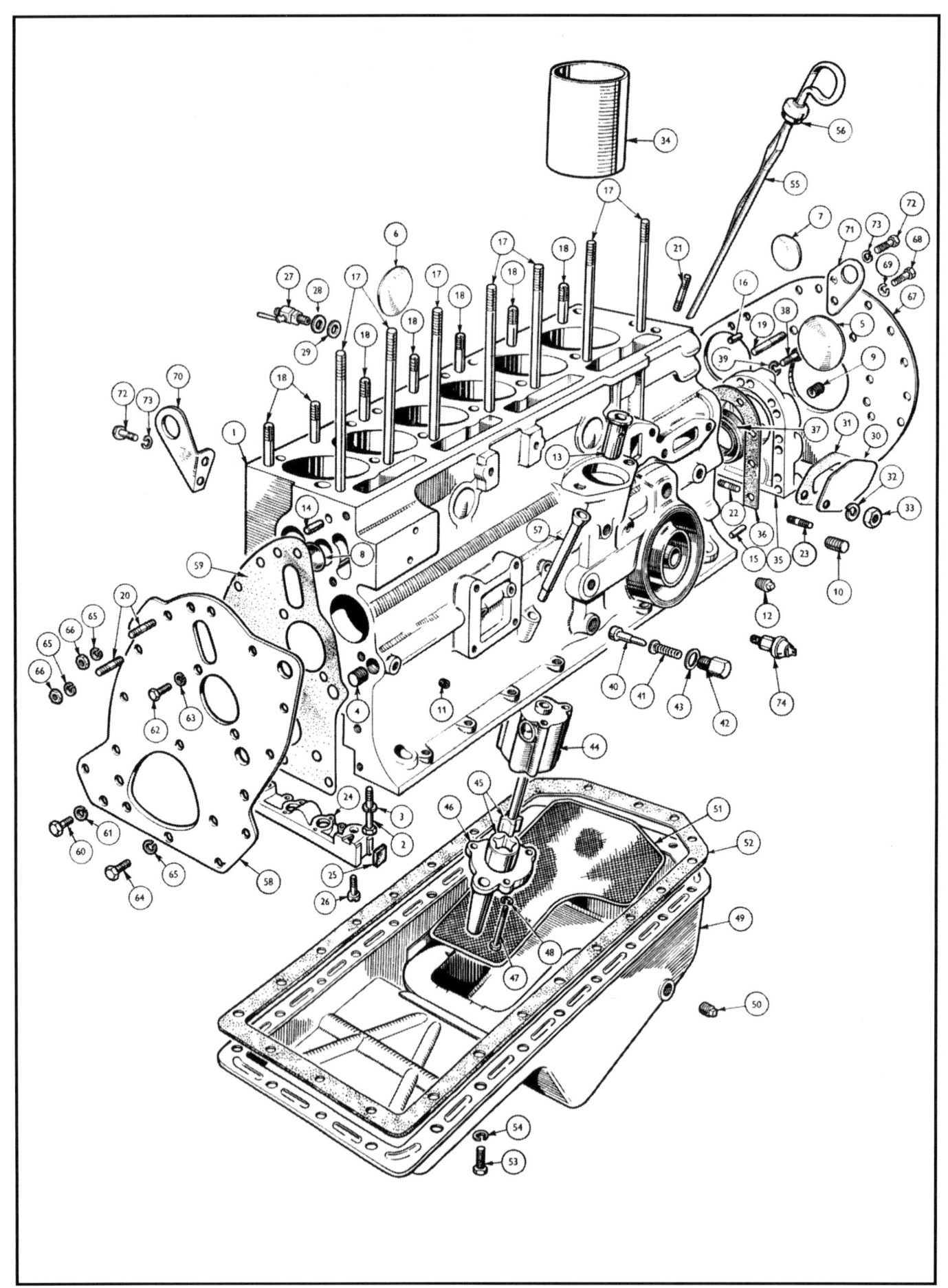

PLATE A

ENGINE

MARK I CARS FITTED UP TO ENGINE No. KC/KD50000E ONLY

Plate No.	Part No.	Description	No. per Unit	Remarks
A49	307039	**OIL SUMP ASSEMBLY**	1	
A50	114774	**Plug,** oil drain	1	
A51	129795	**Gauze,** strainer	1	
A52	211125	**Gasket,** between sump and block	1	
A53	HB0805	**Screw,** set ⎱ Oil sump to	23	
A54	WL0208	**Washer,** lock ⎰ cylinder block	23	
A55	127653	**Dipstick** assembly	1	
A56	32307	**Washer,** felt, on dipstick	1	
A57	127652	**Tube,** dipstick	1	
A58	205456	**FRONT ENGINE PLATE**	1	⎱ Fitted up to Engine No.
A59	212766	**Washer,** joint, front engine plate	1	⎰ KC5000E only
	213777	**FRONT ENGINE PLATE**	1	⎱ Fitted from Engine No.
	213658	**Washer,** joint, front engine plate	1	⎰ KC/KD5001E and future
A60	HU0806	**Screw,** set ⎱ Front engine plate	3	
A61	WL0208	**Washer,** lock ⎰ to cylinder block	3	
A62	HU0807	**Screw,** set ⎱ Front engine plate and camshaft	2	
A63	WL0208	**Washer,** lock ⎰ locating plate to cylinder block	2	
A64	HU0807	**Screw,** set ⎱ Timing cover and	5	
A65	WL0208	**Washer,** lock ⎬ front engine plate	7	
A66	HN2008	**Nut** ⎰ to cylinder block	2	
A67	211514	**REAR ENGINE PLATE**	1	
A68	HU0807	**Screw,** set ⎱ Rear engine plate	7	
A69	WL0208	**Washer,** lock ⎰	7	
		ENGINE LIFTING EYES		
A70	123716	**Eye,** lifting, front	1	
A71	123715	**Eye,** lifting, rear	1	
A72	HU0805	**Screw,** set ⎱ Lifting eyes to	4	
A73	WL0208	**Washer,** lock ⎰ cylinder block	3	
A74	121398	†**OIL PRESSURE SWITCH**	1	

Note:- For Engine Mounting Brackets see Engine Mounting Details.

Note:—Items marked thus † are available on our Factory Exchange Unit Scheme

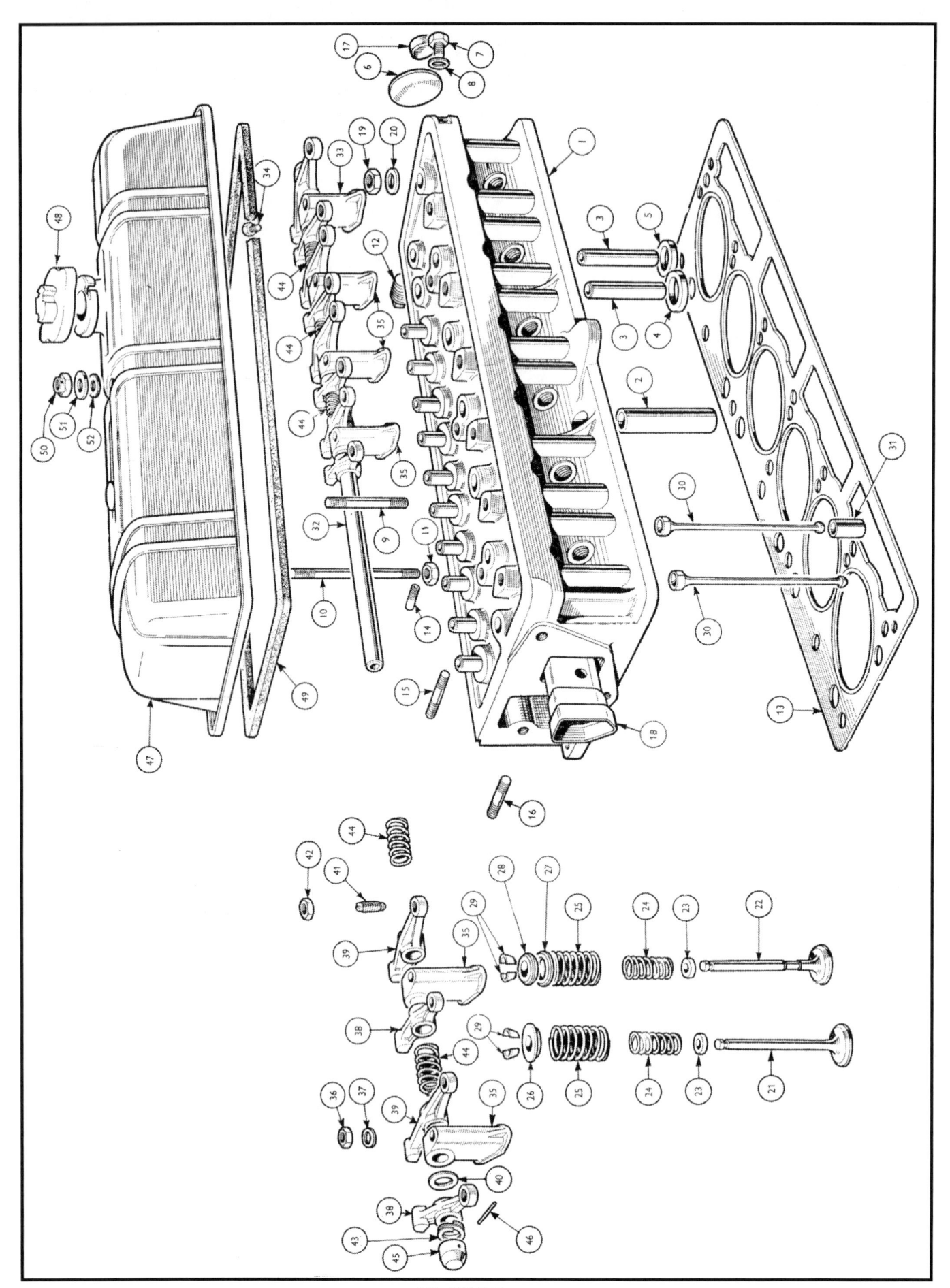

PLATE B

ENGINE

MARK I CARS FITTED UP TO ENGINE No. KC/KD50000E ONLY

Plate No.	Part No.	Description	No. per Unit	Remarks
	515482	**CYLINDER HEAD ASSEMBLY** (With Valves and Springs, less Studs)	1	} High Compression Engines only
B1	515483	**CYLINDER HEAD ASSEMBLY** (Less Valves, Springs and Studs)	1	
	512827	**CYLINDER HEAD ASSEMBLY** (With Valves and Springs, less Studs)	1	} Low Compression Engines only
	515553	**CYLINDER HEAD ASSEMBLY** (Less Valves, Springs and Studs)	1	
	516823	**CYLINDER HEAD ASSEMBLY** (With Valves and Springs, less Studs)	1	} U.S.A. only. Fitted from Engine No. KD6915E and future
	516824	**CYLINDER HEAD ASSEMBLY** (Less Valves, Springs and Studs)	1	
		Note:- The above Assemblies do not include rocker details or inlet and exhaust manifold studs.		
B2	104826	**Tube**, sealing, push rod	12	
B3	119622	**Guide**, valve	12	
B4	130814	**Insert**, valve seat, inlet valve	6	
B5	130813	**Insert**, valve seat, exhaust valve	6	
B6	27378	**Plug**, core, in rear face of head	1	Alternative fitment to 144648
	144648	**Plug**, core, bucket type, in rear face of head	1	Alternative fitment to 27378
B7	101022	**Screw**, set ⎱ Rocker	1	
B8	500469	**Washer**, copper ⎰ oil feed	1	
B9	132495	**Stud**, rocker pedestal	6	
B10	105123	**Stud**, rocker cover, centre and rear	2	
B11	HN2008	**Nut**, stud, to cylinder head	2	
	30123	**Linger**, lead, under nut	A/R	
B12	114774	**Plug**, taper	1	
B13	207102	**Gasket**, cylinder head	1	
B14	127398	**Dowel**, special, inlet manifold attachment	1	
B15	105124	**Stud**, exhaust manifold, outer	2	
B16	101962	**Stud**, inlet manifold	2	
B17	116511	**Plug**, in rear face of head	1	
B18	210829	**Tube** assembly, water delivery	1	
B19	110748	**Nut** ⎱	14	
B20	WP0009	**Washer**, plain ⎰ Cylinder head to cylinder block	14	
	30123	**Linger**, lead ⎰	A/R	

Note:—Items marked thus † are available on our Factory Exchange Unit Scheme

4

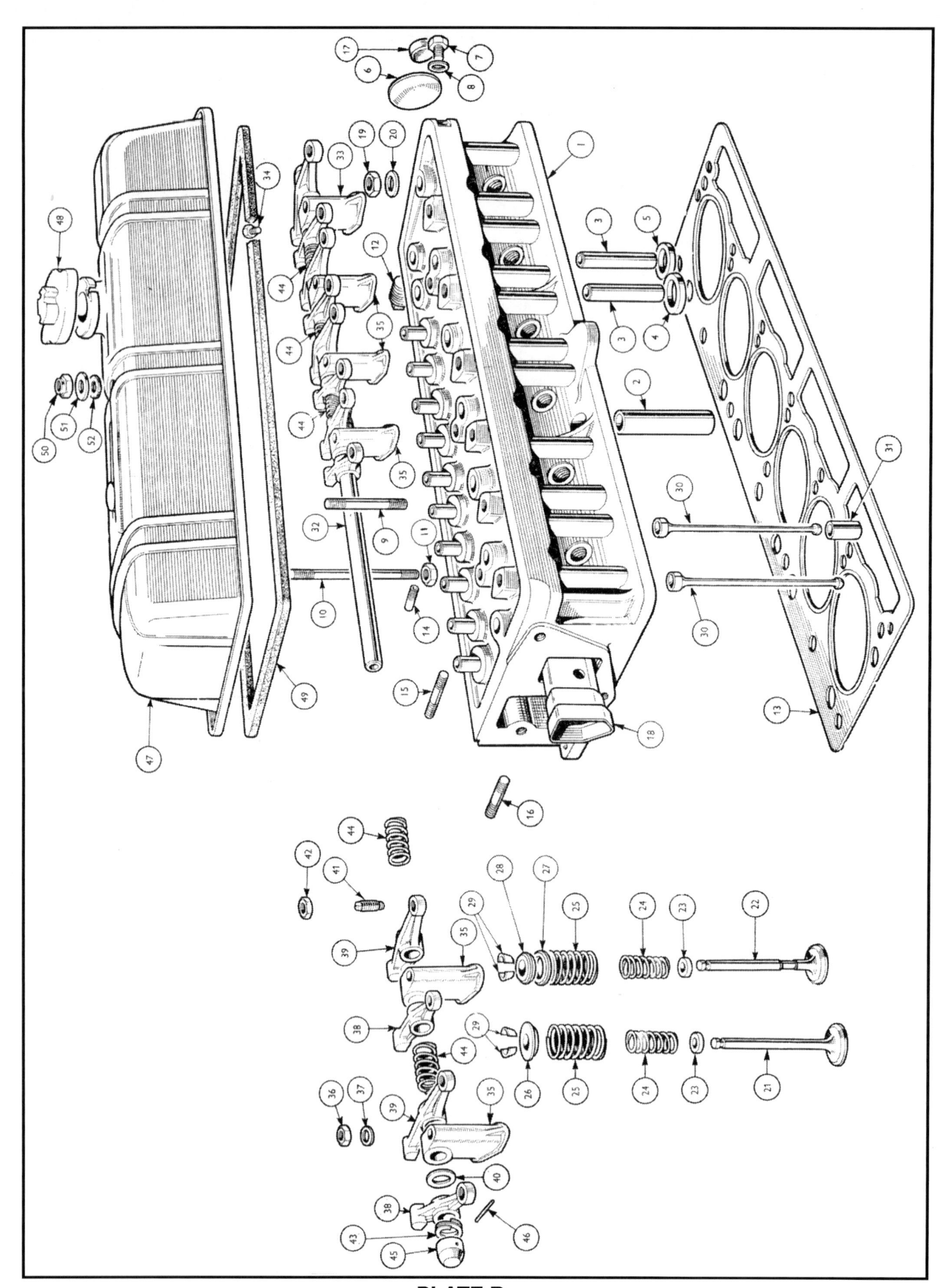

PLATE B

ENGINE
MARK I CARS FITTED UP TO ENGINE No. KC/KD50000E ONLY

Plate No.	Part No.	Description	No. per Unit	Remarks
		VALVES		
B21	122257	**Valve,** inlet	6	
B22	137841	**Valve,** exhaust	6	
	148387	**Valve,** exhaust	6	U.S.A. only. Fitted from Engine No. KD6915E and future
B23	111871	**Collar,** spring, lower	12	
B24	102564	**Spring,** valve, inner	12	
B25	121251	**Spring,** valve, outer	12	
B26	111870	**Collar,** spring, upper (Inlet valve only)	6	
B27	128335	**Collar,** valve, outer (Exhaust only)	6	
B28	128334	**Collar,** valve, inner (Exhaust only)	6	
B29	106663	**Cotter,** split cone	12 prs.	
B30	129058	**PUSH ROD (High Compression)**	12	
	119811	**PUSH ROD (Low Compression)**	12	
B31	143552	**Tappet,** push rod	12	
B32	204736	**ROCKER SHAFT**	1	Alternative to 214562
	214562	**ROCKER SHAFT**	1	Alternative to 204736
B33	128425	**Pedestal,** rocker, drilled	1	Alternative to 104832
B33	104832	**Pedestal,** rocker, drilled	1	Alternative to 128425
B34	104859	**Screw,** locating, shaft to drilled pedestal	1	
B35	128424	**Pedestal,** rocker, plain	5	Alternative to 104831
B35	104831	**Pedestal,** rocker, plain	5	Alternative to 128424
B36	HN2009	**Nut** ⎱ Rocker pedestal	6	
B37	WP0184	**Washer,** plain ⎰ to cylinder head	6	
B38	109023	**Rocker,** No. 1	6	
B39	109024	**Rocker,** No. 2	6	
B40	119759	**Washer,** spacing	12	
B41	109495	**Screw,** adjustment ⎱ Fitted to rockers	12	
B42	57110	**Locknut** ⎰	12	
B43	105322	**Spring,** rocker, outer	2	
B44	119313	**Spring,** rocker, intermediate	5	
B45	104838	**Collar,** on ends of shaft	2	
B46	500975	**Pin,** Mills, securing collar	2	
B47	213496	**ROCKER COVER ASSEMBLY**	1	
B48	143393	**Cap,** oil filler	1	
B49	119322	**Washer,** joint, rocker cover	1	
B50	TN3208	**Nut,** nyloc ⎱	2	
	516134	**Bolt** ⎱ Rocker cover to	1	
B51	WP0008	**Washer,** plain ⎰ cylinder head	3	
B52	WF0508	**Washer,** fibre ⎰	3	

Note:—Items marked thus † are available on our Factory Exchange Unit Scheme

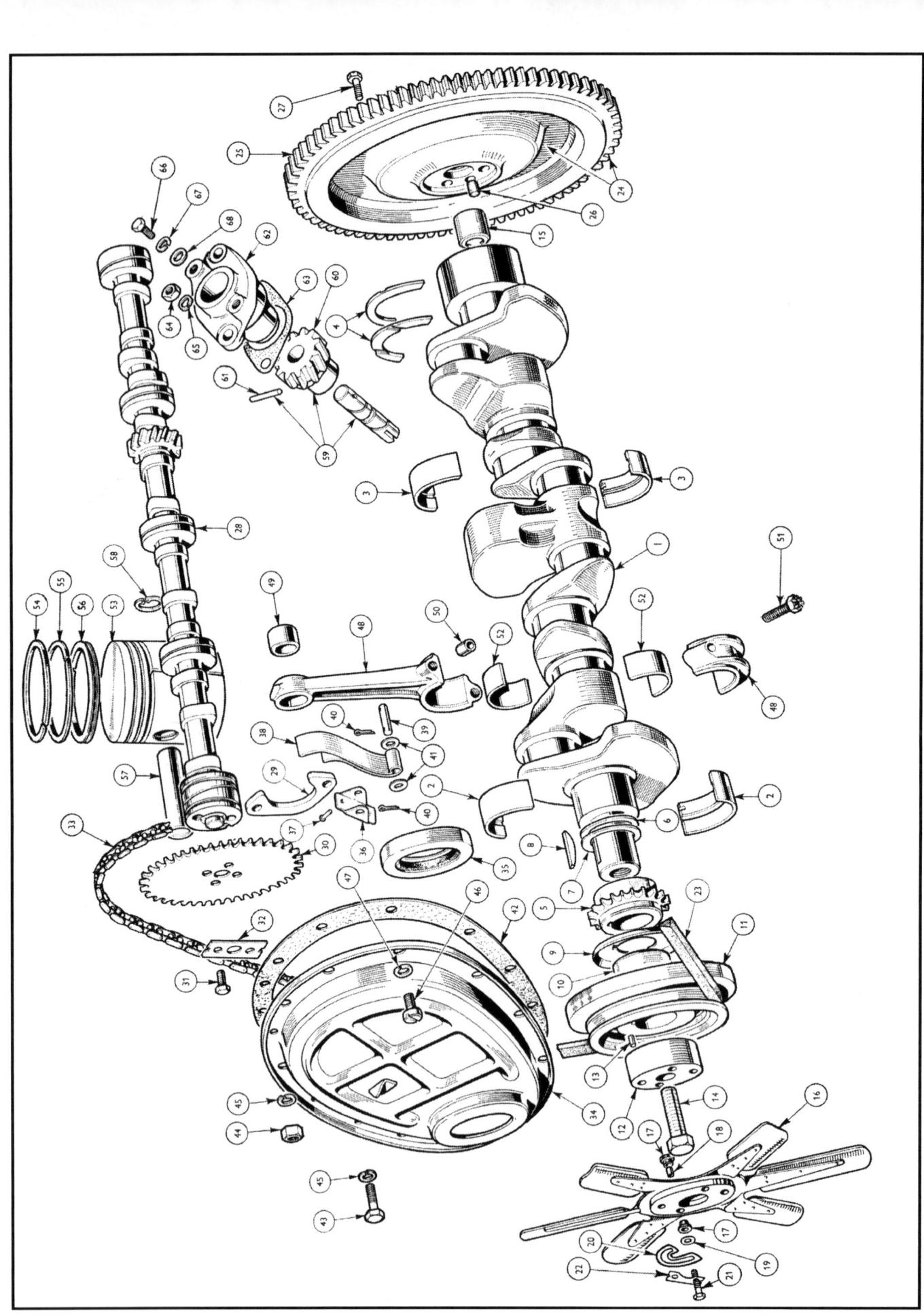

PLATE C

ENGINE
MARK I CARS FITTED UP TO ENGINE No. KC/KD50000E ONLY

Plate No.	Part No.	Description	No. per Unit	Remarks
C1	307718	**CRANKSHAFT**	1	⎫
C2	104819	**Bearing**, main, front and rear	2 prs.	⎬ Fitted up to Engine No.
C3	126938	**Bearing**, main, intermediate	2 prs.	⎬ KC5000E only
C4	104820	**Washer**, thrust (obtainable ·005″ o/s)	2	⎭
	308034	**CRANKSHAFT**	1	⎫
	144194	**Bearing**, main	4 prs.	⎬ Fitted from Engine No.
	149082	**Bearing**, main (Alternative to 144194)	4 prs.	⎬ KC/KD5001E and future
	144195	**Washer**, thrust (obtainable ·005″ o/s)	2	⎭
C5	119389	**Chainwheel**	1	
C6	145275	**Shim**, chainwheel to crankshaft, ·004″ thick	A/R	
C7	145276	**Shim**, chainwheel to crankshaft, ·006″ thick	A/R	
C8	133234	**Key**, locating chainwheel on crankshaft	1	
C9	119390	**Deflector**, oil	1	
C10	133235	**Sleeve**, oil seal	1	
C11	133244	**Pulley and damper** assembly	1	
C12	133238	**Adaptor**, fan	1	
C13	DP0508	**Dowel**, locating adaptor on pulley and damper	2	
C14	HB1316	**Bolt**, securing adaptor and pulley to crankshaft	1	
C15	105143	**Bush**, constant pinion, fitted in end of crankshaft	1	

MAIN BEARINGS are obtainable in the following undersizes:— ·010″, — ·020″, — ·030″. When ordering please quote part number and undersize required.

Plate No.	Part No.	Description	No. per Unit	Remarks
C16	211986	**FAN ASSEMBLY**	1	Fitted up to Engine No. KC/KD9226E only
	308353	**FAN ASSEMBLY**	1	Fitted from Engine No. KC/KD 9227E and future
C17	108496	**Bush** ⎫	8	
C18	108499	**Sleeve** ⎬	4	
C19	108495	**Washer** ⎬ Fan to	4	
C20	107858	**Piece**, balance ⎬ adaptor	1	
C21	HB0810	**Bolt** ⎬	4	
C22	107857	**Washer**, tab ⎭	2	
C23	212683	**Belt**, fan	1	Fitted up to Engine No. KC/KD7905E only
	214314	**Belt**, fan	1	Fitted from Engine No. KC/KD7906E and future

Note:— 214314 Fan belt may be used in conjunction with 147906 Dynamo pulley for all replacements.

Plate No.	Part No.	Description	No. per Unit	Remarks
C24	143689	**FLYWHEEL ASSEMBLY**	1	⎫
C25	201350	**Ring**, gear	1	⎬ Fitted up to Engine No.
	127883	**Dowel** ⎱ Flywheel to	1	⎬ KC5000E only
	138526	**Bolt**, place ⎰ crankshaft	4	⎭
	148042	**FLYWHEEL ASSEMBLY**	1	⎫
	201350	**Ring**, gear	1	⎬ Fitted from Engine No.
	127883	**Dowel** ⎱ Flywheel to	1	⎬ KC/KD5001E and future
	147299	**Bolt**, flywheel ⎰ crankshaft	1	⎭

Note:—Items marked thus † are available on our Factory Exchange Unit Scheme

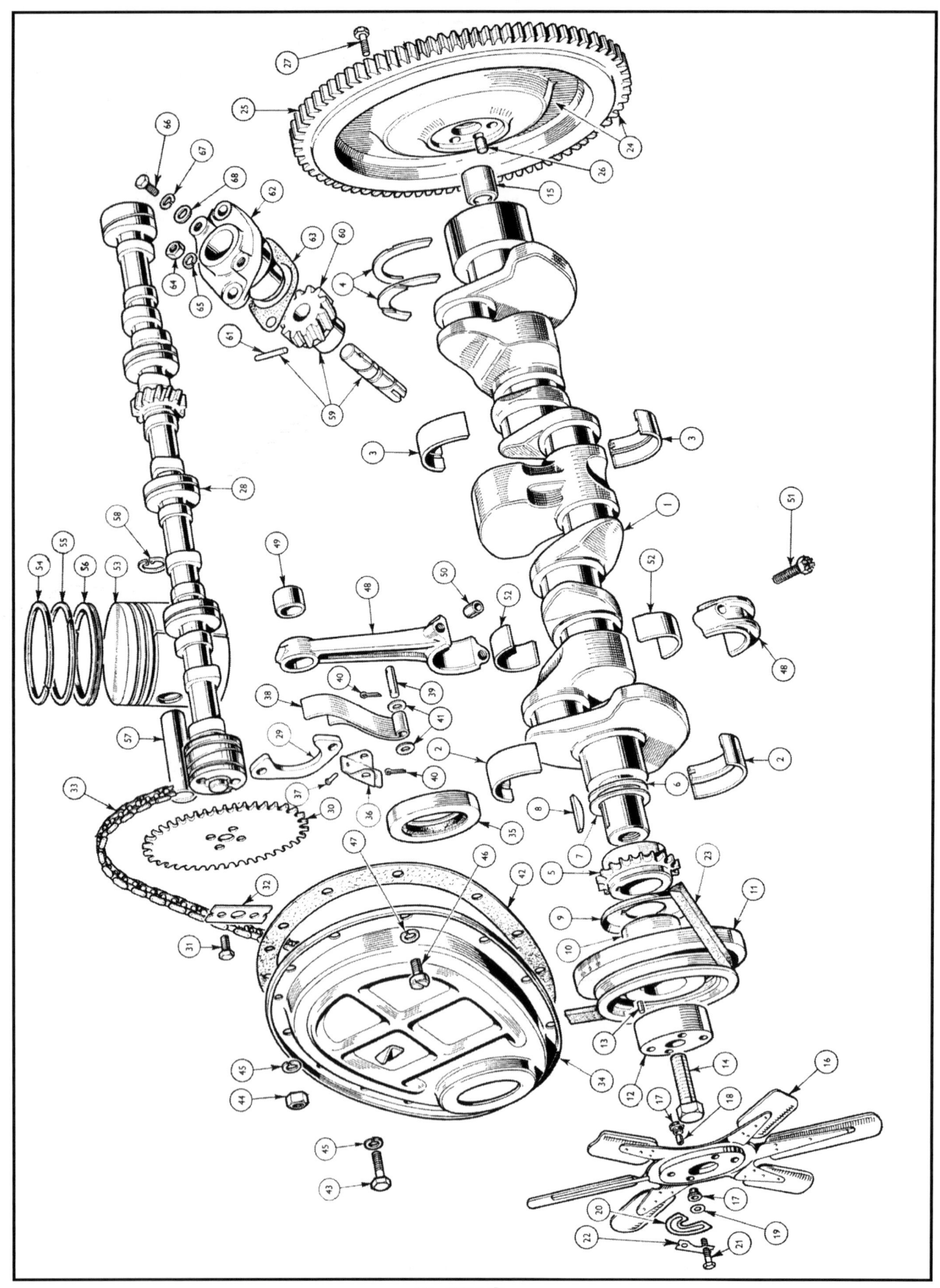

PLATE C

ENGINE
MARK I CARS FITTED UP TO ENGINE No. KC/KD50000E ONLY

Plate No.	Part No.	Description	No. per Unit	Remarks
C28	306785	**CAMSHAFT**	1	
	307621	**CAMSHAFT**	1	U.S.A. only. Fitted from Engine No. KD6915E and future
C29	105114	**Plate**, locating	1	
		Note:- For Locating plate attachment details see Front Engine Plate.		
C30	35960	**Chainwheel**, camshaft	1	
C31	100500	**Screw**, set ⎫ Chainwheel	2	
C32	36411	**Plate**, locking ⎬ to camshaft	1	
C33	105131	**Chain**, timing	1	
C34	207492	**TIMING COVER ASSEMBLY**	1	
C35	125631	**Seal**, oil, in timing cover	1	
C36	43752	**Plate**, anchor, chain tensioner	1	
C37	SP.91.B3	**Rivet**, anchor plate to timing cover	2	
C38	42425	**Tensioner**, chain	1	
C39	33214	**Pin**, anchor, chain tensioner	1	
C40	PC0007	**Pin**, cotter ⎫ Chain tensioner	2	
C41	WP0018	**Washer**, plain ⎬ attachment	2	
C42	211126	**Gasket**, timing cover	1	
C43	HU0807	**Screw**, set ⎫ Timing cover	5	
C44	HN2008	**Nut** ⎬ and front engine plate	2	
C45	WL0208	**Washer**, lock ⎭ to cylinder block	7	
C46	PT0803	**Screw**, set ⎫ Timing cover to	5	
C47	WL0208	**Washer**, lock ⎬ front engine plate	5	
C48	138548	**CONNECTING ROD ASSEMBLY**	6	Fitted up to Engine No. KC5000E only
	146454	**CONNECTING ROD ASSEMBLY**	6	Fitted from Engine No. KC/KD5001E and future
C49	119813	**Bush**, small end	6	
C50	107401	**Dowel**, hollow, connecting rod bolt	12	
C51	138529	**Bolt**, place, connecting rod	12	
C52	128391	**Bearing**, big end	6 prs.	Fitted up to Engine No. KC5000E only
	144193	**Bearing**, big end	6 prs.	Fitted from Engine No. KC/KD5001E and future
	149081	**Bearing**, big end	6 prs.	Alternative to 144193

BIG END BEARINGS are obtainable in the following undersizes:- —·010″, —·020″, —·030″. When ordering, please quote part number and size required.

Note:—Items marked thus † are available on our Factory Exchange Unit Scheme

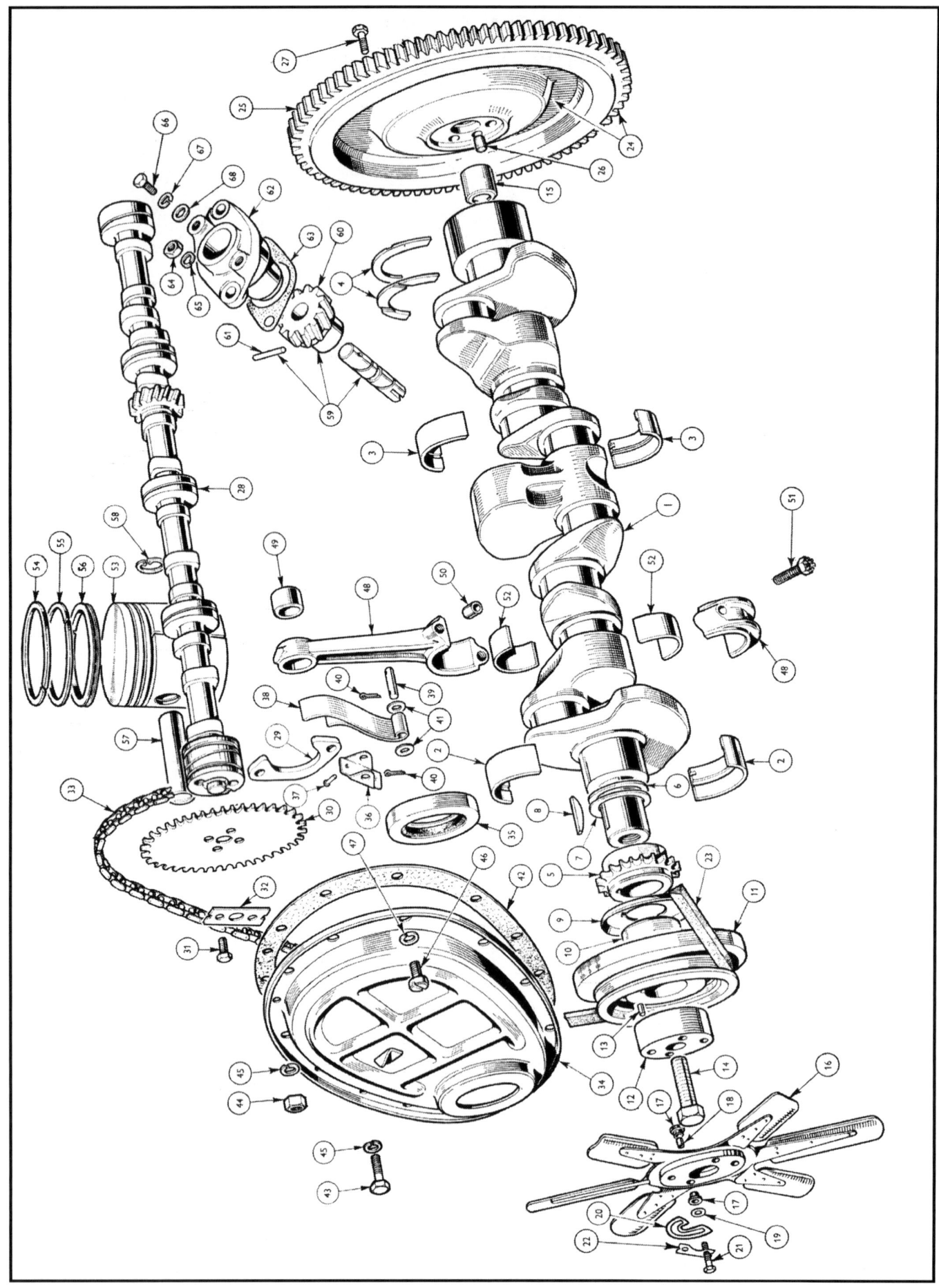

PLATE C

ENGINE

MARK I CARS FITTED UP TO ENGINE No. KC/KD50000E ONLY

Plate No.	Part No.	Description	No. per Unit	Remarks
C53	139809	**PISTON ASSEMBLY (Graded F, G & H)**	6	Fitted up to Engine No. only
	149976	**PISTON ASSEMBLY (Graded F, G & H)**	6	Fitted from Engine No. and future
C54	127262	**Ring,** compression, plated	6	
C55	139810	**Ring,** compression	6	
C56	127264	**Ring,** scraper	6	
C57	127265	**Pin,** gudgeon	6	
C58	508978	**Circlip,** retaining gudgeon pin	12	

PISTONS are obtainable +·020″ oversize.

PISTON RINGS are obtainable in the following oversizes:- +·010″, +·020″, +·030″. When ordering, please quote part number and size required.

Plate No.	Part No.	Description	No. per Unit	Remarks
C59	126786	**DRIVE SHAFT ASSEMBLY, DISTRIBUTOR AND OIL PUMP**	1	
C60	126785	**Gear,** driving, distributor and oil pump	1	
C61	500974	**Pin,** Mills, securing gear	1	
C62	126784	**Pedestal,** distributor	1	
C63	104939	**Washer,** joint, pedestal	1	
C64	HN2008	**Nut** ⎫ Pedestal to cylinder block	2	
C65	WL0208	**Washer,** lock ⎬	2	
C66	HU0704	**Screw,** set ⎭	2	
C67	WL0207	**Washer,** lock ⎫ Distributor to pedestal	1	
C68	WP0035	**Washer,** plain ⎭	2	

Note:- For Details of Distributor see Electrical Section.

Note:—Items marked thus † are available on our Factory Exchange Unit Scheme

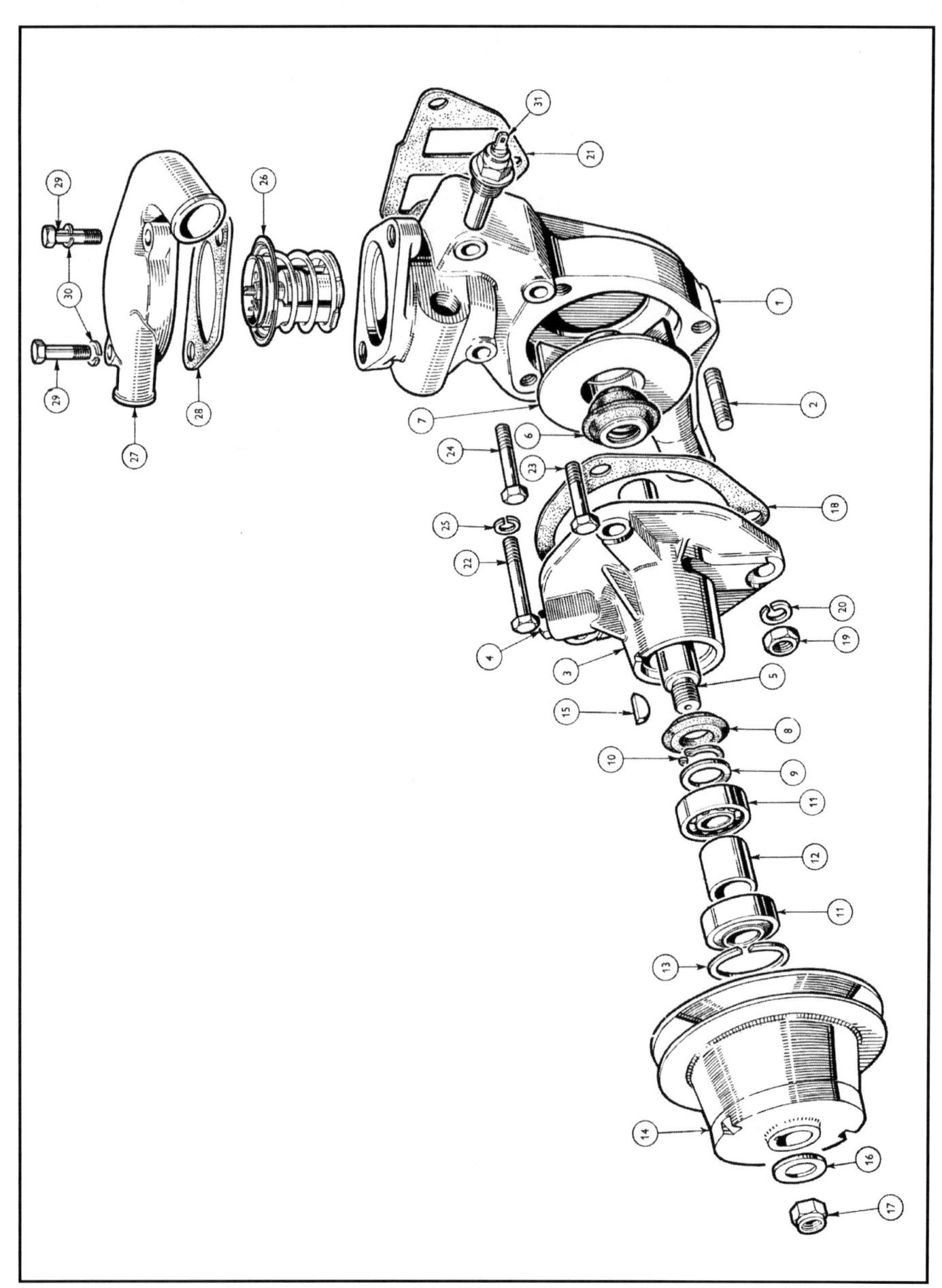

PLATE D

ENGINE
MARK I CARS FITTED UP TO ENGINE No. KC/KD50000E ONLY

Plate No.	Part No.	Description	No. per Unit	Remarks
	514397	**WATER PUMP ASSEMBLY**	1	
D1	307095	**Body,** water pump	1	
D2	101962	**Stud,** bearing housing attachment	3	
	133258	†**Housing,** bearing, assembly	1	
	511813	†**Housing,** bearing, assembly (Reconditioned Unit)	1	
D3	201316	**Housing,** bearing	1	
D4	122115	**Plug**	1	
D5	104839	**Spindle**	1	
D6	148322	**Seal,** between bearing housing and impellor	1	
D7	104840	**Impellor**	1	
D8	60313	**Seal,** bearing	1	
D9	101092	**Washer,** abutment	1	
D10	500047	**Circlip**	1	
D11	100764	**Bearing**	2	
D12	104841	**Piece,** distance, between bearings	1	
D13	100851	**Circlip,** retaining bearing in housing	1	
D14	133239	**Pulley**	1	
D15	KW0420	**Key,** Woodruff, locating pulley on spindle	1	
D16	WP0181	**Washer,** plain ⎫ Pulley to spindle	1	
D17	TN3208	**Nut,** nyloc ⎭	1	
D18	138701	**Gasket** ⎫	1	
D19	HN2008	**Nut** ⎬ Bearing housing to pump body	3	
D20	WL0208	**Washer,** lock ⎭	3	
D21	138792	**Gasket** ⎫	1	
D22	HB0825	**Bolt** ⎪	1	
D23	HB0818	**Bolt** ⎬ Water pump to cylinder head	1	
D24	HB0819	**Bolt** ⎪	1	
D25	WL0208	**Washer,** lock ⎭	3	
D26	140970	†**THERMOSTAT UNIT (82° OPENING)**	1	
	146431	†**THERMOSTAT UNIT (88° OPENING)**	1	Special Order only
D27	212971	**Elbow,** water	1	
D28	57103	**Gasket** ⎫	1	
D29	HB0812	**Bolt** ⎬ Elbow to water pump body	2	
D30	WL0208	**Washer,** lock ⎭	2	
D31	137705	**Temperature transmitter**	1	

Note:—Items marked thus † are available on our Factory Exchange Unit Scheme

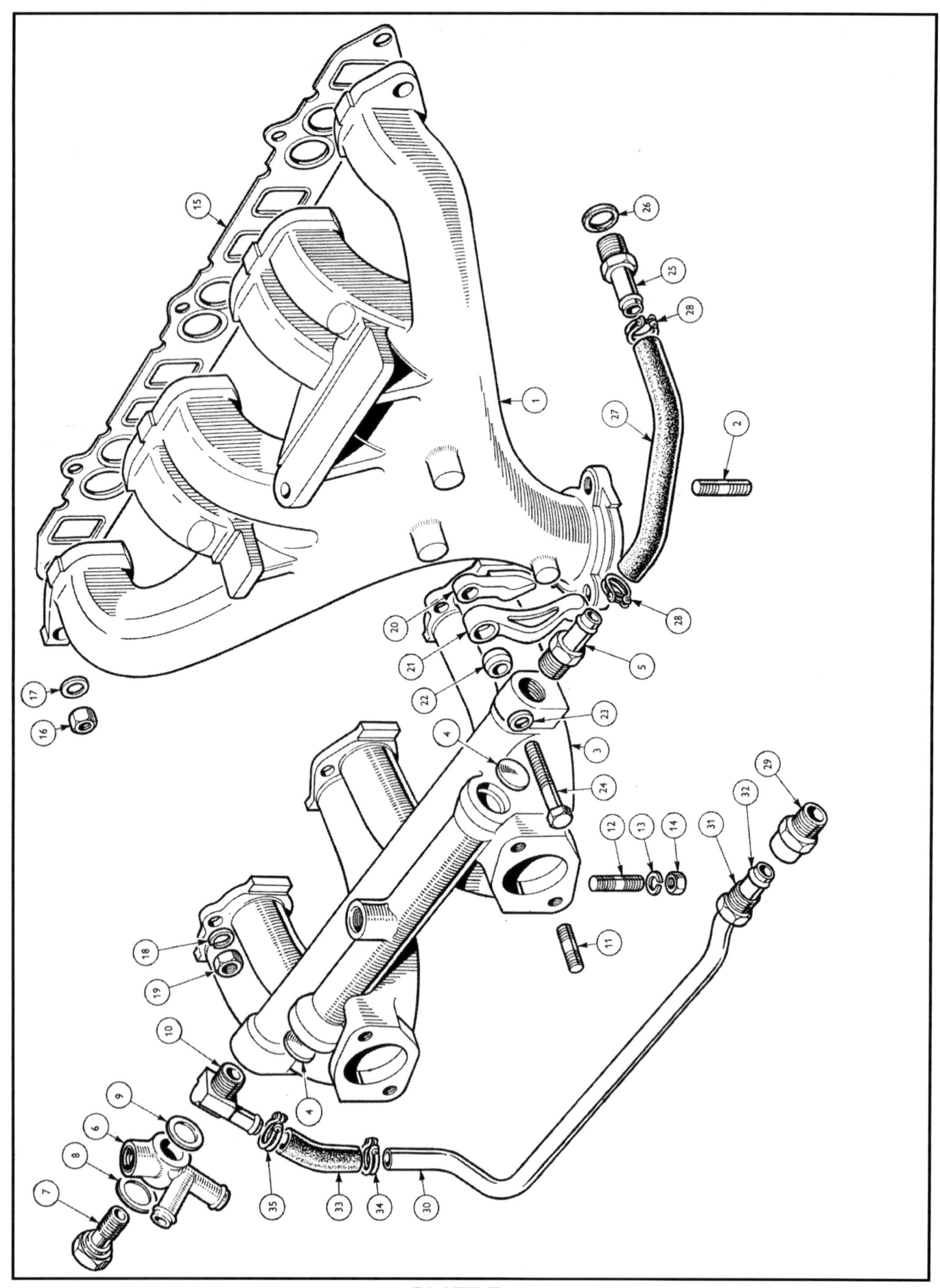

PLATE E

ENGINE
MARK I CARS FITTED UP TO ENGINE No. KC/KD50000E ONLY

Plate No.	Part No.	Description	No. per Unit	Remarks
		MANIFOLDS		
E1	306483	**Manifold,** exhaust	1	
E2	101962	**Stud,** exhaust outlet attachment	3	
E3	212770	**Manifold,** inlet	1	
E4	46172	**Plug,** core	2	
E5	138810	**Adaptor,** front, water feed to manifold	1	
E6	145938	**Adaptor** assembly, water return from manifold and heater ⎫	1	
E7	145155	**Bolt,** banjo ⎬ Adaptor ⎬ Only required when heater is fitted	1	
E8	WF0534	**Washer** (Large hole) ⎬ to	1	
E9	WF0550	**Washer** (Small hole) ⎭ manifold ⎭	1	
E10	138822	**Elbow**—(Only required when heater is not fitted or fresh air kit is fitted)	1	
E11	129383	**Stud,** carburettor attachment	4	
	TD0863	**Stud,** carburettor attachment	4	U.S.A. 'Anti-Smog' vehicles only. Fitted from Engine No. KD10001E and future
E12	129619	**Stud** ⎫	1	
E13	WL0209	**Washer,** lock ⎬ Inlet manifold to exhaust manifold	1	
E14	JN2109	**Nut,** jam ⎭	1	
E15	211555	**Washer,** joint, inlet and exhaust manifold	1	
E16	100498	**Nut** ⎫ Exhaust manifold	2	
E17	WP0036	**Washer,** plain ⎭ to cylinder head	2	
E18	WL0208	**Washer,** lock ⎫ Inlet manifold to	2	
E19	HN2008	**Nut** ⎭ cylinder head	2	
E20	123761	**Plate,** clamp ⎫	6	
E21	123760	**Clamp** ⎬ Exhaust and	6	
E22	119324	**Washer,** spherical ⎬ inlet manifold	6	
E23	WP0036	**Washer,** plain ⎬ to cylinder head	6	
E24	HB0913	**Bolt** ⎭	6	
		MANIFOLD HEATER PIPES		
E25	138530	**Adaptor,** water pump body (To manifold)	1	
E26	WF0524	**Washer,** fibre, between adaptor and water pump body	1	
E27	137876	**Hose,** adaptor to inlet manifold	1	
E28	CS4012	**Clip,** hose attachment	2	
E29	101343	**Adaptor,** water pump body (Return)	1	
E30	210834	**Pipe,** water return	1	
E31	101302	**Nut,** tubing	1	
E32	TL0011	**Sleeve,** tubing	1	
E33	140986	**Hose,** pipe to elbow or adaptor in inlet manifold	1	
E34	CS4013	**Clip,** hose attachment	1	
E35	CS4012	**Clip,** hose attachment	1	

Note:—Items marked thus † are available on our Factory Exchange Unit Scheme

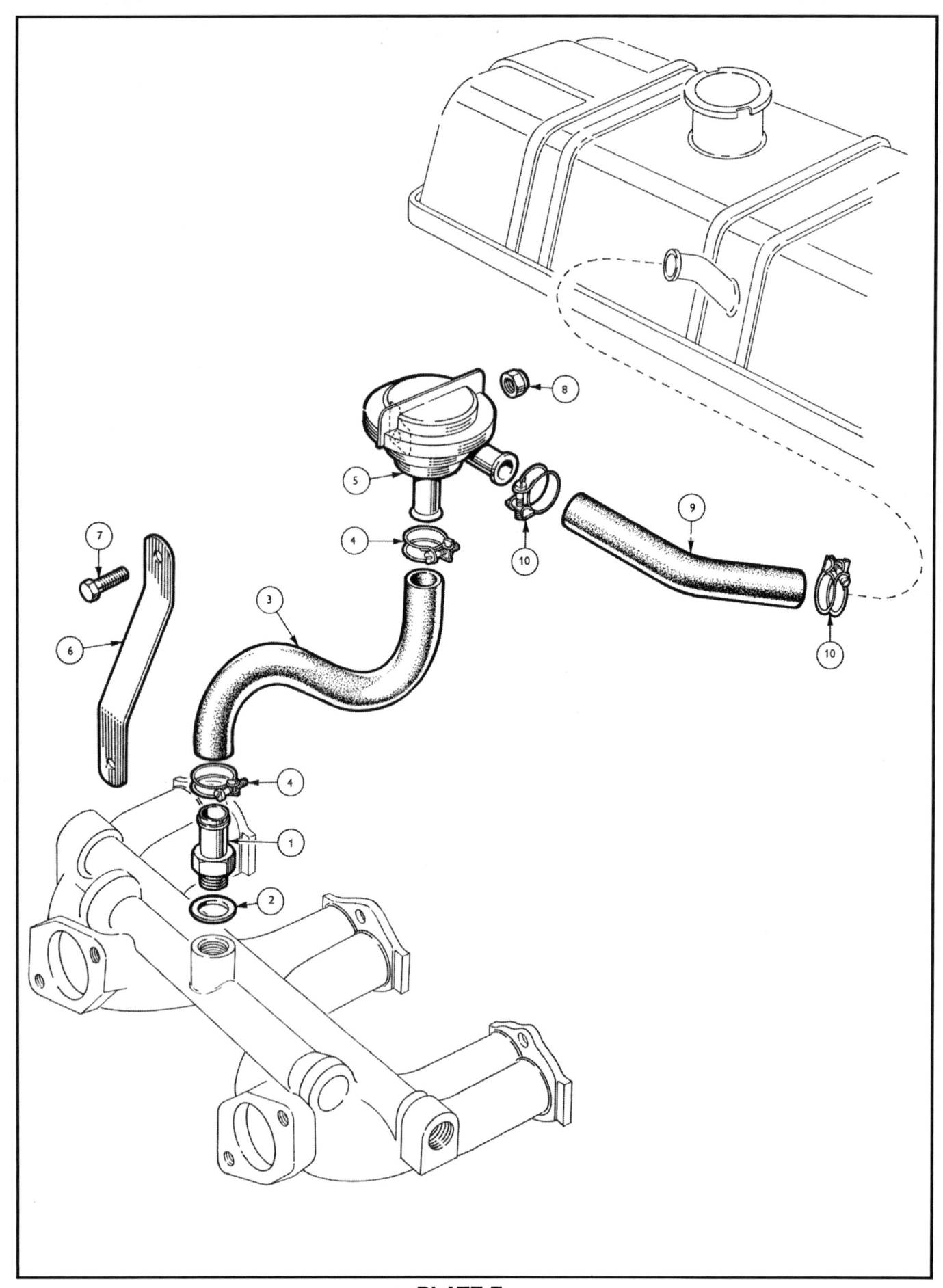

PLATE F

ENGINE

MARK I CARS FITTED UP TO ENGINE No. KC/KD50000E ONLY

Plate No.	Part No.	Description	No. per Unit	Remarks
		BREATHER DETAILS		
F1	138530	**Adaptor,** hose to inlet manifold	1	
F2	WF0513	**Washer,** fibre, on adaptor	1	
F3	143706	**Hose,** inlet manifold adaptor to emission control valve	1	
F4	CS4012	**Clip,** hose attachment	2	
F5	143407	**Valve,** emission control	1	
	516665	**Kit,** emission control valve—Comprising plunger sub assembly, diaphragm and top cover	1	
F6	143313	**Bracket,** control valve, fitted to manifold attachment stud	1	
F7	HU0707	**Screw,** set ⎫ Emission control valve	1	
F8	TN3207	**Nut,** nyloc ⎭ to mounting bracket	1	
F9	143323	**Hose,** emission control valve to rocker cover	1	
F10	CS4012	**Clip,** hose attachment	2	

Note:—Items marked thus † are available on our Factory Exchange Unit Scheme

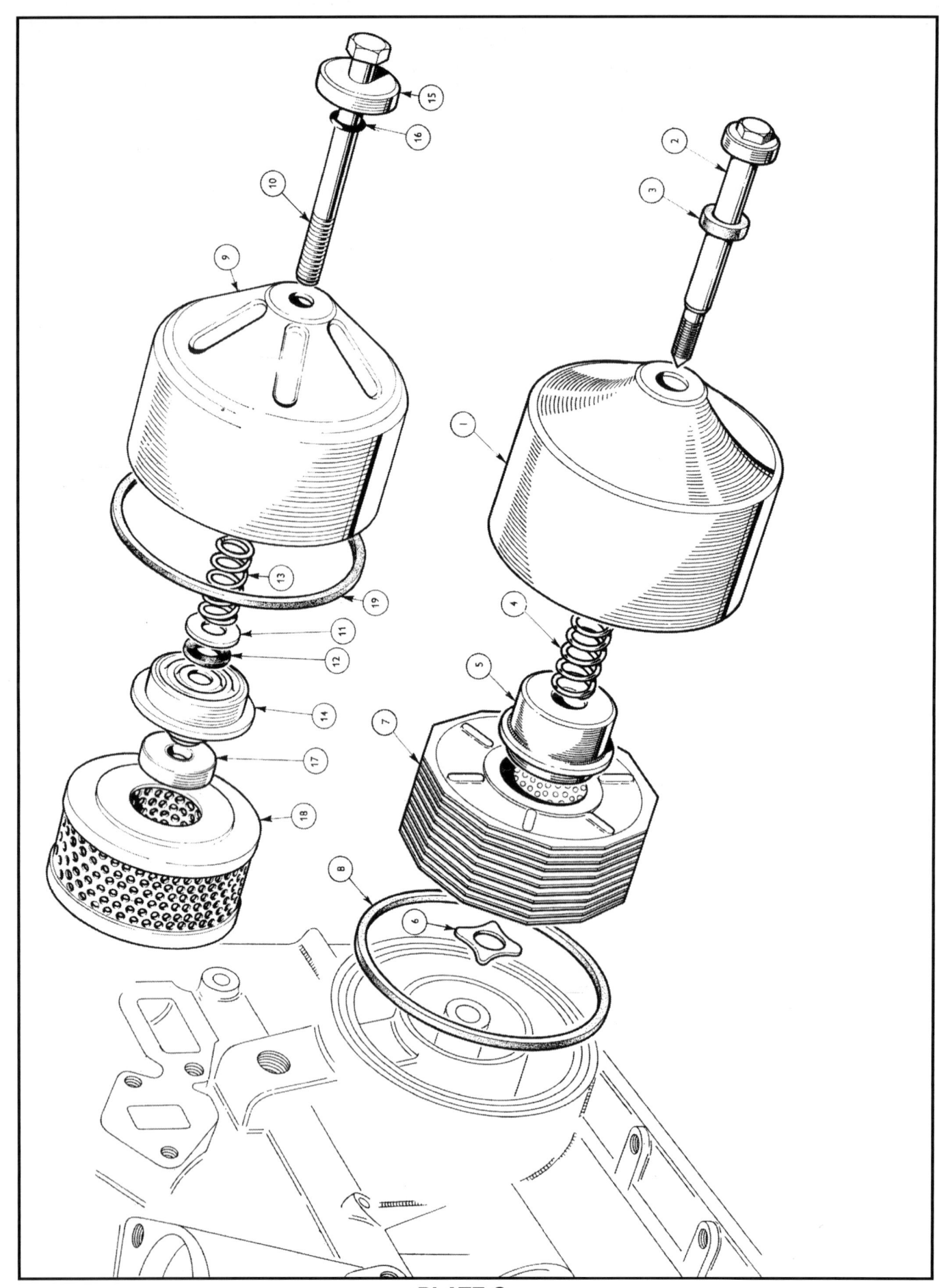

PLATE G

ENGINE
MARK I CARS FITTED UP TO ENGINE No. KC/KD50000E ONLY

Plate No.	Part No.	Description	No. per Unit	Remarks
	125715	**OIL FILTER ASSEMBLY (FULL FLOW)**	1	A.C. Delco. Alternative to Purolator Filter shown below
G1	509878	**Shell** assembly	1	
G2	509879	**Bolt**, centre	1	
G3	509880	**Gasket**, bolt head	1	
G4	509881	**Spring**, element retaining	1	
G5	509882	**Valve** assembly	1	
G6	509883	**Centraliser**, element	1	
G7	125714	**Element**, filter	1	
G8	125531	**Ring**, sealing	1	
	125715	**OIL FILTER ASSEMBLY (FULL FLOW)**	1	Purolator. Alternative to A.C. Delco Filter shown above
G9	517435	**Sump**	1	
G10	517433	**Bolt**, centre	1	
G11	517486	**Washer**	1	
G12	517431	**Seal**, bolt	1	
G13	517432	**Spring**, element retaining	1	
G14	517430	**Valve**, relief, assembly	1	
G15	517428	**Collar**	1	
G16	517429	**'O' ring**	1	
G17	517434	**Plate**, element locating	1	
G18	125713	**Element**, filter	1	
G19	517427	**Ring**, sump sealing	1	

Note:—Items marked thus † are available on our Factory Exchange Unit Scheme

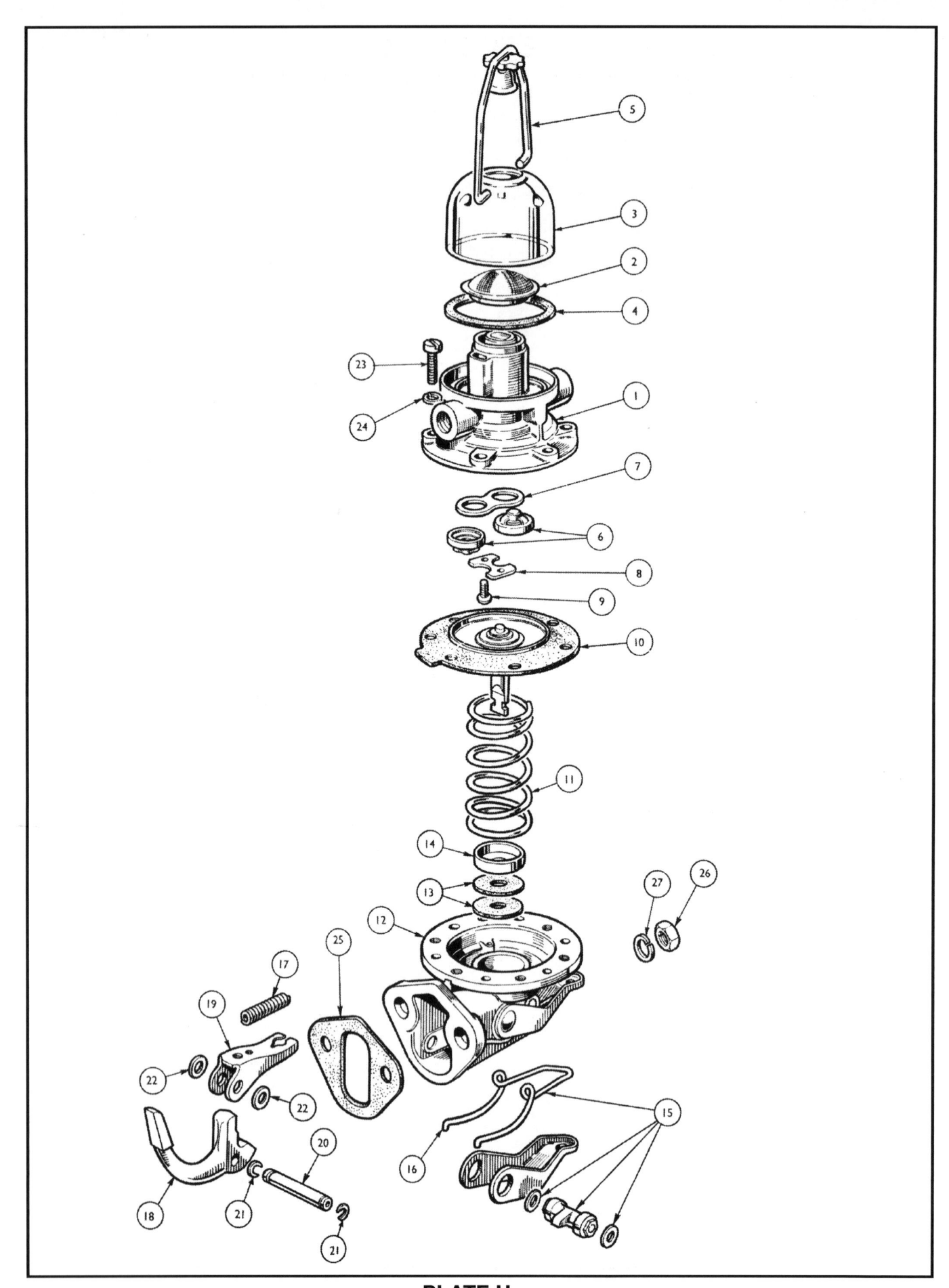

PLATE H

ENGINE
MARK I CARS FITTED UP TO ENGINE No. KC/KD50000E ONLY

Plate No.	Part No.	Description	No. per Unit	Remarks
	206623	**†PETROL PUMP ASSEMBLY**	1	Fitted up to Engine No. KC5000E only
H1	509928	**Casting,** upper	1	
H2	509924	**Screen** assembly	1	
H3	509923	**Bowl,** glass	1	
H4	509930	**Gasket,** between bowl and upper casting	1	
H5	509929	**Bail** assembly, bowl attachment	1	
H6	505239	**Valve and seat** assembly	2	
H7	505241	**Gasket,** valve	1	
H8	505240	**Retainer,** valve	1	
H9	59660	**Screw,** valve retainer to upper casting	2	
H10	501005	**Diaphragm** assembly	1	
H11	509925	**Spring,** diaphragm	1	
H12	509926	**Body and primer** assembly	1	
H13	508981	**Washer,** oil seal	2	
H14	508980	**Retainer,** oil seal	1	
H15	509927	**Primer parts set**	1	
H16	52498	**Spring,** primer	1	
H17	52494	**Spring,** rocker arm	1	
H18	508983	**Arm,** rocker	1	
H19	52479	**Link,** rocker arm	1	
H20	52483	**Pin,** rocker arm and link to body	1	
H21	52484	**Clip,** securing pin	2	
H22	52486	**Washer,** between link and body	2	
H23	52490	**Screw** ⎫ Upper casting to body	6	
H24	57361	**Washer,** spring ⎭	6	
H25	138791	**Gasket,** pump to cylinder block	1	
H26	HN2008	**Nut** ⎫ Pump attachment	2	
H27	WL0208	**Washer,** lock ⎭	2	

Note:—Items marked thus † are available on our Factory Exchange Unit Scheme

13

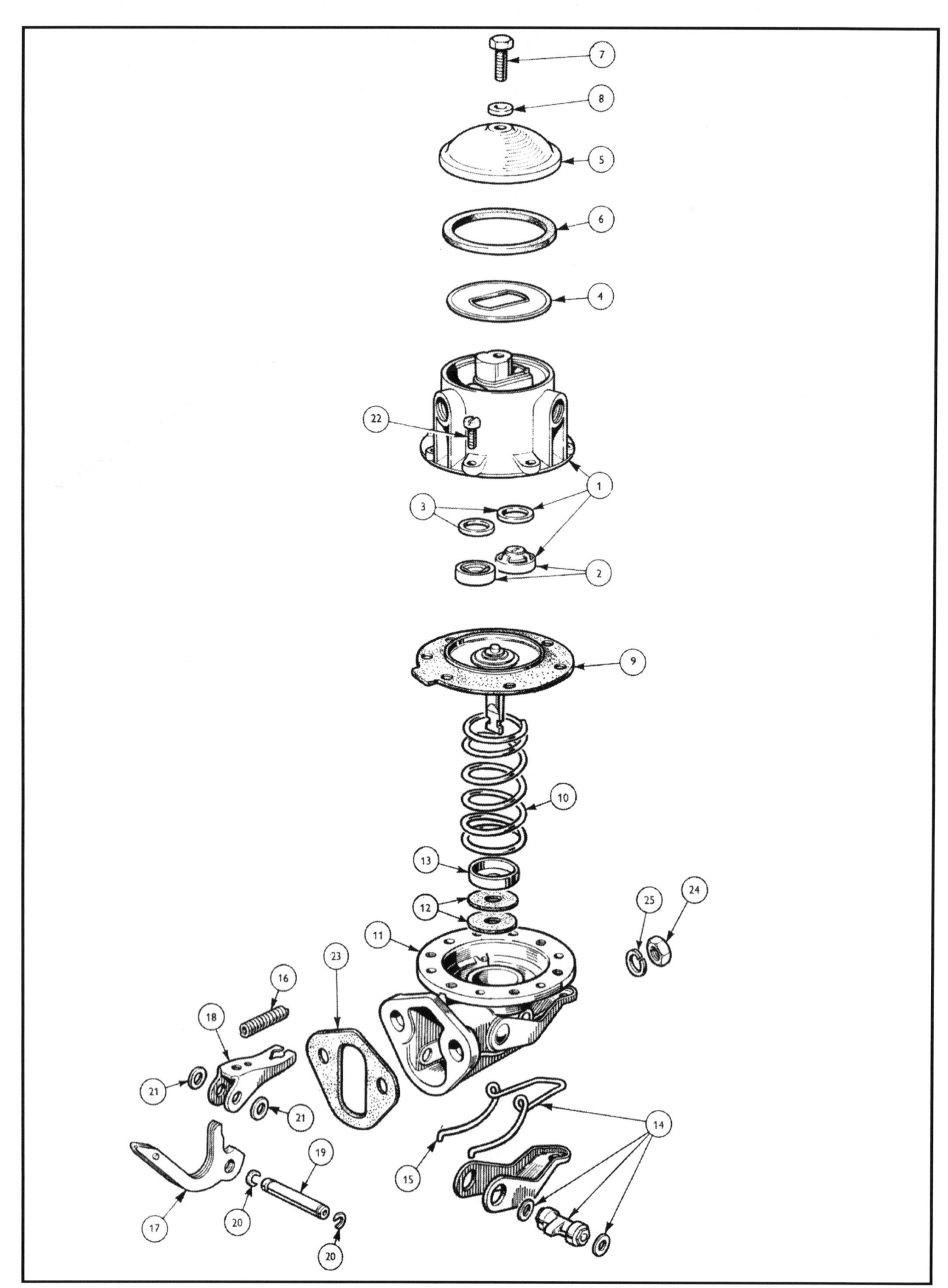

PLATE J

ENGINE

MARK I CARS FITTED UP TO ENGINE No. KC/KD50000E ONLY

Plate No.	Part No.	Description	No. per Unit	Remarks
	213577	**†PETROL PUMP ASSEMBLY**	1	Fitted from Engine No. KC/KD5001E and future
J1	516538	**Casting**, upper, and valves assembly	1	
J2	515036	**Valve** assembly	2	
J3	515037	**Gasket**, valve	2	
J4	516539	**Screw**, filter	1	
J5	59650	**Cover**, filter	1	
J6	516540	**Gasket**, between cover and upper casting	1	
J7	516537	**Bolt** ⎫ Cover to	1	
J8	510498	**Washer** ⎭ upper casting	1	
J9	501005	**Diaphragm** assembly	1	
J10	52492	**Spring**, diaphragm	1	
J11	509926	**Body and primer** sssembly	1	
J12	508981	**Washer**, oil seal	2	
J13	508980	**Retainer**, oil seal	1	
J14	509927	**Primer parts set**	1	
J15	52498	**Spring**, primer	1	
J16	52494	**Spring**, rocker arm	1	
J17	516536	**Rocker arm**	1	
J18	52479	**Link**, rocker arm	1	
J19	52483	**Pin**, rocker arm and link to body	1	
J20	52484	**Clip**, securing pin	2	
J21	52486	**Washer**, between link and body	2	
J22	516541	**Screw**, upper casting to body	6	
	500524	**First aid kit**	1	
	516542	**Repair kit** complete (less rocker arm)	1	

For Attachment Details see page 13.

Note:—Items marked thus † are available on our Factory Exchange Unit Scheme

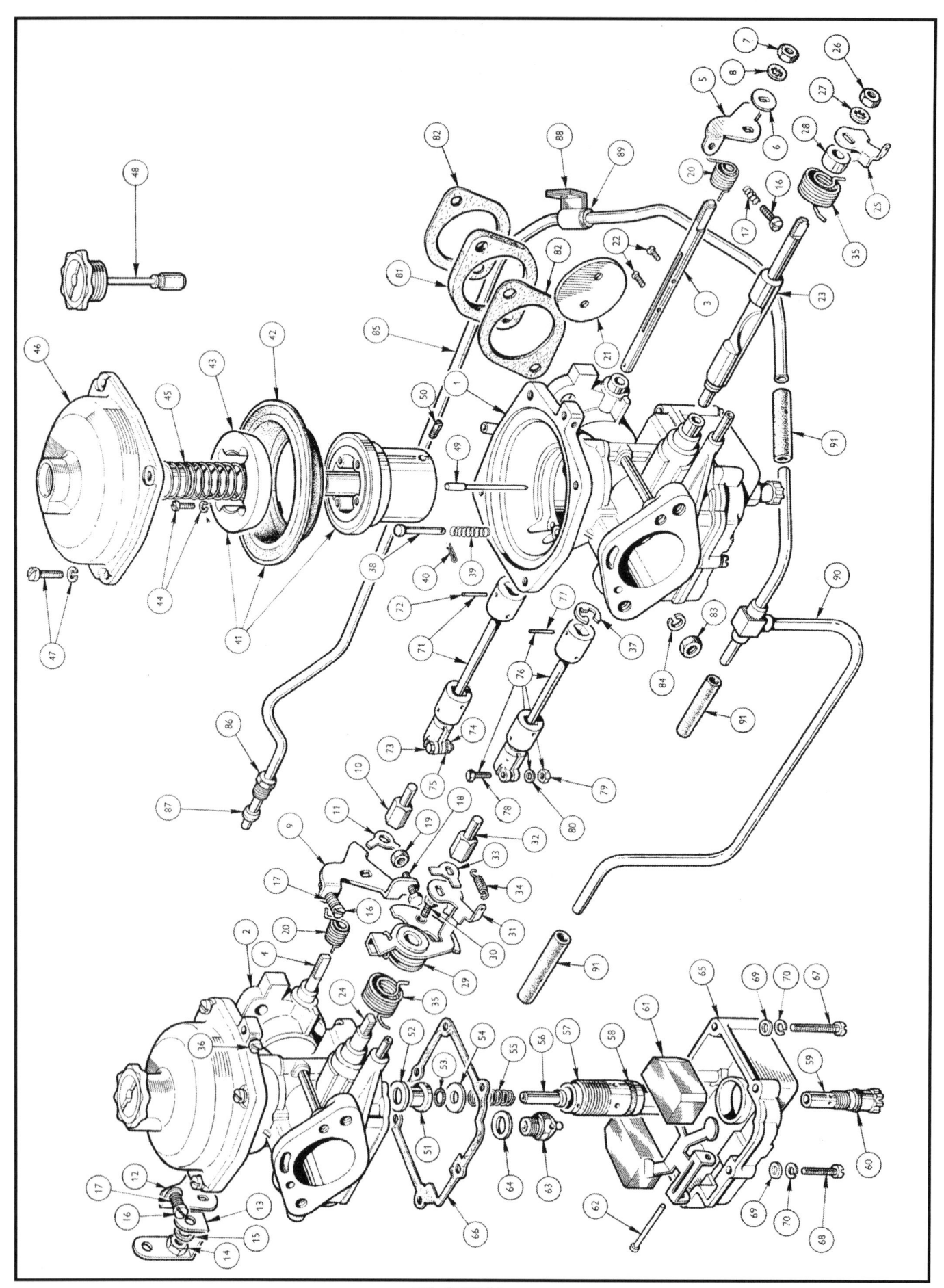

PLATE K

ENGINE

MARK I CARS FITTED UP TO ENGINE No. KC/KD50000E ONLY

Plate No.	Part No.	Description	No. per Unit	Remarks
		NOTE:- For Carburettors fitted to vehicles for U.S.A. from Engine No. KD10001E and future, see pages 18 to 21 inclusive.		
	213502	†CARBURETTOR ASSEMBLY—FRONT	1	
	516062	†CARBURETTOR ASSEMBLY—REAR	1	Supplied less Throttle Lever, Item K13
K1	513683	**Body** assembly, main, front carburettor	1	
K2	513716	**Body** assembly, main, rear carburettor	1	
K3	513684	**Spindle**, throttle, front carburettor	1	
K4	514964	**Spindle**, throttle, rear carburettor	1	
K5	513685	**Stop**, throttle, front carburettor	1	
K6	514977	**Washer**, replacement, between throttle stop and nut, front carburettor	1	
K7	513687	**Nut**, securing throttle stop, front carburettor	1	
K8	513688	**Washer**, shakeproof, under nut	1	
K9	513718	**Stop**, throttle and fast idle lever, rear carburettor	1	
K10	513719	**Nut**, spindle extension, rear carburettor throttle	1	
K11	513720	**Washer**, tab, under nut	1	
K12	514965	**Stop**, throttle, rear carburettor	1	
K13	146186	**Lever**, throttle, rear carburettor	1	Fitted up to Comm. No. KC1114 only
K13	147496	**Lever**, throttle, rear carburettor	1	Fitted from Comm. No. KC1115 and future
K14	513687	**Nut** ⎫ Throttle stop and throttle	1	
K15	513688	**Washer** ⎭ lever to rear carburettor	1	
K16	513697	**Screw**, throttle stop	2	
K17	512282	**Spring**, throttle stop screw	2	
K18	512288	**Screw**, fast idle	1	
K19	512287	**Nut**, lock, fast idle screw	1	
K20	513691	**Spring**, throttle return	2	
K21	513689	**Throttle**	2	
K22	512284	**Screw**, securing throttle	4	
K23	513692	**Bar**, starter, front carburettor	1	
K24	513721	**Bar**, starter, rear carburettor	1	
K25	513693	**Lever**, choke, front carburettor	1	
K26	513687	**Nut**, securing choke lever	1	
K27	513688	**Washer**, shakeproof, under nut	1	
K28	513696	**Bush**, spring retaining, front carburettor	1	
K29	514968	**Lever**, loose, choke and cam lever assembly, rear carburettor	1	
K30	513723	**Screw**, for swivel	1	
K31	513693	**Lever**, choke, rear carburettor	1	
K32	513724	**Nut**, spindle extension, rear carburettor starter bar	1	
K33	513720	**Washer**, tab, under nut	1	
K34	513726	**Spring**, choke lever, rear carburettor	1	
K35	512296	**Spring**, starter bar	2	
K36	513723	**Screw**, clamping control cable, rear carburettor	1	
K37	512298	**Ring**, retaining starter bar	2	
K38	514969	**Pin**, air valve lifting	2	
K39	514970	**Spring**, air valve lifting pin	2	
K40	512324	**Clip**, air valve lifting pin	2	

Note:—Items marked thus † are available on our Factory Exchange Unit Scheme

15

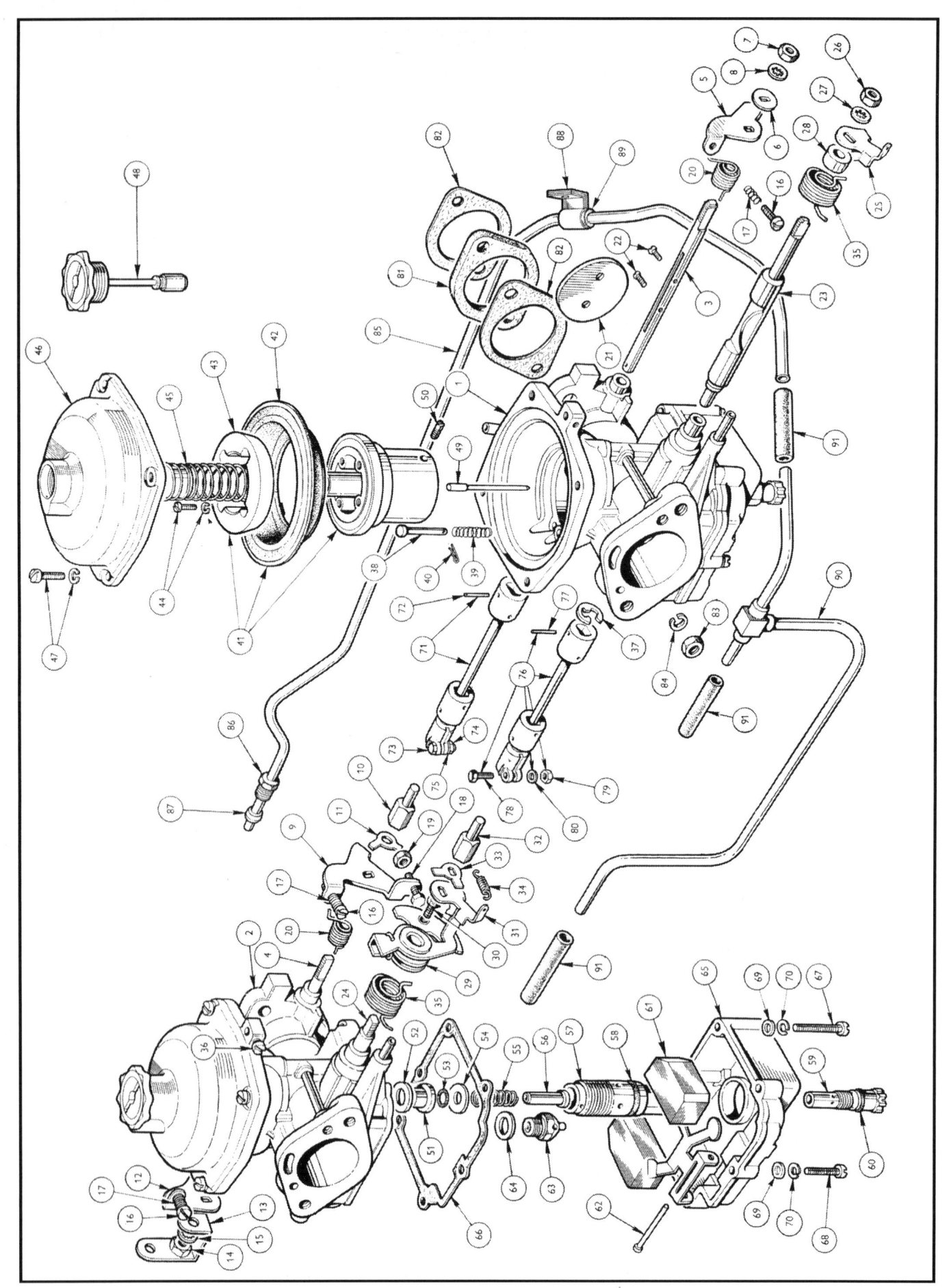

PLATE K

ENGINE

MARK I CARS FITTED UP TO ENGINE No. KC/KD50000E ONLY

Plate No.	Part No.	Description	No. per Unit	Remarks
		CARBURETTOR DETAILS—continued		
K41	515723	**AIR VALVE, SHAFT AND DIAPHRAGM ASSEMBLY**	2	
K42	513694	**Diaphragm,** air valve	2	
K43	515722	**Washer,** retaining diaphragm	2	
K44	512276	**Screw,** complete with spring washer, securing retaining ring	8	
K45	513710	**Spring,** air valve return	2	
K46	515111	**Cover,** suction chamber	2	
K47	512274	**Screw,** complete with spring washer	8	
K48	515112	**Damper** assembly	2	
		JET DETAILS		
K49	515724	**Needle,** metering	2	
K50	512280	**Screw,** locating metering needle in air valve	2	
K51	512318	**Bushing,** jet orifice	2	
K52	512319	**Washer,** bushing	2	
K53	512317	**'O' ring,** fitted in bushing	2	
K54	512316	**Washer,** 'O' ring	2	
K55	512315	**Spring,** jet orifice	2	
K56	513700	**Orifice,** jet	2	
K57	512312	**Screw,** bushing retaining (with 'O' ring)	2	
K58	512311	**'O' ring,** bushing retaining screw	2	
K59	512307	**Screw,** orifice adjusting (with 'O' ring)	2	
K60	512308	**'O' ring,** orifice adjusting screw	2	
K61	515721	**FLOAT AND ARM**	2	
K62	514971	**Pin,** float fulcrum	2	
K63	513702	**Needle seating,** float chamber	2	
K64	512301	**Washer,** needle seating	2	
K65	513706	**Float chamber**	2	
K66	513705	**Gasket,** float chamber	2	
K67	514972	**Screw,** long ⎫	6	
K68	514973	**Screw,** short ⎬ Float chamber	6	
K69	512304	**Washer,** plain ⎭ to main body	12	
K70	514980	**Washer,** spring	12	
		COUPLING DETAILS		
K71	513714	**Coupling** assembly, throttle spindle	1	⎫
K72	513713	**Roll pin**	1	⎬ Alternative fitment
K73	512340	**Bolt,** clamping	1	⎬ to details
K74	512334	**Nut**	1	⎬ listed below
K75	512339	**Washer**	1	⎭
	517388	**Coupling,** spindle, throttle	1	⎫
	512335	**Coupling,** spring, folded	2	⎬
	512340	**Bolt** ⎫	4	⎬ Alternative fitment to
	512334	**Nut** ⎬ Clamping couplings to spindle	4	⎬ details listed above
	512339	**Washer** ⎭	4	⎬
	516987	**Sleeve,** brass	1	⎭
K76	513715	**Coupling** assembly, starter bar	1	
K77	513713	**Roll pin**	1	
K78	512340	**Bolt,** clamping	1	
K79	512334	**Nut**	1	
K80	512339	**Washer**	1	

Note:—Items marked thus † are available on our Factory Exchange Unit Scheme

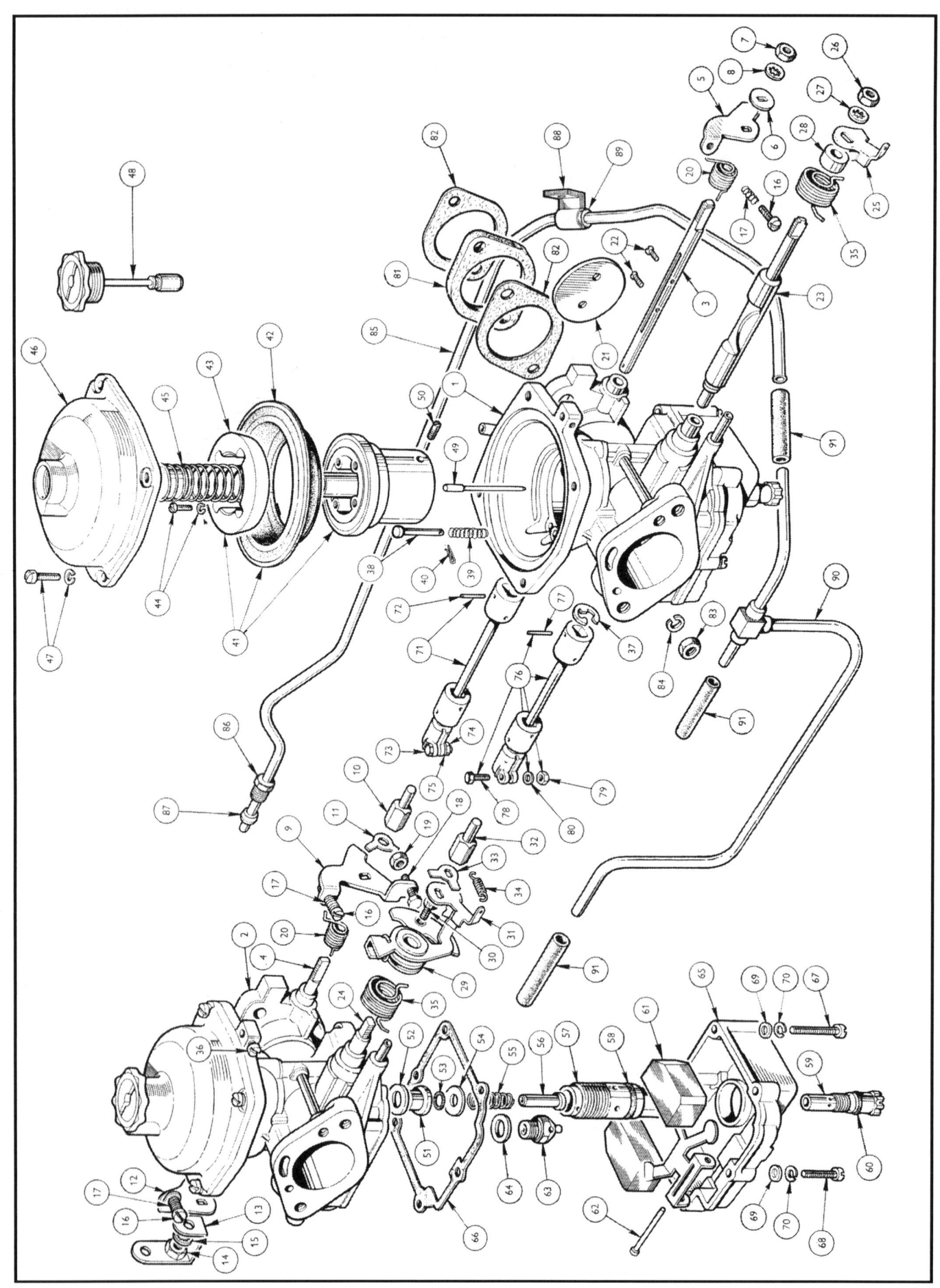

PLATE K

ENGINE
MARK I CARS FITTED UP TO ENGINE No. KC/KD50000E ONLY

Plate No.	Part No.	Description	No. per Unit	Remarks

CARBURETTOR DETAILS—continued

CARBURETTOR ATTACHMENT DETAILS

K81	137882	**Washer,** insulating	2	
K82	137881	**Washer,** joint	4	
K83	HN2008	**Nut** ⎫ Carburettors to manifold	4	
K84	WL0208	**Washer,** lock ⎭	4	
K85	307471	**PETROL PIPE ASSEMBLY—PUMP TO CARBURETTOR**	1	
K86	60176	**Nut,** tubing ⎫ Pipe assembly to pump	1	
K87	102729	**Sleeve** ⎭	1	
K88	138516	**Bracket,** support, pipe to water pump body	1	
K89	114178	**Grommet,** fitted in support bracket	1	
K90	138386	**PETROL PIPE ASSEMBLY—CARBURETTOR TO CARBURETTOR**	1	
K91	120331	**Connection,** flexible, between pipes	3	
	138887	**SUCTION PIPE—CARBURETTOR TO DISTRIBUTOR**	1	
	128262	**Sleeve,** pipe to carburettor and distributor	2	
	138892	**Clip,** suction pipe to petrol pipe	5	

Note:—Items marked thus † are available on our Factory Exchange Unit Scheme

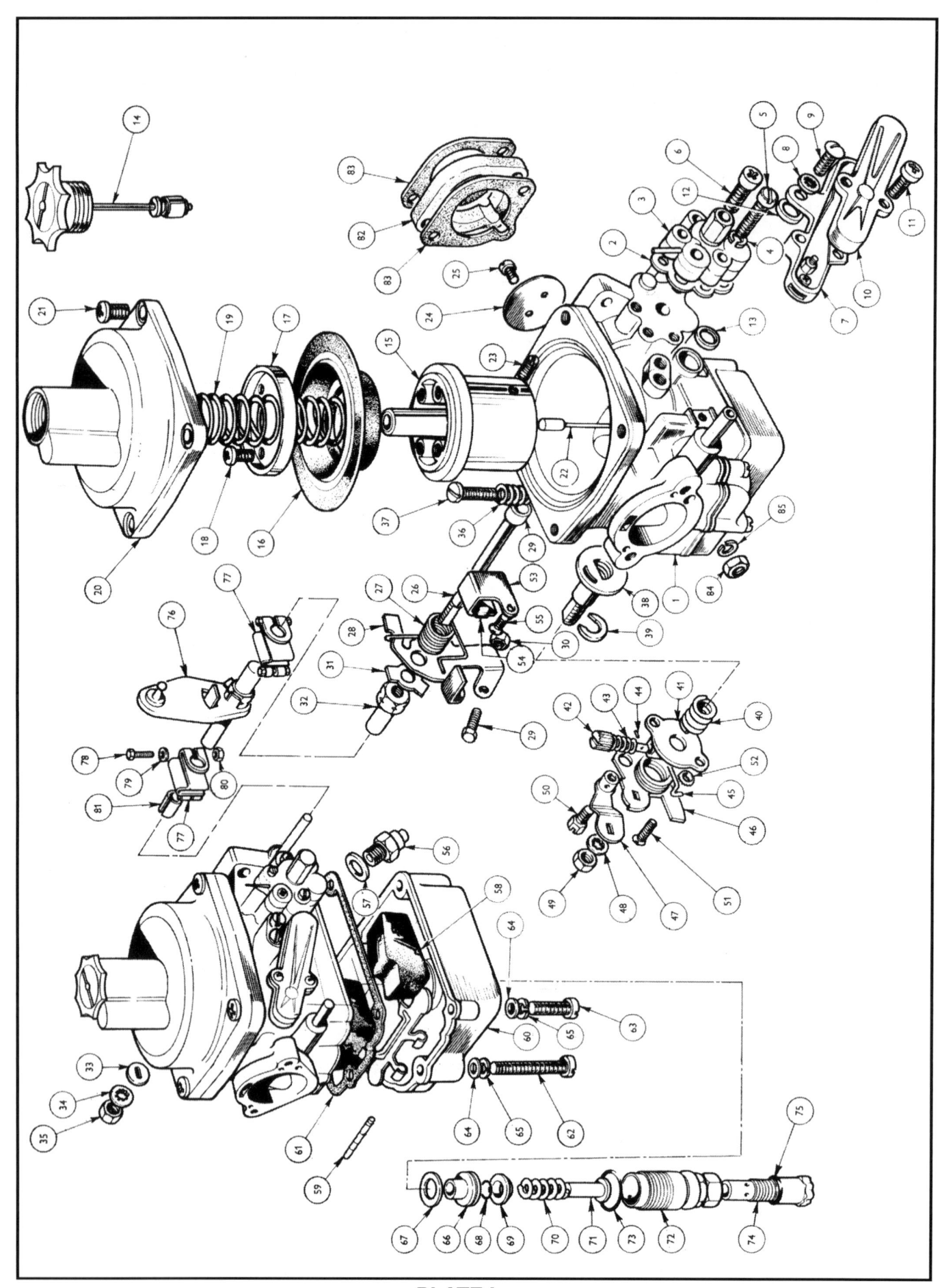

PLATE L

ENGINE
MARK I CARS FITTED UP TO ENGINE No. KC/KD50000E ONLY

Plate No.	Part No.	Description	No. per Unit	Remarks
	308487	†CARBURETTOR ASSEMBLY—FRONT	1	U.S.A. only. Fitted from Engine No. KD10001E and future
	308488	†CARBURETTOR ASSEMBLY—REAR	1	
L1	Not Serviced	Main body assembly		
L2	516967	Gasket, by-pass valve	2	
L3	516966	Valve, by-pass	2	
L4	514980	Washer, lock ⎱ Securing by-pass	6	
L5	514973	Screw ⎰ valve to body	6	
L6	517443	Screw, cover to by-pass body	2	
L7	517444	**TEMPERATURE COMPENSATOR ASSEMBLY**	2	
L8	516974	Washer, shakeproof ⎱ Securing	4	
L9	516973	Screw ⎰ compensator	4	
L10	516968	Cover, temperature compensator	2	
L11	516969	Screw, securing cover	4	
L12	516971	Seal, large, on compensator body	2	
L13	516972	Seal, small, inside carburettors	2	
L14	517449	**DAMPER ASSEMBLY**	2	
L15	Not Serviced	Air valve and shaft		
L16	517448	Diaphragm	2	
L17	Not Serviced	Ring, diaphragm retaining		
L18	517119	Screw, securing diaphragm retaining ring	8	
L19	516945	Spring, air valve return	2	
L20	Not Serviced	Cover assembly, air valve		
L21	512274	Screw, securing cover	8	
L22	517452	Needle, metering	2	
L23	512280	Screw, securing metering needle	2	

Note:—Items marked thus † are available on our Factory Exchange Unit Scheme

18

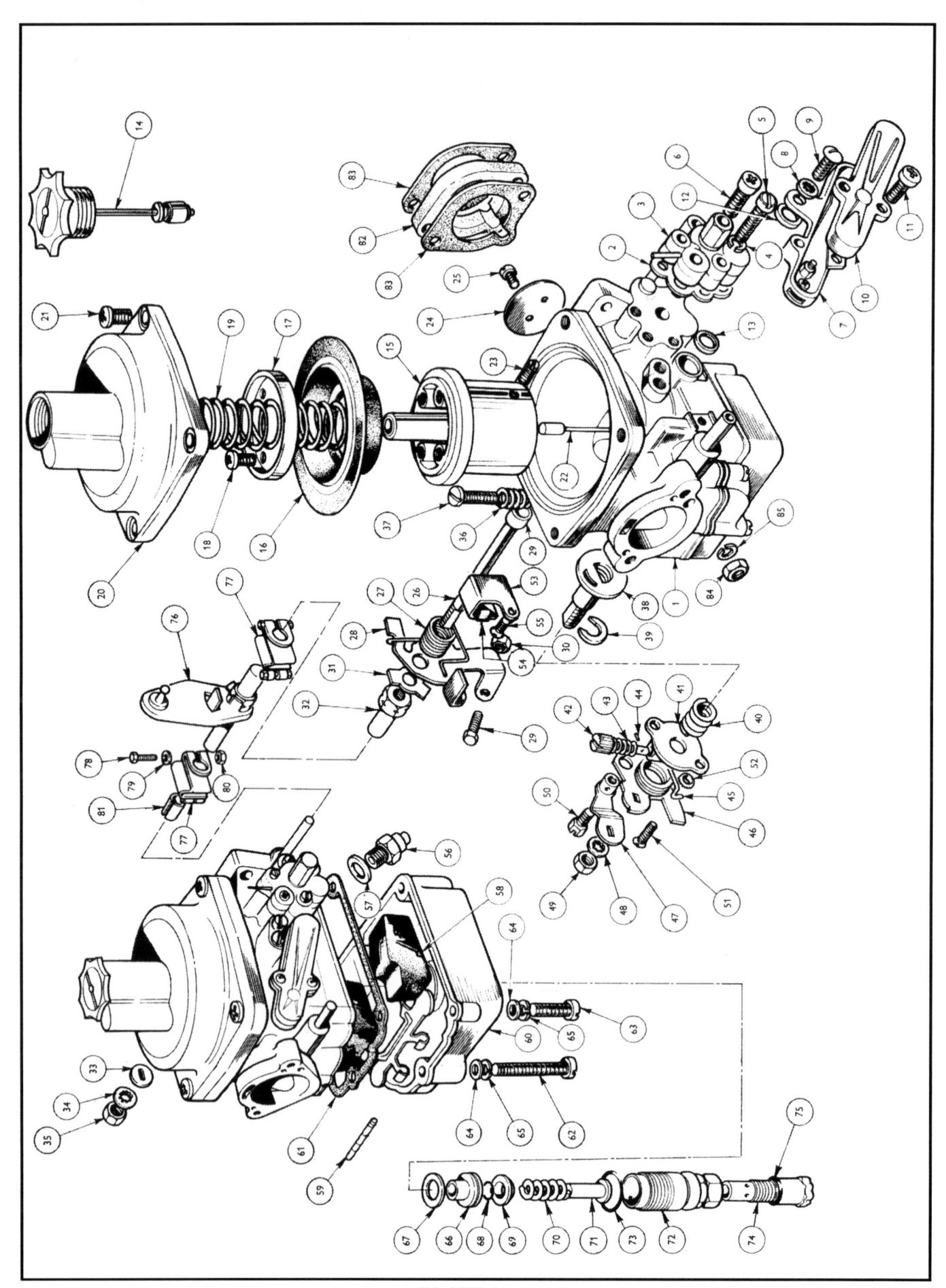

PLATE L

ENGINE
MARK I CARS FITTED UP TO ENGINE No. KC/KD50000E ONLY

Plate No.	Part No.	Description	No. per Unit	Remarks
		CARBURETTORS—continued		
		THROTTLE DETAILS		
L24	513689	**Disc**, throttle	2	
L25	516952	**Screw**, securing disc to spindle	4	Alternative to 512284
L25	512284	**Screw**, securing disc to spindle	4	Alternative to 516952
	516985	**Spindle**, throttle, rear carburettor	1	
L26	516948	**Spindle**, throttle, front carburettor	1	
L27	516951	**Spring**, throttle return	2	
L28	516949	**Lever**, throttle stop and fast idle	2	
L28	516965	**Screw**, fast idler adjustment	2	
L30	512287	**Locknut**, on screw	2	
L31	513720	**Washer**, tab ⎱ Front carburettor	1	
L32	516950	**Nut**, extension ⎰ throttle spindle	1	
L33	514977	**Washer**, spacing ⎱ Rear carburettor	2	
L34	513688	**Washer**, shakeproof ⎬ throttle	1	
L35	513687	**Nut** ⎰ spindle	1	
L36	512282	**Spring**, throttle stop screw	2	
L37	512281	**Screw**, throttle stop	2	
		STARTER BOX		
L38	516954	**Spindle**, starter, assembly	2	
L39	516956	**'C' washer**, on spindle	2	
L40	516955	**Spring**, starter	2	
L41	517442	**Cover**, starter box	2	
L42	Not Serviced	**Stop**, adjuster, cam lever	2	
L43	Not Serviced	**Spring** ⎱ On adjuster	2	
L44	Not Serviced	**Roll pin** ⎰	2	
L45	516957	**Spring**, return	2	
L46	516958	**Cam lever** assembly	2	
L47	516959	**Lever**, starter assembly	2	
L48	513688	**Washer**, shakeproof, securing cam lever	2	
L49	513687	**Nut**, on spindle	2	
L50	513723	**Screw**, swivel	2	
L51	516960	**Screw** ⎱ Securing starter	4	
L52	516961	**Washer**, shakeproof ⎰ to main body	4	
L53	516964	**Bracket**, starter control assembly, with clip	2	
L54	516962	**Clip**, for bracket	2	
L55	516963	**Screw**, securing bracket	2	

Note:—Items marked thus † are available on our Factory Exchange Unit Scheme

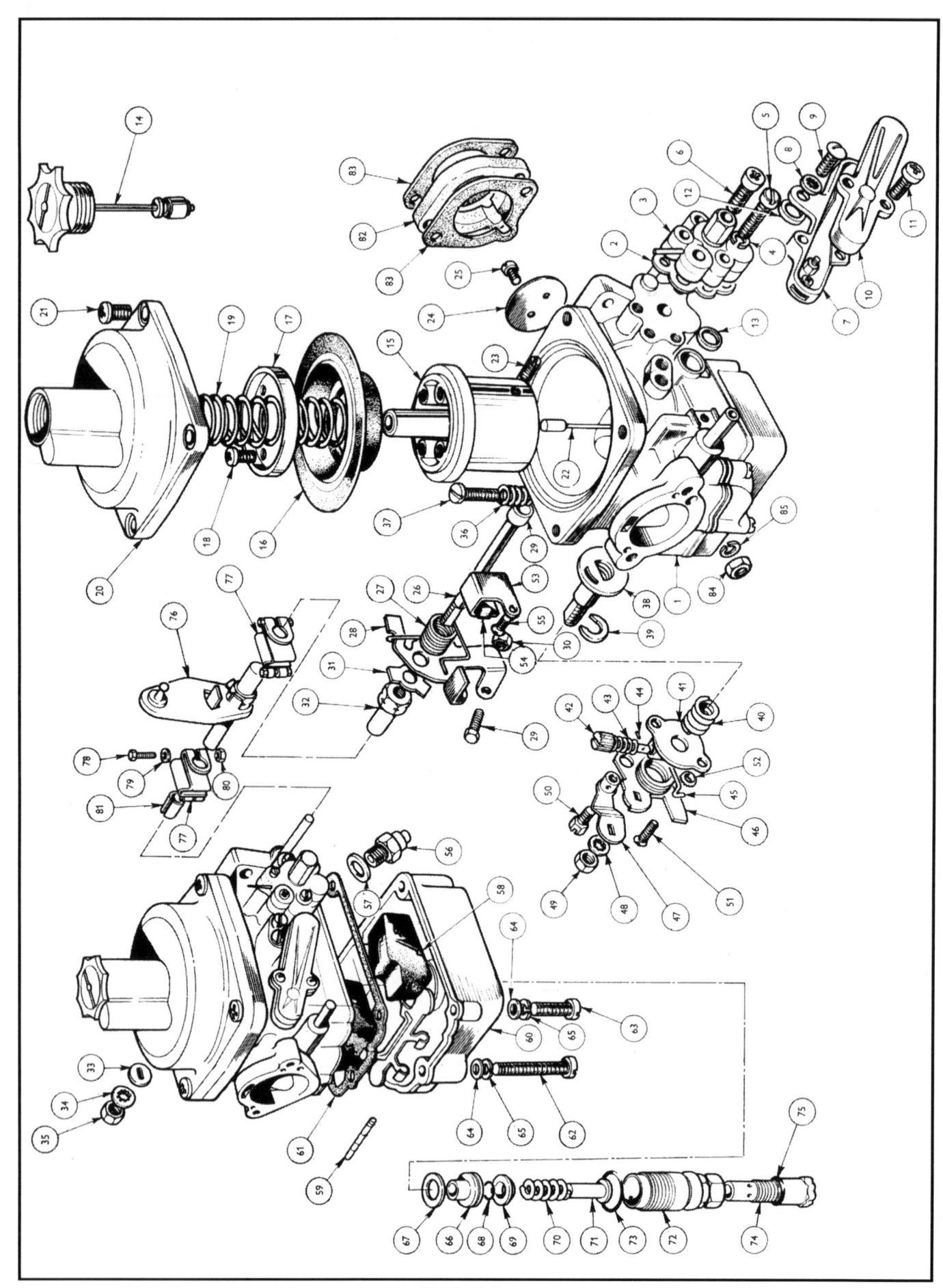

PLATE L

ENGINE
MARK I CARS FITTED UP TO ENGINE No. KC/KD50000E ONLY

Plate No.	Part No.	Description	No. per Unit	Remarks
		CARBURETTORS—continued		
		FLOAT DETAILS		
L56	517453	**Valve**, needle	2	
L57	516005	**Washer**, needle valve	2	
L58	516977	**Float and arm**	2	
L59	517134	**Pin**, float pivot	2	
L60	516981	**Float chamber**	2	
L61	516980	**Gasket**, float chamber	2	
L62	514972	**Screw** ⎫	6	
L63	514973	**Screw** ⎬ Float chamber	6	
L64	512304	**Washer**, plain ⎨ to main body	12	
L65	514980	**Washer**, spring ⎭	12	
L66	512318	**Bushing**, for jet orifice	2	
L67	512319	**Washer**, jet orifice bushing	2	
L68	512317	**'O' ring**	2	
L69	517300	**Bush**, guide	2	
L70	517301	**Spring**, jet orifice	2	
L71	513700	**Jet orifice**	2	
L72	512312	**Screw and 'O' ring** assembly, bushing retaining	2	
L73	512311	**'O' ring**, for screw	2	
L74	517447	**Screw and 'O' ring** assembly, orifice adjusting	2	
L75	512303	**'O' ring**, for screw	2	
	517450	**Clip**, locking, orifice adjuster	2	
	517451	**Wire**, sealing, orifice adjuster	2	
		COUPLING DETAILS		
L76	516986	**Coupling spindle** assembly	1	
L77	512335	**Coupling** assembly	2	
L78	512340	**Screw** ⎫	4	
L79	512339	**Washer** ⎬ Securing couplings to spindle	4	
L80	512334	**Nut** ⎭	4	
L81	516987	**Sleeve**, split	1	
		CARBURETTOR ATTACHMENT DETAILS		
L82	147660	**Washer**, insulating	2	
L83	147659	**Washer**, joint	4	
L84	HN2008	**Nut** ⎱ Carburettors	4	
L85	WL0208	**Washer**, lock ⎰ to manifold	4	
		CARBURETTOR SERVICE AND REPAIR KITS		
	516989	**Lubrication pack**	1	
	516990	**Repair kit**, comprising:-	1	
	516005	**Washer**, needle valve	1	
	512311	**'O' ring**, float chamber	1	
	516980	**Gasket**, float chamber	1	
		Repair kit, comprising:-	1	
	516967	**Gasket**, by-pass valve	2	
	516971	**Washer**, sealing	2	
	516972	**Washer**, sealing	2	
	516005	**Washer**, needle valve	2	
	512311	**'O' ring**	2	
	516980	**Gasket**, float chamber	2	
	517448	**Diaphragm**	2	
	517453	**Valve**, needle	2	

Note:- For Petrol pipe Assemblies, pump to carburettor and carburettor to carburettor, see page 19.
For distributor suction pipes see page 22.

Note:—Items marked thus † are available on our Factory Exchange Unit Scheme

20 and 21

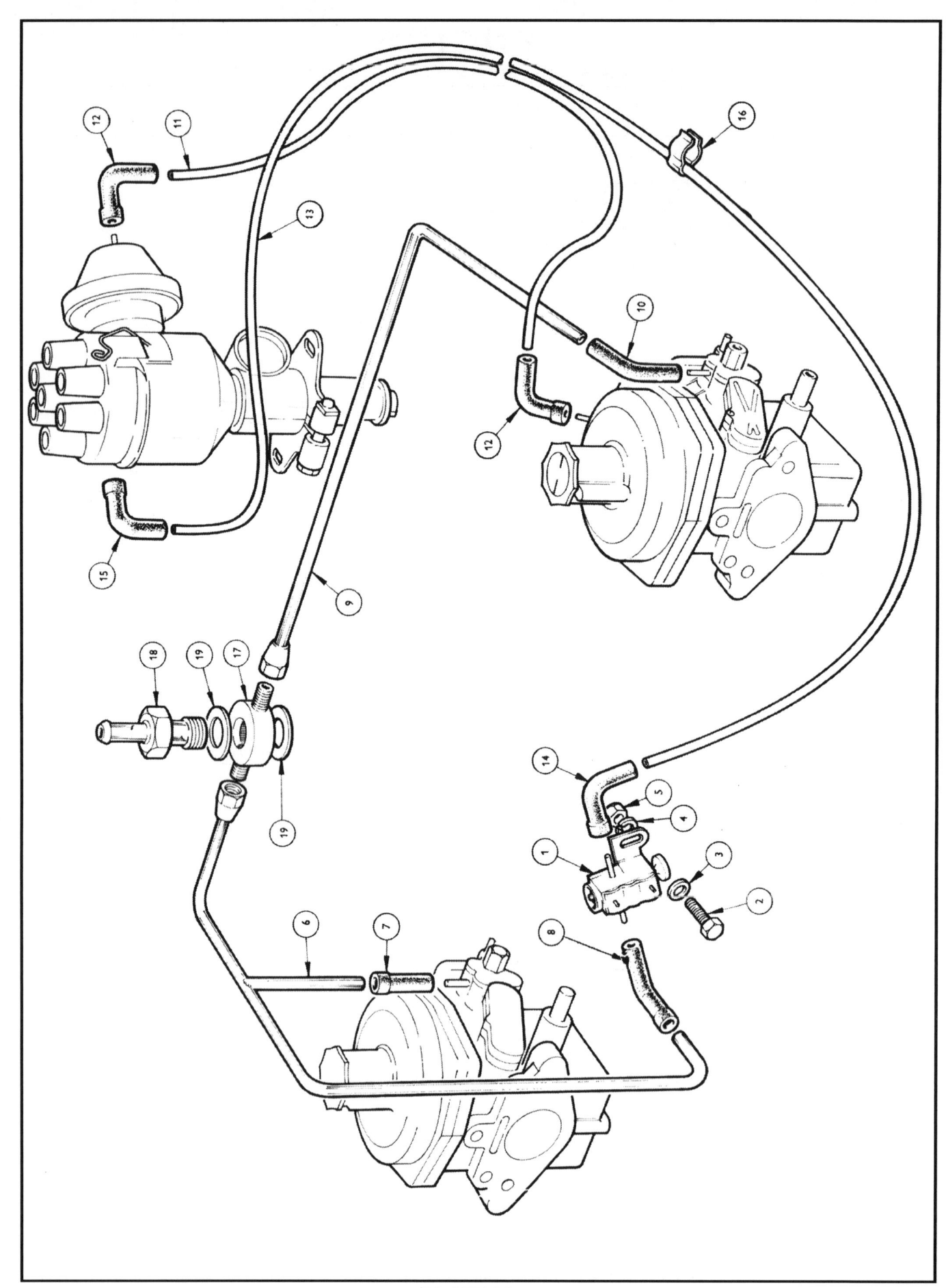

PLATE M

ENGINE
MARK I CARS FITTED UP TO ENGINE No. KC/KD50000E ONLY

Plate No.	Part No.	Description	No. per Unit	Remarks

EMISSION CONTROL DETAILS
(FITTED TO VEHICLES CONFORMING TO ANTI-AIR POLLUTION REGULATIONS—FROM ENGINE No. KD10001E and future)

Plate No.	Part No.	Description	No. per Unit	Remarks
M1	148400	**Valve,** vacuum control	1	
M2	HU0503	**Setscrew**	2	
M3	WP0005	**Washer,** plain — Vacuum control valve to	2	
M4	WL0205	**Washer,** lock — bell crank support bracket	2	
M5	HN2005	**Nut**	2	
M6	149310	**Pipe** assembly, manifold to rear carburettor and vacuum control valve	1	
M7	131211	**Connector,** pipe to rear carburettor	1	
M8	128262	**Sleeve,** connector, pipe to vacuum control valve	1	
M9	149309	**Pipe** assembly, manifold to front carburettor	1	
M10	149381	**Connector,** pipe to front carburettor	1	
M11	138887	**Pipe,** suction, P.V.C., carburettor to distributor (advance)	1	Alternative fitment to items listed below
M12	128262	**Sleeve,** pipe to carburettor and distributor	2	
M13	149386	**Pipe,** suction, P.V.C., vacuum valve to distributor (retard)	1	
M14	149380	**Sleeve,** suction pipe to vacuum valve	1	
M15	128262	**Sleeve,** suction pipe to distributor (retard)	1	
M16	138892	**Clip,** suction pipes to petrol pipe	7	
	151101	**Pipe,** suction, nylon, carburettor to distributor (advance)	1	Alternative fitment to items listed above
	128262	**Sleeve,** pipe to carburettor and distributor	2	
	151100	**Pipe,** suction, nylon, vacuum valve to distributor (retard)	1	
	149380	**Sleeve,** suction pipe to vacuum valve	1	
	128262	**Sleeve,** pipe to distributor (retard)	1	
	100148	**Clip** — Suction pipes to	1	
	138608	**Grommet** — rocker cover centre stud	1	
M17	149362	**Banjo** connector	1	
M18	149361	**Bolt,** banjo (Emission control valve adaptor)	1	
M19	WF0513	**Washer,** fibre, banjo bolt	2	

Note:—Items marked thus † are available on our Factory Exchange Unit Scheme

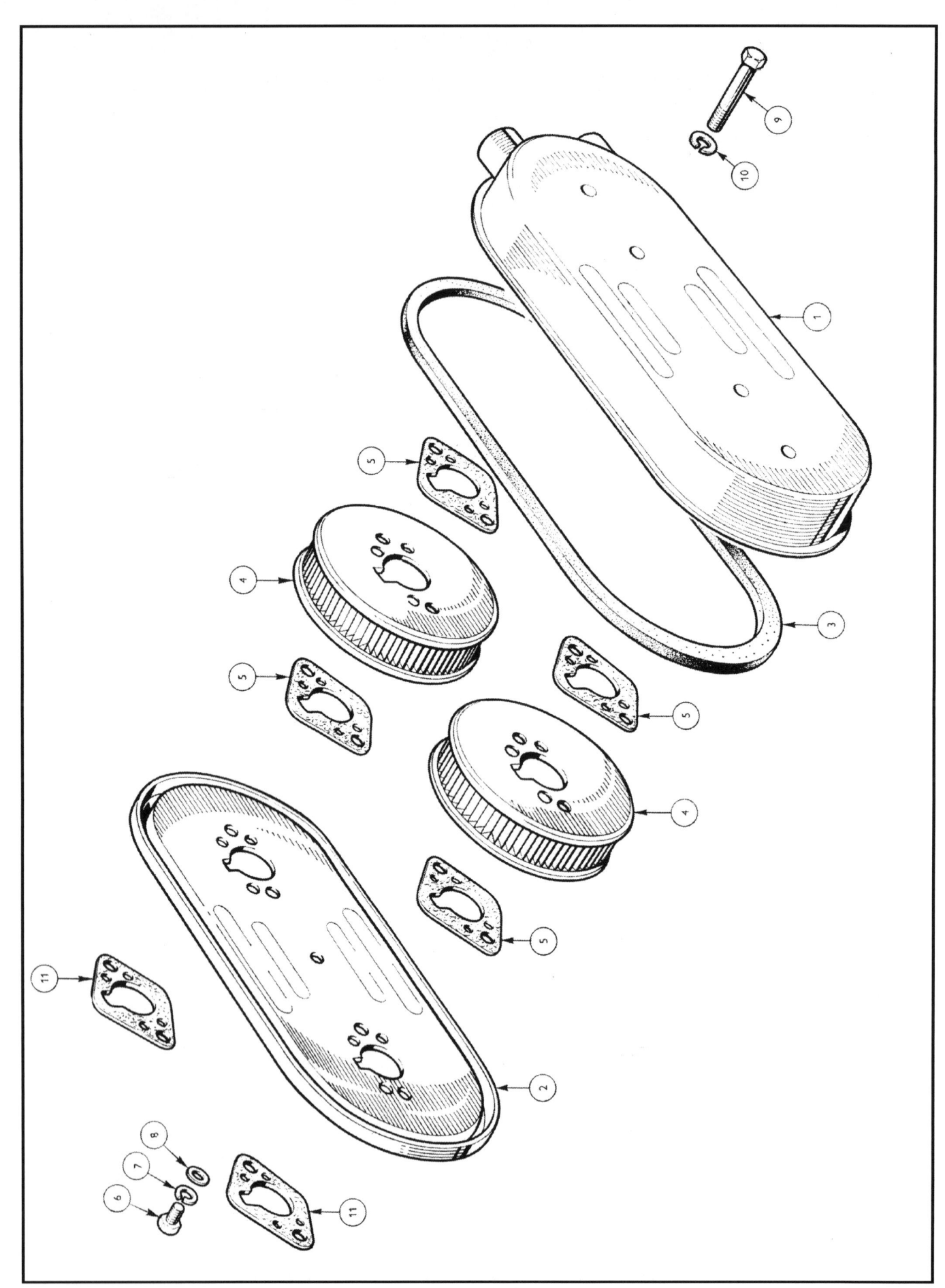

PLATE N

ENGINE
MARK I CARS FITTED UP TO ENGINE No. KC/KD50000E ONLY

Plate No.	Part No.	Description	No. per Unit	Remarks
	214414	**AIR CLEANER AND SILENCER ASSEMBLY**	1	
N1	210943	**Cover,** front, and silencer assembly	1	
N2	214413	**Plate,** back, assembly	1	
N3	138311	**Strip,** sealing	1	
N4	214415	**Element,** filter	2	
N5	148006	**Gasket,** between element, back plate and cover	4	
N6	HU0704	**Screw,** set ⎫	1	
N7	WL0207	**Washer,** lock ⎬ Front cover to back plate	1	
N8	WP0007	**Washer,** plain ⎭	1	
N9	HB0817	**Bolt** ⎫	4	
	HB0867	**Bolt**	4	U.S.A. "Anti-Smog" Vehicles only. Fitted from Engine No. KD10001E and future
		⎬ Air cleaner to carburettor		
N10	WL0208	**Washer,** lock ⎬	4	
N11	148006	**Gasket** ⎭	2	

Note:—Items marked thus † are available on our Factory Exchange Unit Scheme

23

129

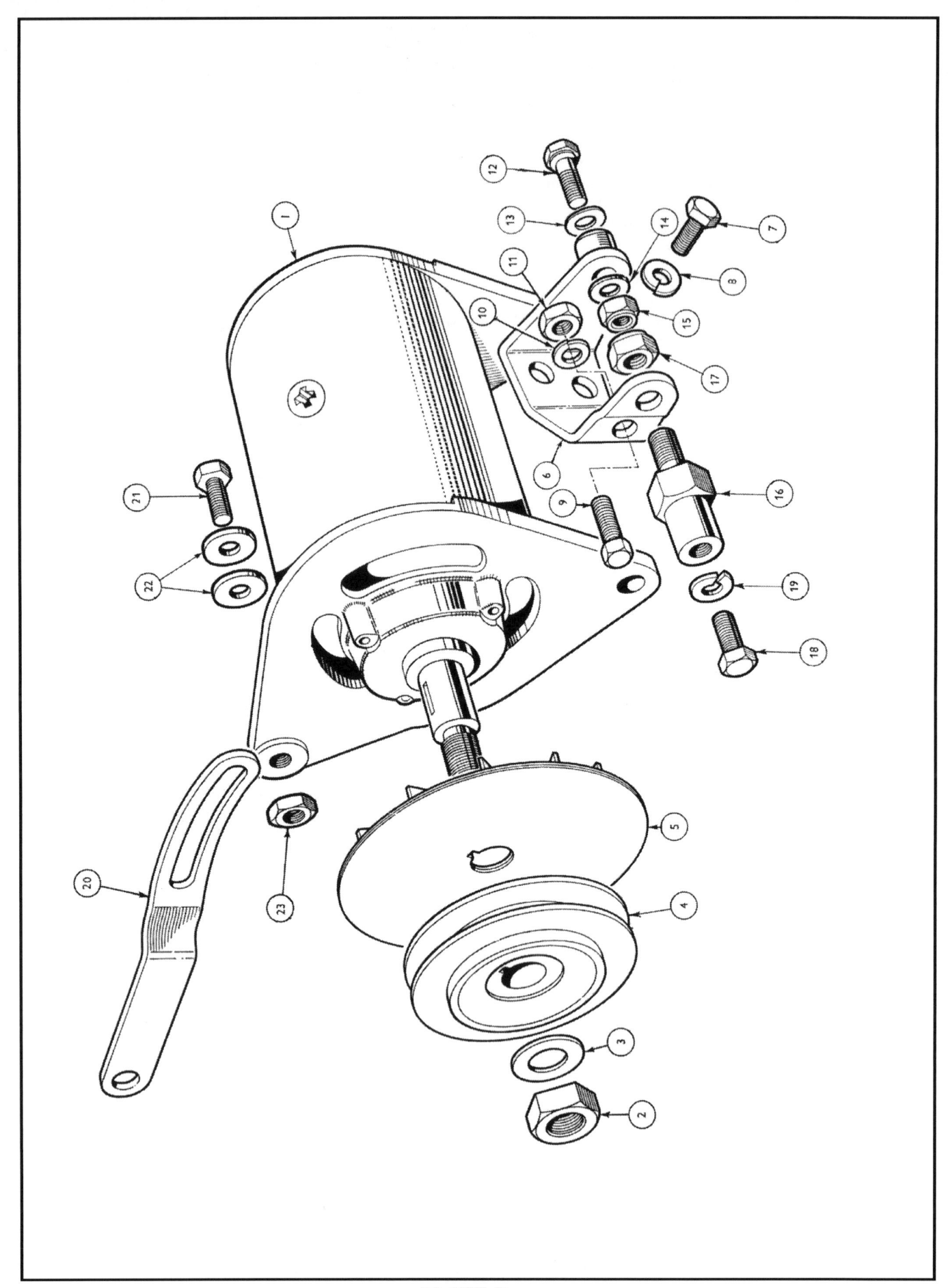

PLATE P

ENGINE

MARK I CARS FITTED UP TO ENGINE No. KC/KD50000E ONLY

Plate No.	Part No.	Description	No. per Unit	Remarks
		DYNAMO MOUNTING DETAILS		
		DYNAMO (Comprising Items P1, P2, P3)		
		For Details see Electrical Section.		
P4	104897	**Pulley,** dynamo	1	Fitted up to Engine No. KC/KD7905E only
	147906	**Pulley,** dynamo	1	Fitted from Engine No. KC/KD7906E and future
P5	147333	**Fan,** dynamo pulley	1	
P6	143437	**Bracket,** dynamo support, assembly	1	
P7	HU0806	**Screw,** set ⎫ Bracket to cylinder block	2	
P8	WL0208	**Washer,** lock ⎭	2	
P9	HU1107	**Screw,** set ⎫	1	
P10	WL0211	**Washer,** lock ⎬ Dynamo bracket to front engine plate	1	
P11	HN2011	**Nut** ⎭	1	
P12	HB0814	**Bolt** ⎫	1	
P13	WP0008	**Washer,** plain ⎬ Dynamo to	A/R	
P14	WP0133	**Washer,** plain ⎱ bracket, rear	A/R	
P15	TN3208	**Nut,** nyloc, thin ⎭	1	
P16	59015	**Pedestal,** dynamo	1	
P17	TN3211	**Nut,** nyloc, pedestal to dynamo bracket	1	
P18	59115	**Bolt** ⎫ Dynamo to pedestal, front	1	
P19	WL0208	**Washer,** lock ⎭	1	
P20	143650	**Link,** dynamo adjusting	1	
P21	HU0857	**Screw,** set ⎫	1	
P22	WP0017	**Washer,** plain ⎬ Link to dynamo	2	
P23	JN2158	**Nut,** jam ⎭	1	

Note:- 147906 Pulley, Dynamo, may be used in conjunction with 214314 Fan Belt for all replacements.

IGNITION

	128404	**Plug,** sparking	6	
	148957	**Plug,** sparking—Champion type UN-12Y	6	Special Order and all U.S.A. fitted from Eng. No. KD6915E and future

H.T. LEADS

	139538	**Engine lead** assembly, No. 1	1	⎫
	139500	**Engine lead** assembly, No. 2	1	⎪
	139539	**Engine lead** assembly, No. 3	1	⎬ Fitted up to Engine No.
	134887	**Engine lead** assembly, No. 4	1	⎪ KC11503E only
	139540	**Engine lead** assembly, No. 5	1	⎪
	139540	**Engine lead** assembly, No. 6	1	⎭
	146113	**Engine lead,** coil to distributor	1	
	150550	**Engine lead** assembly, No. 1	1	⎫
	150551	**Engine lead** assembly, No. 2	1	⎪
	150552	**Engine lead** assembly, No. 3	1	⎬ Fitted from Engine No.
	150553	**Engine lead** assembly, No. 4	1	⎪ KC11504E and future
	150554	**Engine lead** assembly, No. 5	1	⎪
	150555	**Engine lead** assembly, No. 6	1	⎭
	517342	**Engine lead kit**	1	⎫
	150038	**Engine lead** assembly, No. 1	1	⎪
	150030	**Engine lead** assembly, No. 2	1	⎪
	150031	**Engine lead** assembly, No. 3	1	⎬ France only
	150039	**Engine lead** assembly, Nos. 4 and 5	2	⎪
	150032	**Engine lead** assembly, No. 6	1	⎪
	150052	**Engine lead,** coil to distributor	1	⎭

Note:—Items marked thus † are available on our Factory Exchange Unit Scheme

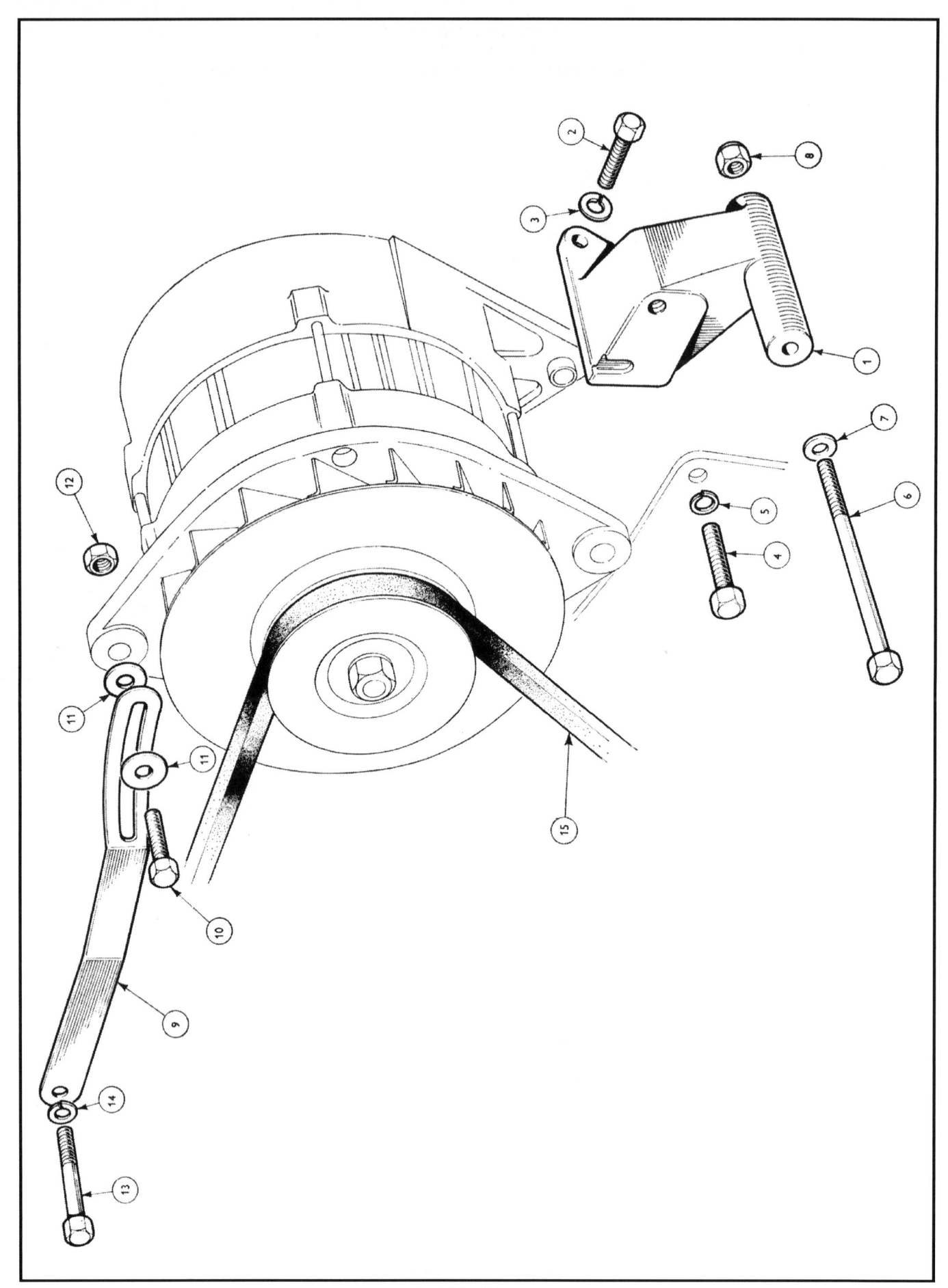

PLATE Q

ENGINE
MARK I CARS FITTED UP TO ENGINE No. KC/KD50000E ONLY

Plate No.	Part No.	Description	No. per Unit	Remarks
		ALTERNATOR ATTACHMENT DETAILS		Special Orders only
		Alternator—For Details see Electrical Section.		
Q1	214268	**Bracket**, alternator mounting	1	
Q2	HU0808	**Screw**, set ⎫ Alternator bracket	2	
Q3	WL0208	**Washer**, lock ⎭ to cylinder block	2	
Q4	HU1108	**Screw**, set ⎫ Alternator bracket to	1	
Q5	WL0211	**Washer**, lock ⎭ front engine plate	1	
Q6	HB0839	**Bolt** ⎫ Alternator	1	
Q7	WP0008	**Washer**, plain ⎬ to	1	
Q8	143802	**Nut**, self locking ⎭ alternator mounting bracket	1	
Q9	147706	**Link**, alternator adjusting	1	
Q10	HU0857	**Setscrew** ⎫	1	
Q11	WP0017	**Washer**, plain ⎬ Adjusting link to alternator	2	
Q12	JN2158	**Nut**, jam ⎭	1	
Q13	HB0819	**Bolt** ⎫ Alternator adjusting link and	1	
Q14	WL0208	**Washer** ⎭ water pump to cylinder head	1	
Q15	214246	**FAN BELT**	1	

Note:—Items marked thus † are available on our Factory Exchange Unit Scheme

25

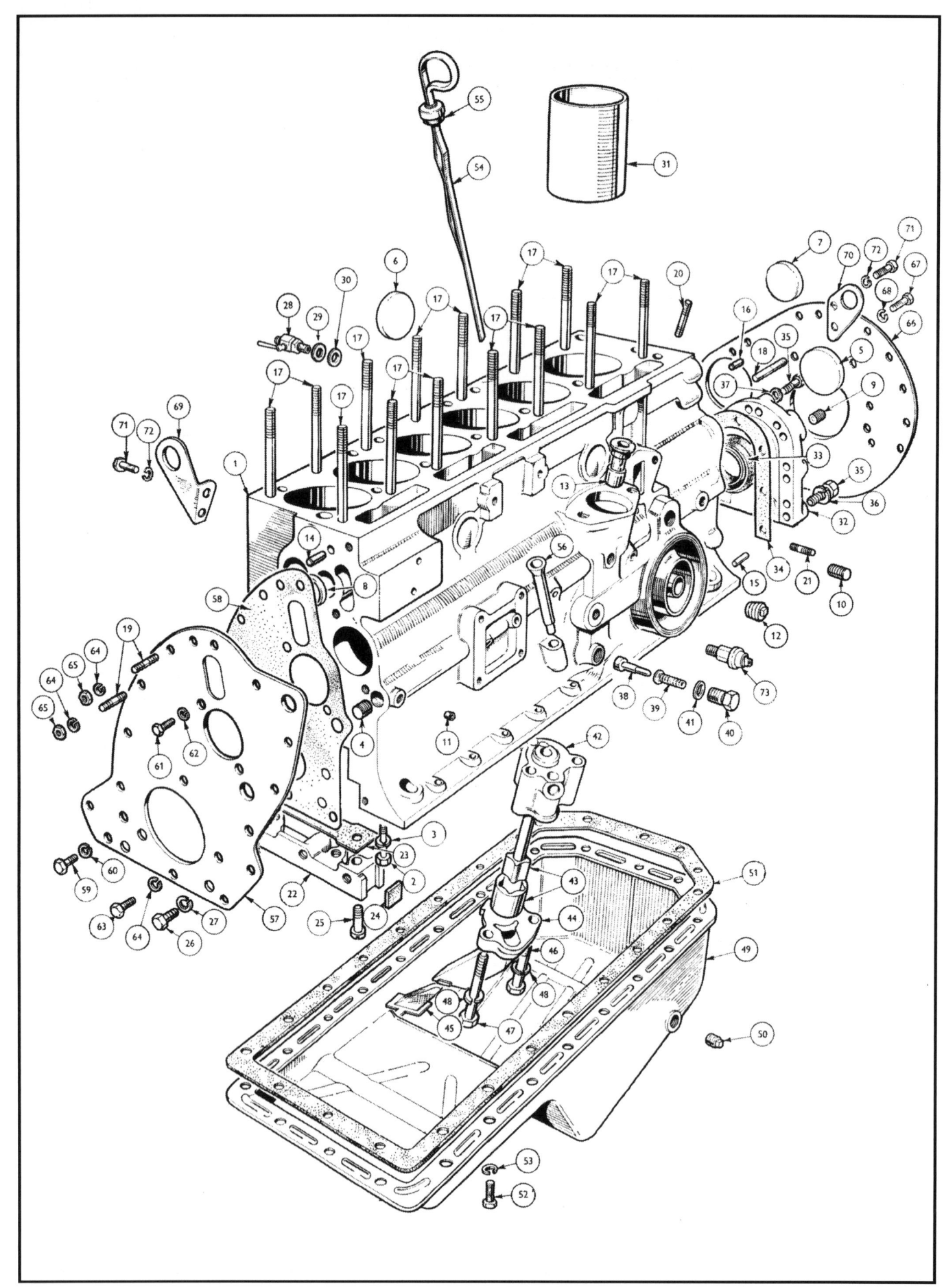

PLATE R

ENGINE

MARK II (G.T.6+) CARS FITTED FROM ENGINE No. KC/KD50001E AND FUTURE

Plate No.	Part No.	Description	No. per Unit	Remarks
	517607	†ENGINE UNIT (9.25 to 1 Compression Ratio)	1	
	517607/R	†ENGINE UNIT (9.25 to 1 Compression Ratio) (RECONDITIONED UNIT)	1	
		Note:- The above Units are supplied less water pump, distributor, dynamo, petrol pump, oil filter, thermostat, exhaust and inlet manifolds, carburettors, and sparking plugs.		
	517613	ENGINE GASKET SET (includes Decarbonising Set)	1	
	517612	DECARBONISING GASKET SET	1	
R1	517611	CYLINDER BLOCK ASSEMBLY	1	
R2	HB1024	Bolt ⎫ Caps to	8	
R3	WL0210	Washer, lock ⎭ block	8	
R4	PS1103	Plug, core, screwed, oil gallery, front	1	
R5	148353	Plug, core, rear of camshaft	1	
R6	144688	Plug, core, front face and R.H. side block	5	
R7	144686	Plug, core, rear face and L.H. side block	3	
R8	144687	Plug, core, front face of block	1	
R9	118632	Plug, dry seal, oil gallery, rear	1	
R10	PU1404	Plug, ¾″, oil gallery	1	
R11	118686	Plug, ⅛″, oil gallery	6	
R12	116511	Plug, oil gallery	1	
R13	137978	Bush, oil pump drive shaft	1	Fitted up to Engine No. only
	149776	Bush, oil pump drive shaft	1	Fitted from Engine No. and future
R14	DP0514	Dowel, timing cover attachment	2	
R15	DP0612	Dowel, rear engine plate attachment	1	
R16	DP0616	Dowel, rear engine plate attachment	1	
R17	146200	Stud, cylinder head attachment	14	
R18	139836	Stud, gearbox and rear engine plate attachment	3	
R19	100433	Stud, timing cover and engine plate	2	
R20	101962	Stud, distributor pedestal attachment	2	
R21	100433	Stud, petrol pump attachment	2	
R22	151134	Block, sealing, front	1	
R23	150531	Gasket, sealing block	1	
R24	36234	Piece, filling ⎫ Sealing block to	2	
R25	100501	Screw ⎭ cylinder block	2	
R26	PT0805	Setscrew ⎫ Sealing block to	2	
R27	WL0208	Washer, lock ⎭ engine plate	2	
R28	61478	Tap, drain	1	
R29	WF0511	Washer, fibre	A/R	
R30	WF0525	Washer, fibre	A/R	
R31	145021	CYLINDER LINER	6	

Note:—Items marked thus † are available on our FACTORY EXCHANGE UNIT SCHEME

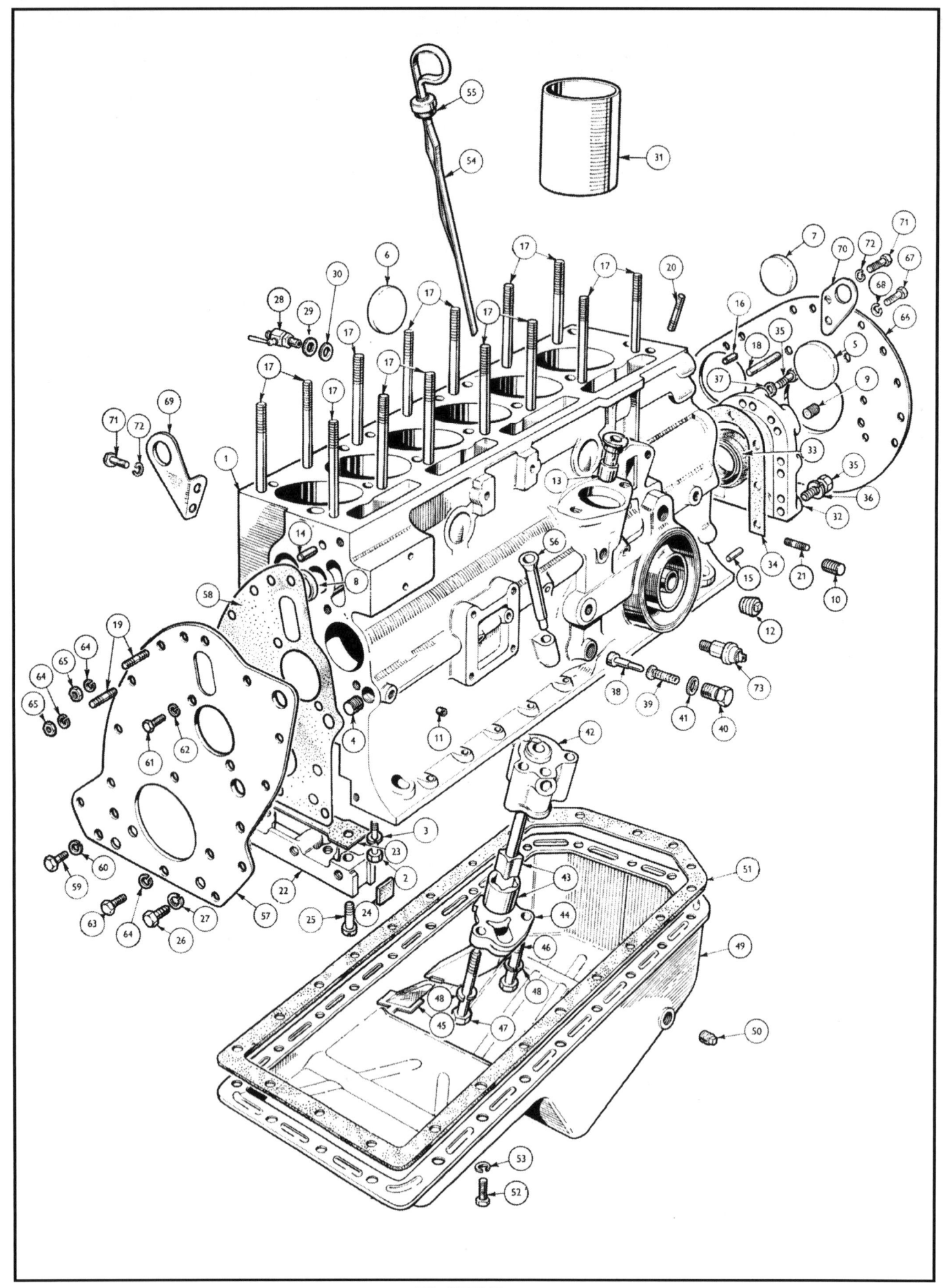

PLATE R

ENGINE
MARK II (G.T.6+) CARS FITTED FROM ENGINE No. KC/KD50001E AND FUTURE

Plate No.	Part No.	Description	No. per Unit	Remarks
R32	212622	**OIL SEAL HOUSING—REAR**	1	
R33	143456	Seal, oil, crankshaft	1	
R34	105321	Washer, joint, between oil seal housing and cylinder block	1	
R35	HB0809	Bolt ⎫ Oil seal housing	7	
R36	WL0208	Washer, lock ⎬ to	6	
R37	500469	Washer, copper ⎭ cylinder block	1	Fitted under head of top bolt
		OIL PRESSURE ADJUSTMENT DETAILS		
R38	132107	Piston, relief valve	1	
R39	131535	Spring	1	
R40	107246	Plug, relief valve	1	
R41	501258	Washer	1	
	149634	**OIL PUMP ASSEMBLY**	1	
R42	127732	Body assembly, oil pump	1	
	104963	Plug, core, oil pump body	1	
R43	508975	Rotor and spindle assembly	1	
R44	214842	Cover, oil pump body	1	
R45	149621	Filter, oil pump	1	
R46	HB0724	Bolt ⎫	2	
R47	HB0727	Bolt ⎬ Oil pump to cylinder block	1	
R48	WL0207	Washer, lock ⎭	3	
R49	308571	**OIL SUMP ASSEMBLY**	1	
R50	114774	Plug, oil drain	1	
R51	211125	Gasket, between sump and block	1	
R52	HB0805	Screw, set ⎫ Oil sump to	23	
R53	WL0208	Washer, lock ⎭ cylinder block	23	
R54	127653	Dipstick assembly	1	
R55	32307	Washer, felt, on dipstick	1	
R56	127652	Tube, dipstick	1	
R57	215349	**FRONT ENGINE PLATE**	1	
R58	215350	Washer, joint, front engine plate	1	
R59	HU0806	Screw, set ⎫ Front engine plate	3	
R60	WL0208	Washer, lock ⎭ to cylinder block	3	
R61	HU0807	Screw, set ⎫ Front engine plate and camshaft	2	
R62	WL0208	Washer, lock ⎭ locating plate to cylinder block	2	
R63	HU0807	Screw, set ⎫ Timing cover and	5	
R64	WL0208	Washer, lock ⎬ front engine plate	7	
R65	HN2008	Nut ⎭ to cylinder block	2	
R66	211514	**REAR ENGINE PLATE**	1	
R67	HU0807	Screw, set ⎫ Rear engine plate	7	
R68	WL0208	Washer, lock ⎭	7	
		ENGINE LIFTING EYES		
R69	123716	Eye, lifting, front	1	
R70	123715	Eye, lifting, rear	1	
R71	HU0805	Screw, set ⎫ Lifting eyes to	4	
R72	WL0208	Washer, lock ⎭ cylinder block	3	
R73	121398	†**OIL PRESSURE SWITCH**	1	

Note:- For Engine Mounting Brackets see Engine Mounting Details.

Note:—Items marked thus † are available on our Factory Exchange Unit Scheme

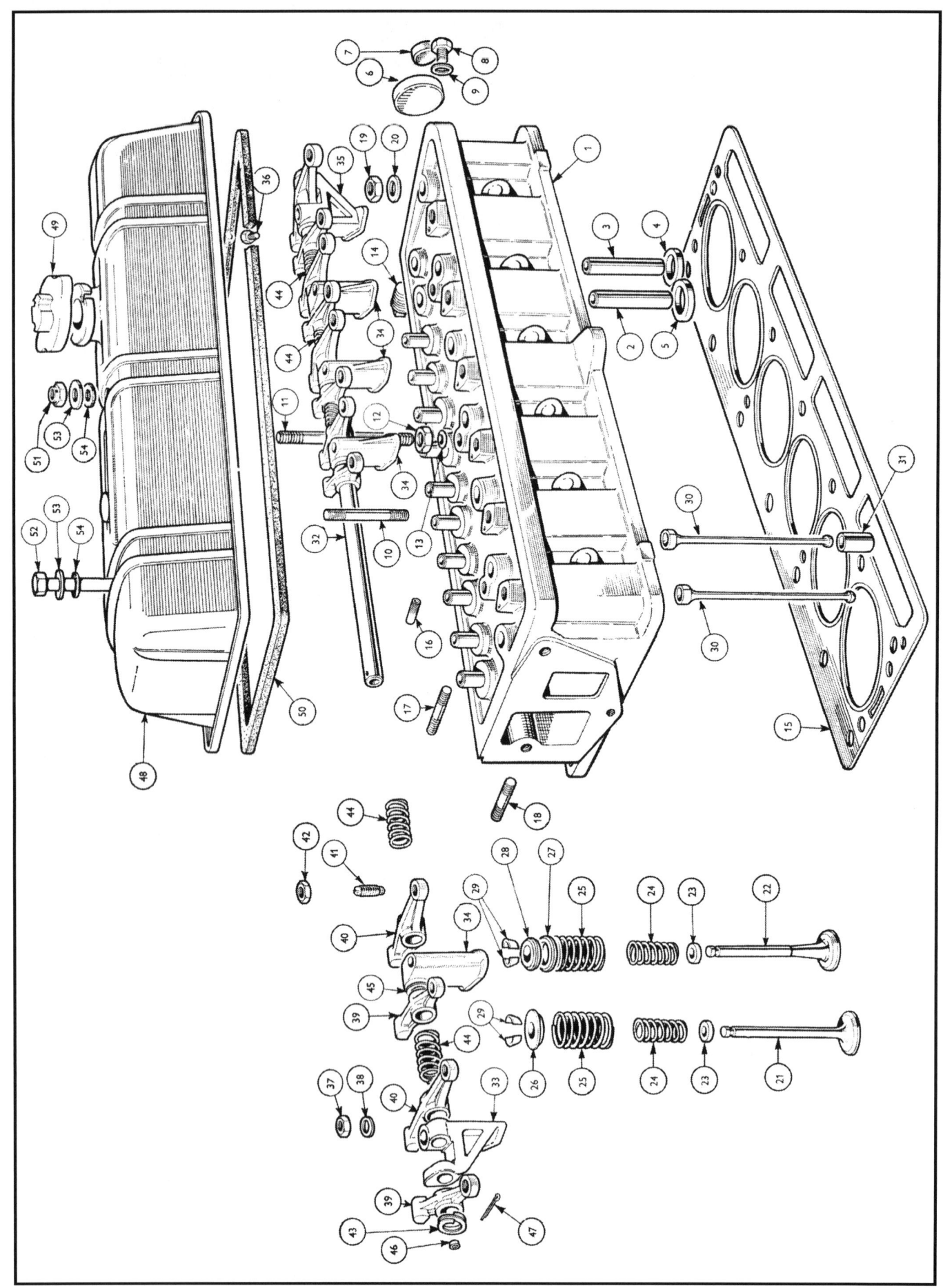

PLATE S

ENGINE

MARK II (G.T.6+) CARS FITTED FROM ENGINE No. KC/KD50001E AND FUTURE

Plate No.	Part No.	Description	No. per Unit	Remarks
	517609	**CYLINDER HEAD ASSEMBLY** (9.25 : 1 Compression Ratio) (With Valves and Springs, less Studs)	1	
S1	517610	**CYLINDER HEAD ASSEMBLY** (9.25 : 1 Compression Ratio) (Less Valves, Springs and Studs)	1	
S2	58923	**Guide**, valve, inlet	6	
S3	111869	**Guide**, valve, exhaust	6	
S4	146497	**Insert**, valve seat, exhaust valve	6	
S5	146496	**Insert**, valve seat, inlet valve	6	
S6	144648	**Plug**, core, bucket type, in rear face of head	1	
S7	144686	**Plug**, core, in rear face of head	1	
S8	101022	**Screw**, set ⎱ Rocker	1	
S9	500469	**Washer**, copper ⎰ oil feed	1	
S10	132495	**Stud**, rocker pedestal	6	
S11	105123	**Stud**, rocker cover, centre and rear	2	
S12	HN2008	**Nut**, stud to cylinder head	2	
S13	30123	**Linger**, lead, under nut	A/R	
S14	114774	**Plug**, taper	1	
S15	213776	**Gasket**, cylinder head	1	
S16	DS3112	**Dowel**, manifold attachment	2	
S17	105124	**Stud**, exhaust manifold, outer	4	
	101962	**Stud**, inlet manifold attachment	3	
S18	105125	**Stud**, inlet manifold attachment	6	
S19	103810	**Nut** ⎱ Cylinder head	14	
S20	508289	**Washer**, plain ⎰ to cylinder block	14	
		VALVES		
S21	146128	**Valve**, inlet	6	
S22	149658	**Valve**, exhaust	6	
S23	149717	**Collar**, spring, lower	12	
S24	102564	**Spring**, valve, inner	12	
S25	149633	**Spring**, valve, outer	12	
S26	111870	**Collar**, spring, upper (Inlet valve only)	6	
S27	128335	**Collar**, valve, outer (Exhaust only)	6	
S28	128334	**Collar**, valve, inner (Exhaust only)	6	
S29	106663	**Cotter**, split cone	12 prs.	
S30	151073	**PUSH ROD**	12	
S31	143552	**Tappet**, push rod	12	

Note:—Items marked thus † are available on our Factory Exchange Unit Scheme

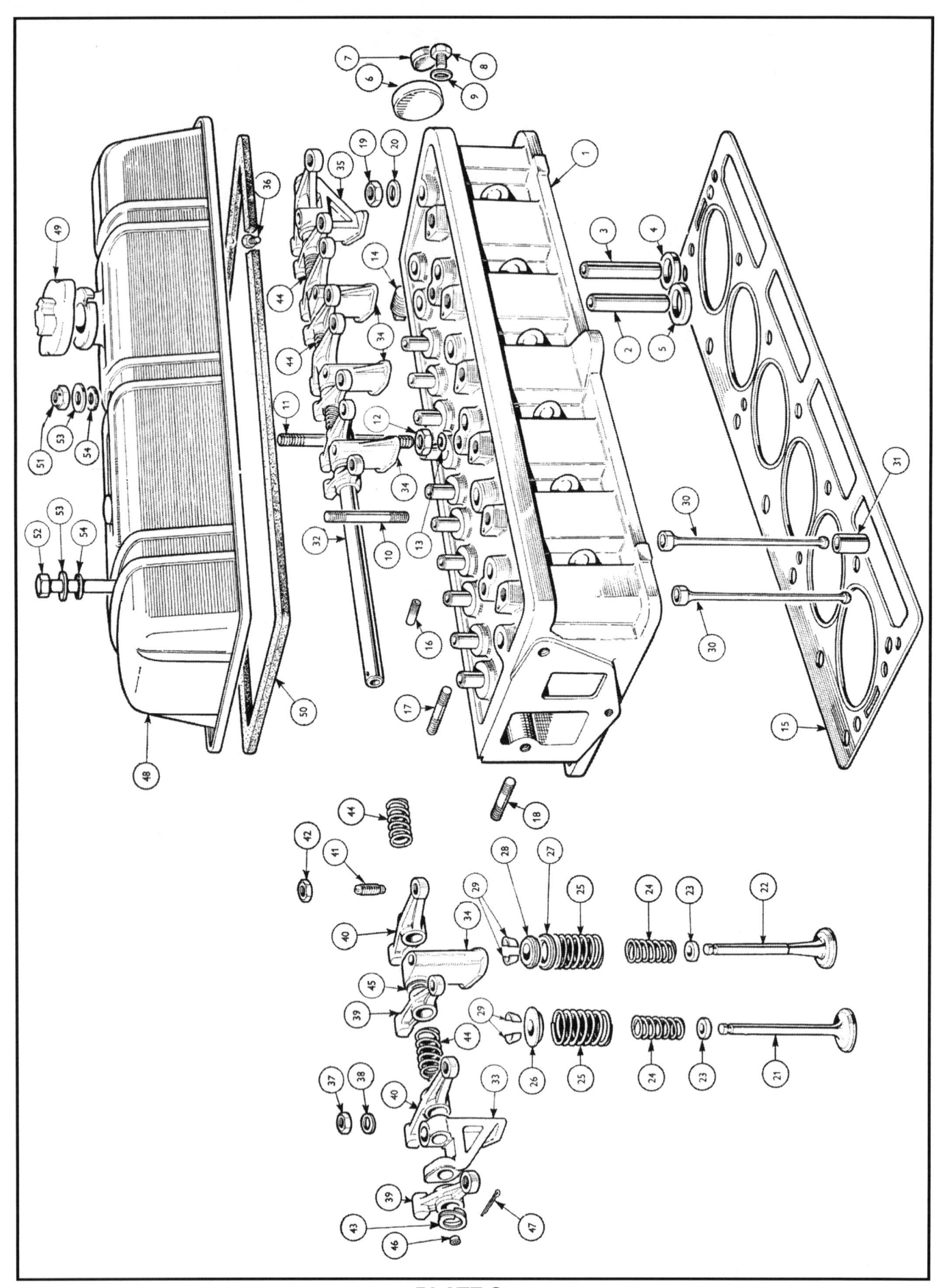

PLATE S

ENGINE

MARK II (G.T.6+) CARS FITTED FROM ENGINE No. KC/KD50001E AND FUTURE

Plate No.	Part No.	Description	No. per Unit	Remarks
S32	214559	**ROCKER SHAFT**	1	
S33	145867	**Pedestal,** No. 1	1	
S34	145868	**Pedestal,** intermediate	4	
S35	145869	**Pedestal,** No. 6	1	
S36	104859	**Screw,** locating shaft to drilled pedestal No. 6	1	
S37	HN2009	**Nut** ⎫ Rocker pedestal	6	
S38	WP0184	**Washer,** plain ⎭ to cylinder head	6	
S39	109023	**Rocker,** No. 1	6	
S40	109024	**Rocker,** No. 2	6	
S41	109495	**Pin,** adjustment ⎫ Fitted in	12	
S42	57110	**Locknut** ⎭ rockers	12	
S43	105322	**Spring,** rocker, fitted with Pedestals No. 1 and 6	2	
S44	119313	**Spring,** rocker, intermediate	5	
S45	WP8013	**Washer,** plain	4	
S46	137811	**Plug,** rocker shaft	2	
S47	PC0010	**Pin,** cotter	1	
S48	210908	**ROCKER COVER ASSEMBLY**	1	
S49	143393	**Cap,** oil filler	1	
S50	119322	**Washer,** joint, rocker cover	1	
S51	TN3208	**Nut,** nyloc ⎫	2	
S52	516134	**Bolt** ⎬ Rocker cover	1	
S53	WP0008	**Washer,** plain ⎬ to cylinder head	3	
S54	WF0508	**Washer,** fibre ⎭	3	

Note:—Items marked thus † are available on our Factory Exchange Unit Scheme

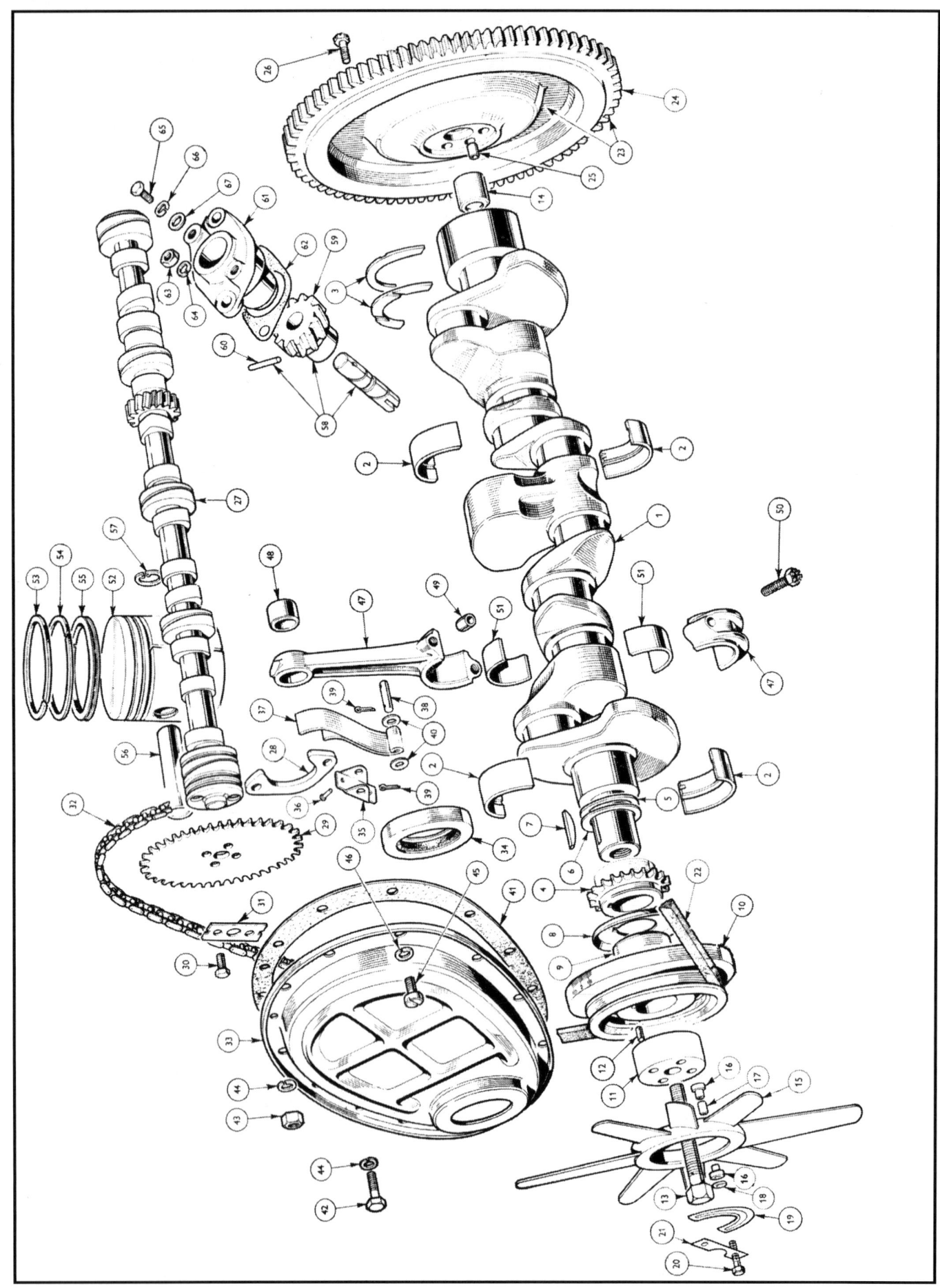

PLATE T

ENGINE
MARK II (G.T.6+) CARS FITTED FROM ENGINE No. KC/KD50001E AND FUTURE

Plate No	Part No	Description	No per Unit	Remarks
T1	308034	**CRANKSHAFT**	1	
T2	149082	Bearing, main	4 prs.	
T3	144195	Washer, thrust (obtainable ·005" o/s)	2	
T4	119389	Chainwheel	1	
T5	145275	Shim, chainwheel to crankshaft, ·004" thick	A/R	
T6	145276	Shim, chainwheel to crankshaft, ·006" thick	A/R	
T7	133234	Key, locating chainwheel on crankshaft	1	
T8	119390	Deflector, oil	1	
T9	133235	Sleeve, oil seal	1	
T10	133244	Pulley and damper assembly	1	
T11	133238	Adaptor, fan	1	
T12	DP0508	Dowel, locating adaptor on pulley and damper	2	
T13	HB1316	Bolt, securing adaptor and pulley to crankshaft	1	
T14	105143	Bush, constant pinion, fitted in end of crankshaft	1	

MAIN BEARINGS are obtainable in the following undersizes:- —·010", —·020", —·030". When ordering please quote part number and undersize required.

Plate No	Part No	Description	No per Unit	Remarks
T15	308353	**FAN ASSEMBLY**	1	
T16	108496	Bush	8	
T17	108499	Sleeve	4	
T18	108495	Washer — Fan to adaptor	4	
T19	107858	Piece, balance	1	
T20	HB0810	Bolt	4	
T21	107857	Washer, tab	2	
T22	214830	Belt, fan	1	
T23	148042	**FLYWHEEL ASSEMBLY**	1	
T24	201350	Ring, gear	1	
T25	127883	Dowel — Flywheel to crankshaft	1	
T26	147299	Bolt, flywheel	1	
T27	308778	**CAMSHAFT**	1	
	307621	**CAMSHAFT**	1	U.S.A. only
T28	105114	Plate, locating	1	

Note:- For Locating Plate Attachment details see Front Engine Plate.

Plate No	Part No	Description	No per Unit	Remarks
T29	35960	Chainwheel, camshaft	1	
T30	100500	Screw, set — Chainwheel to camshaft	2	
T31	36411	Plate, locking	1	
T32	105131	Chain, timing	1	

Note:—Items marked thus † are available on our Factory Exchange Unit Scheme

PLATE T

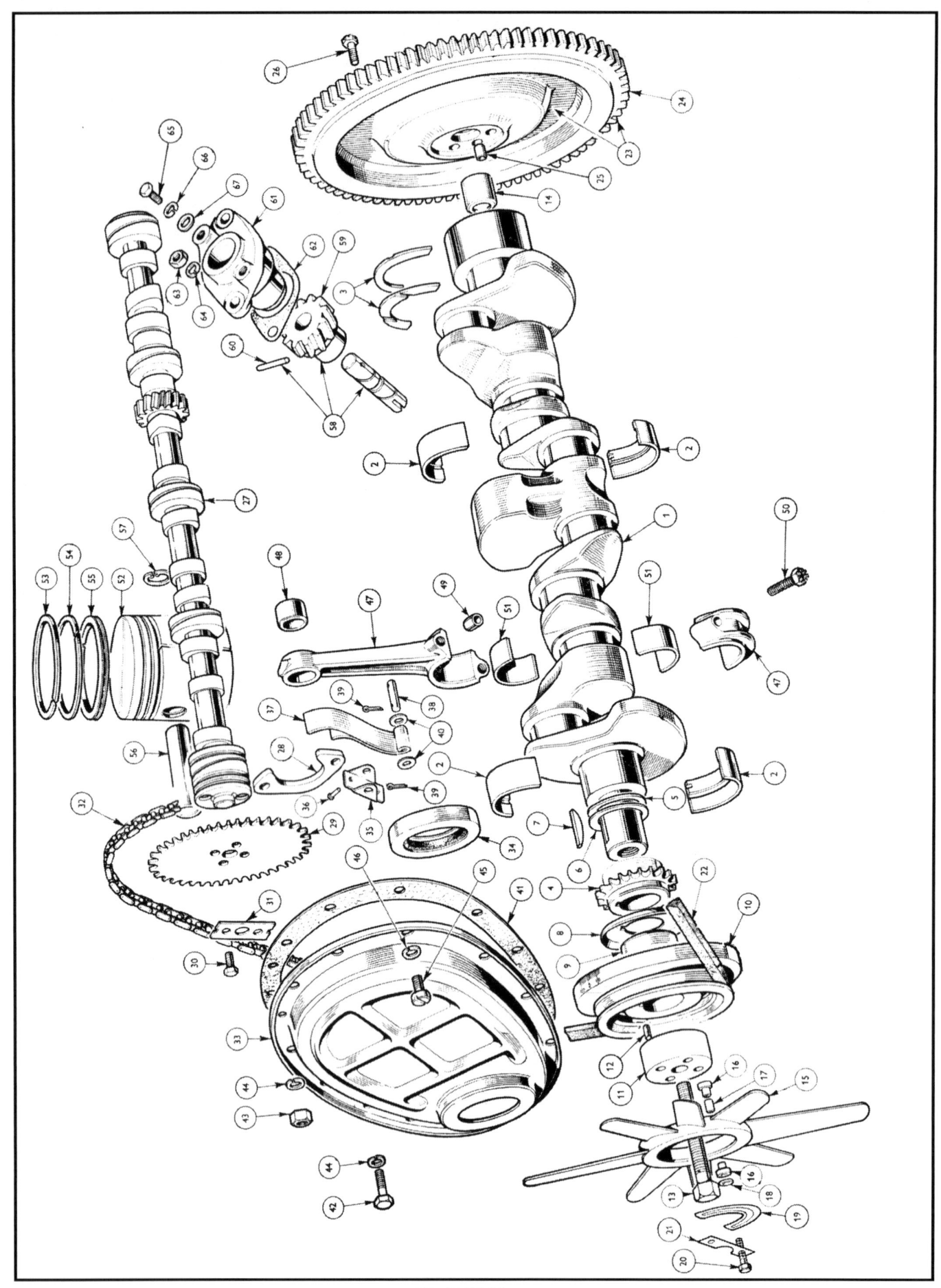

ENGINE

MARK II (G.T.6+) CARS FITTED FROM ENGINE No. KC/KD50001E AND FUTURE

Plate No.	Part No.	Description	No. per Unit	Remarks
T33	207492	**TIMING COVER ASSEMBLY**	1	
T34	125631	**Seal**, oil, in timing cover	1	
T35	43752	**Plate**, anchor, chain tensioner	1	
T36	SP.91.B3	**Rivet**, anchor plate to timing cover	2	
T37	42425	**Tensioner**, chain	1	
T38	33214	**Pin**, anchor, chain tensioner	1	
T39	PC0007	**Pin**, cotter ⎱ Chain tensioner	2	
T40	WP0018	**Washer**, plain ⎰ attachment	2	
T41	211126	**Gasket**, timing cover	1	
T42	HU0807	**Screw**, set ⎫ Timing cover and front engine plate to cylinder block	5	
T43	HN2008	**Nut** ⎬	2	
T44	WL0208	**Washer**, lock ⎭	7	
T45	PT0803	**Screw**, set ⎱ Timing cover to	5	
T46	WL0208	**Washer**, lock ⎰ front engine plate	5	
T47	146454	**CONNECTING ROD ASSEMBLY**	6	
T48	119813	**Bush**, small end	6	
T49	107401	**Dowel**, hollow, connecting rod bolt	12	
T50	138529	**Bolt**, place, connecting rod	12	
T51	149081	**Bearing**, big end	6 prs.	

BIG END BEARINGS are obtainable in the following undersizes:- —·010″, —·020″, —·030″. When ordering, please quote part number and size required.

Plate No.	Part No.	Description	No. per Unit	Remarks
T52	139809	**PISTON ASSEMBLY (Graded F, G & H)**	6	Fitted up to Engine No. only
	149976	**PISTON ASSEMBLY (Graded F, G & H)**	6	Fitted from Engine No. and future
T53	127262	**Ring**, compression, plated	6	
T54	139810	**Ring**, compression	6	
T55	127264	**Ring**, scraper	6	
T56	127265	**Pin**, gudgeon	6	
T57	508978	**Circlip**, retaining gudgeon pin	12	

PISTONS are obtainable +·020″ oversize.

PISTON RINGS are obtainable in the following oversizes:- +·010″, +·020″, +·030″. When ordering, please quote part number and size required.

Plate No.	Part No.	Description	No. per Unit	Remarks
T58	126786	**DRIVE SHAFT ASSEMBLY, DISTRIBUTOR AND OIL PUMP**	1	
T59	126785	**Gear**, driving, distributor and oil pump	1	
T60	500974	**Pin**, Mills, securing gear	1	
T61	126784	**Pedestal**, distributor	1	
T62	104939	**Washer**, joint, pedestal	1	
T63	HN2008	**Nut** ⎱ Pedestal to cylinder block	2	
T64	WL0208	**Washer**, lock ⎰	2	
T65	HU0704	**Screw**, set ⎫	2	
T66	WL0207	**Washer**, lock ⎬ Distributor to pedestal	1	
T67	WP0035	**Washer**, plain ⎭	2	

Note:- For Details of Distributor see Electrical Section.

Note:—Items marked thus † are available on our Factory Exchange Unit Scheme

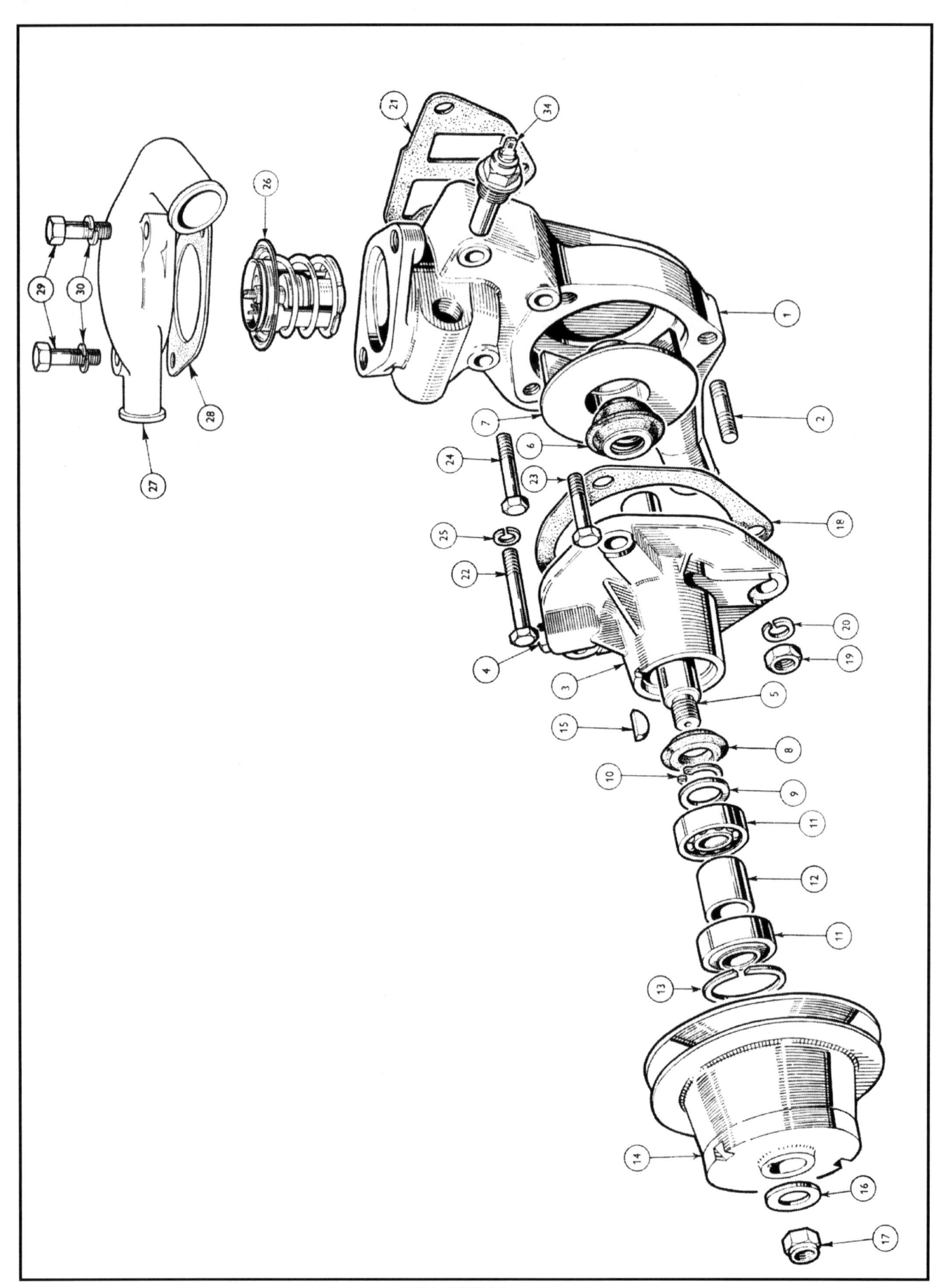

PLATE U

ENGINE

MARK II (G.T.6+) CARS FITTED FROM ENGINE No. KC/KD50001E AND FUTURE

Plate No.	Part No.	Description	No. per Unit	Remarks
	514397	†**WATER PUMP ASSEMBLY**	1	
U1	307095	**Body**, water pump	1	
U2	101962	**Stud**, bearing housing attachment	3	
	133258	†**Housing**, bearing, assembly	1	
	511813	†**Housing**, bearing, assembly (Reconditioned Unit)	1	
U3	201316	**Housing**, bearing	1	
U4	122115	**Plug**	1	
U5	104839	**Spindle**	1	
U6	148322	**Seal**, between bearing housing and impellor	1	
U7	104840	**Impellor**	1	
U8	60313	**Seal**, bearing	1	
U9	101092	**Washer**, abutment	1	
U10	500047	**Circlip**	1	
U11	100764	**Bearing**	2	
U12	104841	**Piece**, distance, between bearings	1	
U13	100851	**Circlip**, retaining bearing in housing	1	
U14	133239	**Pulley**	1	
U15	KW0420	**Key**, Woodruff, locating pulley on spindle	1	
U16	WP0181	**Washer**, plain ⎫ Pulley to spindle	1	
U17	TN3208	**Nut**, nyloc ⎭	1	
U18	138701	**Gasket** ⎫	1	
U19	HN2008	**Nut** ⎬ Bearing housing to pump body	3	
U20	WL0208	**Washer**, lock ⎭	3	
U21	138792	**Gasket** ⎫	1	
U22	HB0825	**Bolt** ⎪	1	
U23	HB0818	**Bolt** ⎬ Water pump to cylinder head	1	
U24	HB0819	**Bolt** ⎪	1	
U25	WL0208	**Washer**, lock ⎭	3	
U26	140970	†**THERMOSTAT UNIT (82° OPENING)**	1	
	146431	†**THERMOSTAT UNIT (88° OPENING)**	1	Special Order only
U27	212971	**Elbow**, water	1	
U28	57103	**Gasket** ⎫	1	
U29	HB0812	**Bolt** ⎬ Elbow to water pump body	2	
U30	WL0208	**Washer**, lock ⎭	2	
U31	137705	**Temperature transmitter**	1	

Note:—Items marked thus † are available on our Factory Exchange Unit Scheme

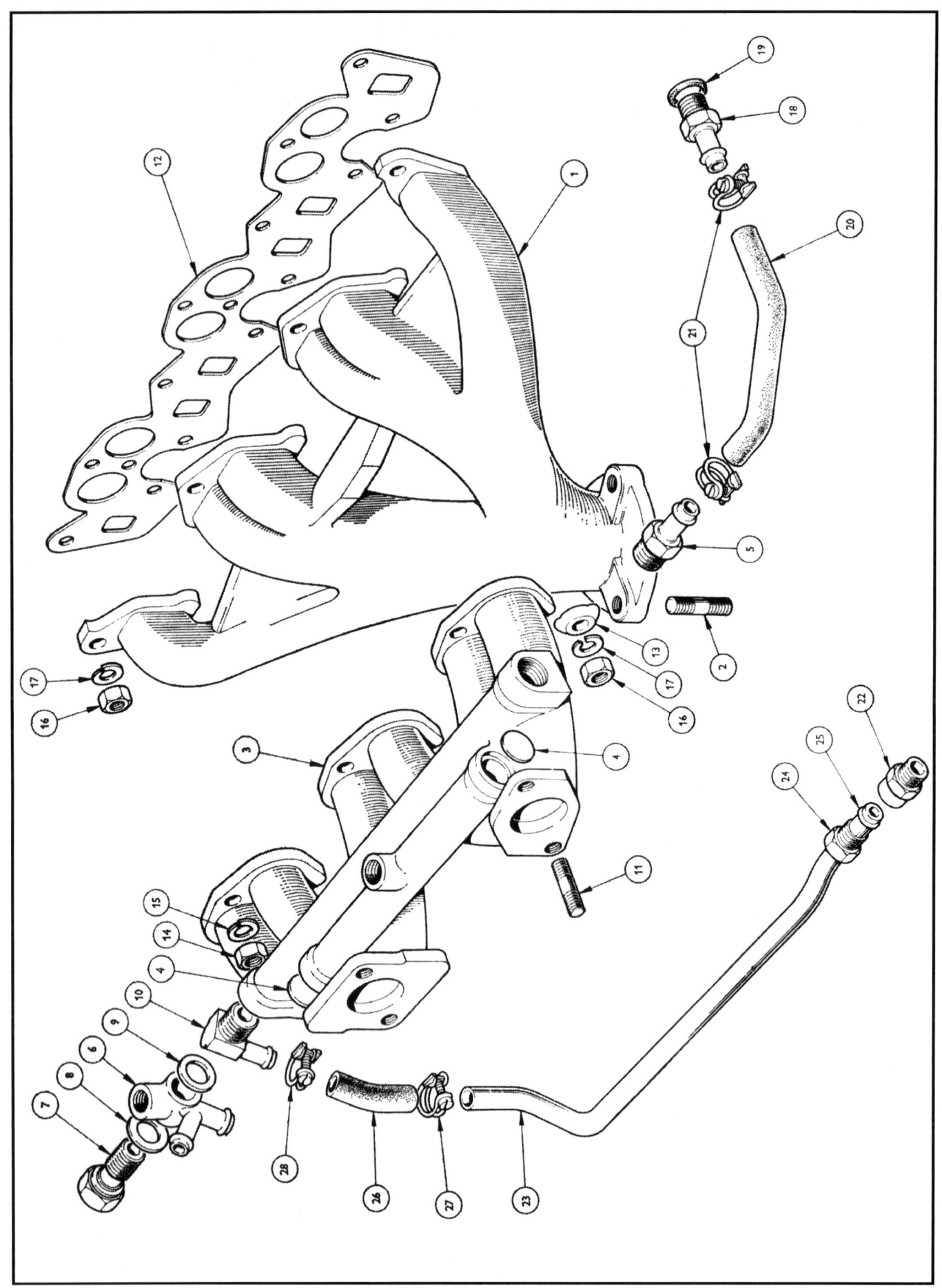

PLATE V

ENGINE
MARK II (G.T.6+) CARS FITTED FROM ENGINE No. KC/KD50001E AND FUTURE

Plate No.	Part No.	Description	No. per No.	Remarks
		MANIFOLDS		
V1	308290	**Manifold**, exhaust	1	
V2	115696	**Stud**, exhaust outlet attachment	3	
V3	308671	**Manifold**, inlet	1	
V4	46172	**Plug**, core	2	
V5	138810	**Adaptor**, front, water feed to manifold	1	
V6	145938	**Adaptor** assembly, water return from manifold and heater ⎫	1	
V7	145155	**Bolt**, banjo ⎬ Adaptor ⎬ Only required when heater is fitted	1	
V8	WF0534	**Washer** (Large hole) ⎬ to	1	
V9	WF0550	**Washer** (Small hole) ⎭ manifold ⎭	1	
V10	138822	**Elbow**—(Only required when heater is not fitted or fresh air kit is fitted)	1	
V11	129383	**Stud**, carburettor attachment	4	
	TD0863	**Stud**, carburettor attachment	4	U.S.A. only
V12	214622	**Washer**, joint, inlet and exhaust manifold	1	
V13	58258	**Clamp** ⎫	6	
V14	HN2008	**Nut** ⎬ Exhaust and inlet	3	
V15	WL0208	**Washer**, lock ⎬ manifold to	3	
V16	100498	**Nut** ⎬ cylinder head	10	
V17	WL0209	**Washer** ⎭	10	
		MANIFOLD HEATER PIPES		
V18	138530	**Adaptor**, water pump body—To manifold	1	
V19	WF0524	**Washer**, fibre, between adaptor and water pump body	1	
V20	137876	**Hose**, adaptor to inlet manifold	1	
V21	CS4012	**Clip**, hose attachment	2	
V22	101343	**Adaptor**, water pump body (Return)	1	
V23	210834	**Pipe**, water return	1	
V24	101302	**Nut**, tubing	1	
V25	TL0011	**Sleeve**, tubing	1	
V26	140986	**Hose**, pipe to elbow or adaptor in inlet manifold	1	
V27	CS4013	**Clip**, hose attachment	1	
V28	CS4012	**Clip**, hose attachment	1	

Note:—Items marked thus † are available on our Factory Exchange Unit Scheme

33

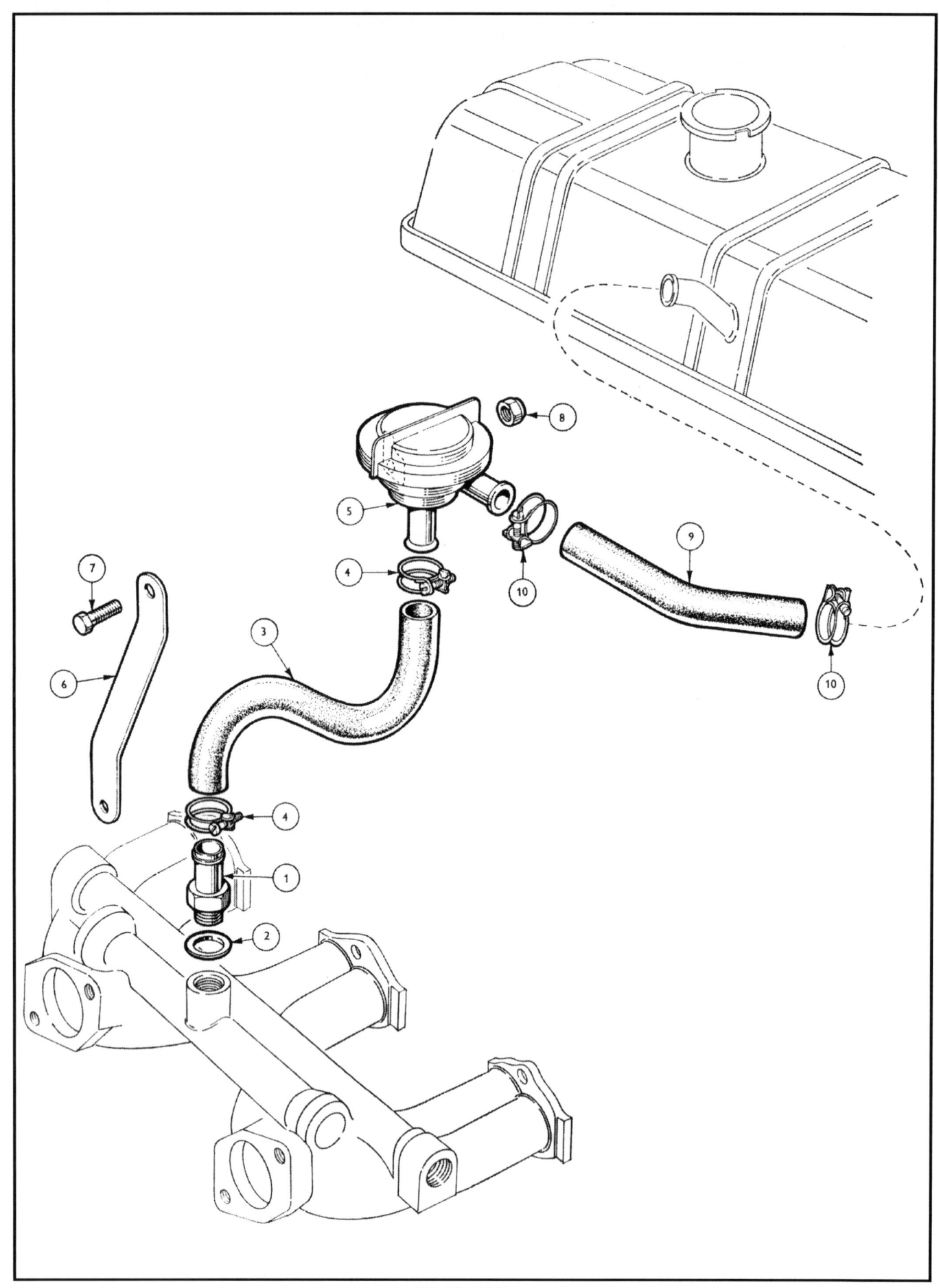

PLATE W

ENGINE

MARK II (G.T.6+) CARS FITTED FROM ENGINE No. KC/KD50001E AND FUTURE

Plate No.	Part No.	Description	No. per Unit	Remarks
		BREATHER DETAILS		
W1	138530	**Adaptor,** hose to inlet manifold	1	
W2	WF0513	**Washer,** fibre, on adaptor	1	
W3	143706	**Hose,** inlet manifold adaptor to emission control valve	1	
W4	CS4012	**Clip,** hose attachment	2	
W5	151658	**Valve,** emission control	1	
	517582	**Kit,** emission control valve, comprising:- Plunger Sub assembly, Diaphragm and Top cover	1	
W6	143313	**Bracket,** control valve, fitted to manifold attachment stud	1	
W7	HU0707	**Screw,** set ⎫ Emission control valve	1	
W8	TN3207	**Nut,** nyloc ⎭ to mounting bracket	1	
W9	143323	**Hose,** emission control valve to rocker cover	1	
W10	CS4012	**Clip,** hose attachment	2	

Note:—Items marked thus † are available on our Factory Exchange Unit Scheme

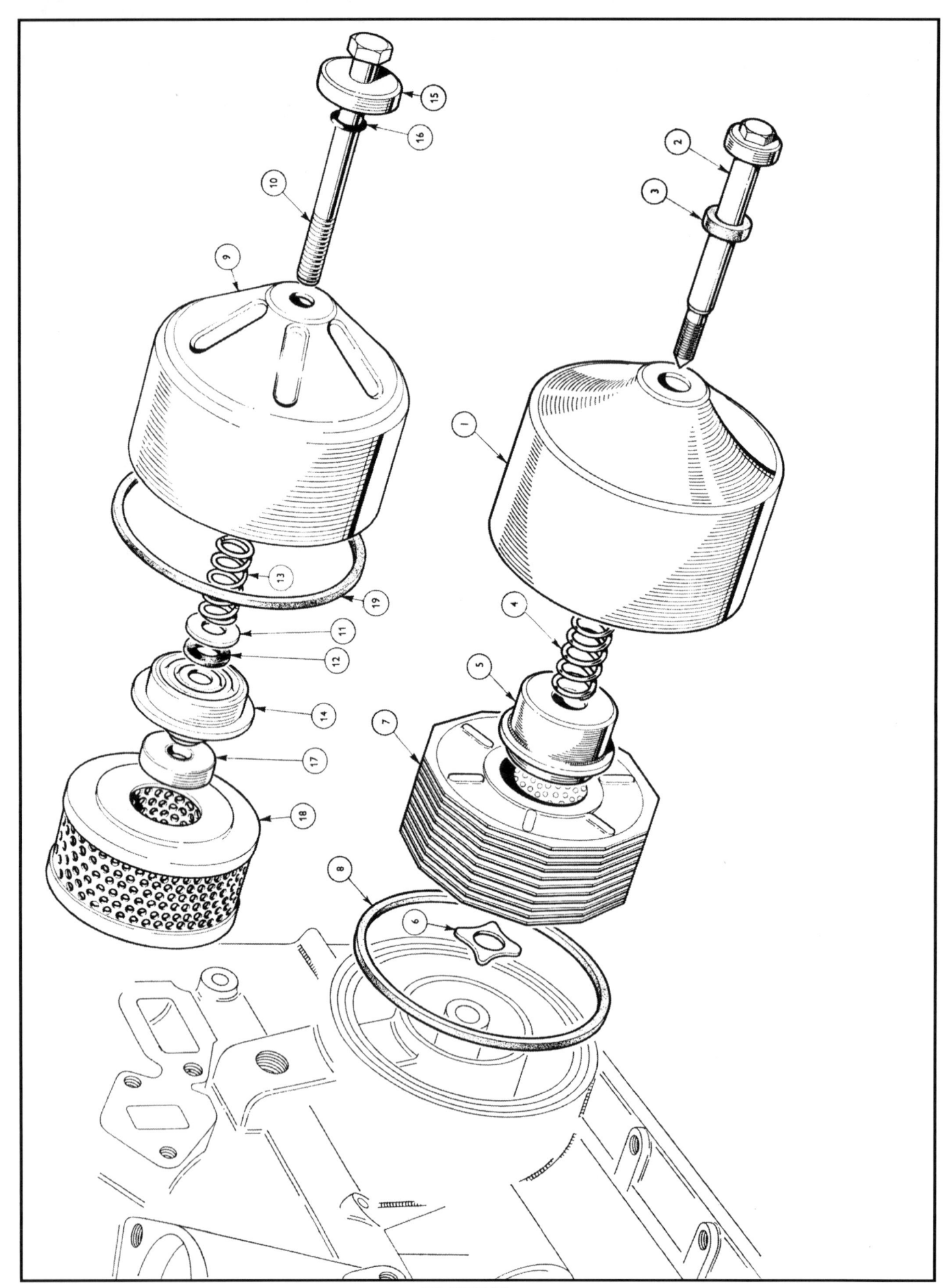

PLATE X

ENGINE
MARK II (G.T.6+) CARS FITTED FROM ENGINE No. KC/KD50001E AND FUTURE

Plate No.	Part No.	Description	No. per Unit	Remarks
	125715	**OIL FILTER ASSEMBLY (FULL FLOW)**	1	A.C. Delco. Alternative to Purolator Filter shown below
X1	509878	**Shell** assembly	1	
X2	509879	**Bolt,** centre	1	
X3	509880	**Gasket,** bolt head	1	
X4	509881	**Spring,** element retaining	1	
X5	509882	**Valve** assembly	1	
X6	509883	**Centraliser,** element	1	
X7	125714	**Element,** filter	1	
X8	125531	**Ring,** sealing	1	
	125715	**OIL FILTER ASSEMBLY (FULL FLOW)**	1	Purolator. Alternative to A.C. Delco Filter shown above
X9	517435	**Sump**	1	
X10	517433	**Bolt,** centre	1	
X11	517486	**Washer**	1	
X12	517431	**Seal,** bolt	1	
X13	517432	**Spring,** element retaining	1	
X14	517430	**Valve,** relief, assembly	1	
X15	517428	**Collar**	1	
X16	517429	**'O' ring**	1	
X17	517434	**Plate,** element locating	1	
X18	125713	**Element,** filter	1	
X19	517427	**Ring,** sump sealing	1	

Note:—Items marked thus † are available on our Factory Exchange Unit Scheme

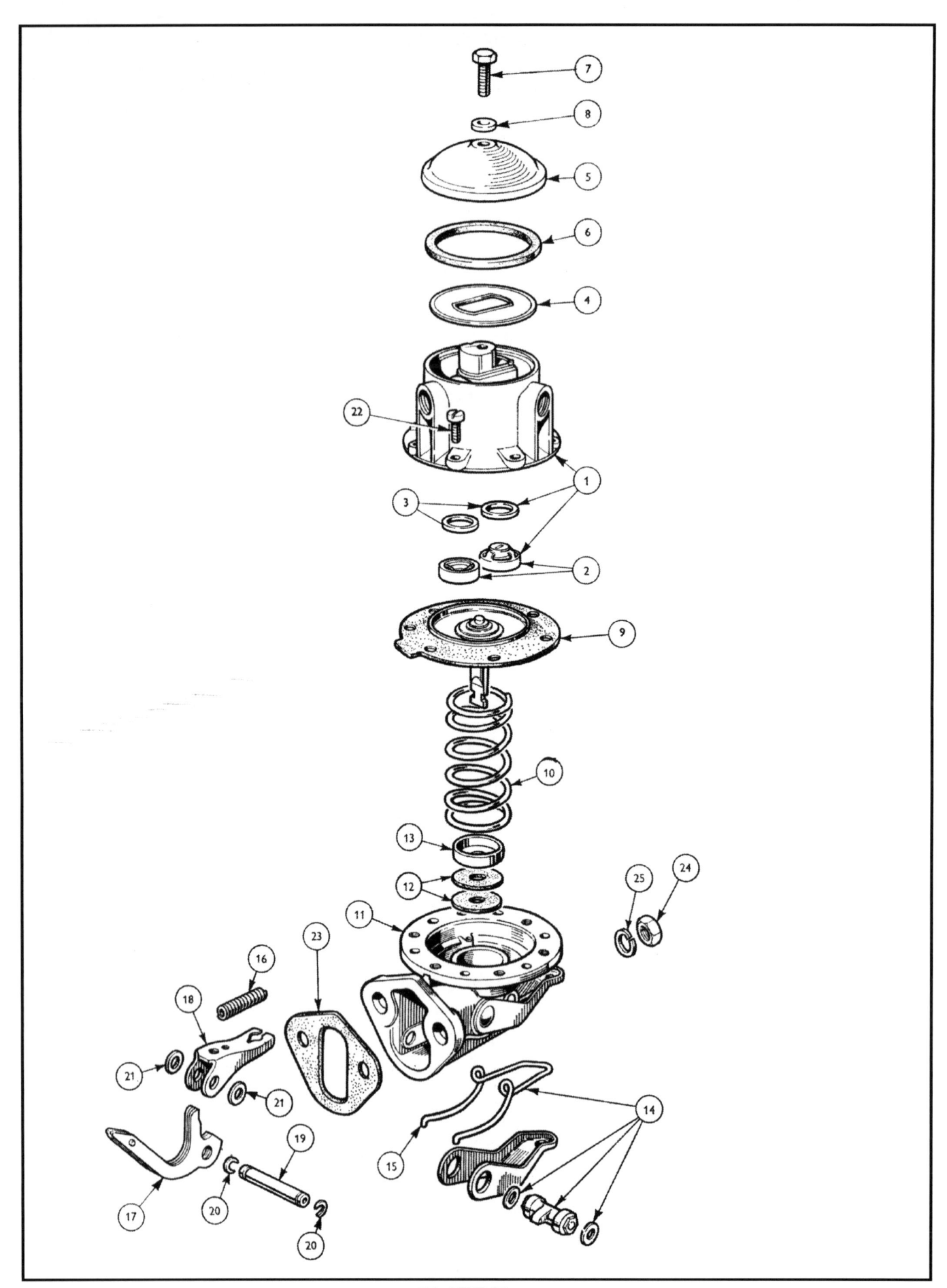

PLATE Y

ENGINE
MARK II (G.T.6+) CARS FITTED FROM ENGINE No. KC/KD50001E AND FUTURE

Plate No.	Part No.	Description	No. per Unit	Remarks
	213577	**PETROL PUMP ASSEMBLY**	1	
Y1	516538	**Casting,** upper, and valves assembly	1	
Y2	515036	**Valve,** assembly	2	
Y3	515037	**Gasket,** valve	2	
Y4	516539	**Screen,** filter	1	
Y5	59650	**Cover,** filter	1	
Y6	516540	**Gasket,** between cover and upper casting	1	
Y7	516537	**Bolt** ⎱ Upper casting	1	
Y8	510498	**Washer** ⎰ to cover	1	
Y9	501005	**Diaphragm** assembly	1	
Y10	52492	**Spring,** diaphragm	1	
Y11	509926	**Body** and primer, assembly	1	
Y12	508981	**Washer,** oil seal	2	
Y13	508980	**Retainer,** oil seal	1	
Y14	509927	**Set,** primer parts	1	
Y15	52498	**Spring,** primer	1	
Y16	52494	**Spring,** rocker arm	1	
Y17	516536	**Rocker** arm	1	
Y18	52479	**Link,** rocker arm	1	
Y19	52483	**Pin,** rocker arm and link to body	1	
Y20	52484	**Clip,** securing pin	2	
Y21	52486	**Washer,** between link and body	2	
Y22	516541	**Screw,** upper casting to body	6	
	500524	**First aid kit**	1	
	516542	**Repair kit,** complete (less rocker arm)	1	
Y23	138791	**Gasket** ⎫	1	
Y24	HN2008	**Nut** ⎬ Securing pump to cylinder block	2	
Y25	WL0208	**Washer,** lock ⎭	2	

Note:—Items marked thus † are available on our Factory Exchange Unit Scheme

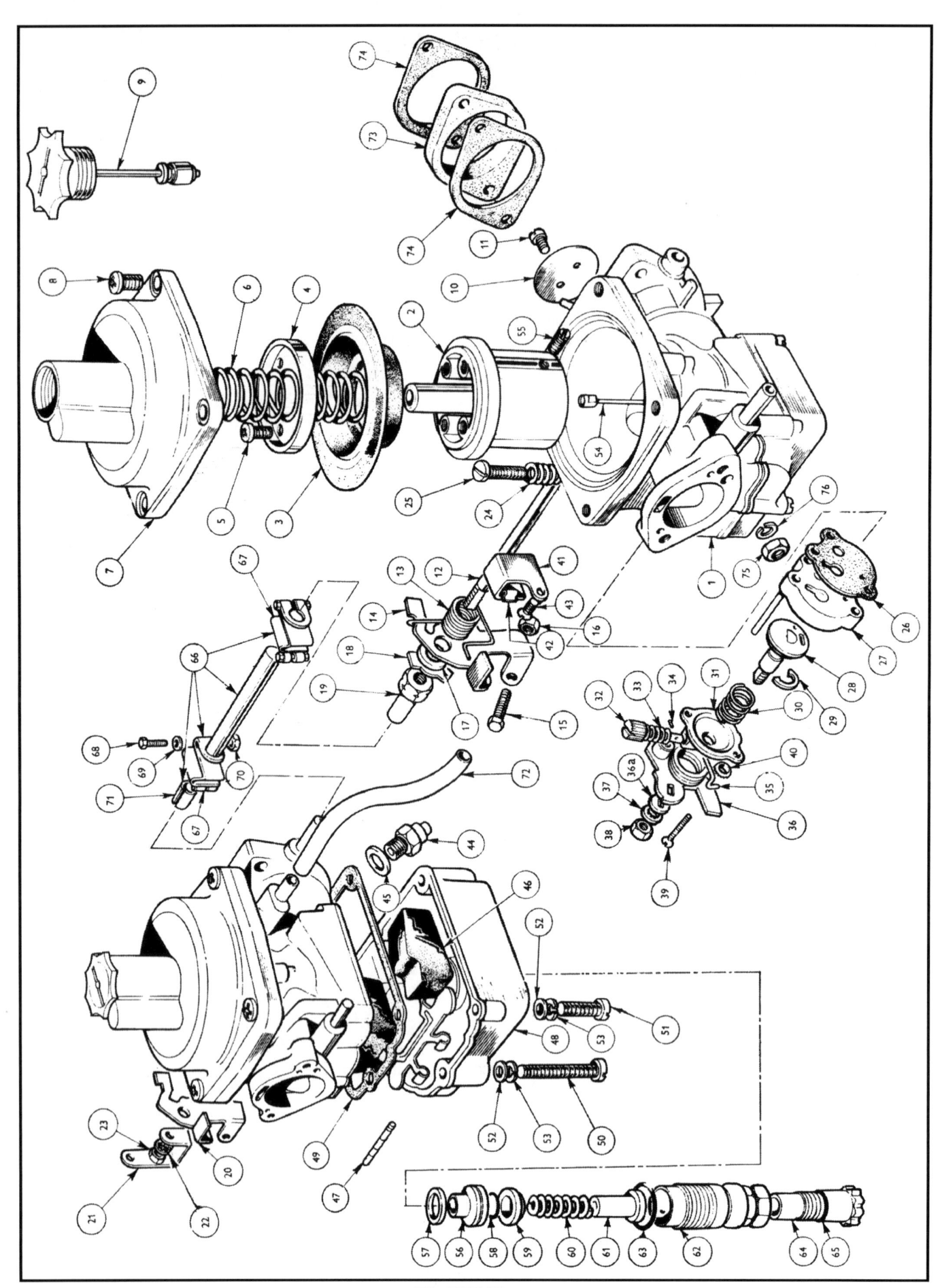

PLATE Z

ENGINE

MARK II (G.T.6+) CARS—U.S.A. ONLY FITTED FROM ENGINE No. KC50001E AND FUTURE

Plate No.	Part No.	Description	No. per Unit	Remarks
	309003	**CARBURETTOR ASSEMBLY—FRONT**	1	
	309004	**CARBURETTOR ASSEMBLY—REAR**	1	
Z1	Not Serviced	**Main body** assembly		
Z2	513708	**Air valve, shaft and diaphragm** assembly	2	
Z3	517448	**Diaphragm**	2	
Z4	513707	**Ring**, diaphragm retaining	2	
Z5	517119	**Screw**, securing diaphragm, retaining ring	8	
Z6	516945	**Spring**, air valve return	2	
Z7	517863	**Cover** assembly, air valve	2	
Z8	512274	**Screw and spring washer**, securing cover	8	
Z9	515112	**DAMPER ASSEMBLY**	2	
		THROTTLE DETAILS		
Z10	513689	**Disc**, throttle	2	
Z11	516952	**Screw**, securing disc to spindle	4	
Z12	513717	**Spindle**, throttle	2	
Z13	517131	**Spring**, throttle return	2	
Z14	517857	**Lever**, throttle stop and fast idle—front carburettor	1	
Z15	516965	**Screw**, fast idle adjustment ⎫ Front carburettor	1	
Z16	512287	**Locknut**, on screw ⎭ only	1	
Z17	514977	**Washer**, spacing ⎫	1	
Z18	513720	**Washer**, tab ⎬ Front carburettor throttle spindle	1	
Z19	513724	**Nut**, extension ⎭	1	
Z20	517865	**Lever**, throttle stop and fast idle—rear carburettor	1	
Z21	147496	**Lever**, throttle—rear carburettor	1	
Z22	513688	**Washer**, shakeproof ⎫ Rear carburettor	1	
Z23	513687	**Nut** ⎭ throttle spindle	1	
Z24	512282	**Spring**, throttle stop screw	2	
Z25	512281	**Screw**, throttle stop	2	
		STARTER BOX—FRONT CARBURETTOR ONLY		
Z26	517858	**Face** assembly, starter	1	
Z27	517859	**Gasket**, starter face assembly	1	
Z28	517860	**Spindle**, starter, assembly	1	
Z29	516956	**'C' Washer**, on spindle	1	
Z30	516955	**Spring**, starter	1	
Z31	516953	**Cover** assembly, starter	1	
Z32	Not Serviced	**Stop**, adjuster, cam lever	1	
Z33	Not Serviced	**Spring** ⎫	1	
Z34	Not Serviced	**Roll pin** ⎬ On adjuster	1	
Z35	516957	**Spring**, cam lever return	1	
Z36	517861	**Cam lever** assembly	1	
Z36a	517000	**Washer**, plain ⎫	1	
Z37	513688	**Washer**, shakeproof ⎬ Securing cam lever	1	
Z38	513687	**Nut** ⎭	1	
Z39	517862	**Screw** ⎫ Starter cover to body	2	
Z40	516961	**Washer**, shakeproof ⎭	2	
Z41	516964	**Bracket**, starter control assembly, with clip	1	
Z42	516962	**Clip**, starter control bracket	1	
Z43	516963	**Screw**, securing bracket	1	

Note:—Items marked thus † are available on our Factory Exchange Unit Scheme

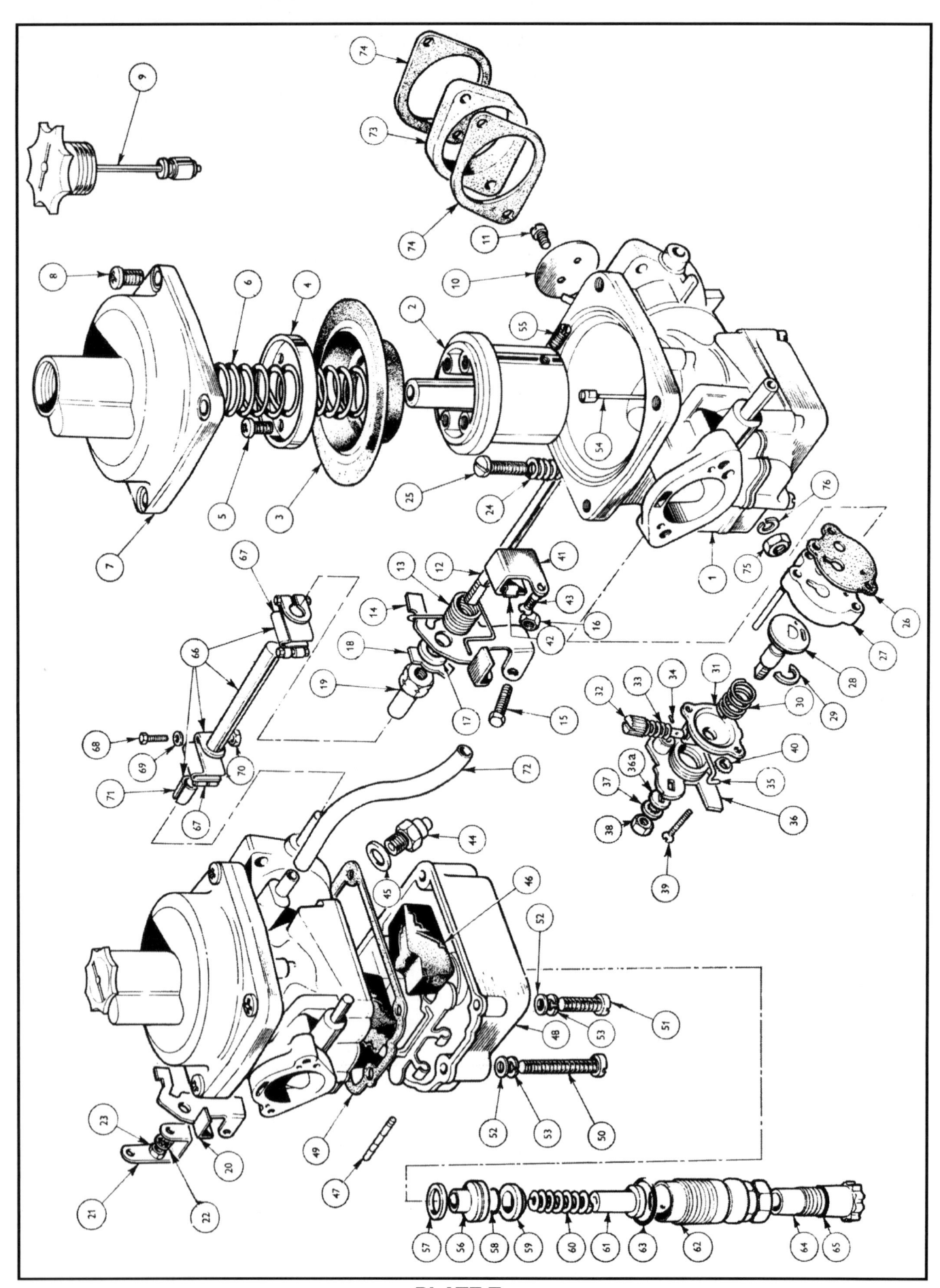

PLATE Z

ENGINE

MARK II (G.T.6+) CARS—U.S.A. ONLY FITTED FROM ENGINE No. KC50001E AND FUTURE

Plate No.	Part No.	Description	No. per Unit	Remarks
		CARBURETTORS—continued		
		FLOAT DETAILS		
Z44	517453	**Valve**, needle	2	
Z45	58529	**Washer**, needle valve	2	
Z46	516977	**Float** and arm	2	
Z47	517134	**Pin**, float pivot	2	
Z48	516981	**Float** chamber	2	
Z49	516980	**Gasket**, float chamber	2	
Z50	514972	**Screw**, long ⎫	8	
Z51	514973	**Screw**, short ⎬ Float chamber	4	
Z52	512304	**Washer**, plain ⎨ to main body	12	
Z53	514980	**Washer**, spring ⎭	12	
		JET DETAILS		
Z54	517864	**Needle**, metering	2	
Z55	512280	**Screw**, securing metering needle	2	
Z56	512318	**Bushing**, jet orifice	2	
Z57	512319	**Washer**, bushing	2	
Z58	512317	**'O' Ring**, fitted in bushing	2	
Z59	512316	**Washer**, 'O' ring	2	
Z60	512315	**Spring**, jet orifice	2	
Z61	513700	**Orifice**, jet	2	
Z62	512312	**Screw**, bushing retaining, assembly	2	
Z63	512311	**'O' Ring**, bushes retaining screw	2	
Z64	512307	**Screw**, orifice adjusting, assembly	2	
Z65	512308	**'O' Ring**, orifice adjusting screw	2	
		COUPLING DETAILS		
Z66	517867	**Coupling spindle** assembly	1	
Z67	512335	**Coupling** assembly	2	
Z68	512340	**Screw** ⎫	4	
Z69	512339	**Washer** ⎬ Securing coupling to spindle	4	
Z70	512334	**Nut** ⎭	4	
Z71	516987	**Sleeve**, split	1	
Z72	517868	**Tube**, starter connection	1	
		CARBURETTOR ATTACHMENT DETAILS		
Z73	137882	**Washer**, insulating	2	
Z74	137881	**Washer**, joint	4	
Z75	HN2008	**Nut** ⎱ Carburettors	4	
Z76	WL0208	**Washer**, lock ⎰ to manifold	4	
	307471	**PETROL PIPE ASSEMBLY—PUMP TO CARBURETTOR**	1	
	60176	**Nut**, tubing	1	
	102729	**Sleeve**	1	
	138516	**Bracket**, support, pipe to water pump body	1	
	114178	**Grommet**, fitted in support bracket	1	
	138386	**PETROL PIPE ASSEMBLY— CARBURETTOR TO CARBURETTOR**	1	
	120331	**Connection**, flexible, between pipes	3	
	151102	**SUCTION PIPE—CARBURETTOR TO DISTRIBUTOR**	1	
	128262	**Sleeve**, pipe to carburettor and distributor	2	
	100148	**Clip**, suction pipe to rocker cover stud	1	
	138608	**Grommet**, fitted in clip	1	

Note:—Items marked thus † are available on our Factory Exchange Unit Scheme

38 and 39

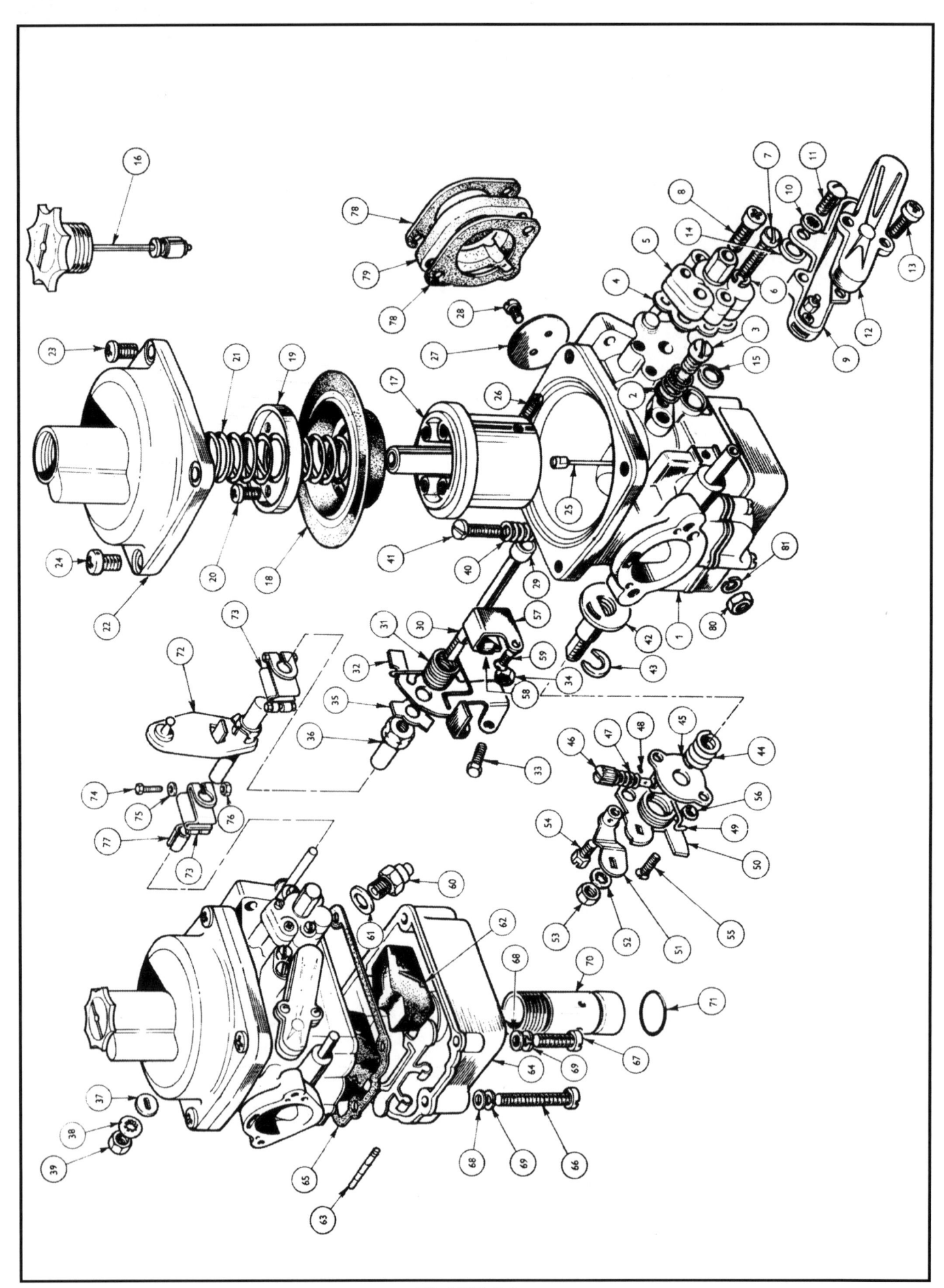

PLATE AA

ENGINE

MARK II (G.T.6+) CARS — U.S.A. ONLY FITTED FROM ENGINE No. KC50001E AND FUTURE

Plate No.	Part No.	Description	No. per Unit	Remarks
	308864	**CARBURETTOR ASSEMBLY, FRONT**	1	
	308865	**CARBURETTOR ASSEMBLY, REAR**	1	
AA1	Not Serviced	**Main body** assembly		
AA2	516976	**Spring,** idler trimming screw	2	
AA3	516975	**Screw,** idler trimming	2	
AA4	517767	**Gasket,** by-pass valve	2	
AA5	517766	**Valve,** by-pass	2	
AA6	514980	**Washer,** lock ⎫ Securing by-pass	6	
AA7	514973	**Screw** ⎭ valve to body	6	
AA8	517765	**Screw,** cover to by-pass body	4	
AA9	517768	**TEMPERATURE COMPENSATOR ASSEMBLY**	2	
AA10	516974	**Washer,** shakeproof ⎫ Securing	4	
AA11	516973	**Screw** ⎭ compensator	4	
AA12	516968	**Cover,** temperature compensator	2	
AA13	516969	**Screw,** securing cover	4	
AA14	516971	**Seal,** large, on compensator body	2	
AA15	516972	**Seal,** small, inside carburettors	2	
AA16	517449	**DAMPER ASSEMBLY**	2	
	516988	**'O' ring,** damper	2	
AA17	Not Serviced	**Air valve and shaft**		
AA18	516984	**Diaphragm**	2	
AA19	Not Serviced	**Ring,** diaphragm retaining		
AA20	517119	**Screw,** securing diaphragm, retaining ring	8	
AA21	516945	**Spring,** air valve return	2	
AA22	Not Serviced	**Cover** assembly, air valve		
AA23	512274	**Screw and spring washer,** securing cover	6	
AA24	517769	**Screw** (drilled for locking) securing cover	2	
AA25	517770	**Needle,** metering	2	
AA26	512280	**Screw,** securing metering needle	2	
		THROTTLE DETAILS		
AA27	513689	**Disc,** throttle	2	
AA28	516952	**Screw,** securing disc to spindle	4	
AA29	516983	**Seal,** throttle spindle	4	
	516985	**Spindle,** throttle, rear carburettor	1	
AA30	516948	**Spindle,** throttle, front carburettor	1	
AA31	516951	**Spring,** throttle return	2	
AA32	516949	**Lever,** throttle stop and fast idle	2	
AA33	516965	**Screw,** fast idle adjustment	2	
AA34	512287	**Locknut,** on screw	2	
AA35	513720	**Washer,** tab ⎫ Front carburettor	1	
AA36	516950	**Nut,** extension ⎭ throttle spindle	1	
AA37	514977	**Washer,** spacing ⎫ Rear carburettor	2	
AA38	513688	**Washer,** shakeproof ⎬ throttle spindle	1	
AA39	513687	**Nut** ⎭	1	
AA40	512282	**Spring,** throttle stop screw	2	
AA41	512281	**Screw,** throttle stop	2	

Note:—Items marked thus † are available on our Factory Exchange Unit Scheme

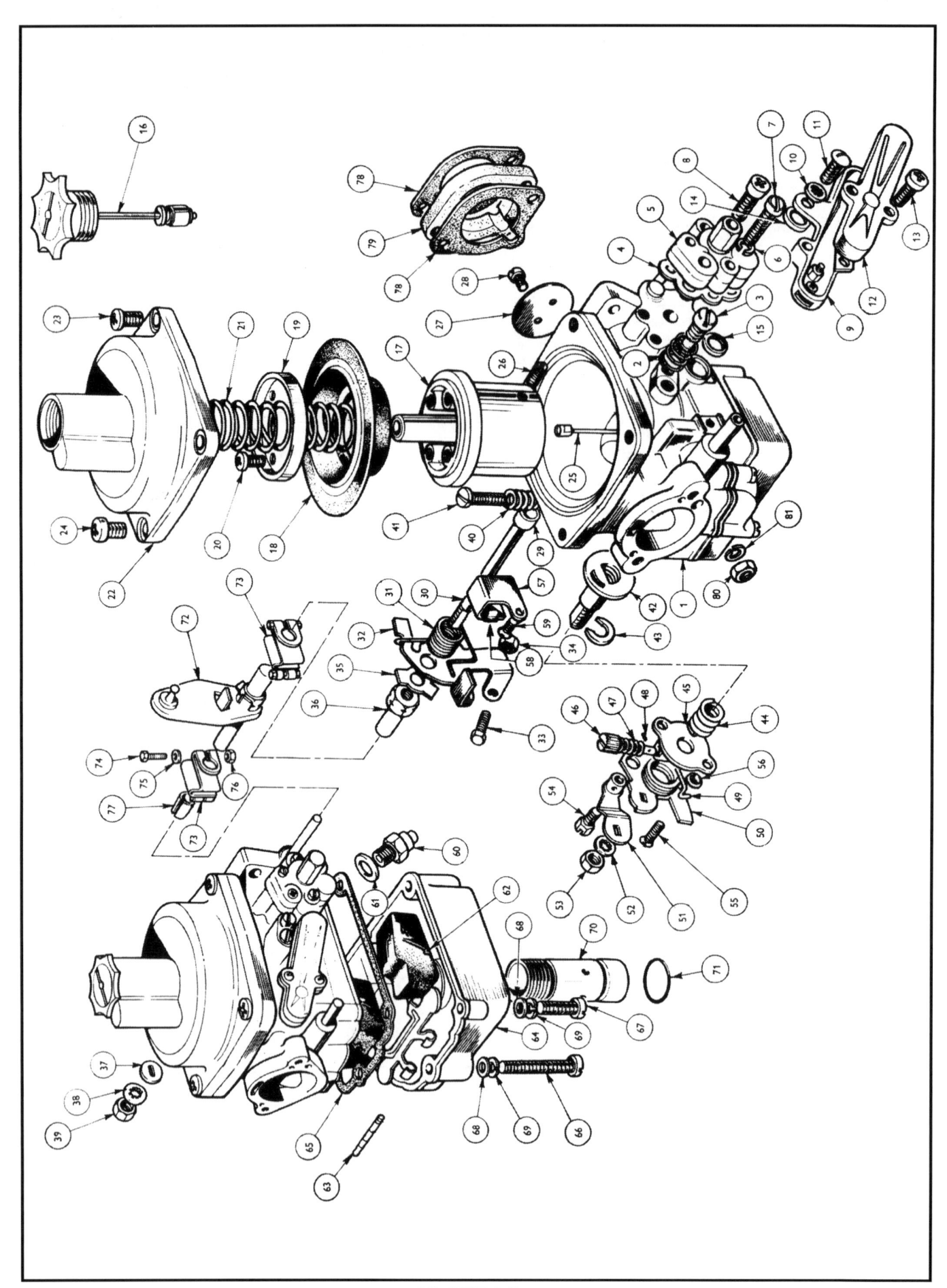

PLATE AA

ENGINE

MARK II (G.T.6+) CARS — U.S.A. ONLY FITTED FROM ENGINE No. KC50001E AND FUTURE

Plate No.	Part No.	Description	No. per Unit	Remarks
		CARBURETTORS—continued		
		STARTER BOX		
AA42	516954	**Spindle,** starter, assembly	2	
AA43	516956	**'C' washer,** on spindle	2	
AA44	516955	**Spring,** starter	2	
AA45	516953	**Cover** assembly, starter	2	
AA46	Not Serviced	**Stop,** adjuster, cam lever	2	
AA47	Not Serviced	**Spring** ⎫ On adjuster	2	
AA48	Not Serviced	**Roll pin** ⎭	2	
AA49	516957	**Spring,** cam lever return	2	
AA50	517764	**Cam lever** assembly	2	
AA51	516959	**Lever,** starter, assembly	2	
AA52	513688	**Washer,** shakeproof ⎫ Securing	2	
AA53	513687	**Nut** ⎭ cam lever	2	
AA54	513723	**Screw,** swivel	2	
AA55	516960	**Screw** ⎫ Securing starter	4	
AA56	516961	**Washer,** shakeproof ⎭ to main body	4	
AA57	516964	**Bracket,** starter control assembly, with clip	2	
AA58	516962	**Clip,** starter control bracket	2	
AA59	516963	**Screw,** securing bracket	2	
		FLOAT DETAILS		
AA60	517453	**Valve,** needle	2	
AA61	516005	**Washer,** needle valve	2	
AA62	516977	**Float and arm**	2	
AA63	517134	**Pin,** float pivot	2	
AA64	516981	**Float chamber**	2	
AA65	516980	**Gasket,** float chamber	2	
AA66	514972	**Screw,** long ⎫	8	
AA67	514973	**Screw,** short ⎬ Float chamber	4	
AA68	512304	**Washer,** plain ⎨ to main body	12	
AA69	514980	**Washer,** spring ⎭	12	
AA70	516979	**Plug** assembly, float chamber sealing	2	
AA71	512311	**'O' ring,** sealing plug	2	
		COUPLING DETAILS		
AA72	516986	**Coupling spindle** assembly	1	
AA73	512335	**Coupling** assembly	2	
AA74	512340	**Screw** ⎫ Securing coupling	4	
AA75	512339	**Washer** ⎬ to	4	
AA76	512334	**Nut** ⎭ spindle	4	
AA77	516987	**Sleeve,** split	1	
		CARBURETTOR ATTACHMENT DETAILS		
AA78	147660	**Washer,** insulating	2	
AA79	147659	**Washer,** joint	4	
AA80	HN2008	**Nut** ⎫ Carburettors	4	
AA81	WL0208	**Washer,** lock ⎭ to manifold	4	

Note:—Items marked thus † are available on our Factory Exchange Unit Scheme

41

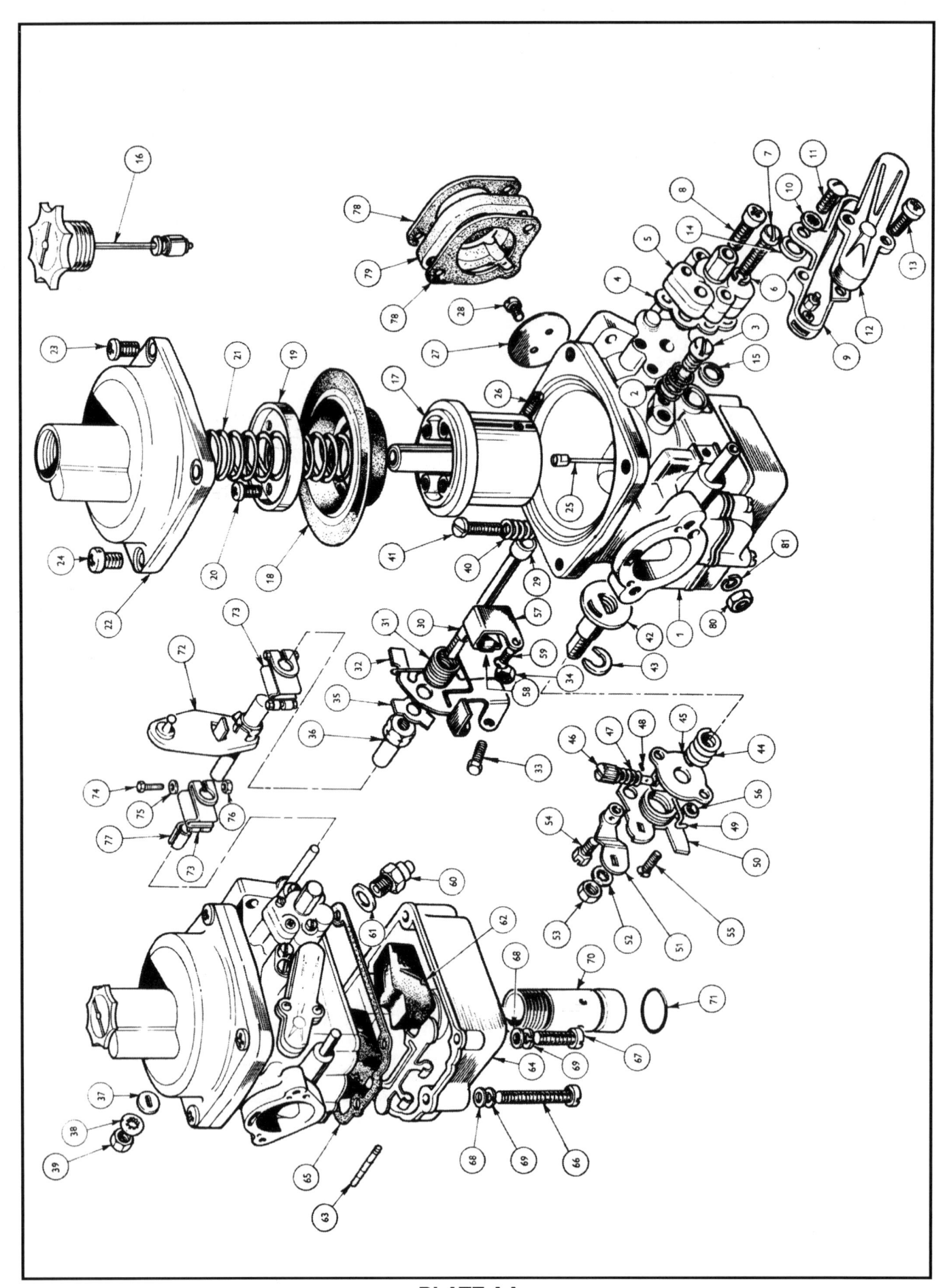

PLATE AA

ENGINE

MARK II (G.T.6+) CARS — U.S.A. ONLY FITTED FROM ENGINE No. KC50001E AND FUTURE

Plate No.	Part No.	Description	No. per Unit	Remarks
		CARBURETTOR SERVICE AND REPAIR KIT		
	516989	**Lubricator pack**	1	
	516990	**Repair kit 'A'**, comprising:-	1	
	516005	**Washer**, needle valve	2	
	512311	**'O' ring**, float chamber plug	2	
	516980	**Gasket**, float chamber	2	
	516991	**Repair kit 'B'**, comprising:-	1	
	516967	**Gasket**, by-pass valve	2	
	516971	**Washer**, sealing	2	
	516972	**Washer**, sealing	2	
	516005	**Washer**, needle valve	2	
	512311	**'O' ring**, sealing plug	2	
	516980	**Gasket**, float chamber	2	
	516983	**Seal**, throttle spindle	2	
	516984	**Diaphragm**	2	
	517453	**Valve**, needle	2	
	516988	**'O' ring**, damper	2	
	307471	**PETROL PIPE ASSEMBLY—PUMP TO CARBURETTOR**	1	
	60176	**Nut**, tubing ⎫ Pipe assembly	1	
	102729	**Sleeve** ⎭ to pump	1	
	138516	**Bracket**, support, pipe to water pump body	1	
	114178	**Grommet**, fitted in support bracket	1	
	138386	**PETROL PIPE ASSEMBLY— CARBURETTOR TO CARBURETTOR**	1	
	120331	**Connection**, flexible, between pipes	3	

Note:- For Carburettor Suction Pipes see page 43

Note:—Items marked thus † are available on our Factory Exchange Unit Scheme

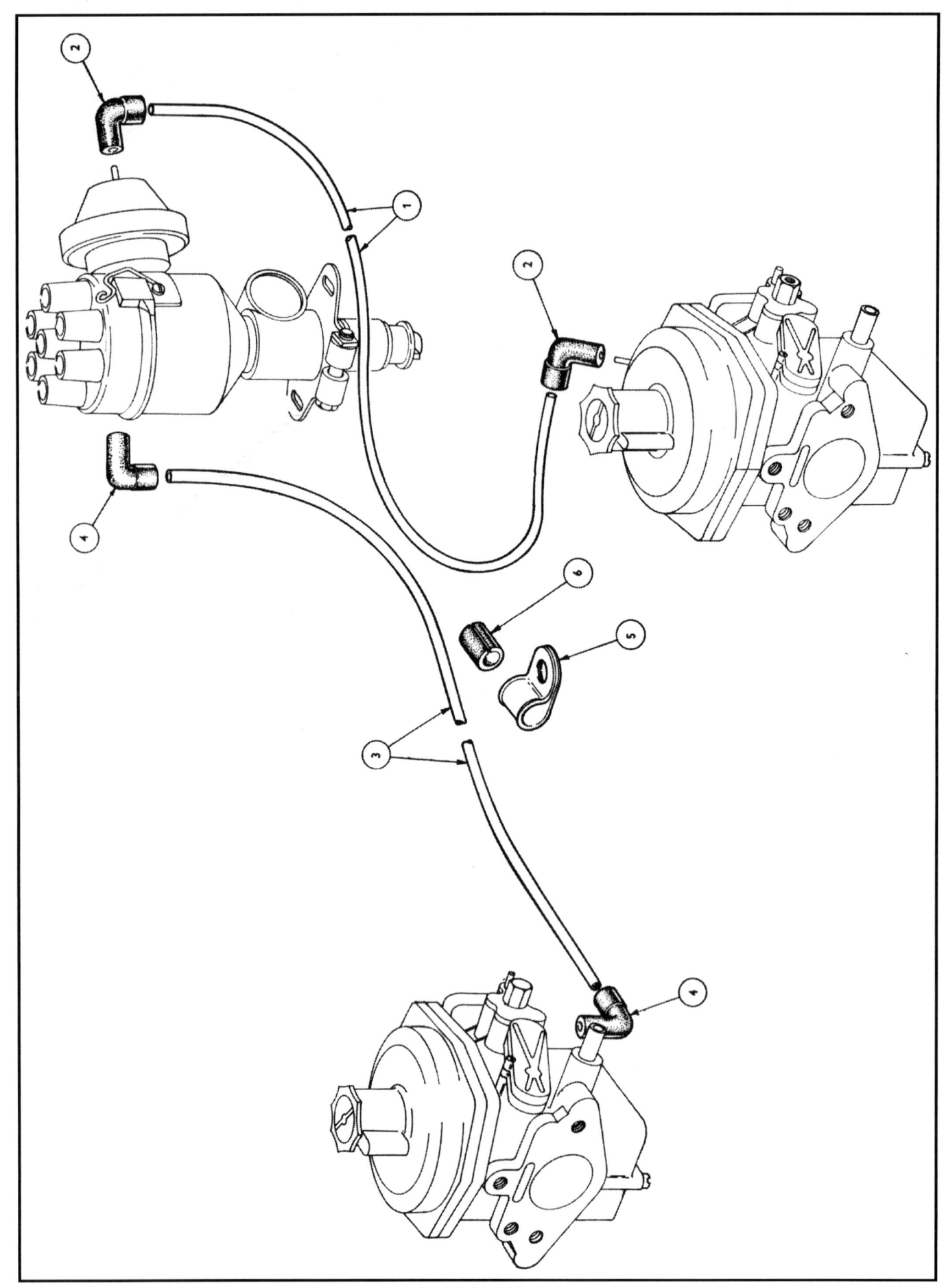

PLATE AB

ENGINE
MARK II (G.T.6+) CARS FITTED FROM ENGINE No. KC/KD50001E AND FUTURE

Plate No.	Part No.	Description	No. per Unit	Remarks

CARBURETTOR SUCTION PIPES
(FITTED TO CARS CONFORMING TO U.S.A. ANTI-AIR POLLUTION REGULATIONS)

Plate No.	Part No.	Description	No. per Unit
AB1	151101	**Pipe,** suction, front carburettor to distributor (Advance)	1
AB2	128262	**Sleeve,** pipe, to front carburettor and distributor (Advance)	2
AB3	151102	**Pipe,** suction, rear carburettor to distributor (Retard)	1
AB4	128262	**Sleeve,** pipe to rear carburettor and distributor (Retard)	2
AB5	100148	**Clip,** suction pipes to rocker cover centre stud	1
AB6	138608	**Grommet**	1

Note:—Items marked thus † are available on our Factory Exchange Unit Scheme

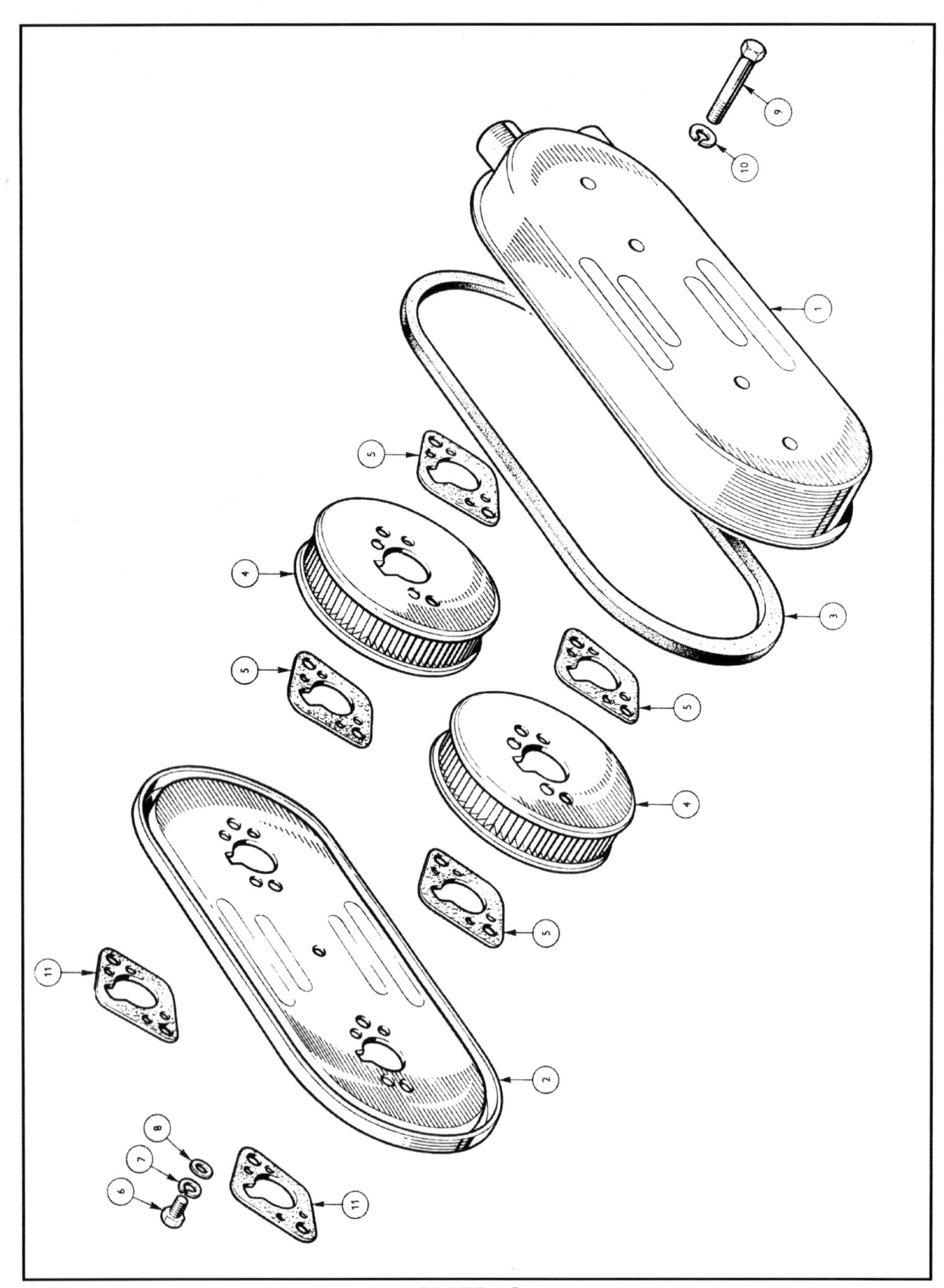

PLATE AC

ENGINE

MARK II (G.T.6+) CARS FITTED FROM ENGINE No. KC/KD50001E AND FUTURE

Plate No.	Part No.	Description	No. per Unit	Remarks
	215496	**AIR CLEANER AND SILENCER ASSEMBLY**	1	
AC1	215497	**Cover**, front, and silencer assembly	1	
AC2	214413	**Plate**, back, assembly	1	
AC3	138311	**Strip**, sealing	1	
AC4	214415	**Element**, filter	2	
AC5	148006	**Gasket**, between element, back plate and cover	4	
AC6	HU0704	**Screw**, set ⎫	1	
AC7	WL0207	**Washer**, lock ⎬ Front cover to back plate	1	
AC8	WP0007	**Washer**, plain ⎭	1	
AC9	HB0867	**Bolt** ⎫	4	
AC10	WL0208	**Washer**, lock ⎬ Air cleaner to carburettor	4	
AC11	148006	**Gasket** ⎭	2	

Note:—Items marked thus † are available on our Factory Exchange Unit Scheme

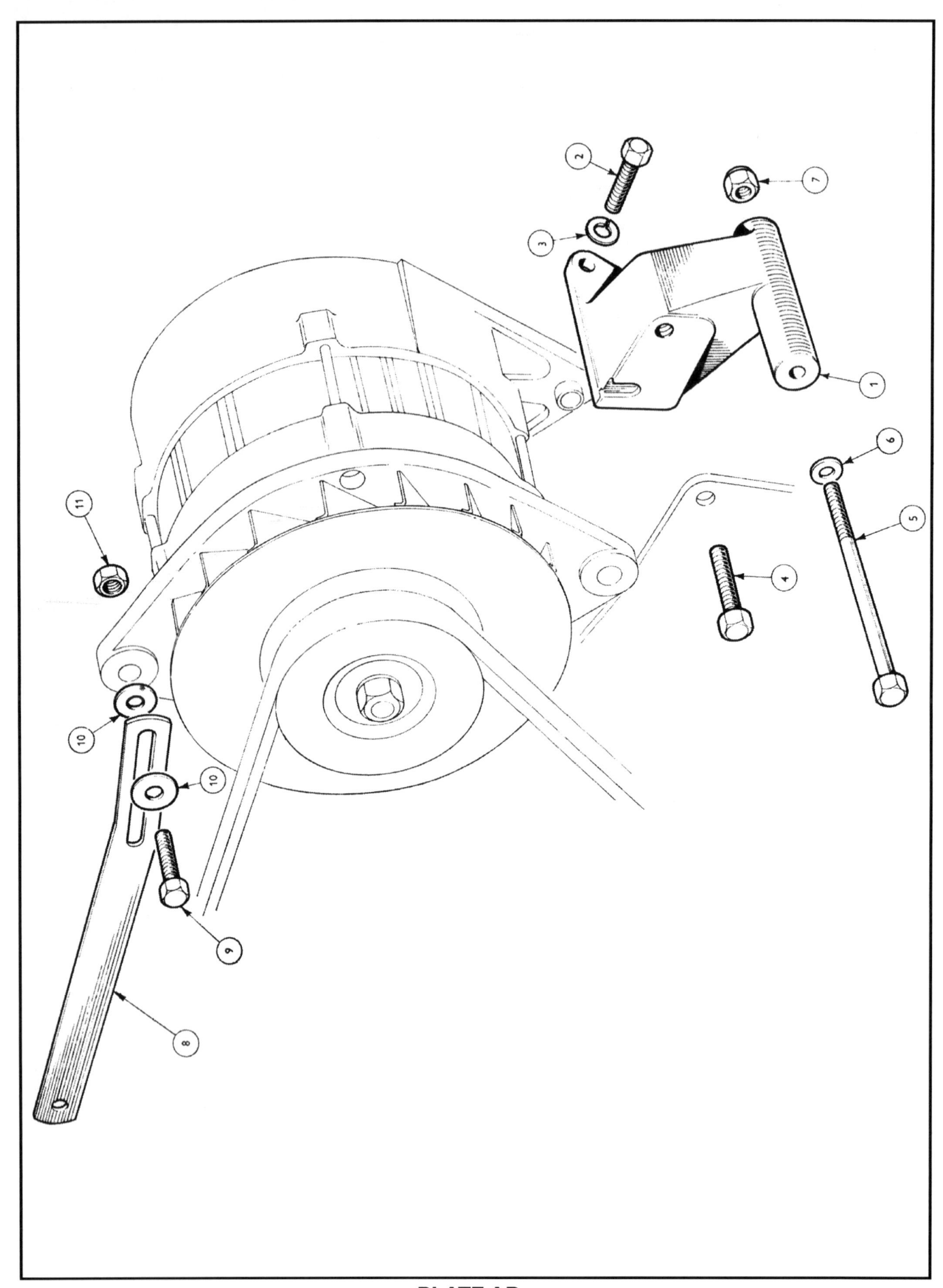

PLATE AD

ENGINE

MARK II (G.T.6+) CARS FITTED FROM ENGINE No. KC/KD50001E AND FUTURE

Plate No.	Part No.	Description	No. per Unit	Remarks
		ALTERNATOR MOUNTING DETAILS		
		Alternator—For Details see Electrical Section.		
AD1	214268	**Bracket**, alternator mounting	1	
AD2	HU0808	**Screw**, set ⎱ Alternator mounting bracket	2	
AD3	WL0208	**Washer**, lock ⎰ to cylinder block	2	
AD4	HU1108	**Screw**, set, alternator bracket to engine plate	1	
AD5	HB0839	**Bolt** ⎫	1	
AD6	WP0139	**Washer**, plain ⎬ Alternator to mounting bracket	1	
AD7	143802	**Nut**, "Cleveloc" ⎭	1	
AD8	150340	**Link**, adjusting, alternator	1	
AD9	HU0857	**Setscrew** ⎫	1	
AD10	WP0017	**Washer**, plain ⎬ Alternator to adjusting link	2	
AD11	JN2158	**Nut**, jam ⎭	1	
		IGNITION		
	128404	**Plug**, sparking	6	
	148957	**Plug**, sparking	6	U.S.A. and Special Order
		H.T. LEADS		
	150550	**Engine lead assembly, No. 1**	1	
	150551	**Engine lead assembly, No. 2**	1	
	150552	**Engine lead assembly, No. 3**	1	
	150553	**Engine lead assembly, No. 4**	1	
	150554	**Engine lead assembly, No. 5**	1	
	150555	**Engine lead assembly, No. 6**	1	
	146113	**Engine lead, coil to distributor**	1	
	517342	**Engine lead kit**	1	⎫
	150038	Engine lead assembly, No. 1	1	⎪
	150030	Engine lead assembly, No. 2	1	⎪
	150031	Engine lead assembly, No. 3	1	⎬ France only
	150039	Engine lead assembly, Nos. 4 and 5	2	⎪
	150032	Engine lead assembly, No. 6	1	⎪
	150052	Engine lead, coil to distributor	1	⎭

Note:—Items marked thus † are available on our Factory Exchange Unit Scheme

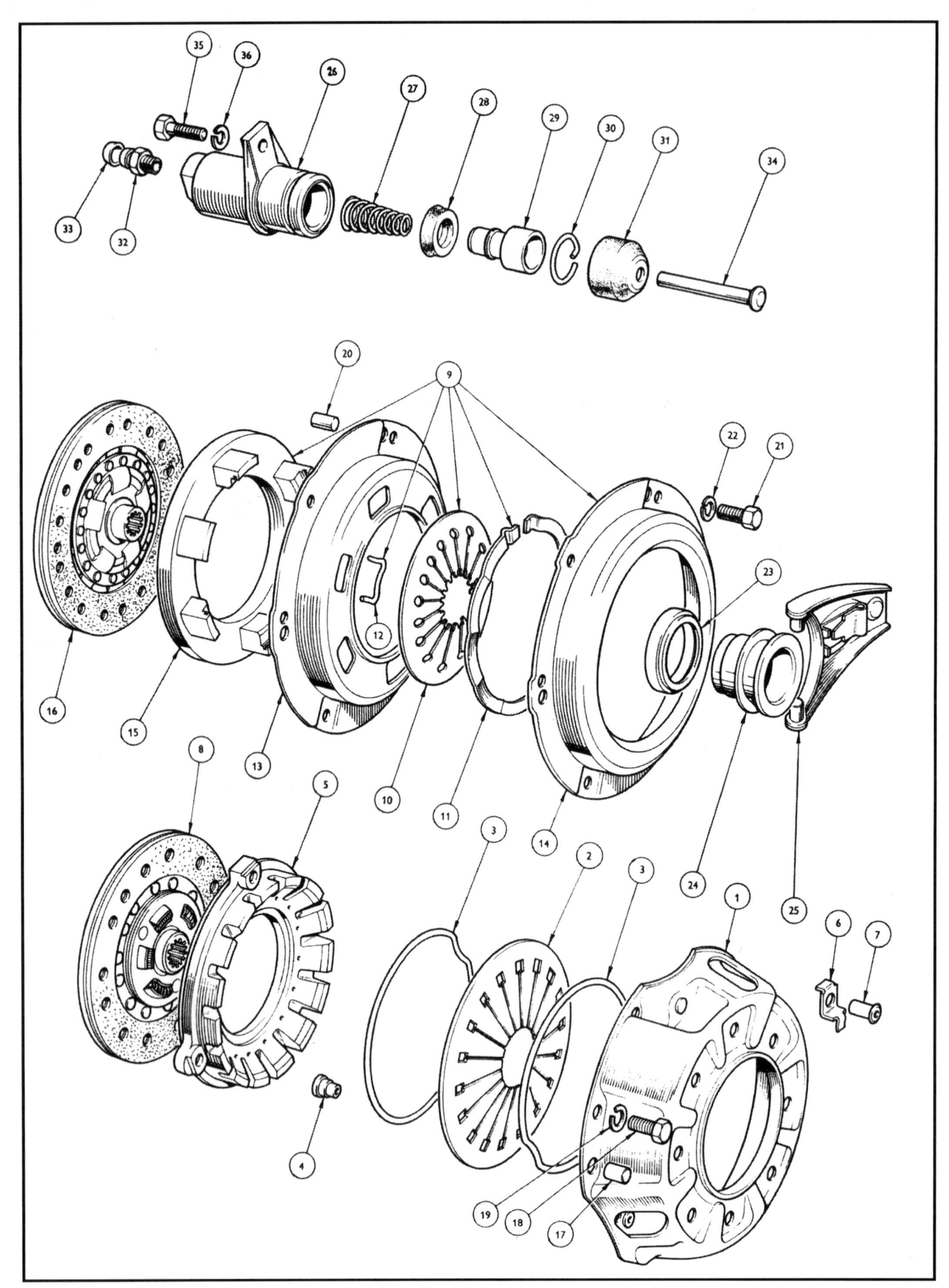

PLATE AE

172

CLUTCH

Plate No.	Part No.	Description	No. per Unit	Remarks
	213501	†CLUTCH COVER ASSEMBLY (BORG & BECK)	1	
AE1	515635	Cover and straps, sub-assembly	1	
AE2	515633	Spring, diaphragm	1	
AE3	515638	Ring, diaphragm spring fulcrum	2	
AE4	515634	Rivet, shouldered, diaphragm spring and fulcrum ring to cover	9	Export only
AE5	515636	Plate, pressure	1	
AE6	515637	Clip, retaining diaphragm spring on pressure plate	3	
AE7	514735	Rivet, clip and strap to pressure plate	3	
	Not Serviced	Weight, balance, clutch cover		
	Not Serviced	Rivet, balance weight to cover		
AE8	145968	DRIVEN PLATE ASSEMBLY (BORG & BECK)	1	
	515640	Facing package	1	
AE9	211146	†CLUTCH COVER ASSEMBLY (LAYCOCK)	1	
AE10	141244	Spring, diaphragm	1	
AE11	512343	Ring, retaining	1	
AE12	512344	Clip, spring	2	
AE13	Not Serviced	Cover, inner	1	
AE14	Not Serviced	Cover, outer	1	
AE15	Not Serviced	Plate, pressure	1	
AE16	150987	DRIVEN PLATE ASSEMBLY (LAYCOCK)	1	
AE17	DP0407	Dowel, locating clutch cover on flywheel	3	Used with Borg & Beck clutches only
AE18	HU0856	Screw, set, clutch cover to flywheel	6	
AE19	WL0208	Washer, lock, on setscrew	6	
AE20	DP0411	Dowel, locating clutch cover on flywheel	3	Used with Laycock clutches only
AE21	HU0857	Screw, set, clutch cover to flywheel	6	
AE22	WL0208	Washer, lock, on setscrew	6	
AE23	141357	CLUTCH THROWOUT BEARING	1	
AE24	143707	Sleeve, clutch throw-out	1	
AE25	132080	CLUTCH OPERATING LEVER ASSEMBLY	1	
	516788	CLUTCH SLAVE CYLINDER ASSEMBLY (Less Push Rod)	1	
AE26	Not Serviced	Body, slave cylinder	1	
AE27	106084	Spring, between body and piston	1	
AE28	516789	Seal, piston	1	
AE29	504848	Piston	1	
AE30	504850	Circlip, retaining piston in body	1	
AE31	516790	Boot, rubber, over end of body	1	
AE32	108756	Screw, bleed, cylinder body	1	
AE33	105676	Cover, dust, over bleed screw	1	
AE34	132239	Rod, push, slave cylinder	1	
AE35	HU0807	Screw, set — Slave cylinder to gearbox casing	2	
AE36	WL0208	Washer, lock — Slave cylinder to gearbox casing	2	
	505704	Service kit, slave cylinder	1	

Note:—Items marked thus † are available on our Factory Exchange Unit Scheme

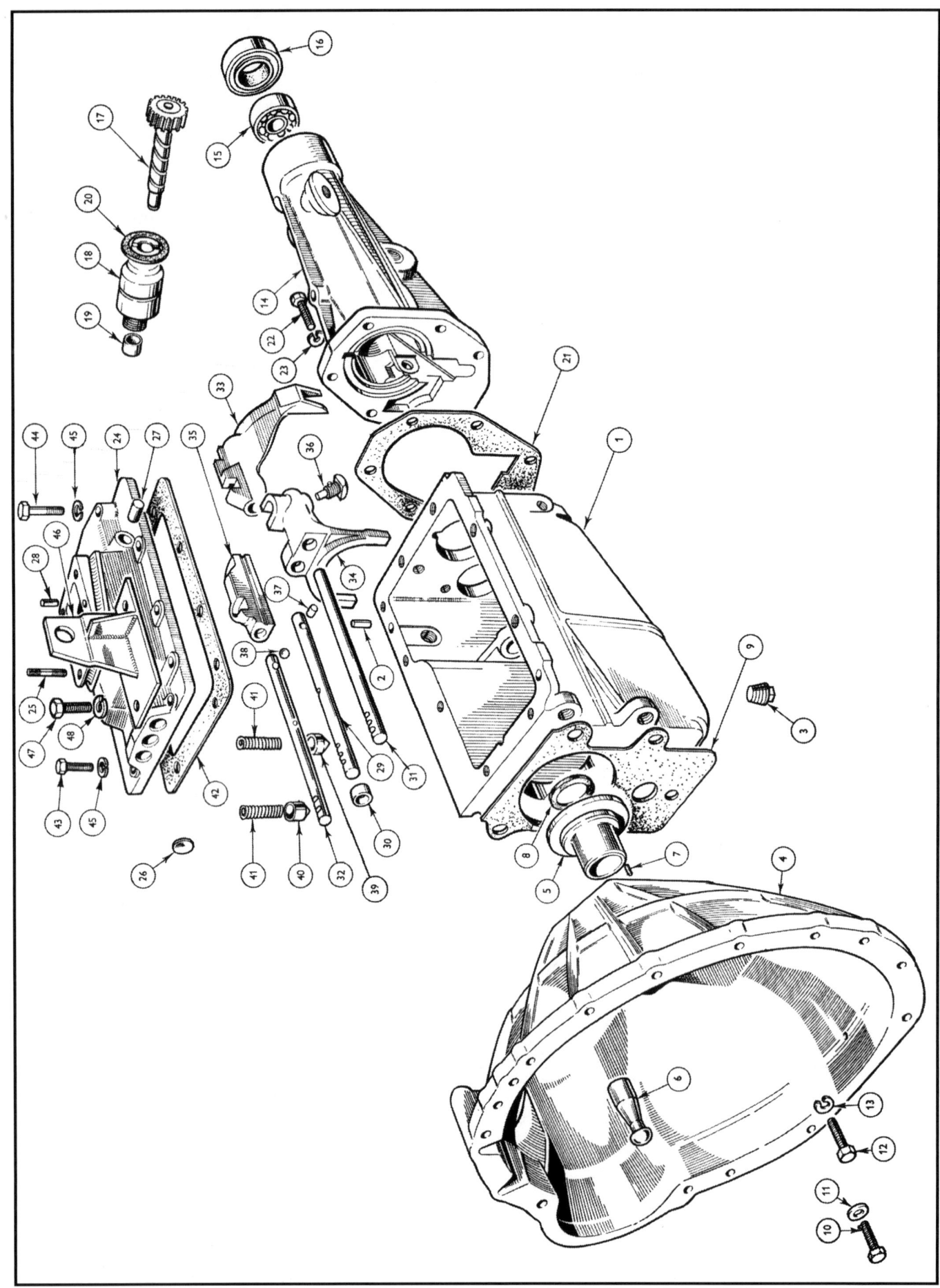

PLATE AF

GEARBOX

Plate No.	Part No.	Description	No. per Unit	Remarks	
	515450	†GEARBOX ASSEMBLY	1		Fitted up to Gearbox No. KC3761 only
	515452	†GEARBOX ASSEMBLY	1	Only required when Overdrive is fitted	
	515741	†GEARBOX ASSEMBLY (Reconditioned Unit)	1		
	515742	†GEARBOX ASSEMBLY (Reconditioned Unit)	1	Only required when Overdrive is fitted	
	516110	†GEARBOX ASSEMBLY	1		Fitted from Gearbox No. KC3762 and future
	516111	†GEARBOX ASSEMBLY	1	Only required when Overdrive is fitted	
	516112	†GEARBOX ASSEMBLY (Reconditioned Unit)	1		
	516113	†GEARBOX ASSEMBLY (Reconditioned Unit)	1	Only required when Overdrive is fitted	

The above assemblies are less Top Cover Extension and Hand Lever Assembly.

Plate No.	Part No.	Description	No. per Unit
AF1	306468	**GEARBOX CASE**	1
AF2	DP0411	**Dowel,** top cover locating	2
AF3	114774	**Plug,** oil level and drain	2
AF4	132077	**CLUTCH HOUSING AND FRONT END COVER ASSEMBLY**	1
AF5	132078	**Cover,** front end	1
AF6	132079	**Pin,** fulcrum	1
AF7	DP0205	**Dowel,** front end cover to clutch housing	1
AF8	132292	**Seal,** oil, front end cover	1
AF9	122569	**Washer,** paper ⎫	1
AF10	509860	**Bolt,** wedglok ⎪	1
AF11	500464	**Washer,** copper ⎬ Clutch housing to gearbox case	1
AF12	HU0908	**Bolt** ⎪	4
AF13	WL0209	**Washer,** lock ⎭	4
AF14	209590	**GEARBOX EXTENSION ASSEMBLY**	1
	119096	**Bearing,** end thrust, speedo drive shaft	1
AF15	117511	**Bearing,** mainshaft, in end of extension	1
AF16	117510	**Seal,** oil, extension end	1
AF17	119100	**Gear,** speedo driven, assembly	1
AF18	144621	**Bearing,** speedo, assembly	1
AF19	108757	**Seal,** oil	1
AF20	119099	**'O' ring**	2
	56305	**Screw,** locking ⎫ Speedo driven gear	1
	WL0208	**Washer,** lock ⎭ to gearbox extension	1
AF21	106437	**Gasket** (Paper) ⎫	1
AF22	HU0807	**Screw,** set ⎬ Extension to gearbox	7
AF23	WL0208	**Washer,** lock ⎭	7

Note:—Items marked thus † are available on our Factory Exchange Unit Scheme

47

175

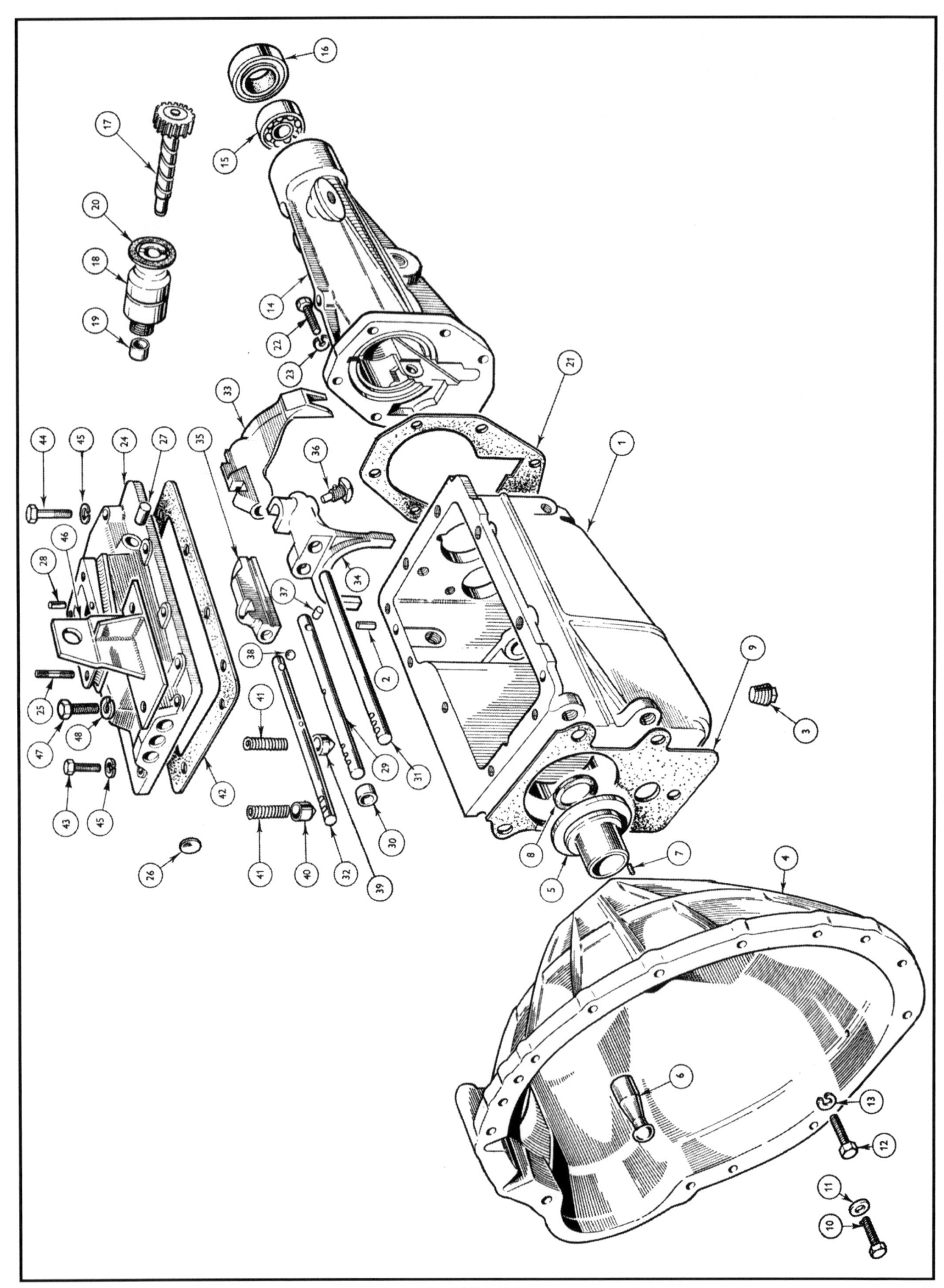

PLATE AF

GEARBOX

Plate No.	Part No.	Description	No. per Unit	Remarks
	515979	**TOP COVER ASSEMBLY**	1	Fitted up to Gearbox No. KC3761 only
	516099	**TOP COVER ASSEMBLY**	1	Fitted from Gearbox No. KC3762 and future
AF24	134761	**Cover**, top, sub-assembly	1	Fitted up to Gearbox No. KC3761 only
	147775	**Cover**, top, sub-assembly	1	Fitted from Gearbox No. KC3762 and future
AF25	106957	**Stud**, extension attachment	4	
AF26	104449	**Plug**, core, selector shaft holes	6	
AF27	107099	**Plug**, interlock hole	1	
AF28	DP0411	**Dowel**, top cover extension	2	
AF29	146240	**Shaft**, selector, 1st/2nd	1	
AF30	146241	**Sleeve**, 1st/2nd selector shaft	1	
AF31	108021	**Shaft**, selector, 3rd/Top	1	
AF32	147395	**Shaft**, selector, reverse actuator	1	
AF33	113868	**Fork**, selector, 1st/2nd	1	
AF34	106268	**Fork**, selector, 3rd/Top	1	
AF35	147394	**Actuator**, reverse gear	1	
AF36	122653	**Screw**, set, wedglok, selector to shafts	3	
AF37	106478	**Pin**, interlock ⎫ Fitted in top cover	1	
AF38	BL0020	**Ball**, interlock ⎭	2	
AF39	106481	**Plunger**, selector shafts (Forward) ⎫ Fitted	2	
AF40	136990	**Plunger**, selector shafts (Reverse) ⎬ in	1	
AF41	106489	**Spring**, plunger ⎭ top cover	3	
AF42	106269	**Washer**, joint ⎫	1	⎫
AF43	HU0707	**Screw**, set, short ⎬ Top cover to	5	⎬
AF44	HB0711	**Bolt**, long ⎬ gearbox casing	2	⎬ Fitted up to
AF45	WL0207	**Washer**, lock ⎭	7	⎬ Gearbox No.
AF46	126746	**Bracket**, reverse light switch	1	⎬ KC3761 only
AF47	HU0708	**Screw**, set ⎫ Reverse light switch bracket	2	⎬
AF48	WL0207	**Washer**, lock ⎭ and top cover to gearbox casing	2	⎭
	106269	**Washer**, joint ⎫	1	⎫
	HU0707	**Screw**, set, short ⎬ Top cover to	7	⎬ Fitted from Gearbox No.
	HB0711	**Bolt**, long ⎬ gearbox casing	2	⎬ KC3762 and future
	WL0207	**Washer**, lock ⎭	9	⎭
	147374	**Rivet**, blanking breather hole in gearbox top cover	1	Must be used when Overdrive is fitted

GEARBOX ATTACHMENT DETAILS

	HN2008	**Nut** ⎫	12	
	WL0208	**Washer**, lock ⎬	12	
	HB0812	**Bolt** ⎬ Gearbox to rear	9	
	HN2009	**Nut** ⎬ engine plate and engine	1	
	WL0209	**Washer**, lock ⎬	1	
	132872	**Bolt**, dowel ⎭	1	

Note:—Items marked thus † are available on our Factory Exchange Unit Scheme

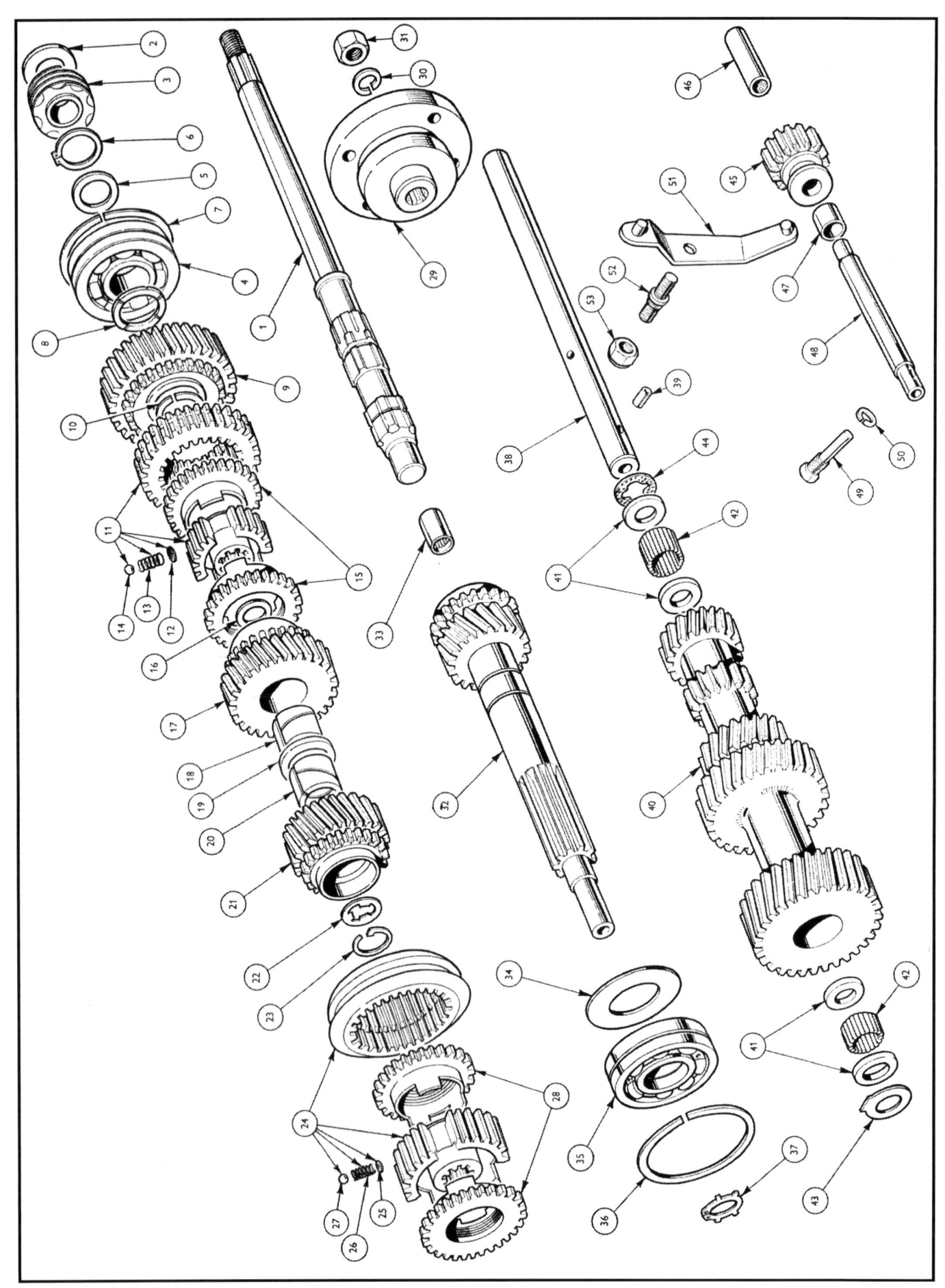

PLATE AG

GEARBOX

Plate No.	Part No.	Description	No. per Unit	Remarks
	213018	**MAINSHAFT**	1	
AG1	213561	**MAINSHAFT**	1	Only required when Overdrive is fitted
AG2	117509	**Washer,** end of mainshaft	1	
AG3	119131	**Gear,** speedo driving	1	
AG4	104433	**Bearing,** ball, mainshaft centre	1	
AG5	143289	**Washer,** ·093″/·091″ thick ⎤	A/R	
AG5	143290	**Washer,** ·096″/·094″ thick ⎬ Between centre bearing	A/R	
AG5	143291	**Washer,** ·099″/·097″ thick ⎨ and circlip	A/R	
AG5	143292	**Washer,** ·102″/·100″ thick ⎦	A/R	
AG6	500872	**Circlip,** retaining bearing on mainshaft	1	
AG7	112654	**Ring,** snap, retaining bearing in casing	1	
AG8	137775	**Washer,** between centre bearing and 1st gear	1	
AG9	144627	**Gear,** 1st speed	1	
AG10	137834	**Collar,** split, 1st speed gear	2 halves	
AG11	515377	**Sleeve** assembly, synchro and operating, 1st/2nd and reverse gears	1	
AG12	37948	**Shim,** under synchro spring	A/R	
AG13	106388	**Spring,** synchro sleeve	3	
AG14	BL0016	**Ball,** synchro	3	
AG15	148409	**Cup,** synchro, 1st and 2nd gears	2	
AG16	106262	**Washer,** mainshaft, between 1st speed sleeve and 2nd gear	1	
AG17	137615	**Gear,** 2nd speed	1	
AG18	147354	**Bush,** 2nd speed gear	1	
AG19	111422	**Washer,** thrust ⎤ Fitted between	1	⎤
	149963	**Washer,** thrust ⎬ 2nd and 3rd	1	⎬ Alternatives
	131843	**Washer,** thrust ⎦ speed gears	1	⎦
AG20	147354	**Bush,** 3rd speed gear	1	
AG21	132097	**Gear,** 3rd speed	1	
AG22	140727	**Washer** ⎤ 3rd speed gear	1	
AG23	112394	**Circlip** ⎦ to mainshaft	1	
AG24	509651	**Sleeve** assembly, synchro and operating, 3rd and Top gears	1	
AG25	37948	**Shim,** under spring	A/R	
AG26	104445	**Spring,** synchro sleeve	3	
AG27	BL0016	**Ball,** synchro	3	
AG28	113797	**Cup,** synchro, 3rd and Top gears	2	
AG29	144690	**FLANGE & STONEGUARD—MAINSHAFT**	1	
AG30	WQ0312	**Washer,** lock ⎤ Flange to mainshaft	1	
AG31	HN2012	**Nut** ⎦	1	
AG32	213113	**CONSTANT PINION SHAFT**	1	
AG33	144782	**Bearing,** needle roller	1	
AG34	106365	**Flinger,** oil, fitted on constant pinion shaft	1	
AG35	104433	**Bearing,** ball	1	
AG36	112654	**Ring,** snap, retaining bearing in casing	1	
AG37	129839	**Circlip,** retaining bearing on constant pinion shaft	1	

Note:—Items marked thus † are available on our Factory Exchange Unit Scheme

PLATE AG

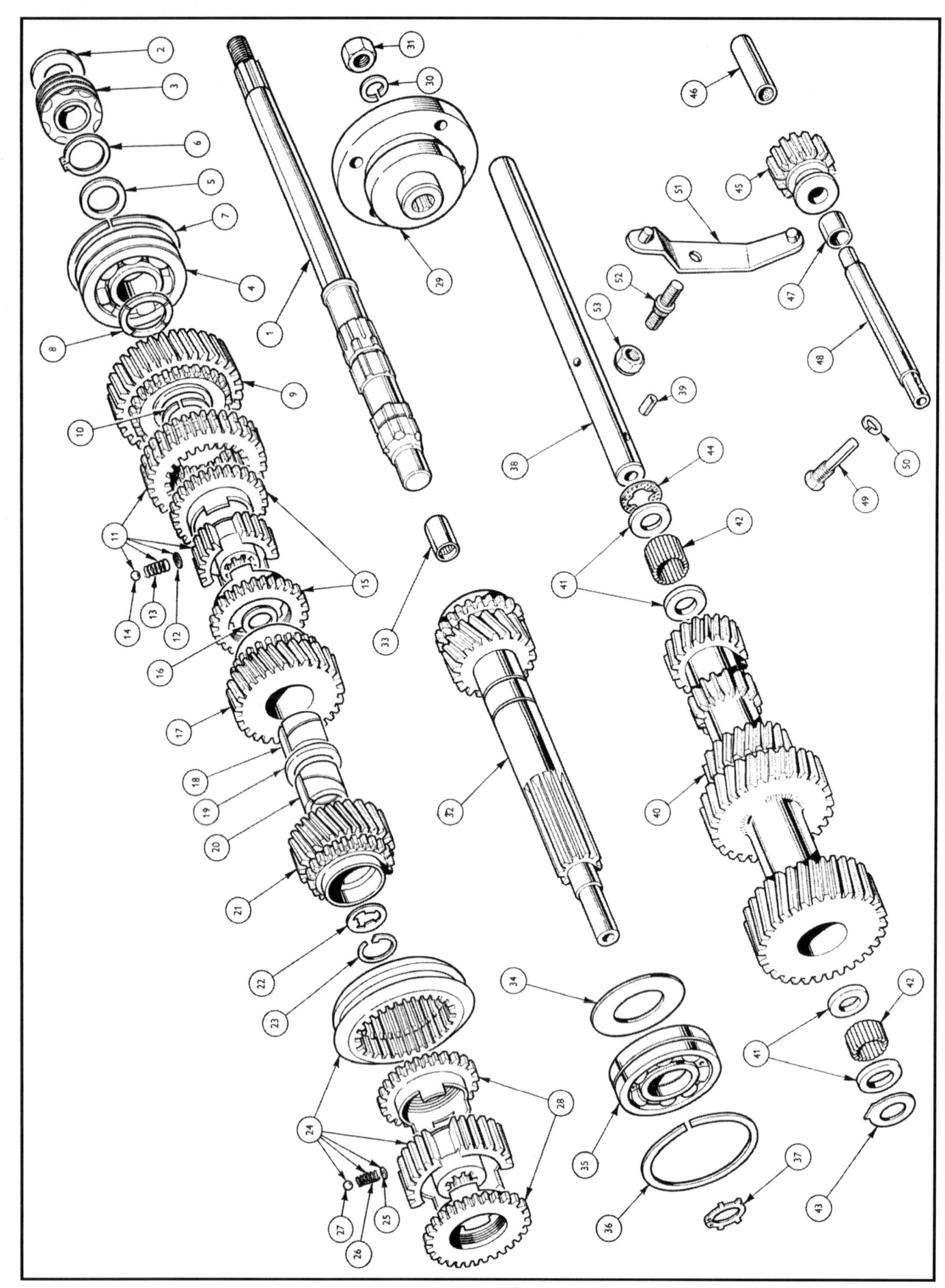

GEARBOX

Plate No.	Part No.	Description	No. per Unit	Remarks
AG38	144595	**COUNTERSHAFT**	1	
AG39	DS1908	**Dowel,** spring tension, countershaft locating	1	
AG40	212993	**Gear cluster**	1	
AG41	119891	**Ring,** retaining, needle rollers	4	
AG42	119893	**Roller,** needle	50	
AG43	113229	**Washer,** thrust, front of countershaft	1	
AG44	106270	**Washer,** thrust, rear of countershaft	1	
	137532	**Spring,** countershaft gear cluster	3	Fitted from Gearbox No. KC57 and future
AG45	144580	**REVERSE IDLER GEAR ASSEMBLY**	1	
AG46	104420	**Bush,** in reverse idler gear	1	
AG47	137687	**Piece,** distance, reverse idler gear	1	
AG48	113071	**Spindle,** reverse idler gear	1	
AG49	106477	**Screw** } Locating spindle in casing	1	
AG50	WL0208	**Washer,** lock }	1	
AG51	106254	**REVERSE OPERATING LEVER ASSEMBLY**	1	
AG52	106448	**Fulcrum,** reverse operating lever	1	
AG53	TN3209	**Nut,** nyloc, fulcrum to gearbox	1	

Note:—Items marked thus † are available on our Factory Exchange Unit Scheme

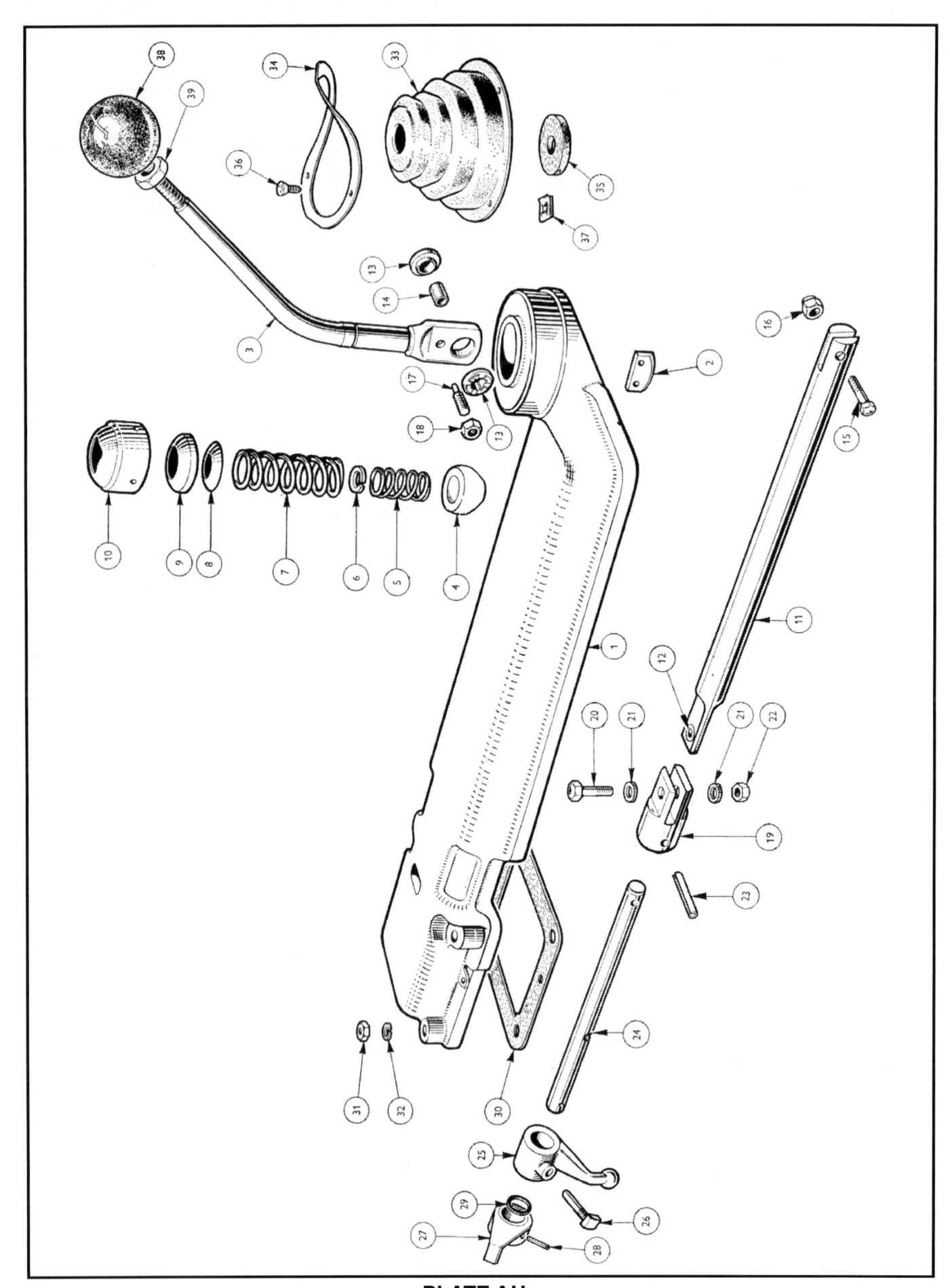

PLATE AH

GEAR SHIFT MECHANISM

Plate No.	Part No.	Description	No. per No.	Remarks
	515379	**TOP COVER EXTENSION AND HAND LEVER ASSEMBLY**	1	Fitted up to Gearbox No. KC3761 only
	516100	**TOP COVER EXTENSION AND HAND LEVER ASSEMBLY**	1	Fitted from Gearbox No. KC3762 and future
	515517	**TOP COVER EXTENSION AND HAND LEVER ASSEMBLY** (OVERDRIVE CONDITION)	1	

Note:— To convert 515379 to 515517 (Overdrive Condition) remove Operating Arm, Part No. 126750, and replace it with 133771.
To convert 516100 to 515517 (Overdrive Condition) replace Gear Lever Shaft 118041 by 127740 and replace Operating Arm 127650 by 133771.

Plate No.	Part No.	Description	No. per No.	Remarks
AH1	306152	**Extension**, top cover	1	
AH2	120307	**Plate**, reverse baulk	1	
	TK4503	**Screw**, baulk plate attachment	2	} Alternative fitment
	RF2607	**Rivet**, baulk plate attachment	2	
AH3	146906	**Lever**, hand, assembly	1	
AH4	138685	**Bush**, spherical	1	
AH5	119252	**Spring**, reverse baulk	1	
AH6	119263	**Circlip**, retaining spring on lever	1	
AH7	119251	**Spring**, cap retainer	1	
AH8	128373	**Washer**, dished, inner	1	
AH9	119573	**Washer**, dished, outer	1	
AH10	126607	**Cap**, top cover extension	1	
	126754	**Dowel**, cap to top cover extension	2	
AH11	129952	**Shaft**, operating assembly	1	
AH12	119262	**Bush**, operating shaft	1	
AH13	138686	**Bush**, hand lever	2	
	146303	**Washer**, plain, hand lever to operating shaft	2	
AH14	129119	**Sleeve**, pinch, in hand lever	1	
AH15	125054	**Bolt** ⎱ Operating shaft	1	
AH16	TN3207	**Nut**, nyloc ⎰ to hand lever	1	
AH17	118054	**Screw**, reverse stop, attached to hand lever	1	
AH18	JN2108	**Nut**, jam, locking screw	1	
AH19	127741	**Coupling**, gear lever shaft	1	
AH20	HB0709	**Bolt** ⎱	1	
AH21	147474	**Washer**, alum ⎬ Coupling to operating shaft	2	
AH22	TN3207	**Nut**, nyloc ⎰	1	
AH23	DS2516	**Dowel**, coupling to gear lever shaft	1	
AH24	127740	**Shaft**, gear lever	1	Fitted up to Gearbox No. KC3761 only
	118041	**Shaft**, gear lever	1	Fitted from Gearbox No. KC3762 and future
AH25	118040	**Lever**, gear, internal	1	
AH26	122653	**Screw**, set, taper (Wedglok), gear lever to shaft	1	
AH27	126750	**Arm** assembly, reverse switch operating	1	Fitted up to Gearbox No. KC3761 only
	133771	**Arm** assembly, reverse switch and overdrive switch operating	1	For use with Overdrive only
AH28	52413	**Pin**, Mills, arm to gear lever shaft	1	
AH29	118053	**Seal**, oil, gear lever shaft	2	

Note:—Items marked thus † are available on our Factory Exchange Unit Scheme

51

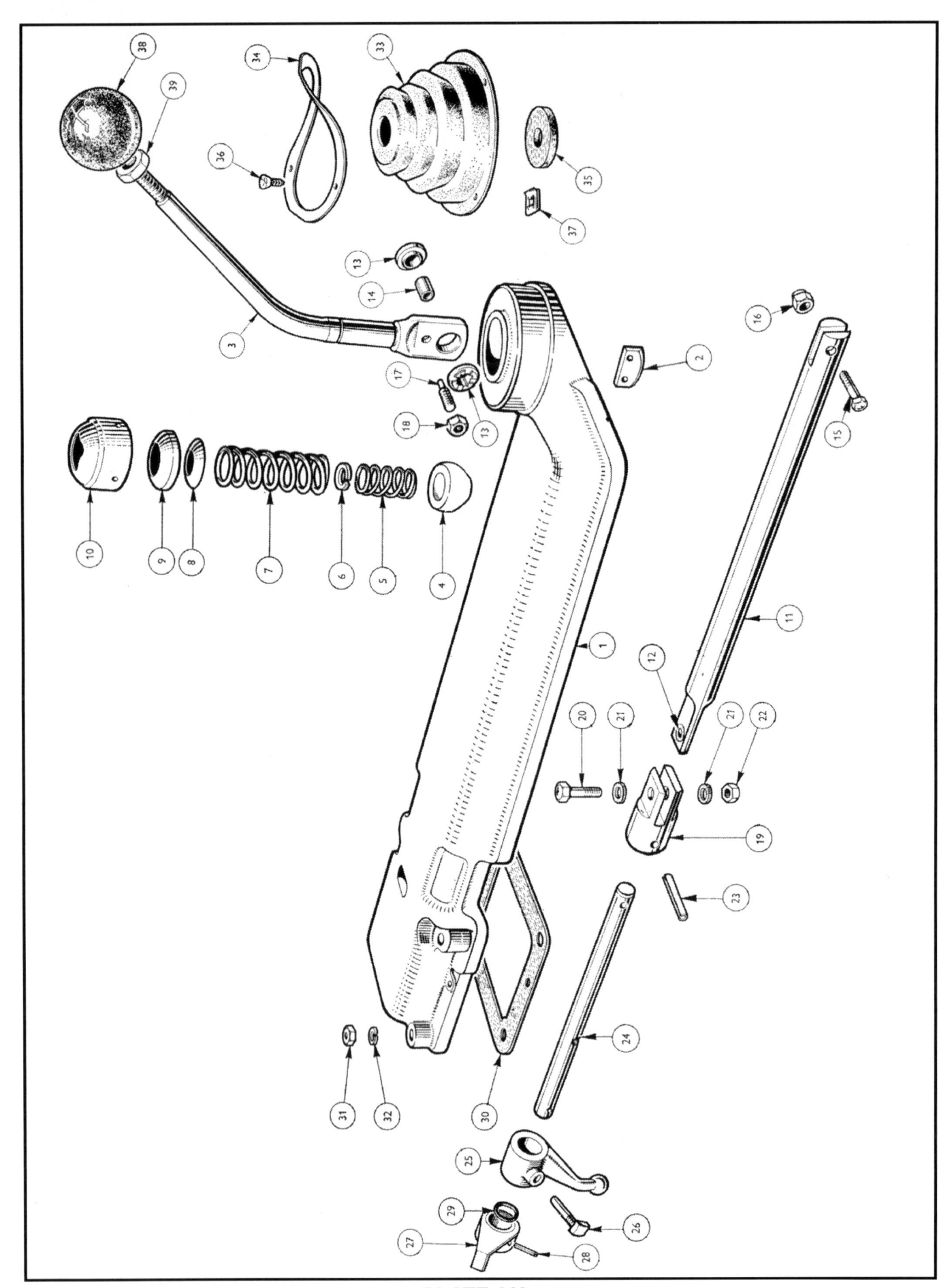

PLATE AH

GEAR SHIFT MECHANISM

Plate No.	Part No.	Description	No. per Unit	Remarks
		TOP COVER EXTENSION AND HAND LEVER ASSEMBLY—continued		
AH30	120305	**Washer**, joint ⎫ Top cover extension and	1	
AH31	HN2008	**Nut** ⎬ hand lever assembly	4	
AH32	WL0208	**Washer**, lock ⎭ to top cover	4	
AH33	710820	**Grommet**, gear lever, fitted to floor	1	
AH34	613607	**Ring**, retaining, gear lever grommet	1	
AH35	611177	**Washer**, rubber, gear lever	1	
AH36	YZ3405	**Screw**, self tapping ⎫ Retaining ring and grommet	4	
AH37	FU2569/4	**Nut**, fix ⎭ to gearbox cover	4	
AH38	144095	**Knob**, gear lever	1	
	150383	**Knob**, gear lever	1	U.S.A. only
AH39	506157	**Nut**, locking knob on lever	1	

Note:—Items marked thus † are available on our Factory Exchange Unit Scheme

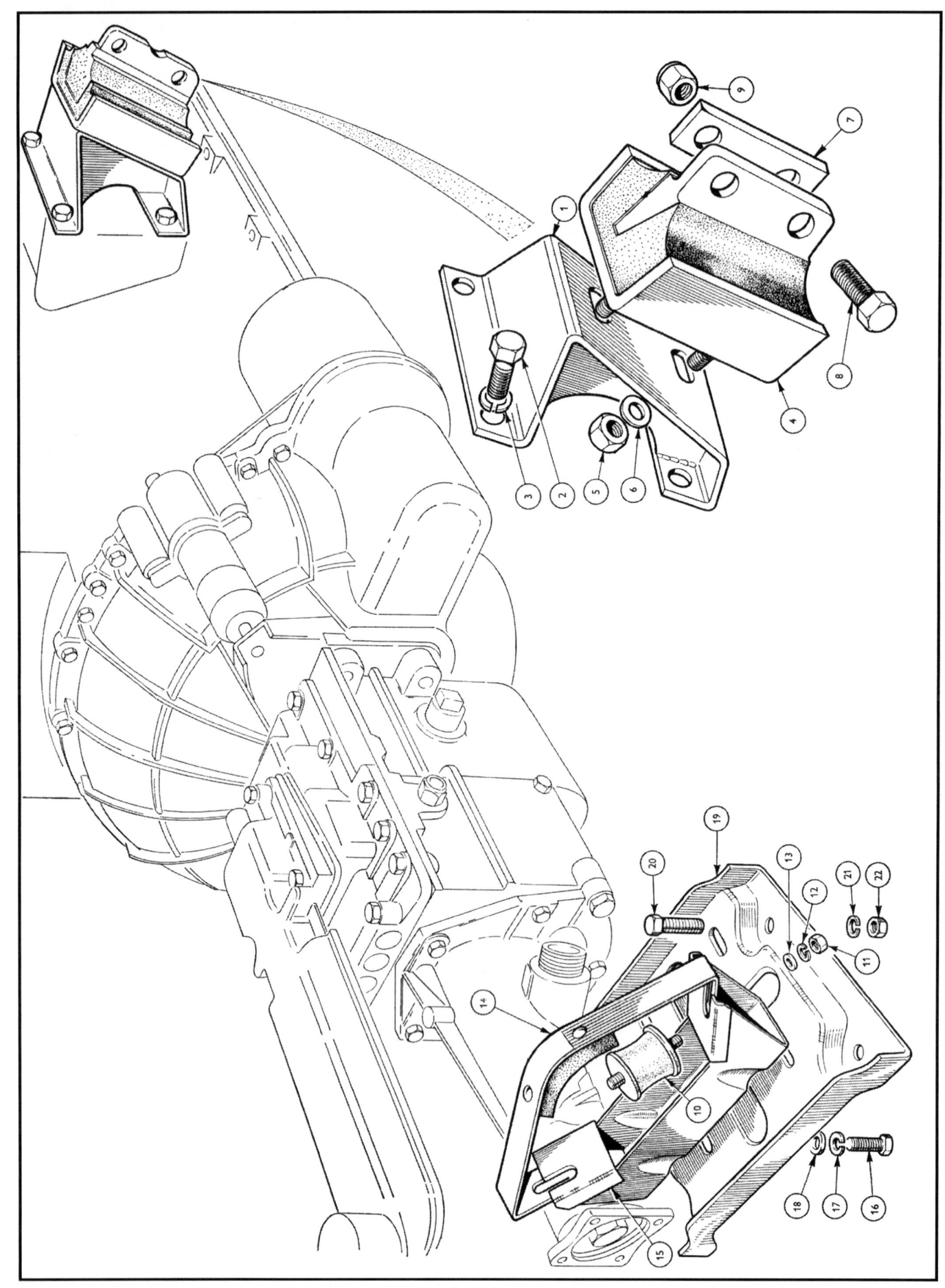

PLATE AJ

ENGINE MOUNTING

Plate No.	Part No.	Description	No. per Unit	Remarks
AJ1	133284	**FRONT ENGINE MOUNTING BRACKET ASSEMBLY—R.H.**	1	
	133285	**FRONT ENGINE MOUNTING BRACKET ASSEMBLY—L.H.**	1	
AJ2	HU0906	**Screw,** set ⎫ Mounting bracket to engine	8	
AJ3	WL0209	**Washer,** lock ⎭	8	
AJ4	132669	**Mounting,** engine, front	2	
AJ5	TN3209	**Nut,** nyloc ⎫ Engine mounting to	4	
AJ6	WP0009	**Washer,** plain ⎭ mounting bracket	4	
AJ7	145199	**Piece,** distance ⎫	2	
AJ8	HB0912	**Bolt** ⎬ Engine mounting to chassis frame bracket	4	
AJ9	YN2909	**Nut,** nyloc ⎭	4	
AJ10	122689	**REAR ENGINE MOUNTING**	2	
AJ11	HN2008	**Nut** ⎫	2	
AJ12	WL0208	**Washer,** lock ⎬ Rear engine mounting to bracket	2	
AJ13	WF0008	**Washer,** plain ⎭	2	
AJ14	137801	**Stop,** rebound, assembly, gearbox extension mounting	1	Heavy Duty only
AJ15	136890	**Bracket** assembly, gearbox mounting	1	
AJ16	HU0805	**Screw,** set ⎫ Mounting bracket to	2	
AJ17	WL0208	**Washer,** lock ⎬ rear engine mounting platform	2	
AJ18	WF0008	**Washer,** plain ⎭	2	
AJ19	209018	**Platform,** rear engine mounting	1	
AJ20	HU0805	**Screw,** set ⎫	4	
AJ21	WL0208	**Washer,** lock ⎬ Engine mounting platform to chassis frame	4	
AJ22	HN2008	**Nut** ⎭	4	

Note:—Items marked thus † are available on our Factory Exchange Unit Scheme

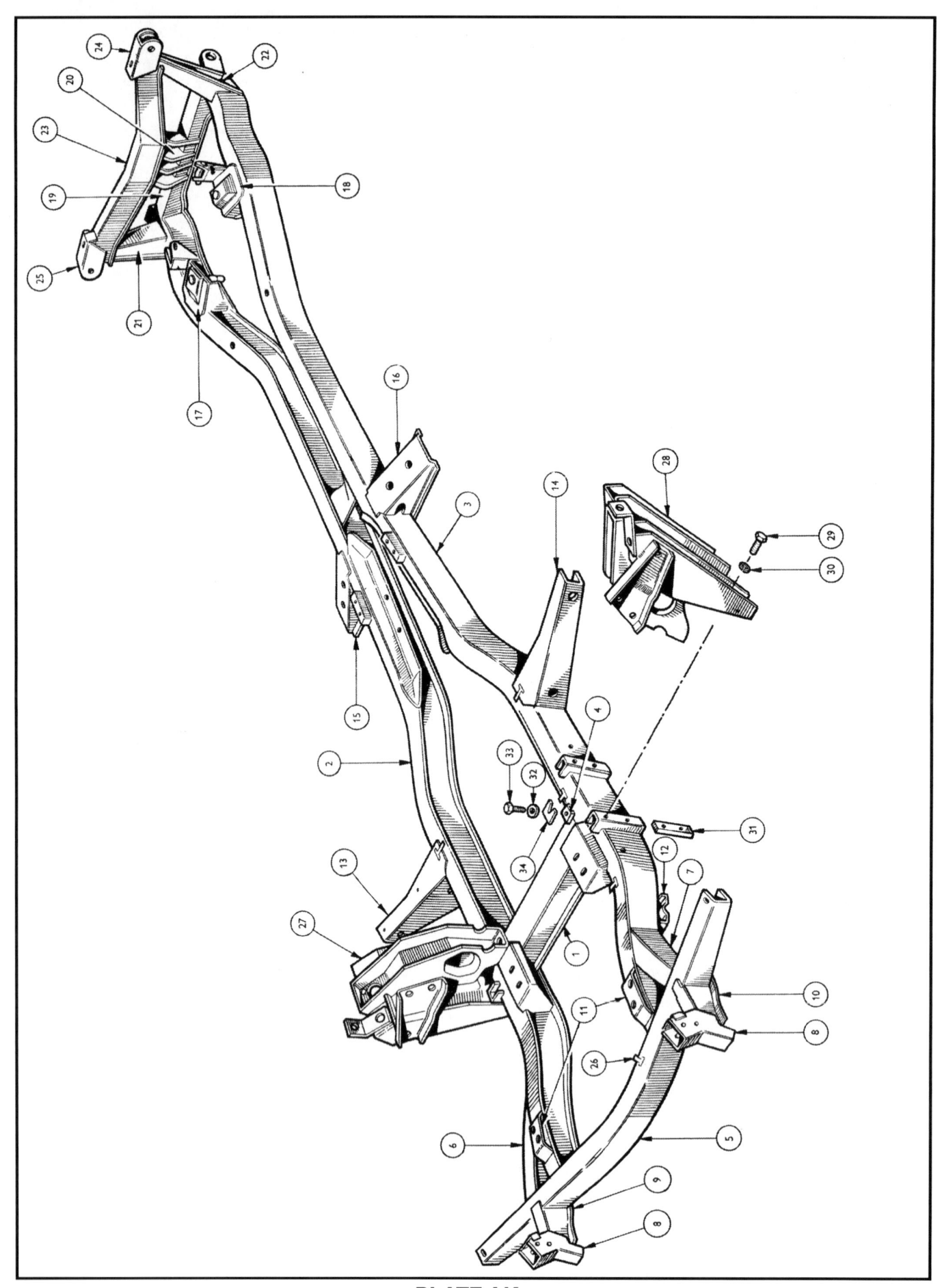

PLATE AK

CHASSIS FRAME

Plate No.	Part No.	Description	No. per Unit	Remarks
	402572	**CHASSIS FRAME COMPLETE**	1	Fitted up to Commission No. KC50000 only
	402644	**CHASSIS FRAME COMPLETE**	1	Fitted from Commission No. KC50001 and future
AK1	Not Serviced	**Crossmember** assembly, front	1	
AK2	Not Serviced	**Sidemember** assembly—R.H.	1	
AK3	Not Serviced	**Sidemember** assembly—L.H.	1	
	132104	**Bracket,** support, inner, suspension—R.H.	1	
AK4	132105	**Bracket,** support, inner, suspension—L.H.	1	
	517303	**Crossmember** assembly, valance support (includes items AK8, AK9, AK10)	1	Fitted up to Commission No. KC50000 only
AK5	209438	**Crossmember** assembly, front valance support	1	Fitted from Commission No. KC50001 and future
AK6	209439	**Gusset** assembly, valance member—R.H.	1	
AK7	209440	**Gusset** assembly, valance member—L.H.	1	
AK8	134295	**Link pivot,** assembly, bonnet	2	⎫ Fitted up to
AK9	133868	**Support,** pivot bracket—R.H.	1	⎬ Commission No.
AK10	133869	**Support,** pivot bracket—L.H.	1	⎭ KC50000 only
	147788	**Support** assembly, pivot bracket—R.H.	1	⎱ Fitted from Commission No.
	147789	**Support** assembly, pivot bracket—L.H.	1	⎰ KC50001 and future
AK11	142224	**Bracket** assembly, radiator support	2	
AK12	134580	**Bracket,** mounting, anti-roll bar	2	
	114210	**Bracket,** mounting, four-way or front three-way piece	1	
	133122	**Bracket,** exhaust pipe mounting, welded to intermediate crossmember	1	
AK13	209398	**Outrigger** assembly, front—R.H.	1	
AK14	209399	**Outrigger** assembly, front—L.H.	1	
AK15	134399	**Outrigger** assembly, intermediate—R.H.	1	
AK16	134400	**Outrigger** assembly, intermediate—L.H.	1	
AK17	209466	**Bracket** assembly, rear axle mounting, and handbrake cable guide—R.H.	1	⎫ Fitted up to Commission No.
AK18	209465	**Bracket** assembly, rear axle mounting, and handbrake cable guide—L.H.	1	⎬ KC50000 only
	149991	**Bracket** assembly, rear axle mounting	2	⎭
	214645	**Bracket** mounting, rear lower wishbone—R.H.	1	⎱ Fitted from Commission No.
	214646	**Bracket** mounting, rear lower wishbone—L.H.	1	⎰ KC50001 and future
	210601	**Rear crossmember and axle mounting** assembly	1	
AK19	Not Serviced	**Crossmember** assembly, rear	1	
AK20	132435	**Bracket,** rear—Rear axle mounting	2	
	136868	**Piece,** distance—Rear axle mounting	1	
AK21	208935	**Bracket,** damper support—R.H.	1	
AK22	209331	**Bracket** assembly, damper support—L.H.	1	⎫ Fitted up to Commission No.
	114210	**Bracket,** rear three-way piece mounting	1	⎭ KC50000 only
	208934	**Bracket,** damper support—L.H.	1	⎱ Fitted from Commission No.
	114210	**Bracket,** mounting, rear three-way piece (welded to sidemember)	1	⎰ KC50001 and future

Note:—Items marked thus † are available on our Factory Exchange Unit Scheme

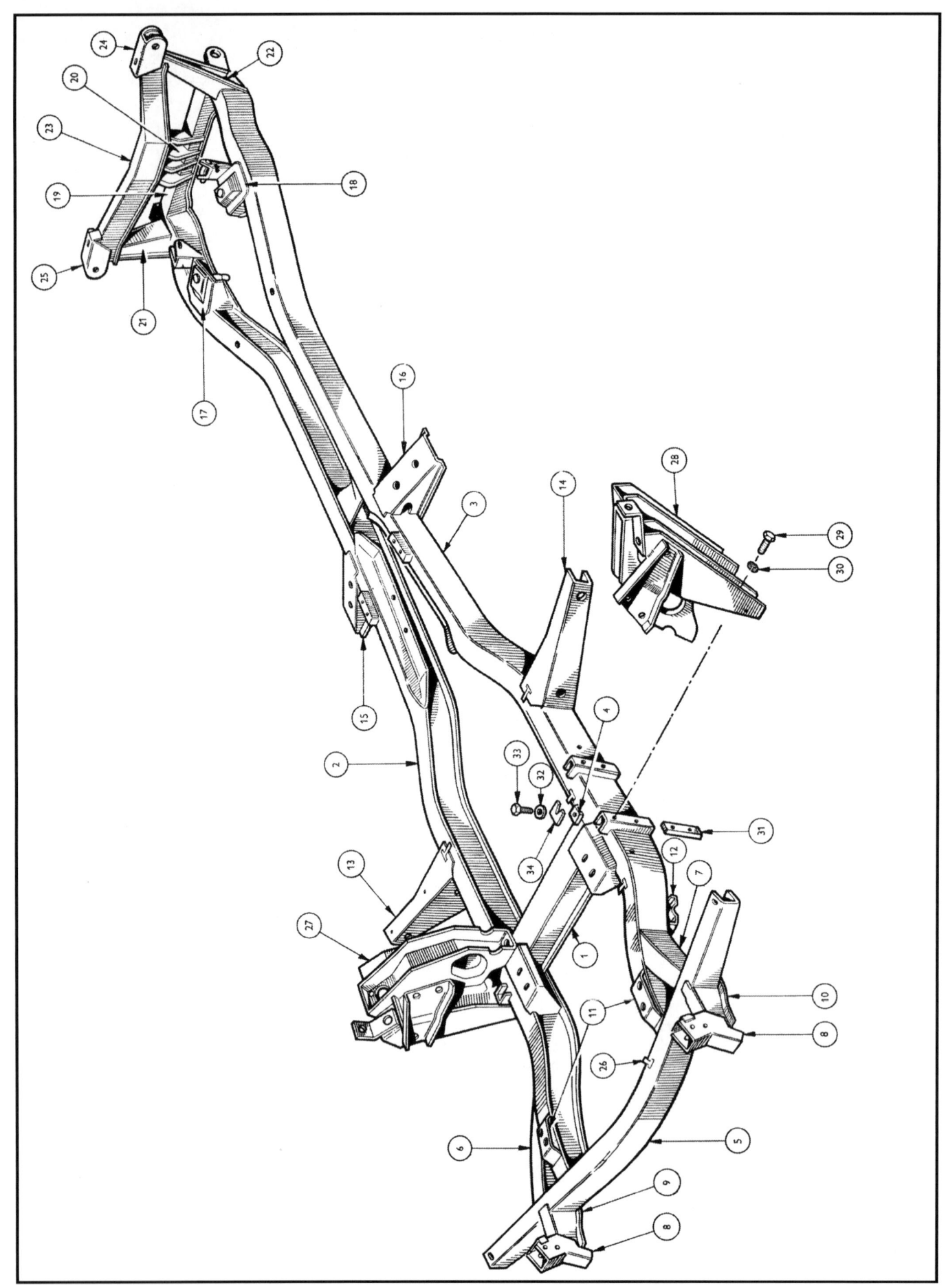

PLATE AK

CHASSIS FRAME

Plate No.	Part No.	Description	No. per Unit	Remarks
		CHASSIS FRAME COMPLETE—continued		
	139521	**Bracket**, mounting, rear brake hose—R.H.	1	⎫ Fitted up to Commission No.
	139522	**Bracket**, mounting, rear brake hose—L.H.	1	⎭ KC8321 only
	149650	**Bracket** assembly, mounting, rear brake hose—R.H.	1	⎫ Fitted from Commission No.
	149649	**Bracket** assembly, mounting, rear brake hose—L.H.	1	⎭ KC8322 up to KC50000 only
	149945	**Bracket**, mounting, rear brake hose—R.H.	1	Fitted from Commission No. KC50001 and future
AK23	208943	**Crossmember** assembly, rear damper mounting	1	
AK24	132819	**Bracket** assembly, rear body mounting (fitted to rear damper crossmember)—L.H.	1	
AK25	132754	**Bracket** assembly, rear body mounting (fitted to rear damper crossmember)—R.H.	1	
AK26	122747	**Clip**, wiring	7	
AK27	305592	**Bracket** assembly, front suspension and engine mounting—R.H.	1	
AK28	305593	**Bracket** assembly, front suspension and engine mounting—L.H.	1	
	123203	**Plate**, stiffener	4	
AK29	HU0908	**Screw**, set ⎫	8	
AK30	118977	**Washer**, lock ⎪	8	
AK31	129650	**Plate**, tapping ⎬ Front suspension mounting	4	
AK32	WP0020	**Washer**, plain ⎪ brackets to chassis frame	2	
AK33	HU0909	**Bolt** ⎪	2	
AK34	128356	**Shim** ⎭	A/R	
		Platform, rear engine mounting—For Details see Engine Mounting Section.		
	308263	**SKID PLATE ASSEMBLY**	1	⎫
	144326	**Bracket**, clamp and weld bolt assembly	2	⎪
	HN2009	**Nut** ⎫ Skid plate	2	⎬ Special Order only
	WL0209	**Washer**, lock ⎭ attachment	2	⎪
	TN3208	**Nut**, nyloc, skid plate attachment, front	4	⎭

Note:—Items marked thus † are available on our Factory Exchange Unit Scheme

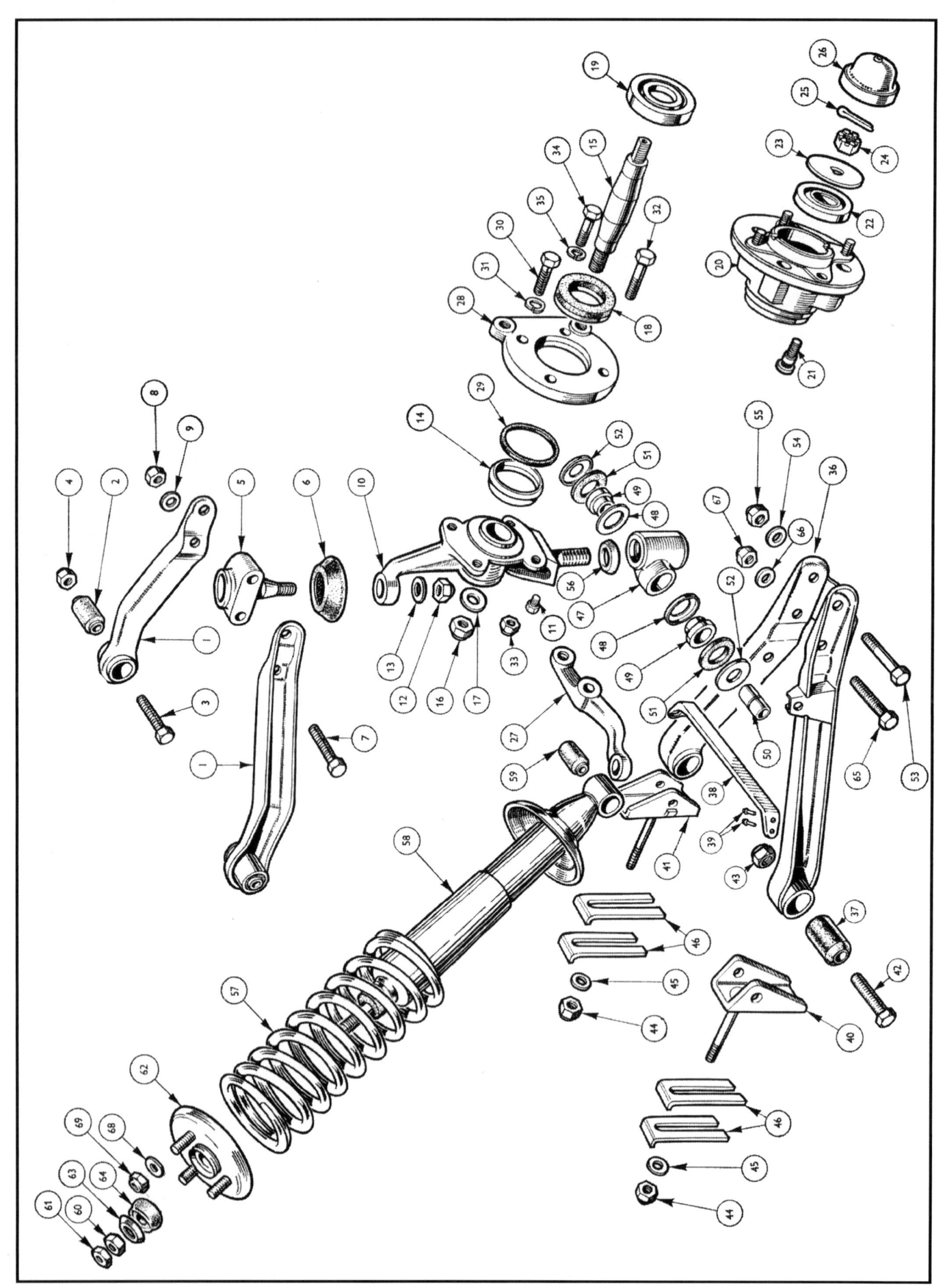

PLATE AL

FRONT SUSPENSION

Plate No.	Part No.	Description	No. per Unit	Remarks
	515329	**FRONT SUSPENSION UNIT—R.H.**	1	
	515330	**FRONT SUSPENSION UNIT—L.H.**	1	
	515953	**FRONT SUSPENSION UNIT—R.H.** } SPECIAL ORDER—FITTED WITH GREASE NIPPLES	1	
	515954	**FRONT SUSPENSION UNIT—L.H.**	1	
		The above Units comprise:- Lower fulcrum, upper and lower wishbones, vertical link, ball joint, stub axle, hub, brake unit and steering tie rod levers		
AL1	119272	**TOP WISHBONE ARM AND BUSH ASSEMBLY**	4	
AL2	119451	**Bush,** rubber	4	
AL3	HB0918	**Bolt,** fulcrum ⎫	2	
	HB0920	**Bolt,** fulcrum ⎬ Top wishbone and hose bracket attachment	2	
AL4	YN2909	**Nut,** nyloc ⎪	4	Alternative to AN3509
	AN3509	**Nut,** Philidas ⎭	4	Alternative to YN2909
AL5	136604	**BALL JOINT ASSEMBLY, UPPER WISHBONE**	2	
AL6	512419	**Gaiter and spring** assembly	2	
	104552	**BALL JOINT ASSEMBLY, UPPER WISHBONE** (Fitted with grease nipples)	2	Special Order
	56934	**Nipple,** grease	2	
	58261	**Gaiter**	2	
AL7	HB0818	**Bolt** ⎫	4	
AL8	YN2908	**Nut,** nyloc ⎬ Ball assembly to upper wishbone	4	
AL9	WP0107	**Washer,** plain ⎭	4	
	209072	**VERTICAL LINK—R.H.**	1	
AL10	209073	**VERTICAL LINK—L.H.**	1	
AL11	129242	**Plug,** grease, vertical link	2	
AL12	YN2910	**Nut,** nyloc ⎫ Ball pin to vertical link	2	
AL13	WP0010	**Washer,** plain ⎭	2	
AL14	138559	**Shield,** water	2	

Note:—Items marked thus † are available on our Factory Exchange Unit Scheme

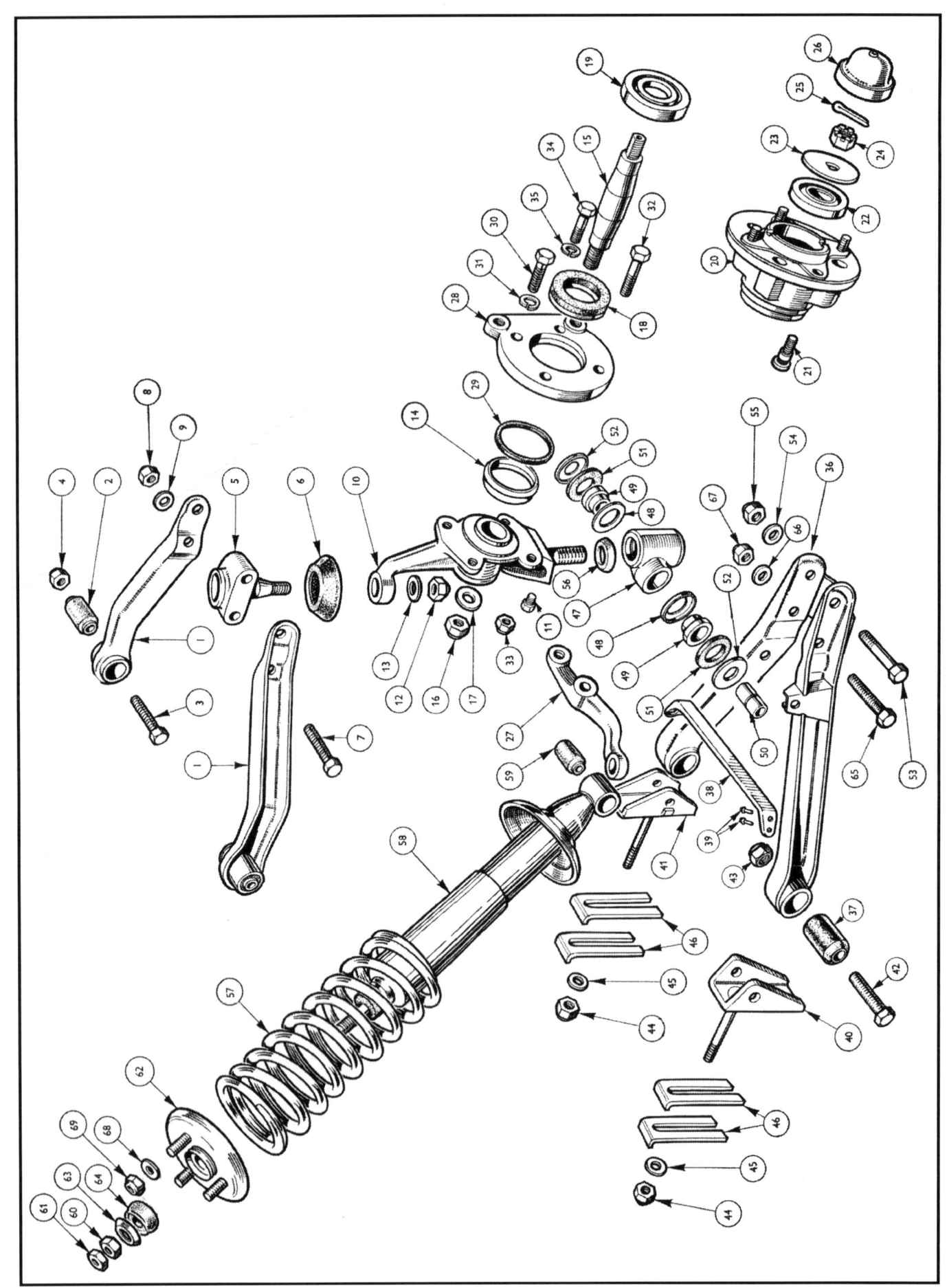

PLATE AL

FRONT SUSPENSION

Plate No.	Part No.	Description	No. per Unit	Remarks
AL15	132065	**STUB AXLE**	2	
AL16	YN2912	**Nut,** nyloc ⎫ Stub axle to	2	
AL17	WP0012	**Washer,** plain ⎬ vertical link	2	
AL18	132664	**Seal,** oil, assembly, between vertical link and inner bearing	2	
	132668	**Seal,** felt	2	
AL19	132066	**Bearing,** inner hub	2	
AL20	145007	**Hub and stud** assembly, front	2	
AL21	112429	**Stud,** wheel	8	
AL22	129897	**Bearing,** hub, outer	2	
AL23	132666	**Washer,** 'D' ⎫	2	
AL24	LN2211	**Nut,** slotted ⎬ Hubs to stub axles	2	
AL25	PC0020	**Pin,** cotter ⎭	2	
AL26	132665	**Cover,** hub end	2	
	205504	**TIE ROD LEVER—R.H.**	1	
AL27	205505	**TIE ROD LEVER—L.H.**	1	
	145106	**Plate,** mounting, brake caliper—R.H.	1	
AL28	145107	**Plate,** mounting, brake caliper—L.H.	1	
AL29	138051	**Ring,** sealing	2	
AL30	HU0806	**Screw,** set ⎫	4	
AL31	WL0208	**Washer,** lock ⎬	4	
AL32	123312	**Bolt** ⎬ Mounting plates and tie rod	2	
AL33	YN2909	**Nut** ⎬ levers to vertical link	2	
AL34	HB0910	**Bolt** ⎬	2	
AL35	WQ0309	**Washer** ⎭	2	
	206685	**LOWER WISHBONE ASSEMBLY—R.H.**	1	
AL36	206686	**LOWER WISHBONE ASSEMBLY—L.H.**	1	
AL37	119451	**Bush,** rubber	4	
AL38	125733	**Strut,** lower wishbone	2	
AL39	SP.91.D2	**Rivet**	8	
AL40	130757	**LOWER WISHBONE FULCRUM BRACKET—FRONT**	1	
AL41	130758	**LOWER WISHBONE FULCRUM BRACKET—REAR**	1	
AL42	HB0919	**Bolt** ⎫ Fulcrum brackets	4	
AL43	YN2909	**Nut,** nyloc ⎬ to lower wishbones	4	
AL44	YN2909	**Nut,** nyloc ⎫	4	Alternative to AN3509
	AN3509	**Nut,** Philidas ⎬ Wishbone fulcrum	4	Alternative to YN2909
AL45	WP0009	**Washer,** plain ⎬ bracket to frame	4	
AL46	122022	**Shim** ⎭	A/R	

Note:—Items marked thus † are available on our Factory Exchange Unit Scheme

57

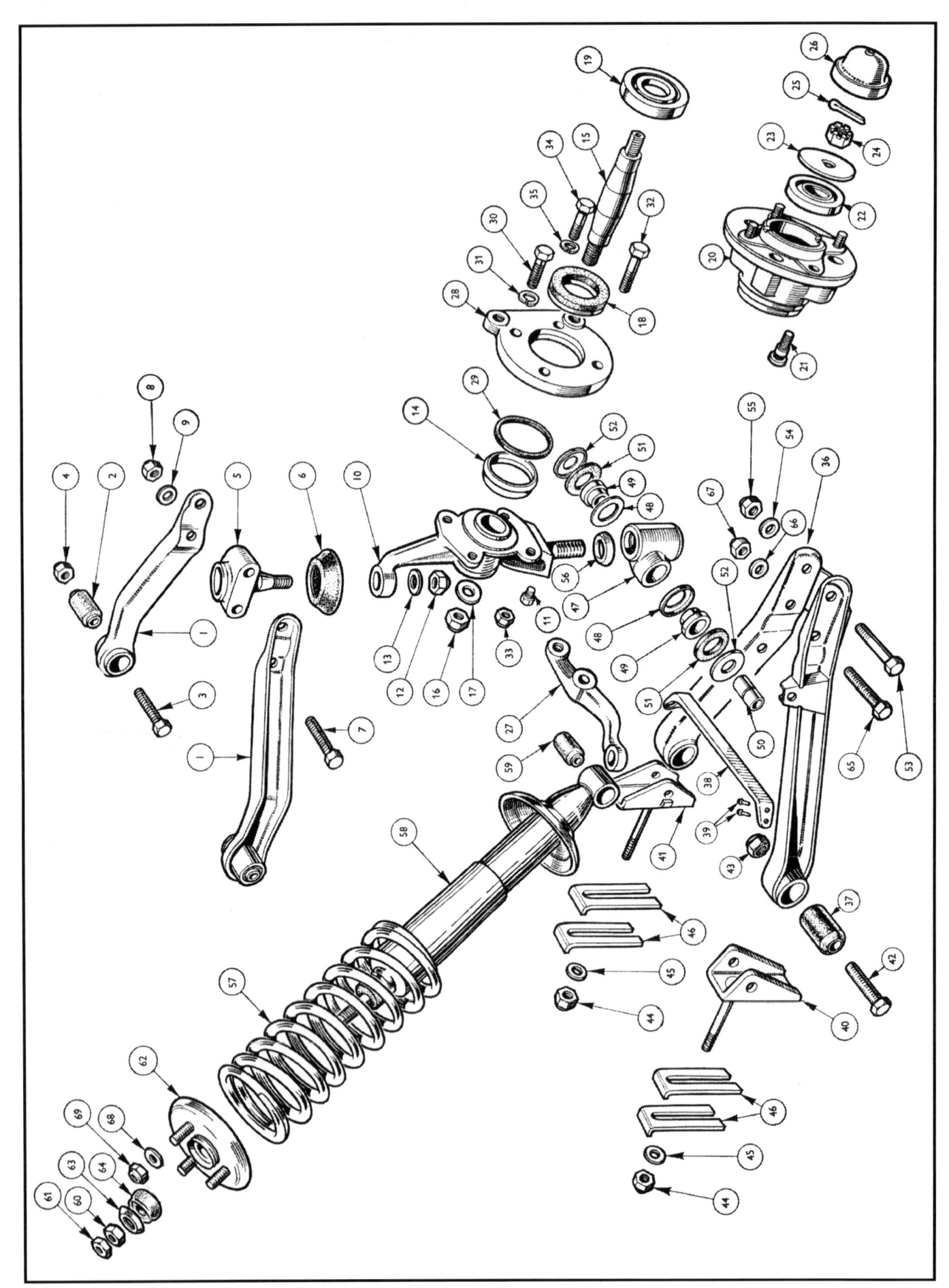

PLATE AL

FRONT SUSPENSION

Plate No.	Part No.	Description	No. per Unit	Remarks
	140919	**BOTTOM TRUNNION ASSEMBLY—R.H.**	1	
AL47	140920	**BOTTOM TRUNNION ASSEMBLY—L.H.**	1	
AL48	140894	**Shield**, water, inner	4	
AL49	140892	**Bearing**	4	
AL50	140893	**Piece**, distance	2	
AL51	122534	**Seal**, dirt, lower trunnion	4	
AL52	140895	**Shield**, water, outer	4	
AL53	119142	**Bolt** ⎫	2	
AL54	WP0010	**Washer**, plain ⎬ Trunnion to wishbone	2	
AL55	YN2910	**Nut**, nyloc ⎭	2	
AL56	122126	**Seal**, oil, trunnion to vertical link	2	
	212938	**FRONT DAMPER AND ROAD SPRING COMPLETE ASSEMBLY**	2	Fitted up to Commission No. KC50000 only
	215418	**FRONT DAMPER AND ROAD SPRING COMPLETE ASSEMBLY**	2	Fitted from Commission No. KC50001 and future
AL57	212425	**Spring**, road, front	2	
AL58	208022	**Damper**, front	2	Fitted up to Commission No. KC50000 only
	215398	**Damper**, front	2	Fitted from Commission No. KC50001 and future
AL59	119450	**Bush**, rubber	2	
AL60	Not Serviced	**Nut** ⎫ Front damper upper		
AL61	separately	**Nut**, lock ⎭ plate attachment		
AL62	122137	**Plate** assembly, spring retaining, upper	2	
AL63	123231	**Cap**, spring plate	4	
AL64	509260	**Bush**, rubber, top	4	
	125441	**Packing**, front road spring, L.H.—L.H.S.	1	
		FRONT DAMPER AND SPRING ATTACHMENT DETAILS		
AL65	HB1020	**Bolt** ⎫	2	
AL66	WP0010	**Washer**, plain ⎬ Front damper lower attachment	2	
AL67	YN2910	**Nut**, nyloc ⎭	2	
AL68	WP0035	**Washer**, plain ⎫ Front damper	6	
AL69	YN2907	**Nut**, nyloc ⎭ upper attachment	6	

Note:—Items marked thus † are available on our Factory Exchange Unit Scheme

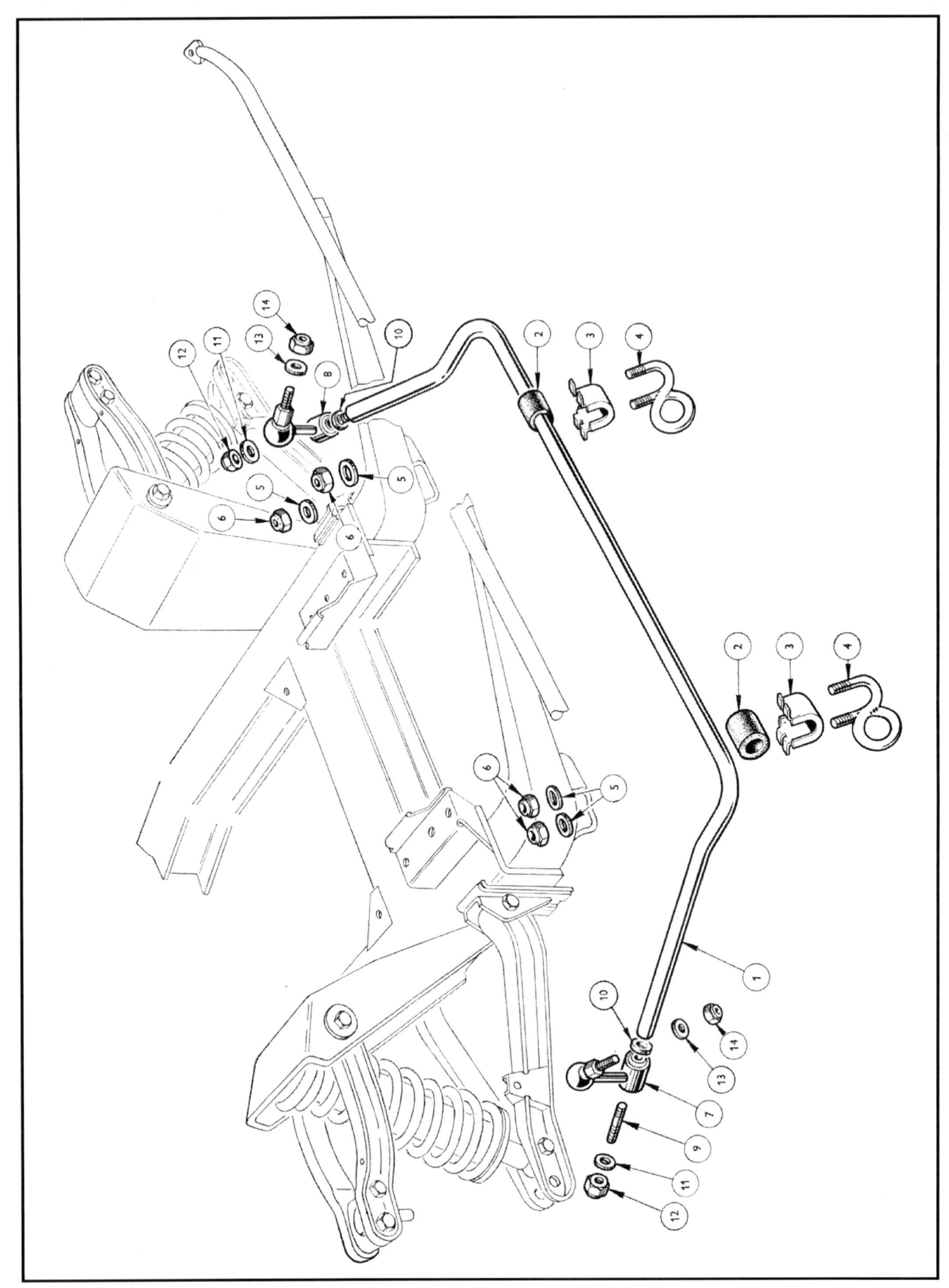

PLATE AM

ANTI-ROLL BAR

Plate No.	Part No.	Description	No. per Unit	Remarks
AM1	207093	**ANTI-ROLL BAR**	1	
AM2	123998	**Bush,** rubber	2	
AM3	123502	**Bracket,** clamp	2	
AM4	139126	**Bracket,** stowage	2	
AM5	WP0107	**Washer,** plain ⎫	4	
AM6	YN2908	**Nut,** nyloc ⎬ Anti-roll bar to mounting brackets	4	Alternative to AN3508
AM6	AN3508	**Nut,** Philidas ⎭	4	Alternative to YN2908
AM7	125481	**Link** assembly—R.H.	1	
AM8	125482	**Link** assembly—L.H.	1	
AM9	125074	**Stud** ⎫	2	
AM10	WP0036	**Washer,** plain ⎬ Link assembly to anti-roll bar	2	
AM11	WP0110	**Washer,** plain	2	
AM12	YN2909	**Nut,** nyloc ⎭	2	
AM13	WP0046	**Washer,** plain ⎱ Link assembly to	2	
AM14	YN2910	**Nut,** nyloc ⎰ lower wishbone	2	

Note:—Items marked thus † are available on our Factory Exchange Unit Scheme

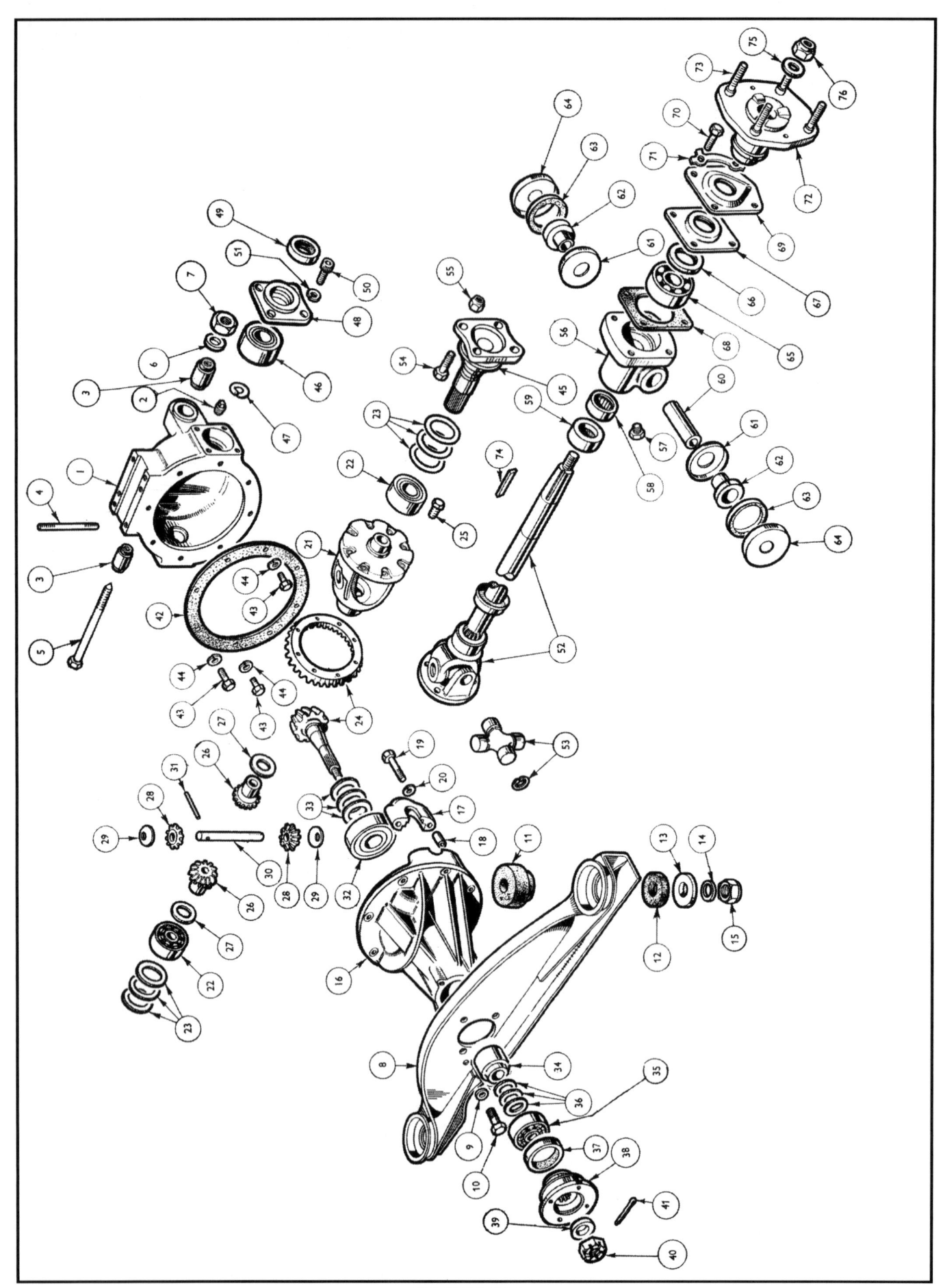

PLATE AN

REAR AXLE

Plate No.	Part No.	Description	No. per Unit	Remarks
	515492	†REAR AXLE CENTRE ASSEMBLY	1	
	515743	†REAR AXLE CENTRE ASSEMBLY (RECONDITIONED UNIT)	1	
	515507	†REAR AXLE CENTRE ASSEMBLY	1	Only required when Overdrive is fitted
	515744	†REAR AXLE CENTRE ASSEMBLY (RECONDITIONED UNIT)	1	

Note:- Replacement Overdrive Rear Axle Centre Assembly Part No. 515507 may have a serial number with Prefix Letters "FD," "HC" or "KD" stamped on the casing. This is to facilitate production build programmes and does not affect the Spares Unit, therefore a unit with any of the above Prefix Letters may be fitted.

Plate No.	Part No.	Description	No. per Unit	Remarks
AN1	213469	**Housing,** assembly, axle	1	
	118826	**Plug,** core	1	
AN2	114774	**Plug,** filler	1	
AN3	147993	**Bush,** mounting	2	
	510408	**Pin,** cotter	1	
AN8	211819	**Plate,** mounting, assembly, rear axle nose	1	Fitted up to Commission No. KC50000 only
	215537	**Plate,** mounting, assembly, rear axle nose	1	Fitted from Commission No. KC50001 and future
AN9	WN0710	**Washer** } Mounting plate to	4	
AN10	132856	**Bolt** } hypoid housing	4	
AN16	515382	**Housing** assembly, hypoid	1	
AN17	Not Serviced	**Cap,** bearing	2	
AN18	60070	**Bush,** bearing cap	4	
AN19	104554	**Bolt** } Bearing cap	4	
AN20	WL0209	**Washer,** lock } attachment	4	

Note:- For items AN4, AN5, AN6, AN7, AN11, AN12, AN13, AN14 and AN15, see end of Rear Axle Centre Assembly Details.

Plate No.	Part No.	Description	No. per Unit	Remarks
AN21	307642	**DIFFERENTIAL CASING**	1	
	305778	**DIFFERENTIAL CASING**	1	Required when Overdrive is fitted and when Crown Wheel and Pinion Assemblies 516274 or 516275 are fitted
AN22	130355	**Bearing** assembly, differential casing	2	
AN23	123817	**Shim,** adjusting differential bearing (·020″)	A/R	
AN23	123815	**Shim,** adjusting differential bearing (·014″)	A/R	
AN23	123814	**Shim,** adjusting differential bearing (·013″)	A/R	
AN23	123813	**Shim,** adjusting differential bearing (·009″)	A/R	
AN24	515129	**Crown wheel and pinion** assembly (3·27 : 1 ratio)	1 pair	
	514201	**Crown wheel and pinion** assembly (3·89 : 1 ratio)	1 pair	Only required when Overdrive is fitted
	516274	**Crown wheel and pinion** assembly (4·1 : 1 ratio)	1 pair	For Competition purposes and must be used in conjunction with Diff. Casing, 305778
	516275	**Crown wheel and pinion** assembly (4·55 : 1 ratio)	1 pair	

Note:—Items marked thus † are available on our Factory Exchange Unit Scheme

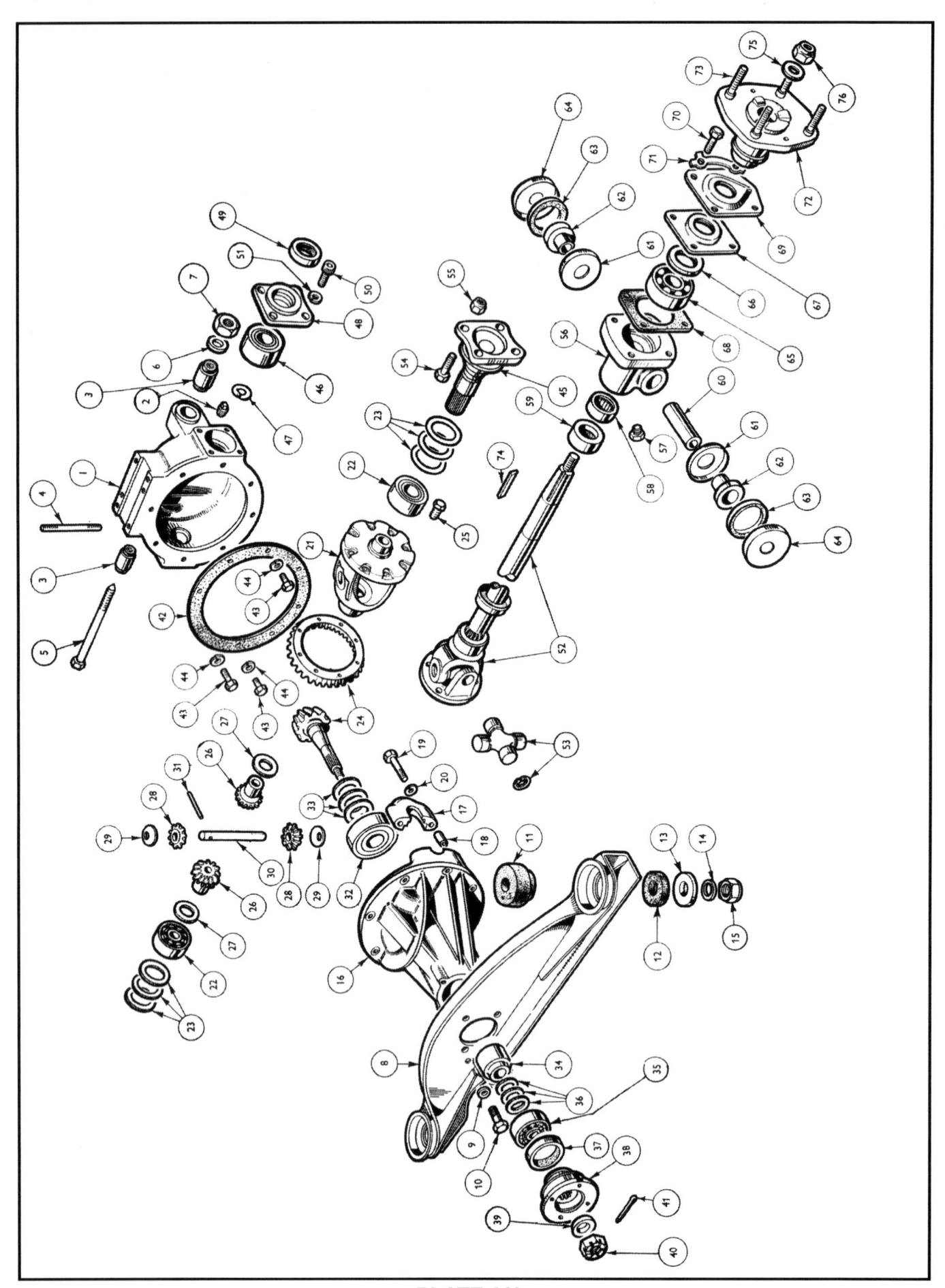

PLATE AN

REAR AXLE

Plate No.	Part No.	Description	No. per Unit	Remarks
		REAR AXLE CENTRE ASSEMBLY—cont.		
AN25	144668	**Bolt,** crown wheel to differential casing	8	For use with Diff. Casing 307642 only
	129781	**Bolt** ⎱ Crown wheel to	8	⎱ For use with Differential Casing
	118977	**Washer,** lock ⎰ differential casing	8	⎰ 305778 only
AN26	134073	**Gear,** differential, 16 teeth	2	
AN27	134075	**Washer,** thrust, flat, for differential gear	2	
AN28	134074	**Pinion,** differential, 10 teeth	2	
AN29	138440	**Washer,** thrust, spherical, pinion gear (·027″)	A/R	
AN29	147249	**Washer,** thrust, spherical, pinion gear (·029″)	A/R	
AN29	134076	**Washer,** thrust, spherical, pinion gear (·030″/·032″)	A/R	
AN29	147250	**Washer,** thrust, spherical, pinion gear (·033″)	A/R	
AN29	138441	**Washer,** thrust, spherical, pinion gear (·035″)	A/R	
AN29	147251	**Washer,** thrust, spherical, pinion gear (·037″)	A/R	
AN29	138442	**Washer,** thrust, spherical, pinion gear (·039″)	A/R	
AN29	148805	**Washer,** thrust, spherical, pinion gear (·041″)	A/R	
AN29	147252	**Washer,** thrust, spherical, pinion gear (·043″)	A/R	
AN30	134072	**Pin,** cross, differential	1	
AN31	110376	**Pin,** locating, cross pin in differential housing	1	
AN32	134065	**Bearing,** roller, pinion head	1	
AN33	145918	**Shim,** adjusting bearing (pinion head), ·075″	A/R	
AN33	148099	**Shim,** adjusting bearing (pinion head), ·077″	A/R	
AN33	145919	**Shim,** adjusting bearing (pinion head), ·0765″	A/R	
AN33	145920	**Shim,** adjusting bearing (pinion head), ·078″	A/R	
AN33	148100	**Shim,** adjusting bearing (pinion head), ·079″	A/R	
AN33	145921	**Shim,** adjusting bearing (pinion head), ·0795″	A/R	
AN33	148101	**Shim,** adjusting bearing (pinion head), ·080″	A/R	
AN33	145922	**Shim,** adjusting bearing (pinion head), ·081″	A/R	
AN33	148102	**Shim,** adjusting bearing (pinion head), ·082″	A/R	
AN33	145923	**Shim,** adjusting bearing (pinion head), ·0825″	A/R	
AN33	148103	**Shim,** adjusting bearing (pinion head), ·083″	A/R	
AN33	145924	**Shim,** adjusting bearing (pinion head), ·084″	A/R	
AN33	148104	**Shim,** adjusting bearing (pinion head), ·085″	A/R	
AN33	145925	**Shim,** adjusting bearing (pinion head), ·0855″	A/R	
AN33	148105	**Shim,** adjusting bearing (pinion head), ·086″	A/R	
AN33	145926	**Shim,** adjusting bearing (pinion head), ·087″	A/R	
AN33	145927	**Shim,** adjusting bearing (pinion head), ·0885″	A/R	
AN33	145928	**Shim,** adjusting bearing (pinion head), ·090″	A/R	
AN33	145929	**Shim,** adjusting bearing (pinion head), ·0915″	A/R	
AN33	145930	**Shim,** adjusting bearing (pinion head), ·093″	A/R	
AN33	145931	**Shim,** adjusting bearing (pinion head), ·0945″	A/R	
AN33	145932	**Shim,** adjusting bearing (pinion head), ·096″	A/R	
AN34	145933	**Spacer,** between bearings	1	
AN35	134070	**Bearing,** roller, pinion nose	1	
AN36	140790	**Shim,** adjusting pinion nose bearing (·030″)	A/R	
AN36	140791	**Shim,** adjusting pinion nose bearing (·010″)	A/R	
AN36	140792	**Shim,** adjusting pinion nose bearing (·005″)	A/R	
AN36	140793	**Shim,** adjusting pinion nose bearing (·003″)	A/R	
AN37	141242	**Seal,** oil, on pinion	1	
AN38	140913	**Flange,** pinion, and stoneguard assembly	1	
AN39	115990	**Washer,** plain, between pinion flange and nut	1	
AN40	112635	**Nut,** slotted, securing flange to pinion	1	
AN41	PC0045	**Pin,** cotter, locking nut	1	
AN42	114749	**Washer,** joint ⎫	1	
AN43	HU0808	**Screw,** set ⎬ Hypoid housing to axle housing	8	
AN44	WL0208	**Washer,** lock ⎭	8	

Note:—Items marked thus † are available on our Factory Exchange Unit Scheme

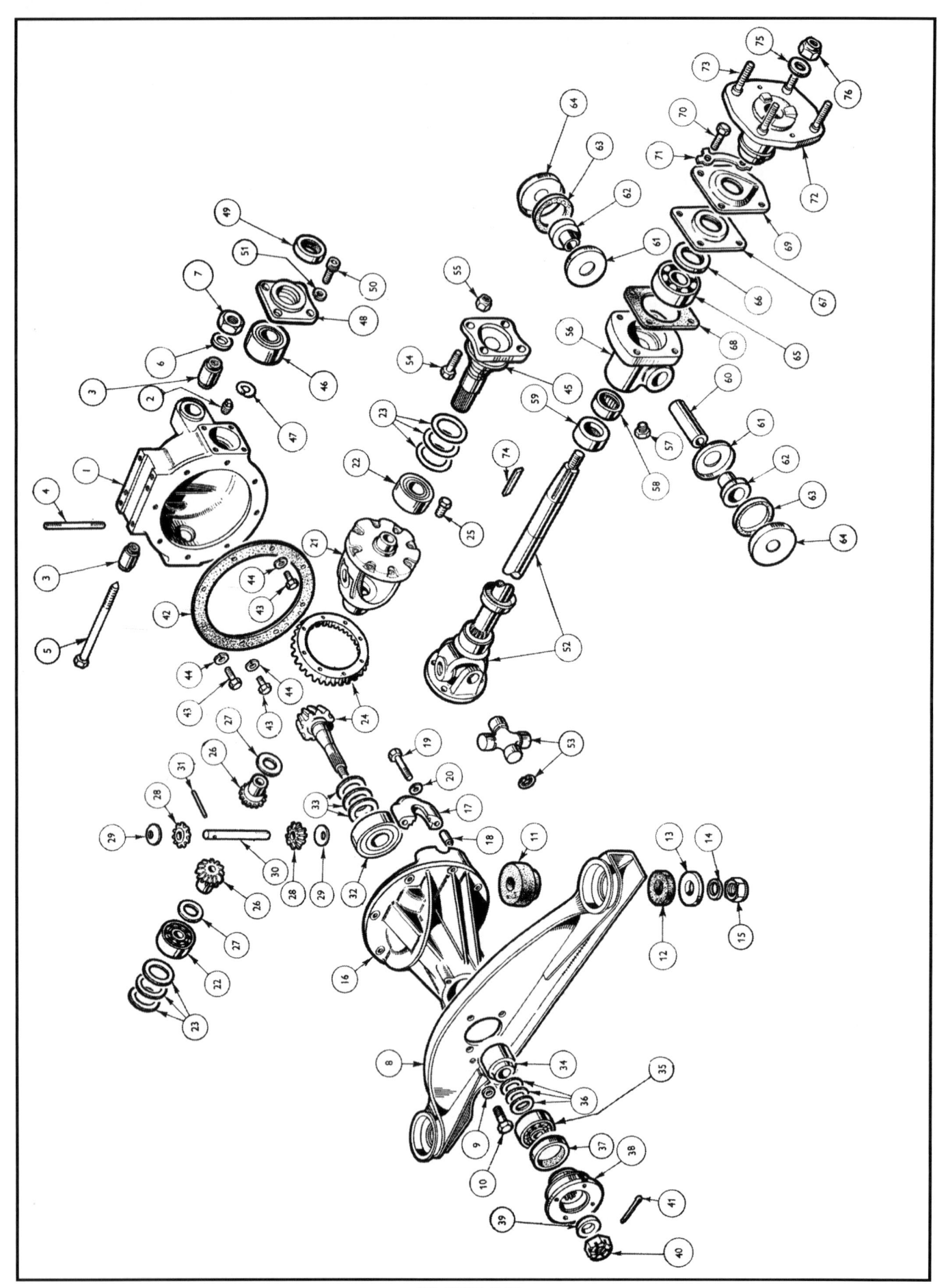

PLATE AN

REAR AXLE

Plate No.	Part No.	Description	No. per Unit	Remarks

REAR AXLE CENTRE ASSEMBLY—cont.

Plate No.	Part No.	Description	No. per Unit	Remarks
AN45	139531	**INNER AXLE SHAFT ASSEMBLY**	2	
AN46	128572	**Bearing**, ball	2	
AN47	139532	**Circlip**	2	
AN48	139530	**Cap**, bearing retaining	2	
AN49	117952	**Seal**, oil	2	
AN50	123803	**Screw** ⎱ Bearing retaining cap	8	
AN51	WL0207	**Washer**, lock ⎰ to housing	8	
AN4	131008	**Stud**, rear road spring	6	Fitted up to Commission No. KC50000 only
	151824	**Stud**, rear road spring	6	Fitted from Commission No. KC50001 and future
AN5	136869	**Bolt** ⎫	1	
AN6	WP0110	**Washer**, plain ⎬ Rear axle to frame	1	
AN7	YN2910	**Nut**, nyloc ⎭	1	
AN11	133568	**Rubber**, mounting, rear axle (Upper) ⎫	2	
AN12	131796	**Rubber**, mounting, rear axle (Lower) ⎬ Axle	2	
AN13	WM0810	**Washer**, medium ⎬ mounting plate	2	
AN14	132419	**Washer**, distance ⎬ to frame	A/R	Fitted up to only
AN15	TN3209	**Nut**, nyloc ⎭	2	
AN52	132300	**OUTER AXLE SHAFT AND FLINGER ASSEMBLY—B.R.D.**	2	⎫
	128135	**Shaft**, yoke, assembly	2	⎪
	132328	**Flange**, yoke	2	⎬ Fitted up to Commission No.
AN53	128133	**Unit package**	2	⎪ KC50000 only
	128469	**Flinger**	2	⎪
AN54	132023	**Bolt** ⎱ Shaft joint to	8	⎪
AN55	511506	**Nut**, nyloc ⎰ inner axle shaft	8	⎭
AN56	204226	**REAR HUB (INNER) ASSEMBLY**	2	⎫
AN57	509539	**Plug**, screwed, inner hub—Alternative to 122115	2	
	122115	**Plug**, screwed, inner hub—Alternative to 509539	2	
AN58	117853	**Bearing**, needle roller	2	
AN59	128978	**Seal**, oil	2	
AN60	141221	**Piece**, distance	2	
AN61	141444	**Shield**, inner	4	
AN62	141218	**Bearing**, nylon, inner hub	4	
AN63	141185	**Seal**, dirt	4	
AN64	141443	**Shield**, outer	4	Fitted up to Commission No.
AN65	104585	**Bearing**, ball, rear hub	2	⎬ KC50000 only
AN66	107193	**Seal**, oil	2	See Page 65 for future
AN67	104773	**Housing**, oil seal	2	
AN68	106664	**Washer**, joint, oil seal housing	2	
AN69	104582	**Catcher**, oil	2	
AN70	121862	**Bolt** ⎱ Oil seal housing and	8	
AN71	121860	**Washer**, tab ⎰ back plate attachment	4	
AN72	131567	**REAR HUB AND STUD ASSEMBLY**	2	⎫
AN73	112429	**Stud**, wheel	8	
AN74	104581	**Key**, axle shaft ⎫	2	
AN75	142333	**Washer**, plain ⎬ Rear hub to axle shaft	2	
AN76	510618	**Nut**, nyloc ⎭	2	⎭

Note:—Items marked thus † are available on our Factory Exchange Unit Scheme

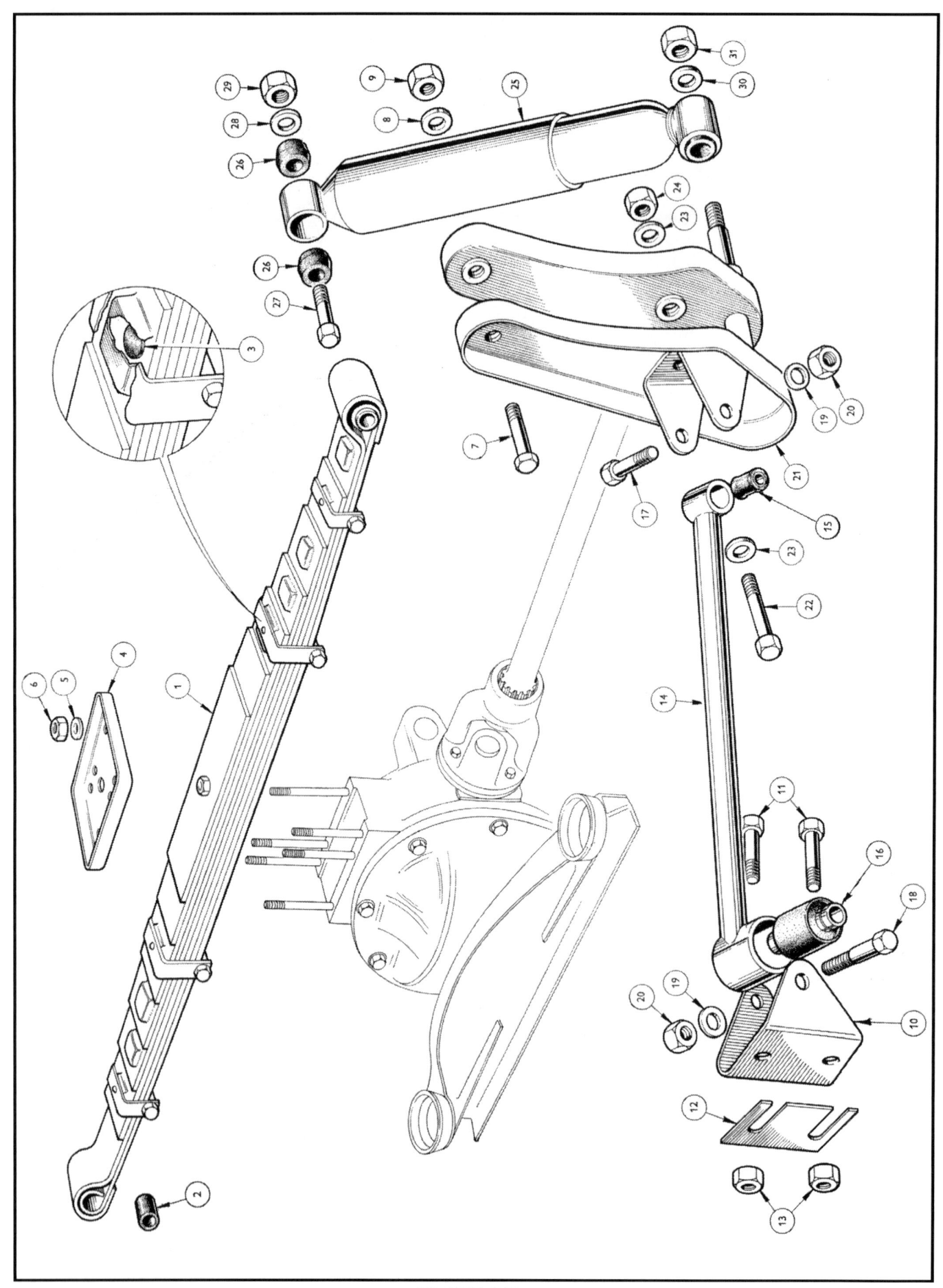

PLATE AP

REAR SUSPENSION
MARK I CARS FITTED UP TO COMMISSION No. KC50000 ONLY

Plate No.	Part No.	Description	No. per Unit	Remarks
AP1	307324	**REAR TRANSVERSE ROAD SPRING ASSEMBLY**	1	
	307324M	**Leaf**, main	1	
AP2	117575	**Bush**, rubber	2	
AP3	114006	**Button**, thrust	8	
AP4	128352	**Plate**, spring	1	
AP5	WP0045	**Washer**, plain ⎫	6	
AP6	YN2909	**Nut**, nyloc ⎬ Spring and plate to axle housing	6	Alternative to AN3509
AP6	AN3509	**Nut**, Philidas ⎭	6	Alternative to YN2909
AP7	HB1027	**Bolt** ⎫ Rear spring ends	2	
AP8	WP0010	**Washer**, plain ⎬ to	2	
AP9	YN2910	**Nut**, nyloc ⎭ vertical link plates	2	
	146315	**Bracket**, pivot, R.H.	1	
AP10	146316	**Bracket**, pivot, L.H.	1	
AP11	HU0914	**Screw**, set, pivot bracket attachment	4	
AP12	133070	**Shim** ⎫ Pivot bracket	A/R	
AP13	JN2109	**Nut**, jam ⎭ to floor panel	4	
AP14	146317	**Radius arm** assembly	2	
AP15	119451	**Bush**, rubber, rear	2	
AP16	146321	**Bush**, rubber, front	2	
AP17	HB0918	**Bolt**, rear ⎫	2	
AP18	HB0921	**Bolt**, front ⎬ Radius arms to bracket	2	
AP19	WP0009	**Washer**, plain ⎬ and vertical link	4	
AP20	YN2909	**Nut**, nyloc ⎬	4	Alternative to AN3509
AP20	AN3509	**Nut**, Philidas ⎭	4	Alternative to YN2909
	132763	**REAR VERTICAL LINK ASSEMBLY—R.H.**	1	
AP21	132764	**REAR VERTICAL LINK ASSEMBLY—L.H.**	1	
AP22	HB1027	**Bolt** ⎫ Vertical link plates	2	
AP23	WP0010	**Washer** ⎬ to	4	
AP24	YN2910	**Nut**, nyloc ⎭ rear hub, inner	2	
AP25	144278	**REAR DAMPER**	2	
AP26	133524	**Bush**, rubber, damper eye	8	
AP27	118599	**Pin**, fulcrum ⎫	2	
AP28	WP0119	**Washer**, plain ⎬ Rear damper upper attachment	2	
AP29	TN3211	**Nut**, nyloc ⎭	2	
AP30	WM0069	**Washer**, plain ⎫ Rear damper	2	
AP31	YN2910	**Nut**, nyloc ⎭ lower attachment	2	

Note:—Items marked thus † are available on our Factory Exchange Unit Scheme

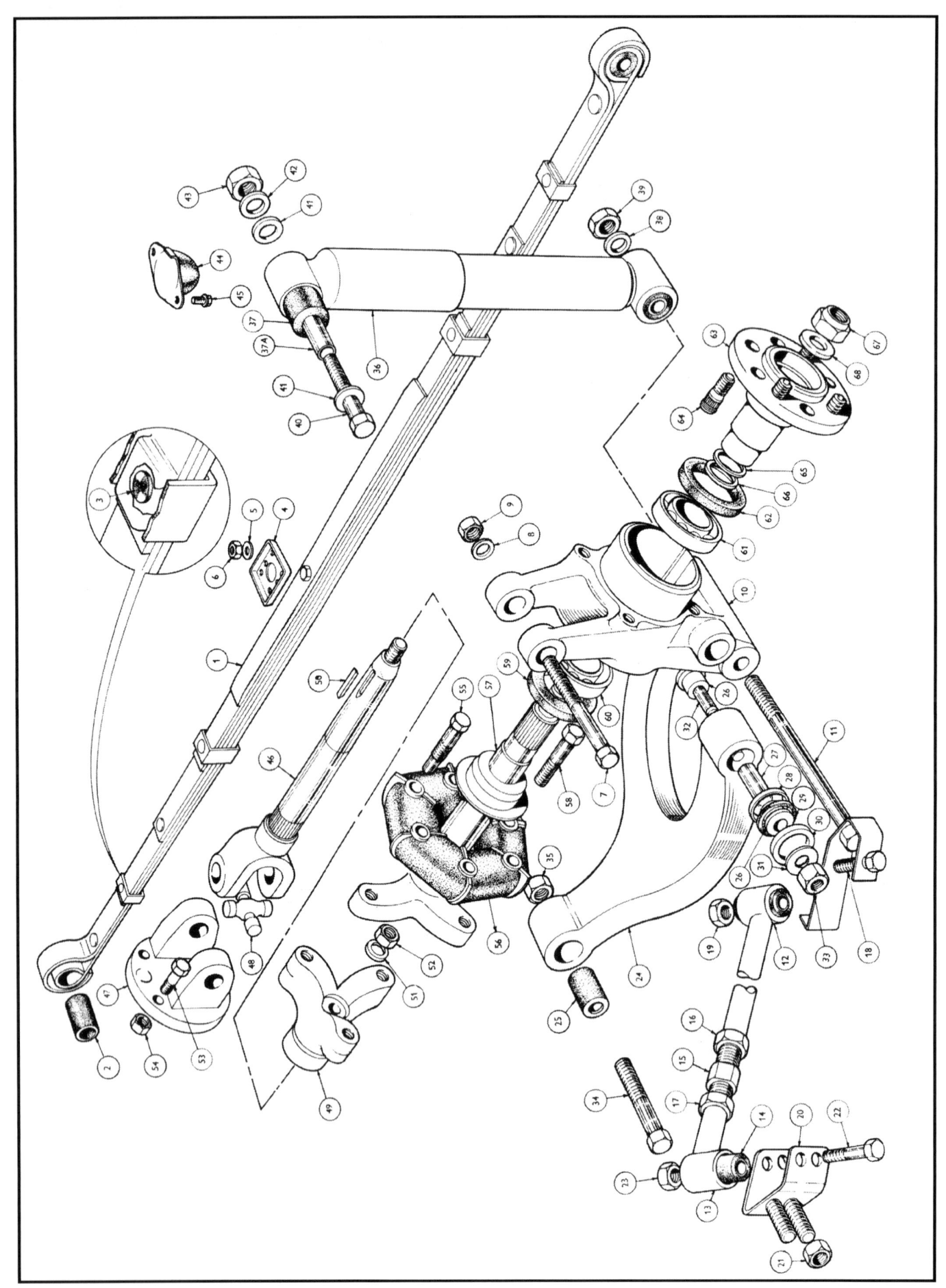

PLATE AQ

REAR SUSPENSION
MARK II (G.T.6+) CARS FITTED FROM COMMISSION No. KC50001 AND FUTURE

Plate No.	Part No.	Description	No. per Unit	Remarks
AQ1	308499	**REAR TRANSVERSE ROAD SPRING ASSEMBLY**	1	
	308499/M	**Leaf**, main	1	
AQ2	117575	**Bush**, rubber	2	
AQ3	114006	**Button**, thrust	8	
AQ4	128352	**Plate**, spring	1	
AQ5	WP0045	**Washer**, plain ⎫	6	
AQ6	YN2909	**Nut**, nyloc ⎬ Spring and plate to axle housing	6	Alternative to AN3509
	AN3509	**Nut**, Philidas ⎭	6	Alternative to YN2909
AQ7	HB1032	**Bolt** ⎫ Rear road spring ends	2	
AQ8	WP0010	**Washer**, plain ⎬ to	2	
AQ9	YN2910	**Nut**, nyloc ⎭ vertical link	2	
	308437	**REAR VERTICAL LINK—R.H.**	1	
AQ10	308438	**REAR VERTICAL LINK—L.H.**	1	
	148975	**Bracket** assembly, mounting, radius arm to vertical link—R.H.	1	
AQ11	148976	**Bracket** assembly, mounting, radius arm to vertical link—L.H.	1	
	151092	**Radius arm** assembly	2	
AQ12	151094	**Eye**, rear, assembly, radius arm	2	
AQ13	151093	**Eye**, front, assembly, radius arm	2	
AQ14	119450	**Bush**, rubber	4	
AQ15	151099	**Adjuster**, radius arm	2	
AQ16	151110	**Nut**, lock ⎫ Adjuster to tubes	2	
AQ17	JN2111	**Nut**, lock ⎭	2	
AQ18	HB1020	**Bolt** ⎫ Radius arm to bracket	2	
AQ19	TN3210	**Nut** ⎭ on vertical link	2	
AQ20	148963	**Bracket** assembly, mounting, radius arm to body floor	2	
AQ21	YN2909	**Nut**, nyloc, radius arm brackets to body floor	4	
AQ22	HB1020	**Bolt** ⎫ Radius arm to	2	
AQ23	TN3210	**Nut**, nyloc ⎭ body floor bracket	2	
	149769	**LOWER WISHBONE ASSEMBLY—R.H.**	1	
AQ24	149770	**LOWER WISHBONE ASSEMBLY—L.H.**	1	
AQ25	148874	**Bush**, lower wishbone	2	
AQ26	148926	**Bush**, outer ⎫	8	
AQ27	148948	**Tube**, distance ⎬	4	
AQ28	148939	**Shield**, water ⎬	8	
AQ29	148950	**Seal**, dirt ⎬ Lower wishbone to	8	
AQ30	148940	**Shield**, water ⎬ vertical link	8	
AQ31	WP8020	**Washer**, plain ⎭	8	
AQ32	149003	**Bolt** ⎫	2	
AQ33	YN2911	**Nut**, nyloc ⎭	2	
AQ34	HB1122	**Bolt** ⎫ Lower wishbone to	2	
AQ35	TN3211	**Nut** ⎭ chassis frame	2	

Note:—Items marked thus † are available on our Factory Exchange Unit Scheme

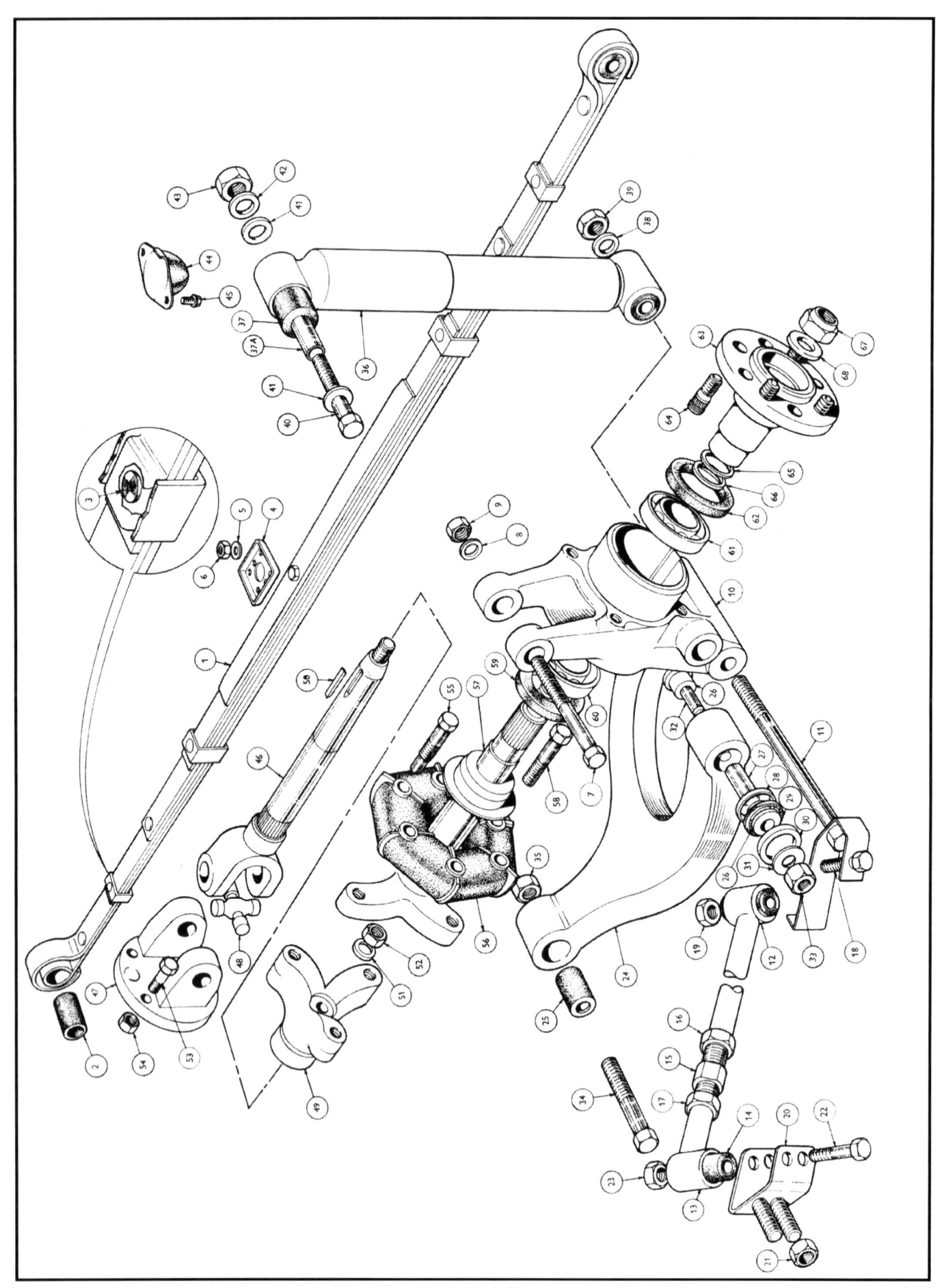

PLATE AQ

REAR SUSPENSION
MARK II (G.T.6+) CARS FITTED FROM COMMISSION No. KC50001 AND FUTURE

Plate No.	Part No.	Description	No. per Unit	Remarks
AQ36	149185	**REAR DAMPER**	2	
AQ37	517666	**Bush**, rubber, damper eye	4	
AQ37a	517667	**Sleeve**, fitted in rubber bush	4	
AQ38	WP8020	**Washer**, plain ⎫ Rear dampers and radius	4	
AQ39	YN2911	**Nut**, nyloc ⎬ arm brackets to vertical link	2	
AQ40	148969	**Bolt** ⎭	2	
AQ41	WP8020	**Washer**, plain ⎫ Rear damper to rear	4	
AQ42	WP0011	**Washer**, plain ⎬ wheelarch bracket	2	
AQ43	YN2911	**Nut**, nyloc ⎭	2	
AQ44	150583	**Rubber**, bump, rear dampers	2	
AQ45	150786	**Screw**, "taptite" bump rubber to wheelarch bracket	4	
AQ46	214623	**INTERMEDIATE DRIVE SHAFT ASSEMBLY**	2	
AQ47	132328	**Flange**, yoke	2	
AQ48	128133	**Unit package**	2	
AQ49	212067	**Flange**, driven	2	
AQ50	144233	**Key** ⎫	2	
AQ51	WP0013	**Washer**, plain ⎬ Driven flange to shaft	2	
AQ52	510618	**Nut**, nyloc ⎭	2	
	128135	**Shaft**, yoke, assembly	2	
AQ53	132023	**Bolt** ⎫ Shaft joint to	8	
AQ54	511506	**Nut**, nyloc ⎭ inner axle shaft	8	
AQ55	144588	**Bolt**, driven flange to rotoflex coupling	6	
AQ56	152273	**ROTOFLEX COUPLING**	2	
AQ57	214614	**DRIVE SHAFT ASSEMBLY, OUTER**	2	
	149865	**Stoneguard**	2	
	148850	**Spacer**	2	
AQ58	141850	**Bolt**, outer drive shaft to rotoflex coupling	6	
AQ59	143826	**Oil seal**, inner ⎫	2	
AQ60	142919	**Bearing**, inner ⎬ Fitted in	2	
AQ61	134589	**Bearing**, outer ⎬ vertical link	2	
AQ62	142337	**Oil seal**, outer ⎭	2	
AQ63	149051	**REAR HUB AND STUD ASSEMBLY**	2	
AQ64	112429	**Stud**, wheel	8	
AQ65	143923	**Piece**, distance .141" thick ⎫	A/R	
AQ65	143924	**Piece**, distance ·148" thick ⎬ Rear hub	A/R	
AQ65	143925	**Piece**, distance ·155" thick ⎬ adjustment	A/R	
AQ66	142340	**Shim** ⎭	A/R	
AQ67	510618	**Nut**, nyloc ⎫ Rear hub to	2	
AQ68	142333	**Washer** ⎭ outer drive shaft	2	

Note:—Items marked thus † are available on our Factory Exchange Unit Scheme

PLATE AR

PROPELLOR SHAFT AND ROAD WHEELS

Plate No.	Part No.	Description	No. per Unit	Remarks
AR1	213150	†PROPELLOR SHAFT (B.R.D.)	1	
	213151	†PROPELLOR SHAFT	1	Only required when Overdrive is fitted
AR2	513800	Unit package (B.R.D.)	2	
AR3	144961	Bolt } Shaft to mainshaft flange	4	
AR4	TN3209	Nut, nyloc	4	
AR5	144961	Bolt } Shaft to hypoid pinion flange	4	
AR6	TN3209	Nut, nyloc	4	
AR7	307405	ROAD WHEEL	5	
AR8	113087	Nut, road wheel	16	
AR9	122806	Plate, nave	4	All markets except U.S.A.
	811419	Wheel Trim	4	Fitted up to Commission No. KC50000 U.S.A. only
	811797	Trim assembly, road wheel	4	Fitted from Commission No. KC50001 and future U.S.A. only
	514517	WIRE WHEEL KIT	1	
AR10	212344	Road wheel, wire	5	
	514930	Spoke, short, wire wheel	40	
	514931	Spoke, long, wire wheel	20	Special Orders for all Markets except Germany, Switzerland and U.S.A. up to Commission No. KC7875 only
	502650	Nipple, spoke	60	
AR11	142597	Adaptor, hub, R.H.	2	
	142598	Adaptor, hub, L.H.	2	
AR12	144504	Nut, securing adaptors to hubs	16	
AR13	107948	Wheel nut, knock-on, R.H.	2	
	107949	Wheel nut, knock-on, L.H.	2	
	108450	Mallet, wheel nuts	1	
	514518	WIRE WHEEL KIT	1	Special Orders for Germany, Switzerland, and U.S.A. up to Commission No. KC7875 only All Markets from Commission No. KC7876 and future
AR14	121295	Wheel nut, octagonal, R.H.	2	
	121296	Wheel nut, octagonal, L.H.	2	
	121297	Spanner, wheel nuts	1	
		For all other Details see Kit No. 514517		

Note:- Inner tubes **must** be fitted to Wire Wheels.

Note:—Items marked thus † are available on our Factory Exchange Unit Scheme

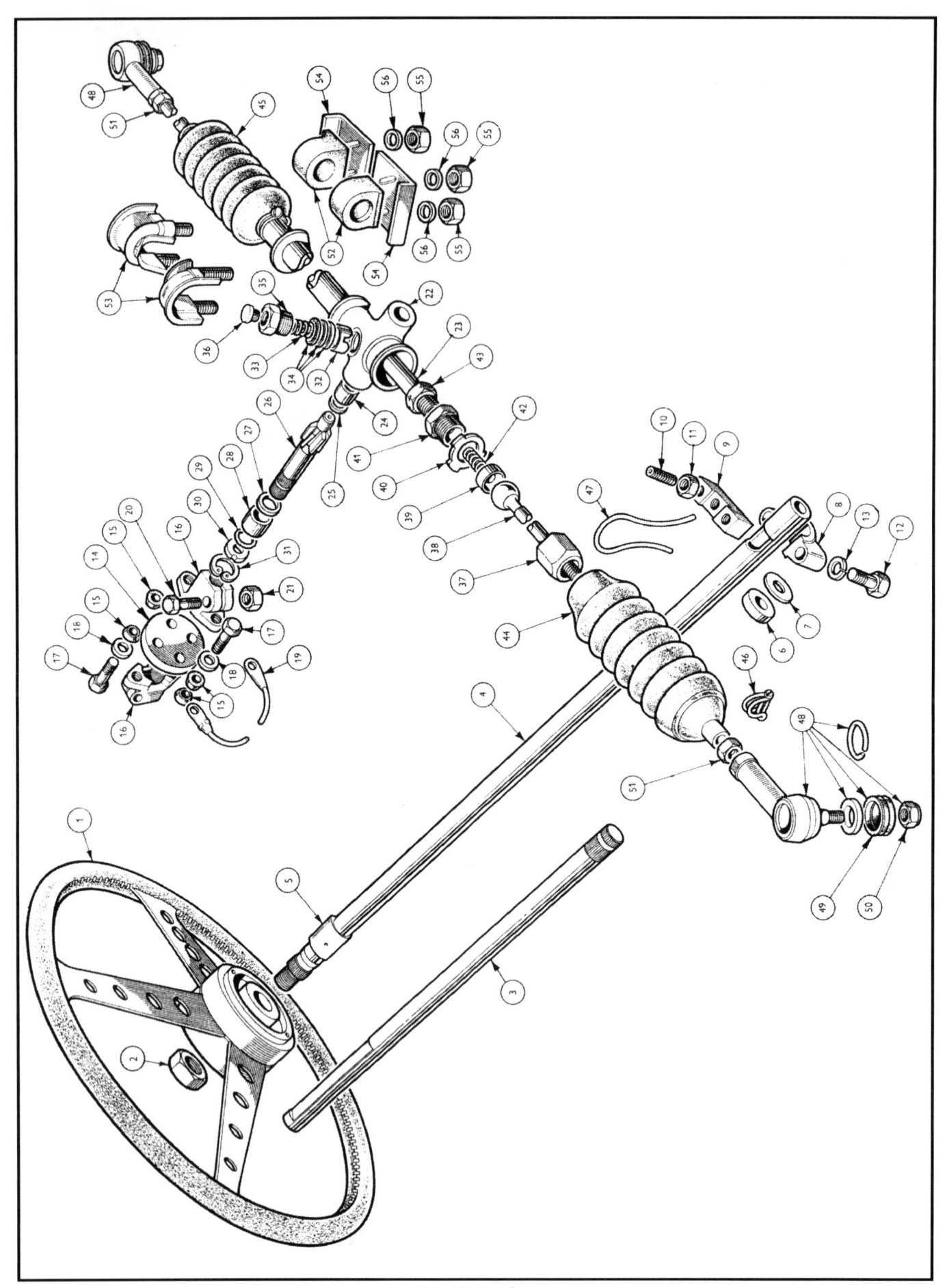

PLATE AS

STEERING

Plate No.	Part No.	Description	No. per Unit	Remarks
AS1	308607	**STEERING WHEEL (Dull Finish Spokes)** Alternative to 307619	1	All markets except U.S.A. up to Commission No. KC50000 only
	307619	**STEERING WHEEL (Polished Spokes)** Alternative to 308607	1	
	812651	**STEERING WHEEL ASSEMBLY (Trimmed)**	1	U.S.A. only up to Commission No. KC50000
	812652	**Trim** assembly, steering wheel	1	
	622275	**Washer**, plate ⎫ Trim to wheel	3	All markets from KC50001 and future
	622276	**Nut**, "Dotloc" ⎭	3	
AS2	105438	**Nut**, steering wheel	1	
AS3	209688	**STEERING COLUMN—LOWER**	1	
AS4	140755	**STEERING COLUMN UPPER ASSEMBLY**	1	
	150064	**STEERING COLUMN UPPER ASSEMBLY (LOCKING)**	1	Special Orders only up to Commission No. KC50000
	151496	**STEERING COLUMN UPPER ASSEMBLY (LOCKING)**	1	Special Orders only from Commission No. KC50001 and future
AS5	140549	**Clip**, cancelling, trafficator	1	
AS6	122718	**Cap**, end, steering column cowl	1	
AS7	122719	**Washer**, bearing	1	
AS8	122669	**Clamp**, steering column	1	
AS9	125782	**Plate**, locating ⎫	1	
AS10	125781	**Screw**, locating ⎪	1	
AS11	JN2110	**Nut**, jam ⎬ Clamp to steering column	1	
AS12	HB0710	**Bolt** ⎪	2	
AS13	WL0207	**Washer**, lock ⎭	2	
	149698	**Tube**, distance, cardboard—L.H.S. only	1	
	142140	**FLEXIBLE JOINT ASSEMBLY**	1	
AS14	110960	**Plate**, flexible joint	1	
AS15	108977	**Bush**, rubber, adaptor plate	8	
AS16	142139	**Adaptor**, steering column	2	
AS17	108976	**Bolt**, plate and bushes to adaptor	4	
AS18	502136	**Washer**, plain, on bolt	4	
AS19	110461	**Strip**, conductor, on bolt	1	
	502148	**Wire**, locking bolt	4	
AS20	HB0810	**Bolt** ⎫ Adaptors to	2	
AS21	TN3208	**Nut**, nyloc ⎭ column and unit	2	
	307830	†**RACK AND PINION ASSEMBLY—R.H.S.**	1	
	307831	†**RACK AND PINION ASSEMBLY—L.H.S.**	1	
	308170	†**RACK AND PINION ASSEMBLY—R.H.S.**	1	Special Order (fitted with grease nipples)
	308171	†**RACK AND PINION ASSEMBLY—L.H.S.**	1	
AS22	Not Serviced	**Rack and pinion body**		
	145108	**Plug**, nylon, fitted in rack and pinion assembly	1	
	128002	**Bush**, rack tube	1	
	128020	**Cover**, end	1	
AS23	208058	**Rack**, steering	1	

Note:—Items marked thus † are available on our Factory Exchange Unit Scheme

67

PLATE AS

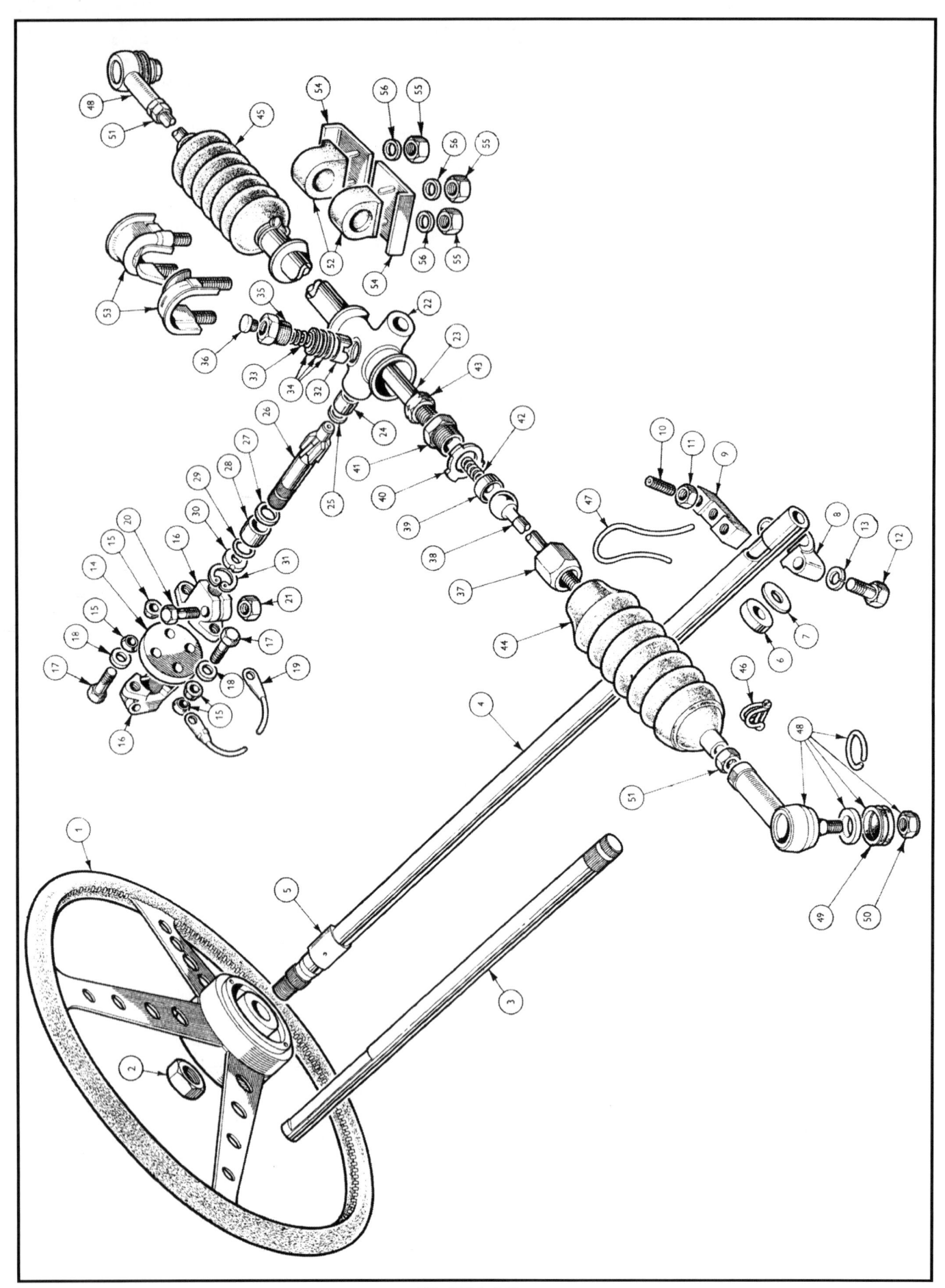

STEERING

Plate No.	Part No.	Description	No. per Unit	Remarks
		RACK AND PINION ASSEMBLY—cont.		
AS24	127997	**Bush,** pinion, lower	1	
AS25	128000	**Washer,** thrust	1	
AS26	213636	**Pinion,** R.H.S.	1	
	213635	**Pinion,** L.H.S.	1	
AS27	127999	**Washer,** thrust	1	
AS28	127998	**Bush,** pinion, upper	1	
	120941	**Shim**	A/R	
AS29	128021	**'O' Ring**	1	
AS30	128001	**Plug,** end	1	
	128008	**Pin**	1	
AS31	509537	**Circlip**	1	
AS32	120946	**Plunger**	1	
	143952	**Washer,** packing, plunger	1	
AS33	126765	**Spring**	1	
AS34	120959	**Shim,** ·002″	A/R	
AS34	120949	**Shim,** ·004″	A/R	
AS34	132055	**Shim,** ·010″	A/R	
AS35	132053	**Cap,** screwed	1	
AS36	133103	**Plug,** grease	1	
	129961	**INNER BALL JOINT ASSEMBLY**	2	
AS37	128024	**Housing,** ball	2	
AS38	128023	**Pin,** ball	2	
AS39	120955	**Socket,** ball	2	
AS40	120957	**Washer,** tab	2	
AS40	130031	**Shim,** ·002″	A/R	
AS40	130032	**Shim,** ·010″	A/R	
AS41	129963	**Sleeve,** adaptor	2	
AS42	120953	**Spring**	2	
AS43	142795	**Locknut**	2	
AS44	128004	**Bellows,** driver's side	1	
AS45	120948	**Bellows,** passenger's side	1	
AS46	CS4009	**Clip,** bellows	2	
	CS4020	**Clip,** bellows, passenger's side	1	
AS47	512781	**Wire,** binding bellows, driver's side	1	
AS48	136600	**Ball joint** assembly, tie rod end	2	
AS49	512420	**Gaiter** assembly	2	
AS50	TN3209	**Nut,** nyloc	2	
	146728	**Ball joint** assembly, tie rod end (fitted with grease nipples)	2	Special Order
	500098	**Nipple,** grease	2	
	WF0541	**Washer,** fibre, grease nipple	2	
	104775	**Seal,** oil, ball joint assembly	2	
	TN3209	**Nut,** nyloc	2	
	WP0045	**Washer,** plain	2	
AS51	128022	**Locknut,** ball joint attachment	2	
AS52	147852	**MOUNTING RUBBER, RACK AND PINION BODY**	2	
AS53	136885	**Clamp** assembly ⎫	2	
AS54	133875	**Plate,** reinforcement ⎬ Rack and pinion	2	
AS55	YN2908	**Nut,** nyloc ⎨ body to frame	4	
AS56	WP0008	**Washer,** plain ⎭	4	

Note:—Items marked thus † are available on our Factory Exchange Unit Scheme

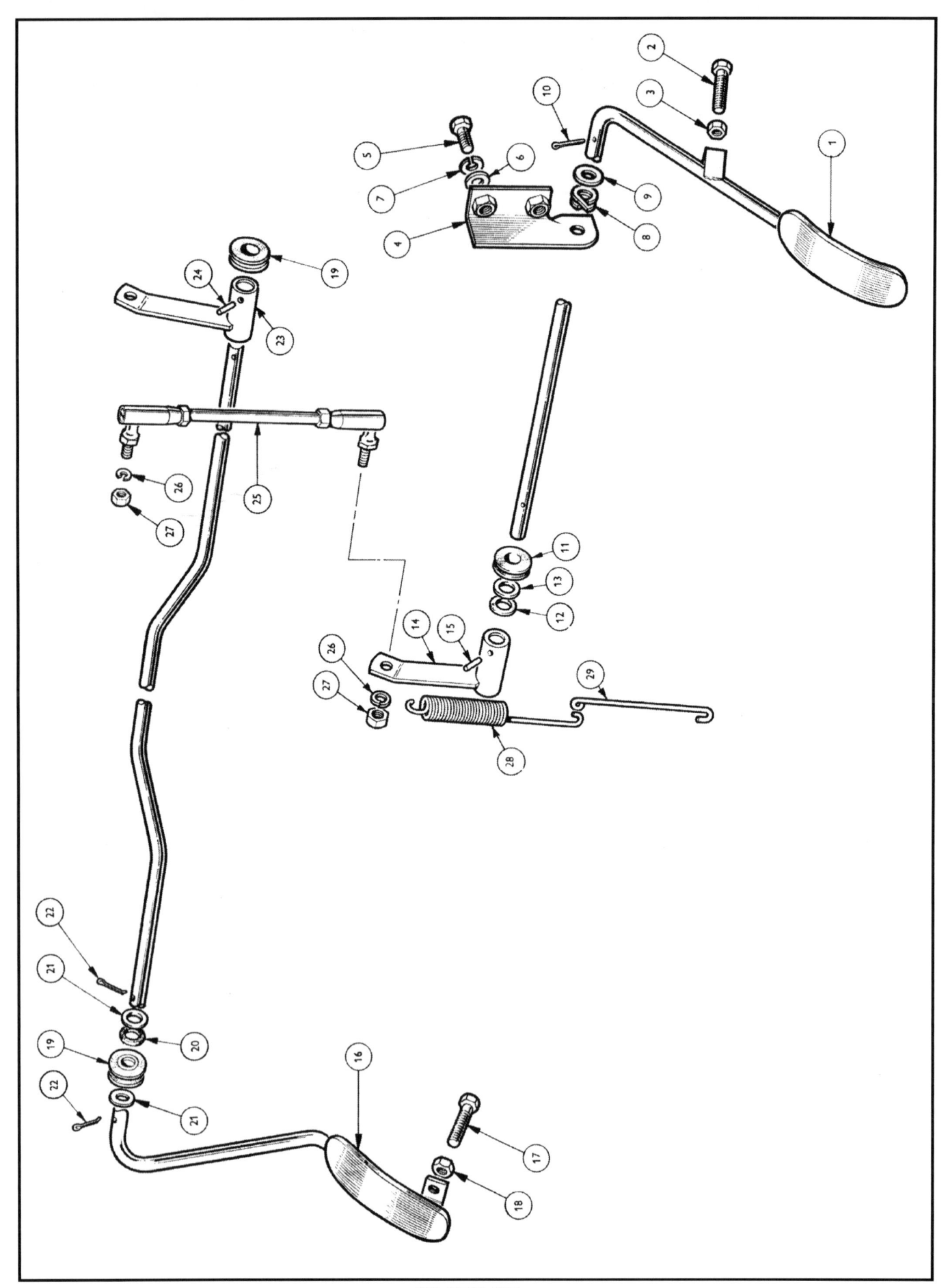

PLATE AT

ACCELERATION CONTROL

Plate No.	Part No.	Description	No. per Unit	Remarks
AT1	212310	**ACCELERATOR PEDAL ASSEMBLY—R.H.S.** (including Item AT14)	1	
AT2	HU0809	Screw, set ⎫ Accelerator stop	1	
AT3	HN2008	Nut ⎭	1	
AT4	137015	Bracket, fulcrum, assembly	1	
AT5	HU0704	Screw, set ⎫	2	
AT6	WP0007	Washer, plain ⎬ Fulcrum bracket to body	2	
AT7	WL0207	Washer, lock ⎭	2	
AT8	WD0159	Washer, lock, double coil ⎫	1	
AT9	WP0009	Washer, plain ⎬ Locating pedal in bearing	1	
AT10	PC0009	Pin, cotter ⎭	1	
AT11	134540	Bearing, accelerator pedal	1	
AT12	134953	Seal, felt, accelerator lever	1	
AT13	WP0009	Washer, plain	1	
AT14	142462	Lever assembly, accelerator operating	1	
AT15	DS1312	Dowel, spring, attaching lever to pedal shaft	1	
AT16	212667	**ACCELERATOR PEDAL ASSEMBLY—L.H.S.** (including Item AT23)	1	
AT17	HU0809	Screw, set ⎫ Accelerator stop	1	
AT18	HN2008	Nut ⎭	1	
AT19	134540	Bearing, accelerator pedal	2	
AT20	134953	Seal, felt, accelerator lever ⎫	1	
AT21	WP0009	Washer, plain ⎬ Locating pedal in bearing	2	
AT22	PC0009	Pin, cotter ⎭	2	
AT23	146297	Lever assembly, accelerator operating	1	
AT24	DS1312	Dowel, spring, attaching lever to pedal shaft	1	
AT25	142519	**THROTTLE OPERATING LINK ROD ASSEMBLY**	1	Fitted up to Commission No. KC1114 only
	134545	**THROTTLE OPERATING LINK ROD ASSEMBLY**	1	Fitted from Commission No. KC1115 up to KC11014 L.H.S. and KC9062 R.H.S. only
	149435	**THROTTLE OPERATING LINK ROD ASSEMBLY**	1	Fitted from Commission No. KC11015 L.H.S. and KC9063 R.H.S. and future
AT26	WL0207	Washer, lock ⎫ Link rod to operating and	2	
AT27	HN2007	Nut ⎭ carburettor levers	2	
AT28	137482	Spring, throttle return	1	
AT29	143747	Link, throttle return spring	1	

Note:- For Acceleration Control Details fitted to U.S.A. Vehicles from Commission No. KC7611, see page 70.

Note:—Items marked thus † are available on our Factory Exchange Unit Scheme

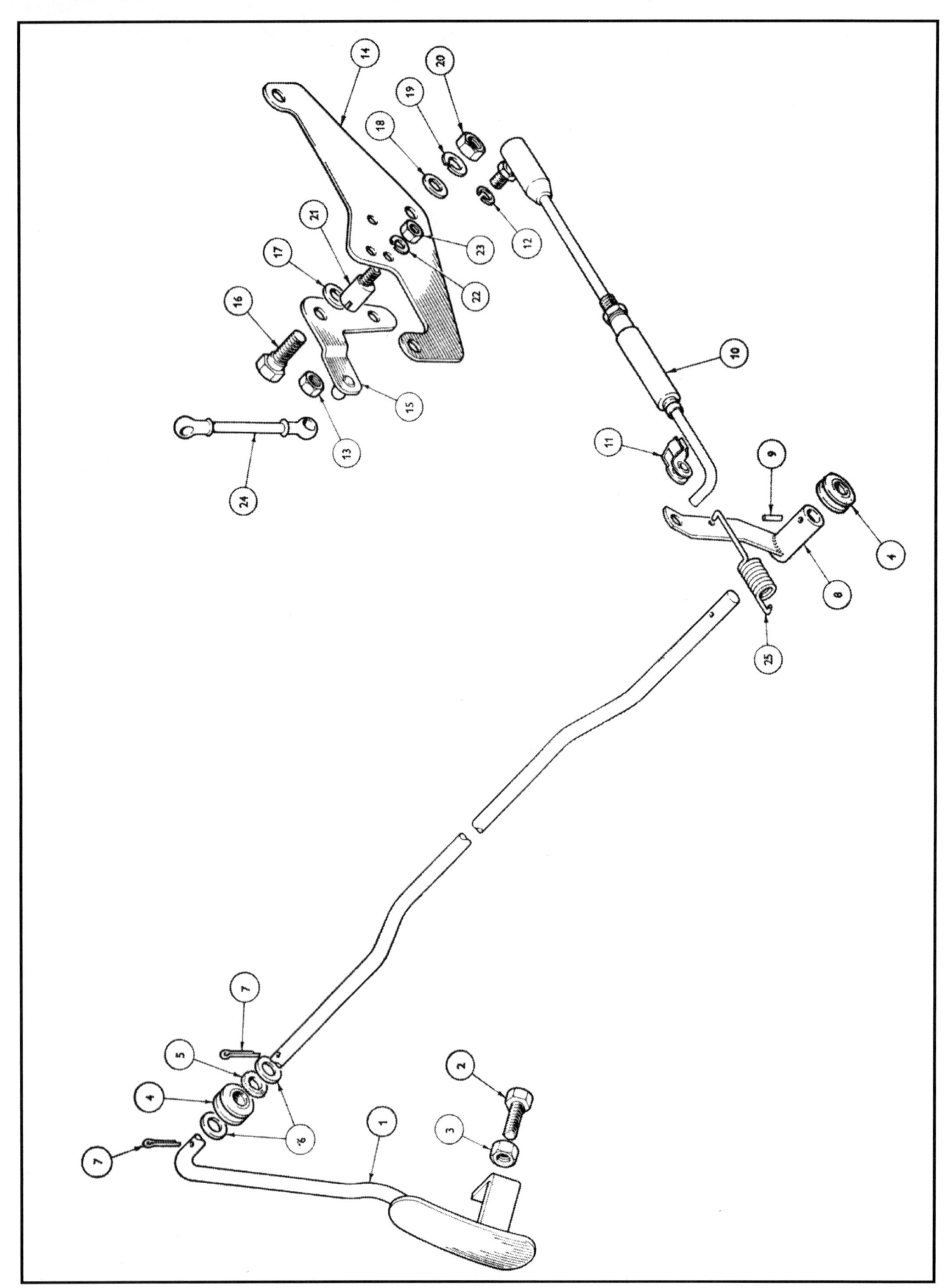

PLATE AU

ACCELERATION CONTROL

Plate No.	Part No.	Description	No. per Unit	Remarks
		ACCELERATION CONTROL DETAILS FOR VEHICLES COMPLYING WITH U.S.A. ANTI-AIR POLLUTION REGULATIONS FROM COMM. No. KC7611—SEE PAGE 69 (L.H.S. ITEMS) FOR DETAILS FITTED TO EARLIER U.S.A. VEHICLES.		
AU1	214666	**ACCELERATOR PEDAL ASSEMBLY—L.H.S.** (including Item No. AU8)	1	
AU2	HU0809	**Screw**, set ⎫ Accelerator stop	1	
AU3	HN2008	**Nut** ⎭	1	
AU4	134540	**Bearing**, accelerator pedal	2	
AU5	134953	**Seal**, felt, accelerator lever	1	
AU6	WP0009	**Washer**, plain	2	
AU7	PC0009	**Pin**, cotter	2	
AU8	149027	**Lever** assembly, accelerator operating	1	
AU9	DS1312	**Dowel**, spring, attaching lever to pedal shaft	1	
AU10	149777	**ADJUSTABLE CONTROL ROD ASSEMBLY —OPERATING LEVER TO BELL CRANK**	1	
AU11	606698	**Clip**, spring, control rod to operating lever	1	
AU12	WL0207	**Washer**, lock ⎫ Control rod to	1	
AU13	HN2007	**Nut** ⎭ bell crank lever	1	
AU14	214665	**Bracket**, support, assembly, bell crank lever (fitted on carburettor studs)	1	
AU15	149030	**Lever**, bell crank	1	
AU16	136482	**Bolt**, shoulder ⎫	1	
AU17	WP0110	**Washer**, plain ⎪ Bell crank lever	1	
AU18	WP0008	**Washer**, plain ⎬ to	1	
AU19	WL0208	**Washer**, lock ⎪ support bracket	1	
AU20	HN2008	**Nut** ⎭	1	
AU21	148972	**Stop**, throttle, adjustable (fitted in bell crank lever bracket)	1	
AU22	WL0203	**Washer**, lock ⎫ Throttle stop to	1	
AU23	HN2053	**Nut** ⎭ support bracket	1	
AU24	149028	**CONNECTING LINK AND SOCKET ASSY. (BELL CRANK TO CARBURETTOR)**	1	
AU25	149025	**Spring**, throttle return	1	

Note:—Items marked thus † are available on our Factory Exchange Unit Scheme

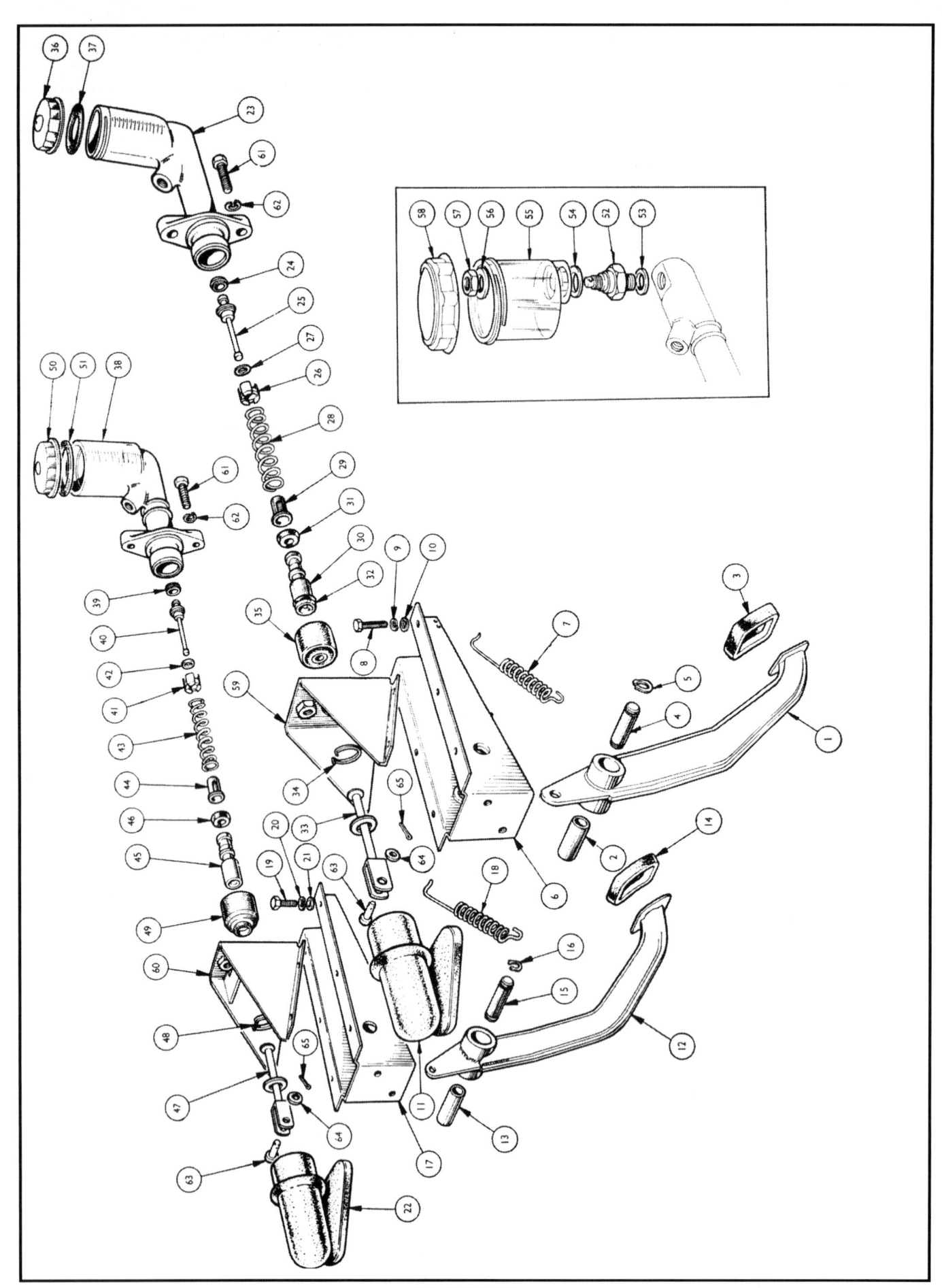

PLATE AV

CLUTCH AND BRAKE PEDALS

Plate No.	Part No.	Description	No. per Unit	Remarks
	209836	**CLUTCH PEDAL AND MOUNTING BRACKET ASSEMBLY**	1	
AV1	134504	**Pedal** assembly, clutch	1	
AV2	105605	**Bush,** pedal to shaft	1	
AV3	122289	**Pad,** rubber, on pedal	1	
AV4	119575	**Shaft,** pedal ⎫ Pedal to	1	
AV5	506542	**Circlip** ⎭ mounting bracket	2	
AV6	137842	**Bracket,** assembly, pedal mounting	1	
AV7	114438	**Spring,** pedal, return	1	
AV8	HU0705	**Screw,** set ⎫	8	
AV9	WL0207	**Washer,** lock ⎬ Pedal mounting bracket to dash	8	
AV10	WM0057	**Washer,** plain ⎭	4	
AV11	125217	**Cover,** dust, clutch pedal	1	
	209837	**BRAKE PEDAL AND MOUNTING BRACKET ASSEMBLY**	1	
AV12	134503	**Pedal** assembly, brake	1	
AV13	105605	**Bush,** pedal to shaft	1	
AV14	122289	**Pad,** rubber, on pedal	1	
AV15	119575	**Shaft,** pedal ⎫ Pedal to	1	
AV16	506542	**Circlip** ⎭ mounting bracket	2	
AV17	134532	**Bracket,** assembly, brake pedal mounting	1	
AV18	114438	**Spring,** pedal return	1	
AV19	HU0705	**Screw,** set ⎫	8	
AV20	WL0207	**Washer,** lock ⎬ Pedal mounting bracket to dash	8	
AV21	WM0057	**Washer,** plain ⎭	4	
AV22	125217	**Cover,** dust, brake pedal	1	

Note:—Items marked thus † are available on our Factory Exchange Unit Scheme

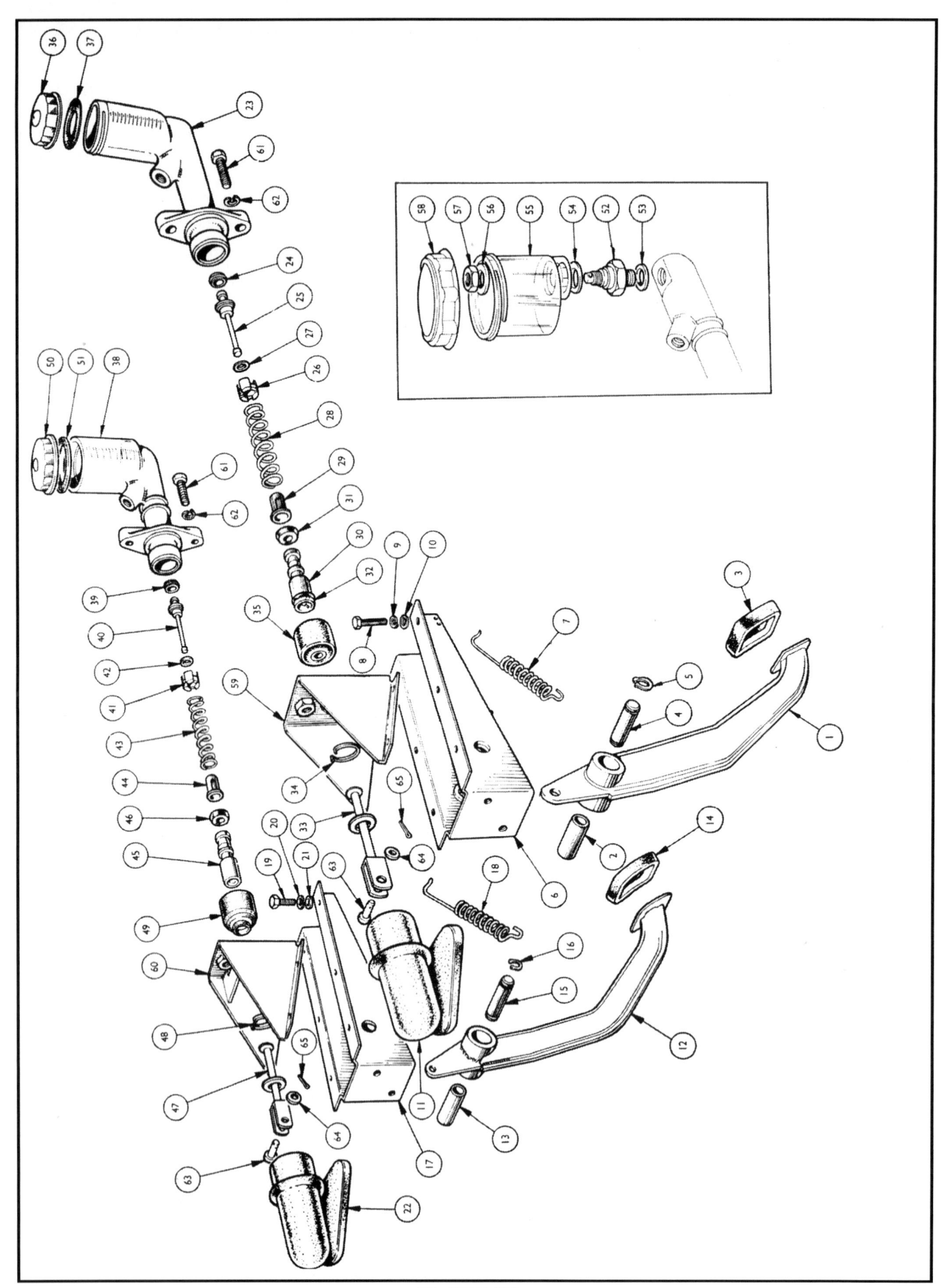

PLATE AV

MASTER CYLINDER

Plate No.	Part No.	Description	No. per Unit	Remarks
	120308	†CLUTCH MASTER CYLINDER ASSEMBLY	1	
AV23	Not Serviced	Body, master cylinder		
AV24	106158	Seal, valve	1	
AV25	106157	Stem, valve	1	
AV26	111163	Spacer, valve	1	
AV27	106090	Washer, spring, valve head	1	
AV28	106156	Spring, plunger	1	
AV29	106088	Retainer, spring	1	
AV30	106155	Plunger, cylinder	1	
AV31	109190	Seal, plunger	1	
AV32	111979	Seal, taper, cylinder plunger	1	
AV33	122296	Rod, push, assembly	1	
AV34	106092	Circlip, push rod retainer	1	
AV35	510940	Cover, dust, rubber, cylinder end	1	
AV36	106094	Lid, reservoir	1	
AV37	106095	Gasket, on reservoir lid	1	
	145232	†BRAKE MASTER CYLINDER ASSEMBLY	1	
	213627	†BRAKE MASTER CYLINDER ASSEMBLY	1	France & Special Orders only
AV38	Not Serviced	Body, master cylinder		
AV39	106158	Seal, valve	1	
AV40	106157	Stem, valve	1	
AV41	111163	Spacer, valve	1	
AV42	106090	Washer, spring, valve head	1	
AV43	106156	Spring, plunger	1	
AV44	106088	Retainer, spring	1	
AV45	511137	Plunger, cylinder	1	
AV46	511138	Seal, gland, plunger	1	
AV47	122296	Rod, push, assembly	1	
AV48	106092	Circlip, push rod retainer	1	
AV49	106093	Cover, dust, cylinder end	1	
AV50	510844	Lid, reservoir	1	Not required France
AV51	510845	Gasket, on reservoir lid	1	
AV52	133580	Adaptor, reservoir to body	1	
AV53	116201	Gasket, adaptor to body	1	
AV54	133582	Seal, adaptor to reservoir	1	
AV55	133579	Reservoir	1	France & Special Orders
AV56	WP0045	Washer, plain ⎱ Reservoir to	1	
AV57	JN2109	Nut, jam ⎰ adaptor attachment	1	
AV58	133581	Cap, filler	1	
AV59	119583	CLUTCH MASTER CYLINDER SUPPORT BRACKET	1	
AV60	138077	BRAKE MASTER CYLINDER SUPPORT BRACKET	1	
	146413	BRAKE MASTER CYLINDER SUPPORT BRACKET	1	France & Special Orders
		Note:- 146413 may be used for all replacements.		
AV61	HU0807	Screw, set ⎱ Master cylinder to	4	
AV62	WL0208	Washer, lock ⎰ support brackets	4	
AV63	PJ8808	Pin ⎱	2	
AV64	WP0008	Washer, plain ⎱ Clutch and brake pedals to master cylinder push rods	2	
AV65	PC0009	Pin, cotter ⎰	2	
	508445	Service kit, clutch master cylinder	1	
	515786	Service kit, brake master cylinder	1	

Note:—Items marked thus † are available on our Factory Exchange Unit Scheme

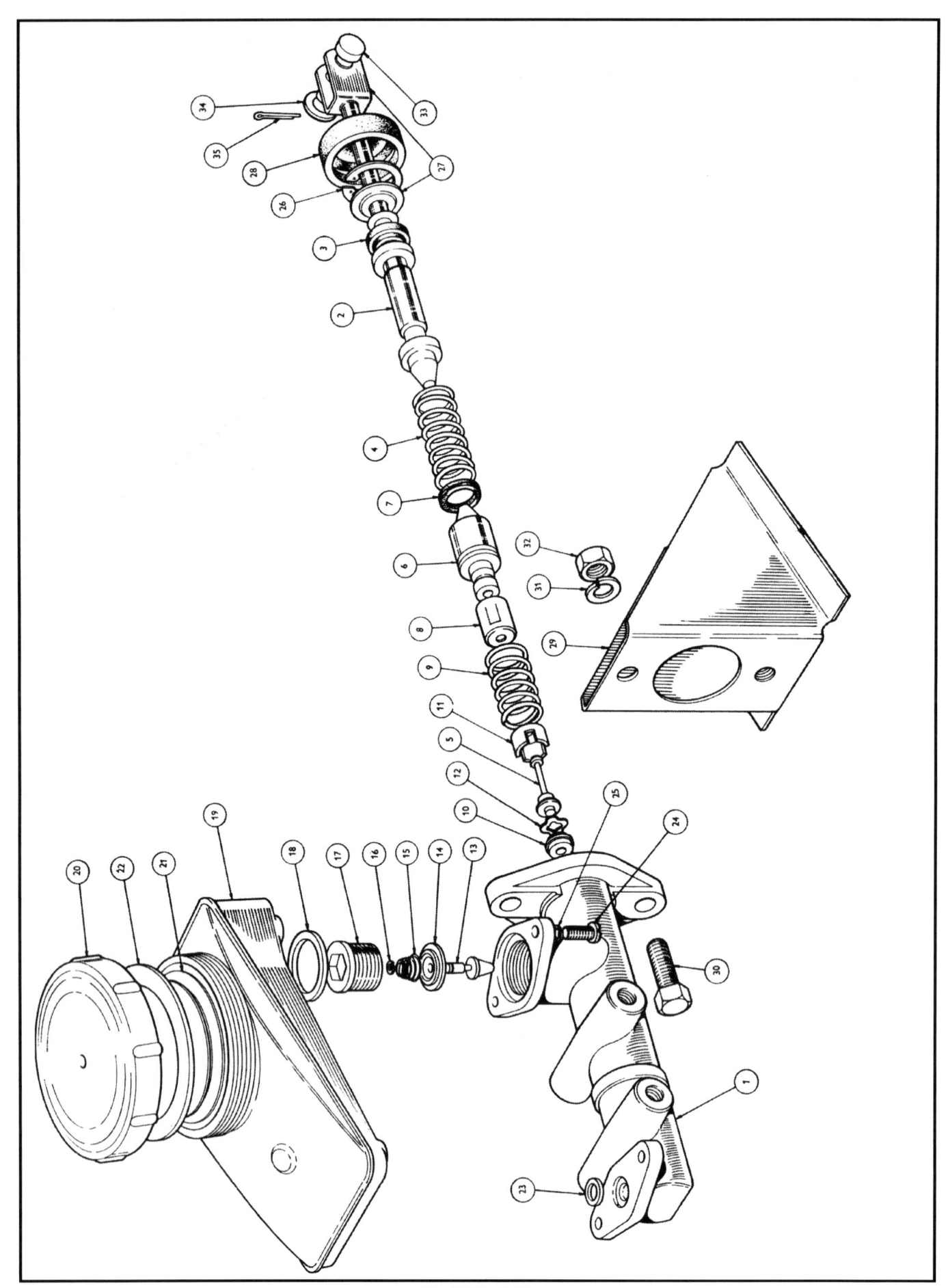

PLATE AW

TANDEM MASTER CYLINDER L.H.S. only

Plate No.	Part No.	Description	No. per Unit	Remarks
	213690	†BRAKE MASTER CYLINDER (TANDEM) ASSEMBLY (L.H.S.) — FITTED TO SPECIAL ORDER ONLY	1	
AW1	Not Serviced	**Body**		
AW2	517016	**Plunger,** primary	1	
AW3	517017	**Seal,** gland	1	
AW4	517028	**Spring**	1	
AW5	517029	**Stem,** valve	1	
AW6	517018	**Plunger,** secondary	1	
AW7	517019	**Seal,** ring, two way	1	
AW8	517030	**Retainer,** spring	1	
AW9	517031	**Spring**	1	
AW10	512802	**Seal**	1	
AW11	517032	**Spacer**	1	
AW12	512803	**Washer,** spring	1	
AW13	517033	**Tipping valve** assembly	1	
AW14	517034	**Seat,** valve	1	
AW15	517035	**Spring,** valve	1	
AW16	517036	**Circlip**	1	
AW17	517037	**Nut,** valve	1	
AW18	517038	**Seal**	1	
AW19	517039	**Reservoir,** fluid, assembly	1	
AW20	517040	**Cap,** filler	1	
AW21	517041	**Baffle**	1	
AW22	517042	**Gasket**	1	
AW23	517043	**Seal**	1	
AW24	517044	**Setscrew**	4	
AW25	517045	**Washer,** spring	4	
AW26	516224	**Circlip**	1	
AW27	517046	**Push rod** assembly	1	
AW28	517020	**Cover,** dust	1	
	517662	**Service kit,** tandem master cylinder	1	
	517333	**Service kit,** reservoir	1	
AW29	148156	**TANDEM BRAKE MASTER CYLINDER SUPPORT BRACKET**	1	
AW30	HU0807	**Setscrew** ⎫	2	
AW31	WL0208	**Washer,** lock ⎬ Master cylinder to support bracket	2	
AW32	HN2008	**Nut** ⎭	1	
AW33	PJ8808	**Pin,** joint ⎫ Brake pedal	1	
AW34	WP0008	**Washer,** plain ⎬ to	1	
AW35	PC0009	**Pin,** cotter ⎭ master cylinder push rod	1	

Note:—Items marked thus † are available on our Factory Exchange Unit Scheme

73

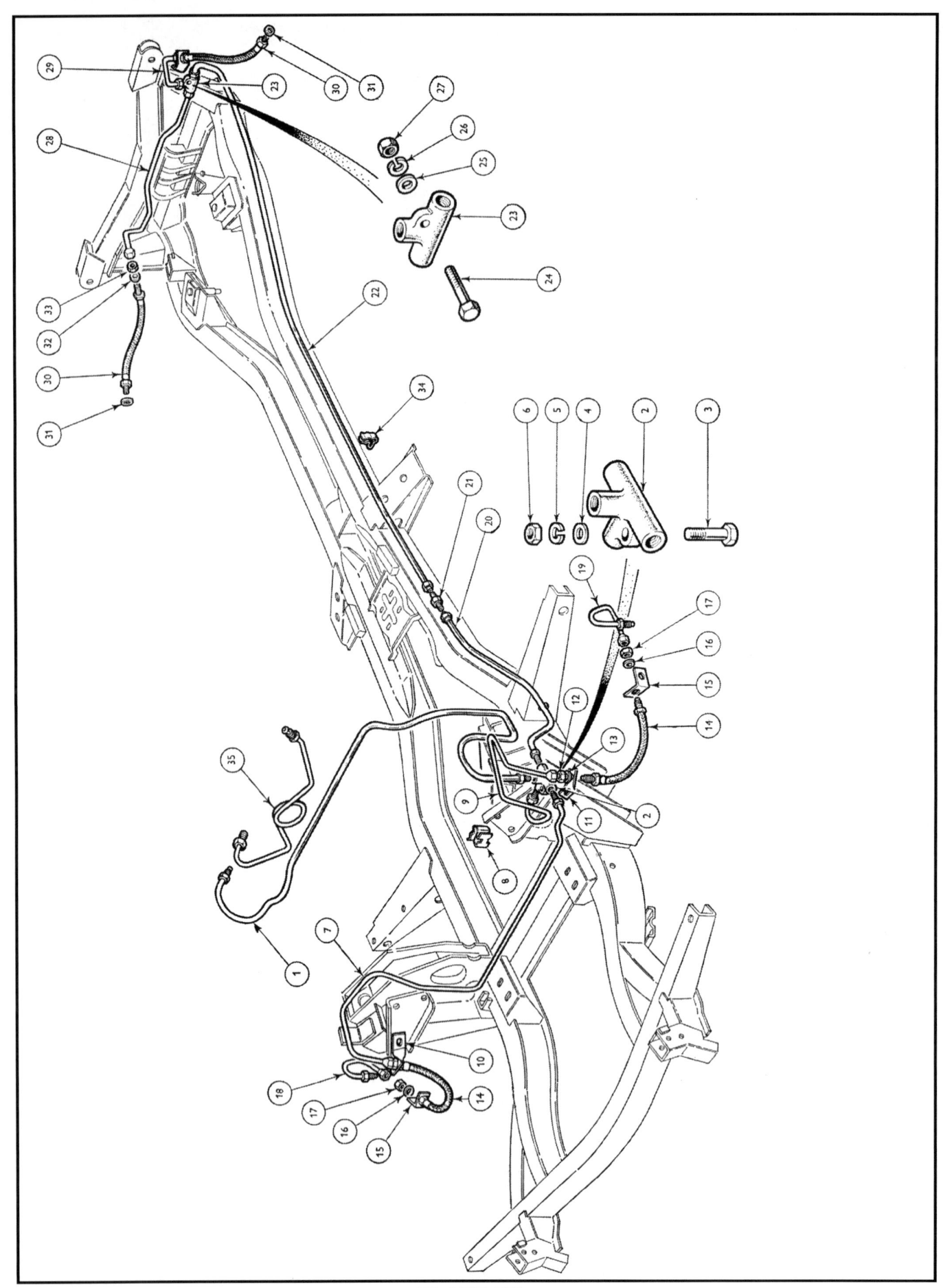

PLATE AX

HYDRAULIC PIPES

Plate No.	Part No.	Description	No. per Unit	Remarks
		HYDRAULIC BRAKE PIPES		
AX1	209755	**Pipe** assembly, master cylinder to four-way connection —R.H.S.	1	
	209754	**Pipe** assembly, master cylinder to four-way connection —L.H.S.	1	Not required when Tandem Brakes fitted
	147748	**Pipe** assembly, tandem master cylinder to pressure differential warning valve—Front—L.H.S. only	1	⎫ Required when Tandem Brakes fitted
	147747	**Pipe** assembly, tandem master cylinder to pressure differential warning valve—Rear—L.H.S. only	1	⎭
	59380	**Clip** ⎱ Pipe to dash shelf	2	
	YA0403	**Screw**, self tapping ⎰ —R.H.S. only	2	
	215104	**Valve** assembly, pressure differential warning	1	⎫
	149971	**Switch**, warning light, pressure differential valve	1	⎬ Required when Tandem Brakes fitted—L.H.S. only
	BL0010	**Ball**	1	
	HB0711	**Bolt** ⎱ Pressure differential valve	1	
	WL0207	**Washer**, lock ⎰ to dash shelf	1	⎭
	136908	**Connection**, three-way	1	
AX2	136939	**Connection**, four-way	1	Not required when Tandem Brakes fitted
AX3	HB0710	**Bolt** ⎱	1	
AX4	WP0007	**Washer**, plain ⎨ Three-way or four-way connection	1	
AX5	WL0207	**Washer**, lock ⎰ to frame bracket	1	
AX6	HN2007	**Nut**	1	
	214176	**Pipe** assembly, pressure differential valve to three-way connection (Front)	1	⎫ Required when Tandem Brakes fitted—L.H.S. only
	308159	**Pipe** assembly, pressure differential valve to double ended union (Rear)	1	⎭
AX7	307755	**Pipe** assembly, three- or four-way to R.H. front hose	1	
AX8	137048	**Clip**, brake pipe to front suspension mounting bracket	2	
AX9	213330	**Pipe** assembly, four-way or three-way to L.H. front hose	1	
AX10	145455	**Bracket**, hose mounting, upper end—R.H.	1	
AX11	145454	**Bracket**, hose mounting, upper end—L.H.	1	
		Note:- Brackets secured by valance panel attachments.		
AX12	516614	**Nut**, jam ⎱ Flexible hose to	2	
AX13	WN0709	**Washer**, shakeproof ⎰ upper bracket	2	
AX14	143320	**Hose**, flexible, front	2	
AX15	145452	**Bracket**, flexible hose, attached to caliper mounting bolt, vertical link	2	
AX16	WN0709	**Washer**, shakeproof ⎱ Flexible hose to	2	
AX17	516614	**Nut**, jam ⎰ lower bracket	2	
AX18	145419	**Pipe** assembly, hose to caliper—R.H.	1	
AX19	145418	**Pipe** assembly, hose to caliper—L.H.	1	
AX20	305764	**Pipe** assembly, four-way to double ended union	1	Not required when Tandem Brakes fitted
AX21	121782	**Connector**, double ended union	1	
AX22	305911	**Pipe** assembly, rear three-way to double ended union	1	Fitted up to Commission No. KC50000 only
	308542	**Pipe** assembly, rear three-way to double ended union	1	Fitted from Commission No. KC50001 and future

Note:—Items marked thus † are available on our Factory Exchange Unit Scheme

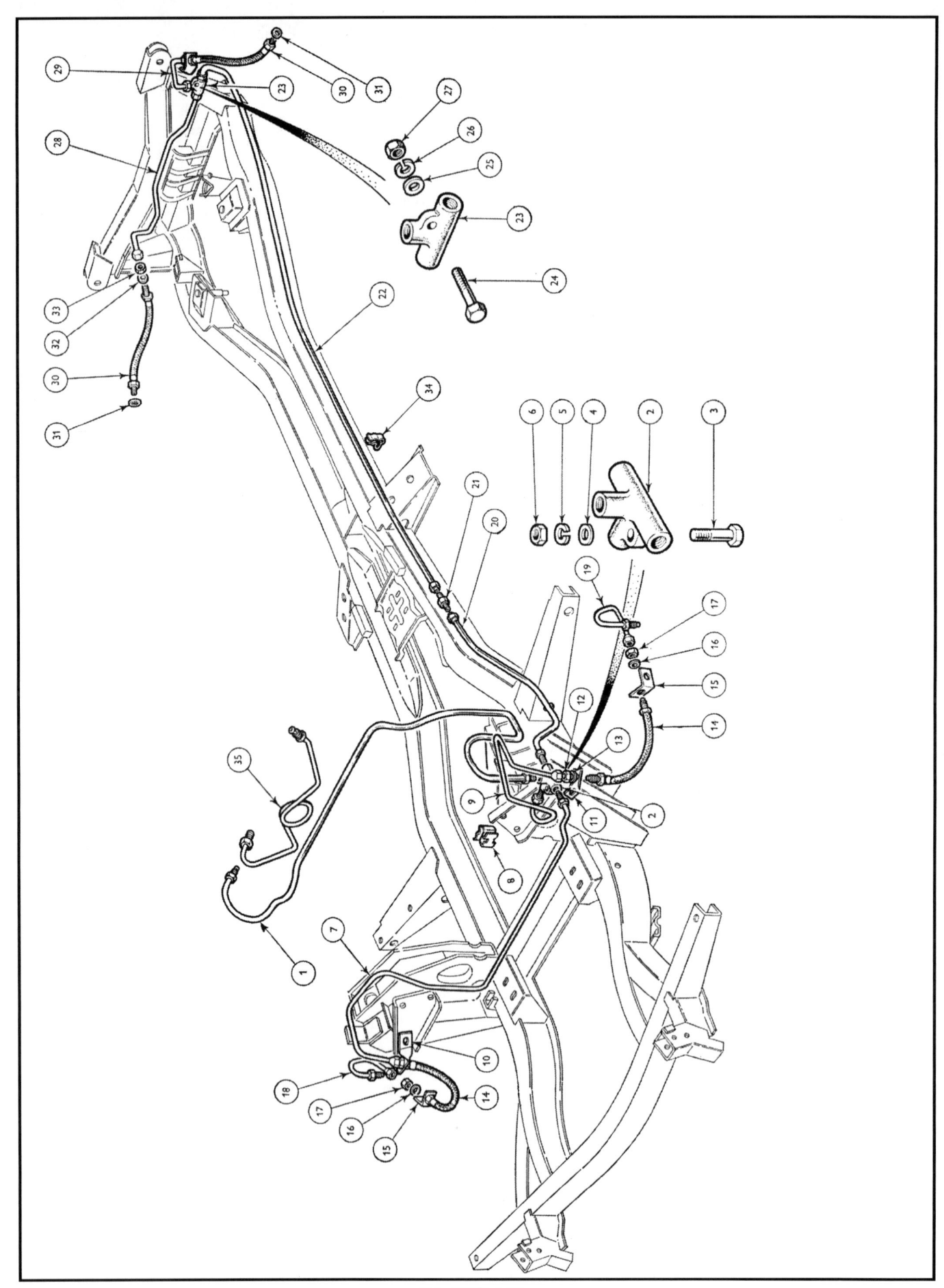

PLATE AX

HYDRAULIC PIPES

Plate No.	Part No.	Description	No. per Unit	Remarks
		HYDRAULIC BRAKE PIPES—continued		
AX23	136908	**Connection**, three-way, rear	1	
AX24	HB0710	**Bolt**	1	
AX25	WP0023	**Washer**, plain ⎫ Three-way connection,	1	
AX26	WL0207	**Washer**, lock ⎬ rear, to bracket	1	
AX27	HN2007	**Nut** ⎭	1	
AX28	211399	**Pipe** assembly, rear three-way to rear hose—R.H.	1	⎫ Fitted up to Commission No.
AX29	139523	**Pipe** assembly, rear three-way to rear hose—L.H.	1	⎭ KC50000 only
	214973	**Pipe** assembly, rear three-way to rear hose—R.H.	1	Fitted from Commission No. KC50001 and future
AX30	115459	**Hose**, flexible, rear	2	⎫
AX31	107072	**Gasket**, hose	2	⎬ Fitted up to Commission No.
AX32	WN0709	**Washer**, shakeproof ⎫ Hose	2	⎭ KC50000 only
AX33	516614	**Nut**, jam ⎬ attachment	2	
	149973	**Hose**, flexible, rear—R.H.	1	
	149977	**Hose**, flexible, rear—L.H.	1	
	107072	**Gasket**, hose	1	Fitted from
	WN0709	**Washer**, shakeproof ⎫ Hose	3	Commission No.
	JN2109	**Nut**, jam ⎬ attachment	3	KC50001 and future
	149974	**Pipe** assembly, R.H. wheel cylinder to R.H. rear flexible hose	1	
	149975	**Pipe** assembly, L.H. wheel cylinder to L.H. rear flexible hose	1	
AX34	59191	**Clip**, brake and petrol pipes	4	
	615707	**Clip**, brake and petrol pipes	1	
	623314	**Clip**, brake and petrol pipes	2	
	503213	**Sleeve**, P.V.C., fitted to brake pipe clip	1	
	623312	**Clip**, brake pipe to heel board reinforcement	2	Fitted from Commission No. KC50001 and future
	517632	**Fluid**, brake and clutch	8 oz. tin	
	517633	**Fluid**, brake and clutch	16 oz. tin	
	517634	**Fluid**, brake and clutch	32 oz. tin	
		HYDRAULIC CLUTCH PIPES		
AX35	146199	**Pipe** assembly, master cylinder to clutch slave cylinder—R.H.S.	1	
	307566	**Pipe** assembly, master cylinder to clutch slave cylinder—L.H.S.	1	Not required when Tandem Brakes fitted
	308158	**Pipe** assembly, master cylinder to clutch slave cylinder—L.H.S.	1	Required when Tandem Brakes fitted
	59380	**Clip** ⎫ Clutch pipe to	2	
	YA0403	**Screw**, self tapping ⎬ dash shelf—L.H.S. only	2	

Note:—Items marked thus † are available on our Factory Exchange Unit Scheme

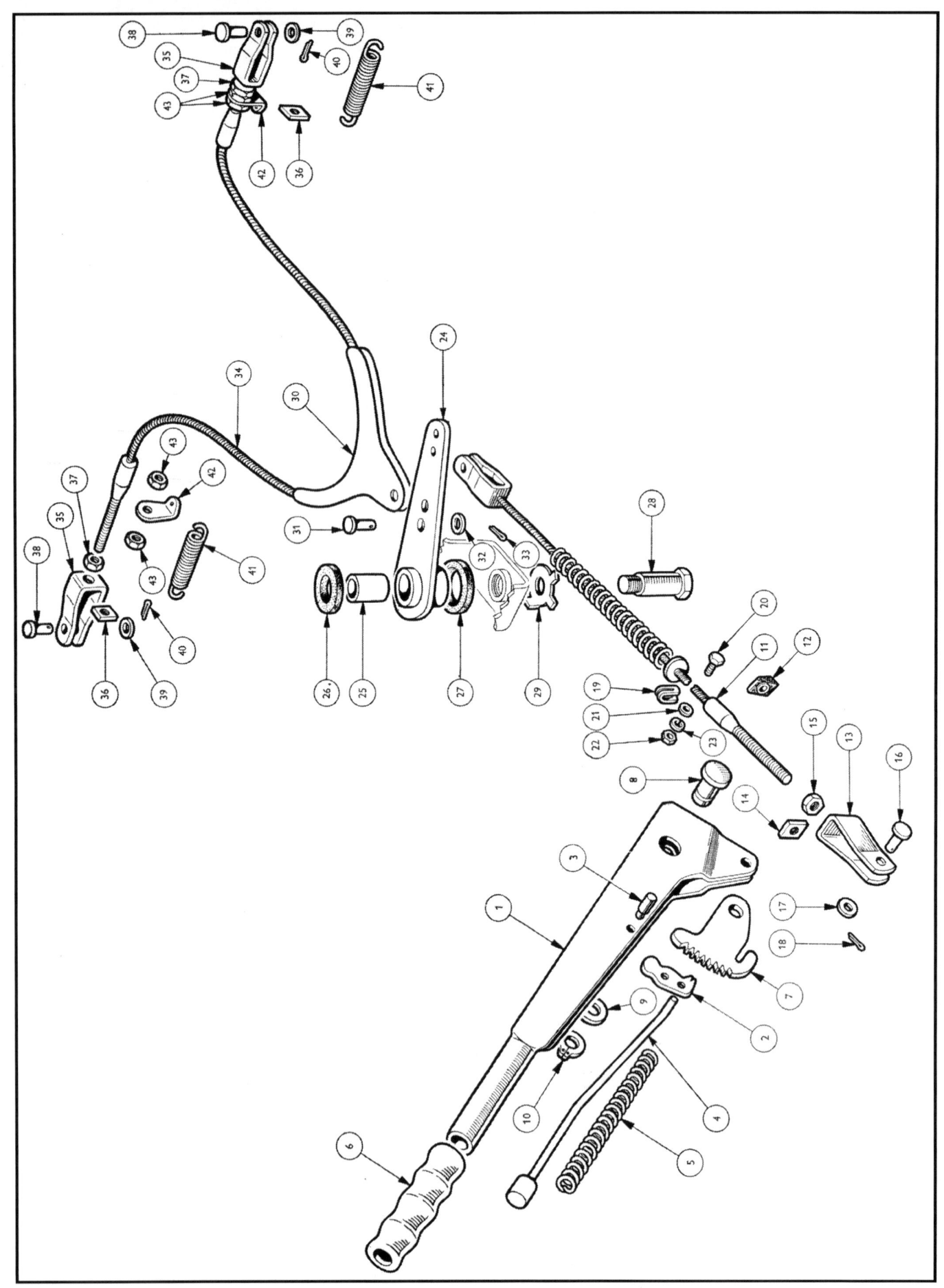

PLATE AY

HANDBRAKE

Plate No.	Part No.	Description	No. per Unit	Remarks
	134253	**HANDBRAKE ASSEMBLY**	1	* See Note below
	132589	**HANDBRAKE ASSEMBLY**	1	‡ See Note below
AY1	132586	**Lever** assembly, handbrake	1	
AY2	134143	**Pawl** ⎫	1	* See Note below
	104737	**Pawl** ⎬ Fitted in lever	1	‡ See Note below
AY3	104738	**Pin** ⎭	1	
AY4	134001	**Rod** assembly, pawl release	1	* See Note below
	132588	**Rod** assembly, pawl release	1	‡ See Note below
AY5	104740	**Spring,** pawl release	1	
AY6	131312	**Grip,** handbrake lever	1	
AY7	104742	**Segment,** ratchet	1	Alternative to 148083
	148083	**Segment,** ratchet	1	Alternative to 104742
AY8	104743	**Pin,** fulcrum ⎫ Handbrake lever	1	
AY9	WP0119	**Washer,** plain ⎬ and ratchet to	1	
AY10	500186	**Ring,** snap ⎭ mounting bracket	1	

Note:— Items marked thus * are fitted up to Commission No. KC9097 and intermittently from KC9098 up to KC9114, R.H.S. only. Fitted up to Commission No. KC11233 and intermittently from KC11234 up to KC11243, L.H.S. only.

Note:— Items marked thus ‡ are fitted intermittently from Commission No. KC9098 up to KC9114 and full incorporation from KC9115 and future—R.H.S. Fitted intermittently from Commission No. KC11234 up to KC11243 and full incorporation from KC11244 and future—L.H.S.

Plate No.	Part No.	Description	No. per Unit	Remarks
AY11	121766	**HANDBRAKE CABLE ASSEMBLY** (Handbrake to relay lever)	1	
AY12	133913	**Grommet,** handbrake cable to floor	1	Fitted up to Body No. 1040KC and on 1047KC, 1052KC, 1065KC and 1217KC only
AY13	104749	**Fork-end,** cable to handbrake	1	
AY14	QN2707	**Nut,** square ⎫ Fork-end attachment	1	
AY15	JN2107	**Nut,** jam ⎭	1	
AY16	104750	**Pin** ⎫	2	
AY17	WP0035	**Washer,** plain ⎬ Cable attachment	2	
AY18	PC0005	**Pin,** cotter ⎭	2	
AY19	106036	**Clip,** handbrake cable	1	
AY20	TF2205	**Screw,** set ⎫	1	
AY21	WP0002	**Washer,** plain ⎬ Clip to	1	
AY22	HN2002	**Nut,** lock ⎬ handbrake cable	1	
AY23	WL0202	**Washer,** lock ⎭	1	

Note:—Items marked thus † are available on our Factory Exchange Unit Scheme

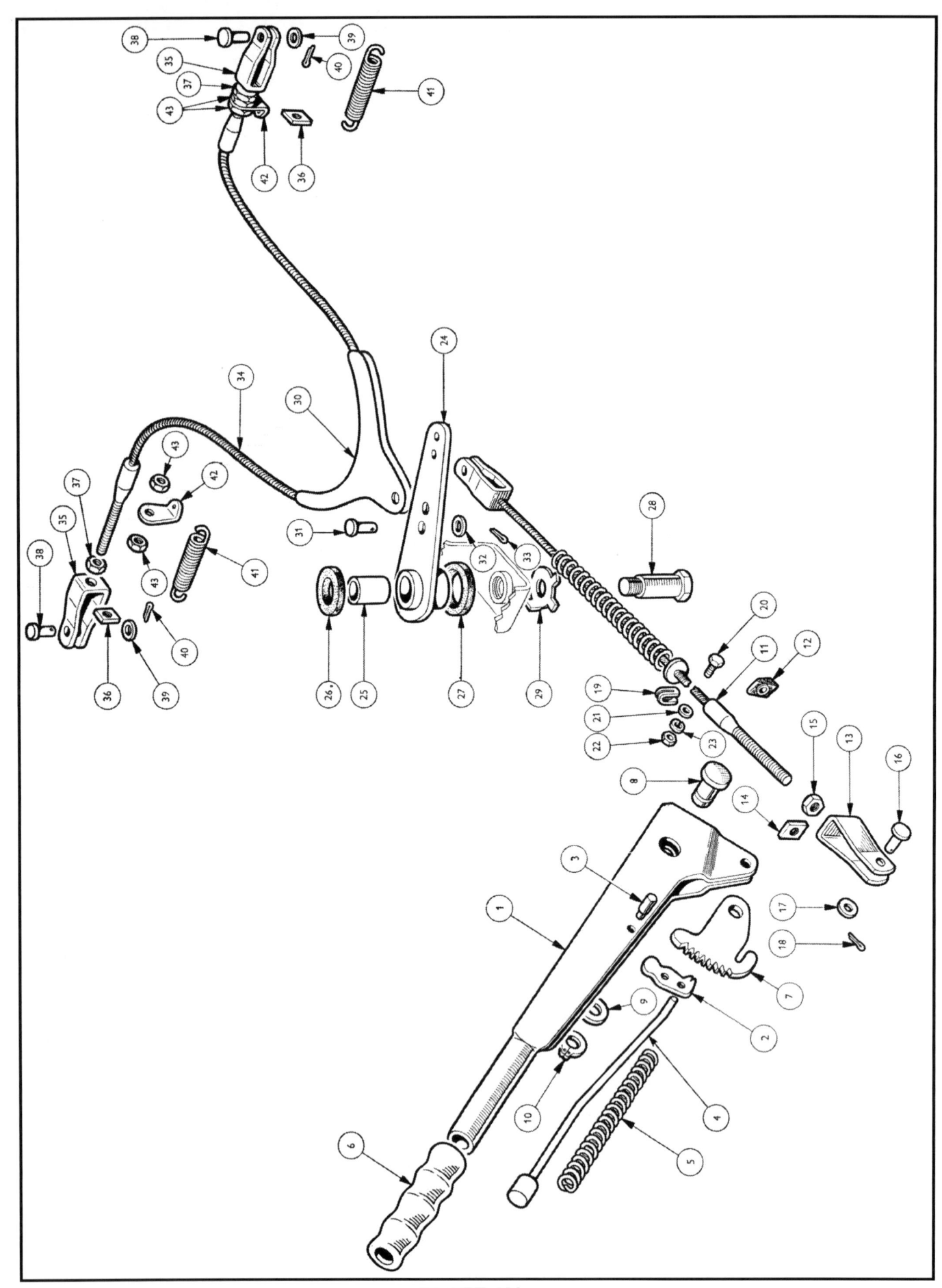

PLATE AY

HANDBRAKE

Plate No.	Part No.	Description	No. per Unit	Remarks
AY24	134862	**RELAY LEVER ASSEMBLY**	1	
AY25	121757	**Bearing**	1	
AY26	121760	**Seal**, felt, relay lever	1	
AY27	121755	**Seal**, dust, rubber	1	
AY28	121759	**Pin**, shouldered ⎫ Relay lever	1	
AY29	121758	**Washer**, tab ⎭ to body	1	
AY30	121699	**COMPENSATING SECTOR**	1	
AY31	PJ8806	**Pin**, joint ⎫	1	
AY32	WP0008	**Washer**, plain ⎬ Compensator to relay lever	1	
AY33	PC0009	**Pin**, cotter ⎭	1	
AY34	133915	**Cable** assembly, compensator to wheel cylinders	1	Fitted up to Commission No. KC50000 only
	149353	**Cable** assembly, compensator to wheel cylinders	1	Fitted from Commission No. KC50001 and future
AY35	104749	**Fork-end**, rear cable	2	
AY36	QN2707	**Nut**, square ⎫ Fork-end	2	
AY37	JN2107	**Nut**, jam ⎭ attachment	2	
AY38	104750	**Pin** ⎫	2	
AY39	WP0007	**Washer**, plain ⎬ Cable to rear brake units	2	
AY40	PC0005	**Pin**, cotter ⎭	2	
AY41	131806	**Spring**, pull-off, handbrake to rear cable	2	
AY42	131807	**Plate**, spring anchor	2	
AY43	HN2007	**Nut**, spring anchor plate to rear cable	4	

Note:—Items marked thus † are available on our Factory Exchange Unit Scheme

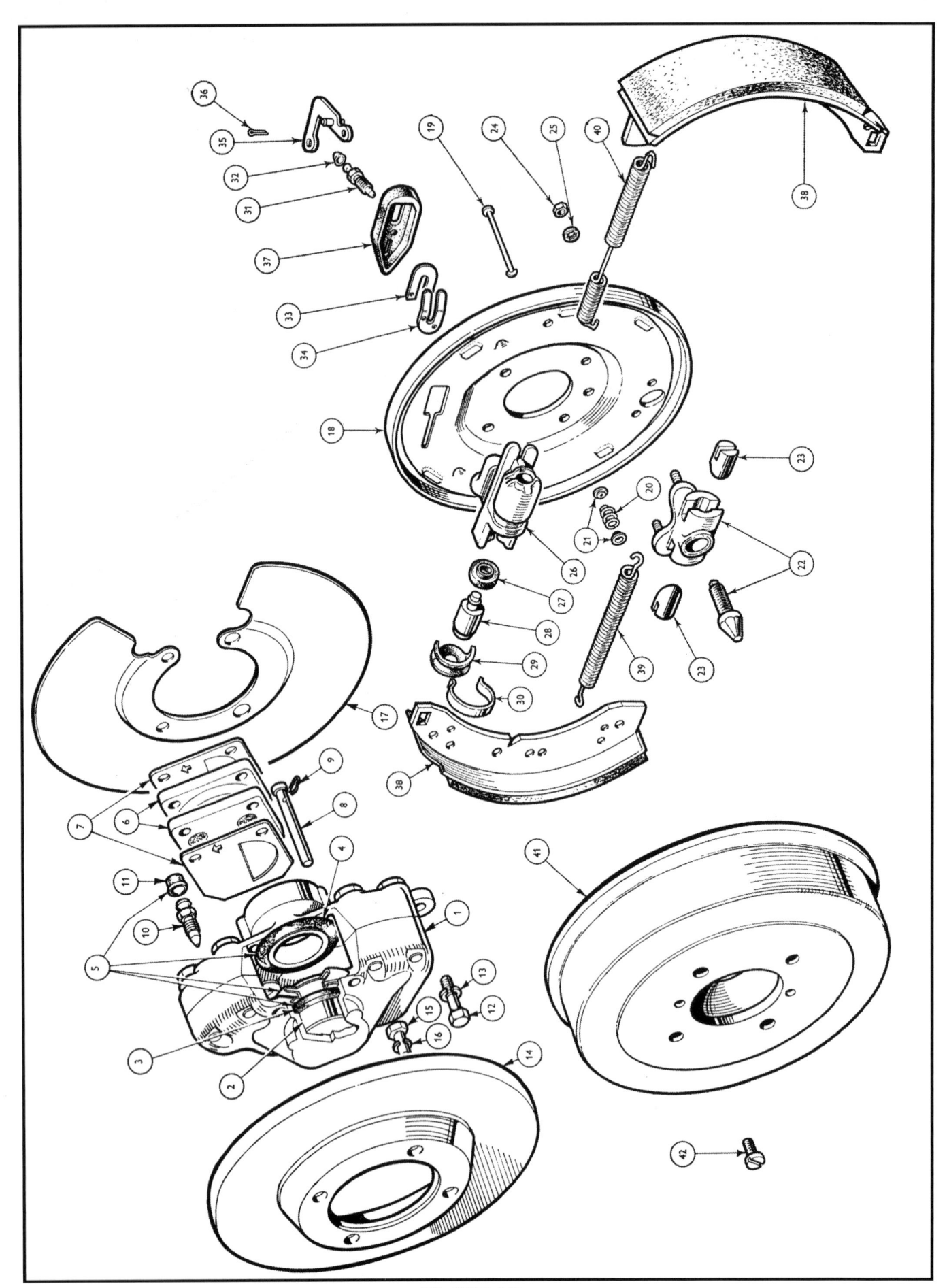

PLATE AZ

BRAKES

Plate No.	Part No.	Description	No. per Unit	Remarks
	307844	**FRONT BRAKE CALIPER ASSEMBLY, R.H.**	1	
AZ1	307843	**FRONT BRAKE CALIPER ASSEMBLY, L.H.**	1	
AZ2	510792	**Piston,** fitted in body	4	
AZ3	504826	**Ring,** piston sealing	4	
AZ4	504827	**Boot,** rubber	4	
AZ5	506667	**Service kit,** front brake caliper	2	
AZ6	146027	**Pad,** lining, assembly	1 set	
	512541	**Pad,** lining (Competition)	1 set	
AZ7	510809	**Shim,** damping	4	
AZ8	509058	**Pin,** pad retaining	4	
AZ9	509059	**Clip,** securing pin in body	4	
AZ10	108756	**Screw,** bleed	2	
AZ11	105676	**Cap,** bleed screw	2	
AZ12	132439	**Bolt** ⎫ Caliper assembly to	4	
AZ13	WL0210	**Washer,** spring ⎭ mounting bracket	4	
AZ14	213227	**FRICTION DISC, FRONT BRAKE CALIPER**	2	
AZ15	113150	**Bolt** ⎫ Friction disc	8	
AZ16	WQ0309	**Washer,** spring ⎭ to front hub	8	
	213232	**Cover,** dust, assembly, R.H.	1	
AZ17	213233	**Cover,** dust, assembly, L.H.	1	
	213540	**REAR BRAKE ASSEMBLY—R.H.**	1	⎫ Fitted up to
	213541	**REAR BRAKE ASSEMBLY—L.H.**	1	⎬ Commission No. KC7278 only
	214638	**REAR BRAKE ASSEMBLY—R.H.**	1	⎫ Fitted from Commission No.
	214639	**REAR BRAKE ASSEMBLY—L.H.**	1	⎬ KC7279 up to Commission No. KC50000 only
	214824	**REAR BRAKE ASSEMBLY—R.H.**	1	⎫ Fitted from Commission No.
	214825	**REAR BRAKE ASSEMBLY—L.H.**	1	⎬ KC50001 and future
	209260	**Back plate** assembly, R.H.	1	⎫ Fitted up to Commission No.
AZ18	209259	**Back plate** assembly, L.H.	1	⎬ KC50000 only
	214817	**Back plate** assembly, R.H.	1	⎫ Fitted from Commission No.
	214818	**Back plate** assembly, L.H.	1	⎬ KC50001 and future
AZ19	120124	**Pin,** shoe hold down ⎫	4	
AZ20	504877	**Spring** ⎬ Shoe to back plate	4	
AZ21	504878	**Washer,** cup ⎭	4	
AZ22	120142	**ADJUSTER UNIT ASSEMBLY**	2	
AZ23	111054	**Tappet,** between wedge and shoe	4	
AZ24	HN2007	**Nut** ⎫ Adjuster unit to	4	
AZ25	WN0707	**Washer,** spring ⎭ back plate	4	

Note:—Items marked thus † are available on our Factory Exchange Unit Scheme

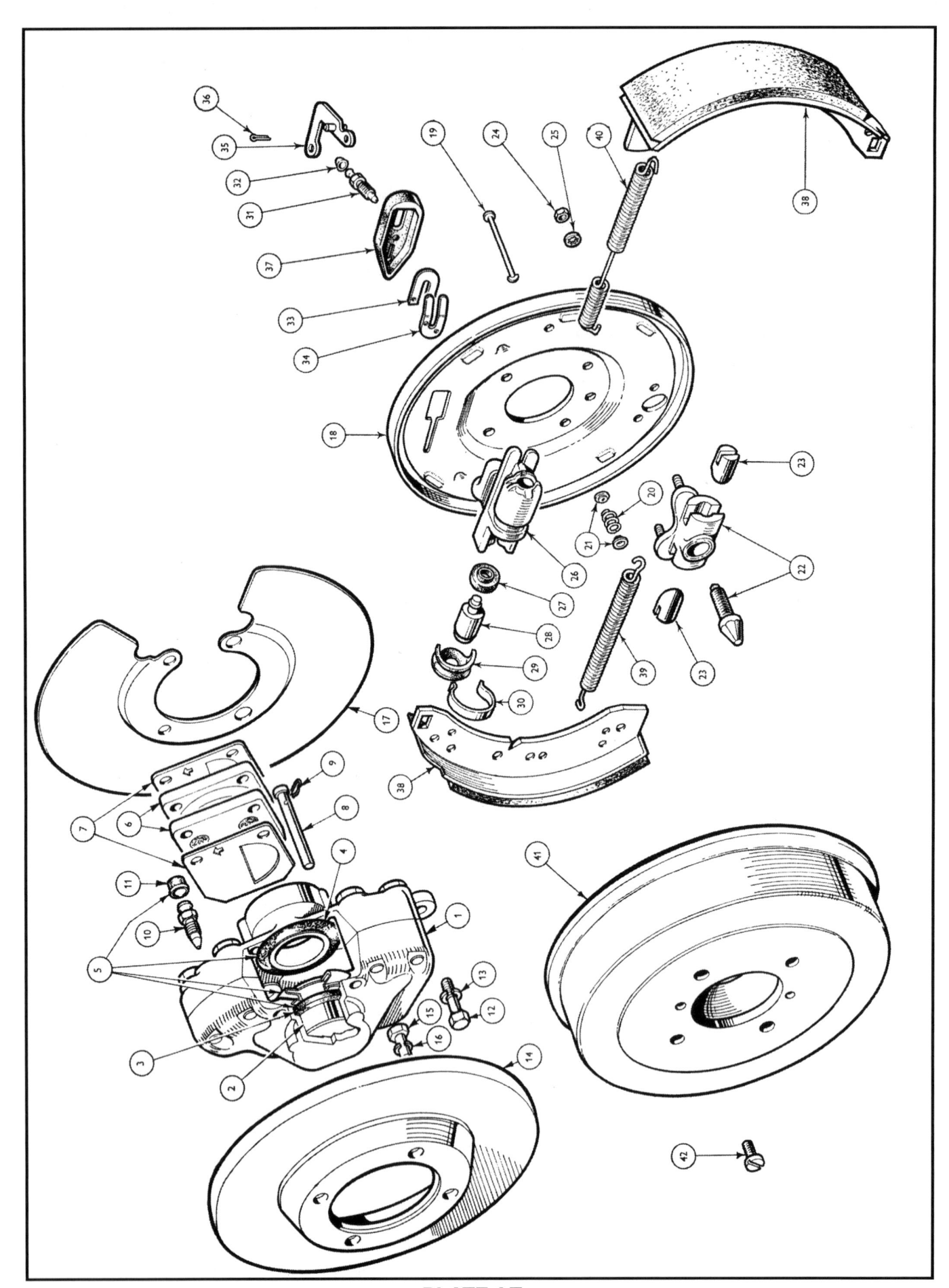

PLATE AZ

BRAKES

Plate No.	Part No.	Description	No. per Unit	Remarks
		REAR BRAKE ASSEMBLY—continued		
	146028	**REAR WHEEL CYLINDER ASSEMBLY**	2	Fitted up to Commission No. KC7278 only
	121174	**REAR WHEEL CYLINDER ASSEMBLY**	2	Fitted from Commission No. KC7279 and future
AZ26	Not Serviced	**Body,** wheel cylinder		
AZ27	107176	**Seal**	2	Fitted up to Commission No. KC7278 only
	506559	**Seal**	2	Fitted from Commission No. KC7279 and future
AZ28	Not Serviced	**Piston**	2	
AZ29	120134	**Cover,** dust	2	
AZ30	120135	**Retainer,** dust cover	2	
AZ31	108756	**Screw,** bleed	2	
AZ32	105676	**Cap,** dust	2	
AZ33	120138	**Plate,** retaining, wheel cylinder	2	
AZ34	120137	**Plate,** spring, wheel cylinder retaining	2	
AZ35	123135	**OPERATING LEVER ASSEMBLY WHEEL CYLINDER**	2	
AZ36	PC0034	**Pin,** cotter, lever retaining	2	
AZ37	120139	**Cover,** dust, wheel cylinder	2	
	507865	**Service kit,** rear wheel cylinder	2	Fitted up to Commission No. KC7278 only
	508433	**Service kit,** rear wheel cylinder	2	Fitted from Commission No. KC7279 and future
AZ38	515495	**BRAKE SHOE ASSEMBLY**	2 prs.	
		BRAKE SHOE ASSEMBLY (Competition)	2 prs.	
AZ39	105689	**Spring,** shoe return, adjuster end	2	
AZ40	105690	**Spring,** shoe return, cylinder end	2	
	HU0907	**Setscrew** ⎫ Rear brake assembly	8	⎫ Fitted from Commission No. KC50001 and future
	149426	**Washer,** tab ⎭ to vertical link	4	⎭

Note:- For Rear Brake attachment details up to Commission No. KC50000 see Rear Axle section page 62.

AZ41	203077	**BRAKE DRUM — REAR**	2	
AZ42	V5435	**Screw,** retaining brake drum	4	

Note:—Items marked thus † are available on our Factory Exchange Unit Scheme

79

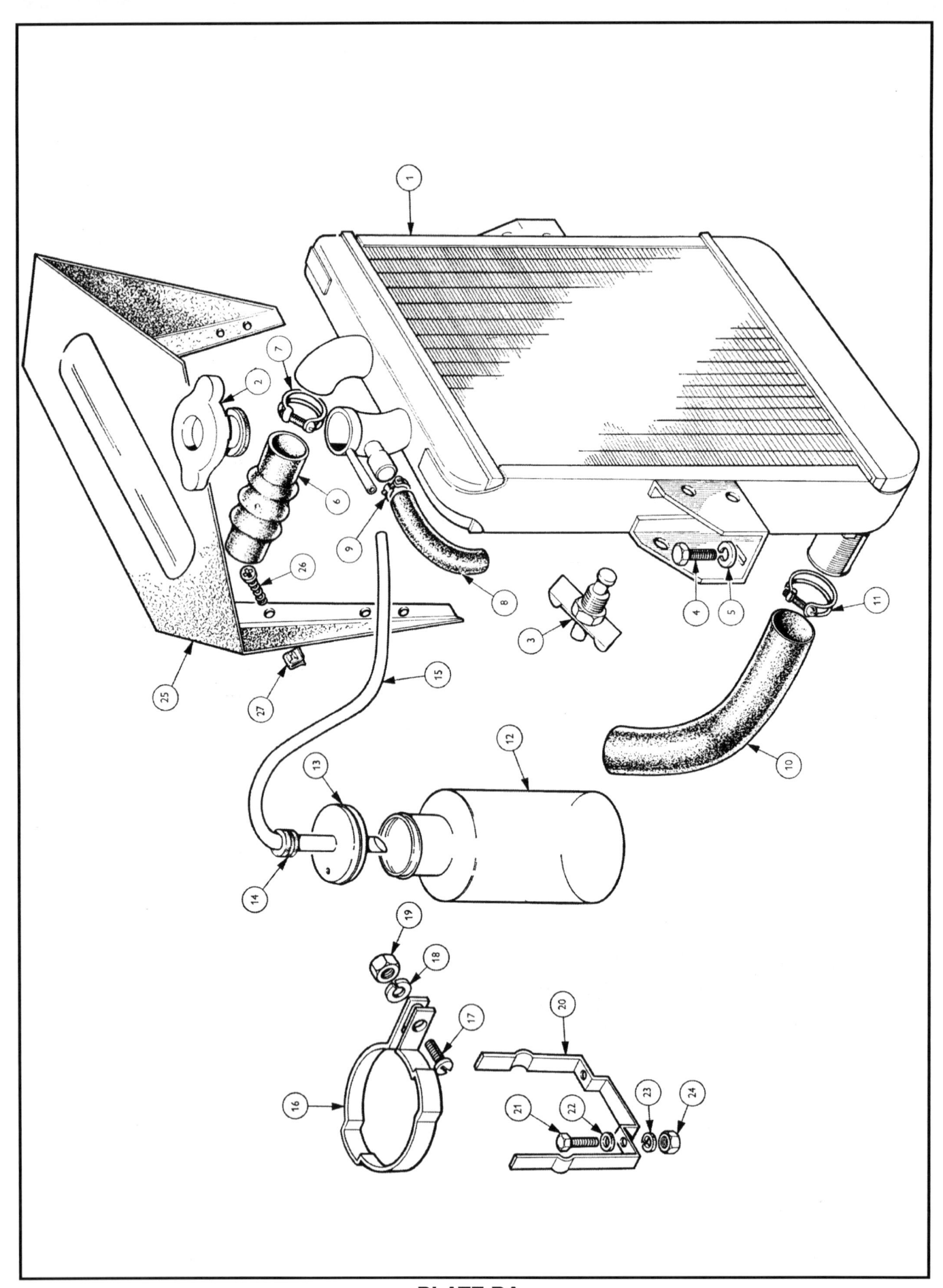

PLATE BA

RADIATOR

Plate No.	Part No.	Description	No. per Unit	Remarks
BA1	307624	†**RADIATOR BLOCK ASSEMBLY**	1	
BA2	137691	**Cap**, filler, assembly	1	
BA3	132565	**Tap**, drain	1	
BA4	HU0805	**Screw**, set ⎫	4	
	WP0107	**Washer**, plain ⎬ Radiator block to frame	4	
BA5	WL0208	**Washer**, lock ⎭	4	
BA6	104903	**Hose**, top, radiator to water elbow	1	
BA7	CS4024	**Clip**, top hose attachment	2	Alternative to CS4025
BA7	CS4025	**Clip**, top hose attachment	2	Alternative to CS4024
BA8	144509	**Hose**, bleed, water elbow to filler neck	1	
BA9	CS4015	**Clip**, bleed hose attachment	2	
BA10	213249	**Hose**, bottom, radiator to water pump	1	
BA11	CS4024	**Clip**, bottom hose attachment	2	Alternative to CS4025
BA11	CS4025	**Clip**, bottom hose attachment	2	Alternative to CS4024
BA12	137632	**RADIATOR OVERFLOW BOTTLE**	1	
BA13	137743	**Cap**, overflow bottle	1	
BA14	616925	**Grommet**, fitted in cap	1	
BA15	142123	**Pipe**, overflow, radiator	1	
BA16	137624	**Strap**, overflow bottle	1	
BA17	PT0508	**Screw** ⎫	1	
BA18	WL0205	**Washer**, lock ⎬ Retaining bottle in strap	1	
BA19	HN2005	**Nut** ⎭	1	
BA20	145671	**Bracket**, mounting, overflow bottle	1	
BA21	HU0704	**Screw**, set ⎫	2	
BA22	WP0007	**Washer**, plain ⎬ Mounting bracket to frame bracket	2	
BA23	WL0207	**Washer**, lock ⎪	2	
BA24	HN2007	**Nut** ⎭	2	
BA25	810334	**RADIATOR COWL ASSEMBLY**	1	
BA26	YF7607	**Screw**, self-tapping ⎫ Radiator cowl	2	
BA27	FU2566/4	**Nut**, fix ⎭ upper attachment	2	

Note:- For Lower Cowl Attachment see Engine Bay Valance Fixings.

Note:—Items marked thus † are available on our Factory Exchange Unit Scheme

80

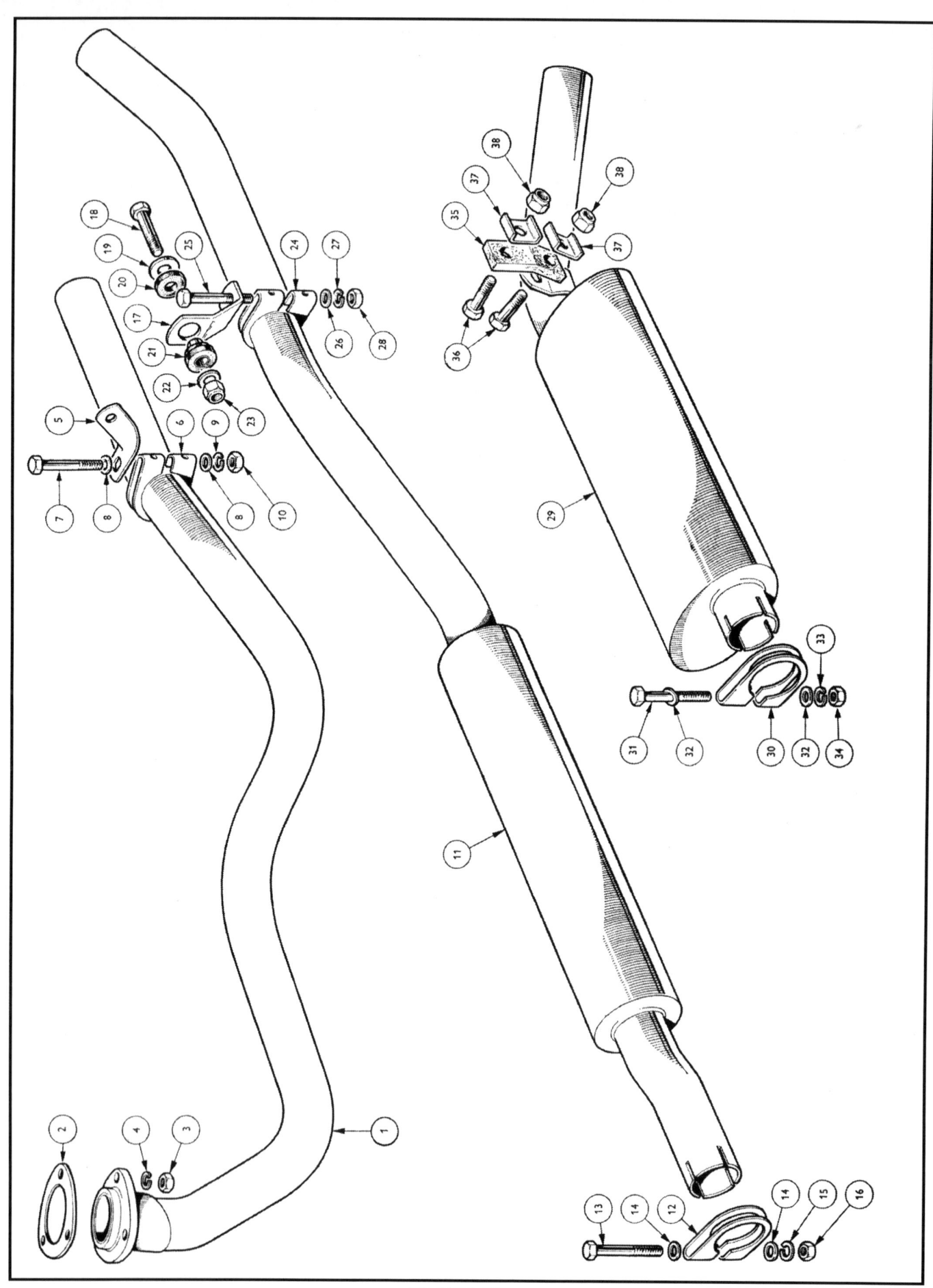

PLATE BB

EXHAUST SYSTEM
MARK I CARS ONLY FITTED UP TO COMMISSION No. KC50000 ONLY

Plate No.	Part No.	Description	No. per Unit	Remarks
BB1	307155	**FRONT EXHAUST PIPE ASSEMBLY**	1	
BB2	123415	**Gasket** ⎫	1	
BB3	100455	**Nut** ⎬ Front exhaust pipe to manifold	3	
BB4	WL0208	**Washer,** lock ⎭	3	
BB5	146163	**Bracket,** front exhaust pipe to rear engine plate attachment	1	
BB6	142281	**Clip,** front exhaust pipe to bracket	1	
BB7	HB0821	**Bolt** ⎫	1	
BB8	WP0107	**Washer,** plain ⎬ Clip to bracket and	2	
BB9	WL0208	**Washer,** lock ⎨ front exhaust pipe	1	
BB10	HN2008	**Nut** ⎭	1	
BB11	307869	**INTERMEDIATE SILENCER AND EXHAUST PIPE ASSEMBLY**	1	
BB12	138807	**Clip** ⎫	1	
BB13	HB0822	**Bolt** ⎬ Front pipe	1	
BB14	WP0107	**Washer,** plain ⎨ to	2	
BB15	WL0208	**Washer,** lock ⎨ intermediate silencer	1	
BB16	HN2008	**Nut** ⎭	1	
BB17	139827	**Bracket,** mounting exhaust pipe to axle mounting plate	1	
BB18	HB0810	**Bolt** ⎫	1	
BB19	WP0017	**Washer,** plain ⎬	1	
BB20	42244	**Grommet,** washer ⎨ Bracket to	1	
BB21	42243	**Grommet** ⎨ axle mounting plate	1	
BB22	WP0107	**Washer,** plain ⎨	1	
BB23	TN3208	**Nut** ⎭	1	
BB24	142281	**Clip,** exhaust pipe attachment	1	
BB25	HB0820	**Bolt** ⎫	1	
BB26	WP0107	**Washer,** plain ⎬ Clip and bracket	1	
BB27	WL0208	**Washer,** lock ⎨ to exhaust pipe	1	
BB28	HN2008	**Nut** ⎭	1	
BB29	307811	**REAR SILENCER AND TAIL PIPE ASSEMBLY**	1	
BB30	138807	**Clip** ⎫	1	
BB31	HB0822	**Bolt** ⎬ Silencer and tail	1	
BB32	WP0107	**Washer,** plain ⎨ pipe assembly to	2	
BB33	WL0208	**Washer,** lock ⎨ intermediate exhaust pipe	1	
BB34	HN2008	**Nut** ⎭	1	
BB35	105292	**Strip,** flexible, tail pipe	1	
BB36	HU0808	**Screw,** set ⎫ Flexible strip to body	2	
BB37	105290	**Plate,** clamp ⎬ and tail pipe brackets	2	
BB38	TN3208	**Nut,** nyloc ⎭	2	

Note:—Items marked thus † are available on our Factory Exchange Unit Scheme

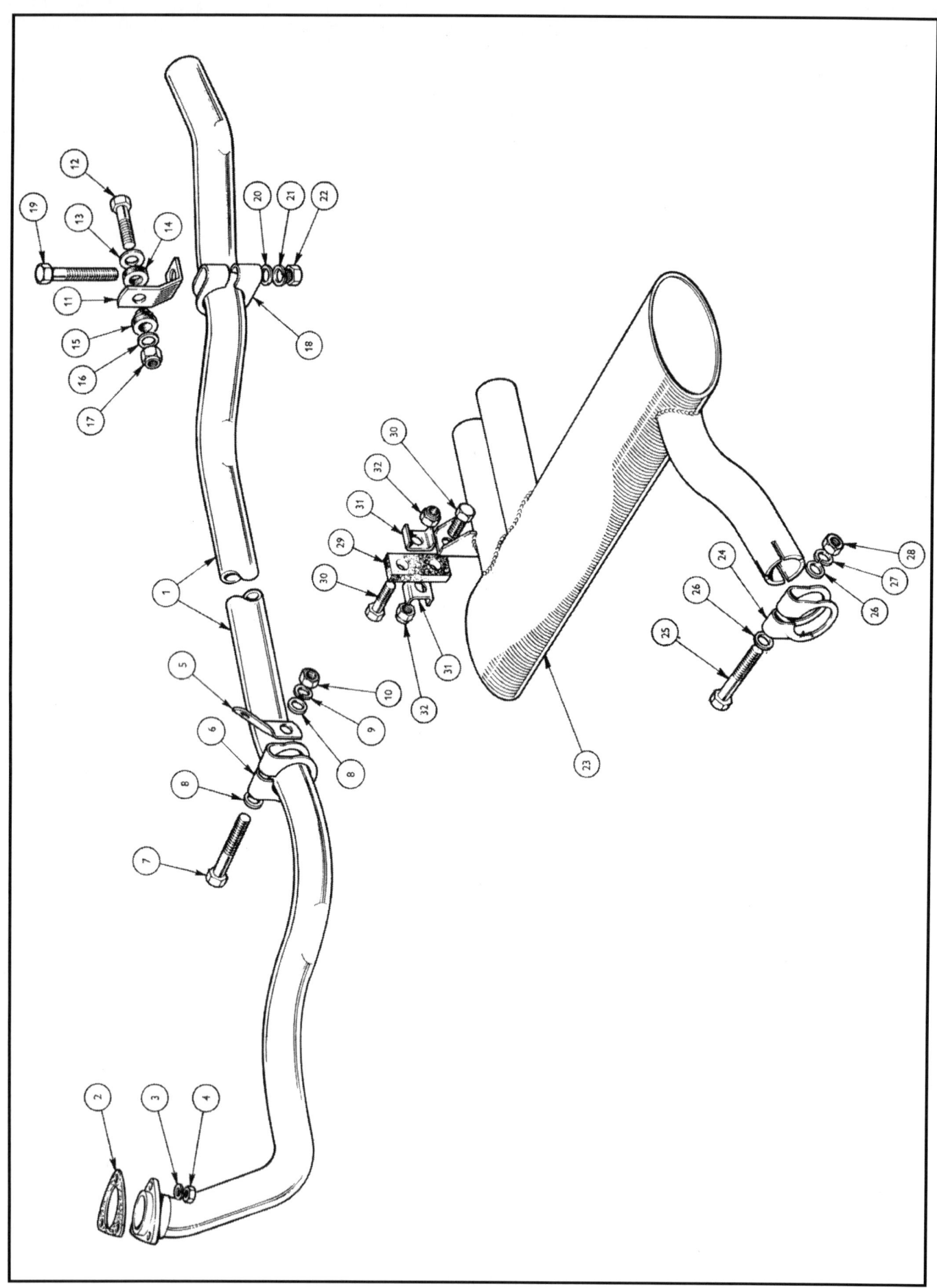

PLATE BC

EXHAUST SYSTEM
MARK II (G.T.6+) CARS FITTED FROM COMMISSION No. KC50001 AND FUTURE

Plate No.	Part No.	Description	No. per Unit	Remarks
BC1	308802	**FRONT EXHAUST PIPE ASSEMBLY**	1	
BC2	106958	**Gasket** ⎫ Front exhaust	1	
BC3	WL0209	**Washer**, lock ⎬ pipe to	3	
BC4	108951	**Nut** ⎭ manifold	3	
BC5	151343	**Bracket**, support, fitted to gearbox extension bolt	1	
BC6	55800	**Clip**, front exhaust pipe support	1	
BC7	HB0823	**Bolt** ⎫	1	
BC8	WP0107	**Washer**, plain ⎬ Front exhaust pipe and	2	
BC9	WL0208	**Washer**, lock ⎨ clip to bracket	1	
BC10	HN2008	**Nut** ⎭	1	
BC11	139827	**Bracket**, mounting, exhaust pipe to axle mounting plate	1	
BC12	HB0810	**Bolt** ⎫	1	
BC13	WP0017	**Washer**, plain ⎬	1	
BC14	42244	**Washer**, grommet ⎨ Bracket to axle	1	
BC15	42243	**Grommet** ⎬ mounting plate	1	
BC16	WP0107	**Washer**, plain ⎨	1	
BC17	TN3208	**Nut** ⎭	1	
BC18	55800	**Clip**, exhaust pipe attachment	1	
BC19	HB0822	**Bolt** ⎫	1	
BC20	WP0107	**Washer**, plain ⎨ Exhaust pipe and clip	1	
BC21	WL0208	**Washer**, lock ⎬ to mounting bracket	1	
BC22	HN2008	**Nut** ⎭	1	
BC23	308804	**SILENCER AND TAIL PIPE**	1	
BC24	108446	**Clip** ⎫	1	
BC25	HB0823	**Bolt** ⎬ Front exhaust pipe	1	
BC26	WP0107	**Washer**, plain ⎬ to	2	
BC27	WL0208	**Washer**, lock ⎨ silencer and tail pipe	1	
BC28	HN2008	**Nut** ⎭	1	
BC29	105292	**Strip**, flexible	1	
BC30	HU0808	**Screw**, set ⎫ Flexible strip to	2	
BC31	105290	**Plate**, clamp ⎬ body and tailpipe	2	
BC32	TN3208	**Nut**, nyloc ⎭ brackets	2	

Note:—Items marked thus † are available on our Factory Exchange Unit Scheme

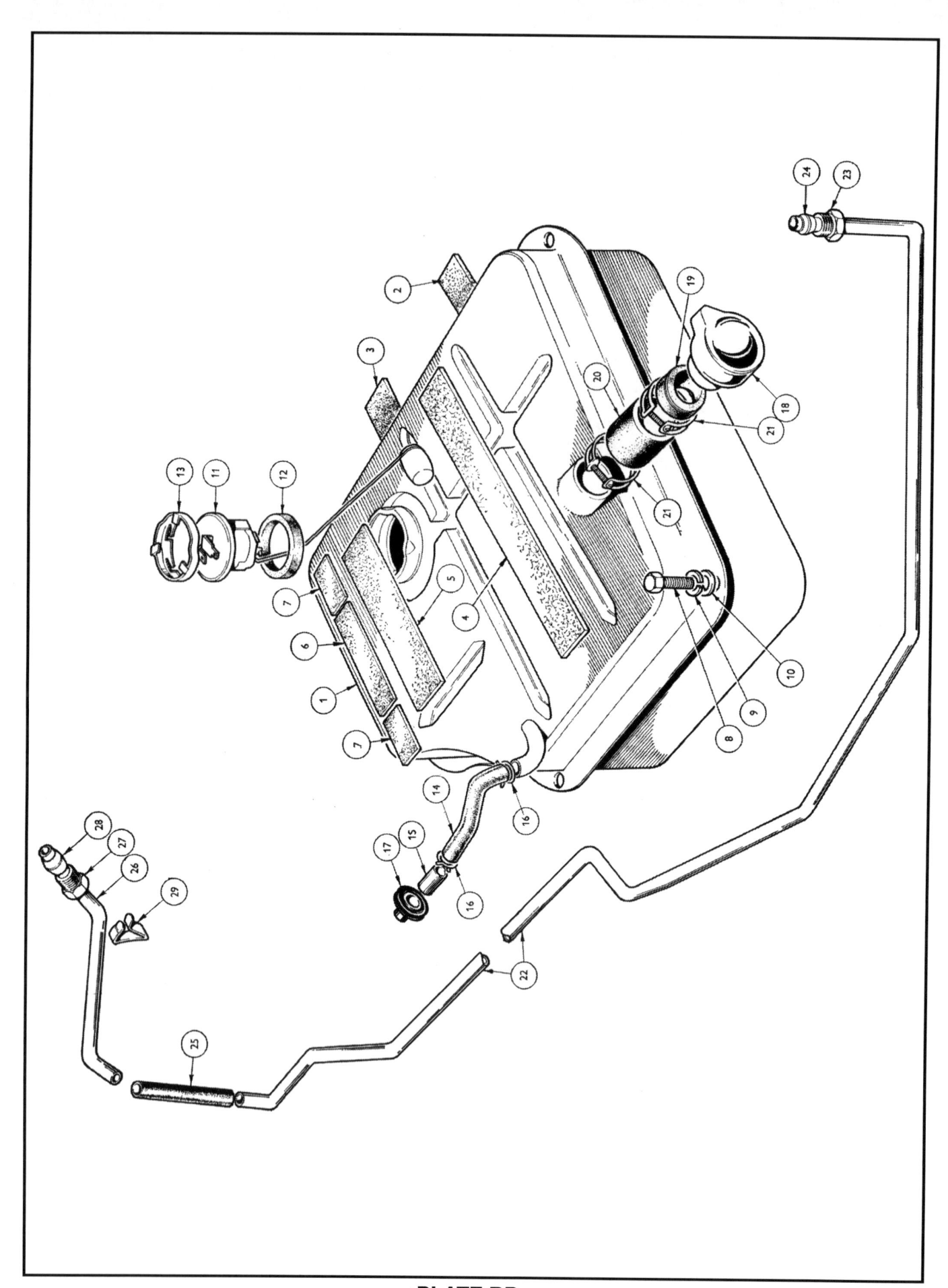

PLATE BD

PETROL SYSTEM
MARK I CARS FITTED UP TO COMMISSION No. KC50000 ONLY

Plate No.	Part No.	Description	No. per Unit	Remarks
BD1	307325	**PETROL TANK ASSEMBLY**	1	
	144510	**Ring**, sealing, petrol feed pipe	1	
BD2	146086	**Felt**, petrol tank to trunk floor	1	
BD3	146088	**Felt**, petrol tank to trunk floor	1	
		Felt strip, petrol tank cover (Items BD4 to BD7 inclusive). For details see Luggage Floor Section.		
BD8	HU0805	**Screw**, set ⎫	3	
BD9	WL0208	**Washer**, lock ⎬ Petrol tank to body	3	
BD10	WP0017	**Washer**, plain ⎭	3	
BD11	307474	†**Gauge**, fuel, tank unit	1	
BD12	134574	**Washer**, gauge unit sealing	1	
BD13	134575	**Ring**, locking, gauge unit	1	
BD14	144817	**Vent pipe**, rubber, tank to outlet pipe	1	⎫ Fitted up to approximately
BD15	144826	**Pipe**, outlet, tank to air	1	⎬ Commission No.
BD16	CC5012	**Clip**, pipe, vent	2	⎬ KC11542 L.H.S.
BD17	131155	**Grommet**, outlet pipe	1	⎭ and KC9145 R.H.S.
	600399	**Plug**, blanking, redundant vent pipe hole	1	Fitted from approximately Commission No. KC11543 L.H.S. and KC9146 R.H.S.
BD18	613506	**Cap**, petrol filler, assembly	1	
BD19	619420	**Grommet**, petrol filler sealing	1	
BD20	144795	**Hose**, petrol filler to tank	1	
BD21	CJ3038	**Clip**, securing hose	2	
BD22	307537	**Pipe** assembly, petrol tank to flexible connector	1	
BD23	60176	**Nut**, tubing ⎫ Pipe to tank	1	
BD24	TL0007	**Sleeve**, tubing ⎭	1	
BD25	115783	**Connector**, flexible, petrol pipe	1	
BD26	212811	**Pipe** assembly, flexible connector to pump	1	
BD27	60176	**Nut**, tubing ⎫ Pipe to pump	1	
BD28	102729	**Sleeve**, tubing ⎭	1	
BD29	59191	**Clip**, petrol and brake pipes	4	
	615707	**Clip**, petrol and brake pipes	1	
	623314	**Clip**, petrol and brake pipes	2	
	149843	**Connector**, top, petrol line filter	1	⎫
	149844	**Connector**, bottom, petrol line filter	1	⎬
	144542	**Pipe** assembly, line filter to pump	1	⎬
	60176	**Nut**, tubing ⎫ Pipe to pump	1	⎬ U.S.A. Only
	102729	**Sleeve**, tubing ⎭	1	⎬ Fitted from Commission No.
	149636	**Filter**, petrol, in-line	1	⎬ and future
	149842	**Clip**, filter attachment	1	⎬ For previous see items BD25,
	PT0504	**Setscrew** ⎫	1	⎬ BD26, BD27 and BD28 above
	WM0055	**Washer**, medium ⎬ Clip to body	1	⎬
	WL0205	**Washer**, lock ⎬	1	⎬
	HN2005	**Nut** ⎭	1	⎭

Note:—Items marked thus † are available on our Factory Exchange Unit Scheme

83

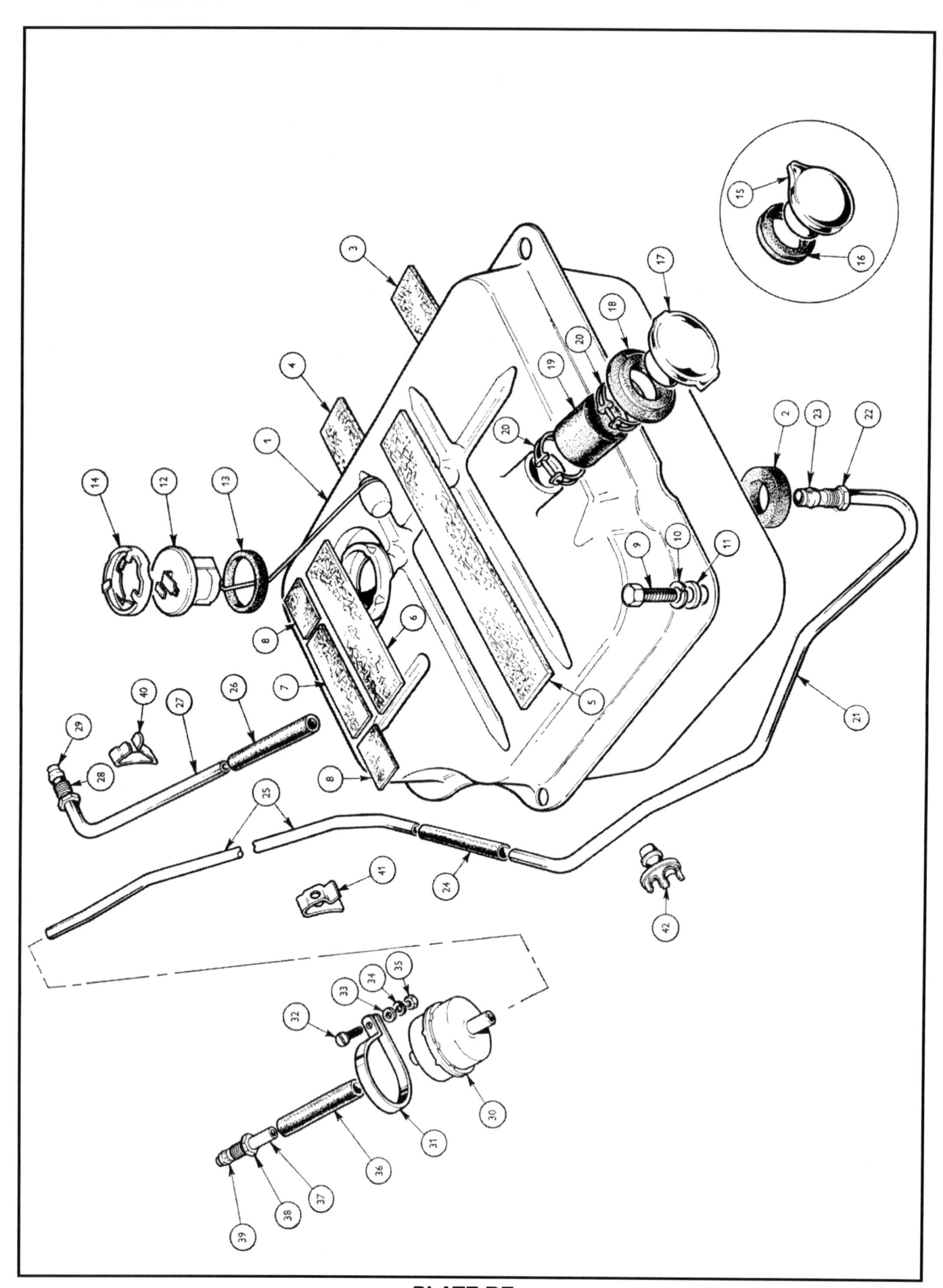

PLATE BE

PETROL SYSTEM

MARK II (G.T.6+) CARS FITTED FROM COMMISSION No. KC50001 AND FUTURE

Plate No.	Part No.	Description	No. per Unit	Remarks
BE1	308678	**PETROL TANK ASSEMBLY**	1	
BE2	144510	**Ring**, sealing petrol feed pipe	1	
BE3	146086	**Felt**, petrol tank to trunk floor	1	
BE4	146088	**Felt**, petrol tank to trunk floor	1	
		Felt strip, petrol tank cover (items BE5 to BE8 inclusive) For details see Luggage Floor Section.		
BE9	HU0805	**Screw**, set ⎫	3	
BE10	WL0208	**Washer**, lock ⎬ Petrol tank to body	3	
BE11	WP0017	**Washer**, plain ⎭	3	
BE12	307474	†**Gauge**, fuel, tank unit	1	
BE13	134574	**Washer**, gauge unit seating	1	
BE14	134575	**Ring**, locking gauge unit	1	
BE15	613506	**Cap**, petrol filler, assembly	1	⎫ All markets
BE16	650247	**Grommet**, petrol filler sealing	1	⎬ except U.S.A.
BE17	714774	**Cap**, petrol filler, assembly	1	⎫ U.S.A. only
BE18	622683	**Grommet**, petrol filler sealing	1	⎭
BE19	144795	**Hose**, petrol filler to tank	1	
BE20	CJ3038	**Clip**, securing hose	2	
BE21	215166	**Pipe assembly**, tank to connector	1	
BE22	60142	**Nut**, tubing ⎫ Pipe to tank	1	
BE23	TL0008	**Sleeve**, tubing ⎭	1	
BE24	115784	**Connector**, flexible, rear pipe to intermediate pipe	1	
BE25	402759	**Pipe**, intermediate	1	
BE26	115784	**Connector**, flexible, intermediate pipe to front pipe or filter	1	
BE27	150593	**Pipe assembly**, connector to pump	1	⎫
BE28	60142	**Nut**, tubing ⎫ Pipe to pump	1	⎬ All markets except U.S.A.
BE29	TL0008	**Sleeve**, tubing ⎭	1	⎭
BE30	149636	**Filter**, petrol, in line	1	⎫
BE31	149842	**Clip**, filter attachment	1	
BE32	PT0504	**Screw**, set ⎫	1	
BE33	WM0055	**Washer**, medium ⎬ Clip to body	1	⎬ U.S.A. only
BE34	WL0205	**Washer**, lock ⎪	1	
BE35	HN2005	**Nut** ⎭	1	
BE36	150698	**Connector**, flexible, filter to front pipe	1	
BE37	150592	**Pipe assembly**, connector to pump	1	
BE38	60142	**Nut**, tubing ⎫ Pipe to pump	1	
BE39	TL0008	**Sleeve**, tubing ⎭	1	⎭
BE40	59191	**Clip** ⎫ Petrol and	4	
BE41	615707	**Clip** ⎬ brake pipe	1	
BE42	623314	**Clip** ⎭ attachment	2	

Note:—Items marked thus † are available on our Factory Exchange Unit Scheme

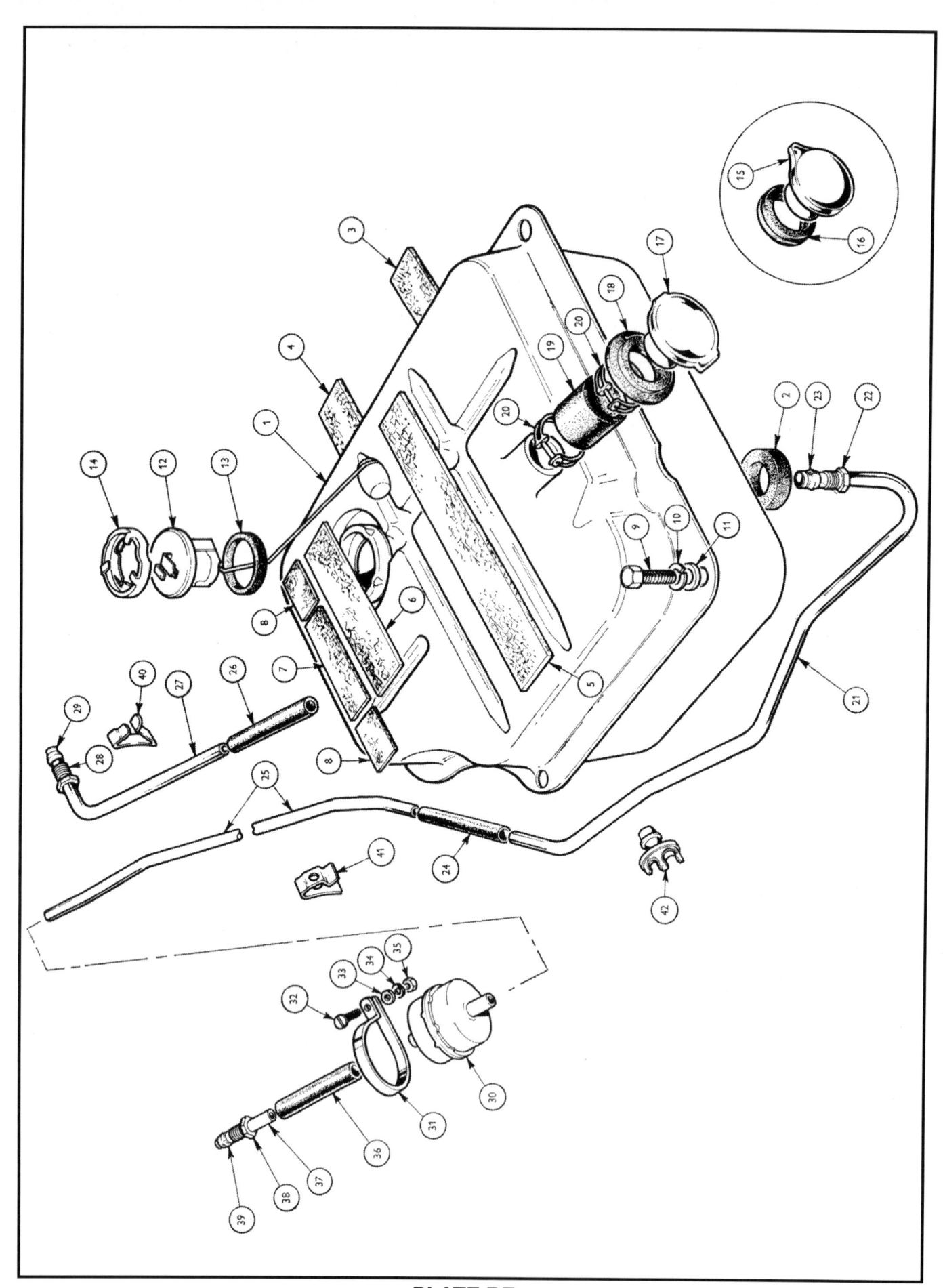

PLATE BE

SERVICE KITS AND TOOLS

Plate No.	Part No.	Description	No. per Unit	Remarks
		SERVICE KITS		
	508445	**Service kit,** clutch master cylinder	1	
	515786	**Service kit,** brake master cylinder	1	
	505704	**Service kit,** slave cylinder	1	
	506667	**Service kit,** front brake caliper	2	
	507865	**Service kit,** rear brake wheel cylinder	2	Fitted up to Commission No. KC7278 only
	508433	**Service kit,** rear brake wheel cylinder	2	Fitted from Commission No. KC7279 and future
	512830	**Gasket set,** decarbonising	1	
	512829	**Gasket set,** engine	1	
	508955	**Repair kit,** water pump	1	
	500524	**First aid kit,** petrol pump	1	Suitable for Petrol Pump 213577 only
	516542	**Repair kit** complete, petrol pump (less rocker arm)	1	
	517632	**Fluid** ⎫	8 oz. tin	
	517633	**Fluid** ⎬ Clutch and brake	16 oz. tin	
	517634	**Fluid** ⎭	32 oz. tin	
	512947	**Workshop Manual**—English	1	
	512948	**Workshop Manual**—French	1	
	512949	**Workshop Manual**—German	1	
	512944	**Owners Handbook**—English	1	
	512945	**Owners Handbook**—French	1	
	512946	**Owners Handbook**—German	1	Mark I vehicles only
	545029	**Owners Handbook**—Flemish	1	
	545057	**Owners Handbook**—English	1	
	545058	**Owners Handbook**—French	1	
	545059	**Owners Handbook**—German	1	Mark II vehicles only
	545060	**Owners Handbook**—Flemish	1	
		TOOLS		
	122746	**Pouch,** tool	1	Not required U.S.A.
	146366	**Pouch,** tool	1	U.S.A. only
	132368	**Spanner,** sparking plug	1	Not required U.S.A.
	59427	**Tool,** combination	1	Fitted up to Commission No. KC50000 only
	134336	**Tool,** nave plate removal	1	Fitted from Commission No. KC50001 and future. All countries except U.S.A.
	503847	**Tool,** combination	1	Fitted from Commission No. KC50001 and future U.S.A. only
	101089	**Spanner,** tube	1	
	122745	**Spanner,** open-ended, $\frac{1}{2}''$ A.F.—$\frac{7}{16}''$ A.F.	1	
	59426	**Spanner,** open-ended, ·50″ A.F.—·56″ A.F. (Alternative to 509361)	1	Not required U.S.A.
	509361	**Spanner,** open-ended, ·50″ A.F.—·56″ A.F. (Alternative to 59426)	1	
	125505	**Gauge,** feeler, assembly	1	
	210926M	**Scissor Jack** assembly ⎫ Alternative to	1	
	210926MH	**Handle,** jack ⎬ 210926P and PH	1	
	210926P	**Scissor Jack** assembly ⎫ Alternative to	1	
	210926PH	**Handle,** jack ⎬ 210926M and MH	1	
		Note:- For Jack Stowage Retaining Strap see Luggage Floor Details.		
	149878	**Special Oil,** rear axle, for topping up	1 qt. tin	
	514639	**Special Grease,** axle shaft	1 lb. tin	

Note:—Items marked thus † are available on our Factory Exchange Unit Scheme

85

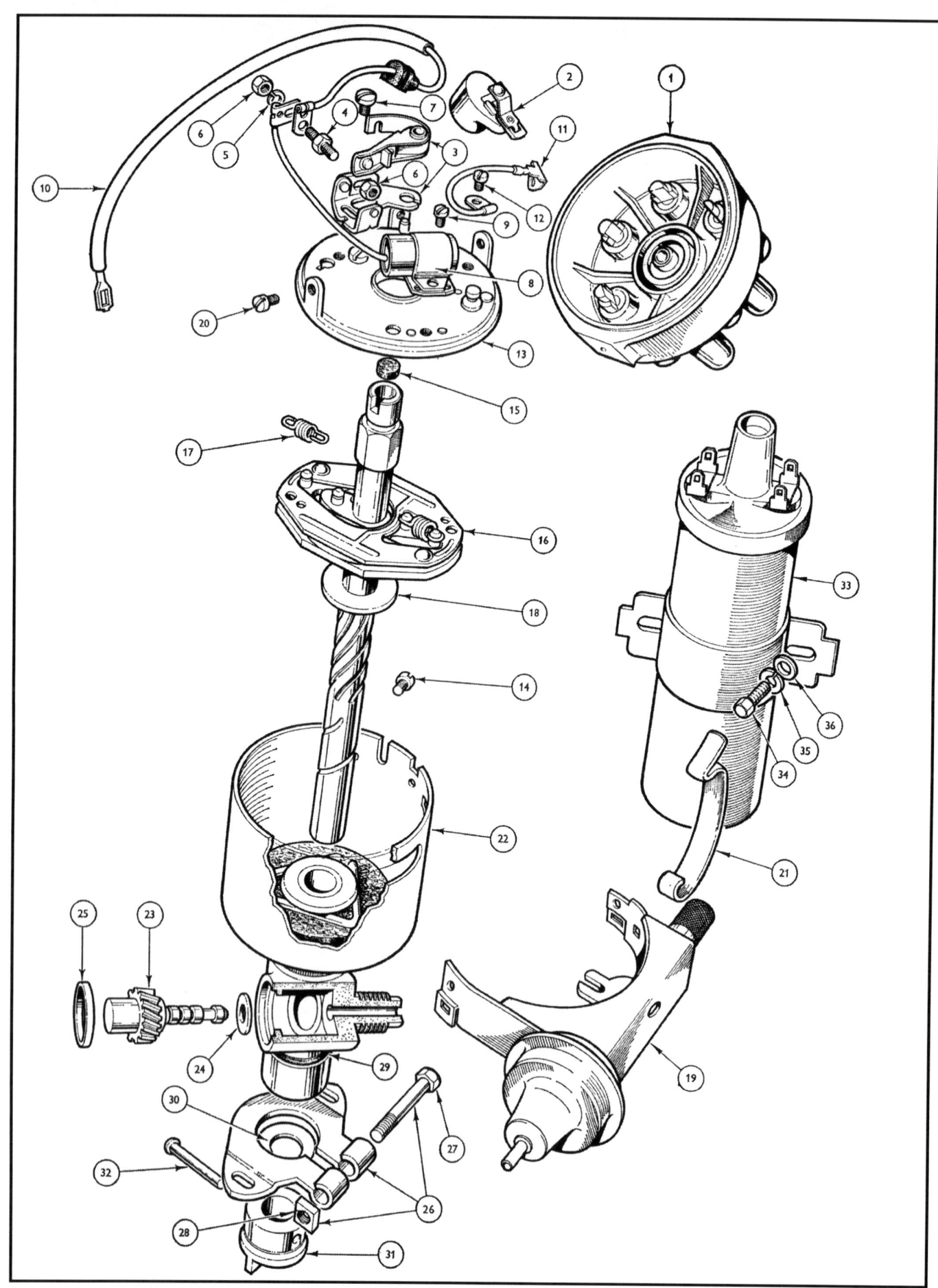

PLATE BF

ELECTRICAL EQUIPMENT

Plate No.	Part No.	Description	No. per Unit	Remarks
	213186	†DISTRIBUTOR ASSEMBLY	1	Fitted up to Commission No. KC50000 only
BF1	513992	**Cap**, distributor	1	
BF2	511837	**Rotor**	1	
BF3	511838	**Contact set**	1	Alternative to 517436
	517436	**Contact set**	1	Alternative to 511838
BF4	511839	**Stud**, contact arm	1	⎫ Only required when
BF5	515710	**Washer**, lock, contact arm stud	1	⎬ contact set 511838
BF6	511841	**Nut**, contact arm	2	⎭ is fitted
BF7	511842	**Screw**, locking, contact point	1	
BF8	511843	**Condenser**	1	
BF9	511844	**Screw**, mounting, condenser	1	
BF10	515711	**Lead**, L.T. (with grommet)	1	
BF11	511846	**Lead**, earth	1	
BF12	511844	**Screw**, earth lead	1	
BF13	511847	**Plate**, breaker, assembly	1	
BF14	511844	**Screw**, breaker plate mounting	1	
BF15	511851	**Wick**, felt, oil	1	
BF16	515712	**Mainshaft and cam** assembly	1	
BF17	515713	**Spring set**, advance weight	1	
BF18	511856	**Washer**, shaft, upper	1	
BF19	515714	**Vacuum control** assembly	1	
BF20	511844	**Screw**, mounting, vacuum control	2	
BF21	511857	**Clip**, cap	2	
BF22	Not Serviced	**Housing** assembly	1	
BF23	511859	**Gear**, tachometer drive	1	
BF24	511860	**Washer**, thrust, drive gear	1	
BF25	511861	**Plug**, housing end, drive gear	1	
BF26	511862	**Clamp**, housing, assembly	1	
BF27	HU0764	**Bolt**, clamp	1	
BF28	NQ2757	**Nut**, clamp	1	
BF29	511863	**Ring**, oil seal	1	
BF30	511864	**Washer**, shaft, lower	1	
BF31	511866	**Coupling**	1	
BF32	511865	**Pin**, coupling	1	
BF33	146112	**IGNITION COIL**	1	
BF34	HU0804	**Screw**, set ⎫	2	
BF35	WL0208	**Washer**, lock ⎬ Ignition coil to cylinder block	2	
BF36	WP0008	**Washer**, plain ⎭	2	
	215511	†DISTRIBUTOR ASSEMBLY	1	Fitted from Commission No. KC50001 and future

Note:- Breakdown details not available.

Note:—Items marked thus † are available on our Factory Exchange Unit Scheme

86

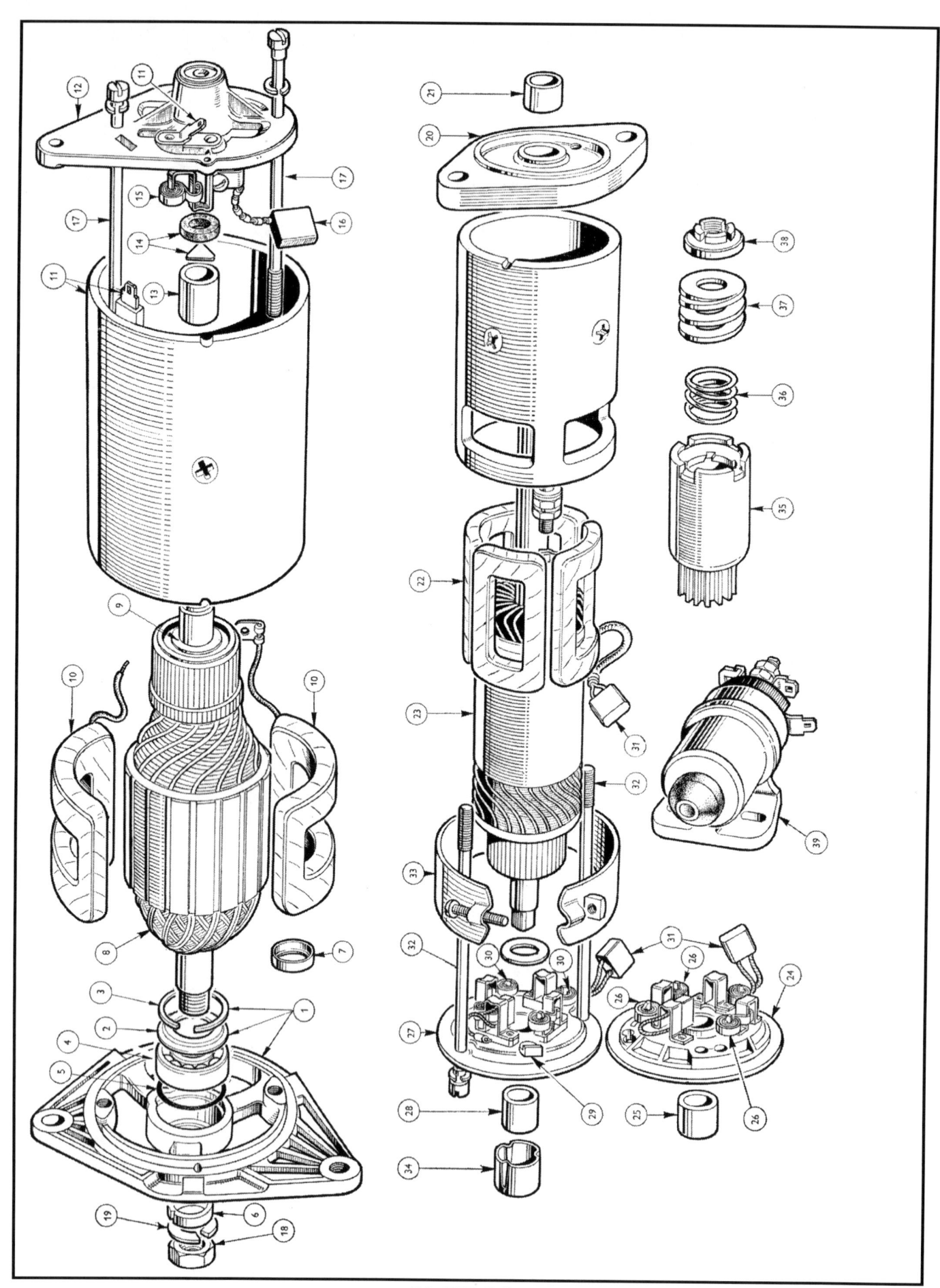

PLATE BG

ELECTRICAL EQUIPMENT

Plate No.	Part No.	Description	No. per Unit	Remarks
	308372/2	†**DISTRIBUTOR ASSEMBLY**	1	U.S.A. (Anti-Smog) only. Fitted from Commission No. KC7611 and future
BG1	513992	**Cap**, distributor	1	
BG2	511837	**Rotor**	1	
BG3	517436	**Contact set**	1	
BG4	517050	**Insulator**	1	
BG5	511842	**Screw**, locking contact point	1	
BG6	516237	**Condenser** assembly	1	
BG7	511844	**Screw**, condenser mounting	1	
BG8	513994	**Lead**, L.T. (with grommet)	1	
BG9	513993	**Lead**, earth	1	
BG10	517437	**Plate**, breaker, assembly	1	
BG11	511844	**Screw**, breaker plate mounting	1	
BG12	511851	**Wick**, felt, oil	1	
BG13	517438	**Mainshaft and cam** assembly	1	
BG14	517439	**Spring set**, advance weight	1	
BG15	511856	**Washer**, shaft, upper	1	
BG16	517440	**Vacuum control** assembly	1	
BG17	511844	**Screw**, vacuum control attachment	1	
BG18	513400	**Clip**, cap	2	
BG19	513999	**Screw**, cap clip and vacuum control	2	
BG20	Not Serviced	**Housing** assembly	1	
BG21	511859	**Gear**, tachometer drive	1	
BG22	511860	**Washer**, thrust, drive gear	1	
BG23	511861	**Plug**, housing end, drive gear	1	
BG24	511862	**Clamp**, housing assembly	1	
BG25	HU0764	**Bolt**, clamp	1	
BG26	NQ2757	**Nut**, clamp	1	
BG27	511863	**Ring**, oil seal	1	
BG28	511864	**Washer**, shaft, lower	1	
BG29	511866	**Coupling**	1	
BG30	511865	**Pin**, coupling	1	

Note:—Items marked thus † are available on our Factory Exchange Unit Scheme

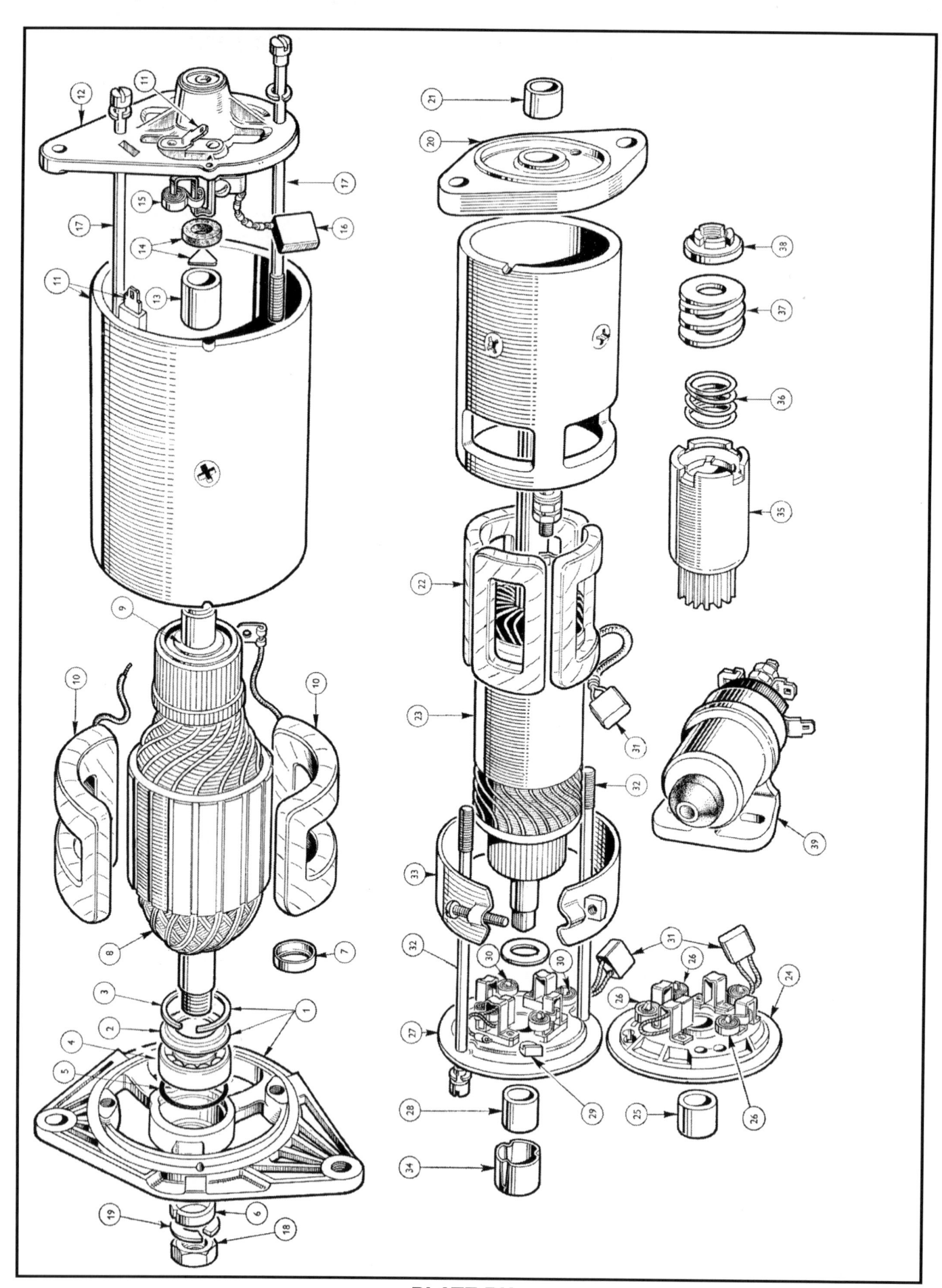

PLATE BH

ELECTRICAL EQUIPMENT

Plate No.	Part No.	Description	No. per Unit	Remarks
	209000	†DYNAMO (Lucas No. 22716J)	1	Fitted up to Commission No. KC50000 only. See Page 91 for Alternator fitted to Mark II (GT.6+) cars
BH1	515590	**Bracket** assembly, drive end, less bearing	1	
BH2	515591	**Plate** ⎫ Retaining drive end bearing	1	
BH3	515592	**Circlip** ⎭	1	
BH4	509307	**Bearing**, drive end bracket	1	
BH5	515593	**Ring**, 'O', oil seal	1	
BH6	509313	**Collar**, drive end bearing	1	
BH7	509312	**Retainer**, bearing ring	1	
BH8	511593	**Armature** assembly	1	
BH9	509314	**Washer**, thrust, commutator end	1	
BH10	511594	**Coil**, field, set	1	
BH11	509315	**Terminal set**, Lucar	1	
BH12	511589	**Bracket** assembly, commutator end	1	
BH13	509304	**Bush**, end bracket	1	
BH14	509305	**Oiler** assembly	1	
BH15	509306	**Spring set**, brush tension	1	
BH16	515589	**Brush set**	1	
BH17	511596	**Bolt**, through end brackets	2	
BH18	509309	**Nut**, shaft	1	
BH19	509310	**Washer**, spring, under shaft nut	1	
	509317	**Set**, sundry parts	1	
	200535	†STARTER MOTOR	1	Lucas No. 25022 or 25079B
BH20	501712	**Bracket** assembly, driving end	1	
BH21	500927	**Bush**, driving end bracket	1	For use with Lucas No. 25022 only
	514025	**Bushing and bearing**	1	For use with Lucas No. 25079B only
BH22	501715	**Coil**, field set	1	
BH23	501714	**Armature** assembly	1	For use with Lucas No. 25022 only
	514026	**Armature** assembly	1	For use with Lucas No. 25079B only
BH24	501706	**Bracket** assembly, commutator end ⎫ Diecast	1	
BH25	500926	**Bush**, commutator bracket ⎬ commutator	1	
BH26	501708	**Spring set**, brush tension ⎭ end bracket	1	
BH27	509817	**Bracket** assembly, commutator end ⎫ Pressed metal	1	
BH28	509818	**Bush**, commutator bracket ⎪	1	
BH29	509820	**Sleeve** ⎬ commutator	1	
BH30	509819	**Spring set**, brush tension ⎭ end bracket	1	
BH31	501705	**Brush set**	1	
BH32	502210	**Bolt**, through end brackets	2	
BH33	57458	**Band**, cover, assembly	1	
BH34	501704	**Cap**, shaft end	1	For use with Lucas No. 25022 only
BH35	500892	**Pinion** and sleeve assembly	1	For use with Lucas No. 25022 only
	511290	**Pinion and barrel**	1	For use with Lucas No. 25079B only
	514023	**Sleeve**, screwed	1	For use with Lucas No. 25079B only
BH36	501711	**Spring**, pinion retaining	1	
BH37	501710	**Spring**, main	1	
BH38	501709	**Nut**, locating	1	For use with Lucas No. 25022 only
	514024	**Cup**, shaft	1	For use with Lucas No. 25079B only
	70391	**Set**, sundry parts	1	

Note:—Items marked thus † are available on our Factory Exchange Unit Scheme

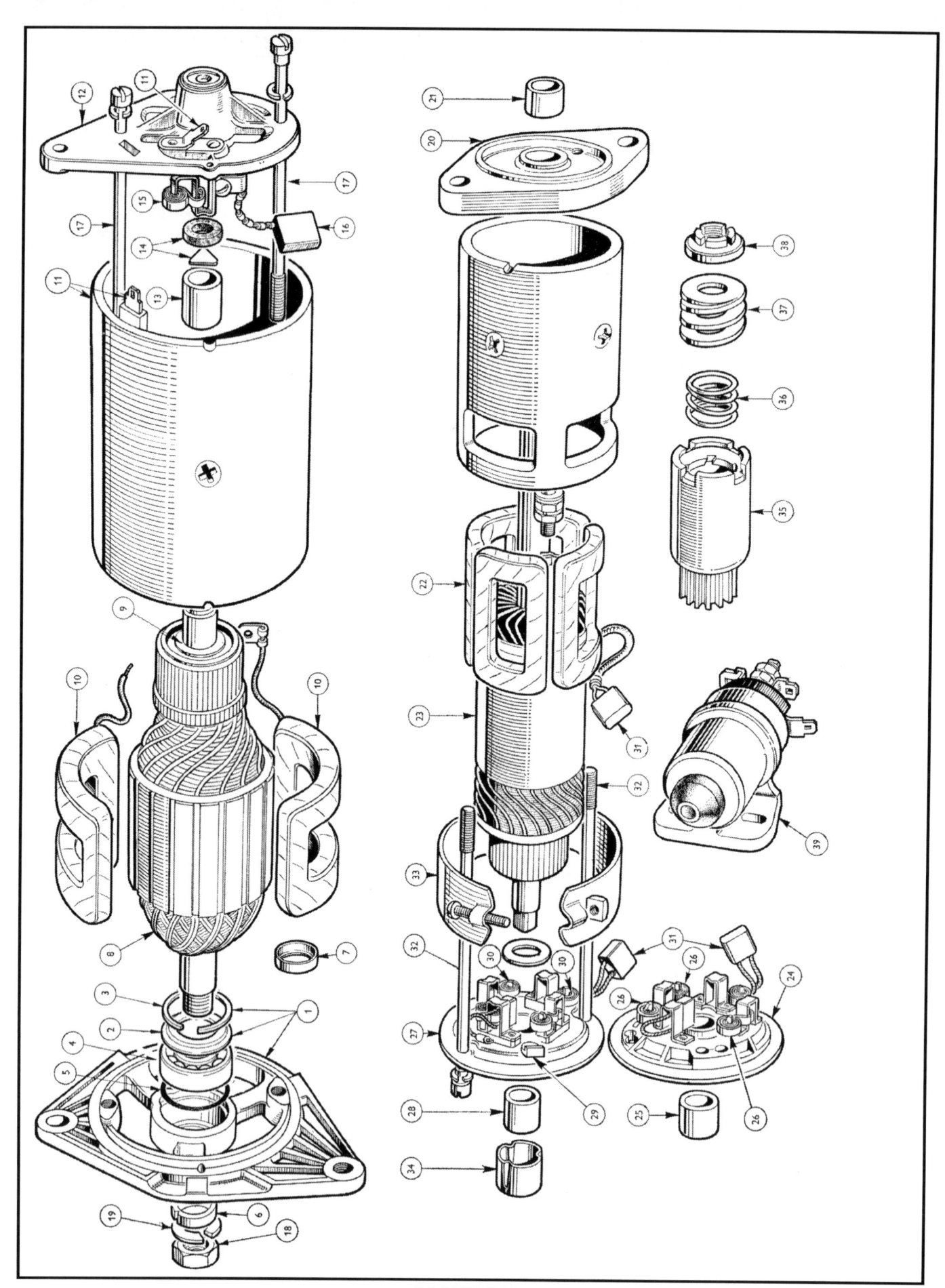

PLATE BH

ELECTRICAL EQUIPMENT

Plate No.	Part No.	Description	No. per Unit	Remarks
		STARTER MOTOR—continued		
	131570	**Packing,** starter motor	1	
	104549	**Shim,** starter motor	A/R	
	HB0917	**Bolt** ⎱	2	
	HN2009	**Nut** ⎰ Starter motor	2	
	WL0209	**Washer,** spring ⎱ attachment	2	
	WE0609	**Washer,** shakeproof ⎰	1	
BH39	121269	**STARTER SOLENOID SWITCH**	1	
	PX0505	**Screw,** set ⎱	2	
	WL0205	**Washer,** lock ⎰ Starter solenoid	2	
	WE0605	**Washer,** shakeproof ⎱ attachment	2	
	WM0055	**Washer,** medium ⎰	2	
	516591	**Nut**	2	Required when starter solenoid switch Lucas 4 ST (No. 76766) is fitted.
	516592	**Washer,** lock	2	

Note:—Items marked thus † are available on our Factory Exchange Unit Scheme

89

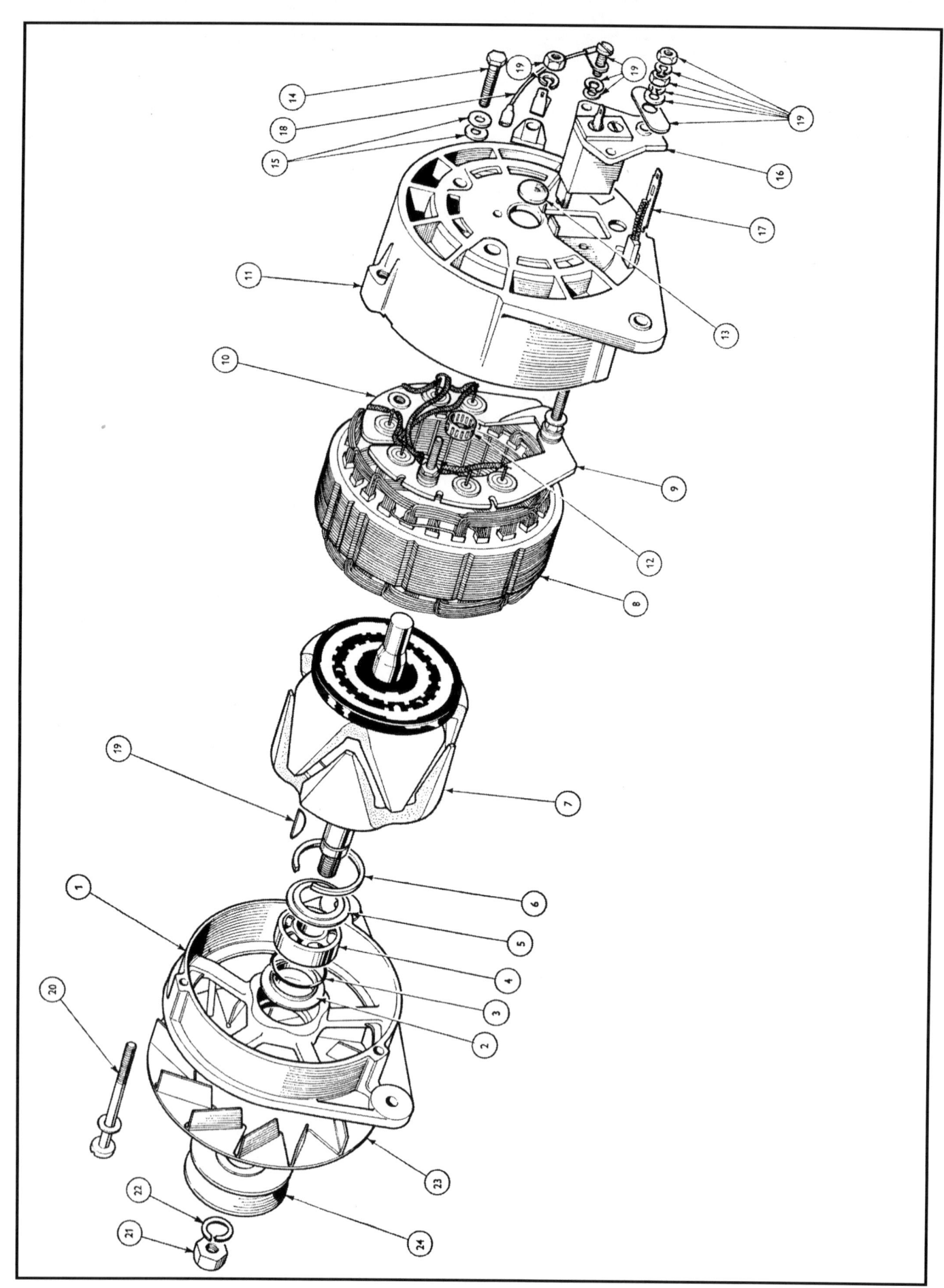

PLATE BJ

ELECTRICAL EQUIPMENT

Plate No.	Part No.	Description	No. per Unit	Remarks
		ALTERNATOR DETAILS FITTED TO MARK I CARS ONLY (UP TO COMMISSION No. KC50000)		
	211962	†**ALTERNATOR**, 11 A.C. — POSITIVE EARTH	1	Fitted to Special Order. only
	213121	†**ALTERNATOR**, 11 A.C. — NEGATIVE EARTH	1	
BJ1	516043	**Bracket**, frame	1	
BJ2	516044	**Washer**, retaining 'O' ring	1	
BJ3	515593	**'O' ring**, oil seal	1	
BJ4	509307	**Bearing**	1	
BJ5	515591	**Plate**, bearing retaining	1	
BJ6	515592	**Circlip**	1	
BJ7	516045	**Rotor**	1	
BJ8	516056	**Stator**	1	
BJ9	516050	**Heatsink**, with anode base diodes } Positive earth	1	
BJ10	516049	**Heatsink**, with cathode base diodes	1	
	516060	**Heatsink**, with anode base diodes } Negative earth	1	
	516059	**Heatsink**, with cathode base diodes	1	
BJ11	516046	**Bracket**, slip ring end	1	
BJ12	516047	**Bearing**, needle roller } Rear, or slip ring end	1	
BJ13	516048	**Seal**, bearing	1	
BJ14	516054	**Screw**, heatsink fixing	1	
BJ15	516055	**Washer**, insulating	2	
BJ16	516052	**Brush box**	1	
BJ17	516051	**Brush**, complete with spring and Lucar blade	2	
BJ18	516053	**Connector**, Lucar, cut-out	1	
BJ19	516057	**Sundry parts set**	1	
BJ20	516042	**Bolt**, through frame	3	
BJ21	509309	**Nut**, shaft	1	
BJ22	509310	**Washer**, shaft	1	
BJ23	143775	**Fan**	1	
BJ24	147530	**Pulley**, alternator	1	

Note:—Items marked thus † are available on our Factory Exchange Unit Scheme

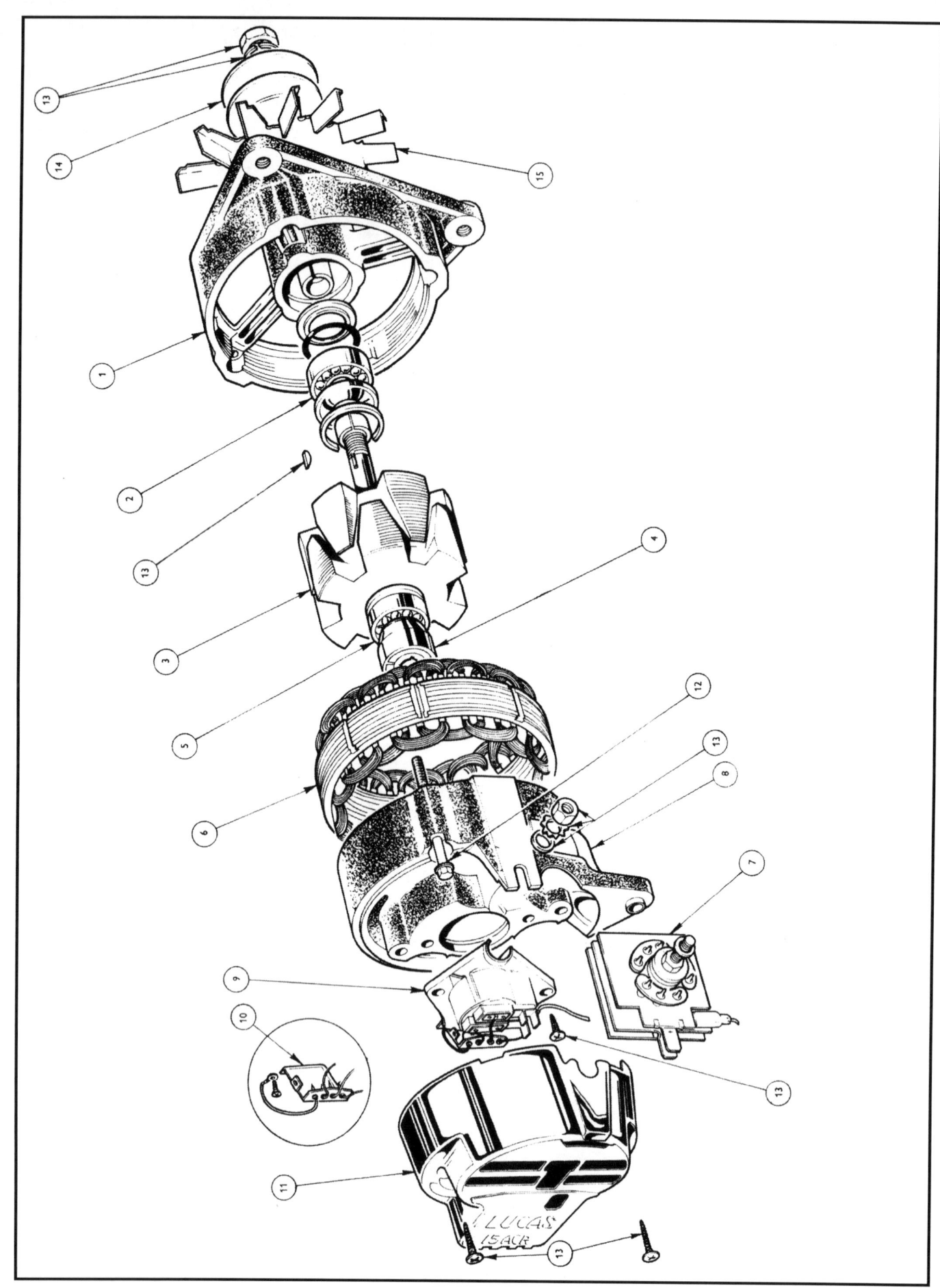

PLATE BK

ELECTRICAL EQUIPMENT

Plate No.	Part No.	Description	No. per Unit	Remarks
		ALTERNATOR DETAILS FITTED TO MARK II CARS ONLY (FROM COMMISSION No. KC50001)		
	215346	†ALTERNATOR, 15 A.C.R. — NEGATIVE EARTH	1	
BK1	517654	**Bracket,** frame, driving end	1	
BK2	517655	**Service kit,** driving end bearing	1	
BK3	517652	**Rotor**	1	
BK4	517653	**Slip ring**	1	
BK5	517657	**Bearing kit,** slip ring end	1	
BK6	517236	**Stator**	1	
BK7	517649	**Rectifier**	1	
BK8	517656	**Bracket,** slip ring end	1	
BK9	517650	**Brush box** assembly (complete with brushes)	1	
	517651	**Brush set**	1	
BK10	517648	**Regulator**	1	
BK11	517647	**Cover**	1	
BK12	517189	**Bolt,** through frame	3	
BK13	517237	**Sundry parts set**	1	
BK14	147530	**Pulley,** alternator	1	
BK15	147990	**Fan,** alternator	1	

Note:—Items marked thus † are available on our Factory Exchange Unit Scheme

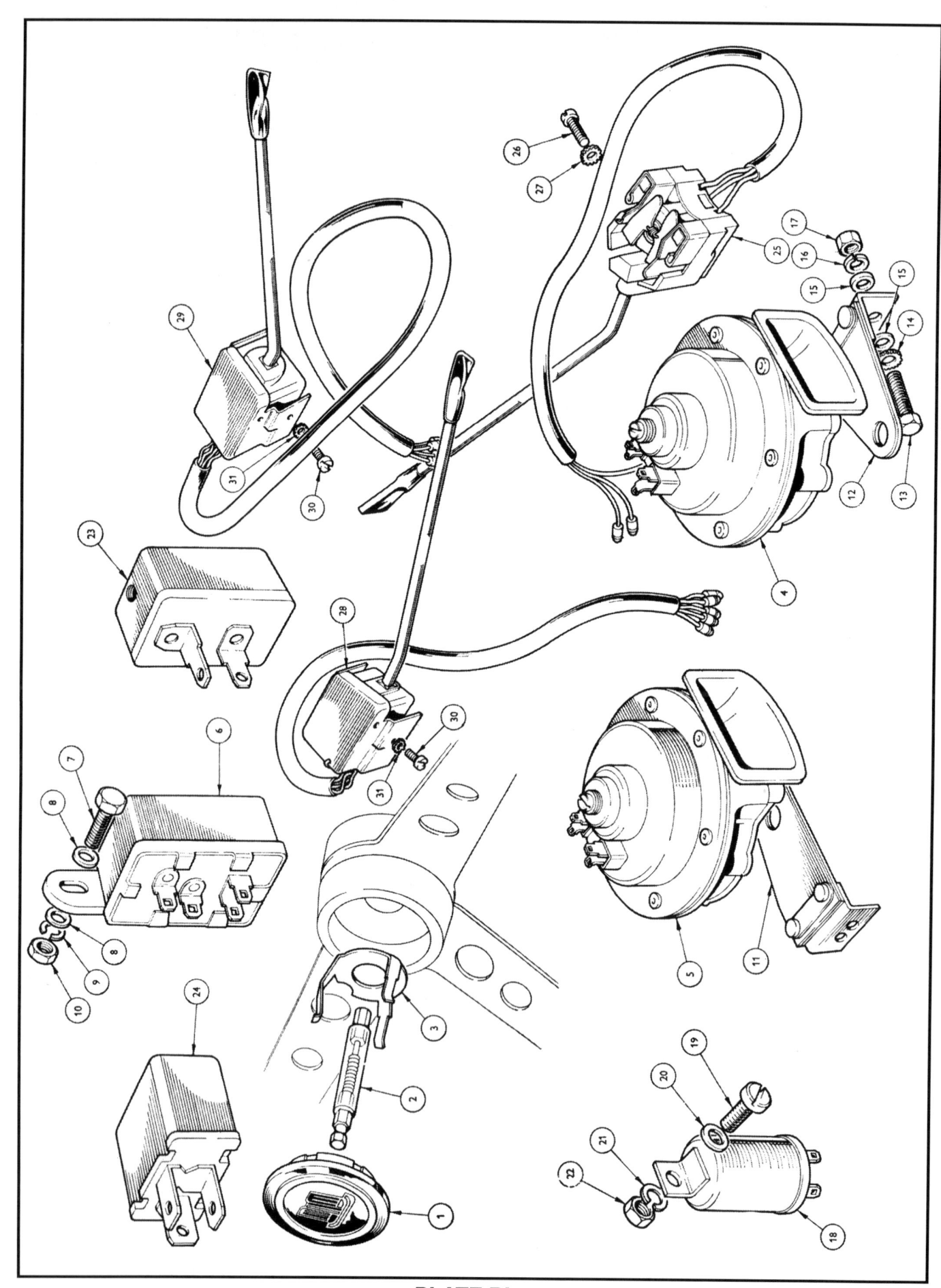

PLATE BL

ELECTRICAL EQUIPMENT

Plate No.	Part No.	Description	No. per Unit	Remarks
BL1	150277	**HORN PUSH ASSEMBLY**	1	
BL2	108657	**Brush,** horn push connection	1	
BL3	204741	**Clip,** horn push assembly	1	
		HORNS		
BL4	143794/1	**Horn**—High note ⎫	1	⎫ Interchangeable in sets
BL5	142301/2	**Horn**—Low note ⎬ Clear Hooters	1	⎬ with 143794/2, 142301/1,
BL6	137747/2	**Relay,** horn ⎭	1	⎭ and 137747/1
	143794/2	**Horn**—High note ⎫	1	⎫ Interchangeable in sets
	142301/1	**Horn**—Low note ⎬ Lucas	1	⎬ with 143794/1, 142301/2,
	137747/1	**Relay,** horn ⎭	1	⎭ and 137747/2
BL7	510503	**Screw,** set ⎫	2	
BL8	508875	**Washer,** plain ⎪ Horn relay	4	
BL9	WL0205	**Washer,** lock ⎨ to dash	2	
BL10	HN2005	**Nut** ⎭	2	
	146250	**Horn,** Super Post ⎫ Clear Hooters	1	⎫ Alternative in car sets
	146711	**Horn,** Post ⎭	1	⎭ to Horns listed above
	144351	**Horn**—High note ⎫	1	
	142301/2	**Horn**—Low note ⎬ Clear Hooters French Markets only	1	
	137747/2	**Relay,** horn ⎭	1	
	133071	**Bracket,** horn mounting (Lucas horns only)	2	⎫
BL11	129915	**Bracket,** horn mounting (Clear Hooter horns only) assembly—R.H.	1	⎬ Supplied as part of the above
BL12	129914	**Bracket,** horn mounting (Clear Hooter horns only) assembly—L.H.	1	⎭ Horn Assemblies
BL13	HU0705	**Screw,** set ⎫	4	
BL14	WE0607	**Washer,** shakeproof ⎪	2	
BL15	WP0023	**Washer,** plain ⎬ Horn attachment	8	
BL16	WL0207	**Washer,** lock ⎪	4	
BL17	HN2007	**Nut** ⎭	4	

Note:—Items marked thus † are available on our Factory Exchange Unit Scheme

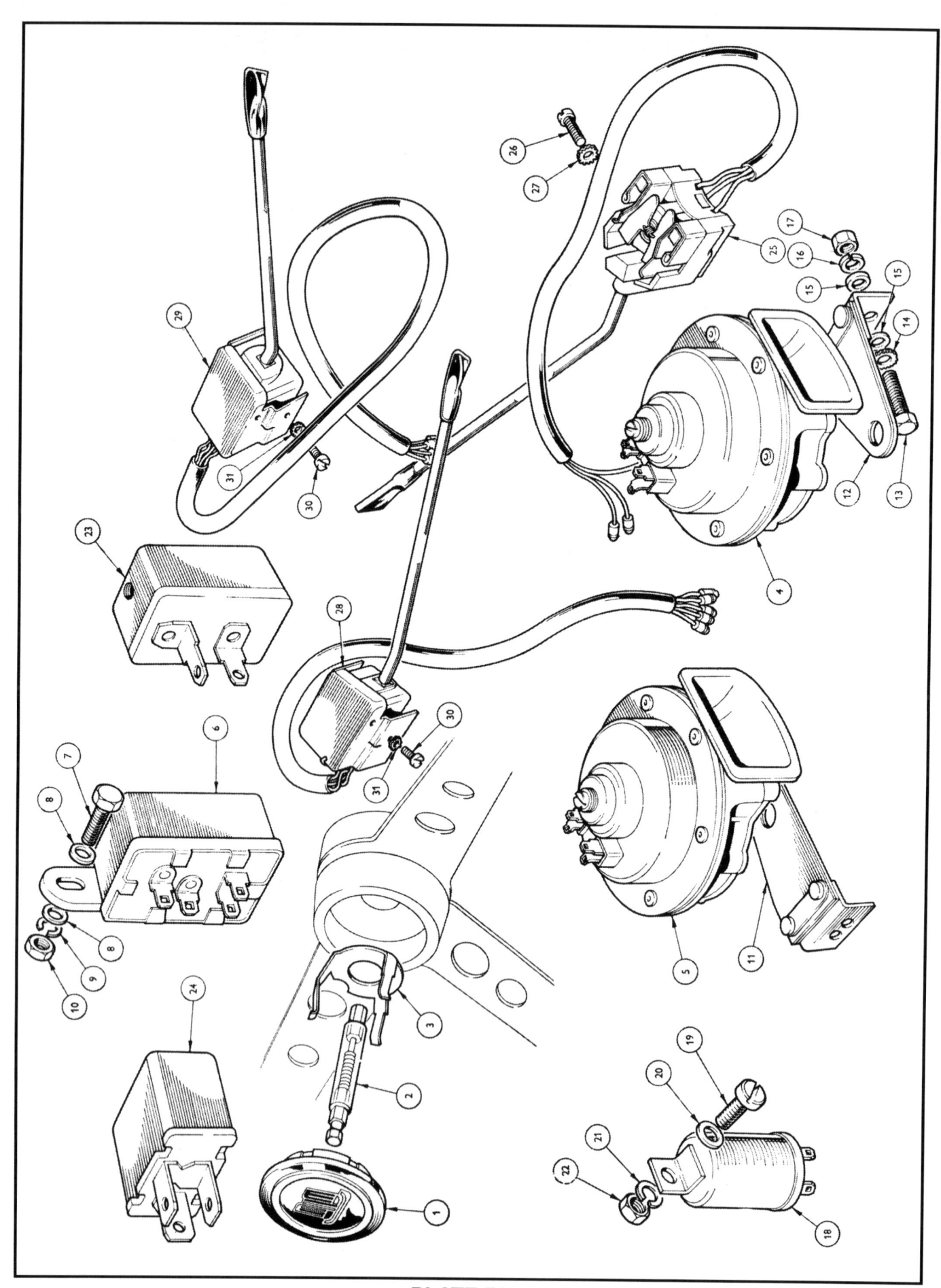

PLATE BL

ELECTRICAL EQUIPMENT

Plate No.	Part No.	Description	No. per Unit	Remarks
BL18	131251	**FLASHER UNIT**	1	Mk. I cars only. Fitted up to Commission No. KC50000
BL19	PT0358	**Screw** ⎫ Flasher unit	1	
BL20	WP0003	**Washer,** plain ⎬ attachment	1	
BL21	WL0203	**Washer,** lock ⎪	1	
BL22	HN2053	**Nut** ⎭	1	
BL23	148644	**FLASHER UNIT**	1	Mk. II cars only. Fitted from Commission No. KC50001
	Not Serviced	**Socket,** flasher unit, part of main harness	1	
	PT0353	**Screw** ⎫ Socket	1	
	WP0003	**Washer,** plain ⎬ attachment	1	
	WL0203	**Washer,** lock ⎪	1	
	HN2053	**Nut** ⎭	1	
BL24	148576	**HAZARD FLASHER UNIT**	1	Mk. II cars only. Fitted from Commission No. KC50001
	Not Serviced	**Socket,** flasher unit, part of main harness	1	
	PT0353	**Setscrew** ⎫ Socket	1	
	WL0203	**Washer,** lock ⎬ attachment	1	
	WP0003	**Washer,** plain ⎪	1	
	HN2053	**Nut** ⎭	1	
BL25	145793	**FLASHER INDICATOR SWITCH**	1	
BL26	TP0402	**Screw** ⎫ Flasher switch	2	
BL27	WE0604	**Washer,** shakeproof ⎭ attachment	2	
	611012	**Label,** instruction, flasher switch—R.H.S.	1	
	611011	**Label,** instruction, flasher switch—L.H.S.	1	
BL28	145794	**LIGHTING SWITCH — HEAD, DIP SIDE AND FLASH — R.H.S.**	1	Fitted up to Commission No. KC50000 only
	145795	**LIGHTING SWITCH — HEAD, DIP SIDE AND FLASH — L.H.S.** (Except Sweden)	1	
	611400	**Label,** instruction, lighting switch—R.H.S.	1	
	611399	**Label,** instruction, lighting switch—L.H.S. (Except Sweden)	1	
	148647	**LIGHTING SWITCH — HEADLAMP DIP AND FLASH — L.H.S.** (Sweden only)	1	
	148646	**Lead,** loop, column switch to panel switch	1	
BL29	148647	**LIGHTING SWITCH — HEADLAMP DIP AND FLASH**	1	Fitted from Commission No. KC50001 and future
BL30	TP0402	**Screw** ⎫ Lighting switch	2	
BL31	WE0604	**Washer,** shakeproof ⎭ attachment	2	

Note:—Items marked thus † are available on our Factory Exchange Unit Scheme

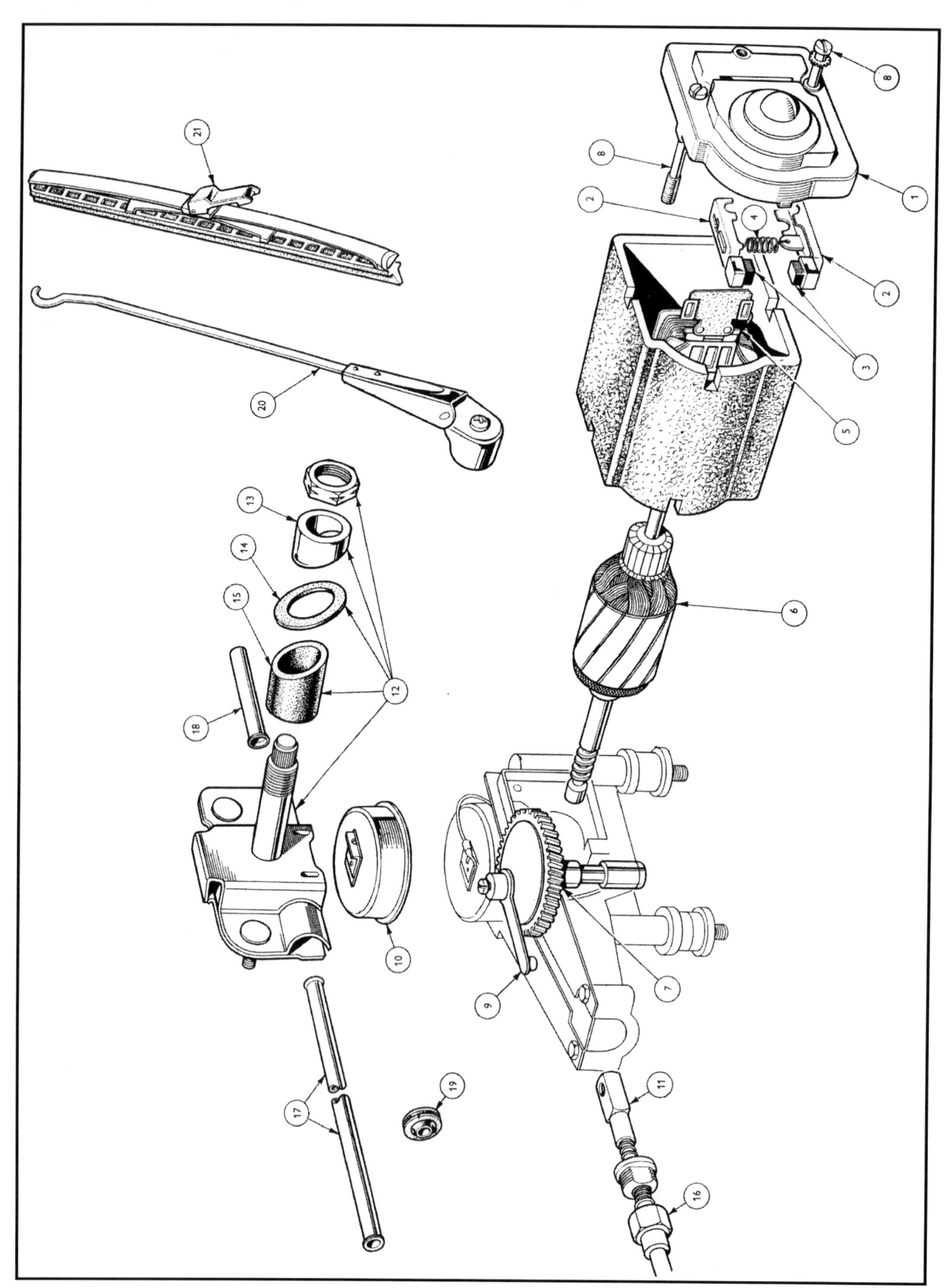

PLATE BM

ELECTRICAL EQUIPMENT

Plate No.	Part No.	Description	No. per Unit	Remarks
		WINDSCREEN WIPER DETAILS (MK. I CARS UP TO COMMISSION No. KC50000 ONLY)		
	515658	†**MOTOR AND GEARBOX**	1	
BM1	511094	Cover and bearing	1	
BM2	508169	**Gear,** brush	1	
BM3	508170	**Brush** set	1	
BM4	57492	**Spring,** brush	1	
BM5	511095	**Coil,** field	1	
BM6	511003	**Armature**	1	
BM7	513962	**Shaft and gear** assembly	1	
	505869	**Set,** sundry parts	1	
BM8	511001	**Bolt,** fixing	2	
	511005	**Stud,** fixing, set	1	
BM9	511096	**Rod,** connecting	1	
BM10	511006	**Switch,** parking	1	
BM11	508182	**CROSSHEAD AND RACK**	1	
BM12	134746	**Wheelbox** assembly	2	
BM13	134747	**Bush,** front, chrome plated	2	
BM14	134751	**Seal,** rubber, wheelbox	2	
BM15	134748	**Bush,** rubber, rear	2	
BM16	706768	**Tubing** assembly, motor to wheelbox	1	
BM17	613656	**Tubing,** wheelbox to wheelbox	1	
BM18	108860	**Extension,** tubing	1	
BM19	131155	**Grommet,** bulkhead	1	
BM20	138479	**Wiper arm**—R.H.S. ⎫	2	
BM21	138478	**Wiper blade**—R.H.S. ⎬ Bright chrome finish	2	
	512955	**Blade,** rubber ⎭	2	
	138480	**Wiper arm**—L.H.S. ⎫	2	Fitted up to Commission No.
	138478	**Wiper blade**—L.H.S. ⎬ Bright chrome finish	2	KC10000 U.S.A. and
	512955	**Blade,** rubber ⎭	2	KC10955 other markets
	149753	**Wiper arm**—L.H.S. ⎫	2	Fitted from Commission No.
	149759	**Wiper blade**—L.H.S. ⎬ Dull finish	2	KC10001 U.S.A. and
	517620	**Blade,** rubber ⎭	2	KC10956 other markets

Note:—Items marked thus † are available on our Factory Exchange Unit Scheme

94

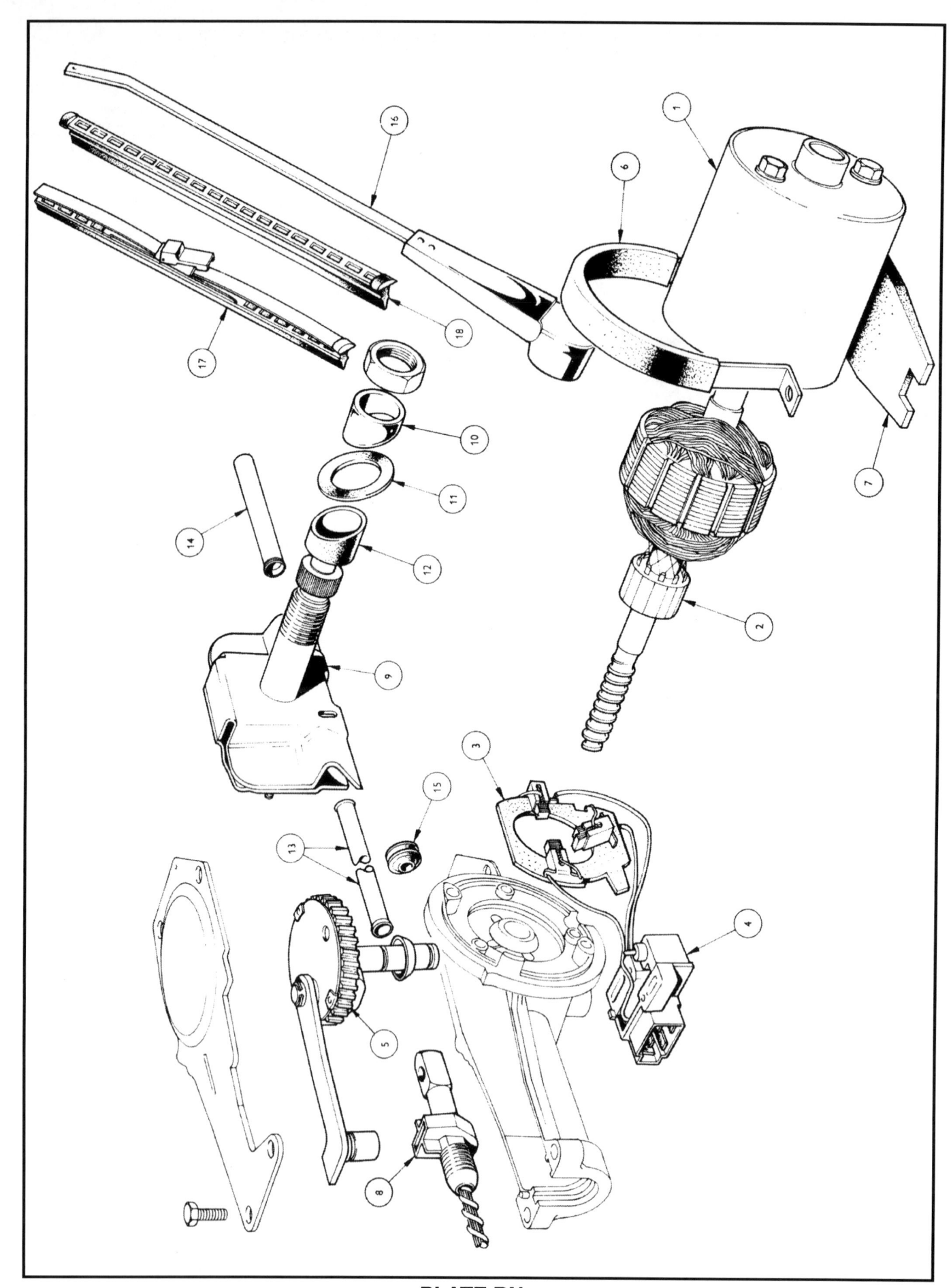

PLATE BN

ELECTRICAL EQUIPMENT

Plate No.	Part No.	Description	No. per Unit	Remarks
		WINDSCREEN WIPER DETAILS (FITTED TO MK. II CARS FROM COMMISSION No. KC50001)		
	517621	**WINDSCREEN WIPER MOTOR (TWO SPEED)**	1	
BN1	Not Serviced	Cover, end	1	
BN2	517643	Armature	1	
BN3	517644	Brush assembly	1	
BN4	517645	Switch, parking	1	
BN5	517646	Gear assembly—R.H.S.	1	
	517622	Gear assembly—L.H.S.	1	
BN6	150846	Strap and sleeve assembly	1	
	150845	Sleeve, rubber	1	
BN7	150844	Pad, fixing, rubber	1	Wiper motor mounting
	HU0704	Screw, set	2	
	WL0207	Washer, lock	2	
	WP0007	Washer, plain	2	
BN8	503604	**CROSSHEAD AND RACK**	1	
BN9	151219	Wheelbox assembly	2	
BN10	134747	Bush, front, chrome plated	2	
BN11	134751	Seal, rubber, wheelbox	2	
BN12	134748	Bush, rubber, rear	2	
	813942	Tubing assembly, motor to wheelbox	1	
BN13	716803	Tubing, wheelbox to wheelbox	1	
BN14	108860	Extension, tubing	1	
BN15	131155	Grommet, bulkhead	1	
BN16	151957	**WIPER ARM—R.H.**	1	
	151956	**WIPER ARM—L.H.**	1	
BN17	151958	**WIPER BLADE**	2	
BN18		Blade, rubber	2	

Note:—Items marked thus † are available on our Factory Exchange Unit Scheme

95

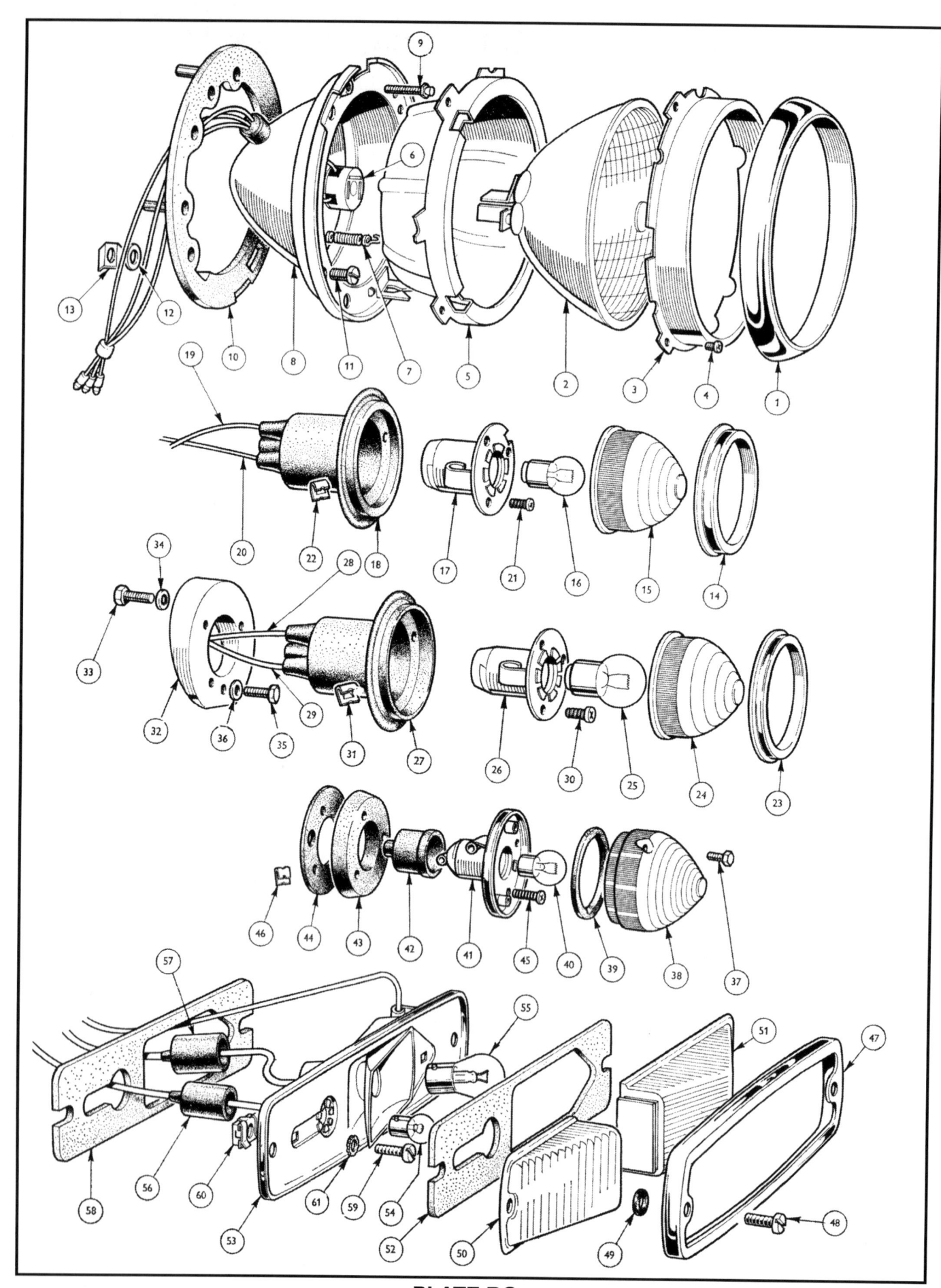

PLATE BO

ELECTRICAL EQUIPMENT

Plate No.	Part No.	Description	No. per Unit	Remarks
	512223	**HEADLAMP ASSEMBLY**	2	
BO1	119072	**Rim**, snap-on	2	
BO2	512231	**Light unit**	2	
BO3	512987	**Plate**, retaining light unit	2	
BO4	507086	**Screw**, securing unit retaining plate	6	
BO5	513265	**Rim**, unit seating	2	
BO6	501478	**Connector and cable** assembly	2	Home and Export (except Sweden)
	504806	**Tube**, P.V.C.	2	L.H. Rule of Road—R.H.S. only
	605953	**Sleeve**, terminal	6	
BO7	513266	**Spring**, fixing unit seating rim	2	
BO8	Not Serviced	**Body**	2	
BO9	513267	**Screw**, trimmer	4	
BO10	512222	**Gasket**, body	2	
BO11	YF7406	**Screw**, set ⎫	8	
BO12	WP0004	**Washer**, plain ⎬ Headlamp to body	8	
BO13	FC2804/4	**Nut** ⎭	8	
	512224	**HEADLAMP ASSEMBLY**	2	
BO1	119072	**Rim**, snap-on	2	
BO2	510892	**Light unit**	2	
	510218	**Bulb**, 12 v., No. 410, 45/40 w.	2	
	510893	**Spring**, retaining bulb	2	
BO3	512987	**Plate**, retaining light unit	2	
BO4	507086	**Screw**, securing unit retaining plate	6	Export only.
BO5	513265	**Rim**, unit seating	2	All R.H. Rule of Road except
BO6	501478	**Connector and cable** assembly	2	U.S.A., Canada and France
	504806	**Tube**, P.V.C.	2	—L.H.S. only
	605953	**Sleeve**, terminal	6	
BO7	513266	**Spring**, fixing unit seating rim	2	
BO8	Not Serviced	**Body**	2	
BO9	513267	**Screw**, trimmer	4	
BO10	512222	**Gasket**, body	2	
BO11	YF7406	**Screw**, set ⎫	8	
BO12	WP0004	**Washer**, plain ⎬ Headlamp to body	8	
BO13	FC2804/4	**Nut** ⎭	8	
	514579	**HEADLAMP ASSEMBLY**	2	
BO1	119072	**Rim**, snap-on	2	
BO2	514578	**Light unit**	2	
BO3	512987	**Plate**, retaining light unit	2	
BO4	507086	**Screw**, securing unit retaining plate	6	
BO5	513265	**Rim**, unit seating	2	
BO6	501478	**Connector and cable** assembly	2	U.S.A. and Canada
	504806	**Tube**, P.V.C.	2	R.H. Rule of Road
	605953	**Sleeve**, terminal	6	—L.H.S. only
BO7	513266	**Spring**, fixing unit seating rim	2	
BO8	Not Serviced	**Body**	2	
BO9	513267	**Screw**, trimmer	4	
BO10	512222	**Gasket**, body	2	
BO11	YF7406	**Screw**, set ⎫	8	
BO12	WP0004	**Washer**, plain ⎬ Headlamp to body	8	
BO13	FC2804/4	**Nut** ⎭	8	

Note:—Items marked thus † are available on our Factory Exchange Unit Scheme

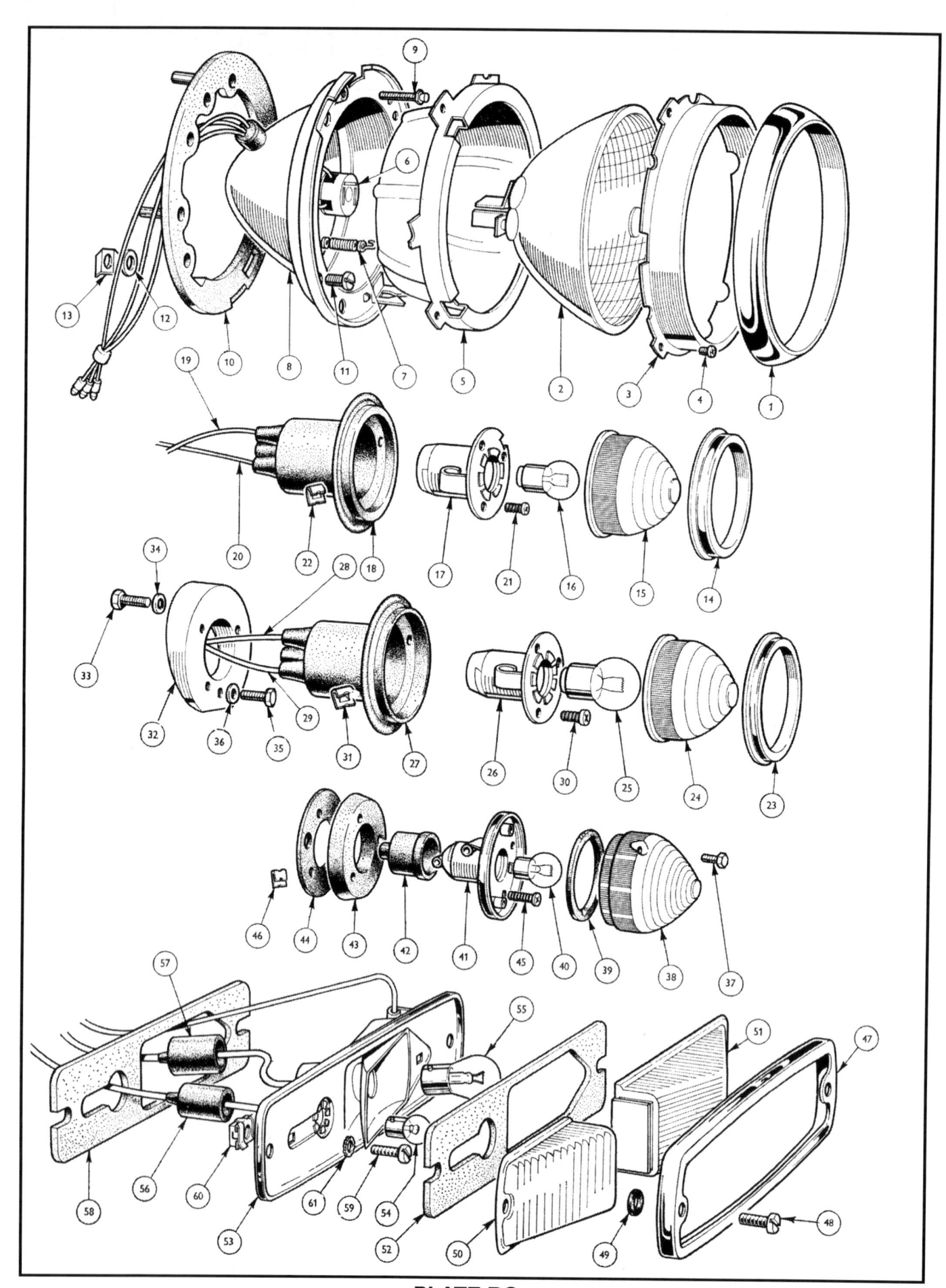

PLATE BO

ELECTRICAL EQUIPMENT

Plate No.	Part No.	Description	No. per Unit	Remarks
	512244	**HEADLAMP ASSEMBLY**	2	
BO1	119072	**Rim**, snap-on	2	
BO2	512241	**Light unit**	2	
	510219	**Bulb**, 12 v., 45/50 w. (Yellow)	2	
	510893	**Spring**, retaining bulb	2	
BO3	512987	**Plate**, retaining light unit	2	
BO4	507086	**Screw**, securing unit retaining plate	6	France, Vietnam and French Countries—R.H. Rule of Road —L.H.S. only
BO5	513265	**Rim**, unit seating	2	
BO6	501478	**Connector and cable** assembly	2	
	504806	**Tube**, P.V.C.	2	
	605953	**Sleeve**, terminal	6	
BO7	513266	**Spring**, fixing unit seating rim	2	
BO8	Not Serviced	**Body**		
BO9	513267	**Screw**, trimmer	4	
BO10	512222	**Gasket**, body	2	
BO11	YF7406	**Screw**, set ⎫	8	
BO12	WP0004	**Washer**, plain ⎬ Headlamp to body	8	
BO13	FC2804/4	**Nut** ⎭	8	
	121355	**SIDE LAMP, FRONT — WHITE LENS**	2	
BO14	505884	**Rim**	2	
BO15	505886	**Lens** (White)	2	
BO16	57591	**Bulb**	2	
BO17	508186	**Bulbholder**	2	
	510907	**Interior**, bulbholder	2	
BO18	508162	**Body**, rubber	2	
BO19	507299	**Lead**, side lamp	2	
BO20	507300	**Lead**, earth	2	
BO21	YA0384	**Screw** ⎫ Side lamps to body	6	All countries except Germany
BO22	FJ2442/9	**Nut**, spire ⎭	6	
	121356	**FRONT FLASHER LAMP — AMBER LENS**	2	
	131995	**FRONT FLASHER LAMP — WHITE LENS**	2	Mk. I cars only Fitted up to Commission No. KC50000 only
BO23	508163	**Rim**	2	
BO24	505887	**Lens** (Amber)	2	
BO24	505886	**Lens** (White)	2	
BO25	502379	**Bulb**, flasher	2	
BO26	508165	**Bulbholder and plate**	2	
	510907	**Interior**, bulbholder	2	
BO27	505883	**Body**, rubber	2	
BO28	507298	**Lead**, flasher	2	
BO29	507300	**Lead**, earth	2	
BO30	YA0384	**Screw** ⎫ Flasher lamps to body	6	All countries except Germany
BO31	FJ2442/9	**Nut**, spire ⎭	6	
BO32	619110	**Plinth**, side and flasher lamps—R.H.	2	
	619109	**Plinth**, side and flasher lamps—L.H.	2	
BO33	XR6402	**Screw**, set (Alternative to TP0402) ⎫ Plinths to body	12	Germany only
BO33	TP0402	**Screw**, set (Alternative to XR6402) ⎭	12	
BO34	WN0704	**Washer**, shakeproof	12	
BO35	TP0403	**Screw**, set (Alternative to TR6403) ⎫ Side and flasher lamps to plinths	12	
BO35	TR6403	**Screw**, set (Alternative to TP0403) ⎬	12	
BO36	WP0004	**Washer**, plain ⎭	12	

Note:—Items marked thus † are available on our Factory Exchange Unit Scheme

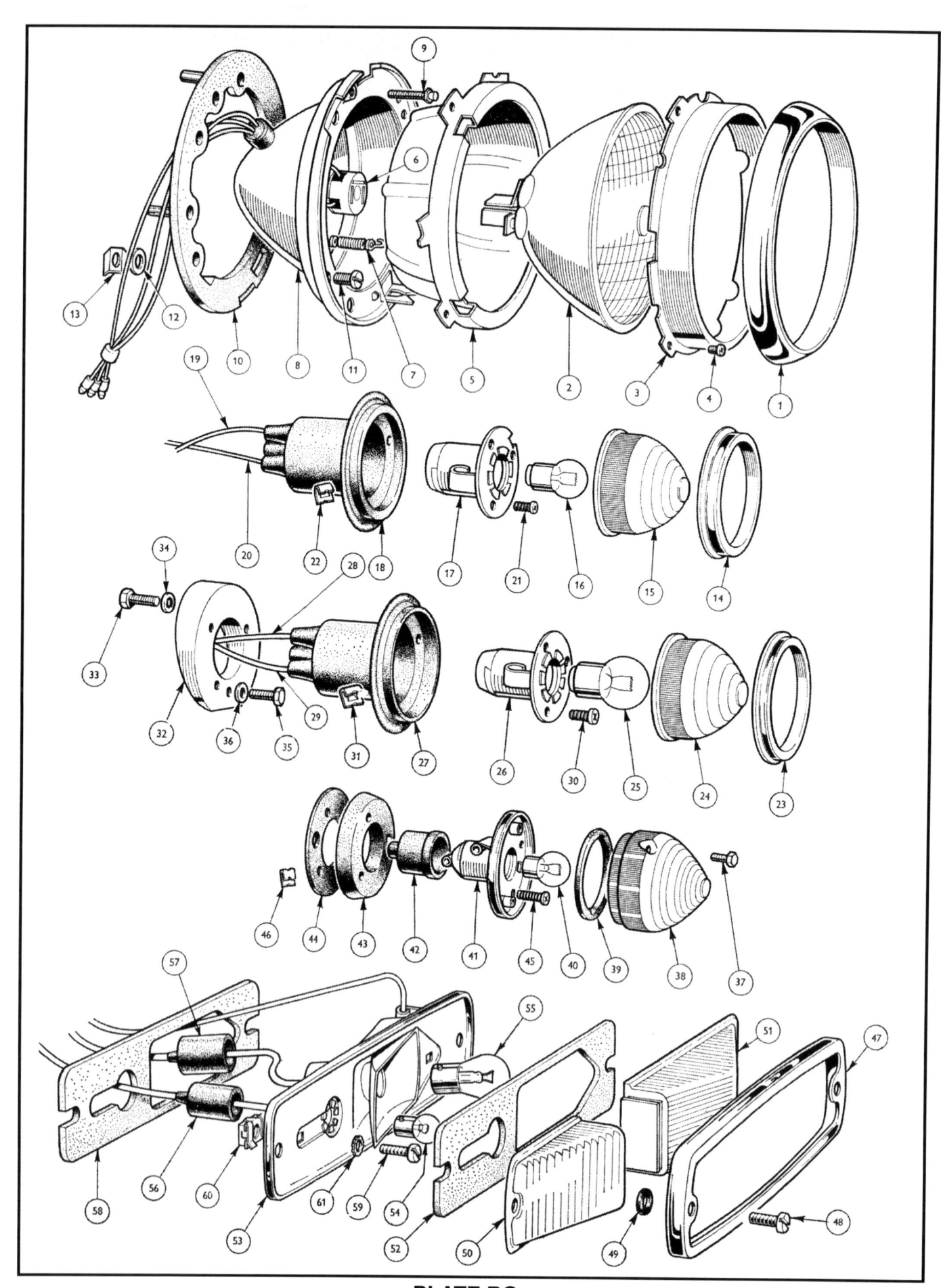

PLATE BO

ELECTRICAL EQUIPMENT

Plate No.	Part No.	Description	No. per Unit		Remarks
	140690	**FRONT FLASHER LAMP AND CABLE ASSEMBLY — WHITE LENS**	2		
BO37	514422	**Screw**, securing lens	4		
BO38	514421	**Lens** (White)	2		
BO39	514065	**Gasket**, lens seating	2		
BO40	502379	**Bulb**	2		
BO41	510907	**Interior**, bulbholder	2	U.S.A. and	Mk. I cars only.
BO42	513730	**Grommet**, cable entry	2	Canada	Fitted up to Comm.
BO43	616415	**Plinth**	2	only	No. KC50000 only
BO44	616416	**Gasket**, lamp seating	2		
	605953	**Sleeve**, terminal	2		
	507298	**Lead**, flasher	2		
	507300	**Lead**, earth	2		
BO45	YX5303	**Screw** ⎫ Lamps to body	6		
BO46	FJ2442/9	**Nut**, spire ⎭	6		
	147547	**SIDE & FLASHER DIRECTION INDICATOR LAMP ASSEMBLY — FRONT (AMBER FLASHER INDICATION LENS)**	2		
	147548	**SIDE & FLASHER DIRECTION INDICATOR LAMP ASSEMBLY — FRONT (WHITE FLASHER INDICATION LENS)**	2		
BO47	516304	**Rim**	2		
BO48	516305	**Screw**, rim fixing	4		
BO49	514064	**Washer**, screw retaining	4		
BO50	516308	**Lens**, side lamp (for use with Amber flasher lens)	2		Mk. II cars only.
BO50	516309	**Lens**, side lamp (for use with White flasher lens)	2		Fitted from Commission No. KC50001 and future
BO51	516306	**Lens**, flasher—Amber	2		
BO51	516307	**Lens**, flasher—White	2		
BO52	147549	**Gasket**, lens seating	2		
BO53	Not Serviced	**Body**	2		
BO54	57591	**Bulb**, side lamp	2		
BO55	502379	**Bulb**, flasher, lamp	2		
BO56	515060	**Grommet**, side lamp	2		
BO57	515061	**Grommet**, flasher lamp	2		
BO58	147549	**Gasket**, body seating	2		
BO59	PT0503	**Screw**, set ⎫	4		
BO60	FZ3404/4	**Retainer**, nut ⎬ Side/Flasher lamp to body	4		
BO61	WE0605	**Washer**, shakeproof ⎭	4		
	151872	**SIDE MARKER ASSEMBLY — FRONT (AMBER)**	2		U.S.A. only.
	625580	**Washer**, special, rubber ⎫ Side	4		Fitted from Commission
	510127	**Washer**, plain ⎬ marker	4		No. KC50001
	508762	**Nut**, hex. ⎭ attachment	4		

Note:—Items marked thus † are available on our Factory Exchange Unit Scheme

98

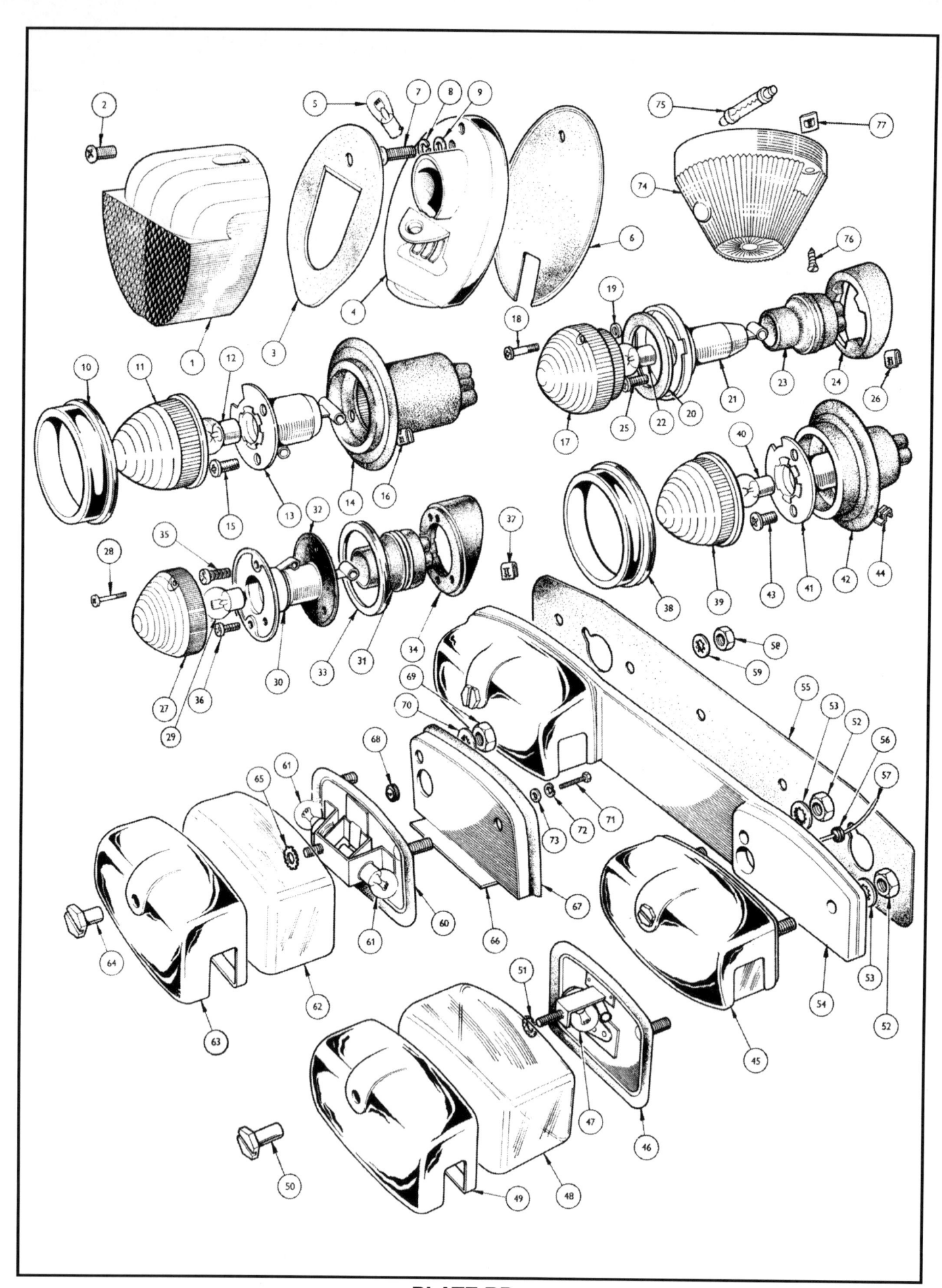

PLATE BP

ELECTRICAL EQUIPMENT

Plate No.	Part No.	Description	No. per Unit	Remarks
	208532	**STOP/TAIL AND REFLEX LAMP (RED GLASS)**	2	
BP1	511800	Lens	2	
BP2	511801	Screw, fixing lens	4	
BP3	511802	Gasket, seating lens	2	
BP4	Not Serviced	Body	2	
	605953	Sleeve, terminal, bulbholder	2	
BP5	502287	Bulb	2	
BP6	511803	Gasket, seating, lamp	2	
BP7	PT0505	Screw, set ⎫	4	
BP8	WL0205	Washer, lock ⎬ Lamps to body	4	
BP9	WP0005	Washer, plain ⎭	4	
	116459	**REAR FLASHER LAMP (RED GLASS)**	2	⎫
	116460	**REAR FLASHER LAMP (AMBER GLASS)**	2	⎪
BP10	508163	Rim	2	⎪
BP11	508822	Glass (Red)	2	⎬ Mk. I cars only.
BP11	508164	Glass (Amber)	2	⎬ Fitted up to Commission
BP12	502379	Bulb, 12 v.	2	⎪ No. KC50000 only
BP13	508165	Bulbholder and plate	2	⎪
	510907	Interior, bulbholder	2	⎪
	605953	Sleeve, terminal	2	⎪
BP14	505883	Body	2	⎪
BP15	YZ3304	Screw ⎫ Rear flasher lamps	6	⎪
BP16	FU2583/4	Nut, spire ⎭ to body	6	⎭
	136581	**REAR FLASHER LAMP**	2	⎫
BP17	514062	Lens	2	⎪
BP18	514063	Screw, lens fixing	4	⎪
BP19	514064	Washer, retaining screw	4	⎪
BP20	514065	Gasket, lens seating	2	⎪
BP21	Not Serviced	Body assembly		⎬ U.S.A. and Canada only.
	514066	Interior, bulbholder	2	⎬ Fitted to Mk. I cars only
BP22	502379	Bulb	2	⎪
BP23	514067	Grommet, cable entry	2	⎪
BP24	613627	Plinth, lamp mounting	2	⎪
BP25	YX5305	Screw ⎫	2	⎪
BP25	YX5308	Screw ⎬ Lamp and plinth to body	4	⎪
BP26	FU2553/4	Nut, fix ⎭	4	⎭

Note:—Items marked thus † are available on our Factory Exchange Unit Scheme

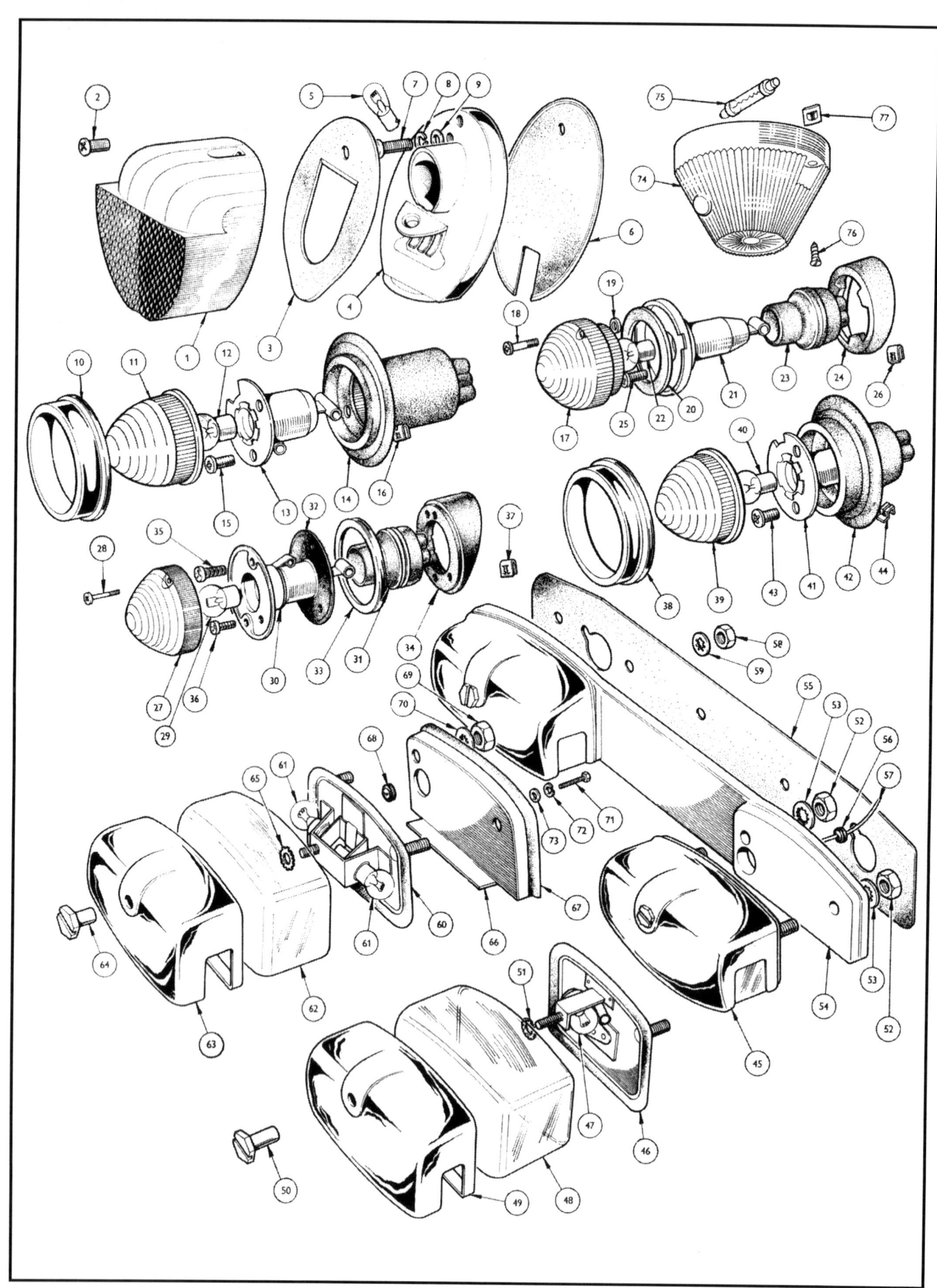

PLATE BP

ELECTRICAL EQUIPMENT

Plate No.	Part No.	Description	No. per Unit	Remarks
	147551	**REAR FLASHER LAMP (AMBER LENS)**	2	⎫
	147550	**REAR FLASHER LAMP (RED LENS)**	2	⎪
BP27	516301	Lens (Amber)	2	⎪
BP27	516302	Lens (Red)	2	⎪
BP28	516303	Screw, lens fixing	4	⎪
	514066	Washer, retaining screw	4	⎬ Mk. II cars only.
BP29	502379	Bulb	2	⎪ Fitted from Commission
BP30	Not Serviced	Body	2	⎪ No. KC50001 and future
BP31	514067	Grommet, cable entry	2	⎪
BP32	147552	Gasket, lamp seating	2	⎪
BP33	147553	Bezel, flasher lamp	2	⎪
BP34	147592	Plinth, flasher lamp	2	⎪
BP35	YZ3310	Screw, self tapping ⎫	2	⎪
	YZ3312	Screw, self tapping ⎬ Lamp and plinth	2	⎪
BP36	YZ3308	Screw, self tapping ⎭ to body	2	⎪
BP37	FU2583/4	Nut, spire fix	6	⎭
	131608	**REVERSE LAMP**	2	
BP38	505884	Rim	2	
BP39	505886	Lens	2	
BP40	502379	Bulb	2	
BP41	508165	Bulbholder and plate assembly	2	
	501823	Interior, bulbholder	2	
BP42	505883	Body	2	
BP43	YZ3344	Screw ⎱ Reverse lamp	6	
BP44	FU2583/4	Nut, spire ⎰ to body	6	
	151873	**SIDE MARKER ASSEMBLY — REAR (RED)**	2	⎫ U.S.A. only.
	625580	Washer, special, rubber ⎫	4	⎪ Fitted from
	510127	Washer, plain ⎬ Side marker attachment	4	⎬ Commission No.
	508762	Nut, hex. ⎭	4	⎭ KC50001

Note:—Items marked thus † are available on our Factory Exchange Unit Scheme

100

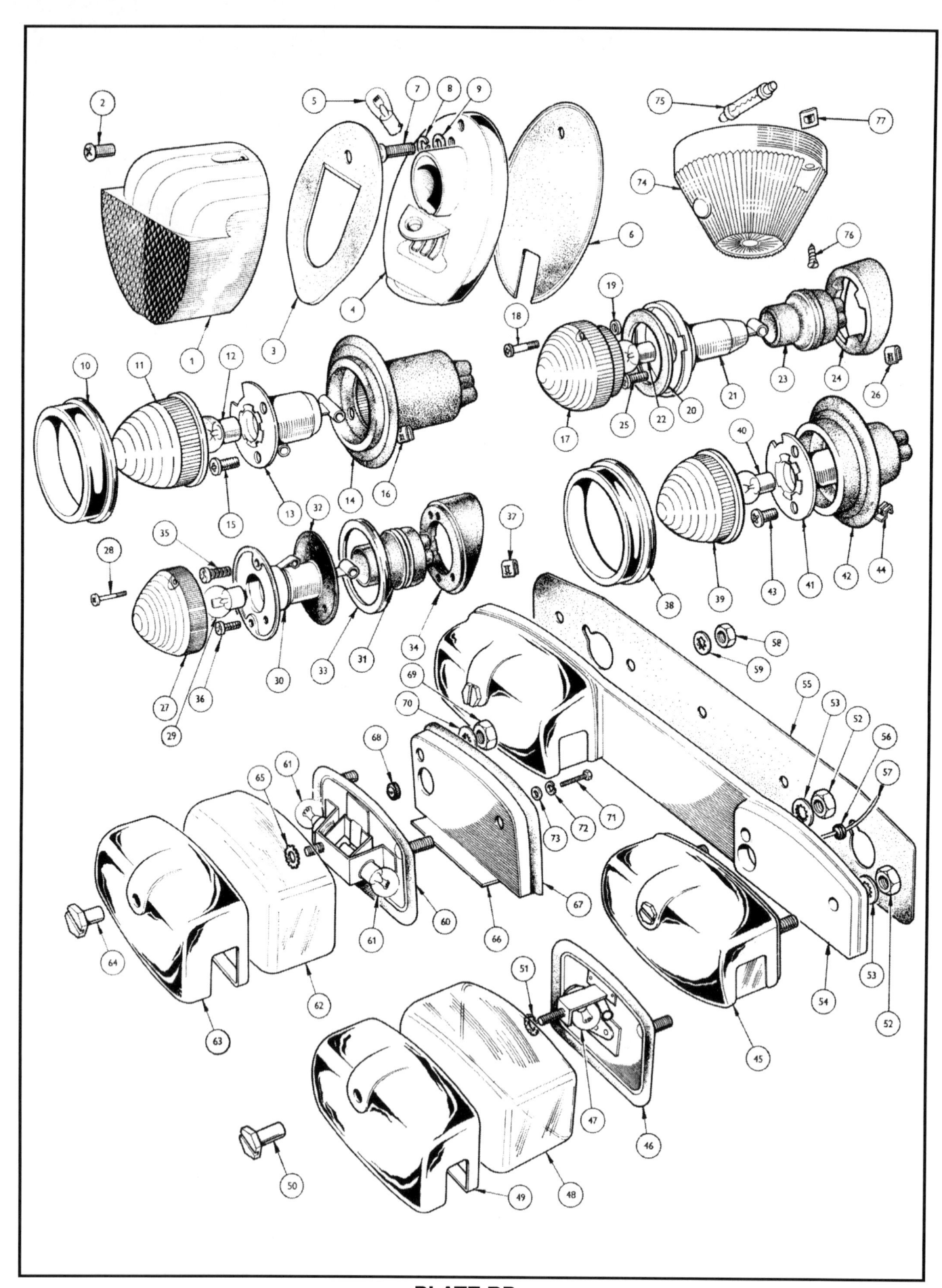

PLATE BP

ELECTRICAL EQUIPMENT

Plate No.	Part No.	Description	No. per Unit	Remarks
BP45	128397	**REAR NUMBER PLATE LAMP**	1	
BP46	Not Serviced	Base		
BP47	59467	**Bulb,** 12 v.	1	
BP48	501362	**Window**	1	All countries except
BP49	502264	**Cover**	1	U.S.A., Canada, Denmark,
BP50	509736	**Nut,** dome, lens fixing	1	and Germany
BP51	WE0605	**Washer,** shakeproof	1	
BP52	HN2005	**Nut,** hex. ⎱ Rear number plate lamp	2	
BP53	WN0705	**Washer,** shakeproof ⎰ attachment	2	
BP45	128397	**REAR NUMBER PLATE LAMP**	2	
BP46	Not Serviced	Base	2	
BP47	59467	**Bulb,** 12 v.	2	
BP48	501362	**Window**	2	
BP49	502264	**Cover**	2	
BP50	509736	**Nut,** dome, lens fixing	2	
BP51	WE0605	**Washer,** shakeproof	2	
BP52	HN2005	**Nut,** hex. ⎱ Rear number plate	4	Germany only
BP53	WN0705	**Washer,** shakeproof ⎰ lamps to plinth	4	
BP54	709845	**Plinth,** number plate lamp	1	
BP55	618789	**Rubber,** plinth mounting	1	
BP56	61917	**Grommet**	2	
BP57	144656	**Cable,** R.H. number plate lamp to R.H. tail lamp	1	
BP58	HN2005	**Nut,** hex. ⎱ Plinth and rubber	6	
BP59	WE0605	**Washer,** shakeproof ⎰ to rear valance panel	6	
	127916	**REAR NUMBER PLATE LAMP**	1	
BP60	Not Serviced	Base		
BP61	501436	**Bulb,** 12 v.	2	
BP62	500492	**Glass**	1	
BP63	502264	**Cover**	1	
BP64	509736	**Nut,** dome	1	
BP65	WE0605	**Washer,** shakeproof	2	
BP66	613093	**Plinth** assembly, rear number plate lamp	1	U.S.A., Canada and
BP67	613110	**Seal,** plinth	1	Denmark only
BP68	61917	**Grommet**	1	
BP69	HN2005	**Nut,** hex. ⎱ Rear number plate	2	
BP70	WN0705	**Washer,** shakeproof ⎰ attachment	2	
BP71	HU0504	**Screw,** set	2	
BP72	WN0705	**Washer,** shakeproof ⎱ Plinth to body attachment	2	
BP73	WP0005	**Washer,** plain ⎰	2	
BP74	617286	**ROOF LAMP ASSEMBLY**	1	Fitted up to Commission No. KC50000 only
	625616	**ROOF LAMP ASSEMBLY**	1	Fitted from Commission No. KC50001 and future
BP75	59897	**Bulb,** festoon, roof lamp	1	
BP76	YA0326	**Screw,** self tapping ⎱ Roof lamp and	2	
BP77	FJ2463/8	**Fix,** spire ⎰ hinge cover fixing	2	

Note:—Items marked thus † are available on our Factory Exchange Unit Scheme

101

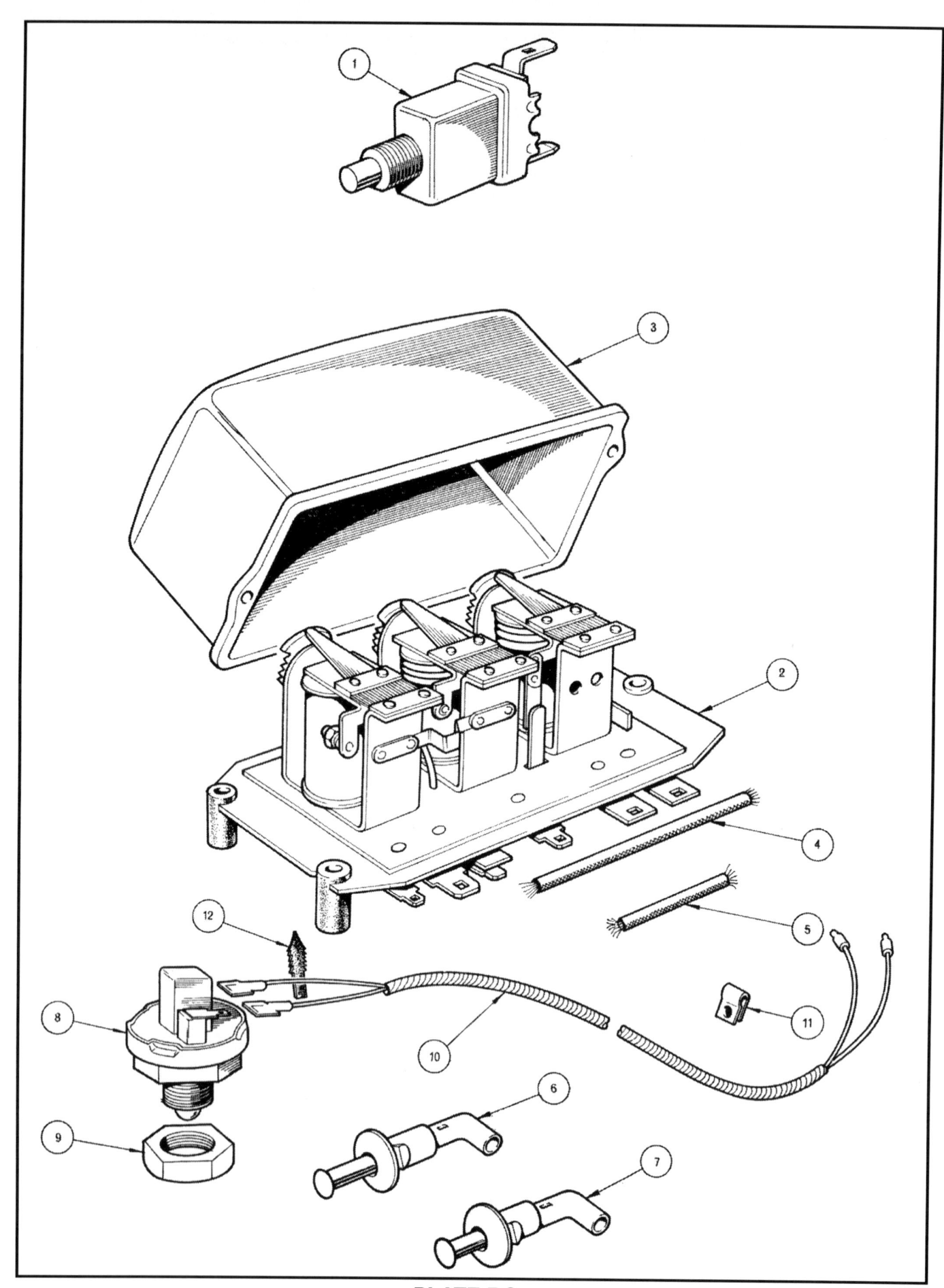

PLATE BQ

ELECTRICAL EQUIPMENT

Plate No.	Part No.	Description	No. per Unit	Remarks
BQ1	134529	**STOP LIGHT SWITCH** (Operated by Brake Pedal)	1	
	JN2111	**Nut,** jam ⎫ Switch to bracket	1	
	WN0711	**Washer,** shakeproof ⎭	1	
BQ2	208952	†**CONTROL BOX**	1	⎫ Mk. I cars only.
BQ3	511585	**Cover**	1	⎪ Fitted up to
BQ4	511586	**Resistance,** swamp, 55 ohms.	1	⎬ Commission No.
BQ5	511587	**Resistance,** point, 60 ohms.	1	⎪ KC50000 only
	YC5520	**Screw** ⎫ Control box attachment	3	⎭
	WL0205	**Washer** ⎭	3	
		Note. The control box fitted to Mk. II cars is part of Alternator No. 215346. See page 91 for details.		
		FUSE BOX (PART OF MAIN HARNESS ASSEMBLY)		
	58465	**Fuse,** 35 amp.	5	
	516506	**Cover,** fuse box	1	
	515186	**BATTERY, DRY CHARGED**	1	
	143796	**BODY HARNESS**	1	⎫ Mk. I cars only.
	144353	**Lead,** interior light	1	⎬ Fitted up to Commission No. KC50000 only
	150461	**BODY HARNESS**	1	⎫
	150516	**Harness,** interior light and heated backlight	1	⎪ Mk. II cars only.
	150804	**Extension,** earth lead, heated backlight	1	⎬ Fitted from Commission No. KC50001
	WE0607	**Washer,** shakeproof, earth lead extension, heated backlight to rear door hinge	1	⎭
	600396	**Grommet,** tail lamp leads (Rear wing)	2	
	59813	**Screw,** self tapping ⎫ Battery leads	2	Alternative to 131169
	131169	**Screw,** self tapping ⎭ to battery	2	Alternative to 59813
	511551	**Sleeve,** wiring clips to frame	6	
	503213	**Sleeve,** wiring clips to body	38	
	511541	**Sleeve,** harness to grille clip	1	
	503213	**Sleeve,** wiring clips to frame	1	
	307518	**MAIN HARNESS AND FUSE BOX—R.H.S.**	1	⎫
	307519	**MAIN HARNESS AND FUSE BOX—L.H.S.**	1	⎬ Mark I cars only Fitted up to Commission No. KC50000 only
	308411	**MAIN HARNESS AND FUSE BOX—L.H.S.** (Fitted to cars with a Dual Brake System)	1	⎭

Note:—Items marked thus † are available on our Factory Exchange Unit Scheme

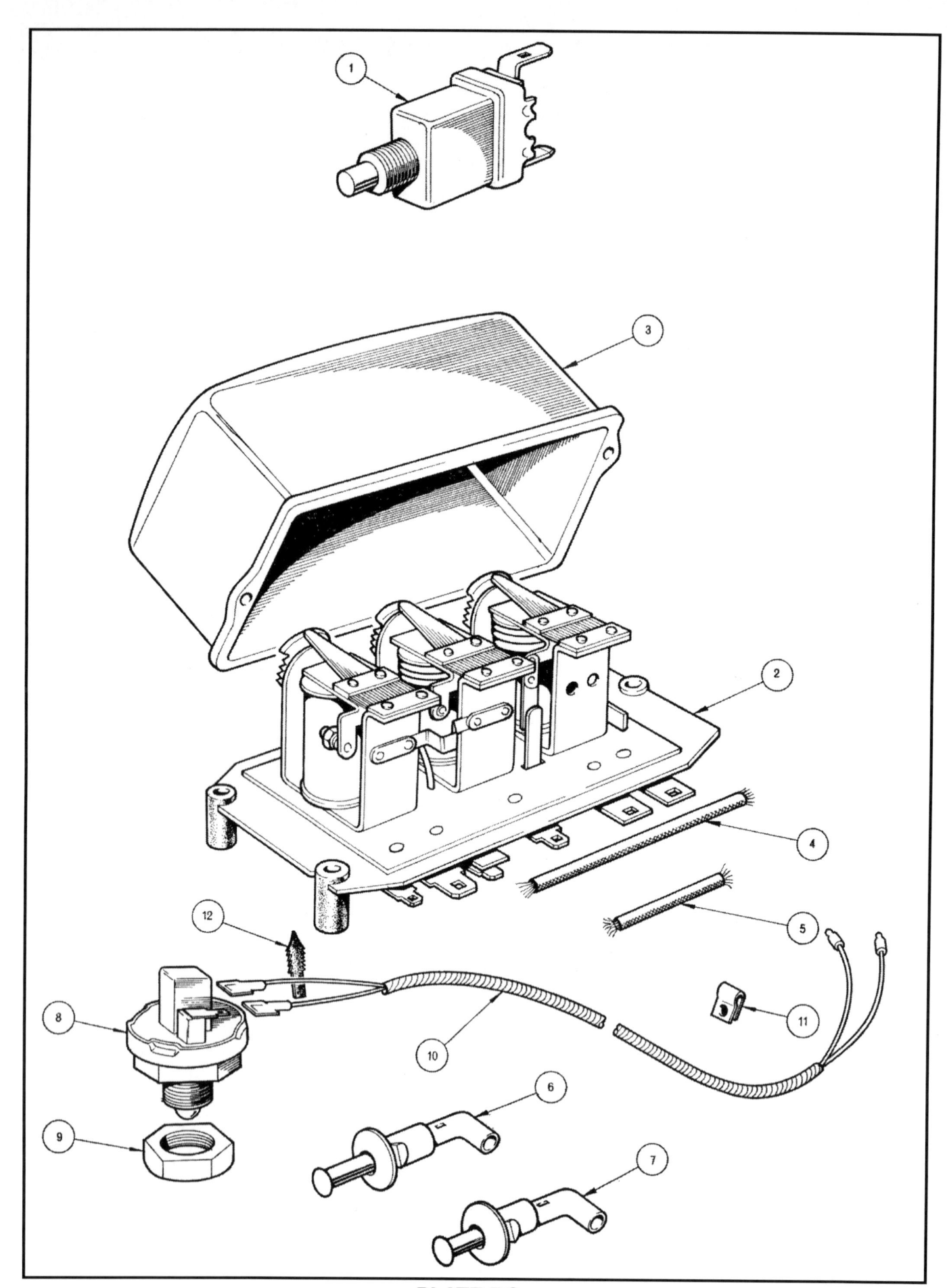

PLATE BQ

ELECTRICAL EQUIPMENT

Plate No.	Part No.	Description	No. per Unit	Remarks
	308682	**MAIN HARNESS AND FUSE BOX ASSEMBLY — R.H.S.**	1	Mk. II cars only. Fitted from Commission No. KC50001
	308601	**MAIN HARNESS AND FUSE BOX ASSEMBLY — L.H.S.**	1	
	144354	**Lead,** extension, horn	1	
	149967	**Lead,** extension, dual brake switch (Fitted to cars with a dual brake system)	1	Fitted up to Commission No. KC50000 only
	615924	**Clip,** cable, dynamo leads (fitted to rear mounting bracket)	1	
	508726	**Clip,** temperature transmitter lead (fitted to Dynamo/Alternator adjusting link)	1	
	134301	**Lead,** earth, steering rack housing to engine front face, R.H.S.	1	
	WN0708	**Washer,** shakeproof, earth lead (Steering box end), R.H.S.	1	
	WN0709	**Washer,** shakeproof, earth lead (Front face end), R.H.S.	1	
	146305	**Lead,** steering column switch to body junction	1	
		ENGINE LEADS		
	509809	**Lead,** bell housing to body earth cable	1	
	514792	**Lead,** starter to solenoid	1	
	514791	**Lead,** battery to earth (Negative)	1	
	514793	**Lead,** battery to solenoid (Positive)—R.H.S.	1	
	515873	**Lead,** battery to solenoid (Positive)—L.H.S.	1	
	HU0704	**Screw,** set ⎫ Battery earth to	1	
	WE0607	**Washer,** shakeproof ⎭ dash—R.H.S. only	1	
	115706	**Boot,** rubber, starter solenoid	1	
	514048	**Clip,** cable lead to bell housing—L.H.S.	1	
	WE0607	**Washer,** shakeproof, bell housing body cable to body	1	
BQ6	606240	**COURTESY LIGHT SWITCH — FRONT DOORS**	2	
BQ7	606239	**COURTESY LIGHT SWITCH — BACK DOOR**	1	
	605953	**Ferrule,** courtesy light switch	3	
BQ8	127380	**REVERSE LIGHT SWITCH**	1	Fitted up to Gearbox No. KC3761 only
BQ9	59474	**Nut,** reverse light switch to bracket	1	
BQ10	146258	**Lead,** reverse light switch	1	
	147471	**REVERSE LIGHT SWITCH**	1	Fitted from Gearbox No. KC3762 and future
	147777	**Lead,** reverse light switch	1	
	100148	**Clip,** 'P', reverse light lead to top cover bolt	1	
	502146	**Washer,** packing, under reverse light switch	A/R	
BQ11	511345	**Clip,** 'P', reverse light lead to gearbox bell housing	1	
BQ12	145890	**Clip,** 'Fir Tree', reverse light lead to engine/body earth lead	1	

Note:—Items marked thus † are available on our Factory Exchange Unit Scheme

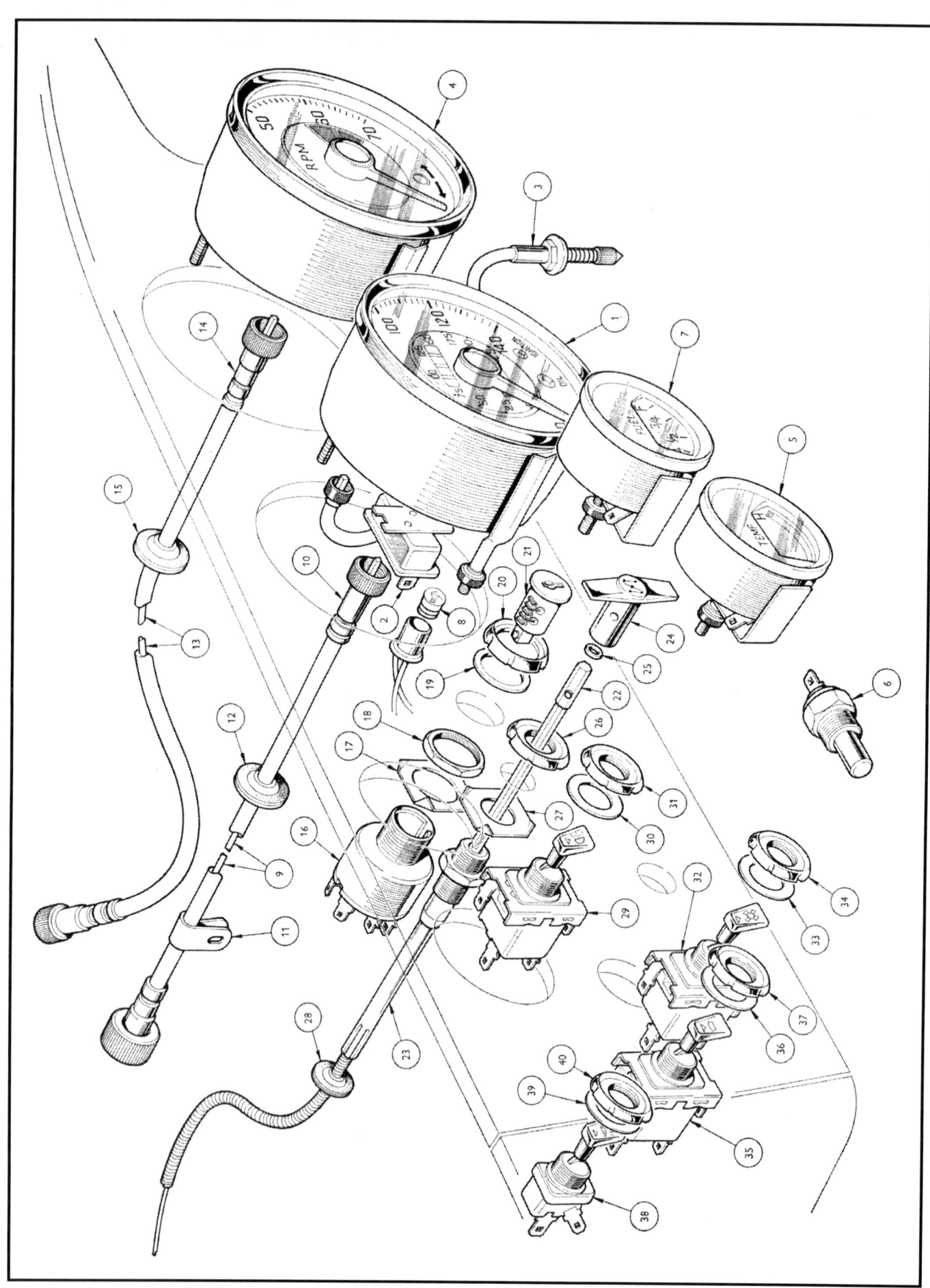

PLATE BR

ELECTRICAL EQUIPMENT

Plate No.	Part No.	Description	No. per Unit	Remarks
		NOTE:- The details on this page are for Mk. I cars only, i.e. Fitted up to Commission No. KC50000 only		
BR1	213514	†SPEEDOMETER — MILE	1	
	213515	†SPEEDOMETER — KILO	1	
	213516	†SPEEDOMETER — MILE	1	Only required when Overdrive is fitted
	213517	†SPEEDOMETER — KILO	1	
BR2	128484	Voltage stabiliser	1	
BR3	134757	Trip, flex, speedometer	1	
BR4	213190	†REVOLUTION COUNTER	1	
BR5	145002	†TEMPERATURE GAUGE	1	
BR6	137705	TEMPERATURE TRANSMITTER	1	
BR7	143577	†FUEL GAUGE	1	
BR8	59492	Bulb, instrument illumination and warning lights	6	
		SPEEDOMETER CABLE ASSEMBLY		
BR9	507223/I	Cable, inner } R.H.S.	1	
BR10	507223/O	Cable, outer }	1	
	504948/I	Cable, inner } L.H.S.	1	
	504948/O	Cable, outer }	1	
BR11	510969	Clip, speedo cable, R.H.S. only (Fitted to valance fixing screw)	1	
	100148	Clip, speedo cable, L.H.S. only	1	
BR12	600396	Grommet, speedo cable	1	
		REV. COUNTER CABLE ASSEMBLY		
BR13	144370/I	Cable, inner } R.H.S.	1	
BR14	144370/O	Cable, outer }	1	
	138316/I	Cable, inner } L.H.S.	1	
	138316/O	Cable, outer }	1	
BR15	600396	Grommet, rev. counter cable	1	
BR16	127651	**IGNITION AND STARTER SWITCH**	1	
BR17	618290	Washer, plate	1	
BR18	510369	Nut, for switch	1	
BR19	616046	Washer, P.V.C., protection	1	
BR20	609793	Bezel	1	
BR21	572540	Barrel, ignition locking	1	
		IGNITION/STARTER SWITCH AND STEERING COLUMN LOCKING DEVICE	1	For details see Accessories section

Note:—Items marked thus † are available on our Factory Exchange Unit Scheme

104

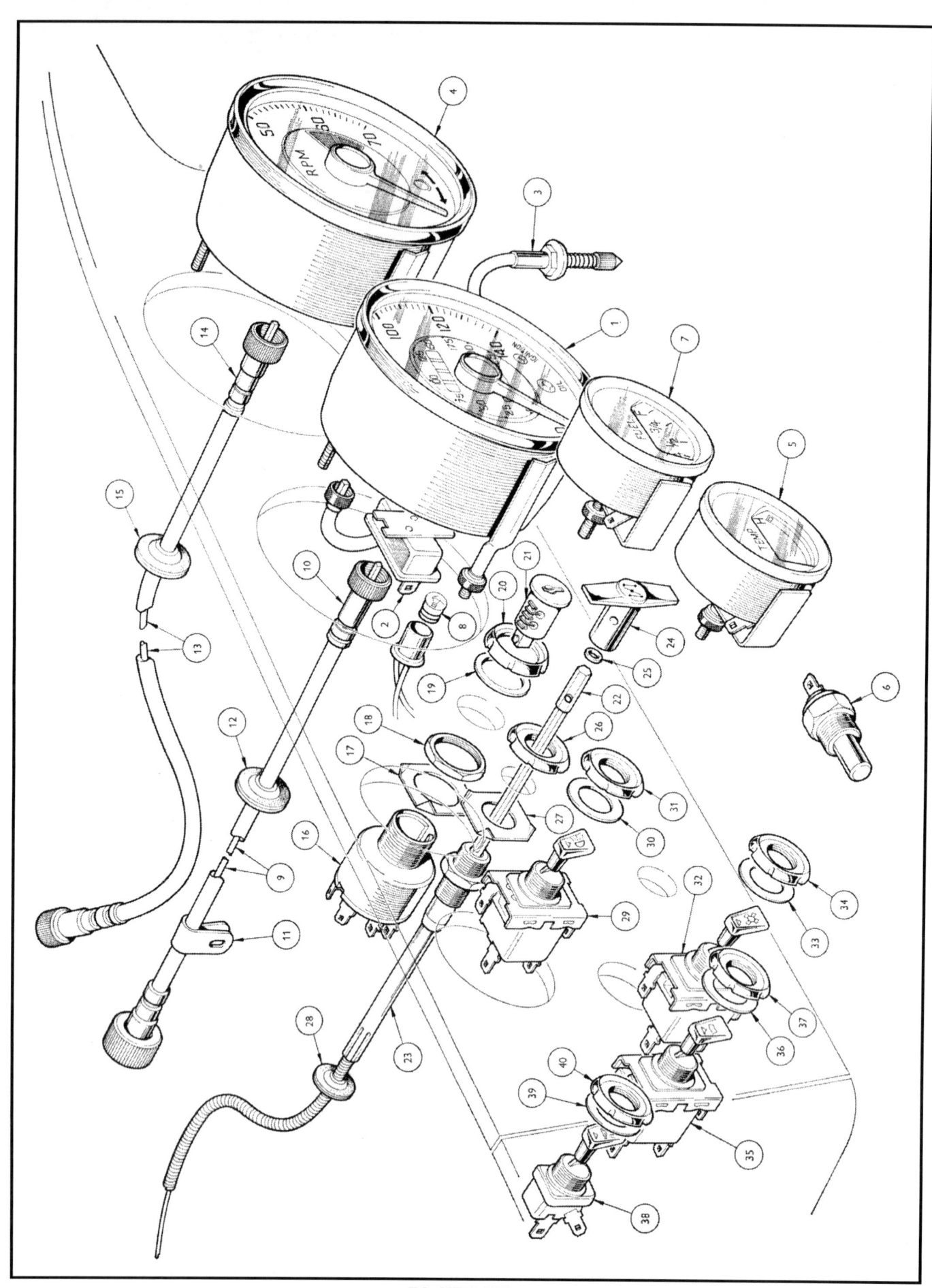

PLATE BR

ELECTRICAL EQUIPMENT

Plate No.	Part No.	Description	No. per Unit	Remarks
		NOTE:- The details on this page are for Mk. I cars only, i.e. Fitted up to Commission No. KC50000 only.		
		CHOKE CONTROL & KNOB ASSEMBLY		
BR22	402397	Cable, inner	1	
BR23	402396	Cable, outer	1	
	214787	Cable assembly, choke control	1	U.S.A. Anti-Smog only. Fitted from Comm. No. KC7611
BR24	143136	Knob	1	
BR25	59445	Washer, knob	1	
BR26	618946	Bezel	1	
BR27	618947	Washer, plate, choke control	1	
BR28	61917	Grommet, choke cable	1	
	616925	Grommet, choke cable	1	U.S.A. Anti-Smog only. Fitted from Comm. No. KC7611
	149137	Tube, P.V.C., heater and choke cable insulating—L.H.S.	1	Fitted from Commission No. KC2795 and future
BR29	145203	**LIGHTING AND INSTRUMENT ILLUMINATION MASTER SWITCH ASSEMBLY**	1	
BR30	616050	Washer, P.V.C.	1	
BR31	609795	Bezel	1	
BR32	144530	**HEATER SWITCH (TWO SPEED)**	1	
BR33	616050	Washer, P.V.C.	1	
BR34	609795	Bezel	1	
BR35	143841	**WINDSCREEN WIPER SWITCH (TWO SPEED)**	1	
BR36	616050	Washer, P.V.C.	1	
BR37	609795	Bezel	1	
BR38	143843	**ROOF LAMP SWITCH**	1	
BR39	616050	Washer, P.V.C.	1	
BR40	609795	Bezel, roof lamp switch	1	
	148830	**DUAL BRAKE WARNING LIGHT AND BEZEL ASSEMBLY**	1	Required when Dual Brake System fitted

Note:—Items marked thus † are available on our Factory Exchange Unit Scheme

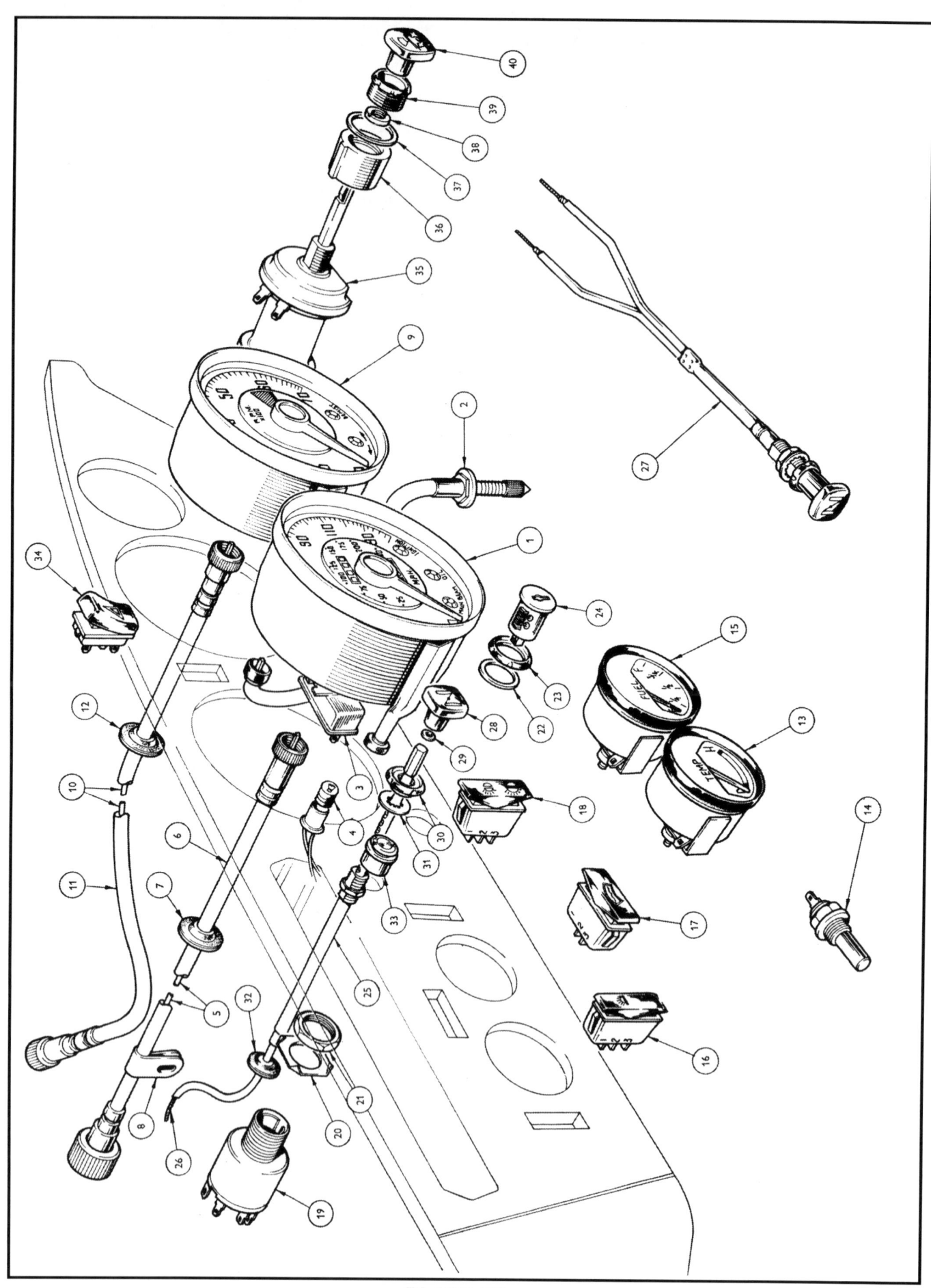

PLATE BS

ELECTRICAL EQUIPMENT

Plate No.	Part No.	Description	No. per Unit	Remarks

NOTE:- The details on this page are for Mk. II cars only, i.e. from Commission No. KC50001.

Plate No.	Part No.	Description	No. per Unit
BS1	215038	†SPEEDOMETER — MILE	1
	215039	†SPEEDOMETER — KILO	1
	215042	†SPEEDOMETER — MILE } OVERDRIVE	1
	215043	†SPEEDOMETER — KILO } ONLY	1
BS2	134757	Trip, flex, speedometer	1
BS3	128484	Voltage stabiliser	1
BS4	59492	Bulb, instrument illumination and warning lights	6

SPEEDOMETER CABLE ASSEMBLY

Plate No.	Part No.	Description	No. per Unit
BS5	507223/I	Cable, inner } R.H.S.	1
BS6	507223/O	Cable, outer }	1
	504948/I	Cable, inner } L.H.S.	1
	504948/O	Cable, outer }	1
BS7	600396	Grommet, speedo cable	1
BS8	510969	Clip, speedo cable, R.H.S. only (Fitted to valance fixing screw)	1
	100148	Clip, speedo cable, L.H.S. only	1
BS9	215044	†REVOLUTION COUNTER (Including flasher and back door window heater warning lights)	1

REV. COUNTER CABLE ASSEMBLY

Plate No.	Part No.	Description	No. per Unit
BS10	144370/I	Cable, inner } R.H.S.	1
BS11	144370/O	Cable, outer }	1
	138316/I	Cable, inner } L.H.S.	1
	138316/O	Cable, outer }	1
BS12	600396	Grommet, rev. counter cable	1
BS13	150163	†TEMPERATURE GAUGE	1
BS14	137705	TEMPERATURE TRANSMITTER	1
BS15	150162	†FUEL GAUGE	1
BS16	150379	INTERIOR LAMP SWITCH	1
BS17	150377	HEATED BACK DOOR GLASS SWITCH	1
BS18	150380	LIGHTING AND INSTRUMENT ILLUMINATION MASTER SWITCH ASSEMBLY	1

Note:—Items marked thus † are available on our Factory Exchange Unit Scheme

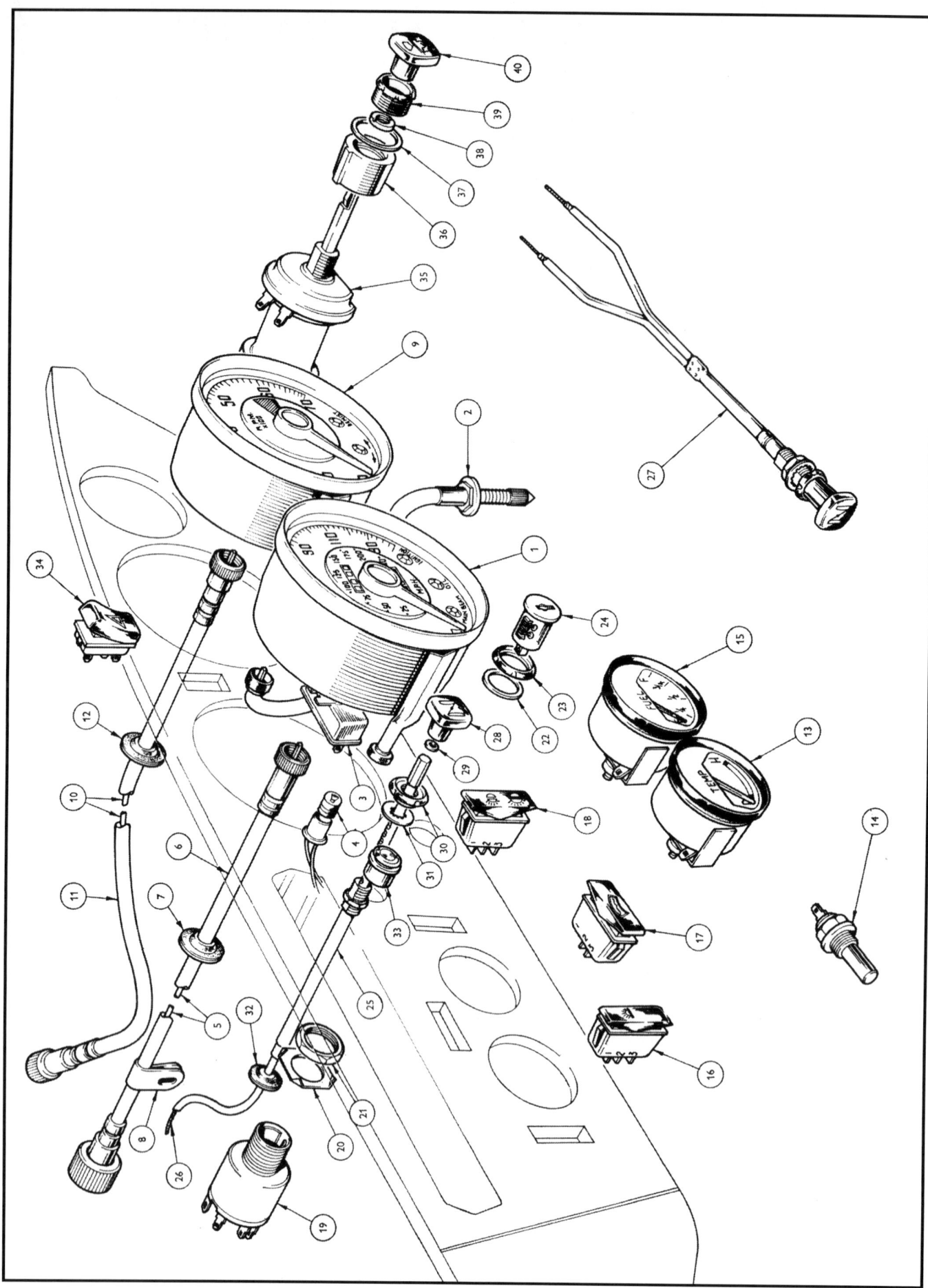

PLATE BS

ELECTRICAL EQUIPMENT

Plate No.	Part No.	Description	No. per Unit	Remarks
		NOTE:- The details on this page are for Mk. II cars only, i.e. from Commission No. KC50001.		
BS19	127651	**IGNITION AND STARTER SWITCH**	1	
BS20	618290	**Washer**, plate	1	
BS21	510369	**Nut**, for switch	1	
BS22	616046	**Washer**, P.V.C., protection	1	
BS23	609793	**Bezel**	1	
BS24	572540	**Barrel**, ignition locking	1	
		IGNITION/STARTER SWITCH AND STEERING COLUMN LOCKING DEVICE	1	For details see Accessories Section
BS25	517599	**CHOKE CONTROL CABLE OUTER ASSEMBLY — R.H.S.**	1	
BS26	517600	**CHOKE CONTROL CABLE INNER ASSEMBLY — R.H.S.**	1	
	517601	**CHOKE CONTROL CABLE OUTER ASSEMBLY — L.H.S.**	1	
	517602	**CHOKE CONTROL CABLE INNER ASSEMBLY — L.H.S.**	1	
BS27	215502	**CHOKE CONTROL COMPLETE ASSEMBLY — L.H.S.** (Includes items BS28, BS29, BS30, BS31)	1	U.S.A. Anti-Smog only
BS28	712907	**Knob**	1	
BS29	59445	**Washer**, knob	1	
BS30	618946	**Bezel**	1	
BS31	WN0711	**Washer**, shakeproof, internal	1	
BS32	61917	**Grommet**, choke cable	1	
	149137	**Tube**, P.V.C., heater and choke cable insulating, L.H.S.	1	
	148830	**DUAL BRAKE WARNING LIGHT AND BEZEL ASSEMBLY**	1	Required when Dual Brake System fitted
BS33	148830	**HAZARD WARNING LIGHT**	1	
BS34	150381	**HAZARD WARNING LIGHT SWITCH**	1	
BS35	150378	**WINDSCREEN WIPER AND WASHER SWITCH (2 SPEED)**	1	
BS36	621510	**Spacer**	1	
BS37	616048	**Washer**, P.V.C.	1	
BS38	622682	**Nut**, spacer	1	
BS39	622443	**Bezel**	1	
BS40	712913	**Knob**	1	
		Heater switch (Integral part of ventilator lever—see Heater details)	1	

Note:—Items marked thus † are available on our Factory Exchange Unit Scheme

107

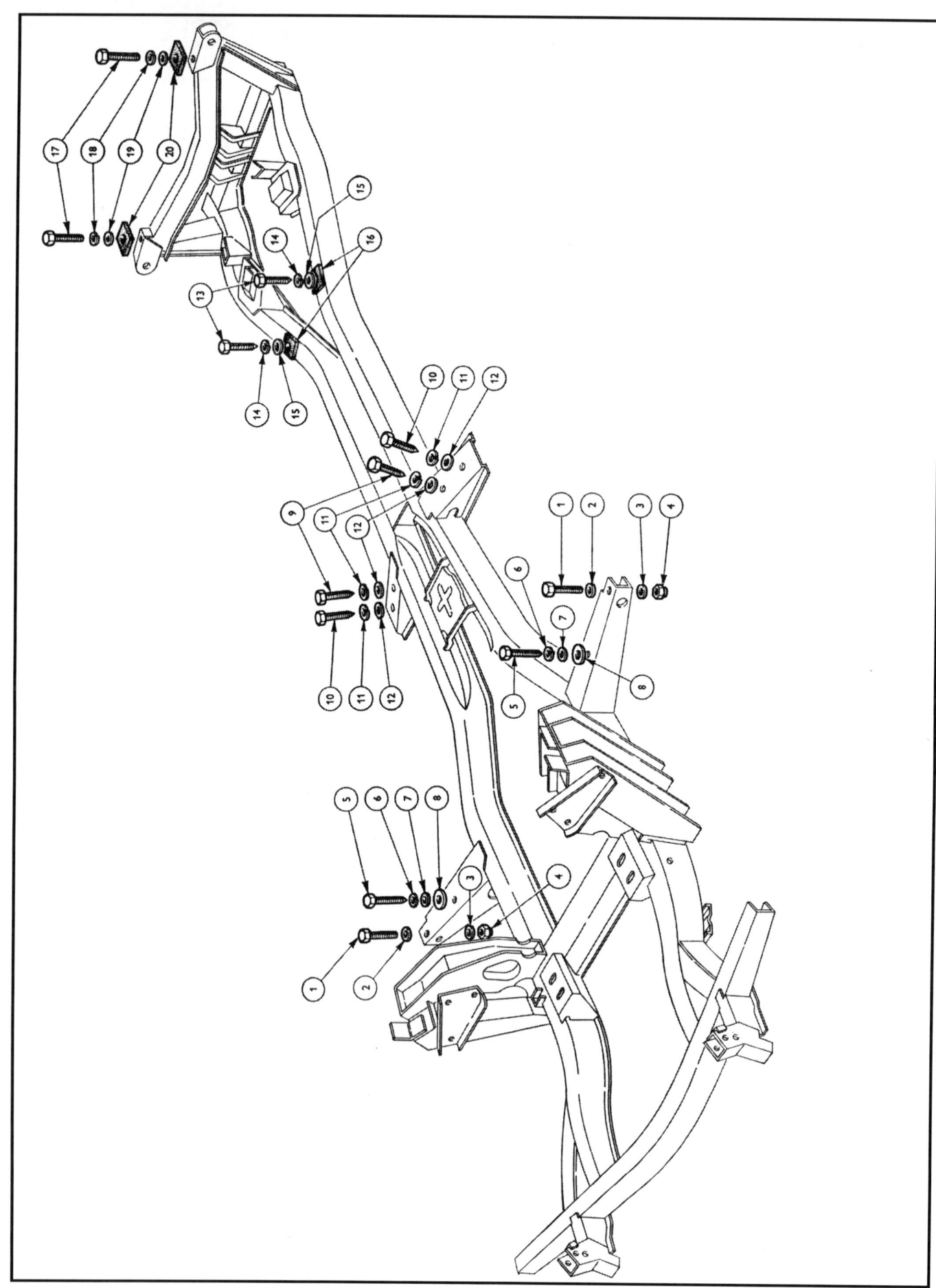

PLATE BT

BODY AND FITTINGS

Plate No.	Part No.	Description	No. per Unit	Remarks
	573673	BODY COMPLETE, PAINTED & TRIMMED (INCLUDING SEATS)—R.H.S.	1	
	573675	BODY COMPLETE, PAINTED & TRIMMED (INCLUDING SEATS)—L.H.S.	1	Mk. I Cars only Fitted up to Body No. 50000KC
	573674	BODY COMPLETE, PAINTED & TRIMMED (LESS SEATS)—R.H.S.	1	
	573676	BODY COMPLETE, PAINTED & TRIMMED (LESS SEATS)—L.H.S.	1	
	575172	BODY COMPLETE, PAINTED & TRIMMED (INCLUDING SEATS)—R.H.S.	1	
	575173	BODY COMPLETE, PAINTED & TRIMMED (INCLUDING SEATS)—L.H.S.	1	Mk. II Cars only Fitted from Body No. 50001KC
	575174	BODY COMPLETE, PAINTED & TRIMMED (LESS SEATS)—R.H.S.	1	
	575175	BODY COMPLETE, PAINTED & TRIMMED (LESS SEATS)—L.H.S.	1	
	575326	BODY COMPLETE, PAINTED & TRIMMED (INCLUDING SEATS)—L.H.S.	1	Mk. II Cars U.S.A. only Fitted from Body No. 50001KC
	575327	BODY COMPLETE, PAINTED & TRIMMED (LESS SEATS)—L.H.S.	1	

Note:- The above assemblies are supplied less the following items:-
Facia Ash Tray, Cubby Box, Steering Column Brackets and Cowl, Veneered Facia Panel, Heater, Bumpers, Electrical Equipment, Instruments, Master Cylinder and Screen Washer.

Plate No.	Part No.	Description	No. per Unit	Remarks
	571451	BODY SHELL, PRIME FINISH—R.H.S. (Complete with Doors, Bonnet and Front Valance)	1	
	571450	BODY SHELL, PRIME FINISH—L.H.S. (Complete with Doors, Bonnet and Front Valance)	1	Mk. I Cars only Fitted up to Body No. 50000KC
	619012	BODY SHELL, PRIME FINISH—R.H.S. (Less Doors, Bonnet and Front Valance)	1	
	619013	BODY SHELL, PRIME FINISH—L.H.S. (Less Doors, Bonnet and Front Valance)	1	
	575170	BODY SHELL, PRIME FINISH—R.H.S. (Complete with Doors, Bonnet and Front Valance)	1	
	575171	BODY SHELL, PRIME FINISH—L.H.S. (Complete with Doors, Bonnet and Front Valance)	1	Mk. II Cars only Fitted from Body No. 50001KC
	575324	BODY SHELL, PRIME FINISH—R.H.S. (Less Doors, Bonnet and Front Valance)	1	
	575323	BODY SHELL, PRIME FINISH—L.H.S. (Less Doors, Bonnet and Front Valance)	1	

Note:—Items marked thus † are available on our Factory Exchange Unit Scheme

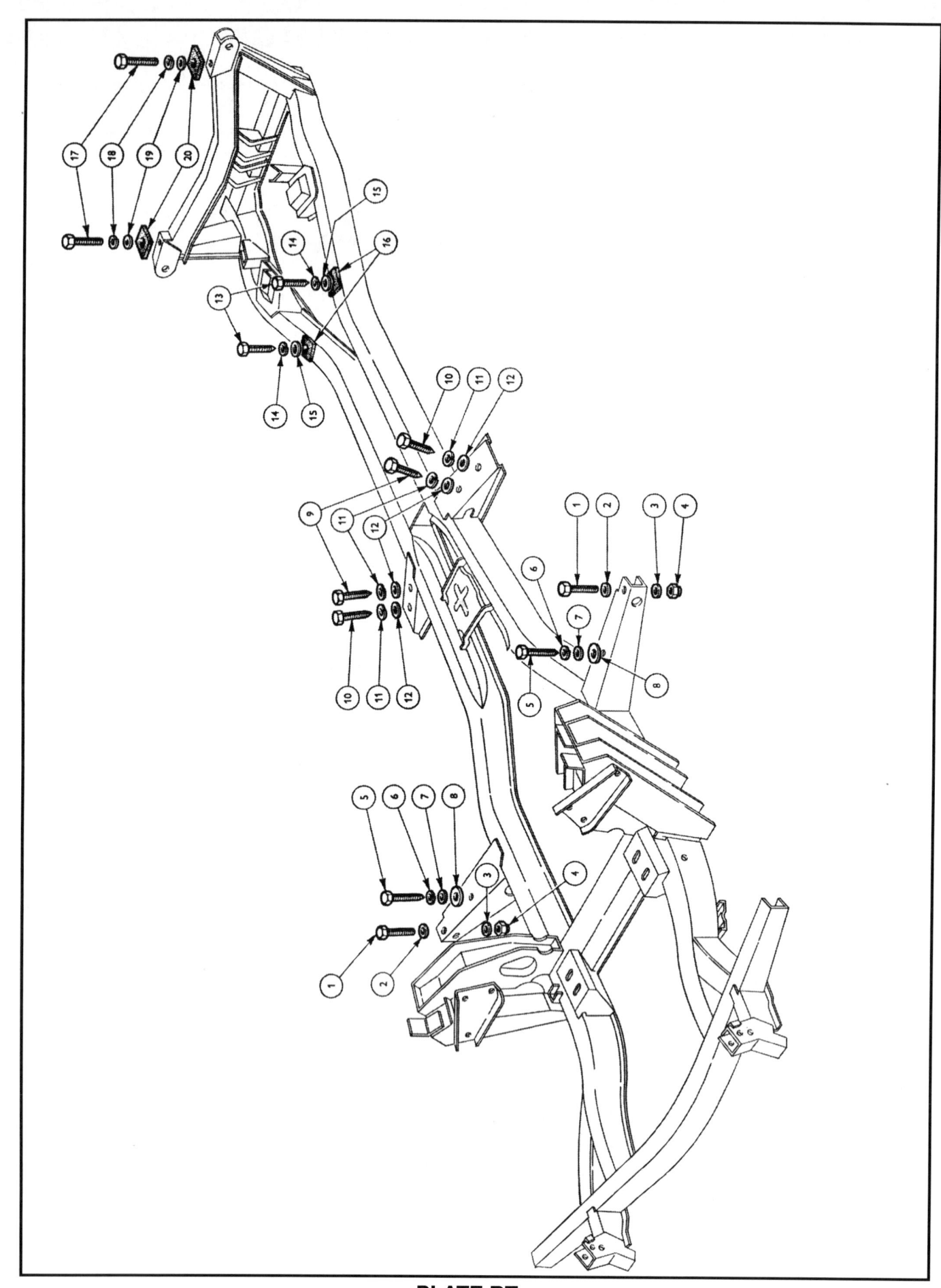

PLATE BT

BODY AND FITTINGS

Plate No.	Part No.	Description		No. per Unit	Remarks
	574245	**BODY MOUNTING PACK**		1	
BT1	HB0826	**Bolt**	⎫	2	
BT2	WM0058	**Washer,** plain	⎪ Dash front outer to	2	
BT3	WP0019	**Washer,** plain	⎬ chassis frame front outrigger	2	
BT4	YN2908	**Nut,** nyloc	⎭	2	
BT5	HU0808P	**Screw,** set	⎫	2	
BT6	WL0208	**Washer,** lock	⎬ Body to mounting	2	
BT7	WM0058	**Washer,** plain	⎭ brackets, dash front	2	
BT8	613178	**Block,** mounting		2	
BT9	HB0816P	**Bolt**	⎫	2	
BT10	HB0824P	**Bolt**	⎬ Main floor to	2	
BT11	WL0208	**Washer,** lock	⎬ chassis outrigger	4	
BT12	WM0058	**Washer,** plain	⎭	4	
BT13	HB0828P	**Bolt**	⎫	2	
BT14	WL0208	**Washer,** lock	⎬ Heelboard crossmember to chassis	2	
BT15	WP0105	**Washer,** plain	⎭	2	
BT16	621101	**Pad,** mounting		2	
BT17	HB0914P	**Bolt**	⎫	2	
BT18	WQ0309	**Washer,** lock	⎬ Seat pan to chassis crossmember	2	
BT19	WM0075	**Washer,** medium	⎭	2	
BT20	621101	**Pad,** mounting		2	
	613178	**Pad,** mounting		2	

Note:—Items marked thus † are available on our Factory Exchange Unit Scheme

109

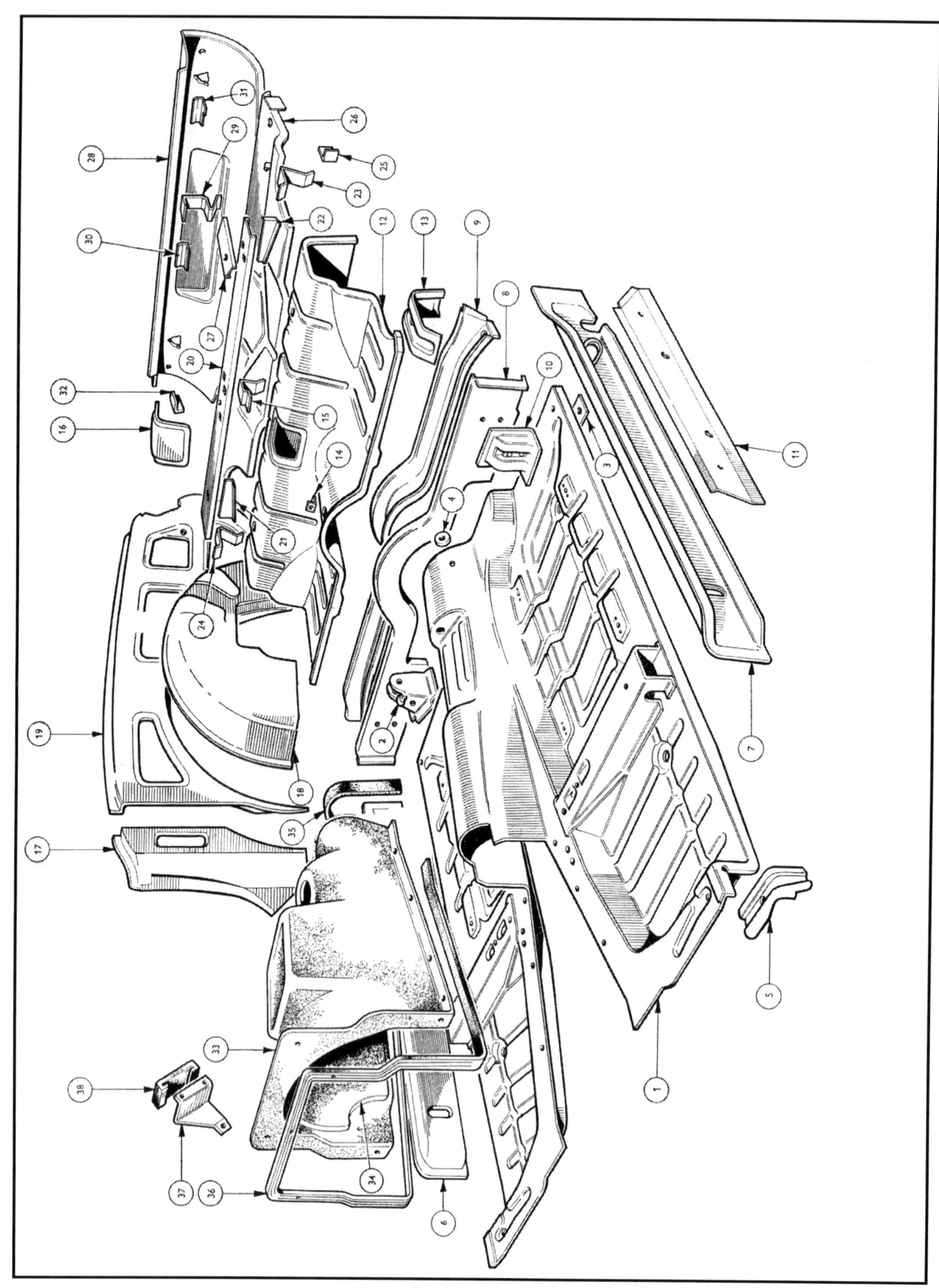

PLATE BU

BODY AND FITTINGS

Plate No.	Part No.	Description	No. per Unit	Remarks
		FLOOR PANEL DETAILS		
BU1	809915	**Floor** assembly, main	1	
BU2	121765	**Bracket,** pivot, handbrake	1	
	612577	**Angle,** sill, reinforcement	1	
	603559	**Clip,** wiring	3	
BU3	615980	**Plate,** reinforcement, assembly, safety harness attachment	2	
BU4	615981	**Washer** assembly, tunnel reinforcement, safety harness attachment	2	Fitted up to Body No 1040KC only, and on 1047KC, 1052KC, 1065KC, and 1217KC
	612528	**Bracket,** mounting, dash front, outer—R H	1	
BU5	612527	**Bracket,** mounting, dash front, outer—L.H.	1	
BU6	806639	**Panel,** sill, inner—R.H.	1	
BU7	806638	**Panel,** sill, inner—L.H.	1	
BU8	903134	**Panel,** heelboard	1	
BU9	807104	**Crossmember** assembly, heelboard	1	
	133919	**Bracket** assembly, handbrake relay mounting	1	
BU10	613344	**Bracket** assembly, radius arm mounting	2	Fitted up to Body No. No. 50000KC only
	623796	**Bracket** assembly, radius arm mounting	2	Fitted from
	715085	**Bracket** assembly, guide, handbrake cable—R.H.	1	Body No. 50001KC
	715084	**Bracket** assembly, guide, handbrake cable—L.H.	1	and future
	806635	**Panel,** sill reinforcement, rear—R.H.	1	
BU11	806634	**Panel,** sill reinforcement, rear—L.H.	1	
BU12	904713	**Seat pan** assembly, rear	1	Fitted up to Body No. 50000KC only
	909820	**Seat pan** assembly, rear	1	Fitted from Body No. 50001KC and future
	706160	**Reinforcement** assembly, body mounting—R.H.	1	
BU13	706159	**Reinforcement** assembly, body mounting—L.H.	1	
BU14	618399	**Bracket** assembly, channel, luggage floor to seat pan	1	Fitted up to Body No. 50000KC only
BU15	618403	**Bracket** assembly, front inner, tank to seat pan	1	
BU16	613812	**Cover,** rear spring access	1	
	FU2585	**Nut,** fix } Cover	2	
	YN8505	**Screw,** self-tapping } attachment	2	
BU17	903147	**Panel,** front outer, rear wheelarch—R.H.	1	
	903146	**Panel,** front outer, rear wheelarch—L.H.	1	
BU18	705788	**Panel,** wheelarch, inner—R.H.	1	Fitted up to Body No. 1040KC, and on 1047KC, 1052KC, 1065KC, and 1217KC only
	705787	**Panel,** wheelarch, inner—L.H.	1	
	712391	**Panel,** wheelarch, inner assembly—R.H.	1	Fitted from Body No. 1041KC up to Body No. 50000KC only, except Body No. 1047KC, 1052KC, 1065KC and 1217KC
	712390	**Panel,** wheelarch, inner assembly—L.H.	1	
	621112	**Plate,** reinforcement, assembly, safety harness (welded to wheelarch)	2	
	715089	**Panel** assembly, wheelarch, inner—R.H.	1	
	715088	**Panel** assembly, wheelarch, inner—L.H.	1	Fitted from Body No. 50001KC and future
	714656	**Bracket** assembly, bump stop and damper mounting, R.H.	1	
	714655	**Bracket** assembly, bump stop and damper mounting, L.H.	1	
	621112	**Plate,** reinforcement assembly, safety harness	2	
BU19	903149	**Panel,** wheelarch, outer—R.H.	1	
	903148	**Panel,** wheelarch, outer—L.H.	1	
BU20	809677	**Rail,** support, assembly, luggage floor	1	Fitted up to Body No. 50000KC only
	814012	**Rail,** support, assembly, luggage floor	1	Fitted from Body No. 50001KC and future

Note:—Items marked thus † are available on our Factory Exchange Unit Scheme

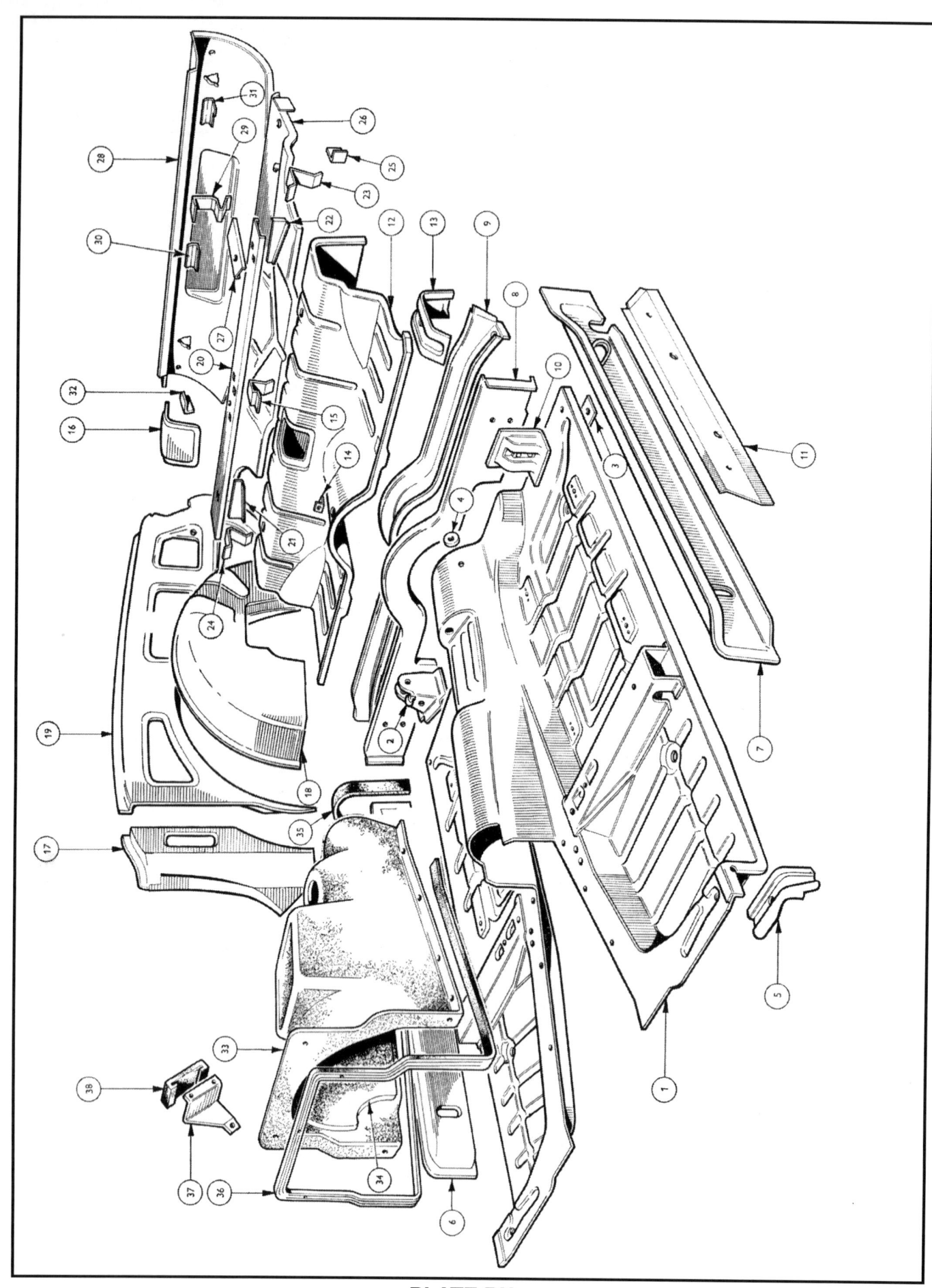

PLATE BU

BODY AND FITTINGS

Plate No.	Part No.	Description	No. per Unit	Remarks
		FLOOR PANEL DETAILS—continued		
BU21	710450	**Gusset**, support rail to inner wheelarch—R.H.	1	
BU22	710449	**Gusset**, support rail to inner wheelarch—L.H.	1	
BU23	618401	**Bracket**, mounting, assembly, front outer petrol tank to L.H. rear wheelarch	1	
BU24	618420	**Bracket**, outer, luggage front floor to R.H. inner wheelarch	1	
BU25	618398	**Bracket**, support, petrol tank side inner to L.H. inner wheelarch	1	
	612297	**Reinforcement** assembly, overrider support, upper, rear	2	
	603559	**Clip**, wiring	4	
BU26	809675	**Floor** assembly, trunk	1	
	615810	**Reinforcement**, overrider attachment	2	
BU27	709564	**Bracket**, reinforcing, spare wheel mounting	1	
	619950	**Bracket**, retaining, jack stowage	1	
	613478	**Bracket**, support, rear exhaust pipe	1	
BU28	709807	**Panel**, rear valance assembly	1	Fitted up to Body No. 50000KC only
	717006	**Panel**, rear valance assembly	1	Fitted from Body No. 50001KC only
BU29	618407	**Bracket**, mounting, assembly, rear inner, petrol tank to rear valance	1	
BU30	618397	**Bracket**, fixing, luggage floor, rear	3	
BU31	618960	**Bracket**, fixing, luggage floor, rear—L.H.	1	
	603559	**Clip**, wiring	4	
BU32	612938	**Angle**, rear valance to wheelarch	2	
BU33	709862	**Cover**, gearbox, assembly	1	
BU34	806357	**Pad**, sound insulation	1	
BU35	608563	**Seal**, gearbox cover, rear	1	
BU36	611957	**Seal**, gearbox cover, top and sides	1	
	FU2569/4	**Nut**, fix, gear lever grommet attachment	4	
	YH6507	**Screw**, self-tapping ⎫	12	
	WP0005	**Washer**, plain ⎪	12	
	608383	**Plate**, retaining ⎬ Gearbox cover attachment	12	
	FU2549/4	**Nut**, spire ⎪	10	
	FF2545/4	**Nut**, fix ⎭	2	
BU37	710498	**Footrest**, gearbox cover	1	
BU38	611822	**Pad**, footrest, rubber	1	
	PX0504	**Screw**, set ⎫ ⎫	3	
	WP0156	**Washer**, plain ⎪ Footrest ⎬ R.H.S. Driver's side only	3	
	WL0205	**Washer**, lock ⎬ attachment ⎪	3	
	HN2005	**Nut** ⎭ ⎭	3	

Note:—Items marked thus † are available on our Factory Exchange Unit Scheme

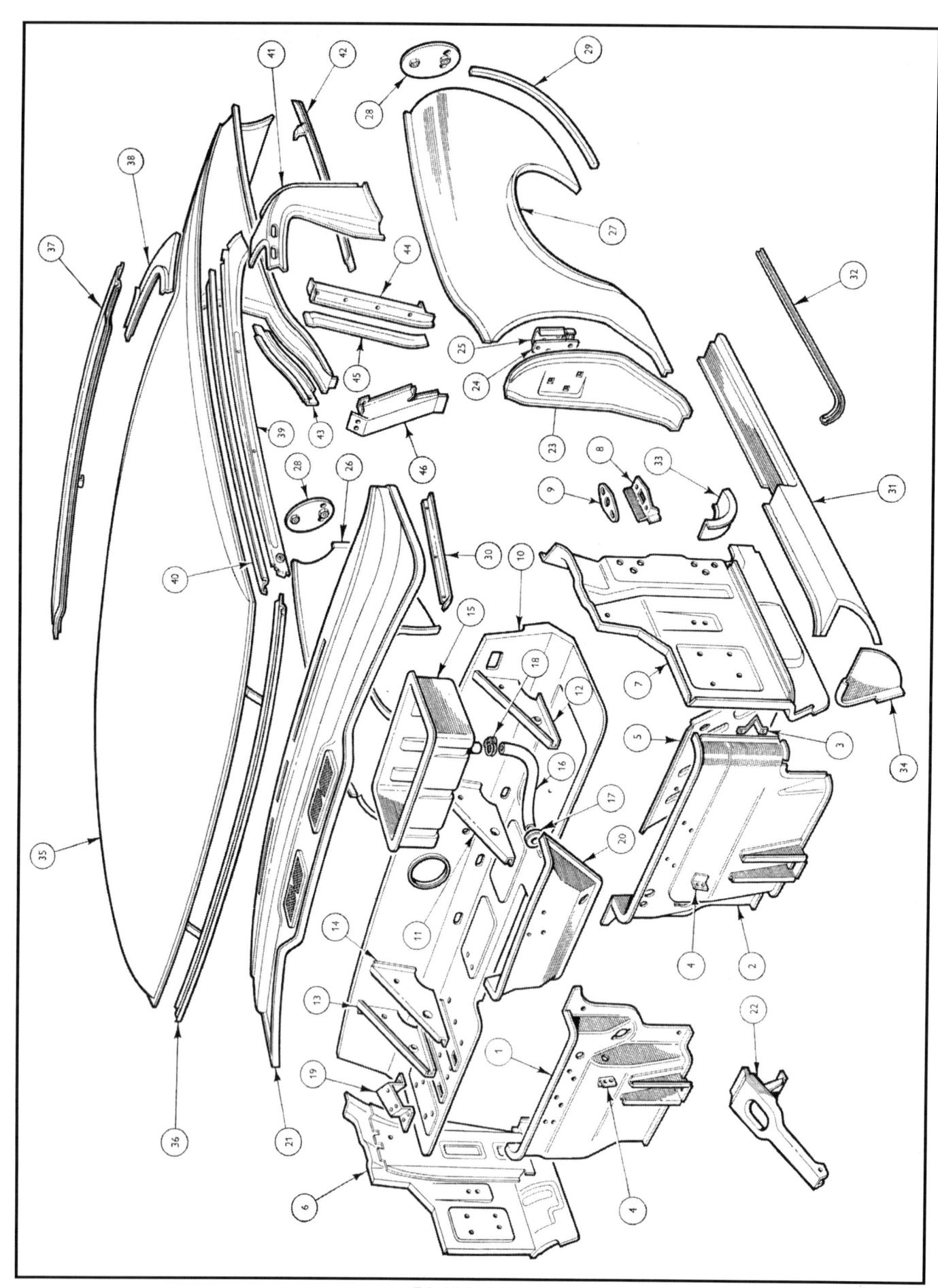

PLATE BV

BODY AND FITTINGS

Plate No.	Part No.	Description	No. per Unit	Remarks
		DASH, BODY SIDE AND ROOF PANELS		
BV1	809741	**Panel,** assembly, dash front, R.H. steering—R.H.	1	
BV2	809739	**Panel,** assembly, dash front, R.H. steering—L.H.	1	
	809742	**Panel,** assembly, dash front, L.H. steering—R.H.	1	
	809740	**Panel,** assembly, dash front, L.H. steering—L.H.	1	
	603559	**Clip,** wiring	3	
	603559	**Clip,** battery drain tube	1	
	607621	**Bracket,** mounting, dash front	2	
	607637	**Plate,** mounting bracket	2	
BV3	620121	**Bracket,** footrest panel, passenger's side	2	
BV4	615706	**Bracket,** engine bay valance, rear	2	
BV5	810252	**Panel,** footrest, passenger side only—R.H.S.	1	
	810253	**Panel,** footrest, passenger side only—L.H.S.	1	
	YA0404	**Screw,** self-tapping ⎫ Footrest panel to	4	
	WP8005	**Washer,** plain ⎬ mounting brackets	4	
	FJ2484	**Nut,** fix ⎭ and floor	2	
BV6	809927	**Panel** assembly, 'A' post and sill reinforcement—R.H.	1	
BV7	809926	**Panel** assembly, 'A' post and sill reinforcement—L.H.	1	
BV8	612616	**Bracket,** bonnet location	2	
	613351	**Bracket** assembly, check strap—R.H.	1	
	613350	**Bracket** assembly, check strap—L.H.	1	
	603344	**Spring,** guide, check strap	2	
	556141	**Rivet,** spring guide attachment	4	
	603559	**Clip,** wiring	4	
BV9	612617	**Plate,** bonnet peg locating	2	
	PX0454/P	**Screw,** set ⎫	4	
	WM0054	**Washer,** plain ⎪ Locating plate to	8	
	WL0204	**Washer,** lock ⎬ bonnet locating bracket	4	
	HN2054	**Nut** ⎭	4	
BV10	809799	**Panel,** dash shelf—R.H.S. (Alternative to 813096)	1	⎫ Fitted up to Commission
	813096	**Panel,** dash shelf—R.H.S. (Alternative to 809799)	1	⎭ KC50000 only
	809800	**Panel,** dash shelf—L.H.S.	1	Fitted up to Commission No. KC7050 only
	813097	**Panel,** dash shelf—L.H.S.	1	Fitted from Commission No. KC7051 up to KC50000 only
	813945	**Panel,** dash shelf—R.H.S.	1	⎫ Fitted from Commission No.
	813944	**Panel,** dash shelf—L.H.S.	1	⎭ KC50001 and future
	603559	**Clip,** wiring	5	
BV11	613687	**Gusset,** battery box, dash shelf—R.H.	1	
BV12	613686	**Gusset,** battery box, dash shelf—L.H.	1	
BV13	613685	**Gusset,** pedals, dash shelf—R.H.—R.H.S.	1	
	612982	**Gusset,** pedals, dash shelf—R.H.—L.H.S.	1	⎫ Fitted up to Commission No.
BV14	612981	**Gusset,** pedals, dash shelf—L.H.	1	⎭ KC7050 only
	621706	**Gusset,** pedals, dash shelf—L.H.—L.H.S.	1	⎫ Fitted from
	621707	**Gusset,** pedals, dash shelf—R.H.—L.H.S.	1	⎬ Commission No.
	612981	**Gusset,** pedals, dash shelf—L.H.—R.H.S.	1	⎭ KC50001 and future
	612850	**Plate,** support, parcel tray	4	

Note:—Items marked thus † are available on our Factory Exchange Unit Scheme

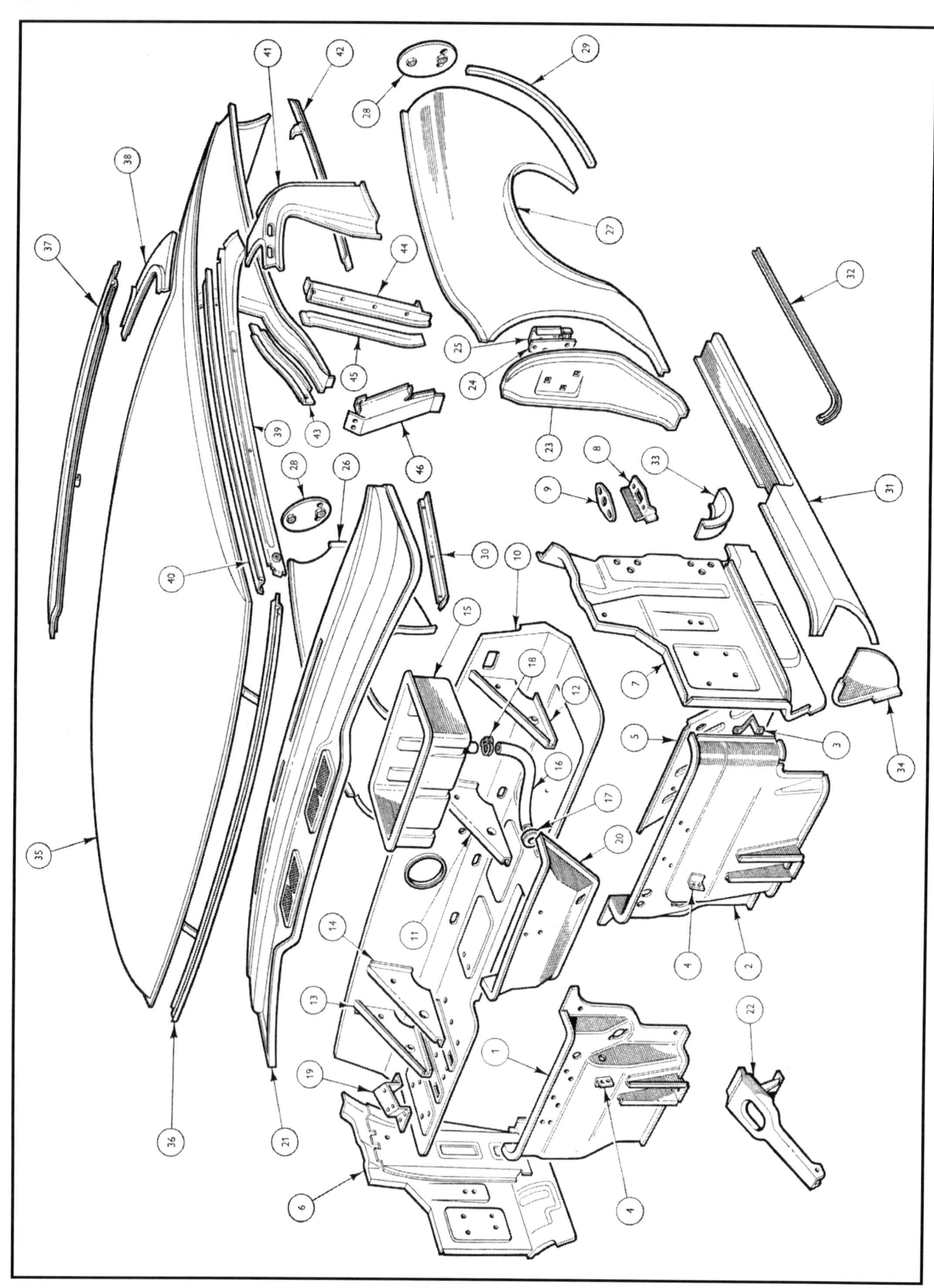

PLATE BV

BODY AND FITTINGS

Plate No.	Part No.	Description	No. per Unit	Remarks
		DASH, BODY SIDE AND ROOF PANELS —continued		
BV15	806707	**Battery box** assembly—R.H.S.	1	
	807030	**Battery box** assembly—L.H.S.	1	
	619864	**Rod,** battery fixing	2	
	621834	**Angle,** battery retaining	1	
	501794	**Washer,** special, battery rod	2	
	132068	**Nut,** wing, securing battery	2	
	613155	**Rubber,** battery shelf	1	
BV16	612970	**Tube,** drain, battery box	1	
BV17	613025	**Grommet,** drain tube	1	
BV18	CS4011	**Clip,** drain tube to battery box	1	Alternative to CS4012
BV18	CS4012	**Clip,** drain tube to battery box	1	Alternative to CS4011
BV19	706550	**Bracket,** dash shelf, windscreen wiper mounting	1	Fitted up to Commission No. KC50000 only
	HU0705	**Screw,** set	4	
	WL0207	**Washer,** lock Motor bracket to dash shelf	4	
	WM0057	**Washer,** plain	4	
BV20	809747	**Air box** assembly	1	Fitted up to Commission No. KC50000 only
	813946	**Air box** assembly	1	Fitted from Commission No. KC50001 and future
	622150	**Clip,** heater hose, foot level vent	1	
	619482	**Reinforcement,** dash shelf, centre	1	
	611665	**Reinforcement,** dash shelf	2	
BV21	809803	**Panel** assembly, front deck	1	
BV22	809785	**Channel** assembly, steering column support—R.H.S.	1	
	809786	**Channel** assembly, steering column support—L.H.S.	1	
	809510	**Panel** assembly, 'B' post, outer—R.H.	1	Fitted up to Comm. No. KC9999 L.H.S. and Body No. 21736 R.H.S. only
BV23	809509	**Panel** assembly, 'B' post, outer—L.H.	1	
	813366	**Panel** assembly, 'B' post, outer—R.H.	1	Fitted from Comm. No. KC10000 L.H.S. and Body No. 21737 R.H.S. and future
	813365	**Panel** assembly, 'B' post, outer—L.H.	1	
	619100	**Plate,** tapped, lock striker—R.H.	1	
BV24	619099	**Plate,** tapped, lock striker—L.H.	1	
	618275	**Retainer,** lock striker—R.H.	1	
BV25	618274	**Retainer,** lock striker—L.H.	1	
BV26	903096	**Panel,** outer, rear wing—R.H.	1	Fitted up to Body No. 50000KC only
BV27	903095	**Panel,** outer, rear wing—L.H.	1	
	907078	**Panel,** outer, rear wing—R.H.	1	Fitted from Body No. 50001KC only
	907077	**Panel,** outer, rear wing—L.H.	1	
BV28	618493	**Plate** assembly, filler, rear side lamp	2	
BV29	706600	**Finisher,** lower rear wing joint	2	
BV30	709662	**Support,** outer, spare wheel board—R.H.	1	
	903098	**Panel,** sill, outer—R.H.	1	
BV31	903097	**Panel,** sill, outer—L.H.	1	
	711538	**Retainer,** sill sealing rubber—R.H.	1	
BV32	711537	**Retainer,** sill sealing rubber—L.H.	1	
	706289	**Panel,** 'A' post outer, lower—R.H.	1	
BV33	706288	**Panel,** 'A' post outer, lower—L.H.	1	
	706423	**Panel,** filler, sill front—R.H.	1	
BV34	706422	**Panel,** filler, sill front—L.H.	1	

Note:—Items marked thus † are available on our Factory Exchange Unit Scheme

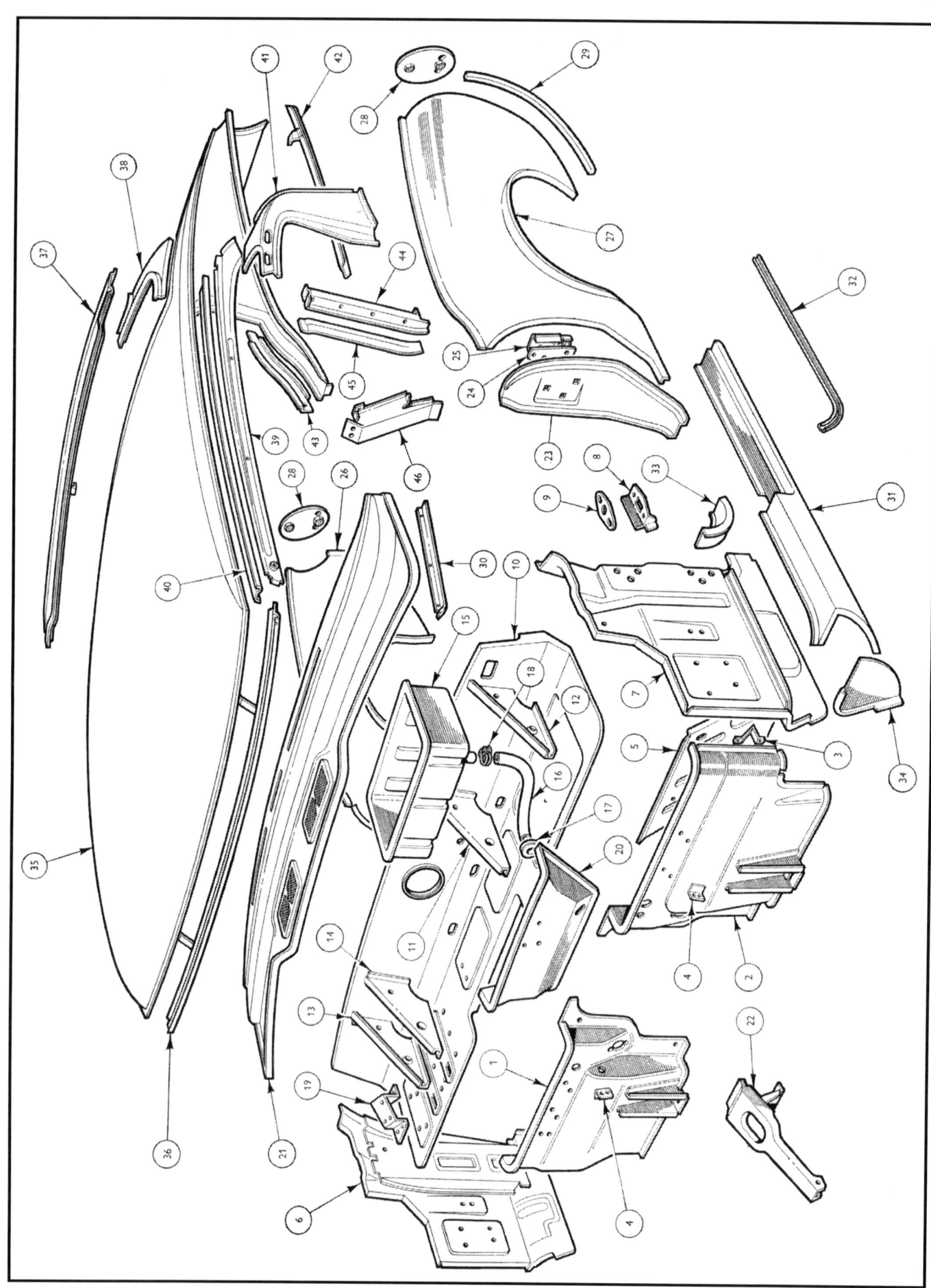

PLATE BV

BODY AND FITTINGS

Plate No.	Part No.	Description	No. per Unit	Remarks
		DASH, BODY SIDE AND ROOF PANELS —continued		
BV35	904471	**Roof panel** assembly, complete	1	Mk. I Cars only. Fitted up to Commission No. KC50000
	714199	**Roof panel** assembly, complete	1	Mk. II Cars only. Fitted from Commission No. KC50001
BV36	809516	**Stiffener** assembly, roof, front	1	
BV37	618179	**Panel** assembly, rear header	1	
	809403	**Panel**, closing, rear member—R.H.	1	
BV38	809402	**Panel**, closing, rear member—L.H.	1	
	904479	**Panel**, cantrail—R.H.	1	
BV39	904478	**Panel**, cantrail—L.H.	1	
	904481	**Panel**, drip moulding—R.H.	1	
BV40	904480	**Panel**, drip moulding—L.H.	1	
	904483	**Panel**, reinforcement, rear quarterlight—R.H.	1	
BV41	904482	**Panel**, reinforcement, rear quarterlight—L.H.	1	
	809947	**Rail**, support, assembly, trim board, rear quarter—R.H.	1	
BV42	809946	**Rail**, support, assembly, trim board, rear quarter—L.H.	1	
	619048	**Bracket**, rear headlining, trim board	4	
	709282	**Panel**, closing, waistrail—R.H.	1	
BV43	709281	**Panel**, closing, waistrail—L.H.	1	
	709284	**Panel**, 'B' post, upper—R.H.	1	
BV44	709283	**Panel**, 'B' post, upper—L.H.	1	
	709286	**Panel**, closing, 'B' post—R.H.	1	
BV45	709285	**Panel**, closing, 'B' post—L.H.	1	
BV46	709567	**Bracket** assembly, striker, back door lock	1	

Note:—Items marked thus † are available on our Factory Exchange Unit Scheme

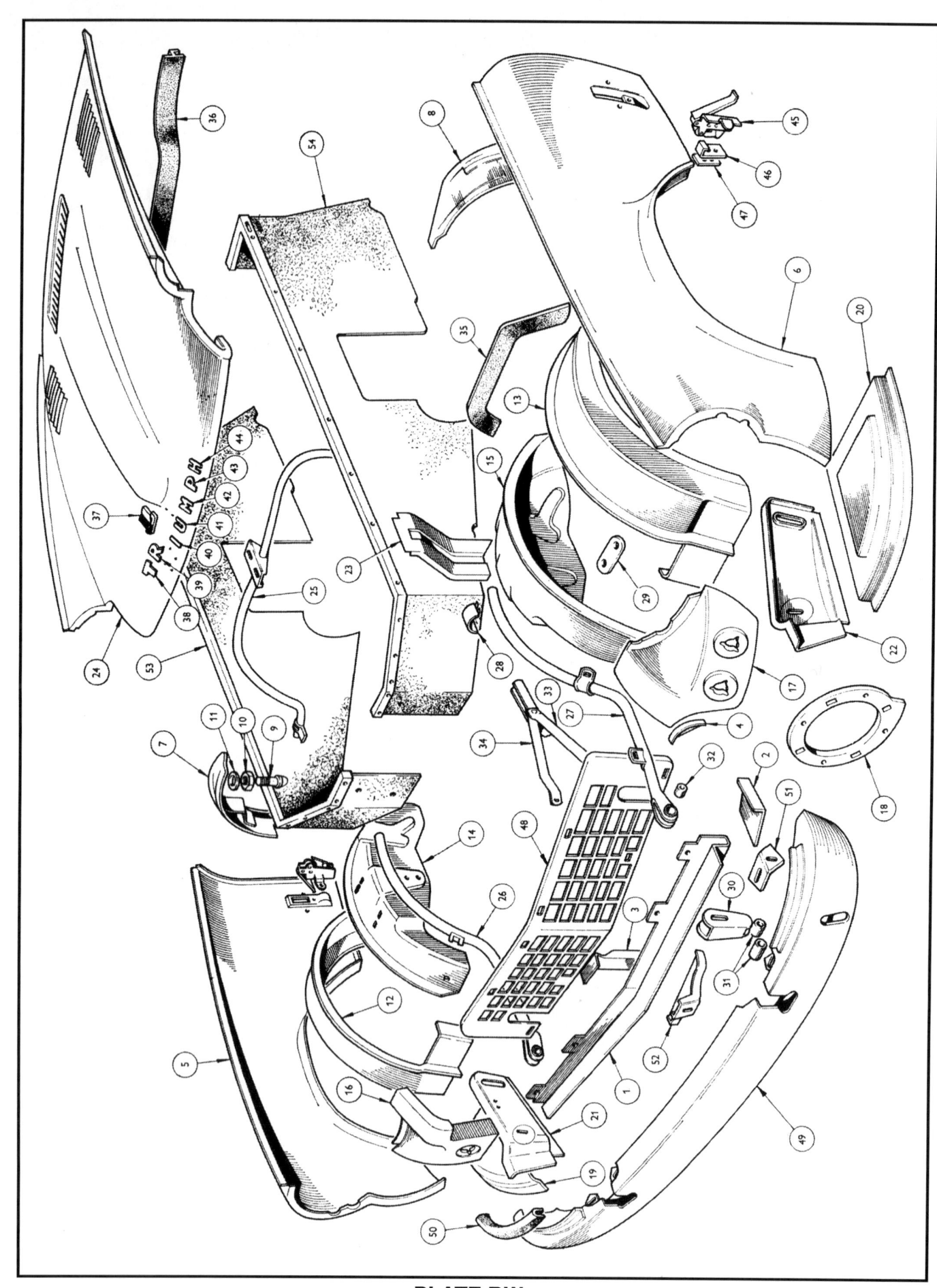

PLATE BW

BODY AND FITTINGS

Plate No.	Part No.	Description	No. per Unit	Remarks
	905302	**BONNET ASSEMBLY**—Mk. I Cars only	1	
BW1	710679	**Channel**, bottom grille aperture	1	
	619740	**Bracket**, bottom channel attachment—R.H.	1	
BW2	619739	**Bracket**, bottom channel attachment—L.H.	1	
BW3	710680	**Strut**, centre, grille aperture	1	
	710715	**Gusset**, grille aperture—R.H.	1	
BW4	710714	**Gusset**, grille aperture—L.H.	1	
BW5	903089	**Side**, front wing—R.H.	1	
BW6	903088	**Side**, front wing—L.H.	1	
BW7	807103	**Reinforcement** assembly, front wing side—R.H.	1	
BW8	807102	**Reinforcement** assembly, front wing side—L.H.	1	
BW9	612962	**Peg**, bonnet location	2	
BW10	JN2108	**Nut**, jam ⎫ Securing bonnet	2	
BW11	WP0008	**Washer**, plain ⎭ location peg	2	
BW12	903138	**Panel**, front wheelarch, outer—R.H.	1	
BW13	903137	**Panel**, front wheelarch, outer—L.H.	1	
BW14	706549	**Panel**, front wheelarch, inner—R.H.	1	
BW15	706548	**Panel**, front wheelarch, inner—L.H.	1	
BW16	903091	**Panel**, nose—R.H.	1	
BW17	903090	**Panel**, nose—L.H.	1	
	612874	**Bracket**, reinforcement, headlamp mounting—R.H.	1	
BW18	612873	**Bracket**, reinforcement, headlamp mounting—L.H.	1	
BW19	706312	**Panel**, filler, nose to wheelarch—R.H.	1	
BW20	706311	**Panel**, filler, nose to wheelarch—L.H.	1	
BW21	810261	**Panel** assembly, closing grille aperture to wheelarch—R.H.	1	
BW22	810260	**Panel** assembly, closing grille aperture to wheelarch—L.H.	1	
	612660	**Support**, front wheelarch to wing—R.H.	1	
BW23	612659	**Support**, front wheelarch to wing—L.H.	1	
	608643	**Packing**, sponge rubber, bonnet	2	
BW24	619011	**Top** assembly, bonnet	1	
	706453	**Reinforcement**, front edge	1	
	603559	**Clip**, wiring	6	
BW25	706539	**Tube** assembly, bonnet, rear	1	
	607628	**Bracket**, bonnet tube	1	
	613076	**Clamp** assembly, bonnet tube, rear	2	
	HU0706	**Screw**, set ⎫	4	
	WP0120	**Washer**, plain ⎬ Rear bonnet tube to wheelarch	4	
	WL0207	**Washer**, lock ⎭	4	
	HN2007	**Nut** ⎫	2	
	WL0207	**Washer**, lock ⎬ Bonnet tube	2	
	WP0120	**Washer**, plain ⎪ to bonnet top	2	
	608643	**Packing**, sponge rubber ⎭	2	
BW26	806883	**Tube** assembly, bonnet hinge—R.H.	1	
BW27	806882	**Tube** assembly, bonnet hinge—L.H.	1	
	607788	**Bush**, pivot, bonnet tube	2	
BW28	607869	**Bracket**, anchor, rear bonnet hinge tube	4	
BW29	607711	**Plate**, backing	4	
	HU0706	**Screw**, set ⎫ Anchor brackets	8	
	WP0007	**Washer**, plain ⎬ to wheelarch	8	
	WL0207	**Washer**, lock ⎭	8	
	HU0706	**Screw**, set ⎫	4	
	WL0207	**Washer**, lock ⎬ Bonnet tube to closing panel	4	
	WP0120	**Washer**, plain ⎭	4	
BW30	612838	**Bracket**, pivot, bonnet hinge tube attachment	2	

Note:—Items marked thus † are available on our Factory Exchange Unit Scheme

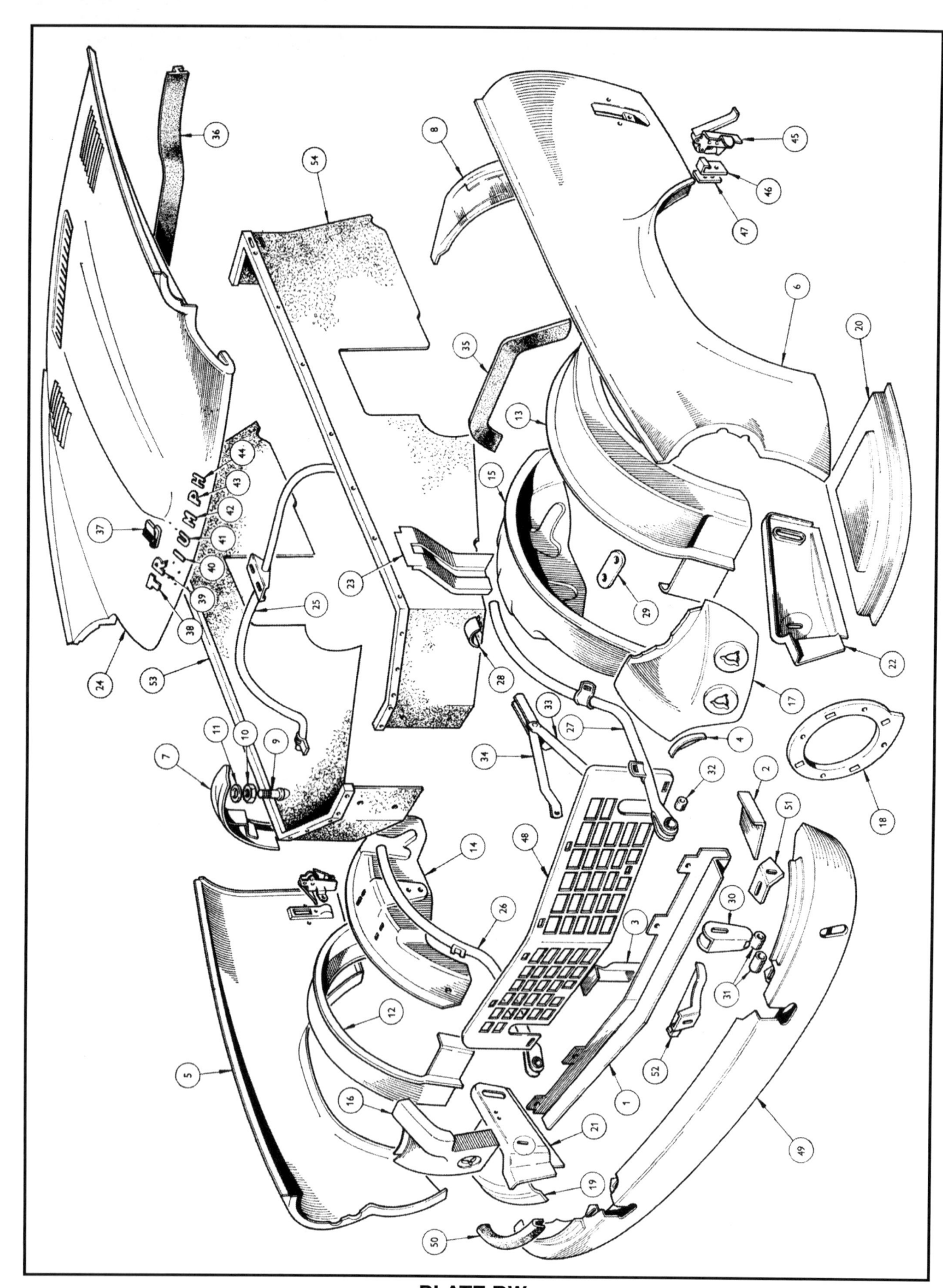

PLATE BW

BODY AND FITTINGS

Plate No.	Part No.	Description	No. per Unit	Remarks
		BONNET ASSEMBLY—Mk. I Cars only —continued		
BW31	612963	**Tube**, distance ⎫	4	
	WM0058	**Washer**, plain ⎬ Bonnet pivot	8	
	TN3208	**Nut**, nyloc ⎬ bracket to frame	4	
	HB0818	**Bolt** ⎭	4	
	HB0916	**Bolt** ⎫	2	
	WP0009	**Washer**, plain ⎬ Bonnet hinge tube	4	
	WP0048	**Washer**, plain ⎬ to	4	
	TN3209	**Nut**, nyloc ⎭ bonnet pivot bracket	2	
BW32	607910	**Spacer**, bonnet fulcrum pin	2	
BW33	613751	**Link** assembly, lower, bonnet stay	1	
BW34	613045	**Link** assembly, upper, bonnet stay	1	
	HB0710	**Bolt** ⎫	1	
	YN2907	**Nut**, nyloc ⎬ Upper link to lower link	1	
	WP0007	**Washer**, plain ⎬	1	
	WP0042	**Washer**, plain ⎭	2	
	145308	**Extension**, bonnet stay bracket	1	⎫
	HU0705	**Screw**, set ⎬ Extension attachment	1	⎬ Fitted up to Body No. 4232KC only
	TN3207	**Nut**, nyloc ⎭	1	⎭
	HB0708	**Bolt**, hex. ⎫	1	
	YN2907	**Nut** ⎬ Attaching lower link to chassis	1	
	WP0007	**Washer**, plain ⎭	1	
	HB0708	**Bolt** ⎫	1	
	YN2907	**Nut**, nyloc ⎬	1	
	WP0007	**Washer**, plain ⎬ Attaching upper link to wheelarch	1	
	WM0816	**Washer**, plain ⎬	1	
	WP0117	**Washer**, plain ⎭	1	
BW35	613666	**Seal**, rear, front wheelarch to dash	2	
	608520	**Clip**, seal attachment	18	
BW36	610675	**Rubber**, sealing, bonnet	1	
BW37	608380	**Badge** assembly, bonnet	1	
	FP1012/4	**Plate**, fix, badge attachment	2	
BW38	703862	**Letter 'T'**	1	
BW39	703863	**Letter 'R'**	1	
BW40	703864	**Letter 'I'**	1	
BW41	703865	**Letter 'U'**	1	
BW42	703866	**Letter 'M'**	1	
BW43	703867	**Letter 'P'**	1	
BW44	703868	**Letter 'H'**	1	
	614006	**Bush**, friction, securing letters to bonnet	14	
BW45	607663	**BONNET CATCH ASSEMBLY—Mk. I Cars only**	2	
	510293	**Screw**, set ⎫	6	
	HN2054	**Nut** ⎬	6	
	WQ0304	**Washer**, lock ⎬ Bonnet catch attachment	6	
	WM0054	**Washer**, medium ⎬	6	
	WN0704	**Washer**, shakeproof ⎭	6	
BW46	607664	**Plate**, catch, bonnet lock, dash side front lower	2	
	613474	**Washer**, catch plate	2	
BW47	609931	**Plate**, tapping	2	
	HU0706	**Screw**, set ⎫ Catch plate	4	
	WP0127	**Washer**, plain ⎬ to dash side	4	
	WN0707	**Washer**, shakeproof ⎭	4	

Note:- For Bonnet Locating Plate Details see page 112.

Note:—Items marked thus † are available on our Factory Exchange Unit Scheme

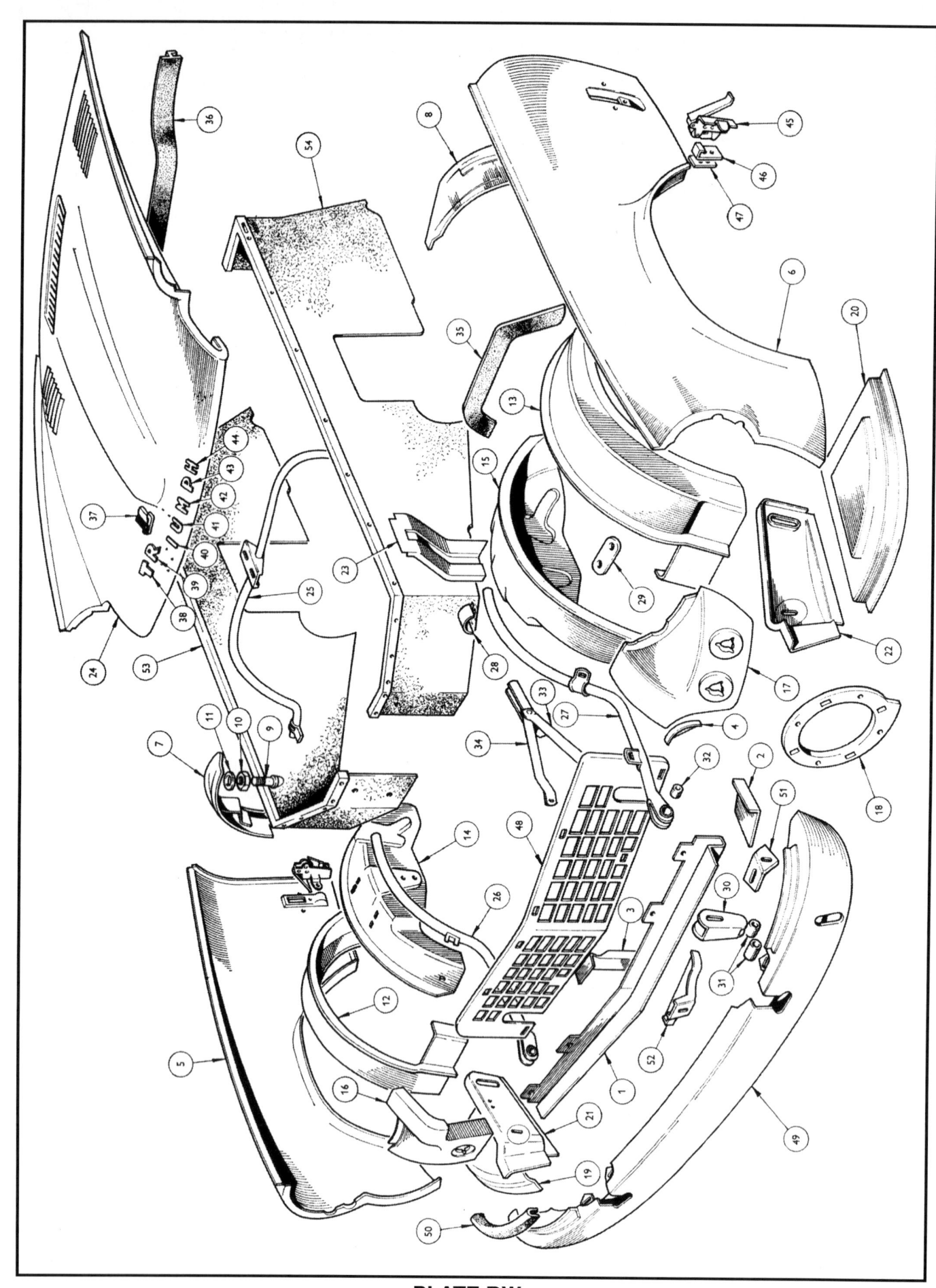

PLATE BW

BODY AND FITTINGS

Plate No.	Part No.	Description	No. per Unit	Remarks
BW48	810402	**RADIATOR GRILLE ASSEMBLY** —Mk. I Cars only	1	
	FZ3404/4	**Nut**, retained ⎫	8	
	512462	**Screw**, set ⎪	6	
	515328	**Screw**, set ⎬ Radiator grille attachment	2	
	514438	**Washer**, plain ⎪	8	
	WL0205	**Washer**, lock ⎪	8	
	WM0816	**Washer**, medium, packing ⎭	4	
BW49	807136	**FRONT VALANCE ASSEMBLY** —Mk. I Cars only	1	
BW50	610676	**Seal**, front valance to bonnet	2	
	612830	**Bracket**, support, front valance, outer—R.H.	1	
BW51	612829	**Bracket**, support, front valance, outer—L.H.	1	
	HU0706P	**Screw**, set ⎫	2	
	WP0120	**Washer**, plain ⎬ Support bracket to valance	2	
	WL0207	**Washer**, lock ⎭	2	
	HU0706P	**Screw**, set ⎫	2	
	WP0120	**Washer**, plain ⎪ Attaching support brackets,	4	
	WL0207	**Washer**, lock ⎬ front valance, outer, to chassis frame	2	
	HN2007	**Nut** ⎭	2	
	706513	**Bracket**, support, front valance—R.H.	1	
BW52	706512	**Bracket**, support, front valance—L.H.	1	
	HU0706P	**Screw**, set ⎫	4	
	WP0007	**Washer**, plain ⎬ Support brackets to valance	4	
	FQ3405/4	**Nut**, retained ⎭	4	
	HU0706P	**Screw**, set ⎫	2	
	WP0007	**Washer**, plain ⎬ Support bracket to overrider mounting bracket	2	
	WL0207	**Washer**, lock ⎭	2	
BW53	905222	**ENGINE BAY VALANCE ASSEMBLY, R.H.**	1	⎫ Mark I Cars only
BW54	905221	**ENGINE BAY VALANCE ASSEMBLY, L.H.**	1	⎭
	573948	**Nut**, twin impression	2	
	RB5404	**Rivet**, twin nut attachment	2	
	YH6506	**Screw**, self-tapping, lower front valance and radiator cowl lower attachment	4	
	HU0505	**Screw**, set ⎫	4	
	WP0005	**Washer**, plain ⎪	8	
	WL0205	**Washer**, lock ⎬ Engine bay valance to dash front	4	
	615699	**Washer**, plate ⎪	2	
	RB5510	**Rivet**, bifurcated ⎪	4	
	WP0028	**Washer**, plain ⎪	4	
	HN2005	**Nut** ⎭	4	
	619822	**Clip**, edge	4	

Note:- For Radiator Cowl see Radiator Section.

Note:—Items marked thus † are available on our Factory Exchange Unit Scheme

117

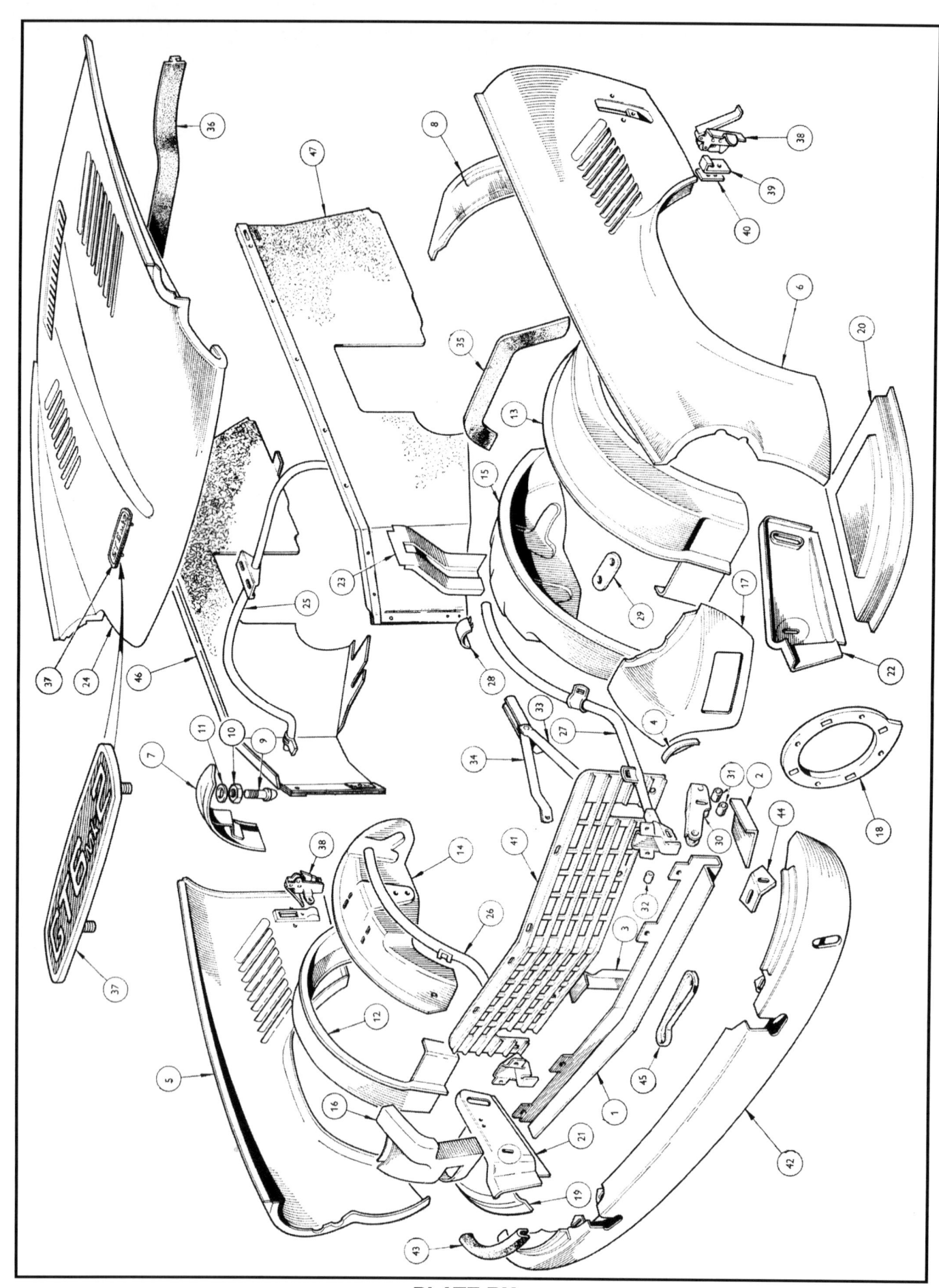

PLATE BX

BODY AND FITTINGS

Plate No.	Part No.	Description	No. per Unit	Remarks
	908116	**BONNET ASSEMBLY—Mk. II Cars only**	1	
BX1	710679	**Channel,** bottom grille aperture	1	
	619740	**Bracket,** bottom channel attachment—R.H.	1	
BX2	619739	**Bracket,** bottom channel attachment—L.H.	1	
BX3	710680	**Strut,** centre, grille aperture	1	
	603559	**Clip,** wiring, centre strut	1	
	710715	**Gusset,** grille aperture—R.H.	1	
BX4	710714	**Gusset,** grille aperture—L.H.	1	
BX5	908114	**Side,** front wing—R.H.	1	
BX6	908113	**Side,** front wing—L.H.	1	
BX7	807103	**Reinforcement** assembly, front wing side—R.H.	1	
BX8	807102	**Reinforcement** assembly, front wing side—L.H.	1	
BX9	612962	**Peg,** bonnet location	2	
BX10	JN2108	**Nut,** jam ⎫ Securing bonnet	2	
BX11	WP0008	**Washer,** plain ⎭ location peg	2	
BX12	903138	**Panel,** front wheelarch, outer—R.H.	1	
BX13	903137	**Panel,** front wheelarch, outer—L.H.	1	
BX14	706549	**Panel,** front wheelarch, inner—R.H.	1	
BX15	706548	**Panel,** front wheelarch, inner—L.H.	1	
BX16	907158	**Panel,** nose—R.H.	1	
BX17	907157	**Panel,** nose—L.H.	1	
	612874	**Bracket,** reinforcement, headlamp mounting—R.H.	1	
BX18	612873	**Bracket,** reinforcement, headlamp mounting—L.H.	1	
BX19	706312	**Panel,** filler, nose to wheelarch—R.H.	1	
BX20	706311	**Panel,** filler, nose to wheelarch—L.H.	1	
BX21	810261	**Panel** assembly, closing grille aperture to wheelarch—R.H.	1	
BX22	810260	**Panel** assembly, closing grille aperture to wheelarch—L.H.	1	
	612660	**Support,** front wheelarch to wing—R.H.	1	
BX23	612659	**Support,** front wheelarch to wing—L.H.	1	
	608643	**Packing,** sponge rubber, bonnet	2	
BX24	622500	**Top** assembly, bonnet	1	
	706453	**Reinforcement,** front edge	1	
	603559	**Clip,** wiring	6	
BX25	706539	**Tube** assembly, bonnet, rear	1	
	607628	**Bracket,** bonnet tube	1	
	613076	**Clamp** assembly, bonnet tube, rear	2	
	HU0706	**Screw,** set ⎫	4	
	WP0120	**Washer,** plain ⎬ Rear bonnet tube to wheelarch	4	
	WL0207	**Washer,** lock ⎭	4	
	HN2007	**Nut** ⎫	2	
	WL0207	**Washer,** lock ⎬ Bonnet tube to	2	
	WP0120	**Washer,** plain ⎨ bonnet top	2	
	608643	**Packing,** sponge rubber ⎭	2	
BX26	811680	**Tube** assembly, bonnet hinge—R.H.	1	
BX27	811679	**Tube** assembly, bonnet hinge—L.H.	1	
BX28	607869	**Bracket,** anchor, rear bonnet hinge tube	4	
BX29	607711	**Plate,** backing ⎫	4	
	HU0706	**Screw,** set ⎬ Anchor brackets	8	
	WP0007	**Washer,** plain ⎨ to wheelarch	8	
	WL0207	**Washer,** lock ⎭	8	

Note:—Items marked thus † are available on our Factory Exchange Unit Scheme

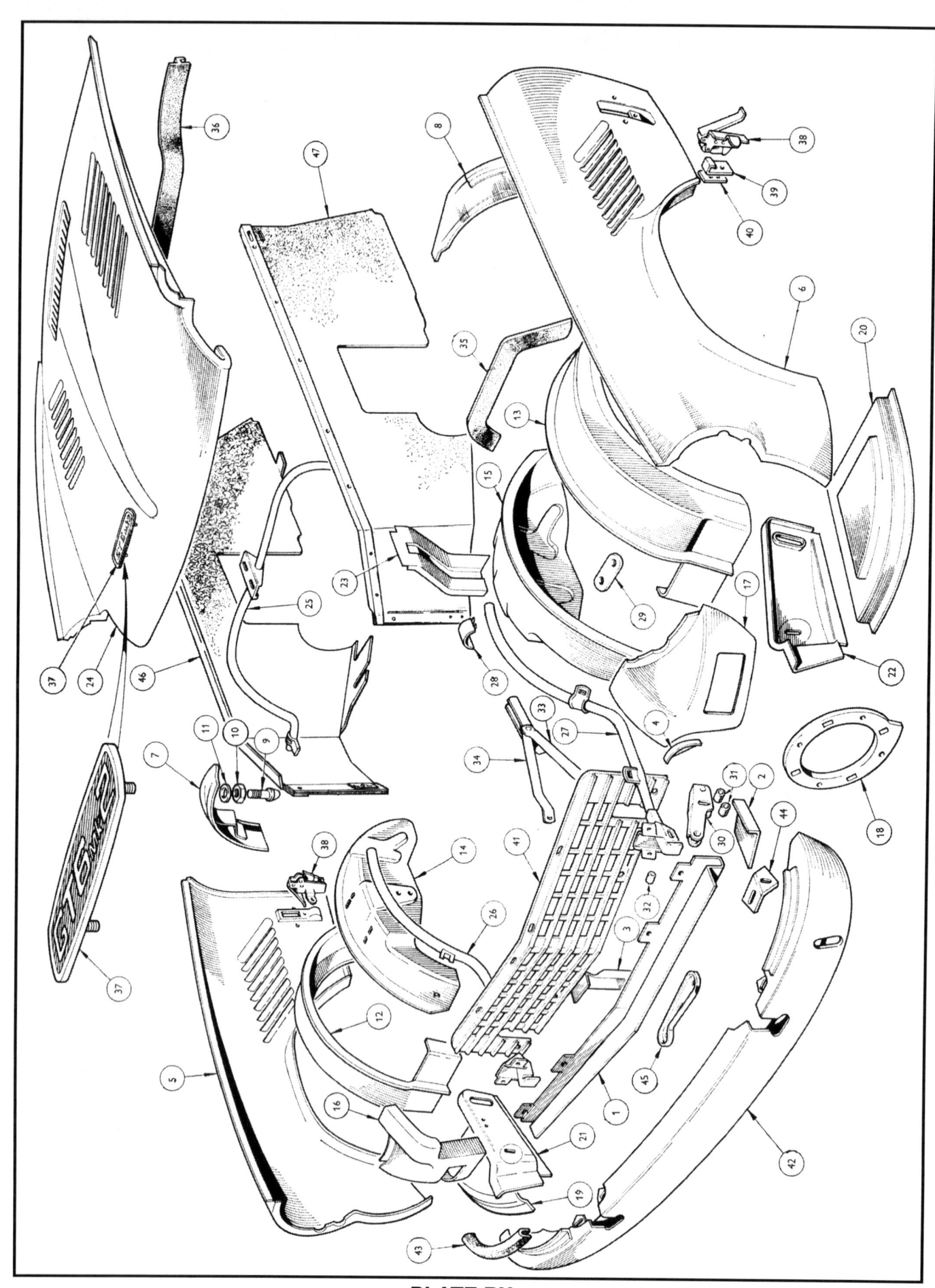

PLATE BX

BODY AND FITTINGS

Plate No.	Part No.	Description		No. per Unit	Remarks
		BONNET ASSEMBLY—Mk. II Cars only			
		—continued			
	HU0706	**Screw,** set	⎫	4	
	WL0207	**Washer,** lock	⎪ Bonnet tube	4	
	WP0120	**Washer,** plain	⎬ to closing panel	4	
	WP0007	**Washer,** plain	⎪ and wheelarch	4	
	HN2007	**Nut**	⎭	4	
BX30	712726	**Bracket,** hinge, assembly, bonnet lower		2	
BX31	621418	**Tube,** distance	⎫	4	
	WM0058	**Washer,** plain	⎪ Bonnet hinge bracket	8	
	TN3208	**Nut,** nyloc	⎬ to frame	4	
	HB0818	**Bolt**	⎭	4	
	HB0919	**Bolt**	⎫	2	
	WP0009	**Washer,** plain	⎪ Bonnet hinge tube	4	
	WP0048	**Washer,** plain	⎬ to	4	
	TN3209	**Nut,** nyloc	⎪ bonnet hinge pivot bracket	2	
BX32	621419	**Spacer,** bonnet fulcrum pin	⎭	2	
BX33	613751	**Link** assembly, lower, bonnet stay		1	
BX34	613045	**Link** assembly, upper, bonnet stay		1	
	HB0710	**Bolt**	⎫	1	
	YN2907	**Nut,** nyloc	⎬ Upper link to lower link	1	
	WP0007	**Washer,** plain	⎪	1	
	WP0042	**Washer,** plain	⎭	2	
	HB0708	**Bolt,** hex.	⎫	1	
	YN2907	**Nut**	⎬ Attaching lower link to chassis	1	
	WP0007	**Washer,** plain	⎭	1	
	HB0708	**Bolt**	⎫	1	
	YN2907	**Nut,** nyloc	⎪	1	
	WP0007	**Washer,** plain	⎬ Attaching upper link to wheelarch	1	
	WM0816	**Washer,** plain	⎪	1	
	WP0117	**Washer,** plain	⎭	1	
BX35	613666	**Seal,** rear, front wheelarch to dash		2	
	608520	**Clip,** seal attachment		18	
BX36	610675	**Rubber,** sealing, bonnet		1	
	622496	**Name plate,** "G.T.6+"		1	U.S.A. only
BX37	623873	**Name plate,** "G.T.6 MK. II"		1	Markets other than U.S.A.
	614006	**Bush,** friction, securing name plate to bonnet		2	
BX38	607663	**BONNET CATCH ASSEMBLY** —Mk. II Cars only		2	
	510293	**Screw,** set	⎫	6	
	HN2054	**Nut**	⎪	6	
	WQ0304	**Washer,** lock	⎬ Bonnet catch attachment	6	
	WM0054	**Washer,** medium	⎪	6	
	WN0704	**Washer,** shakeproof	⎭	6	
BX39	607664	**Plate,** catch, bonnet lock, dash side front lower		2	
	613474	**Washer,** catch plate		2	
BX40	609931	**Plate,** tapping	⎫	2	
	HU0706	**Screw,** set	⎬ Catch plate	4	
	WP0127	**Washer,** plain	⎪ to dash side	4	
	WN0707	**Washer,** shakeproof	⎭	4	

Note:— For Bonnet Locating Plate Details see Dash, Body Side and Roof Panel section.

Note:—Items marked thus † are available on our Factory Exchange Unit Scheme

119

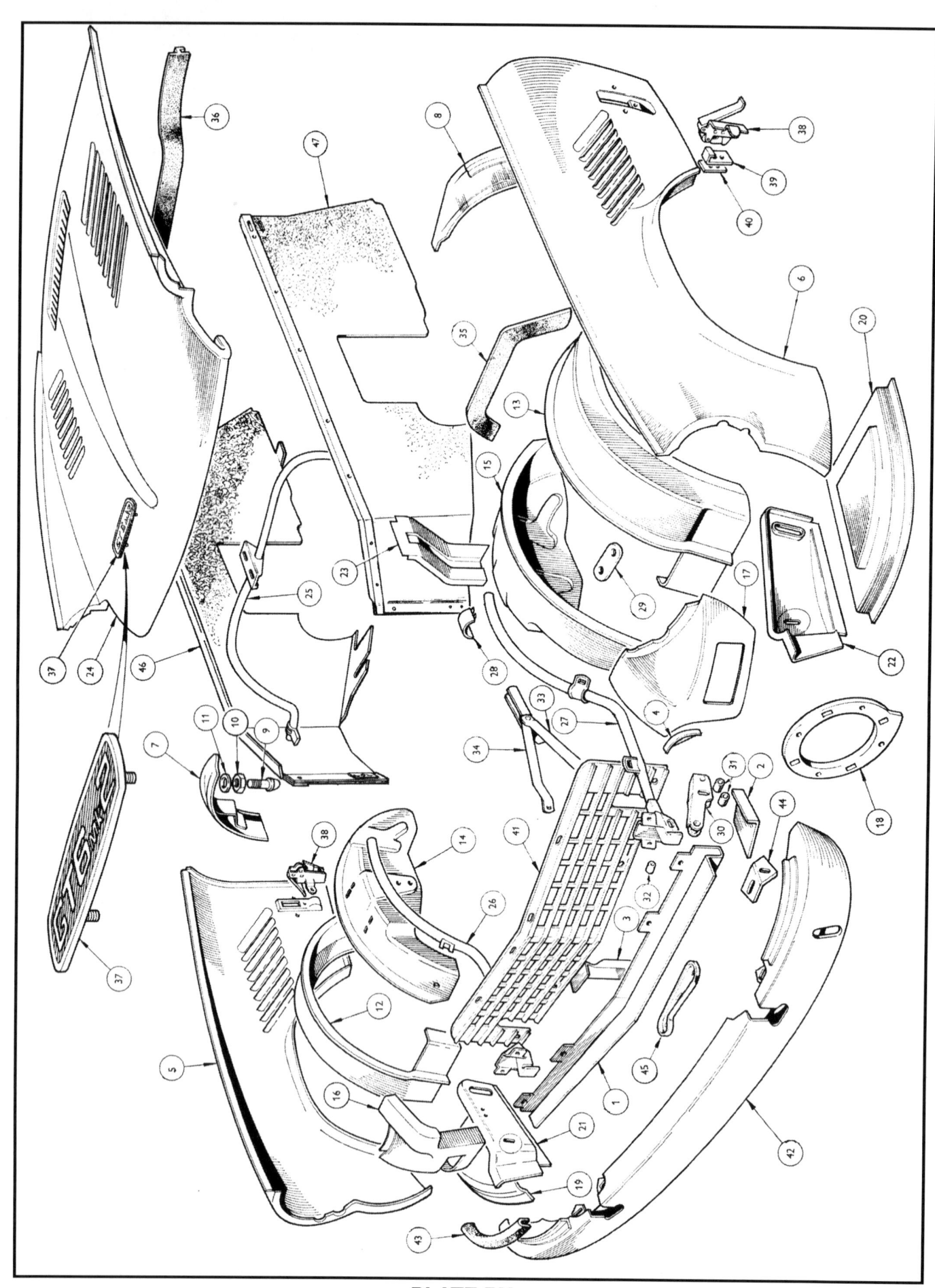

PLATE BX

BODY AND FITTINGS

Plate No.	Part No.	Description	No. per Unit	Remarks
BX41	810402	**RADIATOR GRILLE ASSEMBLY** —Mk. II Cars only	1	
	FZ3404/4	**Nut**, retained ⎫	8	
	512462	**Screw**, set ⎪	6	
	515328	**Screw**, set ⎬ Radiator grille attachment	2	
	514438	**Washer**, plain ⎪	8	
	WL0205	**Washer**, lock ⎪	8	
	WM0816	**Washer**, medium, packing ⎭	2	
BX42	811676	**FRONT VALANCE ASSEMBLY** —Mk. II Cars only	1	
BX43	610676	**Seal**, front valance to bonnet	2	
	612830	**Bracket**, support, front valance, outer—R.H.	1	
BX44	612829	**Bracket**, support, front valance, outer—L.H.	1	
	HU0706P	**Screw**, set ⎫	2	
	WP0120	**Washer**, plain ⎬ Support bracket to valance	2	
	WL0207	**Washer**, lock ⎭	2	
	HU0706P	**Screw**, set ⎫	2	
	WP0120	**Washer**, plain ⎪ Attaching support brackets, front	4	
	WL0207	**Washer**, lock ⎬ valance, outer, to chassis frame	2	
	HN2007	**Nut** ⎭	2	
	712568	**Bracket**, support, front valance—R.H.	1	
BX45	712567	**Bracket**, support, front valance—L.H.	1	
	HU0706P	**Screw**, set ⎫	4	
	WP0007	**Washer**, plain ⎬ Support brackets to valance	4	
	FQ3405/4	**Nut**, retained ⎭	4	
	HU0708P	**Screw**, set ⎫	2	
	WP0007	**Washer**, plain ⎪ Support bracket to	2	
	WL0207	**Washer**, lock ⎬ overrider mounting brackets	2	
	CD26326	**Pad**, mounting ⎪	As Req'd	
	HN2007	**Nut** ⎭	2	
BX46	905222	**ENGINE BAY VALANCE ASSEMBLY, R.H.** (MK. II CARS ONLY)	1	
BX47	910045	**ENGINE BAY VALANCE ASSEMBLY, L.H.** (MK. II CARS ONLY)	1	
	573948	**Nut**, twin impression	2	
	RB5404	**Rivet**, twin nut attachment	2	
	YH6506	**Screw**, self-tapping, lower front valance and radiator cowl lower attachment	4	
	HU0505	**Screw**, set ⎫	4	
	WP0005	**Washer**, plain ⎪	8	
	WL0205	**Washer**, lock ⎬ Engine bay valance to dash front	4	
	615699	**Washer**, plate ⎪	2	
	RB5510	**Rivet**, bifurcated ⎪	4	
	WP0028	**Washer**, plain ⎪	4	
	HN2005	**Nut** ⎭	4	
	619822	**Clip**, edge	4	

Note:- For Radiator Cowl see Radiator section.

Note:—Items marked thus † are available on our Factory Exchange Unit Scheme

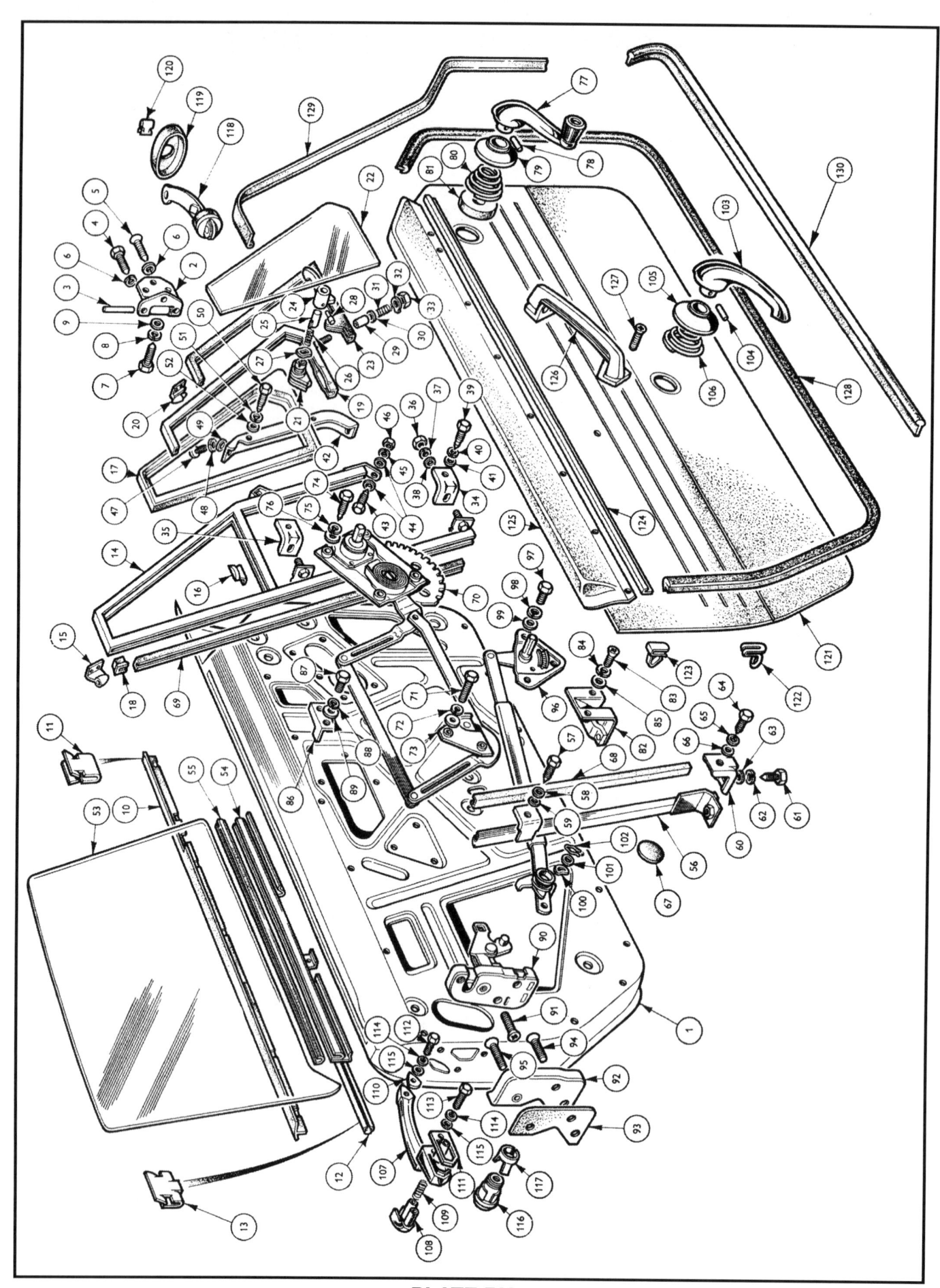

PLATE BY

BODY AND FITTINGS

Plate No.	Part No.	Description	No. per Unit	Remarks
	905231	**FRONT DOOR ASSEMBLY—R.H.**	1	Fitted up to Commission No. KC9999 L.H.S. and Body No. 21736KC R.H.S. only
BY1	905230	**FRONT DOOR ASSEMBLY—L.H.**	1	
	908022	**FRONT DOOR ASSEMBLY—R.H.**	1	Fitted from Commission No. KC10000 L.H.S. and Body No. 21737KC R.H.S., and future
	908021	**FRONT DOOR ASSEMBLY—L.H.**	1	
	617078	**Pad,** sound deadening, door panel	2	
BY2	607824	**Hinge,** door, assembly	4	
BY3	607823	**Pin,** hinge door	4	
BY4	HU0807P	**Screw,** set ⎫	8	
BY5	KX4806P	**Screw,** set ⎬ Hinge to door	4	
BY6	WL0208	**Washer,** lock ⎭	12	
BY7	HU0807P	**Screw,** set ⎫	12	
BY8	WL0208	**Washer,** lock ⎬ Hinge to 'A' post	12	
BY9	610042	**Washer** ⎭	4	
	710574	**Strip,** sealing, rubber, door waist, outer—R.H.	1	
BY10	710573	**Strip,** sealing, rubber, door waist, outer—L.H.	1	
BY11	613169	**Clip,** sealing, rubber attachment	14	
BY12	617321	**Weatherstrip,** waist, inner	2	
BY13	608604	**Clip,** securing waist weatherstrip	8	
	810313	**FRONT DOOR VENTILATOR ASSEMBLY —COMPLETE—R.H.**	1	
	810312	**FRONT DOOR VENTILATOR ASSEMBLY —COMPLETE—L.H.**	1	
	574091	**Surround and guide rail,** assembly—R.H.	1	
BY14	574090	**Surround and guide rail,** assembly—L.H.	1	
	574093	**Pivot,** top, outer—R.H.	1	
BY15	574092	**Pivot,** top, outer—L.H.	1	
	574097	**Screw,** chrome, pivot to surround	4	
	574095	**Plate,** catch locking—R.H.	1	
BY16	574094	**Plate,** catch locking—L.H.	1	
	574096	**Rivet,** catch plate attachment	4	
	574099	**Weatherseal**—R.H.	1	
BY17	574098	**Weatherseal**—L.H.	1	
BY18	574100	**Cover,** top corner	2	
	574102	**Frame assembly,** vent inner, glazed, complete—R.H.	1	
	574101	**Frame assembly,** vent inner, glazed, complete—L.H.	1	
	574104	**Frame assembly,** ventilator—R.H.	1	
BY19	574103	**Frame assembly,** ventilator—L.H.	1	
	574106	**Pivot,** top, inner—R.H.	1	
BY20	574105	**Pivot,** top, inner—L.H.	1	
	574107	**Rivet,** pivot attachment	4	
	574117	**Bracket,** catch handle—R.H.	1	
BY21	574116	**Bracket,** catch handle—L.H.	1	
	574118	**Rivet,** catch bracket	4	
	574064	**Glass,** ventilator—R.H.	1	
BY22	574063	**Glass,** ventilator—L.H.	1	
BY23	574109	**Strip,** glazing	2	
	574111	**Handle,** catch—R.H.	1	
BY24	574110	**Handle,** catch—L.H.	1	
BY25	608540	**Button,** push, handle	2	
BY26	608542	**Spring,** push button	2	
BY27	570220	**Washer,** spring	2	
BY28	573081	**Pin,** Mills, handle retaining	2	

Note:—Items marked thus † are available on our Factory Exchange Unit Scheme

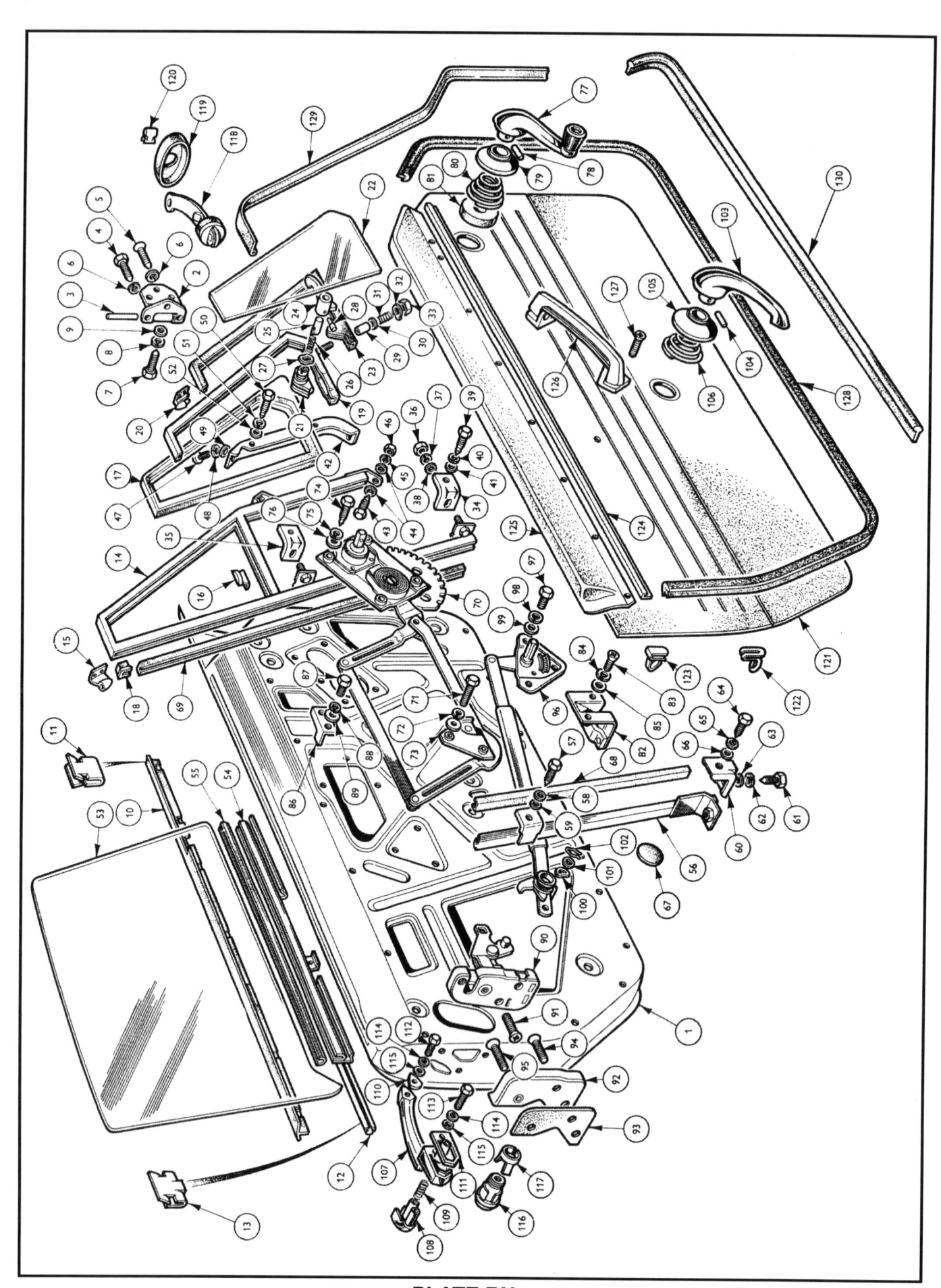

PLATE BY

BODY AND FITTINGS

Plate No.	Part No.	Description	No. per Unit	Remarks

FRONT DOOR DETAILS—continued
FRONT DOOR VENTILATOR ASSEMBLY—cont.

Plate No.	Part No.	Description	No. per Unit	Remarks
BY29	574112	**Tube**, spacer ⎫	2	
BY30	574113	**Washer** ⎬ Lower pivot attachment	2	
BY31	574114	**Spring**, friction ⎬ to outer frame	2	
BY32	574115	**Washer**, tab ⎪	2	
BY33	HN2007	**Nut**, hex. ⎭	2	
BY34	619244	**Bracket** assembly, ventilator support (Bottom front glass channel)	2	
BY35	619242	**Bracket** assembly, ventilator support (Top front glass channel)	2	
BY36	HN2007	**Nut** ⎫ Upper and lower	4	
BY37	WL0207	**Washer**, lock ⎬ ventilator fixing	4	
BY38	WM0057	**Washer**, medium ⎭ to bracket	4	
BY39	HU0705D	**Screw**, set ⎫ Upper and lower	4	
BY40	WL0207	**Washer**, lock ⎬ ventilator support brackets	4	
BY41	WP0139	**Washer**, medium ⎭ to door inner panel	4	
	619250	**Bracket** assembly, front ventilator to door—R.H.	1	
BY42	619249	**Bracket** assembly, front ventilator to door—L.H.	1	
BY43	HU0706D	**Screw**, set ⎫	2	
BY44	WM0057	**Washer**, medium ⎬ Ventilator lower	4	
BY45	WL0207	**Washer**, lock ⎬ fixings to bracket	2	
BY46	HN2007	**Nut** ⎭	2	
BY47	PX0707D	**Screw**, set ⎫	2	
BY48	WL0207	**Washer**, lock ⎬ Ventilator upper fixing to bracket	2	
BY49	WM0057	**Washer**, medium ⎭	2	
BY50	HU0705D	**Screw**, set ⎫ Front ventilator	4	
BY51	WL0207	**Washer**, lock ⎬ fixing bracket to	4	
BY52	WP0139	**Washer**, medium ⎭ door inner panel	4	

DOOR GLASS AND REGULATOR CHANNEL DETAILS

Plate No.	Part No.	Description	No. per Unit	Remarks
	810042	**Glass**, window, front door—R.H.	1	
BY53	810041	**Glass**, window, front door—L.H.	1	
	710620	**Channel** assembly, bottom, window regulator—R.H.	1	⎫ Fitted up to Commission
BY54	710619	**Channel** assembly, bottom, window regulator—L.H.	1	⎬ No. KC8146 only
	713035	**Channel** assembly, bottom, window regulator	2	Fitted from Commission No. KC8147 and future
BY55	617164	**Strip**, glazing	2	
	710195	**Channel**, glass, assembly, rear—R.H.	1	
BY56	710194	**Channel**, glass, assembly, rear—L.H.	1	
BY57	HU0705P	**Screw**, set	2	
BY58	WL0207	**Washer**, lock ⎬ Rear glass channel to door inner panel	2	
BY59	WP0139	**Washer**, medium ⎭	2	
BY60	619242	**Bracket** assembly, bottom, rear glass channel support	2	
BY61	HU0705P	**Screw**, set ⎫	2	
BY62	WL0207	**Washer**, lock ⎬ Bottom support bracket to rear glass channel	2	
BY63	WM0057	**Washer**, plain ⎭	2	
BY64	HU0705P	**Screw**, set ⎫	2	
BY65	WL0207	**Washer**, lock ⎬ Bottom support bracket to door inner panel	2	
BY66	WP0139	**Washer**, plain ⎭	2	
BY67	600421	**Plug**, blanking, door front and rear face	4	
BY68	710650	**Rubber**, glazing, silent run, rear glass channel	2	
BY69	710651	**Rubber**, glazing, silent run, front glass channel	2	

Note:—Items marked thus † are available on our Factory Exchange Unit Scheme

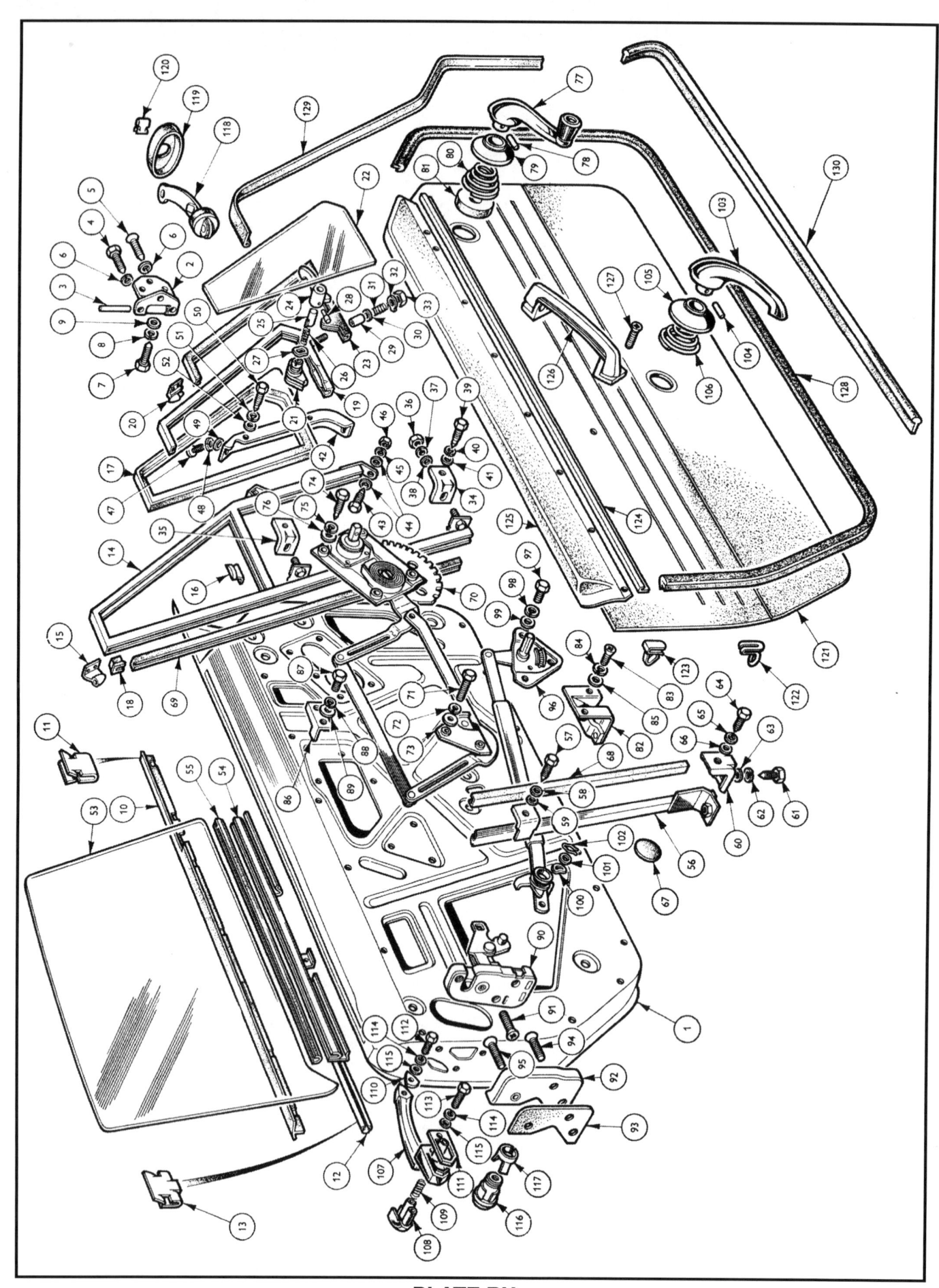

PLATE BY

BODY AND FITTINGS

Plate No.	Part No.	Description	No. per Unit	Remarks
		FRONT DOOR DETAILS—continued		
	810401	**WINDOW REGULATOR ASSEMBLY—R.H.**	1	
BY70	810400	**WINDOW REGULATOR ASSEMBLY—L.H.**	1	
BY71	HU0704	**Screw**, set ⎫ Auxiliary plate,	4	
BY72	WL0207	**Washer**, lock ⎬ window regulator to	4	
BY73	WP0007	**Washer**, plain ⎭ door inner panel	6	
BY74	HU0704	**Screw**, set ⎫	8	
BY75	WL0207	**Washer**, lock ⎬ Window regulator to door inner panel	8	
BY76	WP0007	**Washer**, plain ⎭	8	
BY77	613017	**WINDOW REGULATOR HANDLE**	2	⎫
BY78	600832	**Pin**, handle attachment	2	⎪ Mk. I Cars only.
BY79	650261	**Escutcheon**, handle	2	⎬ Fitted up to Commission
BY80	603382	**Spring**, regulator escutcheon	2	⎪ No. KC50000 only
BY81	609649	**Washer**, sealing rubber	2	⎭
	621811	**WINDOW REGULATOR HANDLE ASSEMBLY**	2	⎫
	623843	**Escutcheon**	2	⎪ Mk. II Cars only.
	603382	**Spring**, escutcheon	2	⎬ Fitted from Commission
	609649	**Washer**, sealing	2	⎪ No. KC50001
	600832	**Pin**, securing handle	2	⎪
	621768	**Knob**, handle	2	⎪
	574581	**Retainer**	2	⎭
BY82	613378	**Bracket** assembly, door glass stop, lower	2	Fitted up to Commission No. KC8146 only
	621672	**Bracket** assembly, door glass stop, lower—R.H.	1	⎫ Fitted from Commission
	621671	**Bracket** assembly, door glass stop, lower—L.H.	1	⎭ No. KC8147 and future
BY83	PX0504	**Screw**, set ⎫	4	Fitted up to Commission No. KC8146 only
	HU0504P	**Screw**, set ⎬ Lower glass stop bracket to door inner panel	4	Fitted from Commission No. KC8147 and future
BY84	WL0205	**Washer**, lock	4	
BY85	WP0005	**Washer**, plain	4	
	619267	**Bracket**, door glass stop, upper—R.H.	1	
BY86	619266	**Bracket**, door glass stop, upper—L.H.	1	
BY87	HU0503P	**Screw**, set ⎫ Upper glass stop bracket	4	
BY88	WL0205	**Washer**, lock ⎬ to door inner panel	4	
BY89	WP0156	**Washer**, plain ⎭	4	
	810292	**DOOR LOCK ASSEMBLY—R.H.**	1	⎫
BY90	810291	**DOOR LOCK ASSEMBLY—L.H.**	1	⎪ Fitted up to
BY91	KT4707	**Screw**, set, lock to door inner panel	6	⎪ Commission No.
	FQ3405	**Nut**, retainer, lock to door inner panel	2	⎬ KC9999 L.H.S., and
	618343	**Striker**, dovetail assembly, door lock—R.H.	1	⎪ Body No. 21736KC
BY92	618342	**Striker**, dovetail assembly, door lock—L.H.	1	⎭ R.H.S. only
BY93	619076	**Washer**, sealing ⎫	2	
BY94	KT4704	**Screw**, set ⎬ Securing striker dovetail to 'B' post	4	
BY95	KT4708	**Screw**, set ⎭	2	

Note:—Items marked thus † are available on our Factory Exchange Unit Scheme

123

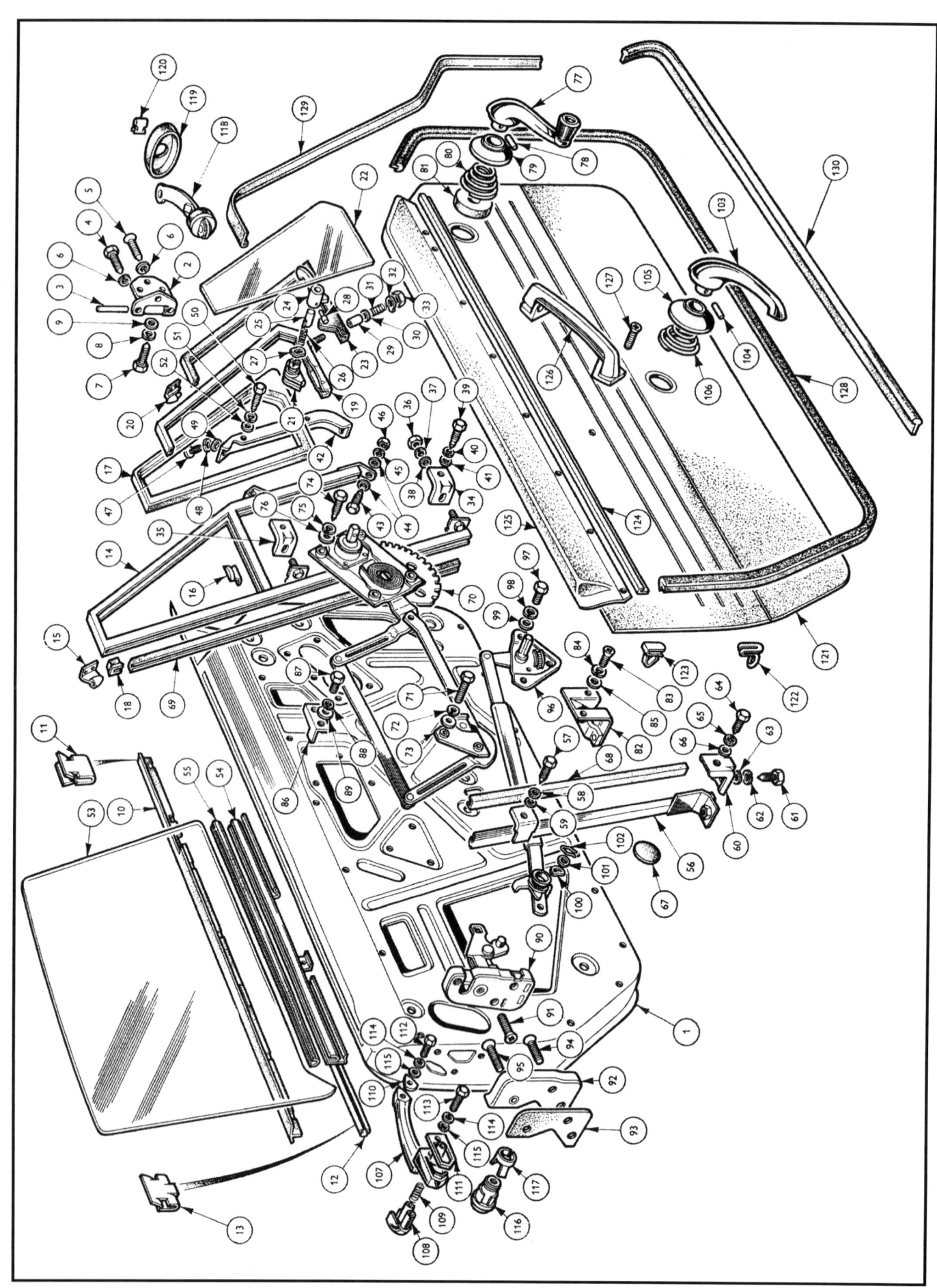

PLATE BY

BODY AND FITTINGS

Plate No.	Part No.	Description	No. per Unit	Remarks
		FRONT DOOR DETAILS—continued		
	907178	**DOOR LOCK ASSEMBLY—R.H.**	1	
	907177	**DOOR LOCK ASSEMBLY—L.H.**	1	Fitted from Commission
	517148	Screw, set, Longlok, lock to door inner panel	6	No. KC10000 L.H.S.
	621877	Striker, dovetail, assembly—R.H.	1	and Body
	621876	Striker, dovetail, assembly—L.H.	1	No. 21737KC R.H.S.
	621714	Shim, packing	2	and future
	517145	Setscrew, Longlok } Securing striker dovetail to 'B' post	4	
	517150	Setscrew, Longlok	4	
	618278	**REMOTE CONTROL MECHANISM AND LINK ASSEMBLY—R.H.**	1	Fitted up to Commission No. KC9999 L.H.S. and
BY96	618277	**REMOTE CONTROL MECHANISM AND LINK ASSEMBLY—L.H.**	1	Body No. 21736KC R.H.S. only
	714651	**REMOTE CONTROL MECHANISM AND LINK ASSEMBLY—R.H.**	1	Fitted from Commission No. KC10000 L.H.S. and Body
	714650	**REMOTE CONTROL MECHANISM AND LINK ASSEMBLY—L.H.**	1	No. 21737KC R.H.S. and future
BY97	HU0503	Screw, set } Remote control mechanism	6	
BY98	WL0205	Washer, lock } to door inner panel	6	
BY99	WP0005	Washer, plain	6	
BY100	550924	Washer, waved	2	
BY101	WP0161	Washer, plain } Remote control link to door lock	4	
BY102	608703	Clip	2	
BY103	608454	Handle, remote control mechanism	2	
BY104	600832	Pin, handle attachment	2	Mk. I Cars only. Fitted up to
BY105	650261	Escutcheon, inside handle	2	Commission No. KC50000 only
BY106	603382	Spring, remote control escutcheon	2	
	621770	Handle, remote control mechanism	2	
	600832	Pin, handle attachment	2	Mk. II Cars only. Fitted from
	623843	Escutcheon, remote control handle	2	Comm. No. KC50001 and future
	603382	Spring, remote control escutcheon	2	
BY107	709386	**OUTSIDE DOOR HANDLE AND PUSH BUTTON ASSEMBLY**	2	
BY108	571286	Push button	2	
BY109	571201	Spring, push button	2	
	571289	Screw, set, lock actuating	2	
	HN2005	Nut, locking setscrew	2	
	571287	Screw, set } Spring retaining	2	
	571288	Washer, shakeproof	2	
BY110	617402	Washer, seating, front	2	
BY111	617403	Washer, seating, rear	2	
BY112	HU0503	Screw, set } Outside handle	2	
BY113	HU0504	Screw, set } to door	2	
BY114	WL0205	Washer, lock	4	
BY115	WP0005	Washer, plain	4	

Note:—Items marked thus † are available on our Factory Exchange Unit Scheme

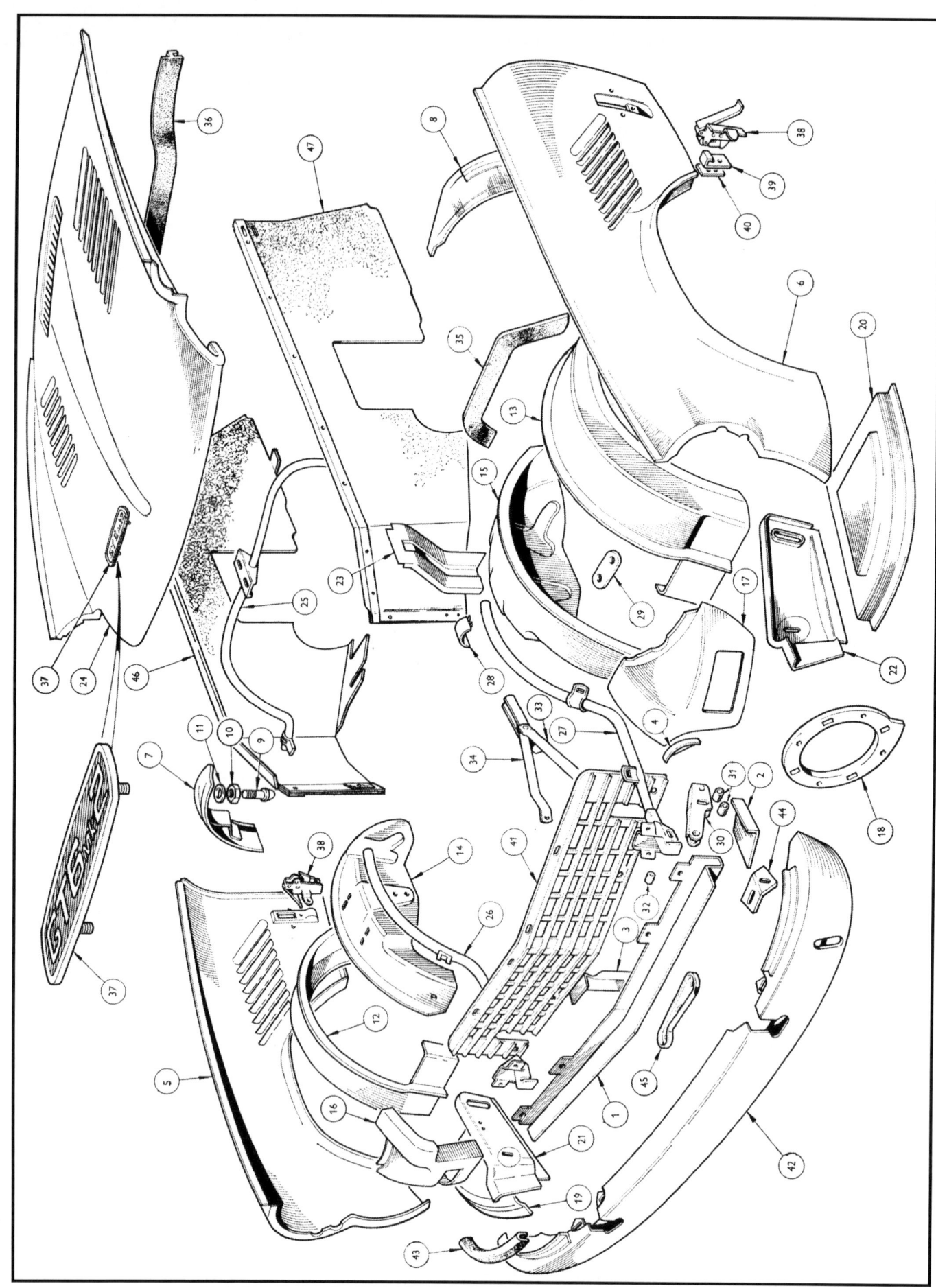

PLATE BY

BODY AND FITTINGS

Plate No.	Part No.	Description	No. per Unit	Remarks
		FRONT DOOR DETAILS—continued		
	618283	**PRIVATE LOCK ASSEMBLY—R.H.**	1	⎫ Fitted up to Commission No. KC4799 only
BY116	618282	**PRIVATE LOCK ASSEMBLY—L.H.**	1	⎬
BY117	616861	Clip, spring, private lock	2	⎭
	621773	**PRIVATE LOCK ASSEMBLY**	2	⎫ Fitted from Commission No. KC4800 and future
	621733	Clip, spring	2	⎬
	621732	Washer, seating	2	⎭
BY118	613024	**CHECK ARM ASSEMBLY, DOOR**	2	
BY119	602821	Seal, check arm	2	
BY120	553121	Clip, seal to door	4	
	613239	Rivet, check arm to body	2	
	710302	**FRONT DOOR TRIM PAD ASSEMBLY (RED)—R.H.**	1	⎫
BY121	710292	**FRONT DOOR TRIM PAD ASSEMBLY (RED)—L.H.**	1	
	710303	**FRONT DOOR TRIM PAD ASSEMBLY (LIGHT TAN)—R.H.**	1	
BY121	710293	**FRONT DOOR TRIM PAD ASSEMBLY (LIGHT TAN)—L.H.**	1	
	710306	**FRONT DOOR TRIM PAD ASSEMBLY (MIDNIGHT BLUE)—R.H.**	1	Fitted up to Commission No. KC9999 L.H.S. and Body No. 21736KC R.H.S. only
BY121	710296	**FRONT DOOR TRIM PAD ASSEMBLY (MIDNIGHT BLUE)—L.H.**	1	
	710307	**FRONT DOOR TRIM PAD ASSEMBLY (SHADOW BLUE)—R.H.**	1	
BY121	710297	**FRONT DOOR TRIM PAD ASSEMBLY (SHADOW BLUE)—L.H.**	1	
	710301	**FRONT DOOR TRIM PAD ASSEMBLY (BLACK)—R.H.**	1	
BY121	710291	**FRONT DOOR TRIM PAD ASSEMBLY (BLACK)—L.H.**	1	⎭

Note:—Items marked thus † are available on our Factory Exchange Unit Scheme

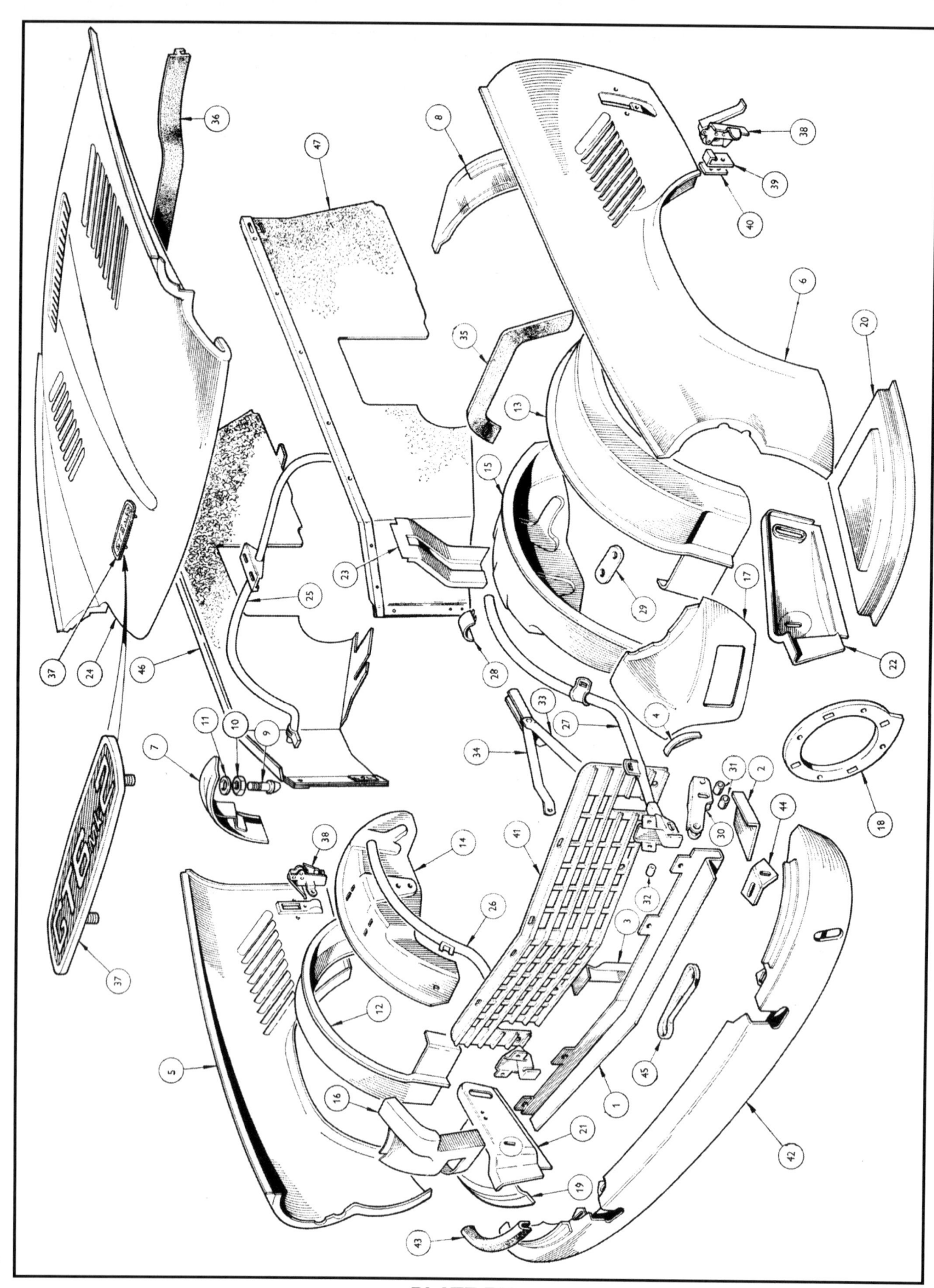

PLATE BY

BODY AND FITTINGS

Plate No.	Part No.	Description	No. per Unit	Remarks
	714502	FRONT DOOR TRIM PAD ASSEMBLY (RED)—R.H.	1	
	714492	FRONT DOOR TRIM PAD ASSEMBLY (RED)—L.H.	1	
	714503	FRONT DOOR TRIM PAD ASSEMBLY (LIGHT TAN)—R.H.	1	
	714493	FRONT DOOR TRIM PAD ASSEMBLY (LIGHT TAN)—L.H.	1	
	714506	FRONT DOOR TRIM PAD ASSEMBLY (MIDNIGHT BLUE)—R.H.	1	Fitted from Commission No. KC10000 L.H.S. and Body No. 21737KC R.H.S. and future
	714496	FRONT DOOR TRIM PAD ASSEMBLY (MIDNIGHT BLUE)—L.H.	1	
	714507	FRONT DOOR TRIM PAD ASSEMBLY (SHADOW BLUE)—R.H.	1	
	714497	FRONT DOOR TRIM PAD ASSEMBLY (SHADOW BLUE)—L.H.	1	
	714501	FRONT DOOR TRIM PAD ASSEMBLY (BLACK)—R.H.	1	
	714491	FRONT DOOR TRIM PAD ASSEMBLY (BLACK)—L.H.	1	
BY122	608511	Clip, trim, pad to door	28	
BY123	608516	Clip, trim, heavy duty, pad to door	14	
	508566	Screw, self-tapping ⎱ Door trim pad	2	
	CD24152	Washer, cup ⎰ attachment	2	
BY124	Not Serviced	Finisher, trim, door, front		
	810651	Capping, front door waist, inner—R.H.	1	
BY125	810641	Capping, front door waist, inner—L.H.	1	
BY126	619680	Door pull assembly	2	
BY127	511664	Screw, set, door pull attachment	4	
	622352	Mirror, exterior, driver's door	1	U.S.A. only
	622351	Head, mirror	1	
	622350	Stem, exterior mirror	1	
		SEALING DETAILS—DOOR APERTURE		
	709864	Door seal, "Neoprene"—R.H.	1	
BY128	709863	Door seal, "Neoprene"—L.H.	1	
BY129	620914	Strip, sealing, 'A' post to door glass	2	Alternative to 612260
	612260	Strip, sealing, 'A' post to door glass	2	Alternative to 620914
BY130	620656	Rubber, sealing, front door sill	2	

Note:—Items marked thus † are available on our Factory Exchange Unit Scheme

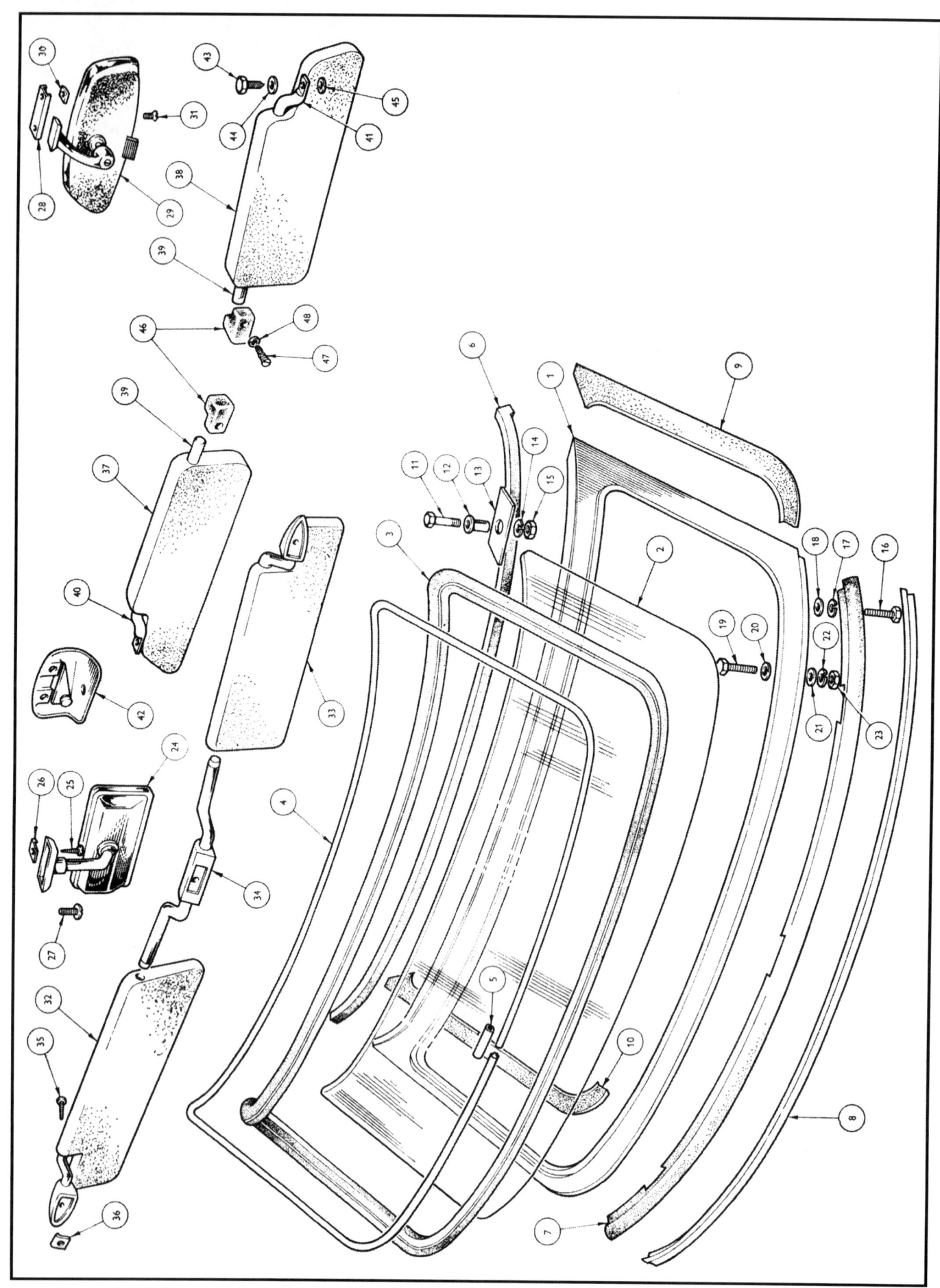

PLATE BZ

BODY AND FITTINGS

Plate No.	Part No.	Description	No. per Unit	Remarks
		WINDSCREEN DETAILS		
BZ1	904719	**Frame** assembly, windscreen	1	Fitted up to Commission No. KC50000 only
	714432	**Frame** assembly, windscreen	1	Fitted from Commission No. KC50001 and future
BZ2	902367	**Glass**, windscreen (Laminated)	1	Special order only
BZ2	903467	**Glass**, windscreen, toughened (Zoned)—R.H.S.	1	
BZ2	903466	**Glass**, windscreen, toughened (Zoned)—L.H.S.	1	
	906707	**Glass**, windscreen—Laminated (High impact interlayer)	1	U.S.A., Sweden and Special orders
BZ3	902369	**Rubber**, glazing, windscreen	1	
BZ4	613954	**Finisher**, windscreen	1	
BZ5	611437	**Clip**, windscreen finisher attachment	1	
BZ6	806144	**Rubber**, sealing, windscreen to header	1	
BZ7	650130	**Rubber**, sealing, windscreen to scuttle	1	
BZ8	708759	**Cover**, trim, windscreen bottom rail	1	
BZ9	620191	**Cover**, trim, windscreen, side (Black)—L.H.	1	
BZ10	620201	**Cover**, trim, windscreen, side (Black)—R.H.	1	
BZ11	KX4818	**Screw**, set	2	
BZ12	619882	**Tube**, distance, assembly	2	
BZ13	619884	**Plate**, reinforcement — Windscreen frame to roof	2	
BZ14	WL0208	**Washer**, lock	2	
BZ15	HN2008	**Nut**	2	
BZ16	HU0708/P	**Screw**, set — Windscreen fixing	2	
BZ17	WL0207	**Washer**, lock — plate outer to	2	
BZ18	WP0120	**Washer**, plain — body outer	2	
BZ19	HU0807	**Screw**, set	3	
BZ20	WM0058	**Washer**, plain — Windscreen attachment	3	
BZ21	WM0058	**Washer**, plain — plate inner to	3	
BZ22	WL0208	**Washer**, lock — front deck panel	3	
BZ23	HN2008	**Nut**	3	
		INTERIOR MIRROR DETAILS		
BZ24	613871	**Interior mirror** assembly	1	All markets except U.S.A. — Fitted up to Commission No. KC50000 only
BZ25	510857	**Screw**, self-tapping — Alternative fitment to 512461 — Mirror attachment	2	
BZ26	FJ2445/9	**Nut**, fix	2	
BZ27	512461	**Setscrew** (Alternative fitment to 510857 and FJ2445/9)	2	
	621767	**Interior mirror** assembly (Non reflective)	1	U.S.A. only
	512461	**Setscrew**, mirror attachment	2	
		Note:— 621767 may be used for replacements in all markets up to Commission No. KC50000.		
BZ28	621704	**Base**, interior mirror	1	Fitted from Commission No. KC50001 and future
BZ29	574937	**Head and stem** assembly	1	
BZ30	621705	**Retainer**, interior mirror	2	
BZ31	512461	**Setscrew**, mirror attachment	2	

Note:—Items marked thus † are available on our Factory Exchange Unit Scheme

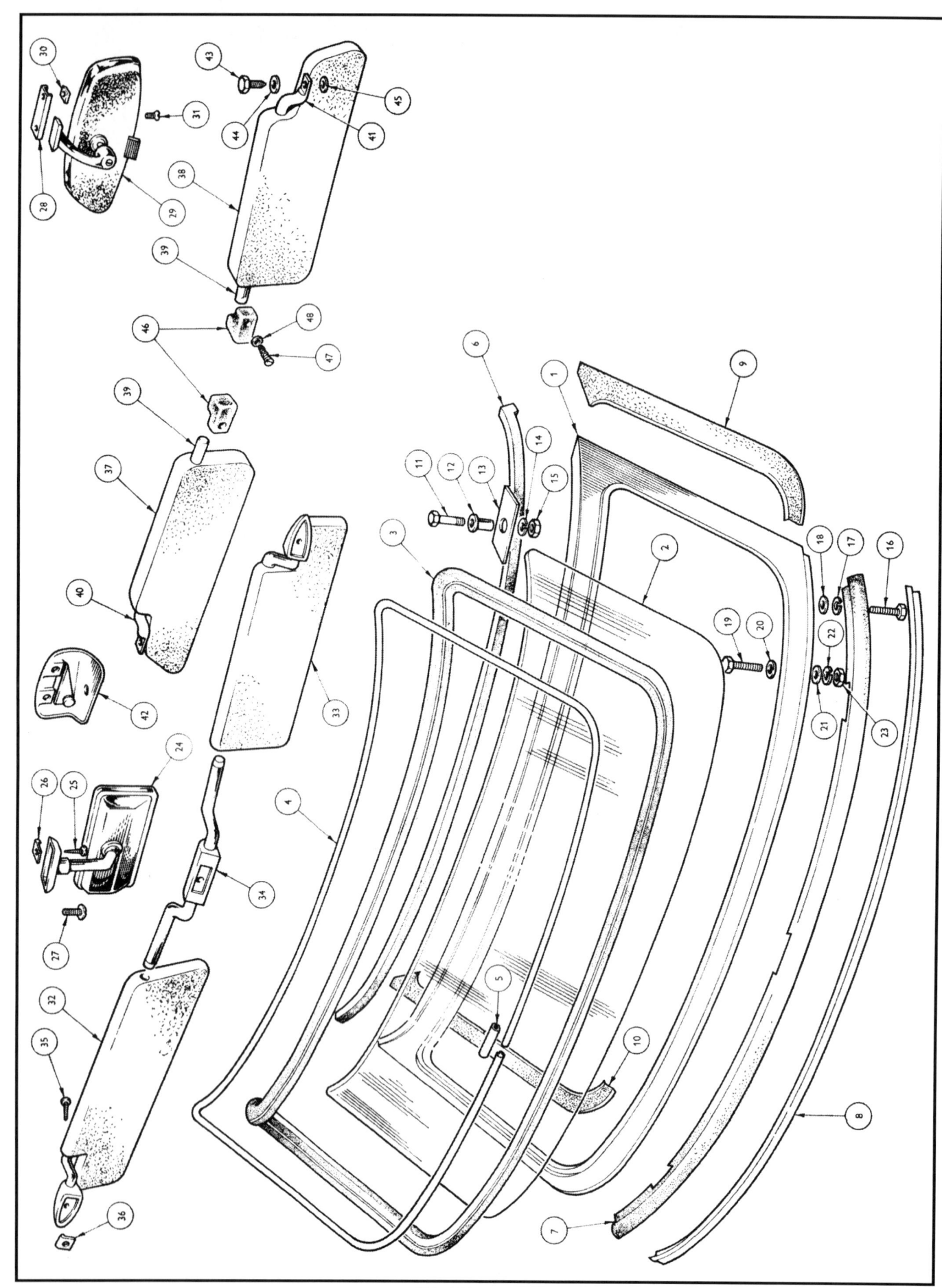

PLATE BZ

BODY AND FITTINGS

Plate No.	Part No.	Description	No. per Unit	Remarks
		SUN VISOR DETAILS FITTED TO MARK I CARS ONLY (UP TO COMMISSION No. KC50000)		
BZ32	711769	SUN VISOR AND OUTER MOUNTING ASSEMBLY (NO MIRROR)—R.H.—R.H.S.	1 1	
BZ33	711759	SUN VISOR AND OUTER MOUNTING ASSEMBLY (WITH MIRROR)—L.H.—R.H.S.	1	
	711789	SUN VISOR AND OUTER MOUNTING ASSEMBLY (WITH MIRROR)—R.H.—L.H.S.	1	All L.H.S. Cars except U.S.A. U.S.A. up to Commission No. KC9999 only
	711769	SUN VISOR AND OUTER MOUNTING ASSEMBLY (NO MIRROR)—R.H.—L.H.S.	1	U.S.A. only from Commission No. KC10000 and future
	711779	SUN VISOR AND OUTER MOUNTING ASSEMBLY (NO MIRROR)—L.H.—L.H.S.	1	
BZ34	710061	**Mounting,** centre, sun visor	1	
BZ35	510125	**Screw,** self-tapping ⎱ Sun visor	3	
BZ36	FJ2445/9	**Nut,** fix ⎰ attachment	3	
		SUN VISOR DETAILS FITTED TO MARK II CARS ONLY (FROM COMMISSION No. KC50001)		
BZ37	812711	SUN VISOR ASSEMBLY—DRIVER'S SIDE (BLACK)	1	
BZ38	812741	SUN VISOR ASSEMBLY—PASSENGER'S SIDE (BLACK)—R.H.S.	1	
	812751	SUN VISOR ASSEMBLY—PASSENGER'S SIDE (BLACK)—L.H.S.	1	
BZ39	812760	**Bar,** mounting, inner	2	
BZ40	812762	**Bar,** mounting, outer—R.H.	1	
BZ41	812761	**Bar,** mounting, outer—L.H.	1	
BZ42	812685	**Bracket,** mounting, sun visor—R.H.	1	
	812684	**Bracket,** mounting, sun visor—L.H.	1	
BZ43	575144	**Bolt,** "Longlok" ⎱	2	
BZ44	WP0007	**Washer,** plain ⎬ Sun visor pivot	2	
BZ45	WP0144	**Washer,** plain ⎰	2	
BZ46	622431	**Retainer,** sun visor	2	
BZ47	511384	**Screw,** self-tapping ⎱ Retainer	4	
BZ48	WP0003	**Washer,** plain ⎰ attachment	4	
	509556	**Screw,** self-tapping ⎱	2	
	570145	**Nut,** fix ⎬ Securing sun visors	2	
	512156	**Screw,** self-tapping ⎰ to windscreen frame	4	
	FC2804	**Nut,** fix	4	

Note:—Items marked thus † are available on our Factory Exchange Unit Scheme

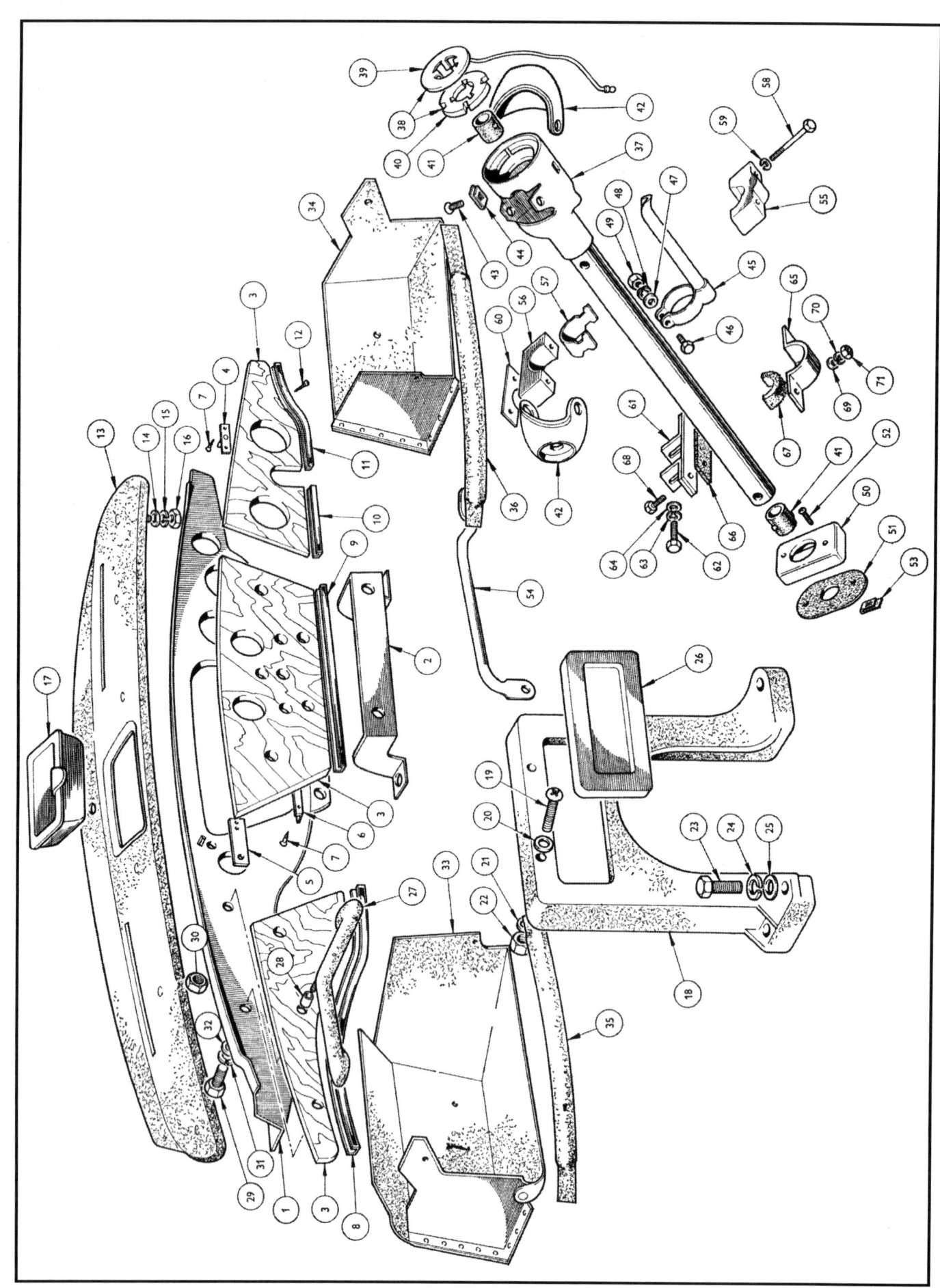

PLATE CA

BODY AND FITTINGS

Plate No.	Part No.	Description	No. per Unit	Remarks
		MARK I CARS ONLY (FITTED UP TO COMMISSION No. KC50000 ONLY)		
CA1	904621	**FACIA PANEL ASSEMBLY—R.H.S.**	1	
	904623	**FACIA PANEL ASSEMBLY—L.H.S.**	1	
	603559	**Clip**, wiring	4	
CA2	709691	**Bracket**, parcel tray support	1	
CA3	905209	**Veneered facing assembly (Facia)**, no heater—R.H.S.	1	
	905210	**Veneered facing assembly (Facia)**, no heater—L.H.S.	1	
	714422	**Veneered facing assembly (Facia)**, no heater—L.H.S.	1	Required when Tandem Brakes are fitted, from Comm. No. KC7051
	905207	**Veneered facing assembly (Facia)**, with heater—R.H.S.	1	
	905208	**Veneered facing assembly (Facia)**, with heater—L.H.S.	1	
	714421	**Veneered facing assembly (Facia)**, with heater—L.H.S.	1	Required when Tandem Brakes are fitted, from Comm. No. KC7051
CA4	618505	**Stud plate** assembly	2	
	618487	**Plate**, attachment—R.H.	1	
CA5	618486	**Plate**, attachment—L.H.	1	
CA6	618488	**Angle**, attachment	1	
CA7	TW0602	**Woodscrew**, plates and angle attachment	11	
CA8	904990	**Moulding**, facia outer (Passenger's side)—R.H.S.	1	
	904991	**Moulding**, facia outer (Passenger's side)—L.H.S.	1	
CA9	904992	**Moulding**, facia centre	1	
CA10	904993	**Moulding**, facia inner (Driver's side)	1	
CA11	904994	**Moulding**, facia outer (Driver's side)—R.H.S.	1	
	904995	**Moulding**, facia outer (Driver's side)—L.H.S.	1	
CA12	514926	**Woodscrew**, facia moulding attachment	12	
	HN2005	**Nut**	2	
	WL0205	**Washer**, lock	2	
	WP0028	**Washer**, plain	4	
	HU0504	**Screw**, set } Veneered facing attachment	2	
	FU2554/4	**Fix**, spire	2	
	CD24153	**Washer**, cup, chrome	2	
	502544	**Screw**, raised head, chrome	2	
CA13	811091	**Crash pad** assembly, facia	1	Fitted up to Comm. No. KC11490 L.H.S. and KC9145 R.H.S. approx.
	813351	**Crash pad** assembly, facia	1	Fitted intermittently from Comm. No. KC11491 L.H.S. and KC9146 R.H.S., and fitted 100% from KC11606 L.H.S. & KC9148 R.H.S.
CA14	WP0197	**Washer**, plain } Crash pad to front deck	6	
CA15	WL0205	**Washer**, lock	6	
CA16	HN2005	**Nut**	6	
CA17	613186	**Ashtray**, facia panel	1	
CA18	810681	**Bracket** assembly, console support, facia to floor	1	
CA19	515279	**Screw**, set	2	
CA20	500309	**Washer**, plain } Support bracket to facia	2	
CA21	WM0057	**Washer**, plain	2	
CA22	YN2907	**Nut**, nyloc	2	
CA23	511930	**Screw**, set, rear	2	
	516288	**Screw**, set, front } Support bracket to floor	2	
CA24	512106	**Washer**, lock	4	
CA25	500172	**Washer**, plain	4	
CA26	709840	**Cover plate** assembly, radio aperture	1	Alternative to 709842
	709842	**Cover plate**, radio aperture	1	Alternative to 709840
	709841	**Plate** assembly, mounting, radio	1	U.S.A. & Canada. Alt. to 709843
	709843	**Plate**, mounting, radio	1	U.S.A. & Canada. Alt. to 709841

Note:—Items marked thus † are available on our Factory Exchange Unit Scheme

129

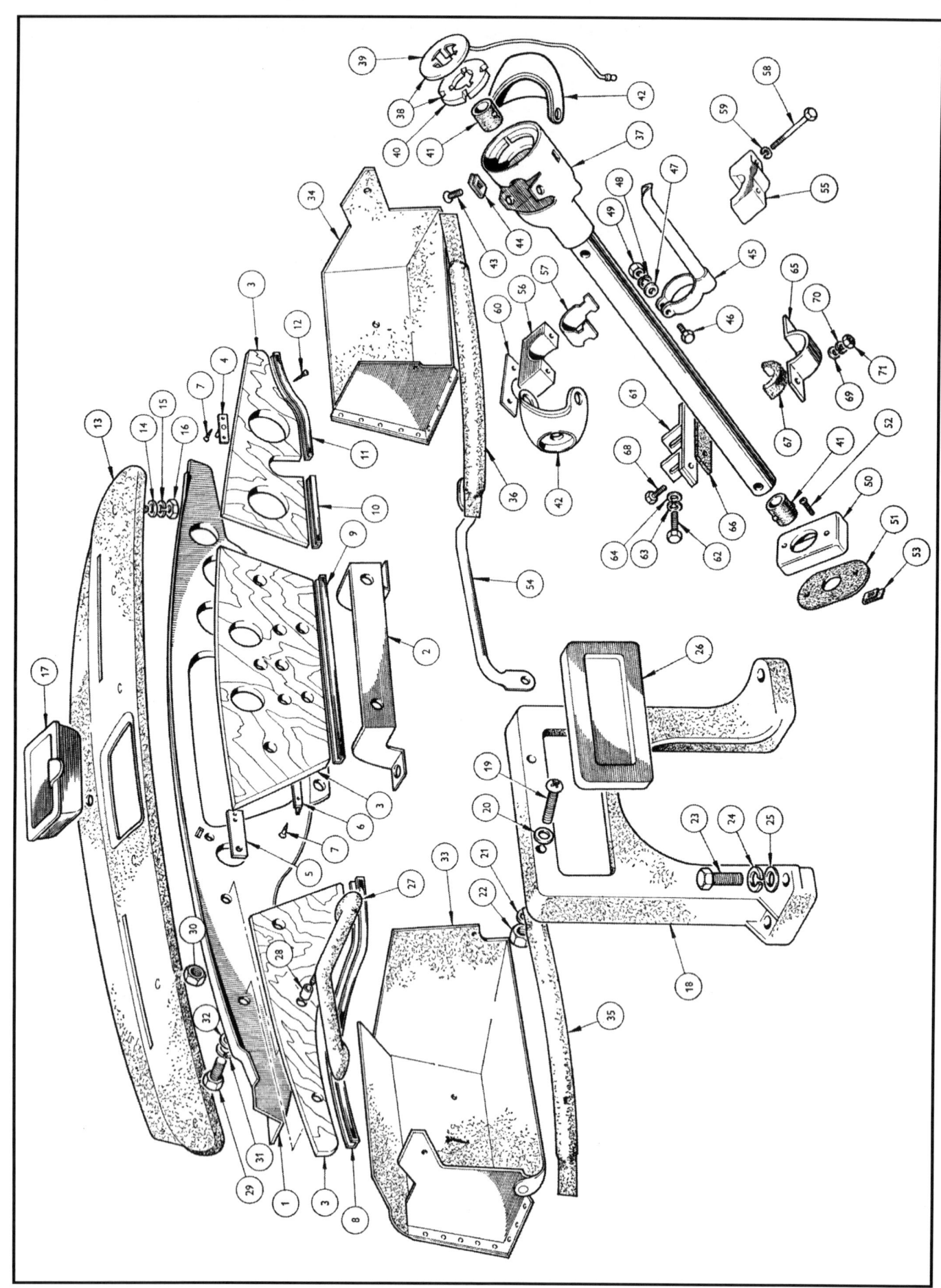

PLATE CA

BODY AND FITTINGS

Plate No.	Part No.	Description	No. per Unit	Remarks

MARK I CARS ONLY
(FITTED UP TO COMMISSION No. KC50000 ONLY)

FACIA PANEL DETAILS—Mark I Cars only—continued

Plate No.	Part No.	Description	No. per Unit	Remarks
CA27	708633	Handle, grab, assembly	1	
CA28	621409	Tube, spacer	1	
	621408	Piece, distance	2	
CA29	HU0707	Screw, set ⎫ Grab handle	1	
CA30	HN2007	Nut ⎬ attachment	1	
CA31	WL0207	Washer, lock	3	
CA32	WP0007	Washer, plain ⎭	3	
CA33	807004	Parcel tray—R.H.S. (Passenger's side)	1	
CA34	809917	Parcel tray—R.H.S. (Driver's side)	1	
	807005	Parcel tray—L.H.S. (Passenger's side)	1	
	809918	Parcel tray—L.H.S. (Driver's side)	1	
	509356	Screw ⎫	4	
	WP0004	Washer, plain ⎬ Parcel tray to dash front	4	
	FU2564/9	Nut, fix ⎭	4	
CA35	709692	Support assembly, parcel tray and crash pad—L.H.	1	
CA36	709693	Support assembly, parcel tray and crash pad—R.H.	1	
	HU0506	Screw, set ⎫	2	
	WP0005	Washer, plain ⎬ Support rail to	4	
	WL0205	Washer, lock ⎨ facia support	2	
	HN2009	Nut ⎭	2	
	HU0505	Screw, set ⎫	3	
	WP0005	Washer, plain ⎬ Support rail to 'A' post and	6	
	WL0205	Washer, lock ⎨ tray to facia (Driver's side)	3	
	HN2009	Nut ⎭	3	
	563032	Plate, back ⎫ Tray to	3	
	565756	Cap, tubular ⎬ support rail	3	
	509356	Screw, self-tapping ⎫	2	
	WP0004	Washer, plain ⎬ Parcel tray to 'A' post	2	
	FU2544/9	Nut, fix ⎭	2	
	603811	Clip, L.H. parcel tray flap to deck stiffener	1	
	622031	**STEERING COLUMN COWL ASSEMBLY (LOCKING)**	1	Germany and Special Orders only
CA37	611364	**STEERING COLUMN COWL ASSEMBLY**	1	
	608135	Support, diaphragm slip ring	1	
	608136	Channel, mounting, column switches	1	
CA38	608462	Slip ring and insulator assembly	1	
CA39	608356	Cable assembly, slip ring	1	
CA40	608139	Insulator, slip ring	1	
	149698	Tube, distance—L.H.S.	1	
CA41	209423	Bearing assembly, steering column	2	
CA42	708479	Escutcheon, flasher and lighting switch	2	
CA43	510273	Screw, self-tapping ⎫ Escutcheon to	2	
CA44	FC2803/9	Nut, fix ⎬ steering column cowl	2	

Note:—Items marked thus † are available on our Factory Exchange Unit Scheme

130

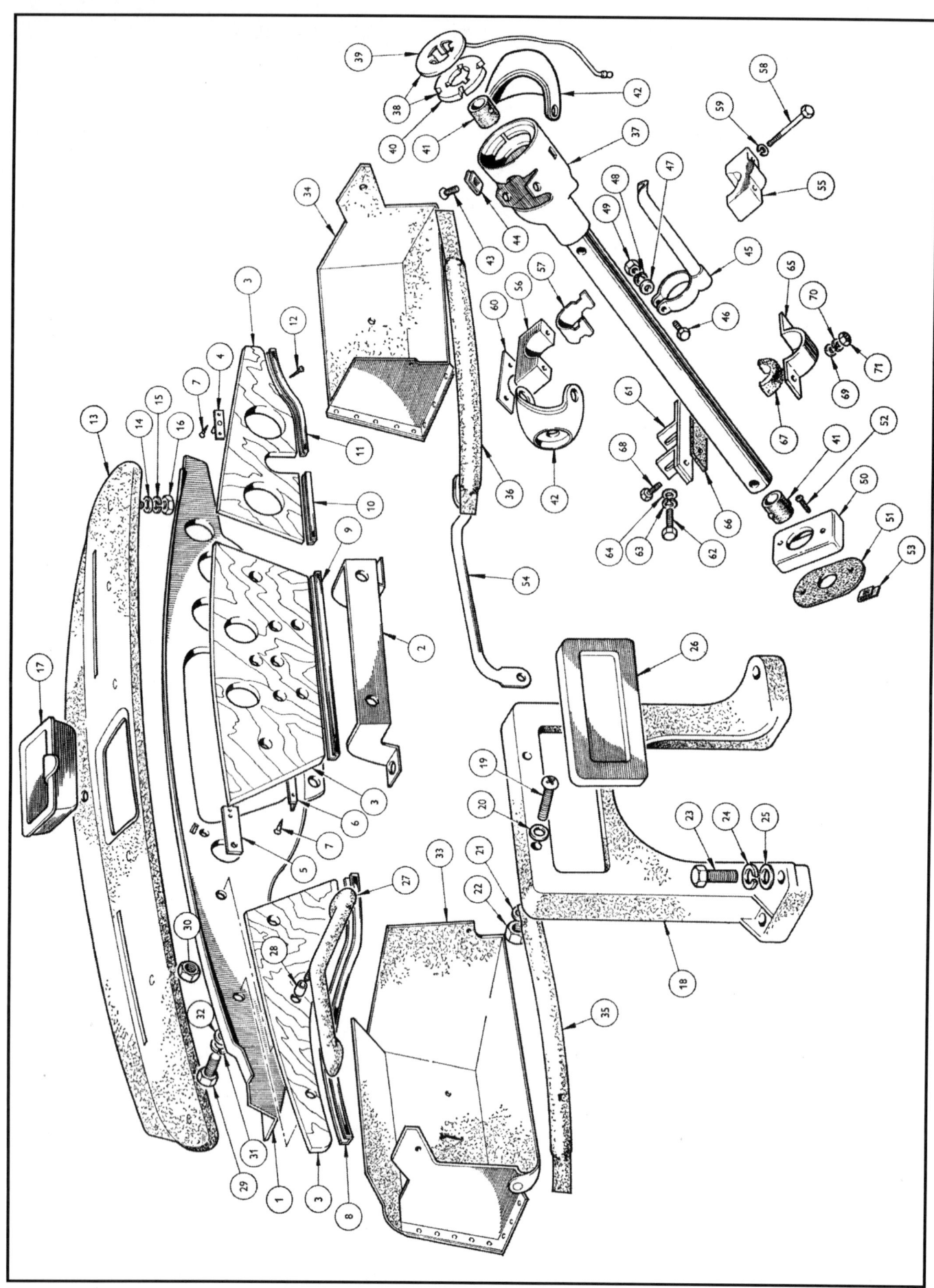

PLATE CA

BODY AND FITTINGS

Plate No.	Part No.	Description	No. per Unit	Remarks

MARK I CARS ONLY
(FITTED UP TO COMMISSION No. KC50000 ONLY)

STEERING COLUMN COWL ASSEMBLY
—continued

CA45	611369	**Cover**, harness, assembly	1	
	609629	**Clip**, harness cover	1	
CA46	TP0504	**Screw**, set ⎫	1	
CA47	WP0138	**Washer**, plain ⎟ Harness cover to	1	
CA48	WL0205	**Washer**, lock ⎟ steering column cowl	1	
CA49	HN2005	**Nut** ⎭	1	
CA50	601597	**Plate**, retaining, steering column	1	
CA51	613466	**Pad**, sealing (Rubber) steering column	1	
CA52	YF7464	**Screw**, self-tapping ⎫ Sealing pad	2	
CA53	FN2044/9	**Nut**, spire ⎭ attachment	2	
CA54	619848	**TIE BAR, STEERING COLUMN CLAMP (UPPER) TO FACIA SUPPORT BRACKET —R.H.S.**	1	
	619849	**TIE BAR, STEERING COLUMN CLAMP (UPPER) TO FACIA SUPPORT BRACKET —L.H.S.**	1	
	HU0706	**Screw**, set ⎫	1	
	WP0007	**Washer**, plain ⎟ Tie bar	1	
	WL0207	**Washer**, lock ⎟ attachment	1	
	HN2007	**Nut** ⎭	1	
CA55	619850	**Clamp**, steering column upper, lower half	1	
CA56	611368	**Clamp**, steering column upper, top half	1	
CA57	609639	**Spring**, steering column clamp	1	
CA58	HB0719	**Bolt** ⎫ Upper and lower clamps	2	
CA59	WL0207	**Washer**, lock ⎭ to mounting brackets	2	
CA60	620547	**Plate**, tapped	1	⎫
	148461	**Strap**, anti-torque	2	⎬ Required when
	HB0720	**Bolt** ⎫ Upper and lower clamps	2	⎬ Locking Steering
	WL0207	**Washer**, lock ⎭ to mounting brackets	2	⎭ is fitted
CA61	612900	**SUPPORT BRACKET ASSEMBLY, STEERING COLUMN (LOWER)**	1	
CA62	HU0715	**Screw**, set ⎫ Support bracket	2	
CA63	WL0207	**Washer**, lock ⎬ to	2	
CA64	WP0007	**Washer**, plain ⎭ channel on dash	2	
CA65	608185	**Clamp**, support bracket, steering column	1	
CA66	608222	**Strip**, felt, support bracket (Body)	1	
CA67	608223	**Strip**, felt, support bracket (Clamp)	1	
CA68	HB0704	**Bolt** ⎫	2	
CA69	WP0122	**Washer**, plain ⎟ Clamp to support	2	
CA70	WL0207	**Washer**, lock ⎟ bracket, lower	2	
CA71	HN2007	**Nut** ⎭	2	

Note:—Items marked thus † are available on our Factory Exchange Unit Scheme

131

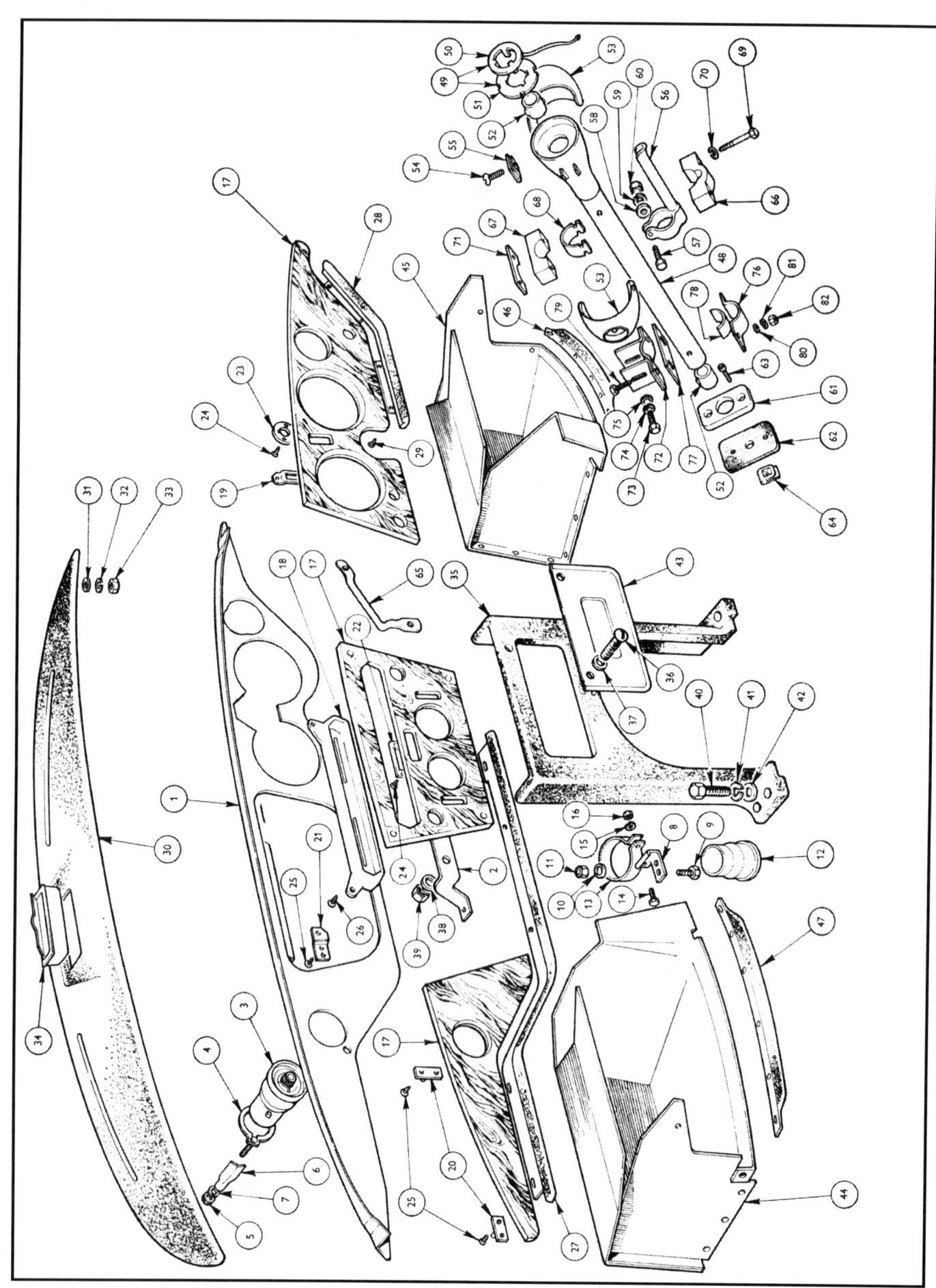

PLATE CB

BODY AND FITTINGS

Plate No.	Part No.	Description	No. per Unit	Remarks
		MARK II CARS ONLY (FITTED FROM COMMISSION No. KC50001)		
CB1	908123	**FACIA PANEL ASSEMBLY—R.H.S.**	1	
	908124	**FACIA PANEL ASSEMBLY—L.H.S.**	1	
	622220	Bracket, mounting, assembly, heater vent control	1	
	603559	Clip, wiring	4	
CB2	709691	Bracket, parcel tray support	1	
CB3	713040	Louvre, face level	2	
CB4	620408	Ring, clamping, assembly ⎫	2	
CB5	620848	Nut, knurled ⎬ Securing louvres	4	
CB6	620847	Clamp ⎬ to facia	4	
CB7	WQ0309	Washer, lock ⎭	4	
	622508	Bracket, foot level vent—R.H.	1	
CB8	622507	Bracket, foot level vent—L.H.	1	
CB9	YX5404	Setscrew ⎫ Foot level vent bracket	4	
CB10	WP0004	Washer, plain ⎬ to	4	
CB11	FU2544/8	Nut, fix ⎭ parcel tray support	4	
CB12	713040	Louvre, foot level vent	2	
CB13	622136	Ring, clamping, foot level vent	2	
CB14	PX0504	Setscrew ⎫ Clamping ring to	2	
CB15	WL0205	Washer, lock ⎬ foot level vent bracket	2	
CB16	HN2005	Nut ⎭	2	
CB17	908121	Veneered facing assembly (Car set)—R.H.S.	1	
	908122	Veneered facing assembly (Car set)—L.H.S.	1	
CB18	713790	Escutcheon, heater controls	1	
CB19	622230	Plate, hazard light switch retainer	1	
CB20	618505	Stud, plate assembly	2	
	618487	Plate, attachment—R.H.	1	
CB21	618486	Plate, attachment—L.H.	1	
CB22	622222	Plate, switch retainer	3	
CB23	622223	Washer, plate, screen washer	1	
CB24	TH4402	Woodscrew, switch plates to facia	10	
CB25	TW0602	Woodscrew, stud and attachment plates to facia	8	
CB26	TW0603	Woodscrew, heater control escutcheon to facia	2	
	HN2005	Nut ⎫	2	
	WL0205	Washer, lock ⎬	2	
	WP0028	Washer, plain ⎬	4	
	HU0504	Screw, set ⎬ Veneered facing	2	
	FU2554/4	Fix, spire ⎬ attachment	2	
	625549	Washer, cup ⎬	4	
	509556	Screw, self-tapping ⎬	4	
	FU2554/4	Fix, spire ⎭	4	
CB27	812981	Padding, assembly, lower facia (Passenger's side)—R.H.S.	1	
CB28	813271	Padding, assembly, lower facia (Driver's side)—R.H.S.	1	
	812991	Padding, assembly, lower facia (Passenger's side)—L.H.S.	1	
	813281	Padding, assembly, lower facia (Driver's side)—L.H.S.	1	
	FJ2443/8	Nut, fix ⎫ Lower facia padding	4	
	YZ3303	Screw, self-tapping ⎬ (Passenger's side) to	4	
	WP0004	Washer, plain ⎭ metal facia panel	4	

Note:—Items marked thus † are available on our Factory Exchange Unit Scheme

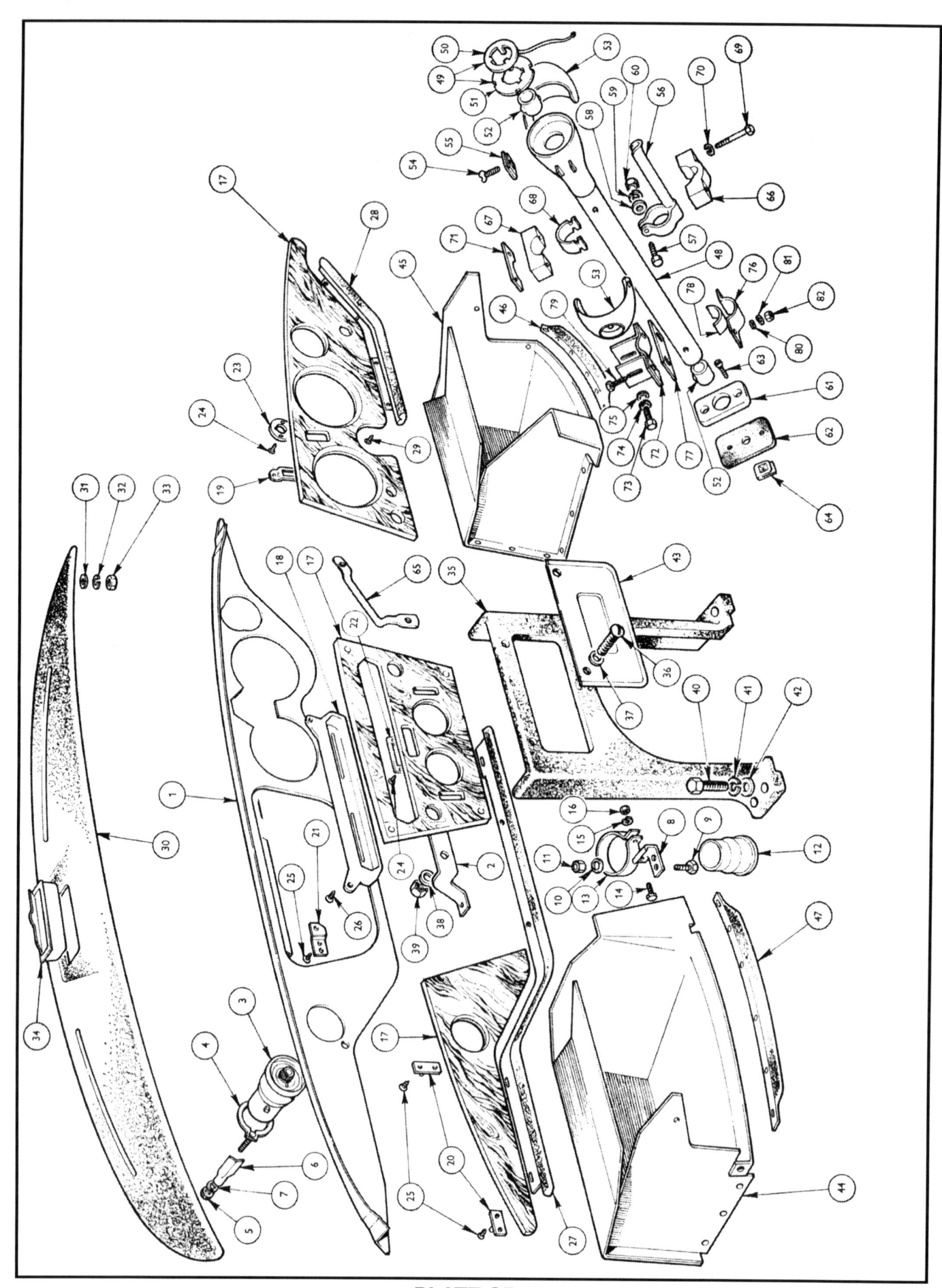

PLATE CB

BODY AND FITTINGS

Plate No.	Part No.	Description	No. per Unit	Remarks

MARK II CARS ONLY
(FITTED FROM COMMISSION No. KC50001)

FACIA PANEL—continued

Plate No.	Part No.	Description	No. per Unit	Remarks
CB29	516762	**Woodscrew**, lower facia padding (Driver's side) to back of wood veneer	3	
CB30	813351	**Crash pad** assembly, facia	1	
CB31	WP0197	**Washer**, plain ⎫	6	
CB32	WL0205	**Washer**, lock ⎬ Crash pad to front deck	6	
CB33	HN2005	**Nut** ⎭	6	
CB34	613186	**Ashtray**, facia panel	1	
CB35	810681	**Bracket** assembly, console support, facia to floor	1	
CB36	515279	**Screw**, set ⎫	2	
CB37	500309	**Washer**, plain ⎪ Support bracket	2	
CB38	WM0057	**Washer**, plain ⎬ to facia	2	
CB39	YN2907	**Nut**, nyloc ⎭	2	
	511930	**Screw**, set, rear ⎫	2	
CB40	516288	**Screw**, set, front ⎪ Support bracket	2	
CB41	512106	**Washer**, lock ⎬ to floor	4	
CB42	500172	**Washer**, plain ⎭	4	
CB43	709842	**Cover plate**, radio aperture	1	
	709843	**Plate**, mounting, radio	1	U.S.A. and Canada
CB44	813753	**Parcel tray** assembly (Passenger's side)—R.H.S.	1	
CB45	813745	**Parcel tray** assembly (Driver's side)—R.H.S.	1	
	813754	**Parcel tray** assembly (Passenger's side)—L.H.S.	1	
	813746	**Parcel tray** assembly (Driver's side)—L.H.S.	1	
	509356	**Screw** ⎫	4	
	WP0004	**Washer**, plain ⎬ Parcel tray to dash front	4	
	FU2564/9	**Nut**, fix ⎭	4	
CB46	709693	**Support** assembly, parcel tray and crash pad—R.H.	1	
CB47	709692	**Support** assembly, parcel tray and crash pad—L.H.	1	
	HU0506	**Screw**, set ⎫	2	
	WP0005	**Washer**, plain ⎪ Support rail to	4	
	WL0205	**Washer**, lock ⎬ facia support	2	
	HN2009	**Nut** ⎭	2	
	HU0505	**Screw**, set ⎫	3	
	WP0005	**Washer**, plain ⎪ Support rail to 'A' post and tray	6	
	WL0205	**Washer**, lock ⎬ to facia (Driver's side)	3	
	HN2009	**Nut** ⎭	3	
	563032	**Plate**, back ⎱ Tray to support rail	3	
	565756	**Cap**, tubular ⎰	3	
	509356	**Screw**, self-tapping ⎫	2	
	WP0004	**Washer**, plain ⎬ Parcel tray to 'A' post	2	
	FU2544/9	**Nut**, fix ⎭	2	
	603811	**Clip**, L.H. parcel tray flap to deck stiffener	1	

Note:—Items marked thus † are available on our Factory Exchange Unit Scheme

133

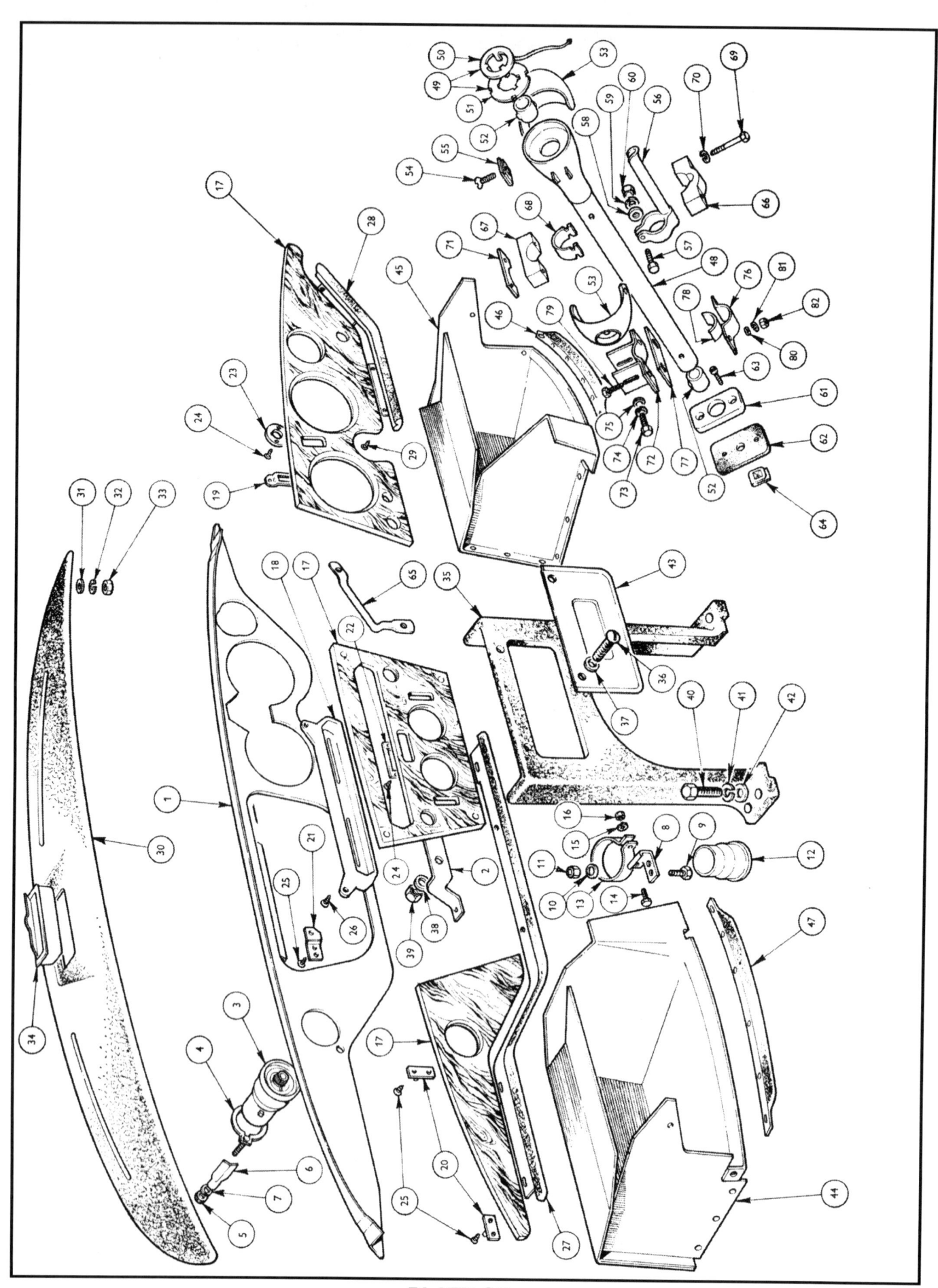

PLATE CB

BODY AND FITTINGS

Plate No.	Part No.	Description	No. per Unit	Remarks
		MARK II CARS ONLY (FITTED FROM COMMISSION No. KC50001)		
	151493	**STEERING COLUMN COWL ASSEMBLY (LOCKING)**	1	Germany and Special Orders
CB48	611364	**STEERING COLUMN COWL ASSEMBLY**	1	
	608135	Support, diaphragm slip ring	1	
	608136	Channel, mounting, column switches	1	
CB49	608462	Slip ring and insulator assembly	1	
CB50	608356	Cable assembly, slip ring	1	
CB51	608139	Insulator, slip ring	1	
	149698	Tube, distance—L.H.S.	1	
CB52	209423	Bearing, assembly, steering column	2	
CB53	708479	Escutcheon, flasher and lighting switch	2	
CB54	510273	Screw, self-tapping ⎱ Escutcheon to	2	
CB55	FC2803/9	Nut, fix ⎰ steering column cowl	2	
CB56	611369	Cover, harness, assembly	1	
	609629	Clip, harness cover	1	
CB57	TP0504	Screw, set	1	
CB58	WP0138	Washer, plain ⎱ Harness cover to	1	
CB59	WL0205	Washer, lock ⎰ steering column cowl	1	
CB60	HN2005	Nut	1	
CB61	601597	Plate, retaining, steering column	1	
CB62	613466	Pad, sealing (Rubber), steering column	1	
CB63	YF7464	Screw, self-tapping ⎱ Sealing pad	2	
CB64	FN2044/9	Nut, spire ⎰ attachment	2	
	716966	**TIE BAR, OUTER, STEERING COLUMN TO FACIA—R.H.S.**	1	
	716967	**TIE BAR, OUTER, STEERING COLUMN TO FACIA—L.H.S.**	1	
	HU0706	Screw, set	2	
	WP0007	Washer, plain ⎱ Outer tie bar	2	
	WL0207	Washer, lock ⎰ attachment	2	
	HN2007	Nut	2	
CB65	623488	**TIE BAR, STEERING COLUMN TO FACIA—R.H.S.**	1	
	623489	**TIE BAR, STEERING COLUMN TO FACIA—L.H.S.**	1	
	HU0706	Screw, set	1	
	WP0007	Washer, plain ⎱ Tie bar attachment	1	
	WL0207	Washer, lock ⎰	1	
	HN2007	Nut	1	
CB66	619850	Clamp, steering column upper, lower half	1	
CB67	611368	Clamp, steering column upper, top half	1	
CB68	609639	Spring, steering column clamp	1	
CB69	HB0719	Bolt ⎱ Upper and lower clamps	2	
CB70	WL0207	Washer, lock ⎰ to mounting brackets	2	
CB71	620547	Plate, tapped	1	

Note:—Items marked thus † are available on our Factory Exchange Unit Scheme

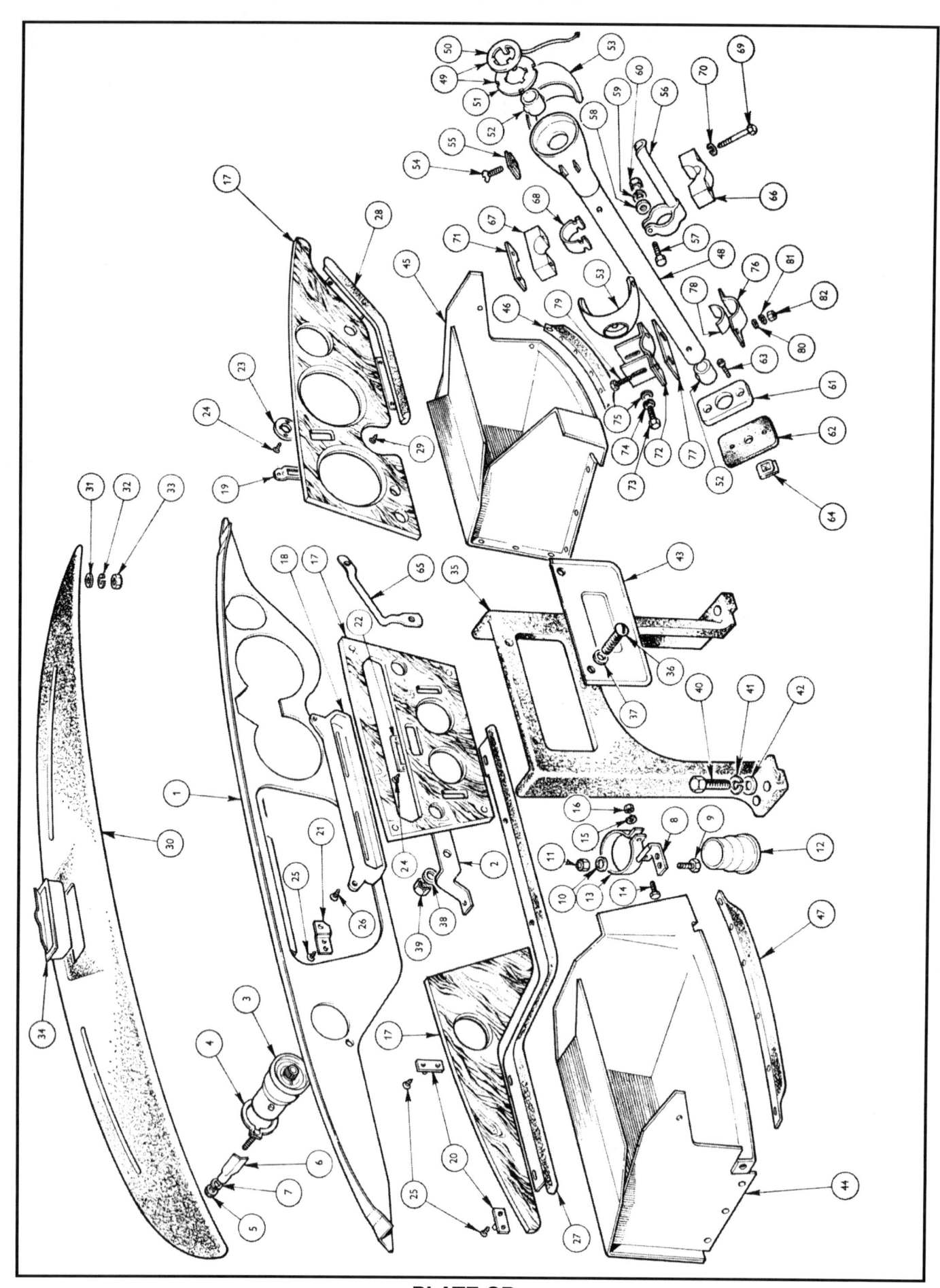

PLATE CB

BODY AND FITTINGS

Plate No.	Part No.	Description	No. per Unit	Remarks
		MARK II CARS ONLY (FITTED FROM COMMISSION No. KC50001)		
	151190	**ANTI-TORQUE STRAP**	2	
	151141	**Plate**, stiffener, anti-torque strap	1	
	HU0706	**Setscrew** ⎫	2	Required when
	WL0207	**Washer**, lock ⎬ Anti-torque straps to stiffener plate	2	Locking Steering Column
	HN2007	**Nut** ⎭	2	is fitted
	HB0720	**Bolt** ⎱ Upper and lower clamps	2	
	WL0207	**Washer**, lock ⎰ to mounting brackets	2	
CB72	622510	**SUPPORT BRACKET ASSEMBLY, STEERING COLUMN (LOWER)**	1	
CB73	HU0715	**Screw**, set ⎱ Support bracket	2	
CB74	WL0207	**Washer**, lock ⎬ to	2	
CB75	WP0007	**Washer**, plain ⎰ channel on dash	2	
CB76	622509	**Clamp**, support bracket, steering column, lower	1	
CB77	623490	**Strip**, felt, support bracket (Body)	1	
CB78	623491	**Strip**, felt, support bracket (Clamp)	1	
CB79	HB0704	**Bolt** ⎫	2	
CB80	WP0122	**Washer**, plain ⎬ Clamp to support	2	
CB81	WL0207	**Washer**, lock ⎨ bracket, lower	2	
CB82	HN2007	**Nut** ⎭	2	

Note:—Items marked thus † are available on our Factory Exchange Unit Scheme

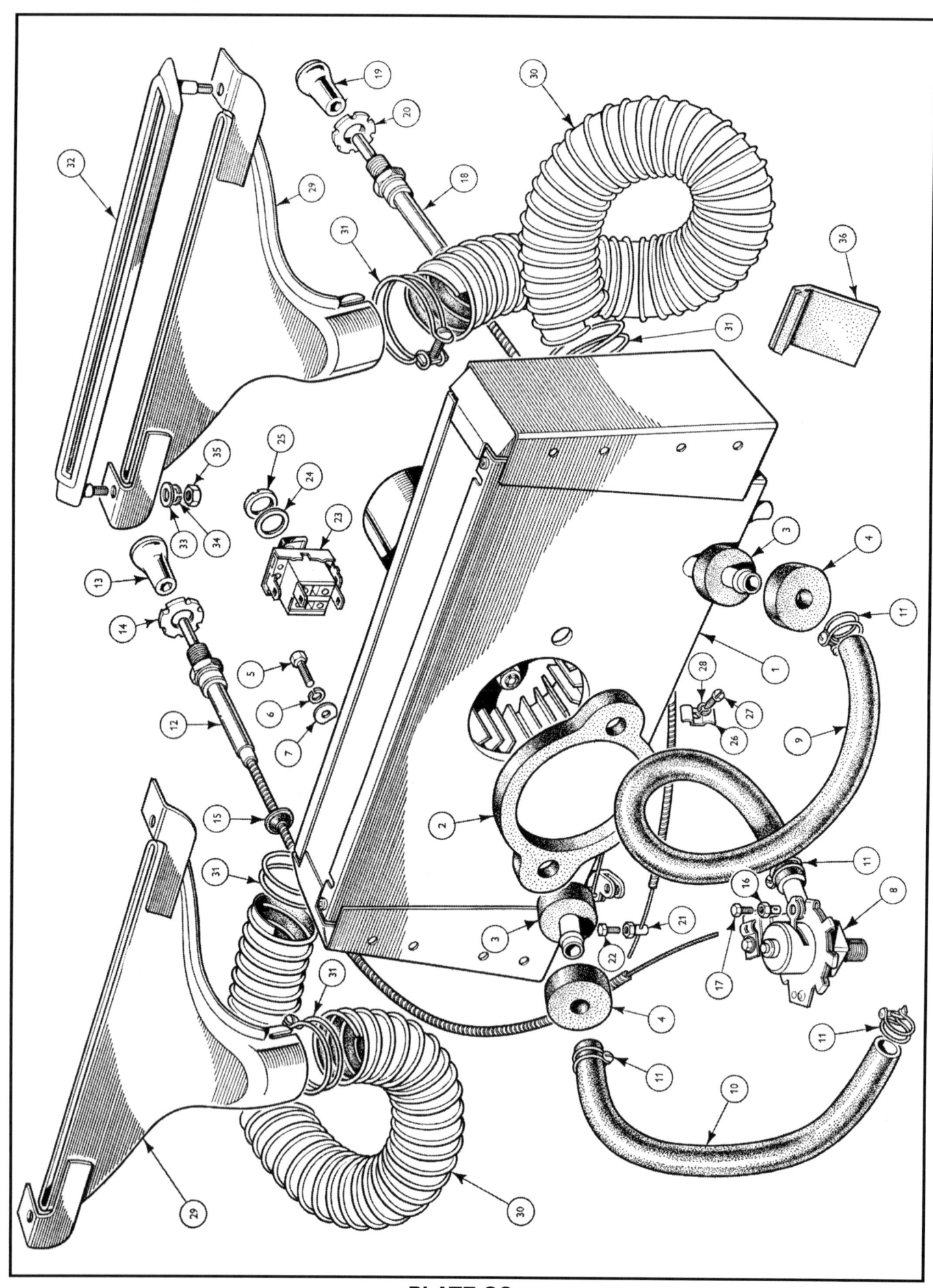

PLATE CC

BODY AND FITTINGS

Plate No.	Part No.	Description	No. per Unit	Remarks
		MARK I CARS ONLY (FITTED UP TO COMMISSION No. KC50000)		
	572534	**HEATER KIT**	1	
CC1	809930	**Heater unit** assembly	1	
CC2	614125	Seal, heater blower	1	
	515828	**Motor and shell**	1	
	515825	**Rotor**, heater motor	1	
	515827	**Resistor**	1	
CC3	613648	Seal, inlet and outlet pipes	2	
CC4	616627	Seal, inlet and outlet pipes	2	
CC5	HU0706	**Screw**, set ⎫	4	
CC6	WL0207	**Washer**, lock ⎬ Heater to dash shelf panel	4	
CC7	613941	'**D**' washer ⎭	4	
CC8	619854	**Valve**, water	1	
CC9	613488	**Hose**, water, valve to heater	1	
CC10	614118	**Hose**, water, return (Heater to manifold)	1	
CC11	CS4012	**Clip**, hose	4	
CC12	619844	**Push/pull control** assembly, water valve	1	
CC13	704884	**Knob**, water valve	1	
	59445	**Washer**, for knob	1	
	610573	**Clip**, securing knob lens	1	
CC14	613314	**Bezel**, push/pull control	1	
CC15	61917	**Grommet**, water valve control to dash	1	
CC16	609123	**Trunnion** ⎫ Water valve control	1	
CC17	559980	**Screw** ⎭ to water valve	1	
CC18	619845	**Push/pull control** assembly, heater outlet	1	
CC19	704881	**Knob**, heater outlet	1	
	59445	**Washer**, for knob	1	
	610573	**Clip**, securing knob lens	1	
CC20	613314	**Bezel**, push/pull control	1	
CC21	609123	**Trunnion** ⎫ Push/pull control	1	
CC22	559980	**Screw** ⎭ (Heater outlet) to heater	1	
CC23	144530	**Switch**, heater (two speed)	1	
CC24	616050	**Washer**, P.V.C.	1	
CC25	609795	**Bezel**, heater switch	1	
CC26	108943	**Clamp**, heater cable	1	
CC27	511765	**Screw**, set ⎫ Clamp attachment	1	
CC28	505307	**Washer**, lock ⎭	1	
CC29	706728	**Nozzle** assembly, demister	2	Fitted up to Comm. No. KC11490 L.H.S. and KC9145 R.H.S. approx.
	714434	**Nozzle** assembly, demister	2	Fitted intermittently from Comm. No. KC11491 L.H.S. and KC9146 R.H.S. Fitted 100% from Comm. No. KC11606 L.H.S. and KC9148 R.H.S.
CC30	602638	**Hose**, demister	2	
CC31	CS4027	**Clip**, hose demister	4	

Note:—Items marked thus † are available on our Factory Exchange Unit Scheme

136

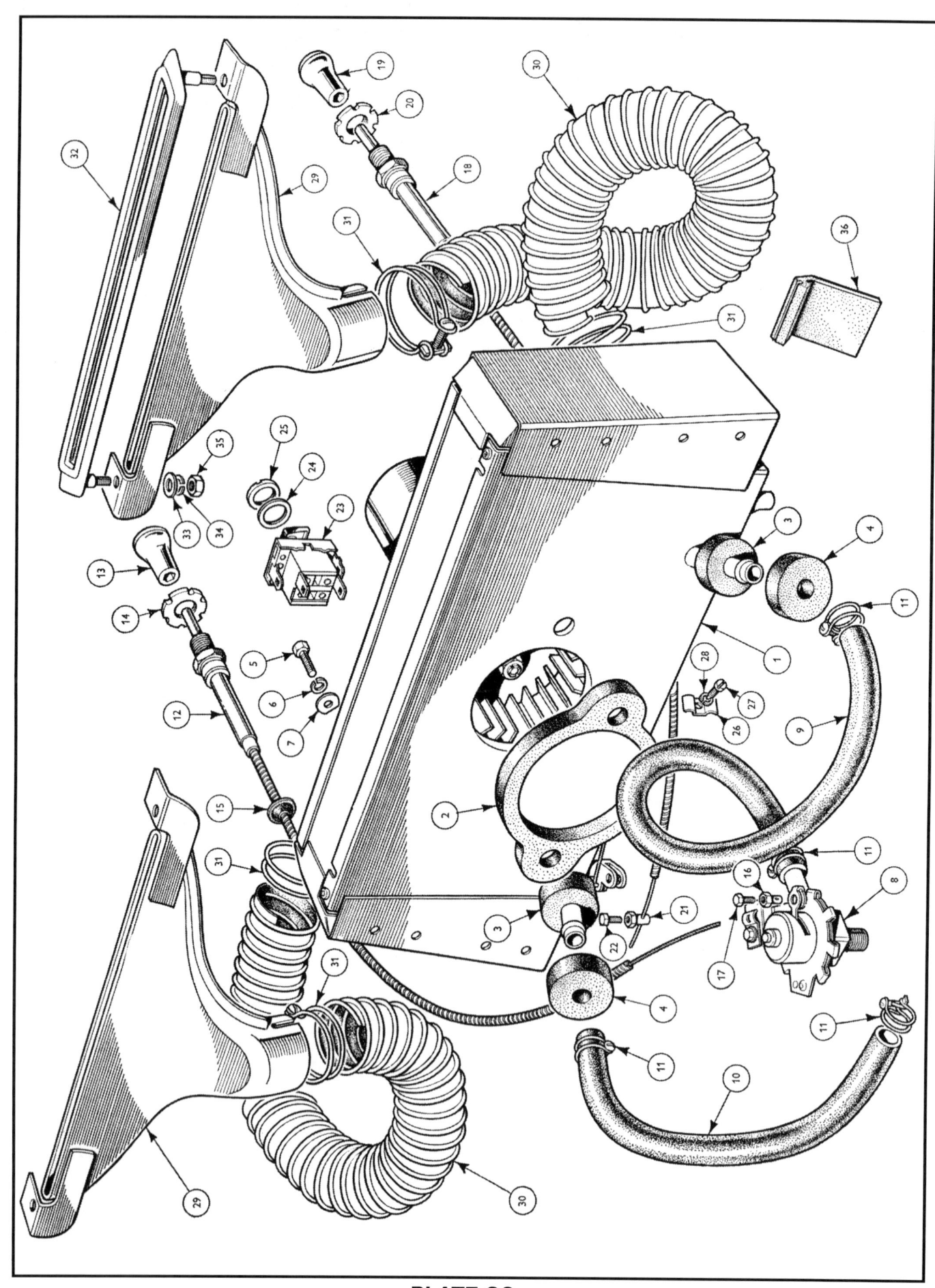

PLATE CC

BODY AND FITTINGS

Plate No.	Part No.	Description	No. per Unit	Remarks
		MARK I CARS ONLY (FITTED UP TO COMMISSION No. KC50000)		
CC32	618954	**DEMISTER OUTLET CAPPING ASSEMBLY**	2	Fitted up to Comm. No. KC11490 L.H.S. and KC9145 R.H.S. approx only
	622812	**DEMISTER OUTLET CAPPING ASSEMBLY**	2	Fitted intermittently from Comm. No. KC11491 L.H.S. and KC9146 R.H.S. Fitted 100% from Comm. No. KC11606 L.H.S. and KC9148 R.H.S.
CC33	WP0138	**Washer**, plain ⎫	4	
CC34	WL0205	**Washer**, lock ⎬ Demister outlet attachment	4	
CC35	HN2005	**Nut** ⎭	4	
	613097	**Plate**, cover, heater aperture on dash	1	⎫ Only required when
	YA0403	**Screw**, cover plate attachment	4	⎭ heater is not fitted
CC36	616206	**Drain flap**, airbox	1	

Note:—Items marked thus † are available on our Factory Exchange Unit Scheme

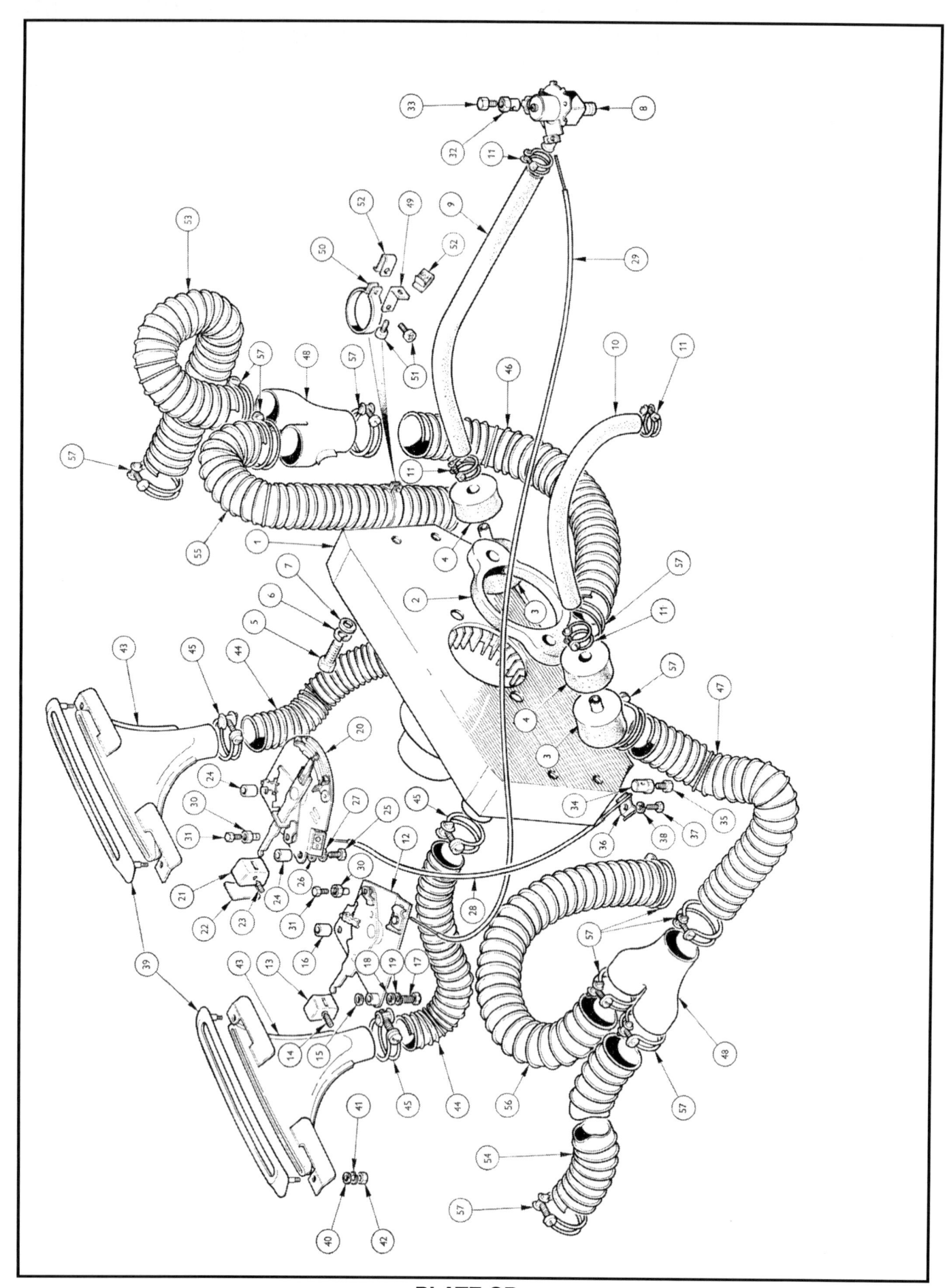

PLATE CD

BODY AND FITTINGS

Plate No.	Part No.	Description	No. per Unit	Remarks

MARK II CARS ONLY
(FITTED FROM COMMISSION No. KC50001)

HEATER DETAILS

Plate No.	Part No.	Description	No. per Unit
CD1	813713	**Heater unit** assembly	1
CD2	614125	**Seal**, heater blower	1
	515828	**Motor and shell**	1
	515825	**Rotor**, heater motor	1
	515827	**Resistor**	1
CD3	613648	**Seal**, inlet and outlet pipes	2
CD4	616627	**Seal**, inlet and outlet pipes	2
CD5	HU0706	**Setscrew** ⎫	4
CD6	WL0207	**Washer**, lock ⎬ Heater to dash shelf panel	4
CD7	613941	**'D' washer** ⎭	4
CD8	619854	**Valve**, water, fitted on inlet manifold water adaptor	1
CD9	613488	**Hose**, water, valve to heater	1
CD10	614118	**Hose**, water, return (Heater to manifold)	1
CD11	CS4012	**Clip**, hose	4
CD12	622237	**Lever**, control, water valve	1
CD13	622228	**Knob** assembly, water valve lever	1
CD14	620750	**Screw**, grub, knob	1
CD15	622235	**Spacer**, thin ⎫	1
CD16	622224	**Spacer**, thick ⎪ Water valve lever	1
CD17	HU0708	**Setscrew** ⎬ control to	2
CD18	WP0007	**Washer**, plain ⎪ facia bracket	2
CD19	WL0207	**Washer**, lock ⎭	2
CD20	622236	**Lever**, control, ventilator and heater motor	1
CD21	622229	**Knob** assembly, ventilator control lever	1
CD22	624276	**Label**, "Pull Boost"	1
CD23	620750	**Screw**, grub, knob	1
CD24	622224	**Spacer**, thick ⎫	2
CD25	HU0708	**Setscrew** ⎬ Ventilator and heater motor	2
CD26	WP0007	**Washer**, plain ⎬ control lever to facia bracket	2
CD27	WL0207	**Washer**, lock ⎭	2
CD28	624193	**Cable** assembly, heater screen	1
CD29	624194	**Cable** assembly, water valve	1
CD30	616034	**Trunnion** ⎱ Cable attachment	2
CD31	559980	**Screw** ⎰ to control levers	2
CD32	609123	**Trunnion** ⎱ Cable assembly	1
CD33	559980	**Screw** ⎰ to water valve	1
CD34	609123	**Trunnion** ⎱ Cable assembly	1
CD35	559980	**Screw** ⎰ (Heater outlet) to heater	1
CD36	108943	**Clamp**, heater cable	1
CD37	511765	**Setscrew** ⎱ Cable clamp	1
CD38	505307	**Washer**, lock ⎰ attachment	1

Note:—Items marked thus † are available on our Factory Exchange Unit Scheme

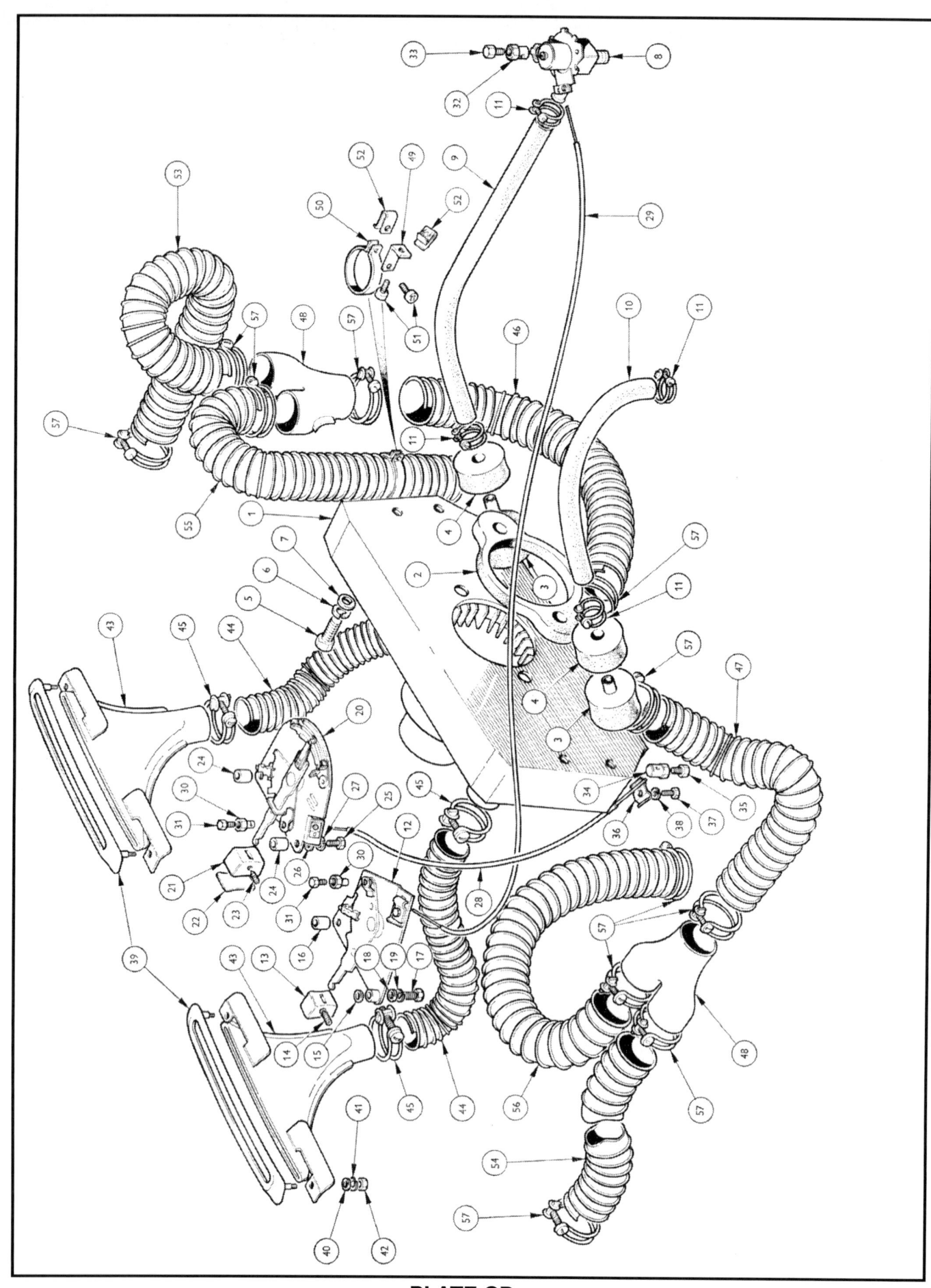

PLATE CD

BODY AND FITTINGS

Plate No.	Part No.	Description	No. per Unit	Remarks

MARK II CARS ONLY
(FITTED FROM COMMISSION No. KC50001)

DEMISTING AND AIR VENTILATION DETAILS

Plate No.	Part No.	Description	No. per Unit	Remarks
CD39	622812	**Capping** assembly, demister outlet	2	
CD40	WP0138	**Washer**, plain ⎫	4	
CD41	WL0205	**Washer**, lock ⎬ Demister capping attachment	4	
CD42	HN2005	**Nut** ⎭	4	
CD43	714434	**Nozzle** assembly, demister	2	
CD44	602638	**Hose**, demister	2	
CD45	CS4027	**Clip**, hose, demister	4	
CD46	614347	**Hose**, heater to 'Y' piece—R.H. ⎫ R.H.S.	1	
CD47	614344	**Hose**, heater to 'Y' piece—L.H. ⎭	1	
	614337	**Hose**, heater to 'Y' piece—R.H. ⎫ L.H.S.	1	
	614338	**Hose**, heater to 'Y' piece—L.H. ⎭	1	
CD48	622138	**Tube** assembly, 'Y' piece	2	
CD49	622553	**Bracket**, 'Y' piece retaining clip	1	
CD50	622566	**Clip**, 'Y' piece retaining R.H.S.	1	
CD51	YX5303	**Setscrew** ⎱ Clip to bracket and	2	
CD52	FU2553/8	**Nut**, fix ⎰ bracket to heater	2	
	622514	**Tube** assembly, 'Y' piece—R.H. ⎫	1	
	622138	**Tube** assembly, 'Y' piece—L.H. ⎬ L.H.S.	1	
	YX5303	**Setscrew** ⎱ R.H. 'Y' piece	1	
	FU2553/8	**Nut**, fix ⎰ to heater	1	
CD53	614346	**Hose**, 'Y' piece to face level vent—R.H. ⎫ R.H.S.	1	
CD54	614348	**Hose**, 'Y' piece to face level vent—L.H. ⎭	1	
	614337	**Hose**, 'Y' piece to face level vent—R.H. ⎫ L.H.S.	1	
	614344	**Hose**, 'Y' piece to face level vent—L.H. ⎭	1	
CD55	614346	**Hose**, 'Y' piece to foot level vent—R.H. ⎫ R.H.S.	1	
CD56	614344	**Hose**, 'Y' piece to foot level vent—L.H. ⎭	1	
	614337	**Hose**, 'Y' piece to foot level vent—R.H. ⎫ L.H.S.	1	
	614345	**Hose**, 'Y' piece to foot level vent—L.H. ⎭	1	
CD57	CS4029	**Clip**, hose ⎱ Hose attachment	12	Alternative to CS4030
	CS4030	**Clip**, hose ⎰	12	Alternative to CS4029

Note:—Items marked thus † are available on our Factory Exchange Unit Scheme

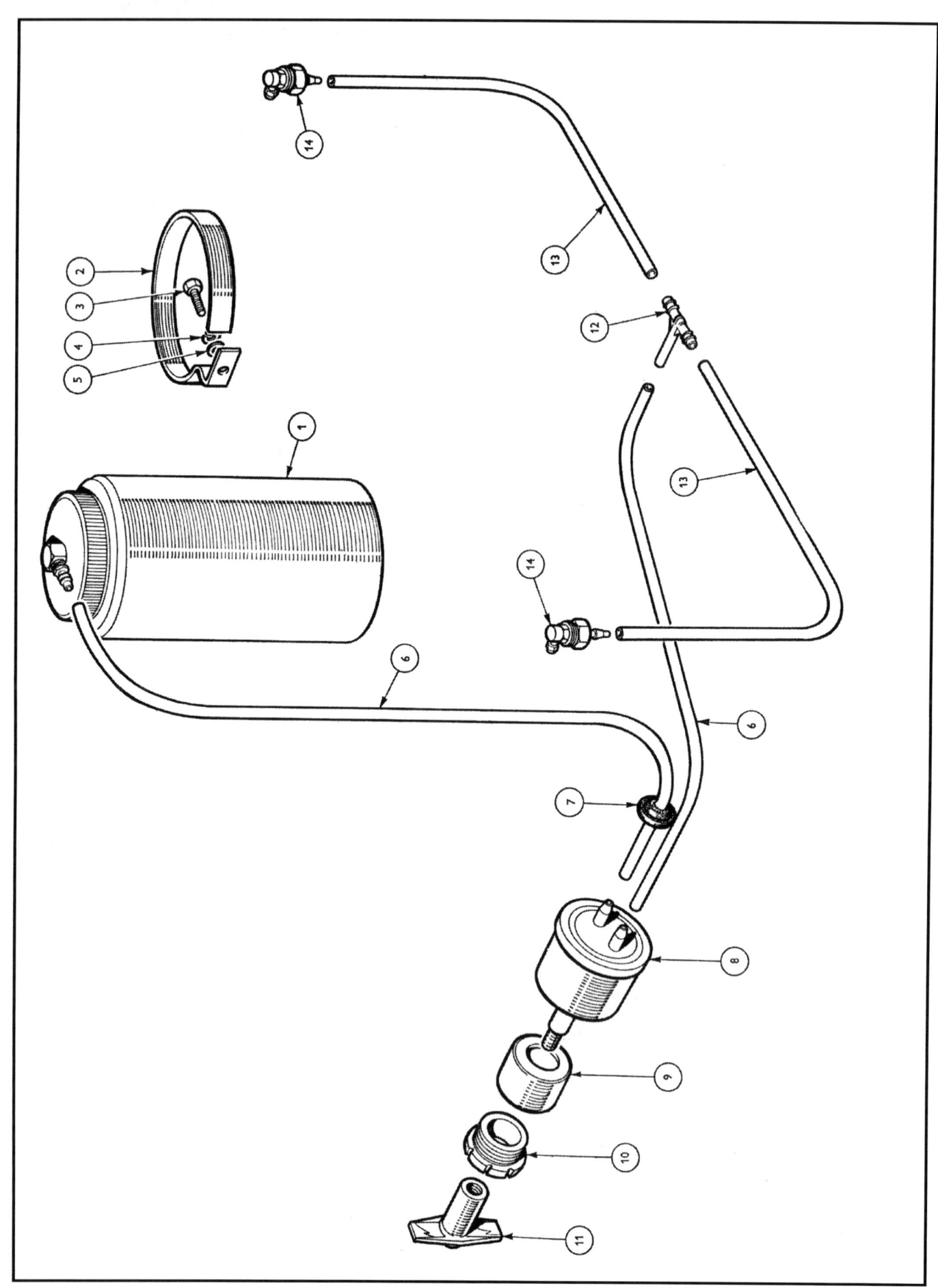

PLATE CE

BODY AND FITTINGS

Plate No.	Part No.	Description	No. per Unit	Remarks
		WINDSCREEN WASHER DETAILS		
CE1	609172	**Container,** water	1	
CE2	614126	**Clip,** water container	1	
CE3	HU0505	**Screw,** set ⎫	1	
CE4	WL0205	**Washer,** lock ⎬ Container attachment	1	
CE5	WP00005	**Washer,** plain ⎭	1	
CE6	604146	**Tubing,** container to plunger and plunger to 'T' piece	A/R	Sold in feet
CE7	61917	**Grommet,** tubing through dash	1	
CE8	609173	**Plunger**	1	⎫ Mark I Cars only.
CE9	609526	**Spacer**	1	⎬ Fitted up to Commission No.
CE10	609919	**Bezel**	1	⎬ KC50000. For future see
CE11	620543	**Knob**	1	⎭ Electrical Equipment, page 107
CE12	612601	**'T' piece**	1	
CE13	604132	**Tubing,** 'T' piece to jets	A/R	Sold in feet
CE14	613650	**Jet mounting** assembly	2	

Note:—Items marked thus † are available on our Factory Exchange Unit Scheme

140

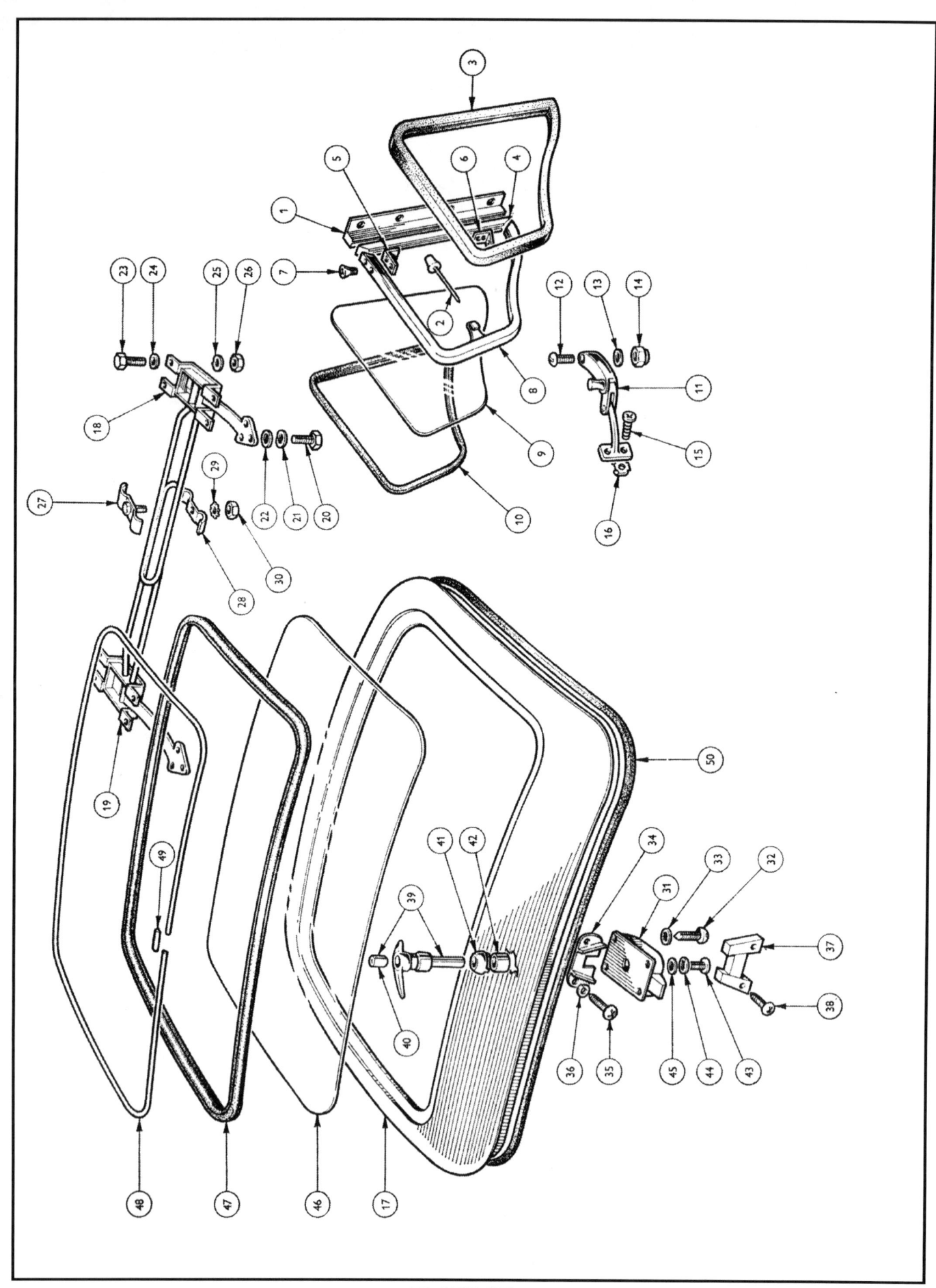

PLATE CF

BODY AND FITTINGS

Plate No.	Part No.	Description	No. per Unit	Remarks
		REAR QUARTER VENTILATOR DETAILS		
	574135	**Hinge** assembly, female portion, rear quarter ventilator, R.H.	1	
CF1	574134	**Hinge** assembly, female portion, rear quarter ventilator, L.H.	1	
CF2	560026	**Rivet**, imex, hinge to 'B' post upper	8	
	810018	**Seal**, rear quarter ventilator—R.H.	1	
CF3	810017	**Seal**, rear quarter ventilator—L.H.	1	
	574121	**Frame** assembly, glazed, rear quarter ventilator—R.H.	1	
	574120	**Frame** assembly, glazed, rear quarter ventilator—L.H.	1	
	574123	**Frame**, front—R.H.	1	
CF4	574122	**Frame**, front—L.H.	1	
CF5	574124	**Bracket**, top, joint	2	
CF6	574125	**Bracket**, bottom, joint	2	
CF7	574126	**Screw**, bracket to front frame	8	
	574128	**Frame**, rear, curved, and toggle bracket assembly—R.H.	1	
CF8	574127	**Frame**, rear, curved, and toggle bracket assembly—L.H.	1	
CF9	573843	**Glass**, toughened	2	
CF10	574129	**Strip**, glazing	2	
	574126	**Screw**, rear frame to front frame attachment	8	
	574131	**Toggle** assembly, rear quarter ventilator—R.H.	1	
CF11	574130	**Toggle** assembly, rear quarter ventilator—L.H.	1	
CF12	574132	**Screw** ⎫	2	
CF13	507261	**Washer** ⎬ Toggle to ventilator attachment	2	
CF14	574133	**Nut**, dome ⎭	2	
CF15	508566	**Screw**, self-tapping ⎫ Toggle to	4	
CF16	FC2803	**Nut**, fix ⎭ rear quarter panel	4	
		BACK DOOR DETAILS		
CF17	809405	**Panel** assembly, back door, complete	1	
CF18	709301	**Hinge** assembly, back door—R.H.	1	⎫ Mark I Cars only. Fitted up to
CF19	709300	**Hinge** assembly, back door—L.H.	1	⎭ Commission No. KC50000
	625609	**Hinge** assembly, back door—R.H.	1	⎫ Mark II Cars only. Fitted from
	625608	**Hinge** assembly, back door—L.H.	1	⎭ Commission No. KC50001
CF20	HN0708	**Bolt** ⎫	6	
CF21	WL0207	**Washer**, lock ⎬ Hinge to back door	6	
CF22	WP0007	**Washer**, plain ⎭	6	
CF23	HB0708	**Bolt** ⎫	4	
CF24	WP0007	**Washer**, plain ⎬ Hinge	8	
CF25	WL0207	**Washer**, lock ⎬ to body	8	
CF26	HN2007	**Nut** ⎭	4	
CF27	574062	**Clamp and bolt** assembly	1	
CF28	574061	**Clamp**, hinge	1	
CF29	WN0708	**Washer**, shakeproof ⎫ Securing clamps	1	
CF30	HN2008	**Nut** ⎭ to torsion bar	1	
CF31	710290	**Lock** assembly, back door	1	
CF32	KX4504P	**Screw**, set ⎫ Lock to door	4	
CF33	WK7605	**Washer**, shakeproof ⎭ inner panel	4	
CF34	619384	**Sleeve**, striker block	1	
CF35	PX0505P	**Screw**, set ⎫ Sleeve to back	2	
CF36	WL0205	**Washer**, lock ⎭ door inner panel	2	
CF37	619383	**Block**, striker	1	
CF38	CX2506/P	**Screw**, set, striker block to platform	2	

Note:—Items marked thus † are available on our Factory Exchange Unit Scheme

141

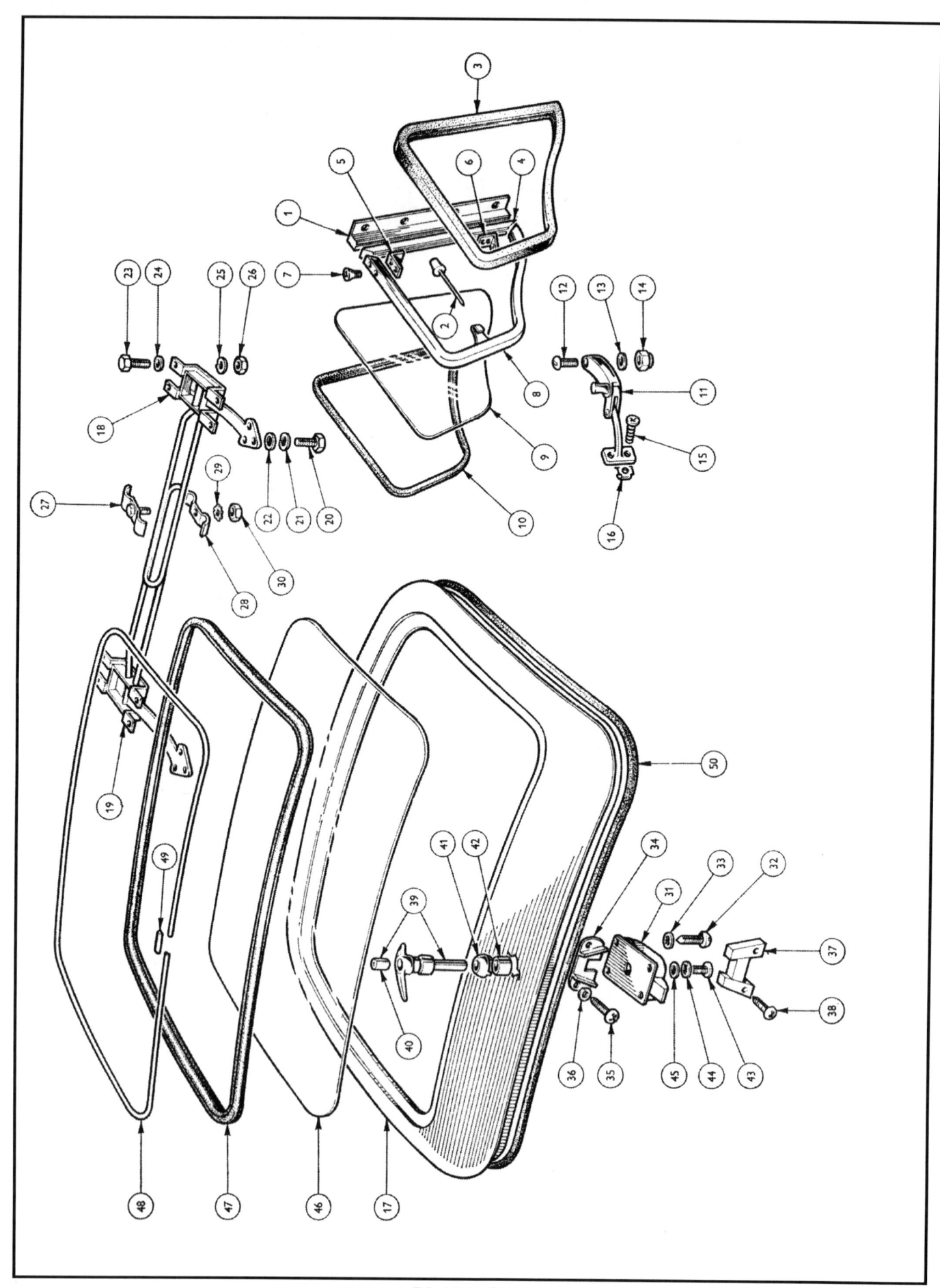

PLATE CF

BODY AND FITTINGS

Plate No.	Part No.	Description	No. per Unit	Remarks
		BACK DOOR DETAILS—continued		
CF39	710497	**Handle** assembly, back door	1	
CF40	574119	**Locking device**, back door handle	1	
CF41	619496	**Escutcheon**, back door handle	1	
CF42	621373	**Washer**, seating, escutcheon, back door handle	1	
CF43	KX4504	**Screw**, set ⎫	1	
CF44	WK7605	**Washer**, shakeproof ⎬ Handle attachment	1	
CF45	WM0055	**Washer**, medium ⎭	1	
CF46	809409	**Glass**, back door	1	Mark I Cars only. Fitted up to Commission No. KC50000 only
	714115	**Glass** (heated), back door	1	All markets except U.S.A. ⎫ Mk. II Cars. Fitted from Comm. No. KC50001
	714571	**Glass** (heated and tinted), back door	1	U.S.A. only ⎭
CF47	904487	**Rubber**, glazing	1	
CF48	613955	**Finisher**, glazing rubber	1	
CF49	611437	**Clip**, finisher attachment	1	
CF50	610657	**Rubber**, sealing, back door aperture	1	

Note:—Items marked thus † are available on our Factory Exchange Unit Scheme

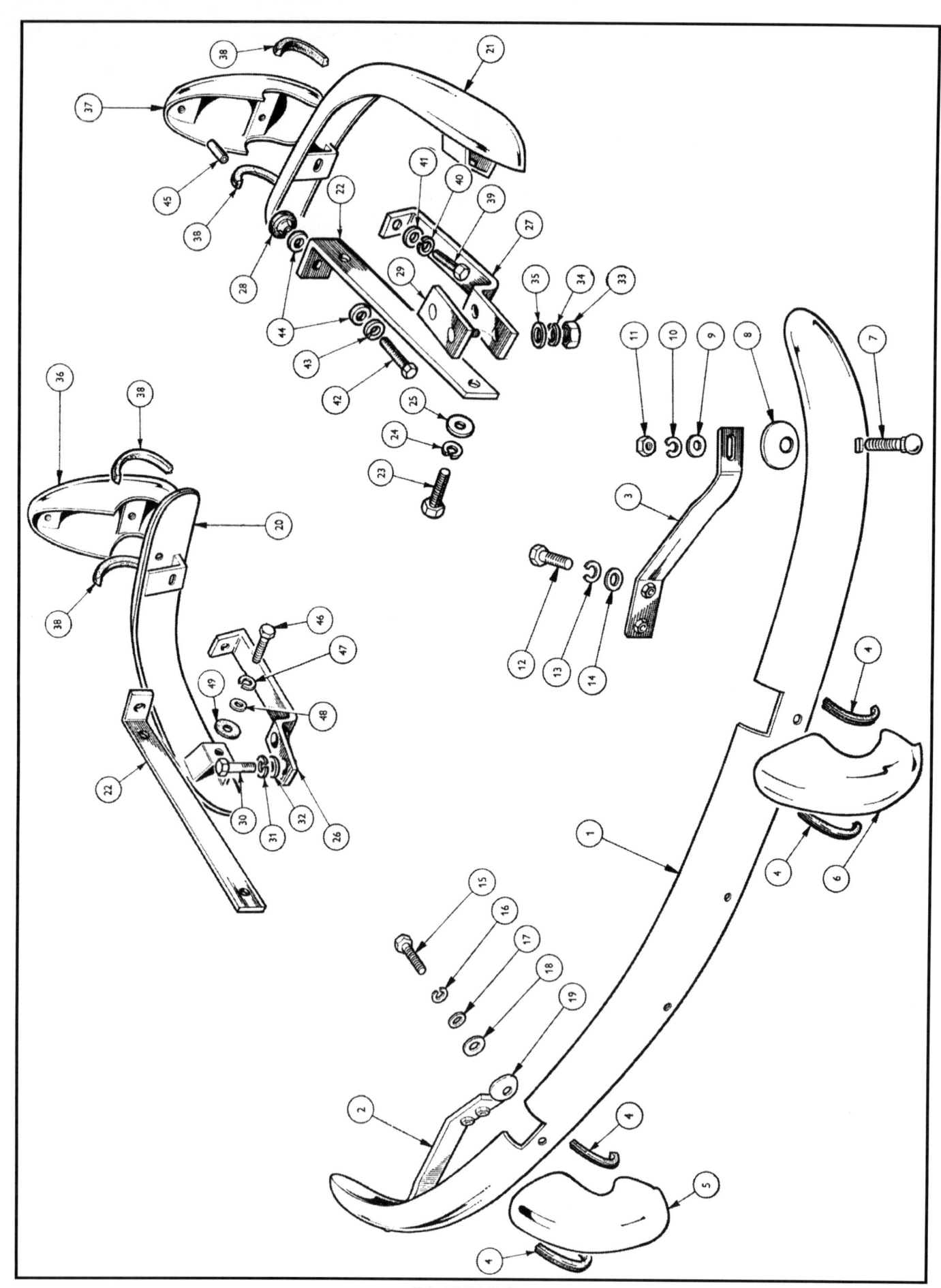

PLATE CG

BODY AND FITTINGS

Plate No.	Part No.	Description	No. per Unit	Remarks
		BUMPER AND OVERRIDER DETAILS **MARK I CARS ONLY (FITTED FROM COMMISSION No. KC50000)**		
CG1	806956	**FRONT BUMPER BAR**	1	
CG2	710706	**Bracket**, support, outer, assembly—R.H.	1	
CG3	710705	**Bracket**, support, outer, assembly—L.H.	1	
CG4	608491	**Moulding**, P.V.C., between bumper and overrider	4	
CG5	710717	**Overrider** assembly, front—R.H.	1	
CG6	710716	**Overrider** assembly, front—L.H.	1	
CG7	554700	**Bolt** ⎫	2	
CG8	607085	**Piece**, packing ⎪	2	
CG9	WP0130	**Washer**, plain ⎬ Securing support bracket to bumper	2	
CG10	WL0209	**Washer**, lock ⎪	2	
CG11	HN2009	**Nut** ⎭	2	
CG12	HU0807	**Screw**, set ⎫ Securing support	4	
CG13	WL0208	**Washer**, lock ⎬ bracket to chassis	4	
CG14	WP0129	**Washer**, plain ⎭ crossmember	4	
CG15	HB0817	**Bolt** ⎫	2	
CG16	WL0208	**Washer**, lock ⎪ Securing overriders	2	
CG17	WM0058	**Washer**, plain ⎬ and bumpers to	2	
CG18	511475	**Spacer** ⎪ chassis brackets	2	
CG19	607085	**Piece**, packing ⎭	2	
CG20	806901	**REAR CORNER BUMPER ASSEMBLY—R.H.**	1	
CG21	806900	**REAR CORNER BUMPER ASSEMBLY—L.H.**	1	
CG22	615825	**Bar**, spring, rear overrider, upper	2	
CG23	HU0908	**Screw**, set ⎫	4	
CG24	WL0209	**Washer**, lock ⎬ Upper spring bar to body	4	
CG25	WM0059	**Washer**, plain ⎭	4	
CG26	615813	**Bar**, spring, assembly, rear overrider, lower—R.H.	1	
CG27	615814	**Bar**, spring, rear overrider, lower—L.H.	1	
CG28	602037	**Grommet**, rubber, rear overrider spring bar	2	
CG29	618410	**Stud plate** assembly, spring bar—L.H.	1	
CG30	HU0908	**Screw**, set ⎫ R.H. lower spring	2	
CG31	WL0209	**Washer**, lock ⎬ bar rear assembly	2	
CG32	WP0155	**Washer**, plain ⎭ to body	2	
CG33	HN2009	**Nut** ⎫	2	
CG34	WL0209	**Washer**, lock ⎬ L.H. lower spring bar, rear, to body	2	
CG35	WP0048	**Washer**, plain ⎭	2	
CG36	706584	**Overrider** assembly, rear—R.H.	1	
CG37	706583	**Overrider** assembly, rear—L.H.	1	
CG38	608491	**Moulding**, P.V.C., between bumper and overrider	4	
CG39	HB0820	**Bolt** ⎫	2	
CG40	WL0208	**Washer**, lock ⎬ Overrider lower mounting to spring bar	2	
CG41	WM0058	**Washer**, plain ⎭	2	
CG42	HB0829	**Bolt** ⎫	2	
CG43	WL0208	**Washer**, lock ⎪ Overrider upper mounting	2	
CG44	WM0808	**Washer**, medium ⎬ bracket to spring bar	4	
CG45	615710	**Tube**, spacer ⎭	2	
CG46	HU0806	**Screw**, set ⎫	2	
CG47	WL0208	**Washer**, lock ⎪ Rear bumper	2	
CG48	WP0139	**Washer**, plain ⎬ side attachment	2	
CG49	610152	**Washer**, rubber ⎭	2	

Note:—Items marked thus † are available on our Factory Exchange Unit Scheme

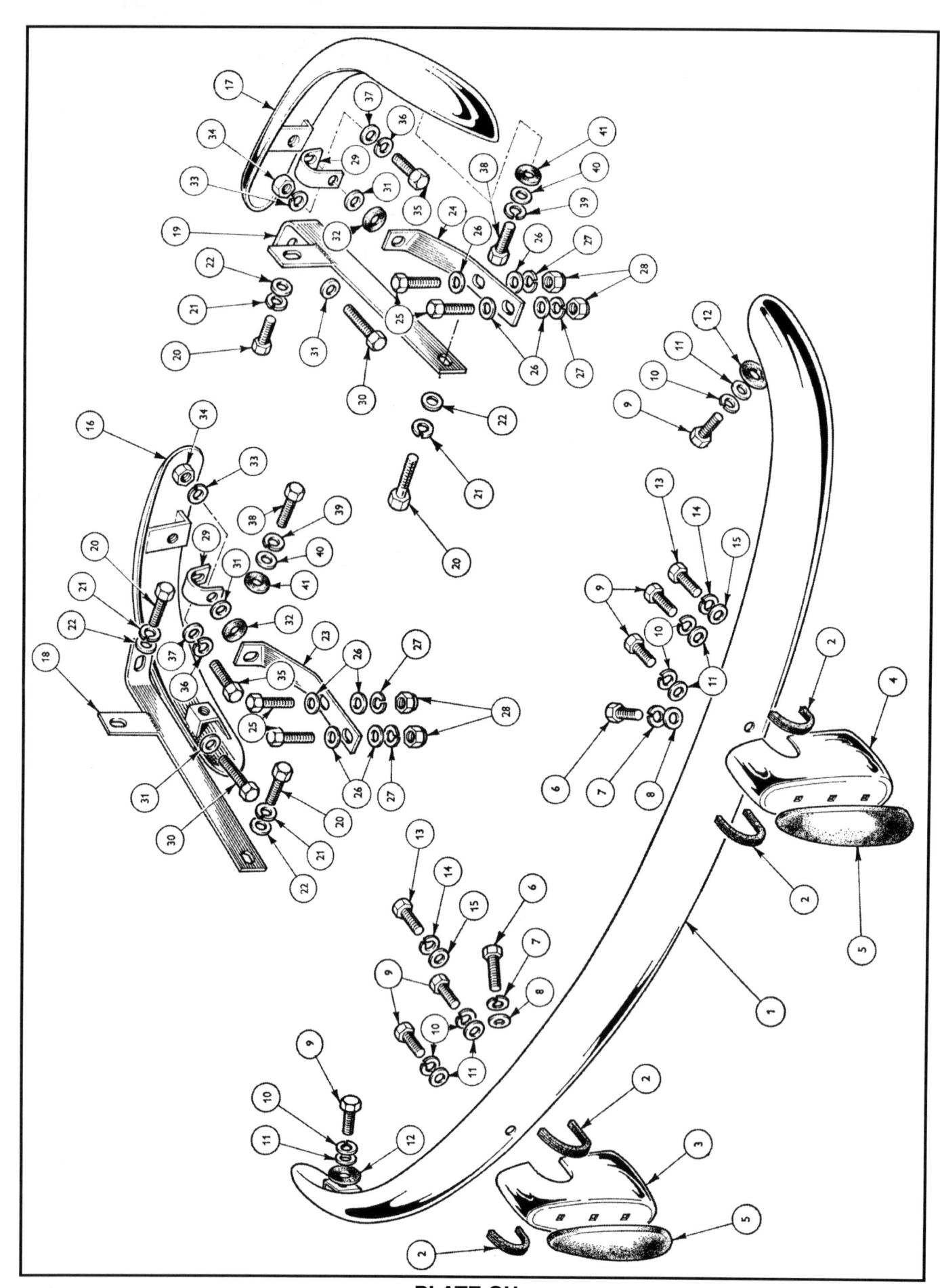

PLATE CH

BODY AND FITTINGS

Plate No.	Part No.	Description	No. per Unit	Remarks
		BUMPER AND OVERRIDER DETAILS MARK II CARS ONLY (FITTED FROM COMMISSION No. KC50001)		
CH1	811660	**FRONT BUMPER BAR ASSEMBLY**	1	
CH2	552218	**Moulding**, P.V.C., between bumper and overrider	4	
CH3	712706	**Overrider** assembly, front—R.H.	1	
CH4	712705	**Overrider** assembly, front—L.H.	1	
CH5	709753	**Buffer**, rubber, assembly, overrider	2	
CH6	HU0907	**Setscrew** ⎫ Overriders to	2	
CH7	WL0209	**Washer**, lock ⎬ front bumper	2	
CH8	WP0009	**Washer**, plain ⎭ —Upper attachment	2	
CH9	HU0806	**Setscrew** ⎫	6	
CH10	WL0208	**Washer**, lock ⎬ Front bumpers to body	6	
CH11	WP0017	**Washer**, plain ⎭	6	
CH12	615829	**Washer**, rubber, bumper to body side panel	2	
CH13	HU0906	**Setscrew** ⎫	2	
CH14	WL0209	**Washer**, lock ⎬ Overrider lower attachment to body	2	
CH15	WP0009	**Washer**, plain ⎭	2	
CH16	811477	**REAR CORNER BUMPER ASSEMBLY—R.H.**	1	
CH17	811476	**REAR CORNER BUMPER ASSEMBLY—L.H.**	1	
CH18	712564	**Bar**, spring, assembly—R.H.	1	
CH19	712563	**Bar**, spring, assembly—L.H.	1	
CH20	HU0908	**Setscrew** ⎫	4	
CH21	WL0209	**Washer**, lock ⎬ Spring bar to rear wheelarch	4	
CH22	WP0009	**Washer**, plain ⎭	4	
CH23	712566	**Support**, rear bumper—R.H.	1	
CH24	712565	**Support**, rear bumper—L.H.	1	
CH25	HU0908	**Setscrew** ⎫	4	
CH26	WP0009	**Washer**, plain ⎬ Support bar	8	
CH27	WL0209	**Washer**, lock ⎬ to trunk floor	4	
CH28	HN2009	**Nut** ⎭	4	
CH29	621252	**Extension**, support, rear bumper	2	
CH30	HU0914	**Setscrew** ⎫	2	
CH31	WP0009	**Washer**, plain ⎪ Spring bar and	4	
CH32	608854	**Washer**, rubber ⎬ support bar to	2	
CH33	WL0209	**Washer**, lock ⎪ rear extension	2	
CH34	HN2009	**Nut** ⎭	2	
CH35	HU0808	**Setscrew** ⎫	2	
CH36	WL0208	**Washer**, lock ⎬ Support extension, rear, to rear bumper	2	
CH37	WP0017	**Washer**, plain ⎭	2	
CH38	HU0806	**Setscrew** ⎫	2	
CH39	WL0208	**Washer**, lock ⎪ Rear bumpers	2	
CH40	WP0105	**Washer**, plain ⎬ to body side	2	
CH41	608854	**Washer**, rubber ⎭	2	

Note:—Items marked thus † are available on our Factory Exchange Unit Scheme

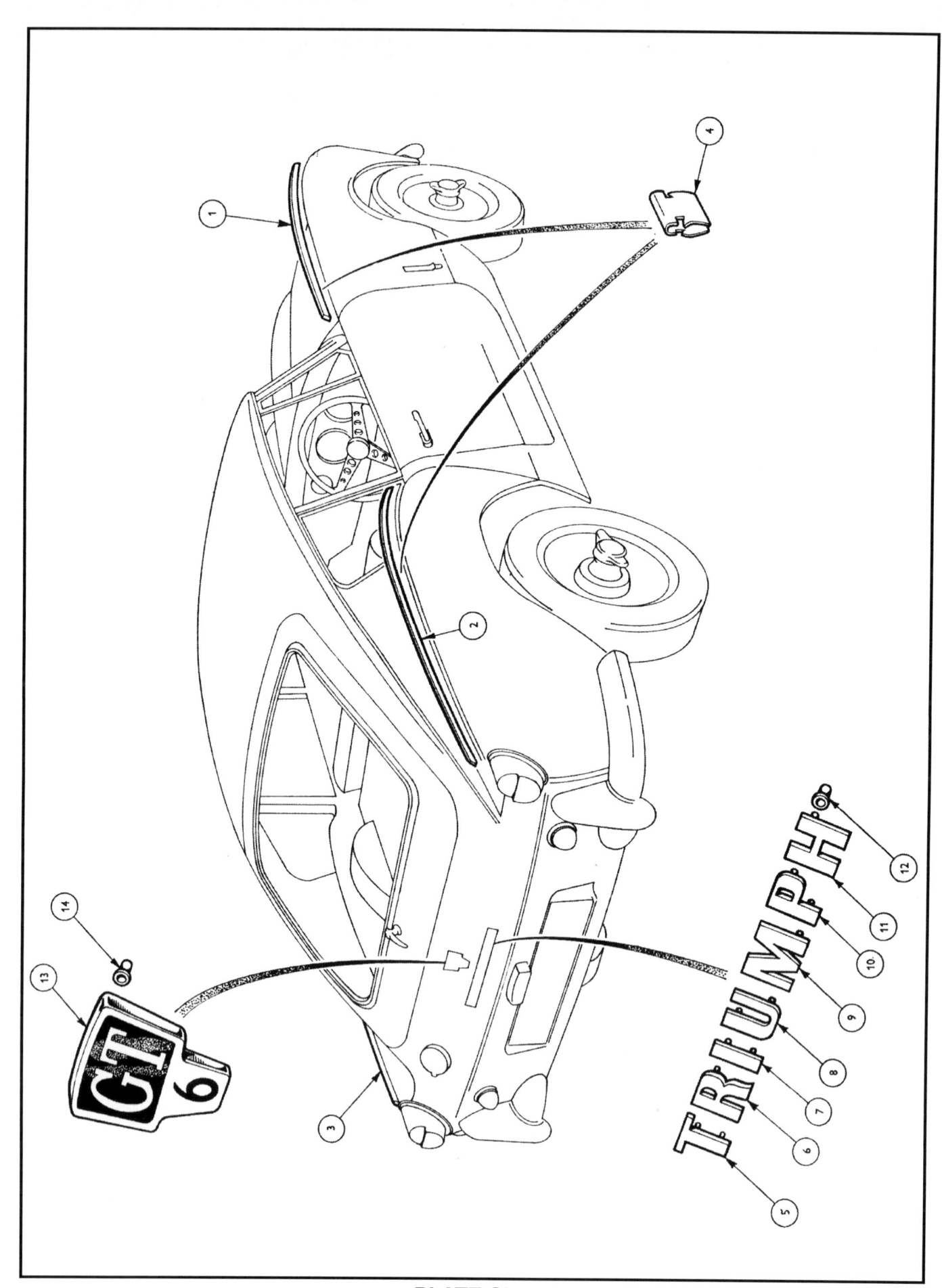

PLATE CI

BODY AND FITTINGS

Plate No.	Part No.	Description	No. per Unit	Remarks

BODY MOULDING DETAILS—Mark I Cars only (FITTED UP TO COMMISSION No. KC50000)

Plate No.	Part No.	Description	No. per Unit
CJ1	710086	**Finisher,** front wing panel joint	2
CJ2	710687	**Finisher,** rear wing, upper—R.H.	1
CJ3	710686	**Finisher,** rear wing, upper—L.H.	1
CJ4	614107	**Clip,** finisher attachment	40
CJ5	703862	**Letter 'T'**	1
CJ6	703863	**Letter 'R'**	1
CJ7	703864	**Letter 'I'**	1
CJ8	703865	**Letter 'U'**	1
CJ9	703866	**Letter 'M'**	1
CJ10	703867	**Letter 'P'**	1
CJ11	703868	**Letter 'H'**	1
CJ12	614006	**Bush,** friction, letters to rear panel	14
CJ13	619860	**Badge,** 'G.T.6.'	1
CJ14	614006	**Bush,** friction, badge to rear panel	2
	712986	**Moulding,** sill, chrome iron—R.H.	1
	712985	**Moulding,** sill, chrome iron—L.H.	1
	621771	**Clip,** beading, moulding attachment	16

Note:—Items marked thus † are available on our Factory Exchange Unit Scheme

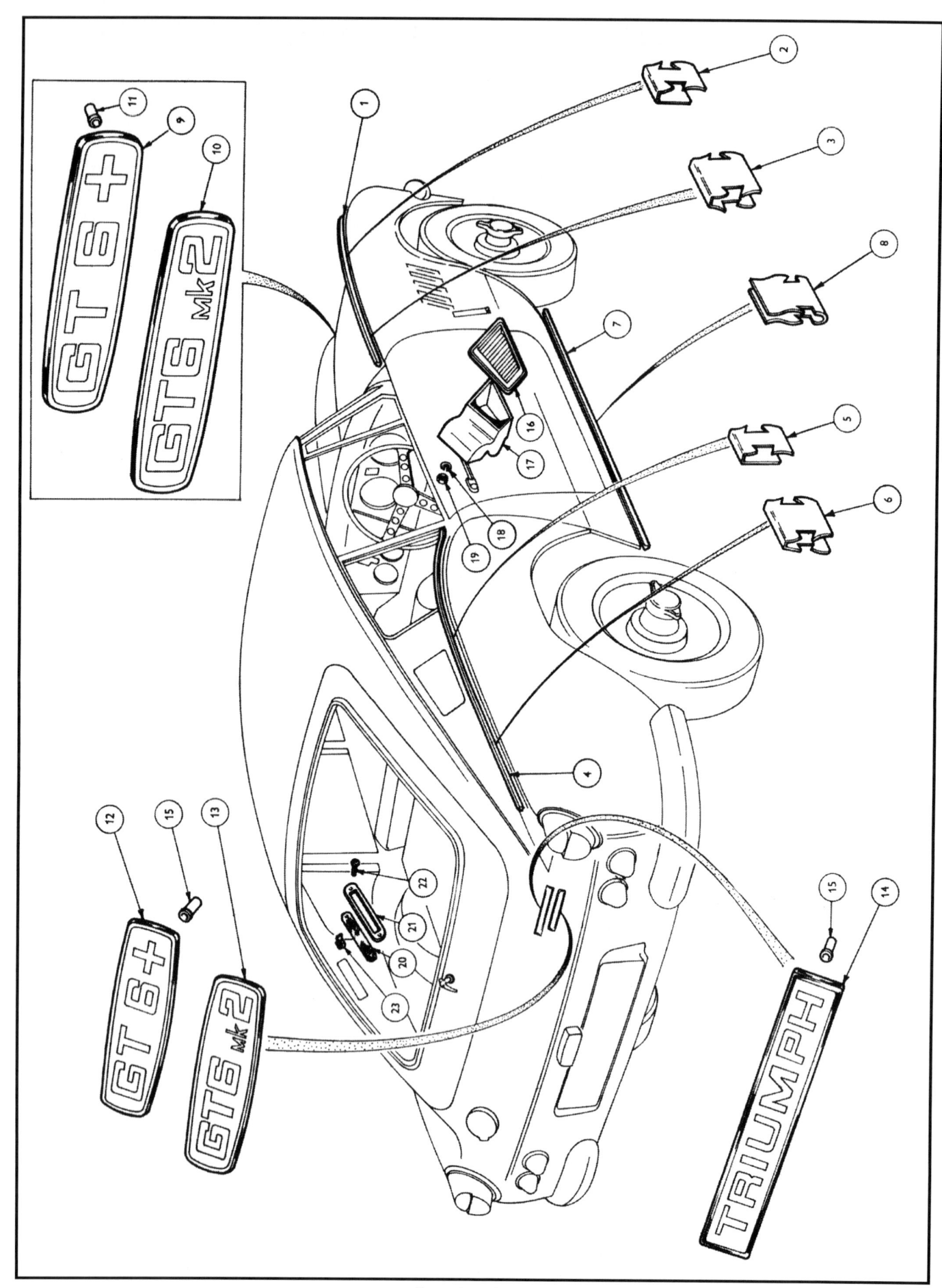

PLATE CK

BODY AND FITTINGS

Plate No.	Part No.	Description	No. per Unit	Remarks
		BODY MOULDINGS, BADGES AND AIR EXTRACTOR GRILLE DETAILS — Mark II Cars only (FITTED FROM COMMISSION No. KC50001)		
CK1	706556	**Finisher**, front wing panel joint	2	
CK2	613766	**Clip** ⎱ Front wing finisher attachment	32	
CK3	613886	**Clip** ⎰	4	
CK4	707319	**Finisher**, rear wing, upper	2	
CK5	613766	**Clip** ⎱ Rear wing finisher attachment	16	
CK6	613886	**Clip** ⎰	4	
CK7	712986	**Moulding**, sill, chrome iron—R.H.	1	
	712985	**Moulding**, sill, chrome iron—L.H.	1	
CK8	621771	**Clip**, beading, moulding attachment	16	
CK9	622496	**Nameplate**—"G.T.6.+" ⎱ Bonnet	1	U.S.A. only
CK10	623873	**Nameplate**—"G.T.6. Mk. II" ⎰ badges	1	All countries except U.S.A.
CK11	614006	**Bush**, friction, nameplate to bonnet attachment	2	
CK12	622497	**Nameplate**—"G.T.6.+" ⎱	1	U.S.A. only
CK13	623872	**Nameplate**—"G.T.6. Mk. II" ⎬ Rear panel badges	1	All countries except U.S.A.
CK14	622260	**Nameplate**—"Triumph" ⎰	1	
CK15	614006	**Bush**, friction, nameplates to rear panel	4	
CK16	813736	**Grille** assembly, air extractor, outer—R.H.	1	
	813735	**Grille** assembly, air extractor, outer—L.H.	1	
CK17	908162	**Duct**, air extractor—R.H.	1	
	908161	**Duct**, air extractor—L.H.	1	
CK18	HN2005	**Nut** ⎱ Air extractor grille and	6	
CK19	WQ0305	**Washer**, lock ⎰ duct to roof panel	6	
CK20	622611	**Grille**, air extractor, inner	2	
CK21	622153	**Bezel**, air extractor duct	2	
CK22	509560	**Screw**, self-tapping ⎱ Bezel attachment	4	
CK23	FU2594/4	**Nut**, spire ⎰	4	

Note:—Items marked thus † are available on our Factory Exchange Unit Scheme

146

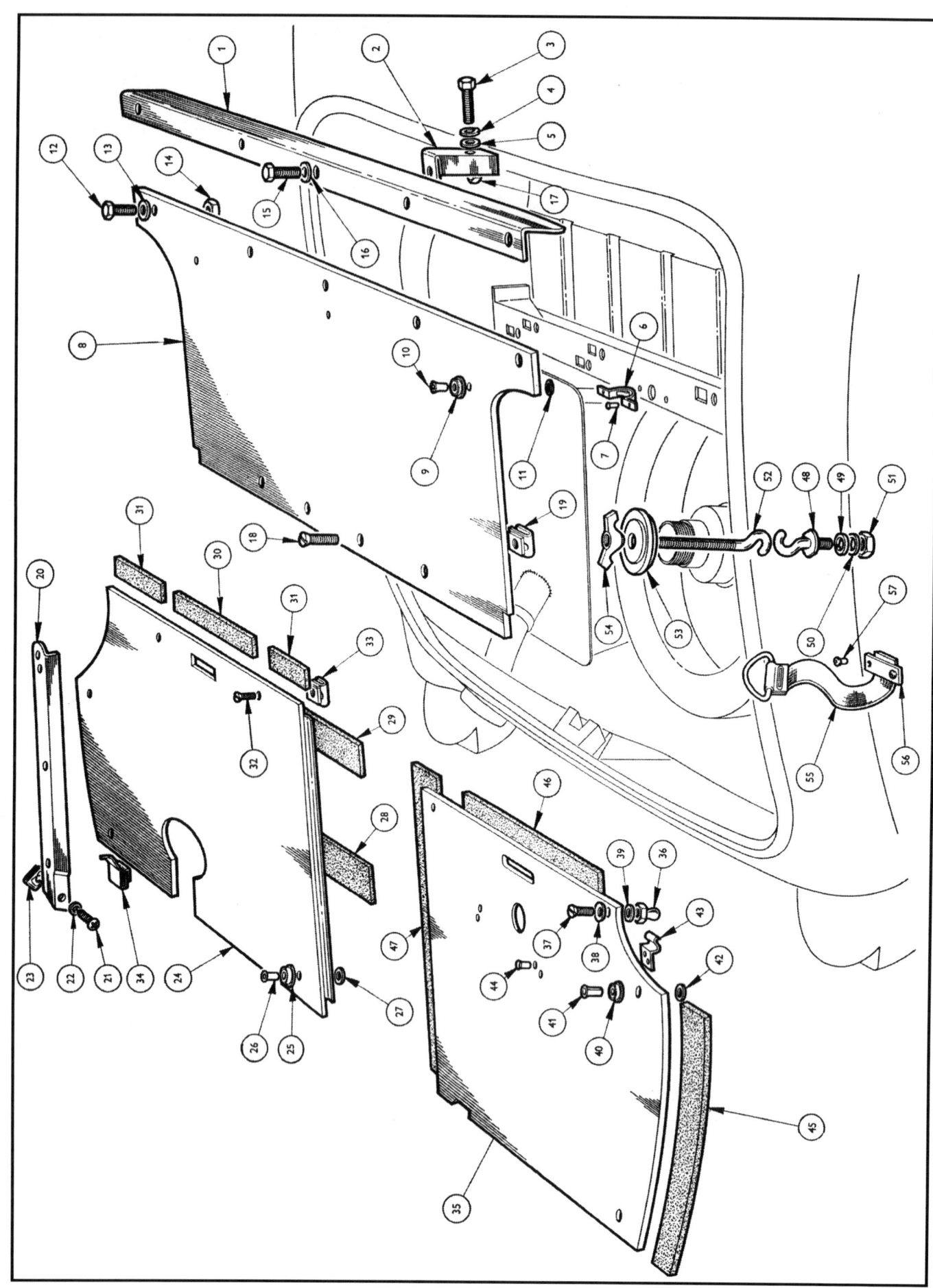

PLATE CL

BODY AND FITTINGS

Plate No.	Part No.	Description	No. per Unit	Remarks
		LUGGAGE FLOOR DETAILS		
CL1	711621	**Angle,** front, trimmed, assembly, luggage floor	1	Not required when Occasional Seat is fitted
CL2	620871	**Channel,** support, trimmed, assembly, front angle	1	⎫ Fitted up to Commission No. KC50000 only
CL3	HU0705	**Screw,** set ⎤ Channel lower fixing to floor	1	⎬
CL4	WL0207	**Washer,** lock ⎬	1	⎪
CL5	WP0007	**Washer,** plain ⎦	1	⎭
	814046	**Rail,** support, assembly, occasional seat	1	⎫
	508271	**Setscrew**	2	⎪
	505307	**Washer,** lock	2	⎪
	508875	**Washer,** plain ⎤ Occasional seat support rail	2	⎬ Only required when Occasional Seat is fitted
	503479	**Setscrew** ⎬ to luggage floor support rail	2	⎪
	502450	**Nut** ⎦	2	⎪
	501795	**Washer,** plain	4	⎪
	510506	**Washer,** lock	2	⎭
		Rail, support, assembly, luggage floor (For details see Floor Panel Section)		
CL6	618430	**Latch,** spring, spire, spare wheel cover attachment	2	
CL7	557922	**Rivet,** spring latch to support rail	4	
CL8	710702	**Luggage floor** assembly, front	1	
CL9	610624	**Stud** ⎤	3	
CL10	563769	**Rivet,** Imex ⎬ Carpet attachment	3	
CL11	WP0109	**Washer,** plain ⎦	3	
CL12	KT4706	**Screw,** set	2	
	KT4708	**Screw,** set ⎤ Front floor to angle ⎤ Not required	2	
CL13	WP0007	**Washer,** plain ⎬ and body brackets ⎬ when occasional	4	
CL14	HN2007	**Nut,** hex. ⎦ ⎦ seat is fitted	4	
CL15	KT4708	**Screw,** set	1	Fitted up to Comm. No. KC50000
	KT4706	**Screw,** set ⎤ Front floor to angle	1	Fitted from Comm. No. KC50001
CL16	WP0007	**Washer,** plain ⎬ and support channel	1	
CL17	HN2007	**Nut,** hex. ⎦	1	
CL18	KT4706	**Screw,** set ⎤ Front floor to	4	
CL19	FQ3405	**Nut,** retainer ⎦ support rail	4	
	716703	**Luggage floor** assembly, centre	1	⎫
	610624	**Stud,** durable	3	⎪ Required when
	565760	**Eyelet,** clinch type	3	⎬ Occasional Seat fitted
	KT4706	**Setscrew** ⎤ Centre luggage floor	4	⎪ to special order
	FQ3405	**Nut,** retainer ⎦ to support rail	4	⎭
CL20	709663	**Support,** outer, petrol tank board	1	
CL21	YZ3404	**Screw,** self-tapping ⎤	2	
CL22	WP8005	**Washer,** plain ⎬ Outer support attachment	2	
CL23	FU2544	**Fix,** spire ⎦	2	
CL24	710703	**Luggage floor** assembly, rear (Petrol tank cover)	1	
CL25	559702	**Stud,** fixing	3	
CL26	563769	**Rivet,** Imex ⎬ Carpet attachment	3	
CL27	WP0109	**Washer,** plain	3	
CL28	146086	**Felt strip,** 14·00" long ⎤	1	
CL29	146087	**Felt strip,** 9·00" long ⎬ Between luggage floor	1	
CL30	619779	**Felt strip,** 7·50" long ⎬ and petrol tank	1	
CL31	619780	**Felt strip,** 2·25" long ⎦	2	

Note:—Items marked thus † are available on our Factory Exchange Unit Scheme

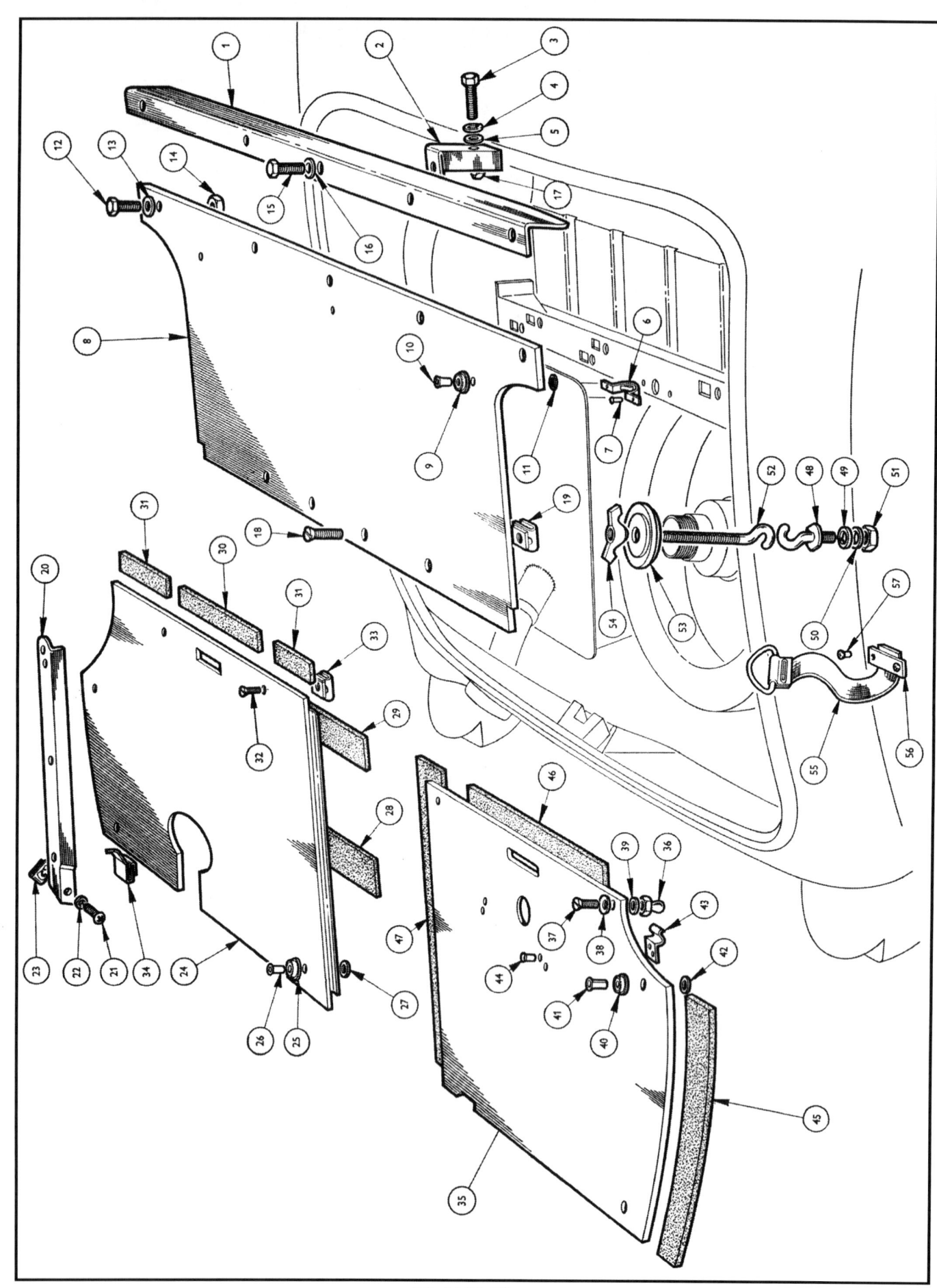

PLATE CL

BODY AND FITTINGS

Plate No.	Part No.	Description	No. per Unit	Remarks
		LUGGAGE FLOOR DETAILS—continued		
CL32	KT4706	**Screw,** set ⎫ Petrol tank cover	2	
CL33	FQ3405	**Nut,** retainer ⎭ to support rail	2	
CL34	617884	**Clip,** spring, petrol tank cover to body brackets	2	
CL35	710704	**Luggage floor** assembly, rear (Spare wheel cover)	1	
CL36	618432	**Stud,** spire, floor to support rail	2	
CL37	SP86D1	**Screw,** countersunk ⎫	2	
CL38	619607	**Washer,** cup ⎬ Stud to luggage floor	2	
CL39	WP0005	**Washer,** plain ⎭	2	
CL40	559702	**Stud,** fixing ⎫	2	
CL41	563769	**Rivet,** Imex ⎬ Carpet attachment	2	
CL42	WP0109	**Washer,** plain ⎭	2	
CL43	620410	**Clip,** spring, jack handle stowage	2	
CL44	618091	**Rivet,** spring clip attachment	2	
CL45	619777	**Felt strip,** Black, 16·50" long ⎫	1	
CL46	619776	**Felt strip,** Black, 13·50" long ⎬ Luggage floor edge	1	
CL47	619778	**Felt strip,** Black, 24·80" long ⎭	1	
CL48	618515	**Hook-bolt** assembly, spare wheel mounting, lower	1	
CL49	WL0208	**Washer,** lock ⎫	1	
CL50	WP0017	**Washer,** plain ⎬ Lower hook to trunk floor	1	
CL51	HN2008	**Nut** ⎭	1	
CL52	650017	**Hook-bolt,** spare wheel mounting, upper	1	
CL53	650016	**Disc,** clamping, spare wheel	1	
CL54	650019	**Nut,** wing	1	
CL55	619946	**Strap** assembly, jack stowage	1	
CL56	619949	**Plate,** retaining, jack stowage strap	1	
CL57	569945	**Rivet,** Imex, plate to bracket	2	

Note:—Items marked thus † are available on our Factory Exchange Unit Scheme

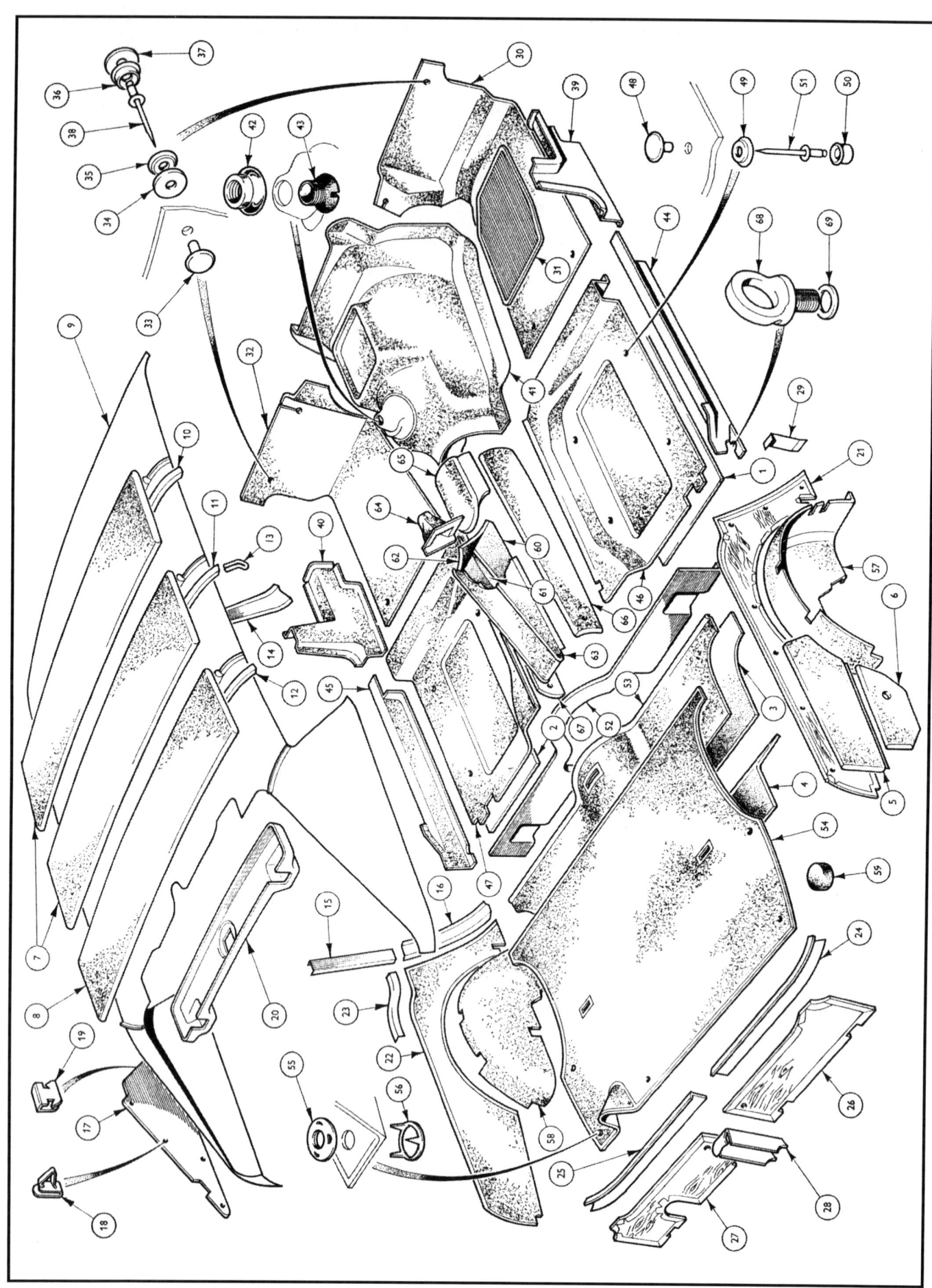

PLATE CM

378

BODY AND FITTINGS

Plate No.	Part No.	Description	No. per Unit	Remarks
		BODY TRIM		
		Note:- Due to wide variation in colour combination and possible deterioration in storage, Trim Assemblies are not held in stock but are manufactured when ordered. To facilitate the matching of Trim Assemblies a sample of the material should be sent together with the Commission and Body numbers of the vehicle.		
		SOUND DEADENING AND INSULATION DETAILS		
CM1	706976	**Pad,** insulation, rear floor, R.H.	1	
CM2	706975	**Pad,** insulation, rear floor, L.H.	1	
		Pad, insulation, gearbox cover (For details see Floor Panel Section)		
CM3	905654	**Pad,** insulation, rear seat pan, lower	1	⎫ Not required when occasional
CM4	810837	**Pad,** insulation, rear seat pan, upper	1	⎭ seat is fitted
CM5	810038	**Pad,** sound insulation, upper, rear quarter, R.H.	1	
	810037	**Pad,** sound insulation, upper, rear quarter, L.H.	1	
CM6	Not Serviced	**Pad,** sound insulation, lower, rear quarter, R.H.	1	
	Not Serviced	**Pad,** sound insulation, lower, rear quarter, L.H.	1	
CM7	905324	**Pad,** sound insulation, roof	2	
CM8	905325	**Pad,** sound insulation, roof, rear	1	
		Pad, sound deadening, doors (For details see Door Section)		
CM9	710909	**HEADLINING ASSEMBLY (WHITE)**	1	Mk. I cars up to Commission No. KC50000
	710901	**HEADLINING ASSEMBLY (BLACK)**	1	Mk. II cars from Commission No. KC50001
CM10	709811	**Listing rail,** front	1	
CM11	709812	**Listing rail,** centre	1	
CM12	709813	**Listing rail,** rear	1	
CM13	608307	**Clip,** locating, listing rail	6	
		TRIM BOARDS AND FINISHERS		
	620181	**Finisher,** trim, 'A' post, upper, R.H.	1	
CM14	620171	**Finisher,** trim, 'A' post, upper, L.H.	1	
	620359	**Finisher,** trim, 'B' post, upper, R.H.	1	
CM15	620349	**Finisher,** trim, 'B' post, upper, L.H.	1	
	620222	**Finisher,** trim, 'B' post, lower, Red, R.H.	1	
CM16	620212	**Finisher,** trim, 'B' post, lower, Red, L.H.	1	
	620223	**Finisher,** trim, 'B' post, lower, Light Tan, R.H.	1	
CM16	620213	**Finisher,** trim, 'B' post, lower, Light Tan, L.H.	1	
	620226	**Finisher,** trim, 'B' post, lower, Midnight Blue, R.H.	1	
CM16	620216	**Finisher,** trim, 'B' post, lower, Midnight Blue, L.H.	1	
	620227	**Finisher,** trim, 'B' post, lower, Shadow Blue, R.H.	1	
CM16	620217	**Finisher,** trim, 'B' post, lower, Shadow Blue, L.H.	1	
	620221	**Finisher,** trim, 'B' post, lower, Black, R.H.	1	
CM16	620211	**Finisher,** trim, 'B' post, lower, Black, L.H.	1	
	810255	**Board,** trim, quarter headlining, R.H.	1	⎫ Fitted up to Commission No.
CM17	810254	**Board,** trim, quarter headlining, L.H.	1	⎭ KC50000
	813742	**Board,** trim, quarter headlining, R.H.	1	⎫ Fitted from Commission No.
	813741	**Board,** trim, quarter headlining, L.H.	1	⎭ KC50001

Note:—Items marked thus † are available on our Factory Exchange Unit Scheme

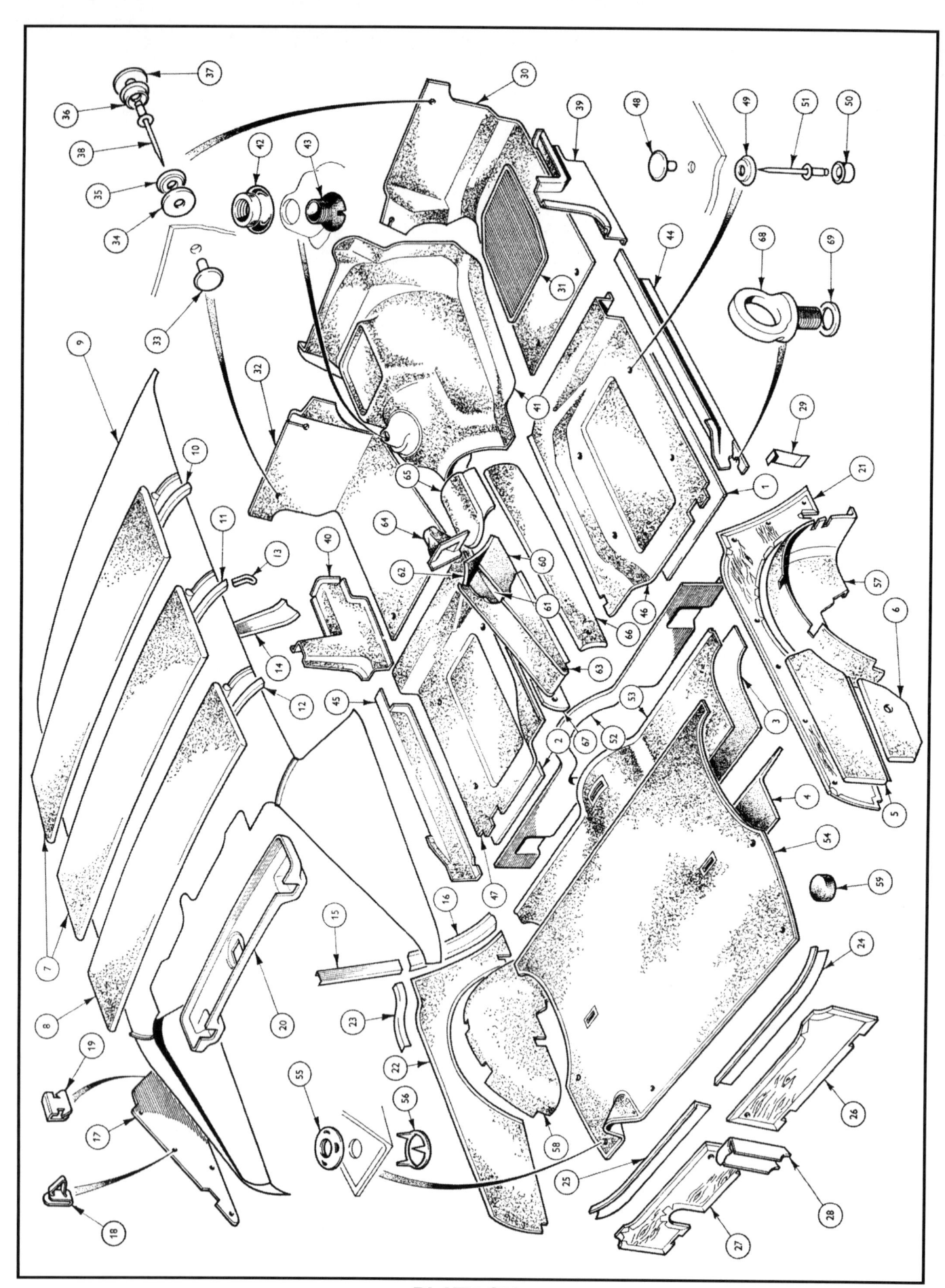

PLATE CM

BODY AND FITTINGS

Plate No.	Part No.	Description	No. per Unit	Remarks
		TRIM BOARDS AND FINISHERS—continued		
CM18	608511	**Clip,** trim ⎫	4	
CM19	608817	**Clip,** edge ⎬ Trim board attachment	2	
	YA0324	**Screw,** self-tapping ⎭	4	
CM20	810699	**Cover,** back door hinge	1	
	515562	**Screw,** hinge cover attachment	2	
	YA0326	**Screw** ⎫ Hinge cover	2	
	FJ2463/8	**Fix,** spire ⎬ and roof	2	
	620889	**Ring,** base, roof lamp ⎭ lamp fixing	2	Fitted up to Body No. 150KC only
CM21	711322	**Trim board** assembly, rear quarter, Red, R.H.	1	
CM22	711312	**Trim board** assembly, rear quarter, Red, L.H.	1	
CM21	711326	**Trim board** assembly, rear quarter, Midnight Blue, R.H.	1	
CM22	711316	**Trim board** assembly, rear quarter, Midnight Blue, L.H.	1	
CM21	711323	**Trim board** assembly, rear quarter, Light Tan, R.H.	1	
CM22	711313	**Trim board** assembly, rear quarter, Light Tan, L.H.	1	
CM21	711327	**Trim board** assembly, rear quarter, Shadow Blue, R.H.	1	
CM22	711317	**Trim board** assembly, rear quarter, Shadow Blue, L.H.	1	
CM21	711321	**Trim board** assembly, rear quarter, Black, R.H.	1	
CM22	711311	**Trim board** assembly, rear quarter, Black, L.H.	1	
	620619	**Clip,** trim, long reach ⎫ Rear quarter	6	
	608516	**Clip,** trim ⎬ trim board	2	
	608511	**Clip,** trim ⎭ attachment	14	
CM23	620389	**Cover,** trim, quarterlight, lower rail	2	
CM24	620372	**Trim,** back door aperture, Red, R.H.	1	
CM25	620362	**Trim,** back door aperture, Red, L.H.	1	
CM24	620373	**Trim,** back door aperture, Light Tan, R.H.	1	
CM25	620363	**Trim,** back door aperture, Light Tan, L.H.	1	
CM24	620376	**Trim,** back door aperture, Midnight Blue, R.H.	1	
CM25	620366	**Trim,** back door aperture, Midnight Blue, L.H.	1	
CM24	620377	**Trim,** back door aperture, Shadow Blue, R.H.	1	
CM25	620367	**Trim,** back door aperture, Shadow Blue, L.H.	1	
CM24	620371	**Trim,** back door aperture, Black, R.H.	1	
CM25	620361	**Trim,** back door aperture, Black, L.H.	1	
CM26	810792	**Trim board** assembly, rear, Red, R.H.	1	
CM27	810782	**Trim board** assembly, rear, Red, L.H.	1	
CM26	810793	**Trim board** assembly, rear, Light Tan, R.H.	1	
CM27	810783	**Trim board** assembly, rear, Light Tan, L.H.	1	
CM26	810796	**Trim board** assembly, rear, Midnight Blue, R.H.	1	
CM27	810786	**Trim board** assembly, rear, Midnight Blue, L.H.	1	
CM26	810797	**Trim board** assembly, rear, Shadow Blue, R.H.	1	
CM27	810787	**Trim board** assembly, rear, Shadow Blue, L.H.	1	
CM26	810791	**Trim board** assembly, rear, Black, R.H.	1	
CM27	810781	**Trim board** assembly, rear, Black, L.H.	1	
	613770	**Clip,** trim, rear trim board attachment	2	
CM28	620321	**Cover,** trim, P.V.C., back door striker platform	1	
CM29	620311	**Cover,** trim, wheelarch, lower front bracket	2	

Note:—Items marked thus † are available on our Factory Exchange Unit Scheme

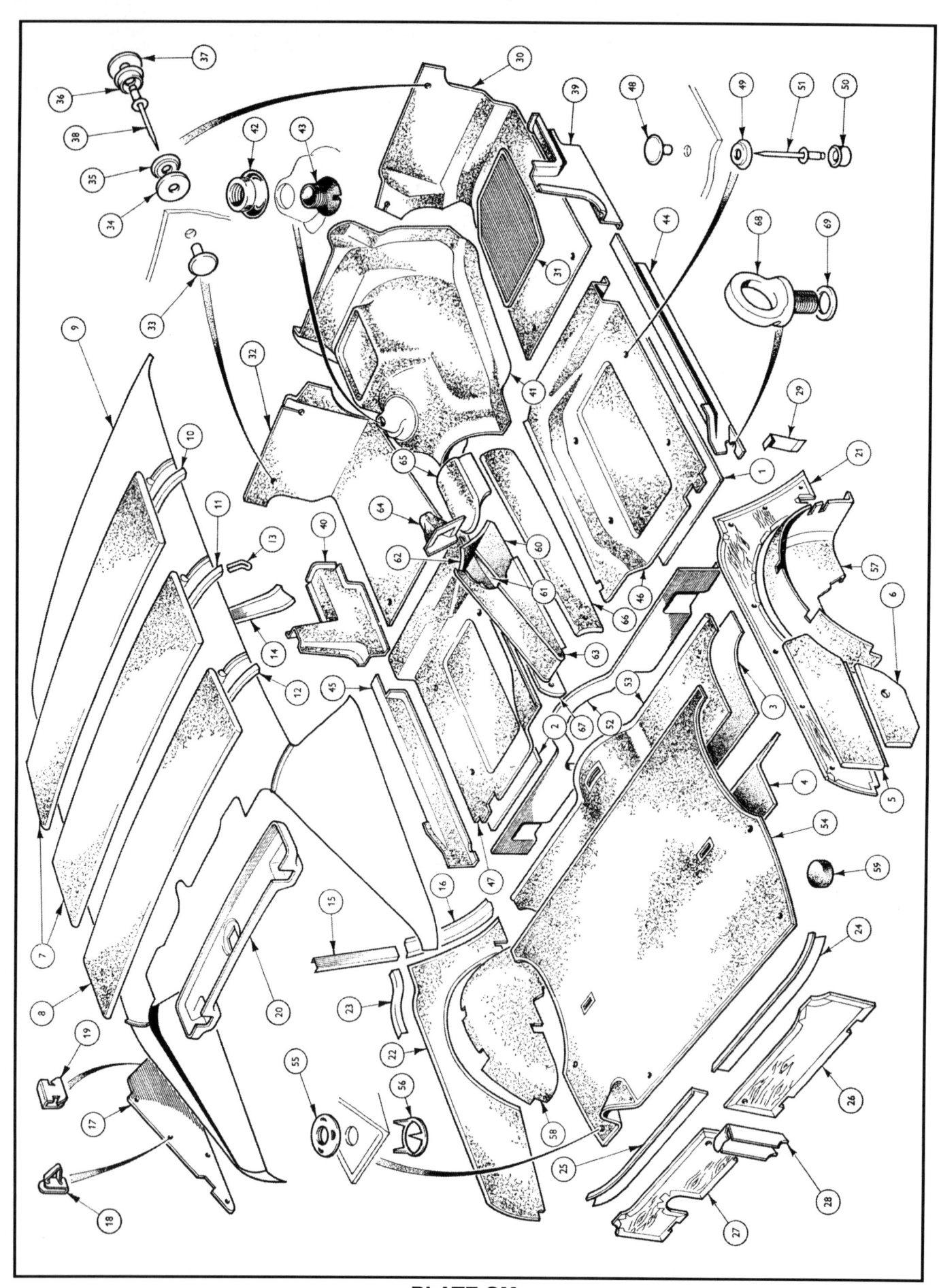

PLATE CM

382

BODY AND FITTINGS

Plate No.	Part No.	Description	No. per Unit	Remarks
		CARPET AND RUBBER MATS		
CM30	711461	**Carpet,** front floor and heel mat assembly, R.H.—R.H.S.	1	
	711481	**Carpet,** front floor and heel mat assembly, L.H.—L.H.S.	1	
CM31	707316	**Heel mat,** R.H.—R.H.S.	1	
	707315	**Heel mat,** L.H.—L.H.S.	1	
CM32	711441	**Carpet,** front floor assembly, L.H.—R.H.S.	1	
	711501	**Carpet,** front floor assembly, R.H.—L.H.S.	1	
CM33	569254	**Button** ⎫	6	
CM34	WP0126	**Washer,** plain ⎬ Carpet attachment	6	
CM35	554517	**Socket** ⎭	6	
CM36	610624	**Stud** ⎫	6	
CM37	WP0126	**Washer,** plain ⎬ Fitted to dash and floor	6	
CM38	561210	**Rivet,** imex ⎭	6	
CM39	620711	**Carpet,** dash side (Formed) R.H.	1	
CM40	620721	**Carpet,** dash side, L.H.	1	
CM41	710841	**Carpet,** gearbox cover assembly—R.H.S.	1	
	710851	**Carpet,** gearbox cover assembly—L.H.S.	1	
CM42	618944	**Ferrule,** gear lever	1	
CM43	619812	**Insert,** ferrule	1	Fitted up to Commission No. KC799 only
	618945	**Insert,** ferrule	1	Fitted from Commission No. KC800 and future
CM44	620781	**Carpet,** sill, R.H. ⎫ Formed type	1	⎫ Alternative fitment in pairs to
CM45	620771	**Carpet,** sill, L.H. ⎭	1	⎬ 813691 and 813681
	813691	**Carpet,** sill, R.H. ⎫ Cut and sewn type	1	⎫ Alternative fitment in pairs to
	813681	**Carpet,** sill, L.H. ⎭	1	⎬ 620781 and 620771
CM46	711391	**Carpet** assembly, rear floor, R.H.	1	⎫ Fitted up to Body No.
CM47	711381	**Carpet** assembly, rear floor, L.H.	1	⎬ 1040KC only, and on
CM48	553252	**Button** ⎫ Carpet attachment	4	⎬ 1047KC, 1052KC,
CM49	554517	**Socket** ⎭	4	⎭ 1065KC and 1217KC
	712571	**Carpet** assembly, rear floor, Black	1	⎫ Fitted from Body No.
	614081	**Grommet** assembly, handbrake	1	⎬ 1041KC and future
	553252	**Button**	4	⎬ except 1047KC, 1052KC,
	554517	**Socket**	4	⎭ 1065KC and 1217KC
CM50	554021	**Stud** ⎫ Rear floor	4	
CM51	563769	**Rivet,** imex ⎭ carpet attachment	4	
CM52	620761	**Carpet,** formed, heelboard	1	
CM53	711351	**Carpet** assembly, rear seat pan	1	Fitted up to Commission No. KC50000 only
	716971	**Carpet** assembly, rear seat pan (Not required when occasional seat is fitted)	1	Fitted from Commission No. KC50001 and future
CM54	810841	**Carpet** assembly, luggage floor	1	Not required when occasional seat is fitted
	814661	**Carpet** assembly, luggage floor	1	Only required when occasional seat is fitted
CM55	CD23803	**Socket** ⎫ Carpet to	8	
CM56	CD23802	**Ring,** pronged ⎭ luggage floor	8	
CM57	620831	**Carpet,** rear wheelarch cover, R.H.	1	
CM58	620821	**Carpet,** rear wheelarch cover, L.H.	1	
CM59	619558	**Pad,** spare wheel to floor	3	

Note:—Items marked thus † are available on our Factory Exchange Unit Scheme

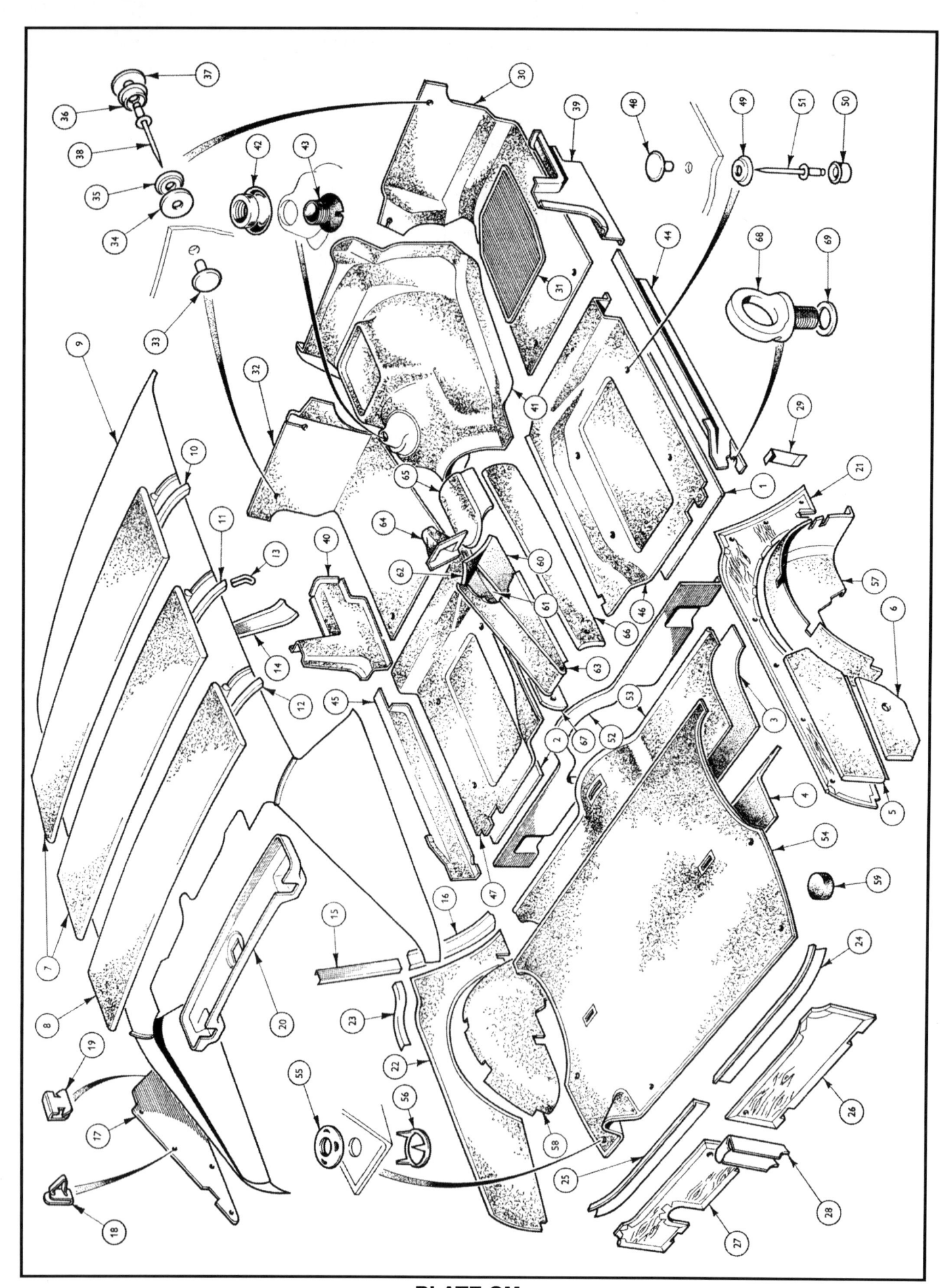

PLATE CM

BODY AND FITTINGS

Plate No.	Part No.	Description	No. per Unit	Remarks
	711082	HANDBRAKE COVER AND CENTRE ARMREST ASSEMBLY, LEATHERCLOTH, RED	1	
	711083	HANDBRAKE COVER AND CENTRE ARMREST ASSEMBLY, LEATHERCLOTH, LIGHT TAN	1	
	711086	HANDBRAKE COVER AND CENTRE ARMREST ASSEMBLY, LEATHERCLOTH, MIDNIGHT BLUE	1	
	711087	HANDBRAKE COVER AND CENTRE ARMREST ASSEMBLY, LEATHERCLOTH, SHADOW BLUE	1	
	711081	HANDBRAKE COVER AND CENTRE ARMREST ASSEMBLY, LEATHERCLOTH, BLACK	1	
	711092	HANDBRAKE COVER AND CENTRE ARMREST ASSEMBLY, LEATHER, RED	1	Special Order only
	711093	HANDBRAKE COVER AND CENTRE ARMREST ASSEMBLY, LEATHER, LIGHT TAN	1	Special Order only
	711096	HANDBRAKE COVER AND CENTRE ARMREST ASSEMBLY, LEATHER, MIDNIGHT BLUE	1	Special Order only
	711097	HANDBRAKE COVER AND CENTRE ARMREST ASSEMBLY, LEATHER, SHADOW BLUE	1	Special Order only
	711091	HANDBRAKE COVER AND CENTRE ARMREST ASSEMBLY, LEATHER, BLACK	1	Special Order only
CM60	619437	**Pad,** foam, handbrake cover, side	2	
CM61	619439	**Pad,** foam, handbrake cover, top	1	
CM62	619440	**Pad,** foam, handbrake cover, front	1	
CM63	711102	**Cover** assembly, handbrake (Centre armrest) leathercloth, Red	1	
CM63	711103	**Cover** assembly, handbrake (Centre armrest) leathercloth, Light Tan	1	
CM63	711106	**Cover** assembly, handbrake (Centre armrest) leathercloth, Midnight Blue	1	
CM63	711107	**Cover** assembly, handbrake (Centre armrest) leathercloth, Shadow Blue	1	
CM63	711101	**Cover** assembly, handbrake (Centre armrest) leathercloth, Black	1	

Note:—Items marked thus † are available on our Factory Exchange Unit Scheme

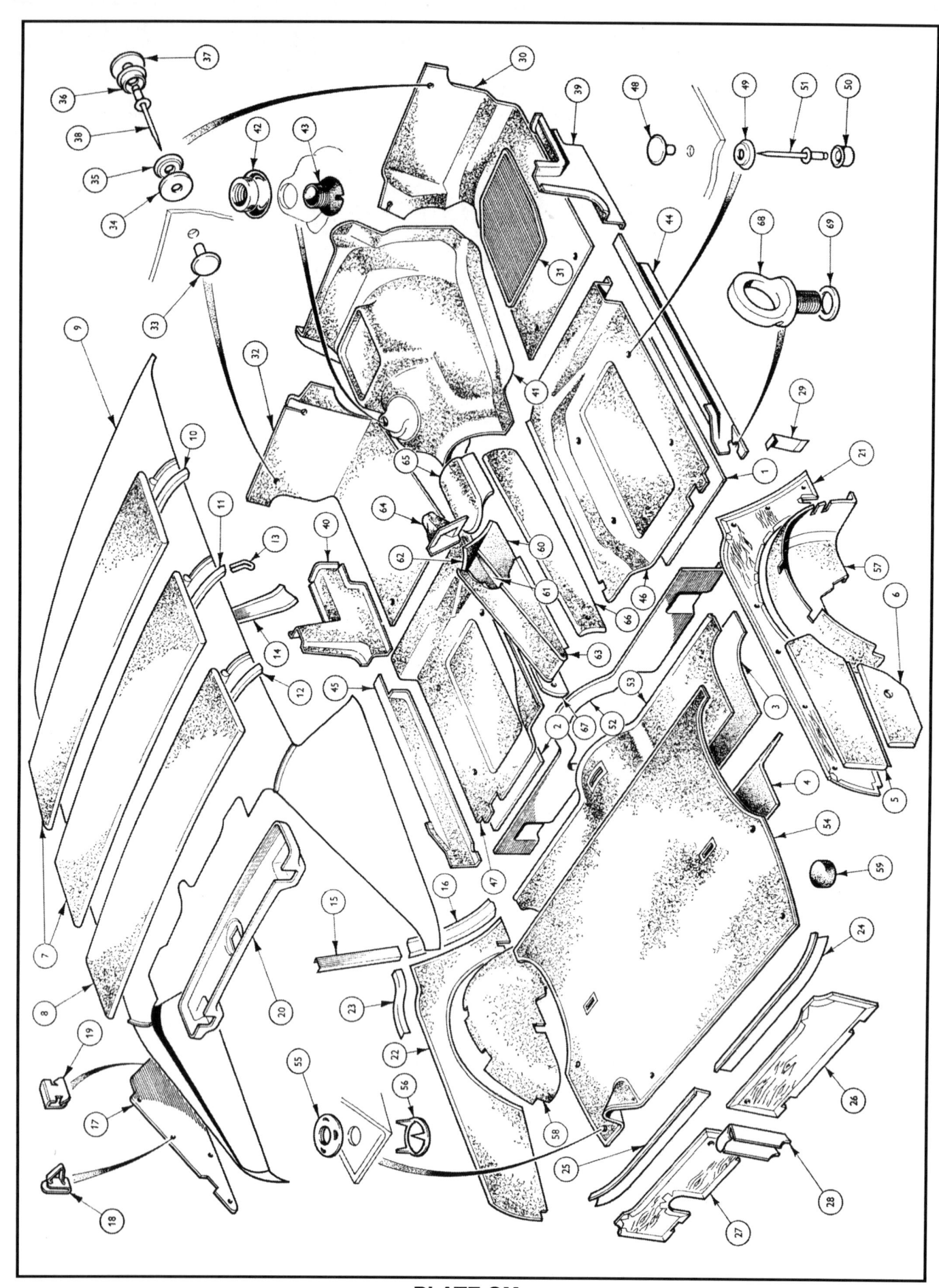

PLATE CM

BODY AND FITTINGS

Plate No.	Part No.	Description	No. per Unit	Remarks
		HANDBRAKE COVER AND CENTRE ARMREST ASSEMBLY—continued		
CM63	711112	**Cover** assembly, handbrake (Centre armrest) leather, Red	1	
CM63	711113	**Cover** assembly, handbrake (Centre armrest) leather, Light Tan	1	
CM63	711116	**Cover** assembly, handbrake (Centre armrest) leather, Midnight Blue	1	
CM63	711117	**Cover** assembly, handbrake (Centre armrest) leather, Shadow Blue	1	
CM63	711111	**Cover** assembly, handbrake (Centre armrest) leather, Black	1	
CM64	620502	**Grommet**, handbrake assembly, leathercloth, Red	1	
CM64	620503	**Grommet**, handbrake assembly, leathercloth, Light Tan	1	
CM64	620506	**Grommet**, handbrake assembly, leathercloth, Midnight Blue	1	
CM64	620507	**Grommet**, handbrake assembly, leathercloth, Shadow Blue	1	
CM64	620501	**Grommet**, handbrake assembly, leathercloth, Black	1	
CM64	620512	**Grommet**, handbrake assembly, leather, Red	1	
CM64	620513	**Grommet**, handbrake assembly, leather, Light Tan	1	
CM64	620516	**Grommet**, handbrake assembly, leather, Midnight Blue	1	Special Order only
CM64	620517	**Grommet**, handbrake assembly, leather, Shadow Blue	1	
CM64	620511	**Grommet**, handbrake assembly, leather, Black	1	
	YZ3304	**Screw**, handbrake cover and centre armrest attachment	6	
		TUNNEL COVERS		
CM65	711022	**Cover** assembly, tunnel, centre, leathercloth, Red	1	
CM65	711023	**Cover** assembly, tunnel, centre, leathercloth, Light Tan	1	
CM65	711026	**Cover** assembly, tunnel, centre, leathercloth, Midnight Blue	1	
CM65	711027	**Cover** assembly, tunnel, centre, leathercloth, Shadow Blue	1	
CM65	711021	**Cover** assembly, tunnel, centre, leathercloth, Black	1	
CM65	711032	**Cover** assembly, tunnel, centre, leather, Red	1	
CM65	711033	**Cover** assembly, tunnel, centre, leather, Light Tan	1	
CM65	711036	**Cover** assembly, tunnel, centre, leather, Midnight Blue	1	Special Order only
CM65	711037	**Cover** assembly, tunnel, centre, leather, Shadow Blue	1	
CM65	711031	**Cover** assembly, tunnel, centre, leather, Black	1	
CM66	711052	**Cover** assembly, tunnel, rear—R.H., leathercloth, Red	1	
CM66	711056	**Cover** assembly, tunnel, rear—R.H., leathercloth, Midnight Blue	1	
CM66	711051	**Cover** assembly, tunnel, rear—R.H., leathercloth, Black	1	
CM66	711072	**Cover** assembly, tunnel, rear—R.H., leather, Red	1	Special Order only
CM66	711076	**Cover** assembly, tunnel, rear—R.H., leather, Midnight Blue	1	Fitted up to Body No. 1040KC only, and on 1047KC, 1052KC, 1065KC and 1217KC
CM66	711071	**Cover** assembly, tunnel, rear—R.H., leather, Black	1	
CM67	711042	**Cover** assembly, tunnel, rear—L.H., leathercloth, Red	1	
CM67	711046	**Cover** assembly, tunnel, rear—L.H., leathercloth, Midnight Blue	1	
CM67	711041	**Cover** assembly, tunnel, rear—L.H., leathercloth, Black	1	
CM67	711062	**Cover** assembly, tunnel, rear—L.H., leather, Red	1	Special Order only
CM67	711066	**Cover** assembly, tunnel, rear—L.H., leather, Midnight Blue	1	
CM67	711061	**Cover** assembly, tunnel, rear—L.H., leather, Black	1	

Note:—Items marked thus † are available on our **Factory Exchange Unit Scheme**

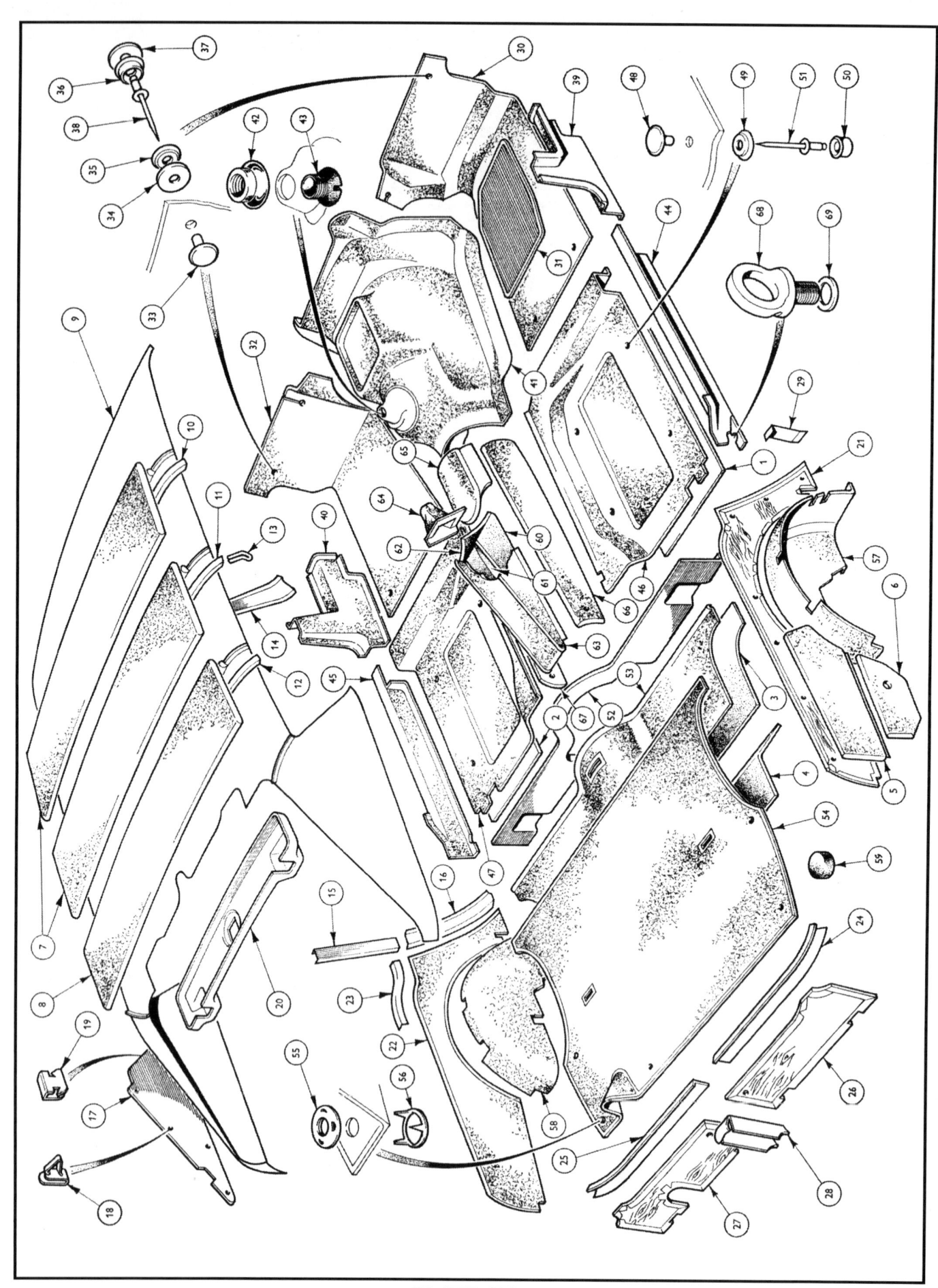

PLATE CM

BODY AND FITTINGS

Plate No.	Part No.	Description	No. per Unit	Remarks
		TUNNEL COVERS—continued		
CM66	712442	**Cover** assembly, tunnel, rear—R.H., leathercloth, Red	1	
CM66	712443	**Cover** assembly, tunnel, rear—R.H., leathercloth, Light Tan	1	
CM66	712446	**Cover** assembly, tunnel, rear—R.H., leathercloth, Midnight Blue	1	
CM66	712447	**Cover** assembly, tunnel, rear—R.H., leathercloth, Shadow Blue	1	
CM66	712441	**Cover** assembly, tunnel, rear—R.H., leathercloth, Black	1	
CM66	712462	**Cover** assembly, tunnel, rear—R.H., leather, Red	1	Special Order only
CM66	712463	**Cover** assembly, tunnel, rear—R.H., leather, Light Tan	1	
CM66	712466	**Cover** assembly, tunnel, rear—R.H., leather, Midnight Blue	1	Fitted from Body No. 1041KC and future, except 1047KC, 1052KC, 1065KC and 1217KC
CM66	712467	**Cover** assembly, tunnel, rear—R.H., leather, Shadow Blue	1	
CM66	712461	**Cover** assembly, tunnel, rear—R.H., leather, Black	1	
CM67	712432	**Cover** assembly, tunnel, rear—L.H., leathercloth, Red	1	
CM67	712433	**Cover** assembly, tunnel, rear—L.H., leathercloth, Light Tan	1	
CM67	712436	**Cover** assembly, tunnel, rear—L.H., leathercloth, Midnight Blue	1	
CM67	712437	**Cover** assembly, tunnel, rear—L.H., leathercloth, Shadow Blue	1	
CM67	712431	**Cover** assembly, tunnel, rear—L.H., leathercloth, Black	1	
CM67	712452	**Cover** assembly, tunnel, rear—L.H., leather, Red	1	Special Order only
CM67	712453	**Cover** assembly, tunnel, rear—L.H., leather, Light Tan	1	
CM67	712456	**Cover** assembly, tunnel, rear—L.H., leather, Midnight Blue	1	
CM67	712457	**Cover** assembly, tunnel, rear—L.H., leather, Shadow Blue	1	
CM67	712451	**Cover** assembly, tunnel, rear—L.H., leather, Black	1	
	502476	**Screw**, self-tapping } Tunnel cover,	2	
	CD24153	**Washer**, cup } front attachment	2	
	510857	**Screw**, self-tapping } Tunnel cover,	2	
	CD24256	**Washer**, cup } rear attachment	2	
	712600	**SAFETY HARNESS**	2	Suitable for fitment to vehicles from Body No. 1041KC and future, except 1047KC, 1052KC, 1065KC and 1217KC
	621421	**Finisher**, safety harness aperture, rear tunnel	2	Fitted from approx. Body No. 1041KC up to Body No. only
	621867	**Finisher**, safety harness aperture, rear tunnel (May be used for all replacements if fitted in pairs)	2	Fitted from Body No. and future
CM68	612531	**Eye bolt** } Safety belt fixing	4	Fitted up to Body No. 1040KC only, and on 1047KC, 1052KC, 1065KC and 1217KC
CM69	WL0210	**Washer**, lock	4	
	621308	**Eye bolt**	4	
	WL0210	**Washer**, lock	4	Floor and tunnel safety harness attachment
	621292	**Washer**, plain (Above mounting pads)	2	Fitted from Body No. 1041KC and future, except 1047KC, 1052KC, 1065KC and 1217KC
	621101	**Pad**, mounting, eye bolts (Fitted between floor and frame)	2	
	621370	**Bolt**, safety harness } Rear wheelarch	2	
	621371	**Spacer** } safety harness	2	
	621374	**Washer**, waved } attachment	2	

Note:—Items marked thus † are available on our Factory Exchange Unit Scheme

154

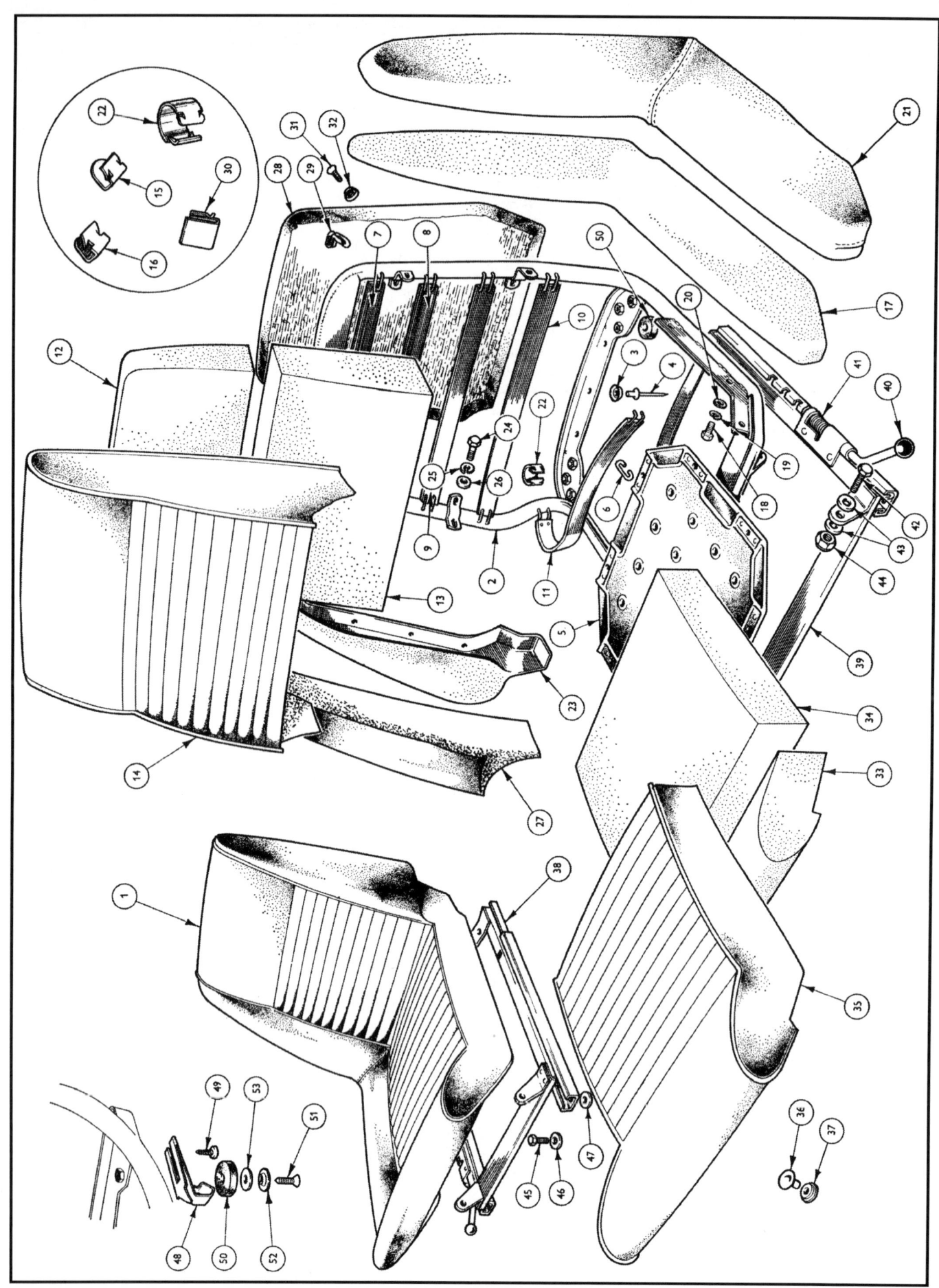

PLATE CN

BODY AND FITTINGS

Plate No.	Part No.	Description	No. per Unit	Remarks
CN1	905482	FRONT SEAT COMPLETE ASSEMBLY, TRIMMED—LEATHERCLOTH (Red)—R.H.	1	
	905472	FRONT SEAT COMPLETE ASSEMBLY, TRIMMED—LEATHERCLOTH (Red)—L.H.	1	
CN1	905483	FRONT SEAT COMPLETE ASSEMBLY, TRIMMED—LEATHERCLOTH (Light Tan)—R.H.	1	
	905473	FRONT SEAT COMPLETE ASSEMBLY, TRIMMED—LEATHERCLOTH (Light Tan)—L.H.	1	
CN1	905486	FRONT SEAT COMPLETE ASSEMBLY, TRIMMED—LEATHERCLOTH (Midnight Blue)—R.H.	1	
	905476	FRONT SEAT COMPLETE ASSEMBLY, TRIMMED—LEATHERCLOTH (Midnight Blue)—L.H.	1	Fitted up to Commission No. KC9999 (U.S.A.) and KC12804 Black trim, KC9012 Blue trim, KC8805 Tan trim, KC12747 Red trim, (other markets) only
CN1	905487	FRONT SEAT COMPLETE ASSEMBLY, TRIMMED—LEATHERCLOTH (Shadow Blue)—R.H.	1	
	905477	FRONT SEAT COMPLETE ASSEMBLY, TRIMMED—LEATHERCLOTH (Shadow Blue)—L.H.	1	
CN1	905481	FRONT SEAT COMPLETE ASSEMBLY, TRIMMED—LEATHERCLOTH (Black)—R.H.	1	
	905471	FRONT SEAT COMPLETE ASSEMBLY, TRIMMED—LEATHERCLOTH (Black)—L.H.	1	
CN1	905502	FRONT SEAT COMPLETE ASSEMBLY, TRIMMED—LEATHER (Red)—R.H.	1	
	905492	FRONT SEAT COMPLETE ASSEMBLY, TRIMMED—LEATHER (Red)—L.H.	1	
CN1	905503	FRONT SEAT COMPLETE ASSEMBLY, TRIMMED—LEATHER (Light Tan)—R.H.	1	
	905493	FRONT SEAT COMPLETE ASSEMBLY, TRIMMED—LEATHER (Light Tan)—L.H.	1	

Note:—Items marked thus † are available on our Factory Exchange Unit Scheme

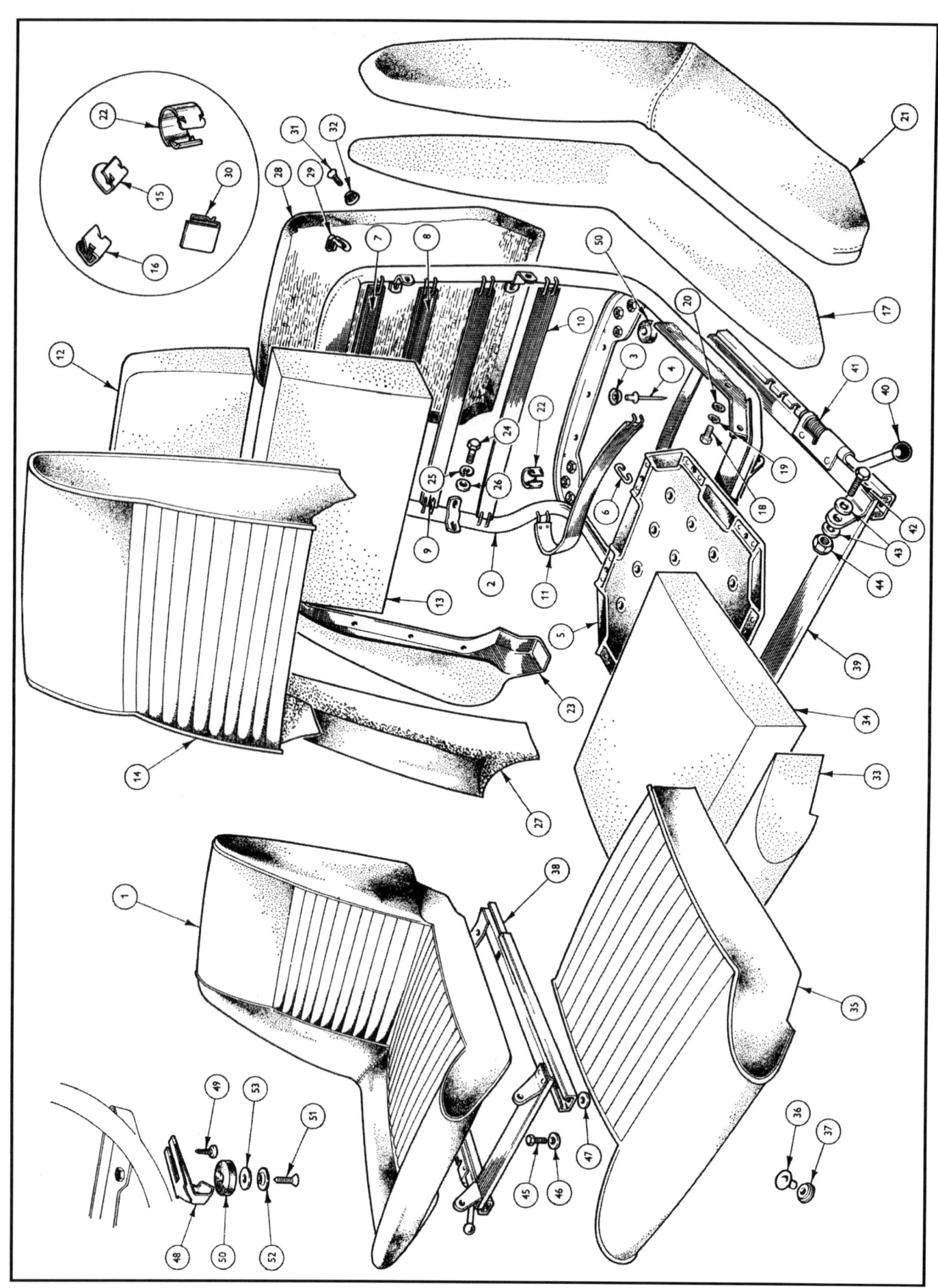

PLATE CN

BODY AND FITTINGS

Plate No.	Part No.	Description	No. per Unit	Remarks
CN1	905506	FRONT SEAT COMPLETE ASSEMBLY, TRIMMED—LEATHER (Midnight Blue)—R.H.	1	
	905496	FRONT SEAT COMPLETE ASSEMBLY, TRIMMED—LEATHER (Midnight Blue)—L.H.	1	
CN1	905507	FRONT SEAT COMPLETE ASSEMBLY, TRIMMED—LEATHER (Shadow Blue)—R.H.	1	
	905497	FRONT SEAT COMPLETE ASSEMBLY, TRIMMED—LEATHER (Shadow Blue)—L.H.	1	
CN1	905501	FRONT SEAT COMPLETE ASSEMBLY, TRIMMED—LEATHER (Black)—R.H.	1	
	905491	FRONT SEAT COMPLETE ASSEMBLY, TRIMMED—LEATHER (Black)—L.H.	1	Fitted up to Commission No. KC9999 (U.S.A.) and KC12804 Black trim, KC9012 Blue trim, KC8805 Tan trim, KC12747 Red trim (other markets) only
	905522	FRONT SEAT FRAME AND SQUAB ASSEMBLY, TRIMMED—LEATHERCLOTH (RED)—R.H.	1	
	905512	FRONT SEAT FRAME AND SQUAB ASSEMBLY, TRIMMED—LEATHERCLOTH (RED)—L.H.	1	
	905523	FRONT SEAT FRAME AND SQUAB ASSEMBLY, TRIMMED—LEATHERCLOTH (LIGHT TAN)—R.H.	1	
	905513	FRONT SEAT FRAME AND SQUAB ASSEMBLY, TRIMMED—LEATHERCLOTH (LIGHT TAN)—L.H.	1	
	905526	FRONT SEAT FRAME AND SQUAB ASSEMBLY, TRIMMED—LEATHERCLOTH (MIDNIGHT BLUE)—R.H.	1	
	905516	FRONT SEAT FRAME AND SQUAB ASSEMBLY, TRIMMED—LEATHERCLOTH (MIDNIGHT BLUE)—L.H.	1	
	905527	FRONT SEAT FRAME AND SQUAB ASSEMBLY, TRIMMED—LEATHERCLOTH (SHADOW BLUE)—R.H.	1	
	905517	FRONT SEAT FRAME AND SQUAB ASSEMBLY, TRIMMED—LEATHERCLOTH (SHADOW BLUE)—L.H.	1	

Note:—Items marked thus † are available on our Factory Exchange Unit Scheme

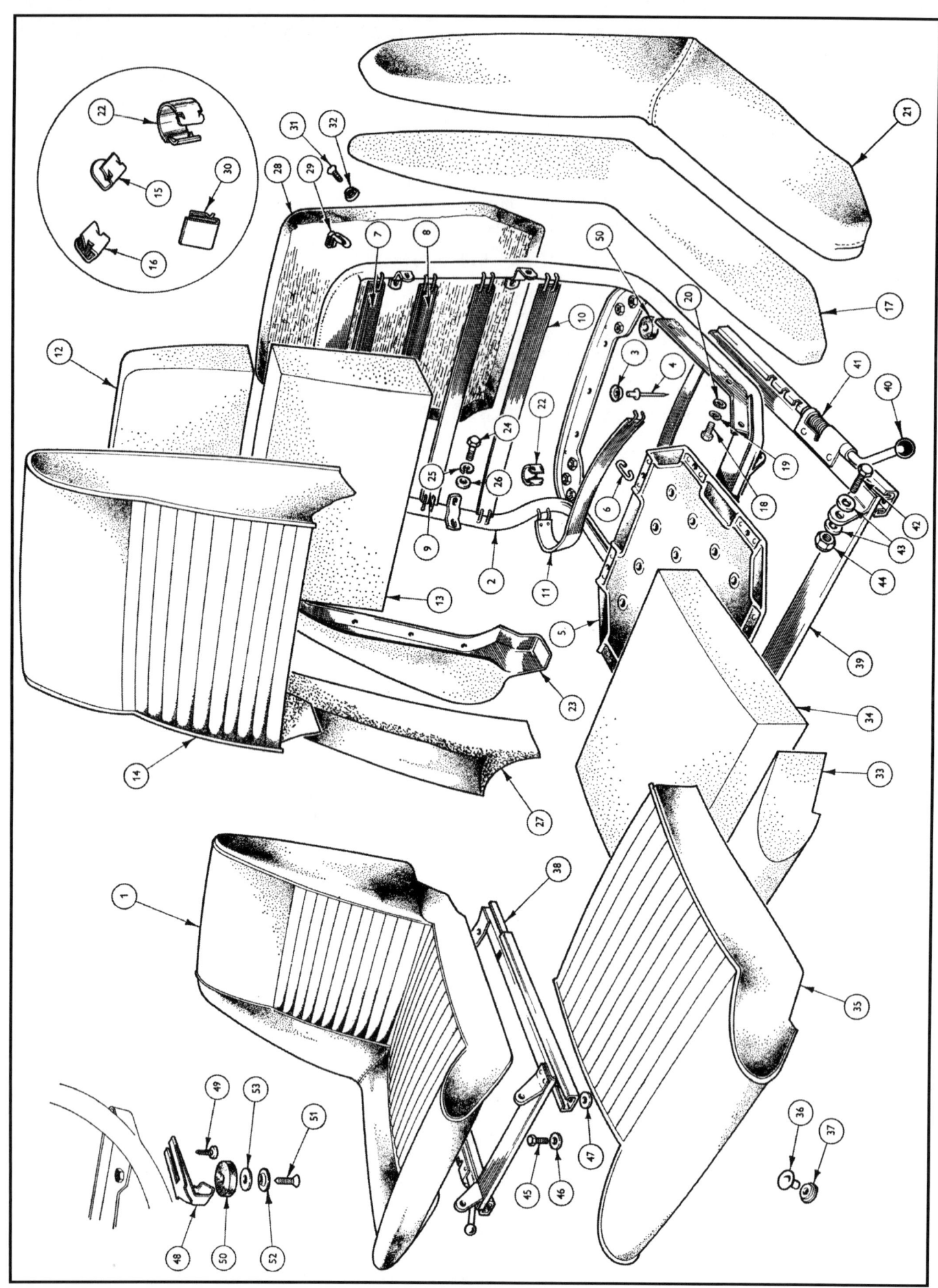

PLATE CN

394

BODY AND FITTINGS

Plate No.	Part No.	Description	No. per Unit	Remarks
	905521	FRONT SEAT FRAME AND SQUAB ASSEMBLY, TRIMMED—LEATHERCLOTH (BLACK)—R.H.	1	
	905511	FRONT SEAT FRAME AND SQUAB ASSEMBLY, TRIMMED—LEATHERCLOTH (BLACK)—L.H.	1	
	905542	FRONT SEAT FRAME AND SQUAB ASSEMBLY, TRIMMED—LEATHER (RED)—R.H.	1	
	905532	FRONT SEAT FRAME AND SQUAB ASSEMBLY, TRIMMED—LEATHER (RED)—L.H.	1	
	905543	FRONT SEAT FRAME AND SQUAB ASSEMBLY, TRIMMED—LEATHER (LIGHT TAN)—R.H.	1	
	905533	FRONT SEAT FRAME AND SQUAB ASSEMBLY, TRIMMED—LEATHER (LIGHT TAN)—L.H.	1	
	905546	FRONT SEAT FRAME AND SQUAB ASSEMBLY, TRIMMED—LEATHER (MIDNIGHT BLUE)—R.H.	1	Fitted up to Commission No. KC9999 (U.S.A.) and KC12804 Black trim, KC9012 Blue trim, KC8805 Tan trim, KC12747 Red trim, (other markets) only
	905536	FRONT SEAT FRAME AND SQUAB ASSEMBLY, TRIMMED—LEATHER (MIDNIGHT BLUE)	1	
	905547	FRONT SEAT FRAME AND SQUAB ASSEMBLY, TRIMMED—LEATHER (SHADOW BLUE)—R.H.	1	
	905537	FRONT SEAT FRAME AND SQUAB ASSEMBLY, TRIMMED—LEATHER (SHADOW BLUE)—L.H.	1	
	905541	FRONT SEAT FRAME AND SQUAB ASSEMBLY, TRIMMED—LEATHER (BLACK)—R.H.	1	
	905531	FRONT SEAT FRAME AND SQUAB ASSEMBLY, TRIMMED—LEATHER (BLACK)—L.H.	1	
	904601	**Frame** assembly, R.H. seat	1	
CN2	904600	**Frame** assembly, L.H. seat	1	
CN3	610624	**Stud**, cushion attachment	6	
CN4	561210	**Rivet**, stud to frame	6	
CN5	573900	**Diaphragm**, seat base	2	
CN6	613966	**Hook**, diaphragm	16	
CN7	619498	**Strap** assembly, squab, 11" long—Top	2	
CN8	619499	**Strap** assembly, squab, 12" long—Top intermediate	2	
CN9	619500	**Strap** assembly, squab, 12.5" long—Centre	2	
CN10	619501	**Strap** assembly, squab, 13.75" long—Bottom intermediate	2	
CN11	619498	**Strap** assembly, squab, 11" long—Bottom	2	
	621340	**Hook**, strap	20	
CN12	810630	**Pad**, squab, upper	2	
	810632	**Pad**, squab, lower, R.H. seat	1	

Note:—Items marked thus † are available on our Factory Exchange Unit Scheme

157

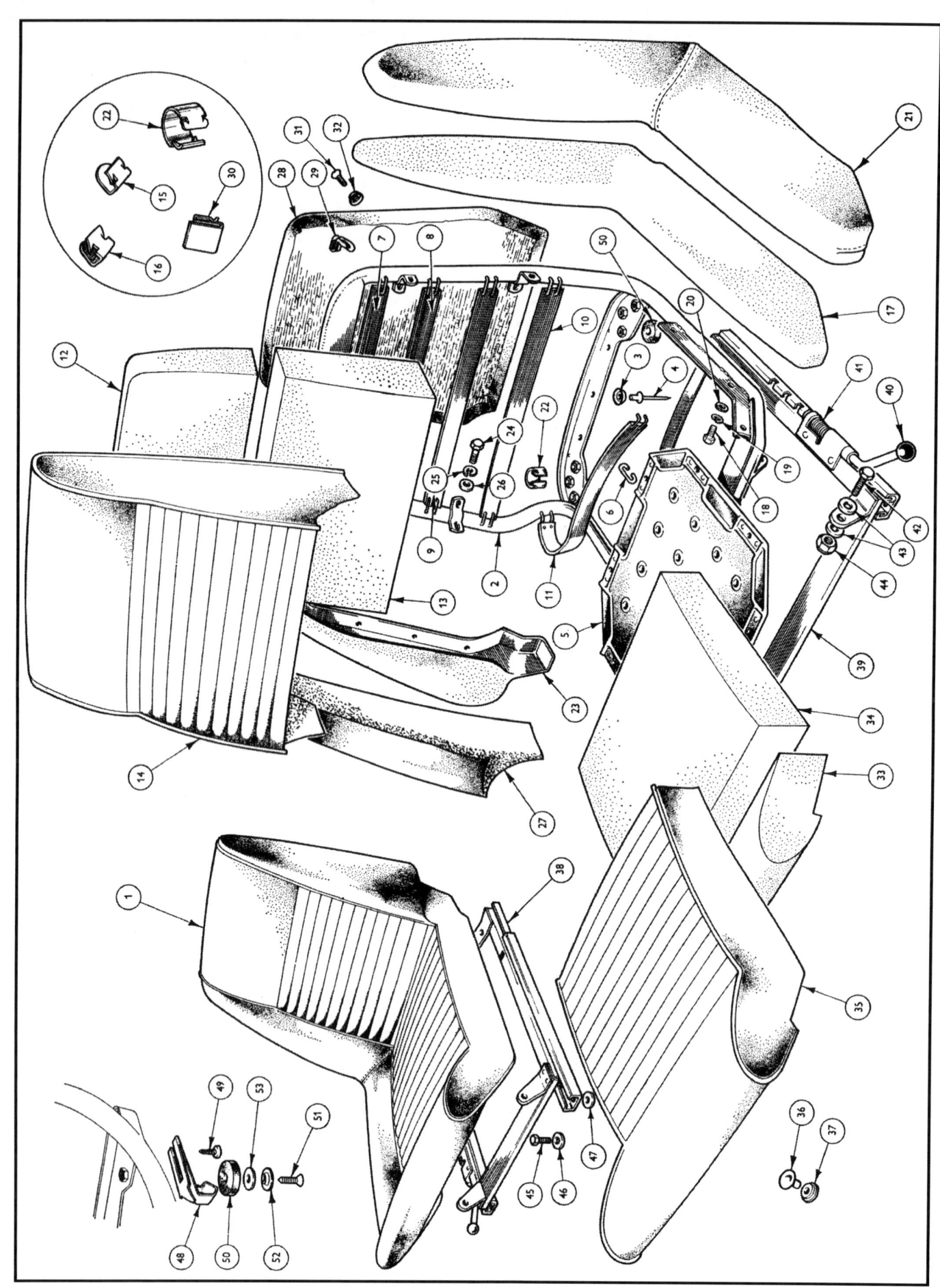

PLATE CN

BODY AND FITTINGS

Plate No.	Part No.	Description	No. per Unit	Remarks
		FRONT SEAT FRAME AND SQUAB ASSEMBLY—continued		
CN13	810631	**Pad**, squab, lower, L.H. seat	1	
	711262	**Cover** assembly, squab, sewn—Leathercloth, Red, R.H. seat	1	
CN14	711252	**Cover** assembly, squab, sewn—Leathercloth, Red, L.H. seat	1	
	711263	**Cover** assembly, squab, sewn—Leathercloth, Light Tan, R.H. seat	1	
CN14	711253	**Cover** assembly, squab, sewn—Leathercloth, Light Tan, L.H. seat	1	
	711266	**Cover** assembly, squab, sewn—Leathercloth, Midnight Blue, R.H. seat	1	
CN14	711256	**Cover** assembly, squab, sewn—Leathercloth, Midnight Blue, L.H. seat	1	
	711267	**Cover** assembly, squab, sewn—Leathercloth, Shadow Blue, R.H. seat	1	
CN14	711257	**Cover** assembly, squab, sewn—Leathercloth, Shadow Blue, L.H. seat	1	
	711261	**Cover** assembly, squab, sewn—Leathercloth, Black, R.H. seat	1	
CN14	711251	**Cover** assembly, squab, sewn—Leathercloth, Black, L.H. seat	1	Fitted up to Commission No. KC9999 (U.S.A.) and KC12804 Black trim, KC9012 Blue trim, KC8805 Tan trim, KC12747 Red trim, (other markets) only
	711282	**Cover** assembly, squab, sewn—Leather, Red, R.H. seat	1	
CN14	711272	**Cover** assembly, squab, sewn—Leather, Red, L.H. seat	1	
	711283	**Cover** assembly, squab, sewn—Leather, Light Tan, R.H. seat	1	
CN14	711273	**Cover** assembly, squab, sewn—Leather, Light Tan, L.H. seat	1	
	711286	**Cover** assembly, squab, sewn—Leather, Midnight Blue, R.H. seat	1	
CN14	711276	**Cover** assembly, squab, sewn—Leather, Midnight Blue, L.H. seat	1	
	711287	**Cover** assembly, squab, sewn—Leather, Shadow Blue R.H. seat	1	
CN14	711277	**Cover** assembly, squab, sewn—Leather, Shadow Blue L.H. seat	1	
	711281	**Cover** assembly, squab, sewn—Leather, Black, R.H. seat	1	
CN14	711271	**Cover** assembly, squab, sewn—Leather, Black, L.H. seat	1	
CN15	610520	**Clip**, trim, squab cover to frame	4	
CN16	608817	**Clip**, trim, squab cover to frame	6	
	905061	**Side panel** assembly, outer (Foamed) R.H.—R.H. seat	1	
CN17	905060	**Side panel** assembly, outer (Foamed) L.H.—L.H. seat	1	
CN18	HU0504	**Screw**, set ⎫	18	
CN19	WL0205	**Washer**, lock ⎬ Outer side panel to frame	18	
CN20	WP0005	**Washer**, plain ⎭	18	

Note:—Items marked thus † are available on our Factory Exchange Unit Scheme

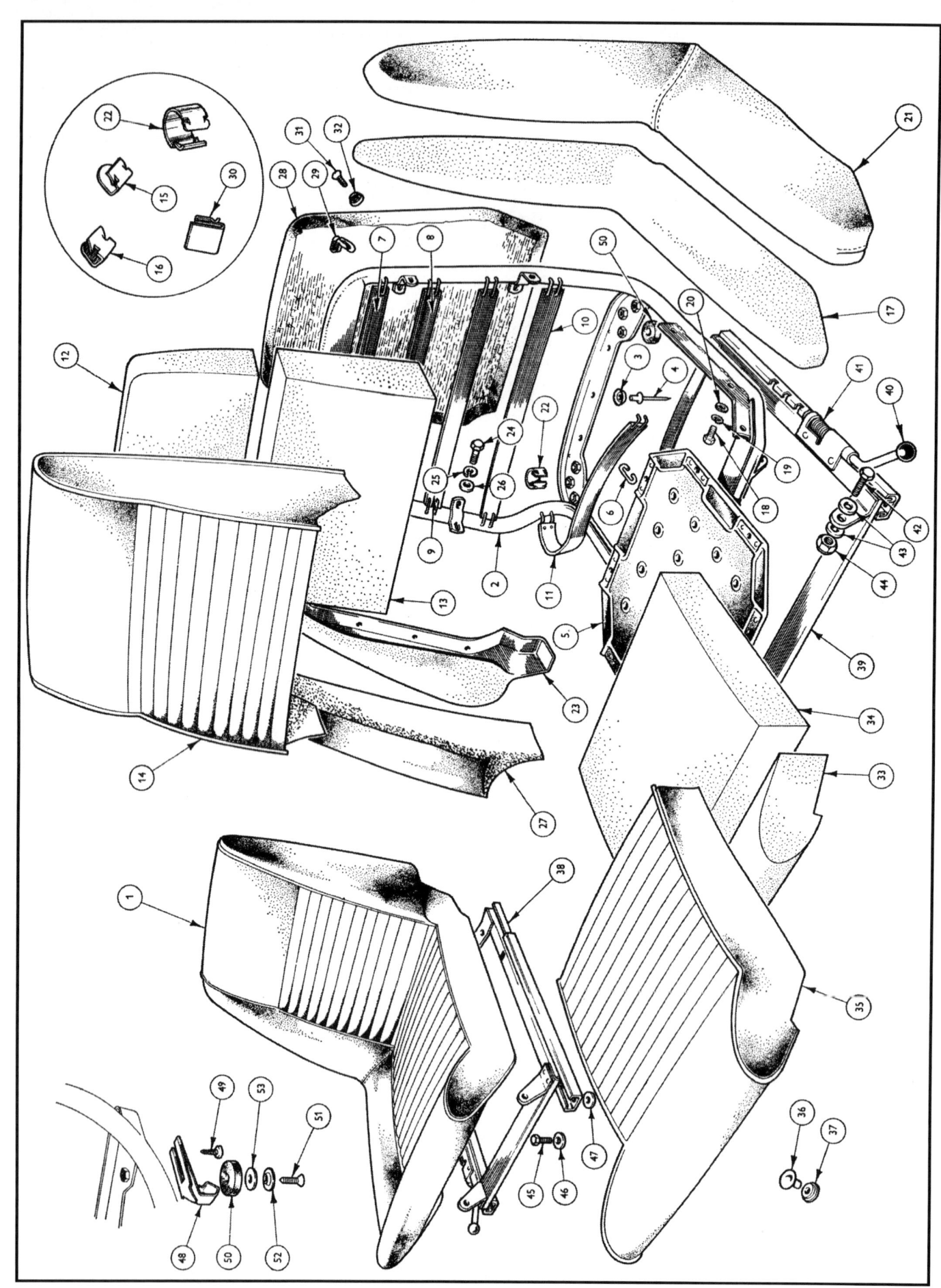

PLATE CN

BODY AND FITTINGS

Plate No.	Part No.	Description	No. per Unit	Remarks
		FRONT SEAT FRAME AND SQUAB ASSEMBLY —continued		
	620422	**Cover** assembly, sewn, side panel, outer —Leathercloth, Red, R.H.—R.H. seat	1	
CN21	620412	**Cover** assembly, sewn, side panel, outer —Leathercloth, Red, L.H.—L.H. seat	1	
	620423	**Cover** assembly, sewn, side panel, outer —Leathercloth, Light Tan, R.H.—R.H. seat	1	
CN21	620413	**Cover** assembly, sewn, side panel, outer —Leathercloth, Light Tan, L.H.—L.H. seat	1	
	620426	**Cover** assembly, sewn, side panel, outer —Leathercloth, Midnight Blue, R.H.—R.H. seat	1	
CN21	620416	**Cover** assembly, sewn, side panel, outer —Leathercloth, Midnight Blue, L.H.—L.H. seat	1	
	620427	**Cover** assembly, sewn, side panel, outer —Leathercloth, Shadow Blue, R.H.—R.H. seat	1	
CN21	620417	**Cover** assembly, sewn, side panel, outer —Leathercloth, Shadow Blue, L.H.—L.H. seat	1	
	620421	**Cover** assembly, sewn, side panel, outer —Leathercloth, Black, R.H.—R.H. seat	1	
CN21	620411	**Cover** assembly, sewn, side panel, outer —Leathercloth, Black, L.H.—L.H. seat	1	Fitted up to Commission No. KC9999 (U.S.A.) and KC12804 Black trim, KC9012 Blue trim, KC8805 Tan trim, KC12747 Red trim, (other markets) only
	620442	**Cover** assembly, sewn, side panel, outer —Leather, Red, R.H.—R.H. seat	1	
CN21	620432	**Cover** assembly, sewn, side panel, outer —Leather, Red, L.H.—L.H. seat	1	
	620443	**Cover** assembly, sewn, side panel, outer—Leather, Light Tan, R.H.—R.H. seat	1	
CN21	620433	**Cover** assembly, sewn, side panel, outer—Leather, Light Tan, L.H.—L.H. seat	1	
	620446	**Cover** assembly, sewn, side panel, outer—Leather, Midnight Blue, R.H.—R.H. seat	1	
CN21	620436	**Cover** assembly, sewn, side panel, outer—Leather, Midnight Blue, L.H.—L.H. seat	1	
	620447	**Cover** assembly, sewn, side panel, outer—Leather, Shadow Blue, R.H.—R.H. seat	1	
CN21	620437	**Cover** assembly, sewn, side panel, outer—Leather, Shadow Blue, L.H.—L.H. seat	1	
	620441	**Cover** assembly, sewn, side panel, outer—Leather, Black, R.H.—R.H. seat	1	
CN21	620431	**Cover** assembly, sewn, side panel, outer—Leather, Black, L.H.—L.H. seat	1	
CN15	610520	**Clip**, trim ⎫ Outer side panel cover	4	
CN16	608817	**Clip**, trim ⎭ to frame and flange	22	
CN22	608862	**Clip**, tube, outer side panel cover to frame	2	
CN23	810100	**Side panel** assembly, inner (Foamed) R.H.—L.H. seat	1	
	810101	**Side panel** assembly, inner (Foamed) L.H.—R.H. seat	1	
CN24	HU0504	**Screw**, set ⎫	12	
CN25	WL0205	**Washer**, lock ⎬ Inner side panel to frame	12	
CN26	WP0005	**Washer**, plain ⎭	12	

Note:—Items marked thus † are available on our Factory Exchange Unit Scheme

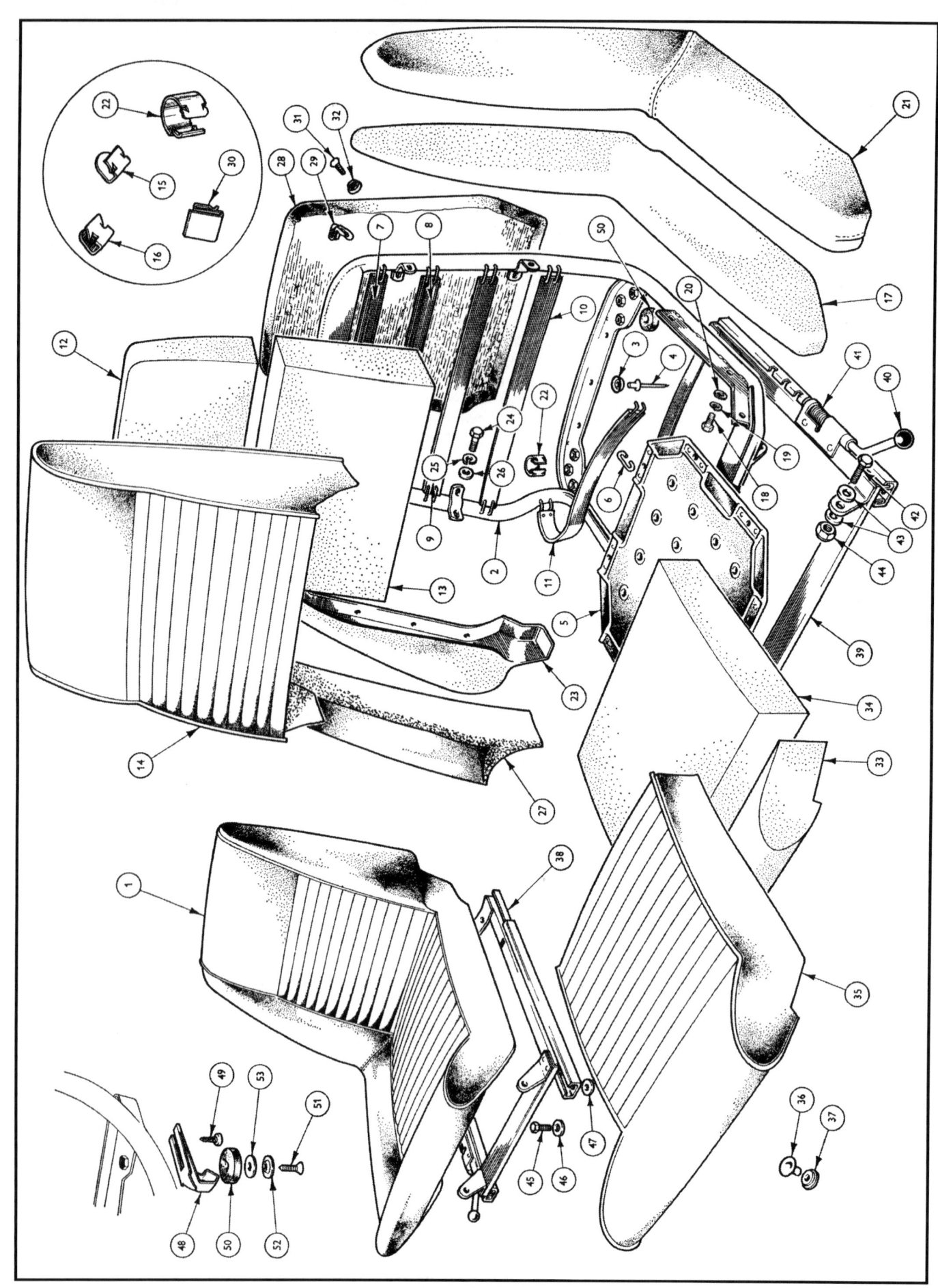

PLATE CN

BODY AND FITTINGS

Plate No.	Part No.	Description	No. per Unit	Remarks
		FRONT SEAT FRAME AND SQUAB ASSEMBLY —continued		
CN27	620452	**Cover** assembly, sewn, side panel, inner, —Leathercloth, Red, R.H.—L.H. seat	1	
	620462	**Cover** assembly, sewn, side panel, inner, —Leathercloth, Red, L.H.—R.H. seat	1	
CN27	620453	**Cover** assembly, sewn, side panel, inner —Leathercloth, Light Tan, R.H.—L.H. seat	1	
	620463	**Cover** assembly, sewn, side panel, inner —Leathercloth, Light Tan, L.H.—R.H. seat	1	
CN27	620456	**Cover** assembly, sewn, side panel, inner —Leathercloth, Midnight Blue, R.H.—L.H. seat	1	
	620466	**Cover** assembly, sewn, side panel, inner —Leathercloth, Midnight Blue, L.H.—R.H. seat	1	
CN27	620457	**Cover** assembly, sewn, side panel, inner —Leathercloth, Shadow Blue, R.H.—L.H. seat	1	
	620467	**Cover** assembly, sewn, side panel, inner —Leathercloth, Shadow Blue, L.H.—R.H. seat	1	
CN27	620451	**Cover** assembly, sewn, side panel, inner —Leathercloth, Black, R.H.—L.H. seat	1	
	620461	**Cover** assembly, sewn, side panel, inner —Leathercloth, Black, L.H.—R.H. seat	1	
CN27	620472	**Cover** assembly, sewn, side panel, inner —Leather, Red, R.H.—L.H. seat	1	Fitted up to Commission No. KC9999 (U.S.A.) and KC12804 Black trim, KC9012 Blue trim, KC8805 Tan trim, KC12747 Red trim, (other markets) only
	620482	**Cover** assembly, sewn, side panel, inner —Leather, Red, L.H.—R.H. seat	1	
CN27	620473	**Cover** assembly, sewn, side panel, inner —Leather, Light Tan, R.H.—L.H. seat	1	
	620483	**Cover** assembly, sewn, side panel, inner —Leather, Light Tan, L.H.—R.H. seat	1	
CN27	620476	**Cover** assembly, sewn, side panel, inner —Leather, Midnight Blue, R.H.—L.H. seat	1	
	620486	**Cover** assembly, sewn, side panel, inner —Leather, Midnight Blue, L.H.—R.H. seat	1	
CN27	620477	**Cover** assembly, sewn, side panel, inner —Leather, Shadow Blue, R.H.—L.H. seat	1	
	620487	**Cover** assembly, sewn, side panel, inner —Leather, Shadow Blue, L.H.—R.H. seat	1	
CN27	620471	**Cover** assembly, sewn, side panel, inner —Leather, Black, R.H.—L.H. seat	1	
	620481	**Cover** assembly, sewn, side panel, inner —Leather, Black, L.H.—R.H. seat	1	
CN15	610520	**Clip**, trim, inner side panel cover to seat frame	4	
CN16	608817	**Clip**, trim, inner side panel cover to flange	10	
CN22	608862	**Clip**, tube, inner side panel cover to seat frame	4	
	810742	**Back panel** assembly, trimmed, Red—R.H. seat	1	
CN28	810732	**Back panel** assembly, trimmed, Red—L.H. seat	1	
	810743	**Back panel** assembly, trimmed, Light Tan—R.H. seat	1	
CN28	810733	**Back panel** assembly, trimmed, Light Tan—L.H. seat	1	
	810746	**Back panel** assembly, trimmed, Midnight Blue —R.H. seat	1	

Note:—Items marked thus † are available on our Factory Exchange Unit Scheme

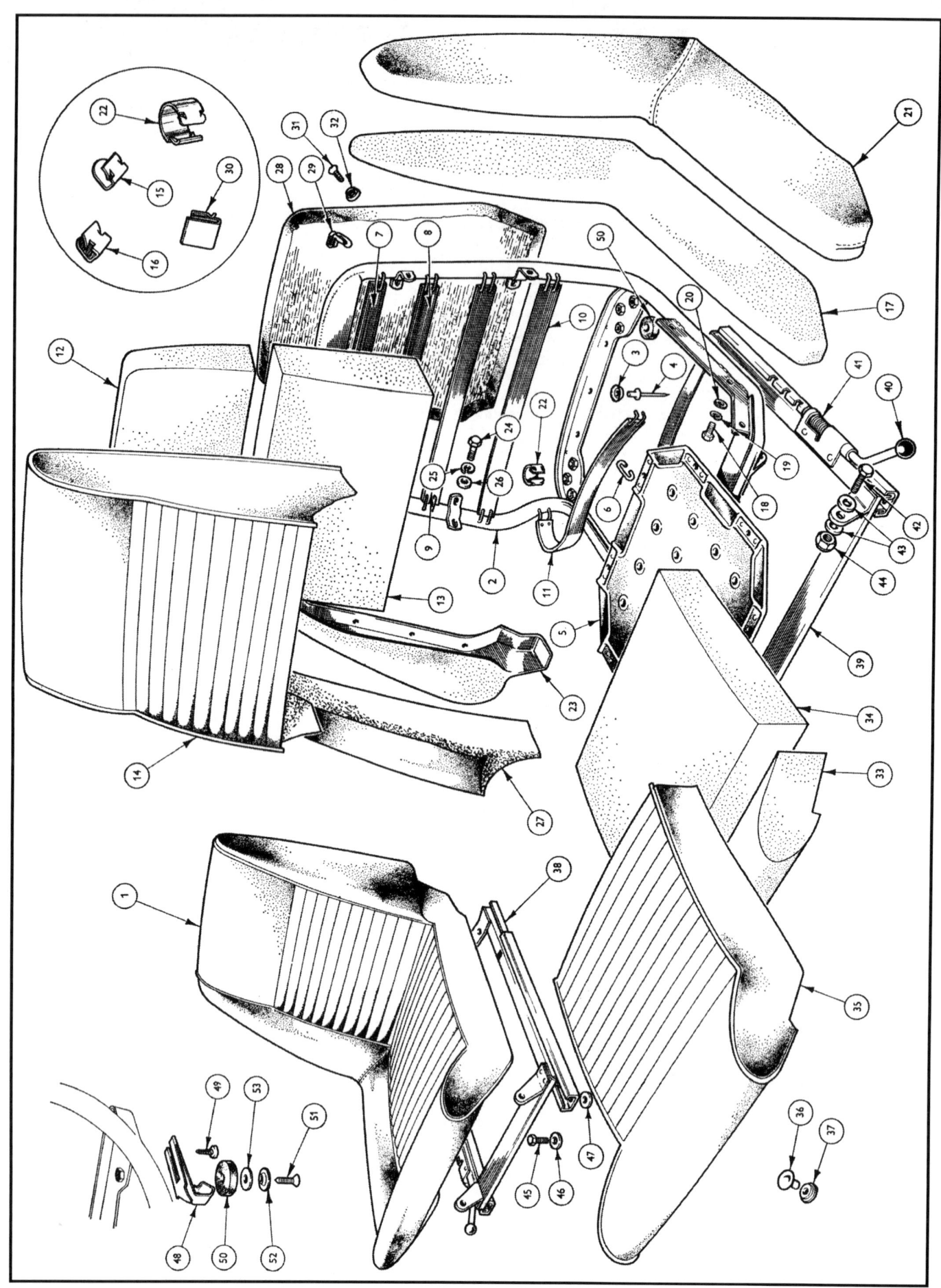

PLATE CN

BODY AND FITTINGS

Plate No.	Part No.	Description	No. per Unit	Remarks
		FRONT SEAT FRAME AND SQUAB ASSEMBLY —continued		
CN28	810736	**Back panel** assembly, trimmed, Midnight Blue —L.H. seat	1	
	810747	**Back panel** assembly, trimmed, Shadow Blue —R.H. seat	1	
CN28	810737	**Back panel** assembly, trimmed, Shadow Blue —L.H. seat	1	
	810741	**Back panel** assembly, trimmed, Black—R.H. seat	1	
CN28	810731	**Back panel** assembly, trimmed, Black—L.H. seat	1	
CN29	613769	**Clip,** trim ⎫ Back panel	12	
CN30	613770	**Clip,** trim ⎭ to frame	4	
CN31	512554	**Screw,** self-tapping, chrome ⎫ Back panel lower	4	
CN32	619618	**Washer,** cup ⎭ attachment	4	
	905562	**CUSHION ASSEMBLY, TRIMMED —LEATHERCLOTH (RED)—R.H. SEAT**	1	
	905552	**CUSHION ASSEMBLY, TRIMMED —LEATHERCLOTH (RED)—L.H. SEAT**	1	
	905563	**CUSHION ASSEMBLY, TRIMMED—LEATHER-CLOTH (LIGHT TAN)—R.H. SEAT**	1	Fitted up to Commission No. KC9999 (U.S.A.) and KC12804 Black trim, KC9012 Blue trim, KC8805 Tan trim, KC12747 Red trim, (other markets) only
	905553	**CUSHION ASSEMBLY, TRIMMED—LEATHER-CLOTH (LIGHT TAN)—L.H. SEAT**	1	
	905566	**CUSHION ASSEMBLY, TRIMMED—LEATHER-CLOTH (MIDNIGHT BLUE)—R.H. SEAT**	1	
	905556	**CUSHION ASSEMBLY, TRIMMED—LEATHER-CLOTH (MIDNIGHT BLUE)—L.H. SEAT**	1	
	905567	**CUSHION ASSEMBLY, TRIMMED—LEATHER-CLOTH (SHADOW BLUE)—R.H. SEAT**	1	
	905557	**CUSHION ASSEMBLY, TRIMMED—LEATHER-CLOTH (SHADOW BLUE)—L.H. SEAT**	1	
	905561	**CUSHION ASSEMBLY, TRIMMED—LEATHER-CLOTH (BLACK)—R.H. SEAT**	1	
	905551	**CUSHION ASSEMBLY, TRIMMED—LEATHER-CLOTH (BLACK)—L.H. SEAT**	1	
	905582	**CUSHION ASSEMBLY, TRIMMED—LEATHER (RED)—R.H. SEAT**	1	
	905572	**CUSHION ASSEMBLY, TRIMMED—LEATHER (RED)—L.H. SEAT**	1	

Note:—Items marked thus † are available on our Factory Exchange Unit Scheme

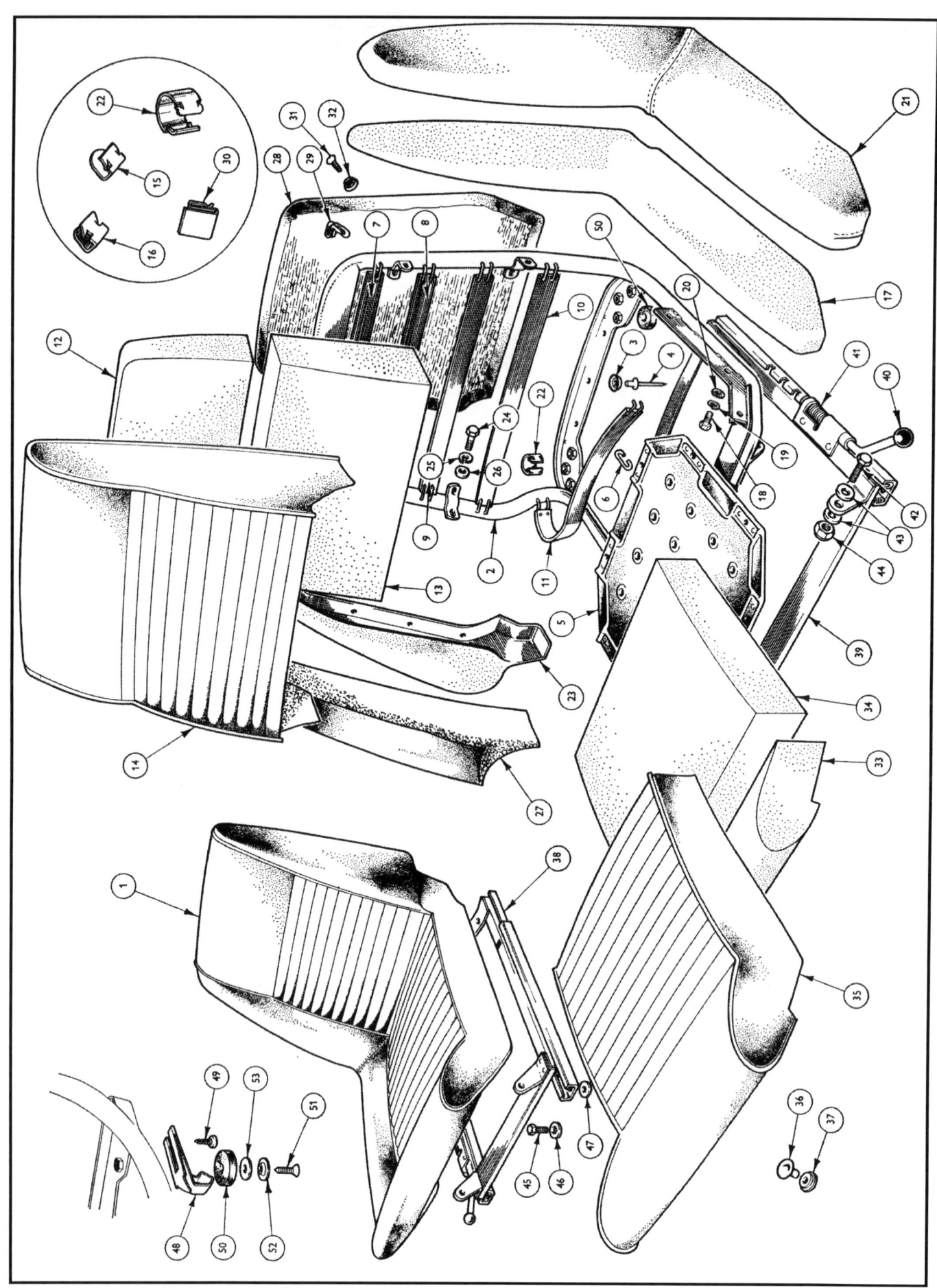

PLATE CN

BODY AND FITTINGS

Plate No.	Part No.	Description	No. per Unit	Remarks
		FRONT SEAT CUSHION ASSEMBLY —TRIMMED—continued		
	905583	CUSHION ASSEMBLY, TRIMMED—LEATHER (LIGHT TAN)—R.H. SEAT	1	
	905573	CUSHION ASSEMBLY, TRIMMED—LEATHER (LIGHT TAN)—L.H. SEAT	1	
	905586	CUSHION ASSEMBLY, TRIMMED—LEATHER (MIDNIGHT BLUE)—R.H. SEAT	1	
	905576	CUSHION ASSEMBLY, TRIMMED—LEATHER (MIDNIGHT BLUE)—L.H. SEAT	1	
	905587	CUSHION ASSEMBLY, TRIMMED—LEATHER (SHADOW BLUE)—R.H. SEAT	1	
	905577	CUSHION ASSEMBLY, TRIMMED—LEATHER (SHADOW BLUE)—L.H. SEAT	1	
	905581	CUSHION ASSEMBLY, TRIMMED—LEATHER (BLACK)—R.H. SEAT	1	
	905571	CUSHION ASSEMBLY, TRIMMED—LEATHER (BLACK)—L.H. SEAT	1	Fitted up to Commission No. KC9999 (U.S.A.) and KC12804 Black trim, KC9012 Blue trim, KC8805 Tan trim, KC12747 Red trim, (other markets) only
	810241	Pad, cushion, front, R.H. seat	1	
CN33	810240	Pad, cushion, front, L.H. seat	1	
	810243	Pad, cushion, rear, R.H. seat	1	
CN34	810242	Pad, cushion, rear, L.H. seat	1	
	711142	Cover assembly, cushion—Leathercloth, Red, R.H. seat	1	
CN35	711132	Cover assembly, cushion—Leathercloth, Red, L.H. seat	1	
	711143	Cover assembly, cushion—Leathercloth, Light Tan, R.H. seat	1	
CN35	711133	Cover assembly, cushion—Leathercloth, Light Tan, L.H. seat	1	
	711146	Cover assembly, cushion—Leathercloth, Midnight Blue, R.H. seat	1	
CN35	711136	Cover assembly, cushion—Leathercloth, Midnight Blue, L.H. seat	1	
	711147	Cover assembly, cushion—Leathercloth, Shadow Blue, R.H. seat	1	
CN35	711137	Cover assembly, cushion—Leathercloth, Shadow Blue, L.H. seat	1	
	711141	Cover assembly, cushion—Leathercloth, Black, R.H. seat	1	
CN35	711131	Cover assembly, cushion—Leathercloth, Black, L.H. seat	1	
	711162	Cover assembly, cushion—Leather, Red, R.H. seat	1	
CN35	711152	Cover assembly, cushion—Leather, Red, L.H. seat	1	

Note:—Items marked thus † are available on our Factory Exchange Unit Scheme

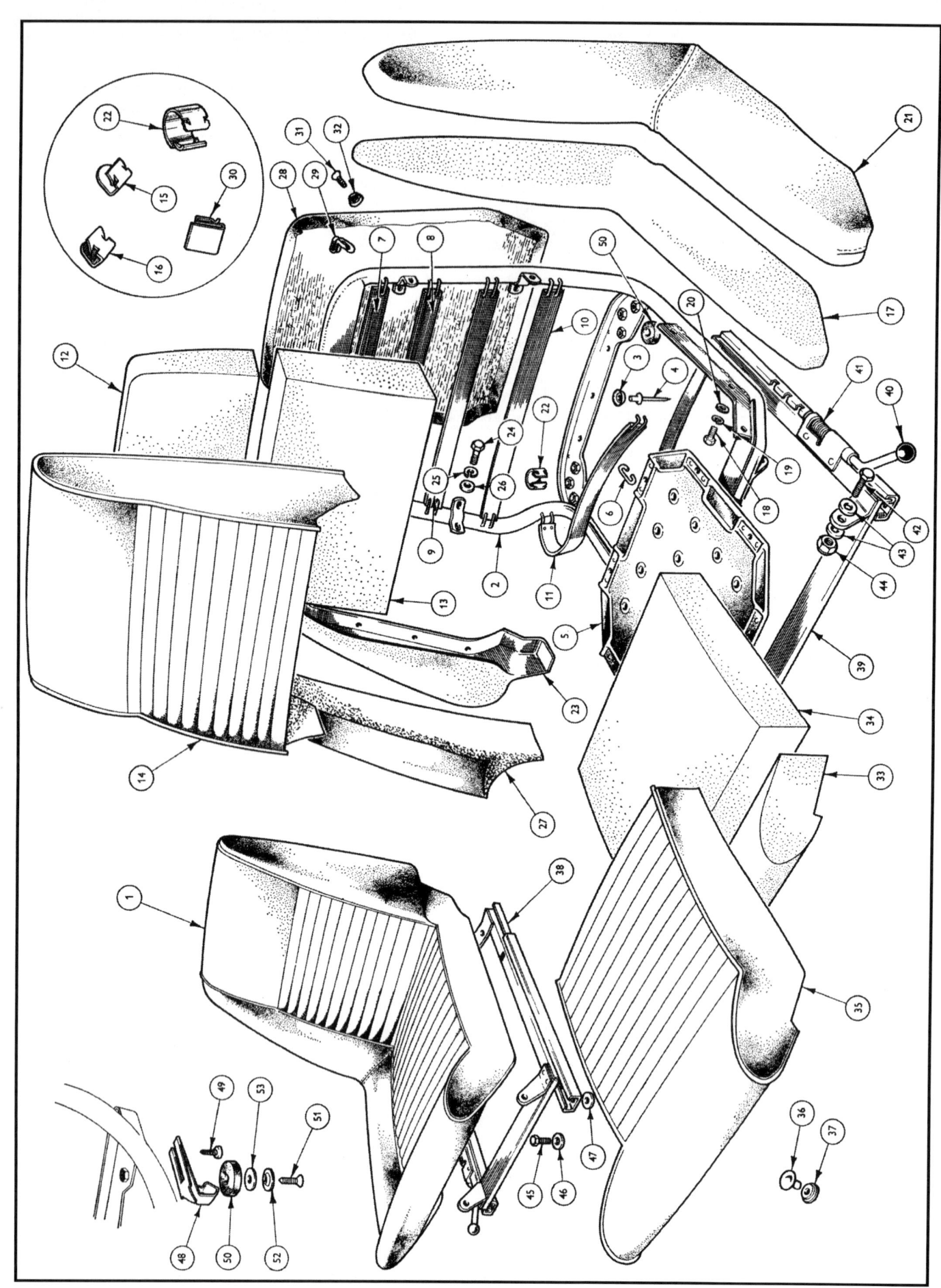

PLATE CN

406

BODY AND FITTINGS

Plate No.	Part No.	Description	No. per Unit	Remarks
		FRONT SEAT CUSHION ASSEMBLY —**TRIMMED**—continued		
	711163	**Cover** assembly, cushion—Leather, Light Tan, R.H. seat	1	
CN35	711153	**Cover** assembly, cushion—Leather, Light Tan, L.H. seat	1	
	711166	**Cover** assembly, cushion—Leather, Midnight Blue, R.H. seat	1	
CN35	711156	**Cover** assembly, cushion—Leather, Midnight Blue, L.H. seat	1	
	711167	**Cover** assembly, cushion—Leather, Shadow Blue, R.H. seat	1	
CN35	711157	**Cover** assembly, cushion—Leather, Shadow Blue, L.H. seat	1	
	711161	**Cover** assembly, cushion—Leather, Black, R.H. seat	1	
CN35	711151	**Cover** assembly, cushion—Leather, Black, L.H. seat	1	Fitted up to Commission No. KC9999 (U.S.A.) and KC12804 Black trim, KC9012 Blue trim, KC8805 Tan trim, KC12747 Red trim, (other markets) only
CN36	565747	**Button** ⎱ Cushion cover	6	
CN37	567642	**Socket** ⎰ to frame	6	
CN38	810374	**SEAT SLIDE ASSEMBLY—R.H. SEAT**	1	
CN39	810373	**SEAT SLIDE ASSEMBLY—L.H. SEAT**	1	
CN40	609966	**Knob**	2	
	609965	**Spring**, catch rod—R.H.	1	
CN41	609964	**Spring**, catch rod—L.H.	1	
CN42	HU0807	**Screw**, set	4	
CN43	WP0150	**Washer**, plain ⎱ Seat slide to seat	8	
CN44	YN2908	**Nut**, nyloc	4	
CN45	HU0706	**Screw**, set ⎱ Seat slide	8	
CN46	WP0023	**Washer**, plain ⎰ to floor	8	
CN47	WP0048	**Washer**, plain, between seat slide and carpet	8	
CN48	613303	**Spring**, seat retaining	2	
CN49	YZ3403	**Screw**, self-tapping, spring to seat	2	
CN50	613746	**Buffer**, rubber	4	
CN51	KX4505	**Screw**, set	4	
CN52	613745	**Washer**, cup ⎱ Buffer to seat	4	
CN53	WP0117	**Washer**, plain ⎰	4	

Note:—Items marked thus † are available on our Factory Exchange Unit Scheme

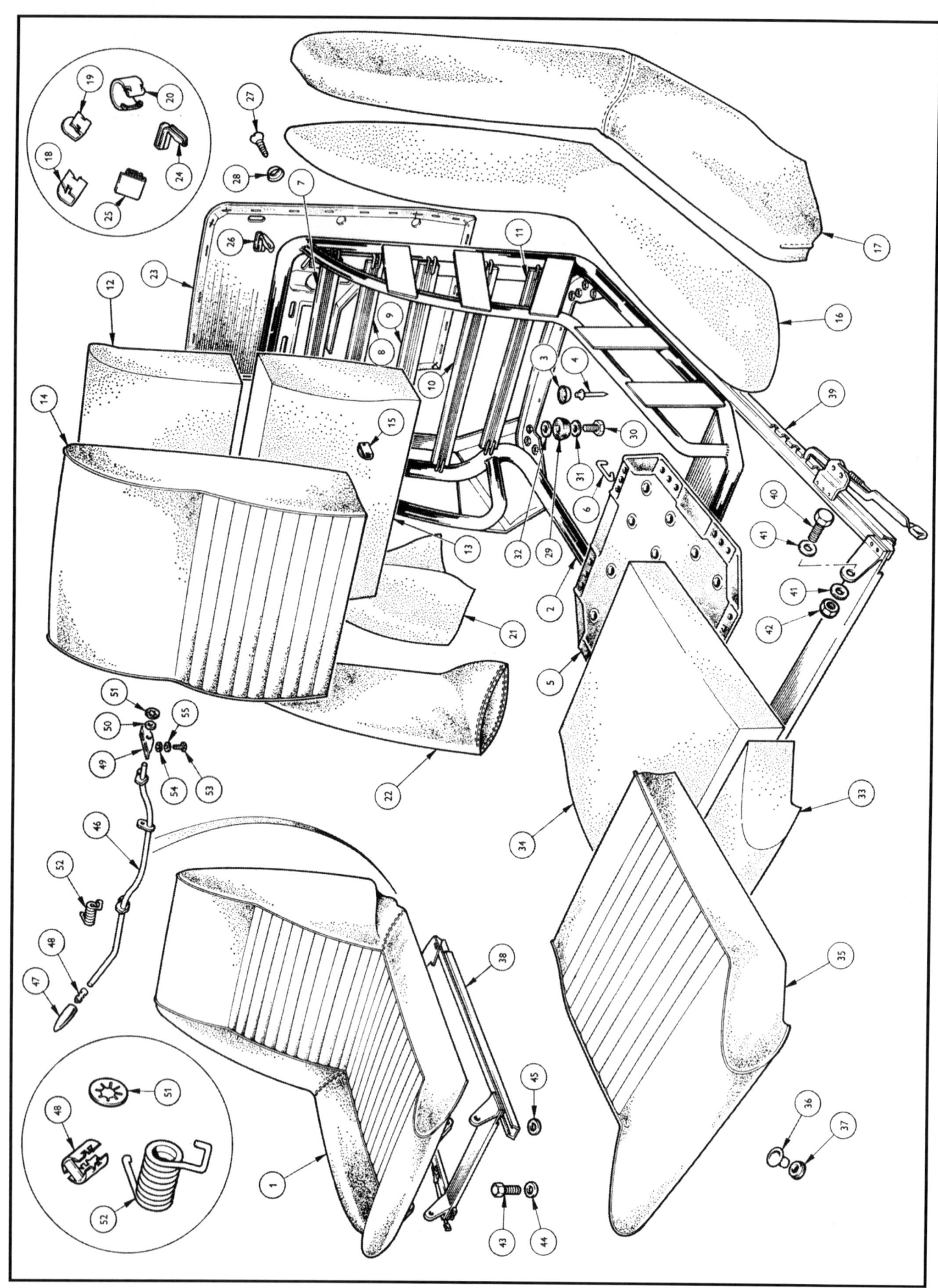

PLATE CP

BODY AND FITTINGS

Plate No.	Part No.	Description	No. per Unit	Remarks
CP1	907952	**FRONT SEAT COMPLETE ASSEMBLY, TRIMMED—LEATHERCLOTH (Red)—R.H.**	1	
	907942	**FRONT SEAT COMPLETE ASSEMBLY, TRIMMED—LEATHERCLOTH (Red)—L.H.**	1	
CP1	907953	**FRONT SEAT COMPLETE ASSEMBLY, TRIMMED—LEATHERCLOTH (Light Tan)—R.H.**	1	
	907943	**FRONT SEAT COMPLETE ASSEMBLY, TRIMMED—LEATHERCLOTH (Light Tan)—L.H.**	1	
CP1	907956	**FRONT SEAT COMPLETE ASSEMBLY, TRIMMED—LEATHERCLOTH (Midnight Blue)—R.H.**	1	
	907946	**FRONT SEAT COMPLETE ASSEMBLY, TRIMMED—LEATHERCLOTH (Midnight Blue)—L.H.**	1	Fitted from Commission No. KC10000 (U.S.A.) and KC12805 Black trim, KC9013 Blue trim, KC8806 Tan trim, KC12748 Red trim, (other markets) up to Commission No. KC50000
CP1	907957	**FRONT SEAT COMPLETE ASSEMBLY, TRIMMED—LEATHERCLOTH (Shadow Blue)—R.H.**	1	
	907947	**FRONT SEAT COMPLETE ASSEMBLY, TRIMMED—LEATHERCLOTH (Shadow Blue)—L.H.**	1	
CP1	907951	**FRONT SEAT COMPLETE ASSEMBLY, TRIMMED—LEATHERCLOTH (Black)—R.H.**	1	
	907941	**FRONT SEAT COMPLETE ASSEMBLY, TRIMMED—LEATHERCLOTH (Black)—L.H.**	1	
CP1	907972	**FRONT SEAT COMPLETE ASSEMBLY, TRIMMED—LEATHER (Red)—R.H.**	1	
	907962	**FRONT SEAT COMPLETE ASSEMBLY, TRIMMED—LEATHER (Red)—L.H.**	1	
CP1	907973	**FRONT SEAT COMPLETE ASSEMBLY, TRIMMED—LEATHER (Light Tan)—R.H.**	1	

Note:—Items marked thus † are available on our Factory Exchange Unit Scheme

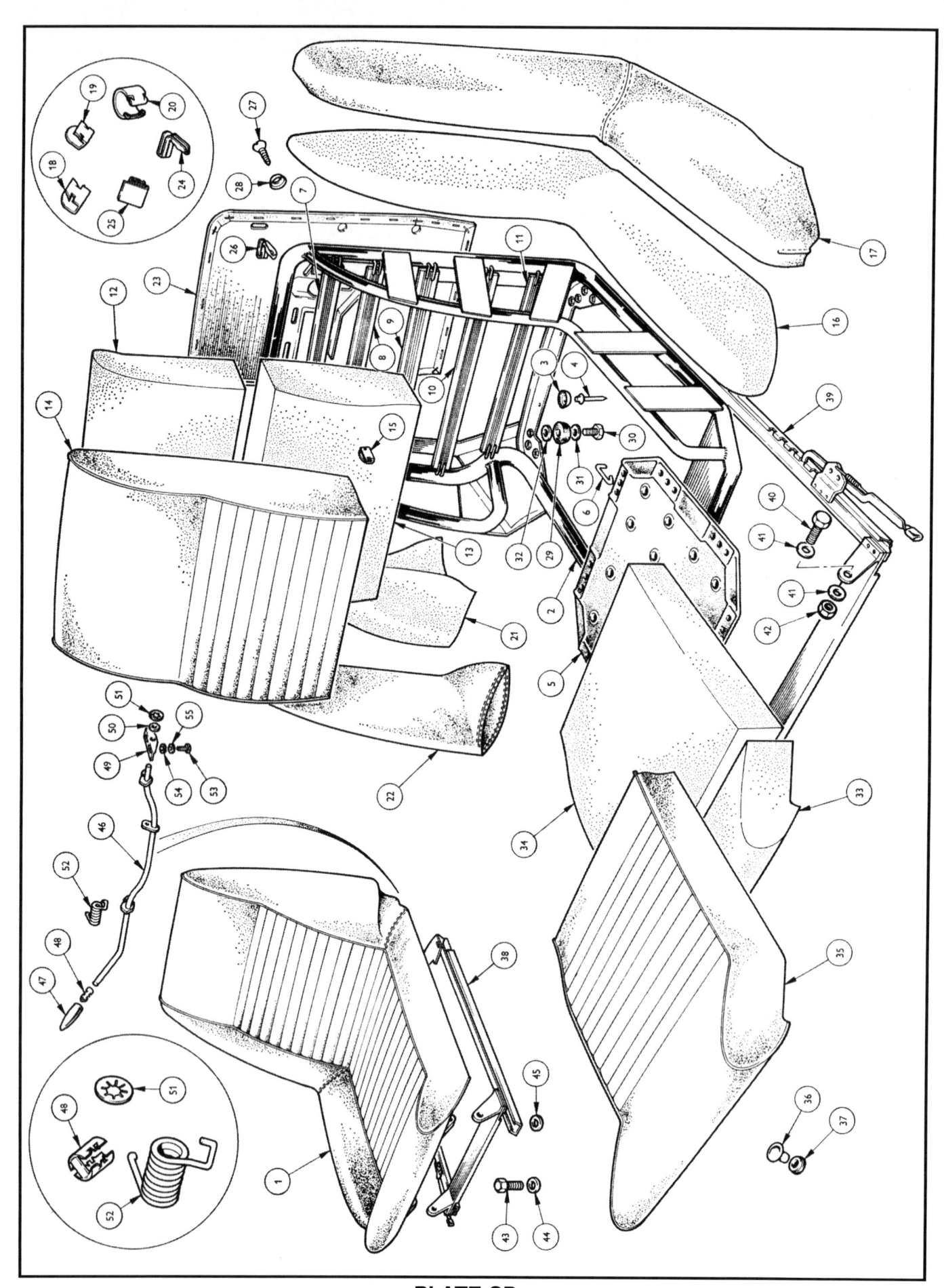

PLATE CP

BODY AND FITTINGS

Plate No.	Part No.	Description	No. per Unit	Remarks
	907963	FRONT SEAT COMPLETE ASSEMBLY, TRIMMED—LEATHER (Light Tan)—L.H.	1	
CP1	907976	FRONT SEAT COMPLETE ASSEMBLY, TRIMMED—LEATHER (Midnight Blue)—R.H.	1	
	907966	FRONT SEAT COMPLETE ASSEMBLY, TRIMMED—LEATHER (Midnight Blue)—L.H.	1	
CP1	907977	FRONT SEAT COMPLETE ASSEMBLY, TRIMMED—LEATHER (Shadow Blue)—R.H.	1	
	907967	FRONT SEAT COMPLETE ASSEMBLY, TRIMMED—LEATHER (Shadow Blue)—L.H.	1	
CP1	907971	FRONT SEAT COMPLETE ASSEMBLY, TRIMMED—LEATHER (Black)—R.H.	1	
	907961	FRONT SEAT COMPLETE ASSEMBLY, TRIMMED—LEATHER (Black)—L.H.	1	Fitted from Commission No. KC10000 (U.S.A.) and KC12805 Black trim, KC9013 Blue trim, KC8806 Tan trim, KC12748 Red trim, (other markets) up to Commission No. KC50000
	907992	FRONT SEAT FRAME AND SQUAB ASSEMBLY, TRIMMED—LEATHERCLOTH (RED)—R.H.	1	
	907982	FRONT SEAT FRAME AND SQUAB ASSEMBLY, TRIMMED—LEATHERCLOTH (RED)—L.H.	1	
	907993	FRONT SEAT FRAME AND SQUAB ASSEMBLY, TRIMMED—LEATHERCLOTH (LIGHT TAN)—R.H.	1	
	907983	FRONT SEAT FRAME AND SQUAB ASSEMBLY, TRIMMED—LEATHERCLOTH (LIGHT TAN)—L.H.	1	
	907996	FRONT SEAT FRAME AND SQUAB ASSEMBLY, TRIMMED—LEATHERCLOTH (MIDNIGHT BLUE)—R.H.	1	
	907986	FRONT SEAT FRAME AND SQUAB ASSEMBLY, TRIMMED—LEATHERCLOTH (MIDNIGHT BLUE)—L.H.	1	
	907997	FRONT SEAT FRAME AND SQUAB ASSEMBLY, TRIMMED—LEATHERCLOTH (SHADOW BLUE)—R.H.	1	
	907987	FRONT SEAT FRAME AND SQUAB ASSEMBLY, TRIMMED—LEATHERCLOTH (SHADOW BLUE)—L.H.	1	

Note:—Items marked thus † are available on our Factory Exchange Unit Scheme

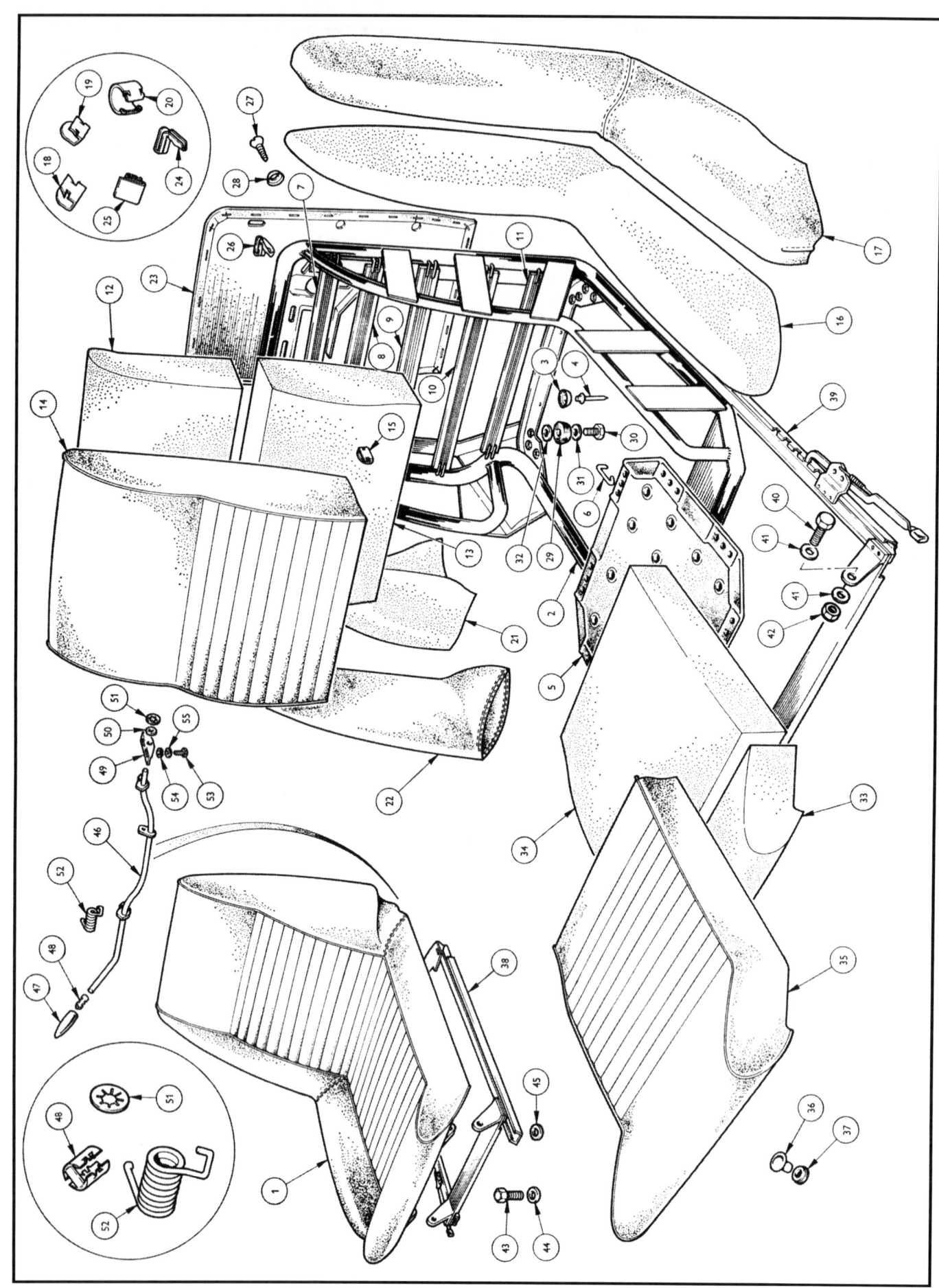

PLATE CP

BODY AND FITTINGS

Plate No.	Part No.	Description	No. per Unit	Remarks
	907991	FRONT SEAT FRAME AND SQUAB ASSEMBLY, TRIMMED—LEATHERCLOTH (BLACK)—R.H.	1	
	907981	FRONT SEAT FRAME AND SQUAB ASSEMBLY, TRIMMED—LEATHERCLOTH (BLACK)—L.H.	1	
	908012	FRONT SEAT FRAME AND SQUAB ASSEMBLY, TRIMMED—LEATHER (RED)—R.H.	1	
	908002	FRONT SEAT FRAME AND SQUAB ASSEMBLY, TRIMMED—LEATHER (RED)—L.H.	1	
	908013	FRONT SEAT FRAME AND SQUAB ASSEMBLY, TRIMMED—LEATHER (LIGHT TAN)—R.H.	1	
	908003	FRONT SEAT FRAME AND SQUAB ASSEMBLY, TRIMMED—LEATHER (LIGHT TAN)—L.H.	1	
	908016	FRONT SEAT FRAME AND SQUAB ASSEMBLY, TRIMMED—LEATHER (MIDNIGHT BLUE)—R.H.	1	
	908006	FRONT SEAT FRAME AND SQUAB ASSEMBLY, TRIMMED—LEATHER (MIDNIGHT BLUE)—L.H.	1	
	908017	FRONT SEAT FRAME AND SQUAB ASSEMBLY, TRIMMED—LEATHER (SHADOW BLUE)—R.H.	1	Fitted from Commission No. KC10000 (U.S.A.) and KC12805 Black trim, KC9013 Blue trim, KC8806 Tan trim, KC12748 Red trim, (other markets) up to Commission No. KC50000
	908007	FRONT SEAT FRAME AND SQUAB ASSEMBLY, TRIMMED—LEATHER (SHADOW BLUE)—L.H.	1	
	908011	FRONT SEAT FRAME AND SQUAB ASSEMBLY TRIMMED—LEATHER (BLACK)—R.H.	1	
	908001	FRONT SEAT FRAME AND SQUAB ASSEMBLY, TRIMMED—LEATHER (BLACK)—L.H.	1	
	907318	Frame assembly—R.H. seat	1	
CP2	907317	Frame assembly—L.H. seat	1	
CP3	610624	Stud, cushion attachment	6	
CP4	561210	Rivet, stud to frame	6	
CP5	573900	Diaphragm, seat base	2	
CP6	613966	Hook, diaphragm	16	
CP7	619498	Strap assembly, squab, 11″ long—Top	2	
CP8	619499	Strap assembly, squab, 12″ long—Top intermediate	2	
CP9	619500	Strap assembly, squab, 12·5″ long—Centre	2	
CP10	619501	Strap assembly, squab, 13·75″ long—Bottom intermediate	2	
CP11	619498	Strap assembly, squab, 11″ long—Bottom	2	
CP12	810630	Pad, squab, upper	2	
	810632	Pad, squab, lower—R.H. seat	2	
CP13	810631	Pad, squab, lower—L.H. seat	2	
	623420	Piece, filler, squab side	4	
	714682	Cover assembly, squab, sewn—Leathercloth, Red—R.H. seat	1	
CP14	714672	Cover assembly, squab, sewn—Leathercloth, Red—L.H. seat	1	
	714683	Cover assembly, squab, sewn—Leathercloth, Light Tan—R.H. seat	1	
CP14	714673	Cover assembly, squab, sewn—Leathercloth, Light Tan—L.H. seat	1	

Note:—Items marked thus † are available on our Factory Exchange Unit Scheme

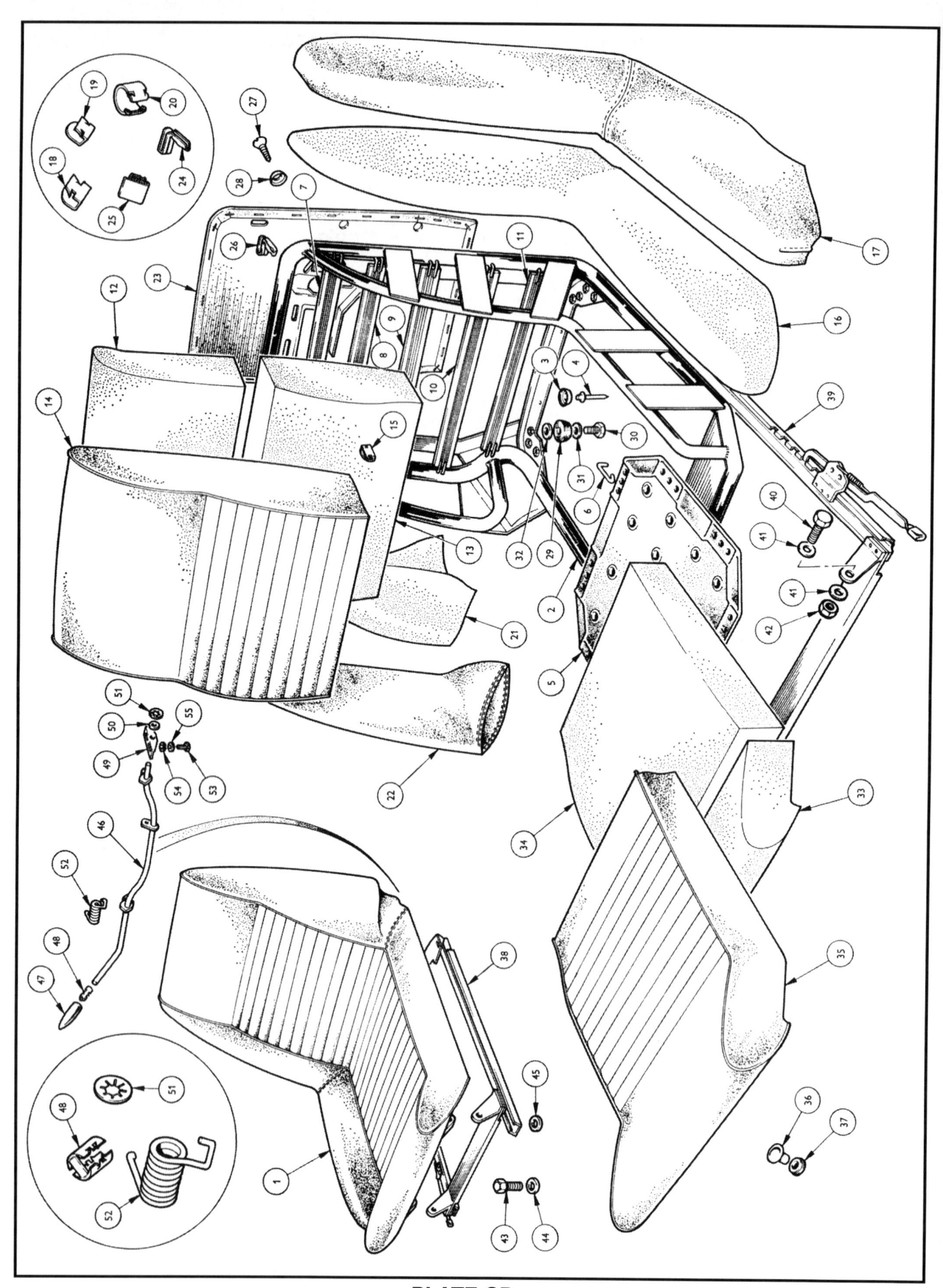

PLATE CP

BODY AND FITTINGS

Plate No	Part No.	Description	No per Unit	Remarks
		FRONT SEAT FRAME AND SQUAB ASSEMBLY, TRIMMED—continued		
	714686	**Cover** assembly, squab, sewn—Leathercloth, Midnight Blue—R.H. seat	1	
CP14	714676	**Cover** assembly, squab, sewn—Leathercloth, Midnight Blue—L.H. seat	1	
	714687	**Cover** assembly, squab, sewn—Leathercloth, Shadow Blue—R.H. seat	1	
CP14	714677	**Cover** assembly, squab, sewn—Leathercloth, Shadow Blue—L.H. seat	1	
	714681	**Cover** assembly, squab, sewn—Leathercloth, Black—R.H. seat	1	
CP14	714671	**Cover** assembly, squab, sewn—Leathercloth, Black—L.H. seat	1	
	714702	**Cover** assembly, squab, sewn—Leather, Red—R.H. seat	1	
CP14	714692	**Cover** assembly, squab, sewn—Leather, Red—L.H. seat	1	
	714703	**Cover** assembly, squab, sewn—Leather, Light Tan—R.H. seat	1	
CP14	714693	**Cover** assembly, squab, sewn—Leather, Light Tan—L.H. seat	1	
	714706	**Cover** assembly, squab, sewn—Leather, Midnight Blue—R.H. seat	1	Fitted from Commission No. KC10000 (U.S.A.) and KC12805 Black trim, KC9013 Blue trim, KC8806 Tan trim, KC12748 Red trim, (other markets) up to Commission No. KC50000
CP14	714696	**Cover** assembly, squab, sewn—Leather, Midnight Blue—L.H. seat	1	
	714707	**Cover** assembly, squab, sewn—Leather, Shadow Blue—R.H. seat	1	
CP14	714697	**Cover** assembly, squab, sewn—Leather, Shadow Blue—L.H. seat	1	
	714701	**Cover** assembly, squab, sewn—Leather, Black—R.H. seat	1	
CP14	714691	**Cover** assembly, squab, sewn—Leather, Black—L.H. seat	1	
CP15	603811	**Clip**, trim, squab cover to frame	8	
	907242	**Padding**, seat side, outer, R.H.—R.H. seat	1	
CP16	907241	**Padding**, seat side, outer, L.H.—L.H. seat	1	
	623392	**Cover** assembly, sewn, side panel, outer—Leathercloth, Red, R.H.—R.H. seat	1	
CP17	623382	**Cover** assembly, sewn, side panel, outer—Leathercloth, Red, L.H.—L.H. seat	1	
	623393	**Cover** assembly, sewn, side panel, outer—Leathercloth, Light Tan, R.H.—R.H. seat	1	
CP17	623383	**Cover** assembly, sewn, side panel, outer—Leathercloth, Light Tan, L.H.—L.H. seat	1	
	623396	**Cover** assembly, sewn, side panel, outer—Leathercloth, Midnight Blue, R.H.—R.H. seat	1	
CP17	623386	**Cover** assembly, sewn, side panel, outer—Leathercloth, Midnight Blue, L.H.—L.H. seat	1	
	623397	**Cover** assembly, sewn, side panel, outer—Leathercloth, Shadow Blue, R.H.—R.H. seat	1	
CP17	623387	**Cover** assembly, sewn, side panel, outer—Leathercloth, Shadow Blue, L.H.—L.H. seat	1	

Note:—Items marked thus † are available on our Factory Exchange Unit Scheme

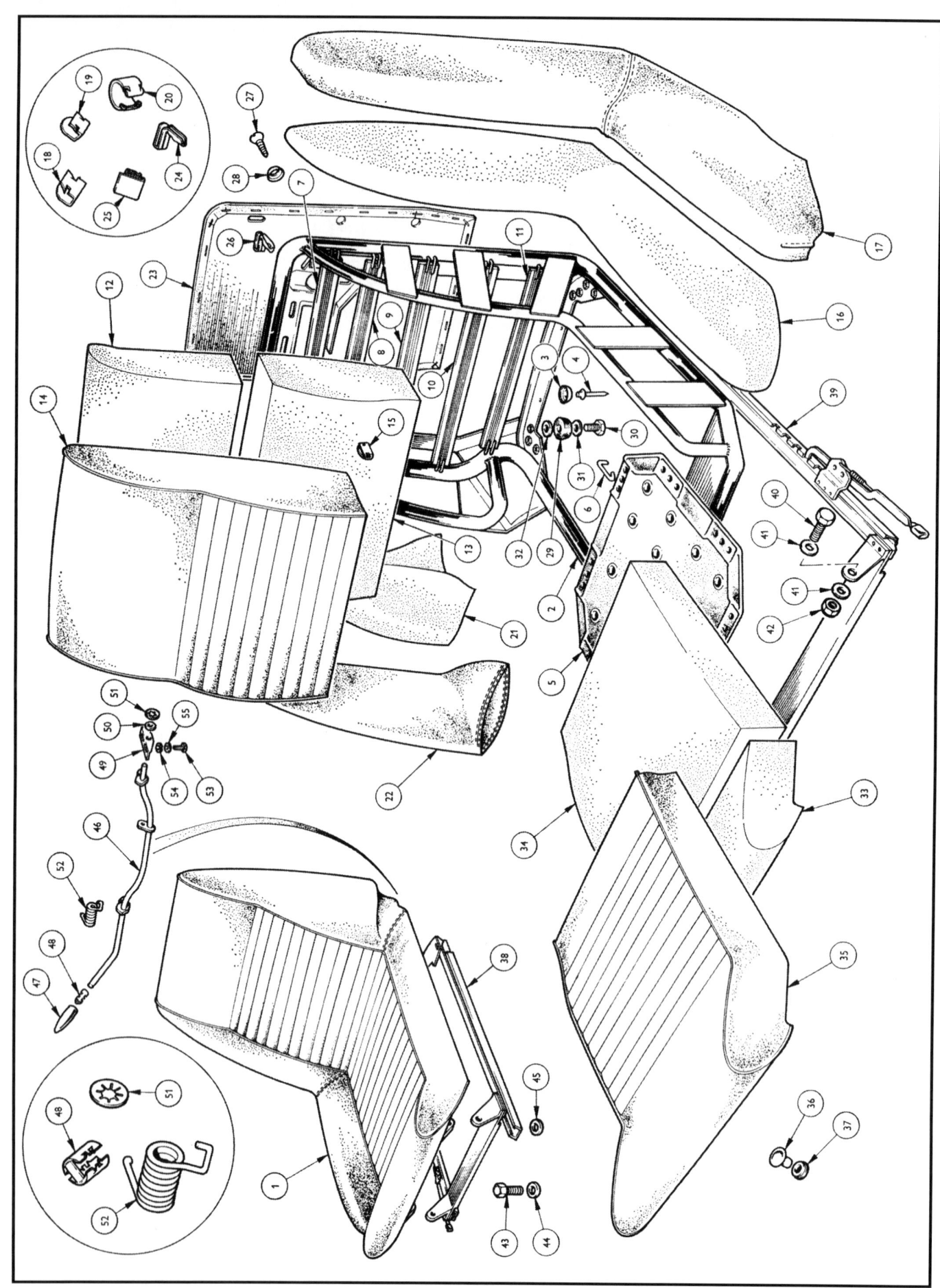

PLATE CP

416

BODY AND FITTINGS

Plate No.	Part No.	Description	No. per Unit	Remarks
		FRONT SEAT FRAME AND SQUAB ASSEMBLY, TRIMMED—continued		
	623391	**Cover** assembly, sewn, side panel, outer—Leathercloth, Black, R.H.—R.H. seat	1	
CP17	623381	**Cover** assembly, sewn, side panel, outer—Leathercloth, Black, L.H.—L.H. seat	1	
	623412	**Cover** assembly, sewn, side panel, outer—Leather, Red, R.H.—R.H. seat	1	
CP17	623402	**Cover** assembly, sewn, side panel, outer—Leather, Red, L.H.—L.H. seat	1	
	623413	**Cover** assembly, sewn, side panel, outer—Leather, Light Tan, R.H.—R.H. seat	1	
CP17	623403	**Cover** assembly, sewn, side panel, outer—Leather, Light Tan, L.H.—L.H. seat	1	
	623416	**Cover** assembly, sewn, side panel, outer—Leather, Midnight Blue, R.H.—R.H. seat	1	
CP17	623406	**Cover** assembly, sewn, side panel, outer—Leather, Midnight Blue, L.H.—L.H. seat	1	
	623417	**Cover** assembly, sewn, side panel, outer—Leather, Shadow Blue, R.H.—R.H. seat	1	
CP17	623407	**Cover** assembly, sewn, side panel, outer—Leather, Shadow Blue, L.H.—L.H. seat	1	Fitted from Commission No. KC10000 (U.S.A.) and KC12805 Black trim, KC9013 Blue trim, KC8806 Tan trim, KC12748 Red trim, (other markets) up to Commission No. KC50000
	623411	**Cover** assembly, sewn, side panel, outer—Leather, Black, R.H.—R.H. seat	1	
CP17	623401	**Cover** assembly, sewn, side panel, outer—Leather, Black, L.H.—L.H. seat	1	
CP18	608817	**Clip**, trim, side panel, outer cover to seat frame (Front trim plate)	4	
	608817	**Clip**, trim, side panel, outer cover to seat frame (Outer lower trim plate)	10	
	608817	**Clip**, trim, side panel, outer cover to seat frame (Outer side trim plate)	6	
CP19	610520	**Clip**, trim, side panel, outer cover to seat frame, lower	4	
CP20	608862	**Clip**, tube, side panel, outer cover to seat frame	2	
	907244	**Padding**, seat side, inner, L.H.—R.H. seat	1	
CP21	907243	**Padding**, seat side, inner, R.H.—L.H. seat	1	
	623352	**Cover** assembly, sewn, side panel, inner—Leathercloth, Red, L.H.—R.H. seat	1	
CP22	623342	**Cover** assembly, sewn, side panel, inner—Leathercloth, Red, R.H.—L.H. seat	1	
	623353	**Cover** assembly, sewn, side panel, inner—Leathercloth, Light Tan, L.H.—R.H. seat	1	
CP22	623343	**Cover** assembly, sewn, side panel, inner—Leathercloth, Light Tan, R.H.—L.H. seat	1	
	623356	**Cover** assembly, sewn, side panel, inner—Leathercloth, Midnight Blue, L.H.—R.H. seat	1	
CP22	623346	**Cover** assembly, sewn, side panel, inner—Leathercloth, Midnight Blue, R.H.—L.H. seat	1	
	623357	**Cover** assembly, sewn, side panel, inner—Leathercloth, Shadow Blue, L.H.—R.H. seat	1	

Note:—Items marked thus † are available on our Factory Exchange Unit Scheme

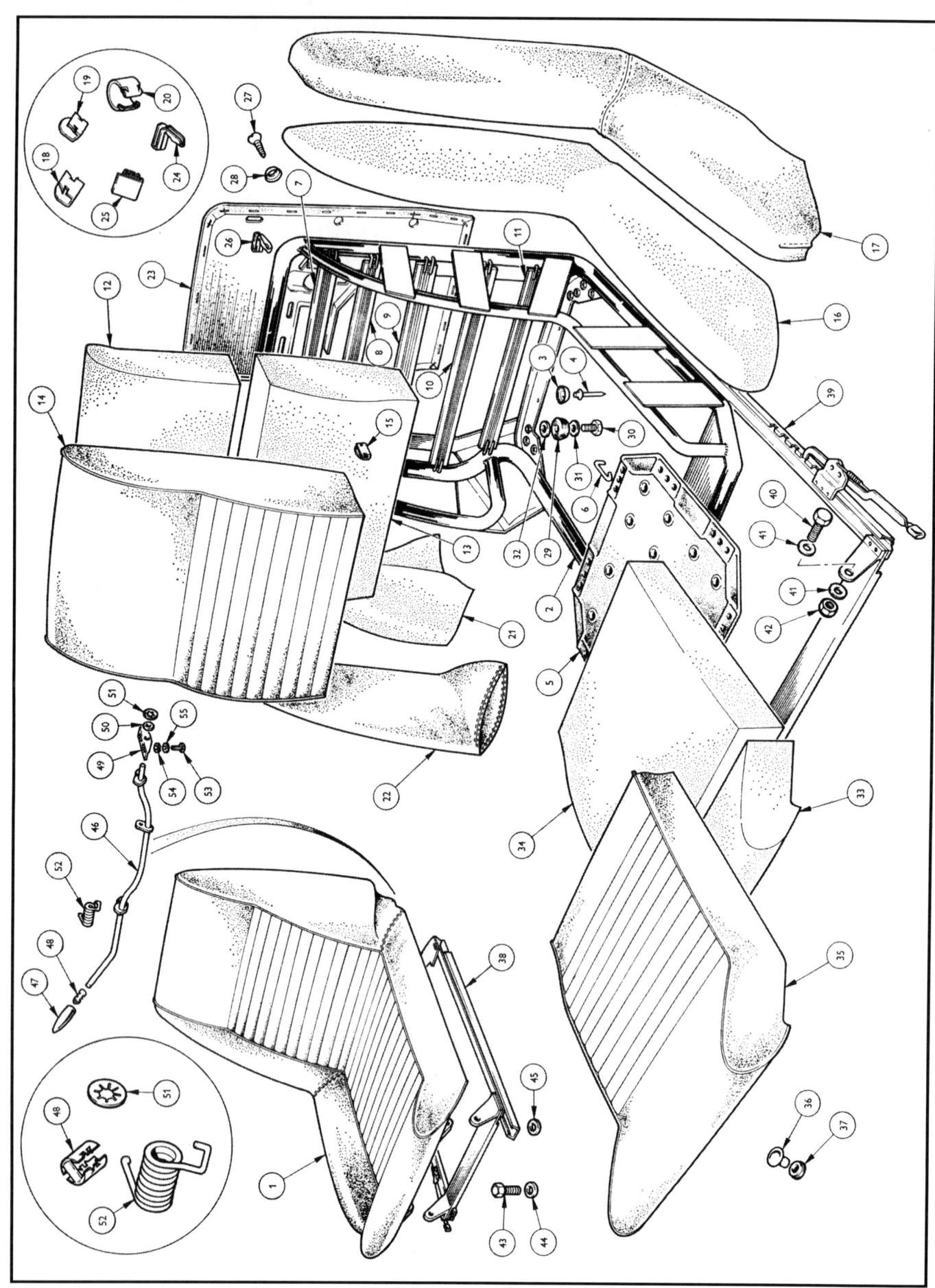

PLATE CP

BODY AND FITTINGS

Plate No.	Part No.	Description	No. per Unit	Remarks
		FRONT SEAT FRAME AND SQUAB ASSEMBLY, TRIMMED—continued		
CP22	623347	Cover assembly, sewn, side panel, inner—Leathercloth, Shadow Blue, R.H.—L.H. seat	1	
	623351	Cover assembly, sewn, side panel, inner—Leathercloth, Black, L.H.—R.H. seat	1	
CP22	623341	Cover assembly, sewn, side panel, inner—Leathercloth, Black, R.H.—L.H. seat	1	
	623372	Cover assembly, sewn, side panel, inner—Leather, Red, L.H.—R.H. seat	1	
CP22	623362	Cover assembly, sewn, side panel, inner—Leather, Red, R.H.—L.H. seat	1	
	623373	Cover assembly, sewn, side panel, inner—Leather, Light Tan, L.H.—R.H. seat	1	
CP22	623363	Cover assembly, sewn, side panel, inner—Leather, Light Tan, R.H.—L.H. seat	1	
	623376	Cover assembly, sewn, side panel, inner—Leather, Midnight Blue, L.H.—R.H. seat	1	
CP22	623366	Cover assembly, sewn, side panel, inner—Leather, Midnight Blue, R.H.—L.H. seat	1	
	623377	Cover assembly, sewn, side panel, inner—Leather, Shadow Blue, L.H.—R.H. seat	1	Fitted from Commission No. KC10000 (U.S.A.) and KC12805 Black trim, KC9013 Blue trim, KC8806 Tan trim, KC12748 Red trim, (other markets) up to Commission No. KC50000
CP22	623367	Cover assembly, sewn, side panel, inner—Leather, Shadow Blue, R.H.—L.H. seat	1	
	623371	Cover assembly, sewn, side panel, inner—Leather, Black, L.H.—R.H. seat	1	
CP22	623361	Cover assembly, sewn side panel, inner—Leather, Black, R.H.—L.H. seat	1	
CP18	608817	Clip, trim, side panel, inner cover to seat frame (Upper and lower side, inner trim plates)	8	
CP19	610520	Clip, trim, side panel, inner cover to seat frame, lower	4	
CP20	608862	Clip, tube, side panel, inner cover to seat frame (Upper and lower)	4	
	811752	Seat back assembly, trimmed, Red—R.H. seat	1	
CP23	811742	Seat back assembly, trimmed, Red—L.H. seat	1	
	811753	Seat back assembly, trimmed, Light Tan—R.H. seat	1	
CP23	811743	Seat back assembly, trimmed, Light Tan—L.H. seat	1	
	811756	Seat back assembly, trimmed, Midnight Blue—R.H. seat	1	
CP23	811746	Seat back assembly, trimmed, Midnight Blue—L.H. seat	1	
	811757	Seat back assembly, trimmed, Shadow Blue—R.H. seat	1	
CP23	811747	Seat back assembly, trimmed, Shadow Blue—L.H. seat	1	
	811751	Seat back assembly, trimmed, Black—R.H. seat	1	
CP23	811741	Seat back assembly, trimmed, Black—L.H. seat	1	
CP24	608516	Clip, trim, seat back to seat frame	4	
CP25	613770	Clip, trim, seat back to seat frame (Back, upper, trim plate)	4	
CP26	613769	Clip, trim, seat back to seat frame	8	

Note:—Items marked thus † are available on our Factory Exchange Unit Scheme

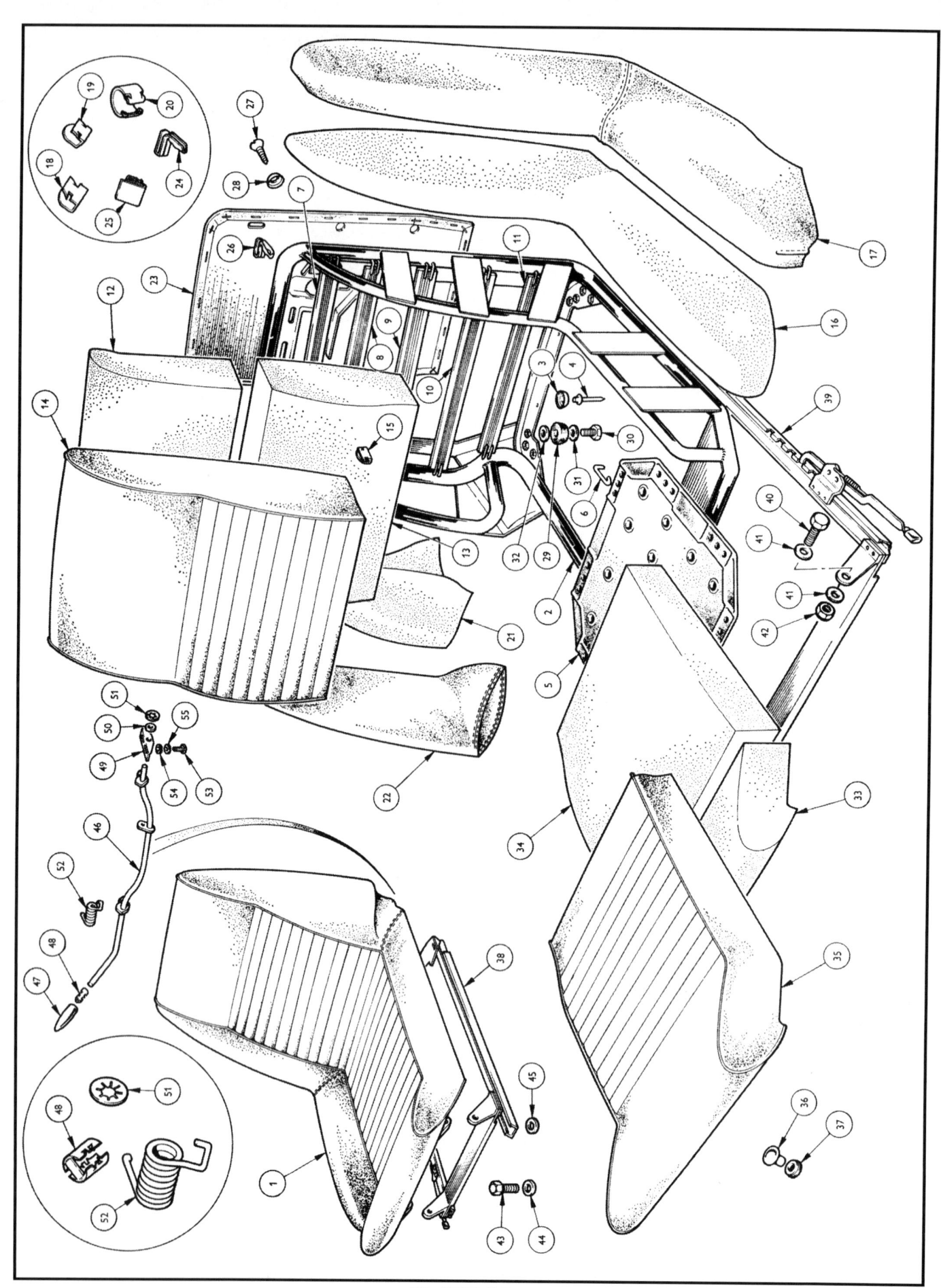

PLATE CP

BODY AND FITTINGS

Plate No.	Part No.	Description	No. per Unit	Remarks
		FRONT SEAT FRAME AND SQUAB ASSEMBLY, TRIMMED—continued		
CP27	512554	**Screw**, self-tapping, chrome ⎫ Seat back, lower	4	
CP28	619618	**Washer**, cup ⎭ attachment	4	
CP29	621515	**Buffer**, rubber	4	
CP30	509140	**Setscrew** ⎫ Rubber buffer	4	
CP31	516834	**Washer**, plain ⎬ to	4	
CP32	503923	**Washer**, plain ⎭ seat frame, lower	4	
	905562	**CUSHION ASSEMBLY, TRIMMED—LEATHER-CLOTH (RED)—R.H. SEAT**	1	
	905552	**CUSHION ASSEMBLY, TRIMMED—LEATHER-CLOTH (RED)—L.H. SEAT**	1	
	905563	**CUSHION ASSEMBLY, TRIMMED—LEATHER-CLOTH (LIGHT TAN)—R.H. SEAT**	1	
	905553	**CUSHION ASSEMBLY, TRIMMED—LEATHER-CLOTH (LIGHT TAN)—L.H. SEAT**	1	Fitted from Commission No. KC10000 (U.S.A.) and KC12805 Black trim, KC9013 Blue trim, KC8806 Tan trim, KC12748 Red trim, (other markets) up to Commission No. KC50000
	905566	**CUSHION ASSEMBLY, TRIMMED—LEATHER-CLOTH (MIDNIGHT BLUE)—R.H. SEAT**	1	
	905556	**CUSHION ASSEMBLY, TRIMMED—LEATHER-CLOTH (MIDNIGHT BLUE)—L.H. SEAT**	1	
	905567	**CUSHION ASSEMBLY, TRIMMED—LEATHER-CLOTH (SHADOW BLUE)—R.H. SEAT**	1	
	905557	**CUSHION ASSEMBLY, TRIMMED—LEATHER-CLOTH (SHADOW BLUE)—L.H. SEAT**	1	
	905561	**CUSHION ASSEMBLY, TRIMMED—LEATHER-CLOTH (BLACK)—R.H. SEAT**	1	
	905551	**CUSHION ASSEMBLY, TRIMMED—LEATHER-CLOTH (BLACK)—L.H. SEAT**	1	
	905582	**CUSHION ASSEMBLY, TRIMMED—LEATHER (RED)—R.H. SEAT**	1	
	905572	**CUSHION ASSEMBLY, TRIMMED—LEATHER (RED)—L.H. SEAT**	1	
	905583	**CUSHION ASSEMBLY, TRIMMED—LEATHER (LIGHT TAN)—R.H. SEAT**	1	
	905573	**CUSHION ASSEMBLY, TRIMMED—LEATHER (LIGHT TAN)—L.H. SEAT**	1	

Note:—Items marked thus † are available on our Factory Exchange Unit Scheme

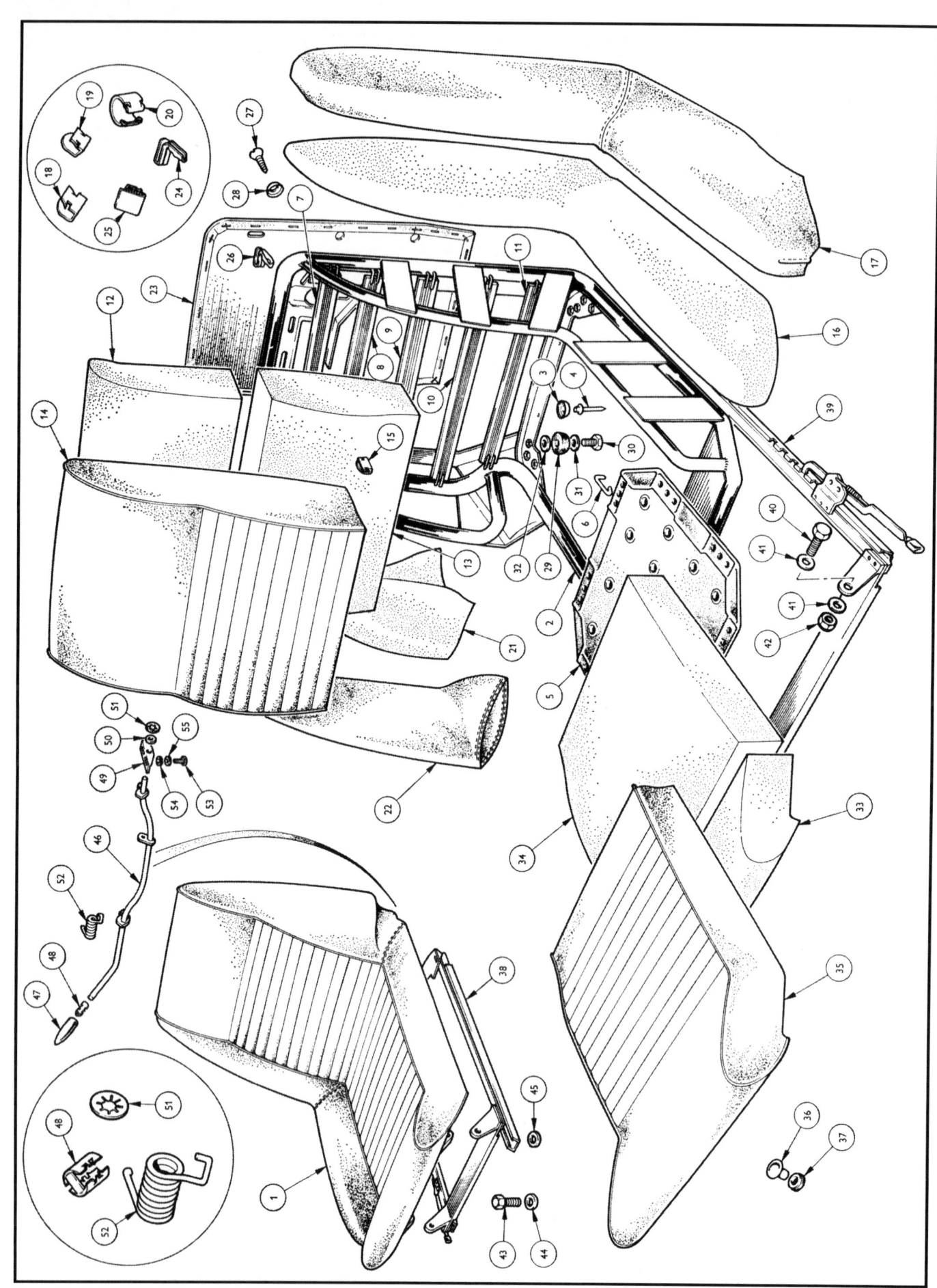

PLATE CP

BODY AND FITTINGS

Plate No.	Part No.	Description	No. per Unit	Remarks
		FRONT SEAT CUSHION ASSEMBLY—continued		
	905586	CUSHION ASSEMBLY, TRIMMED—LEATHER (MIDNIGHT BLUE)—R.H. SEAT	1	
	905576	CUSHION ASSEMBLY, TRIMMED—LEATHER (MIDNIGHT BLUE)—L.H. SEAT	1	
	905587	CUSHION ASSEMBLY, TRIMMED—LEATHER (SHADOW BLUE)—R.H. SEAT	1	
	905577	CUSHION ASSEMBLY, TRIMMED—LEATHER (SHADOW BLUE)—L.H. SEAT	1	
	905581	CUSHION ASSEMBLY, TRIMMED—LEATHER (BLACK)—R.H. SEAT	1	
	905571	CUSHION ASSEMBLY, TRIMMED—LEATHER (BLACK)—L.H. SEAT	1	
	810241	Pad, cushion, front,—R.H. seat	1	
CP33	810240	Pad, cushion, front,—L.H. seat	1	
	810243	Pad, cushion, rear,—R.H. seat	1	
CP34	810242	Pad, cushion, rear,—L.H. seat	1	Fitted from Commission No. KC10000 (U.S.A.) and KC12805 Black trim, KC9013 Blue trim, KC8806 Tan trim, KC12748 Red trim, (other markets) up to Commission No. KC50000
	711142	Cover assembly, cushion—Leathercloth, Red—R.H. seat	1	
CP35	711132	Cover assembly, cushion—Leathercloth, Red—L.H. seat	1	
	711143	Cover assembly, cushion—Leathercloth, Light Tan—R.H. seat	1	
CP35	711133	Cover assembly, cushion—Leathercloth, Light Tan—L.H. seat	1	
	711146	Cover assembly, cushion—Leathercloth, Midnight Blue—R.H. seat	1	
CP35	711136	Cover assembly, cushion—Leathercloth, Midnight Blue—L.H. seat	1	
	711147	Cover assembly, cushion—Leathercloth, Shadow Blue—R.H. seat	1	
CP35	711137	Cover assembly, cushion—Leathercloth, Shadow Blue—L.H. seat	1	
	711141	Cover assembly, cushion—Leathercloth, Black—R.H. seat	1	
CP35	711131	Cover assembly, cushion—Leathercloth, Black—L.H. seat	1	
	711162	Cover assembly, cushion—Leather, Red—R.H. seat	1	
CP35	711152	Cover assembly, cushion—Leather, Red—L.H. seat	1	
	711163	Cover assembly, cushion—Leather, Light Tan—R.H. seat	1	
CP35	711153	Cover assembly, cushion—Leather, Light Tan—L.H. seat	1	
	711166	Cover assembly, cushion—Leather, Midnight Blue—R.H. seat	1	
CP35	711156	Cover assembly, cushion—Leather, Midnight Blue—L.H. seat	1	
	711167	Cover assembly, cushion—Leather, Shadow Blue—R.H. seat	1	

Note:—Items marked thus † are available on our Factory Exchange Unit Scheme

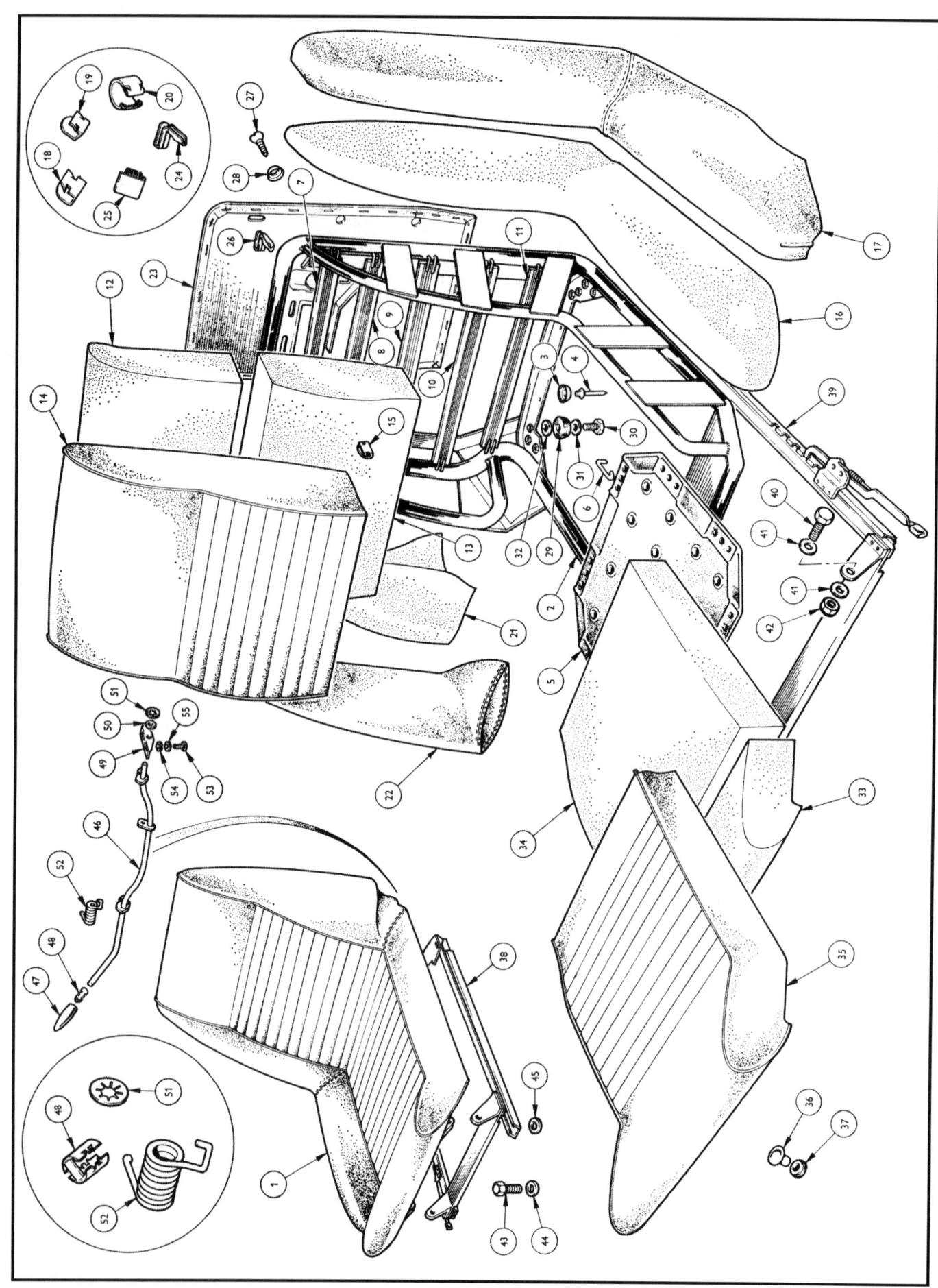

PLATE CP

BODY AND FITTINGS

Plate No.	Part No.	Description	No. per Unit	Remarks
		FRONT SEAT CUSHION ASSEMBLY—continued		
CP35	711157	Cover assembly, cushion—Leather, Shadow Blue—L.H. seat	1	
	711161	Cover assembly, cushion—Leather, Black—R.H. seat	1	
CP35	711151	Cover assembly, cushion—Leather, Black—L.H. seat	1	Fitted from Commission No. KC10000 (U.S.A.) and KC12805 Black trim, KC9013 Blue trim, KC8806 Tan trim, KC12748 Red trim, (other markets) up to Commission No. KC50000
CP36	565747	Button ⎫ Cushion cover	6	
CP37	567642	Socket ⎭ to frame	6	
CP38	812683	**SEAT SLIDE ASSEMBLY—R.H. SEAT**	1	
CP39	812682	**SEAT SLIDE ASSEMBLY—L.H. SEAT**	1	
CP40	HU0807	Screw, set ⎫	4	
CP41	WP0150	Washer, plain ⎬ Seat slide to seat	8	
CP42	YN2908	Nut, nyloc ⎭	4	
CP43	HU0706	Screw, set ⎫ Seat slide	8	
CP44	WP0023	Washer, plain ⎭ to floor	8	
CP45	WP0048	Washer, plain, between seat slide and carpet	8	
CP46	712732	**SEAT SAFETY CATCH AND CONTROL LEVER ASSEMBLY—R.H.**	1	
	712731	**SEAT SAFETY CATCH AND CONTROL LEVER ASSEMBLY—L.H.**	1	
CP47	621458	Knob, control lever	2	
CP48	621776	Clip, knob fixing	2	U.S.A. only fitted from Commission No. KC10000 up to KC50000 only
CP49	621266	Bracket, attachment, safety catch and lever	4	
CP50	503661	Washer, plain spacing	4	
CP51	574841	Fix, multi-prong, securing bracket	2	
CP52	623486	Spring, tension, between link and frame—R.H.	1	
	623485	Spring, tension, between link and frame—L.H.	1	
CP53	506731	Setscrew ⎫ Safety catch	8	
CP54	508875	Washer, plain ⎬ and control lever	8	
CP55	505307	Washer, lock ⎭ to seat	8	

Note:—Items marked thus † are available on our Factory Exchange Unit Scheme

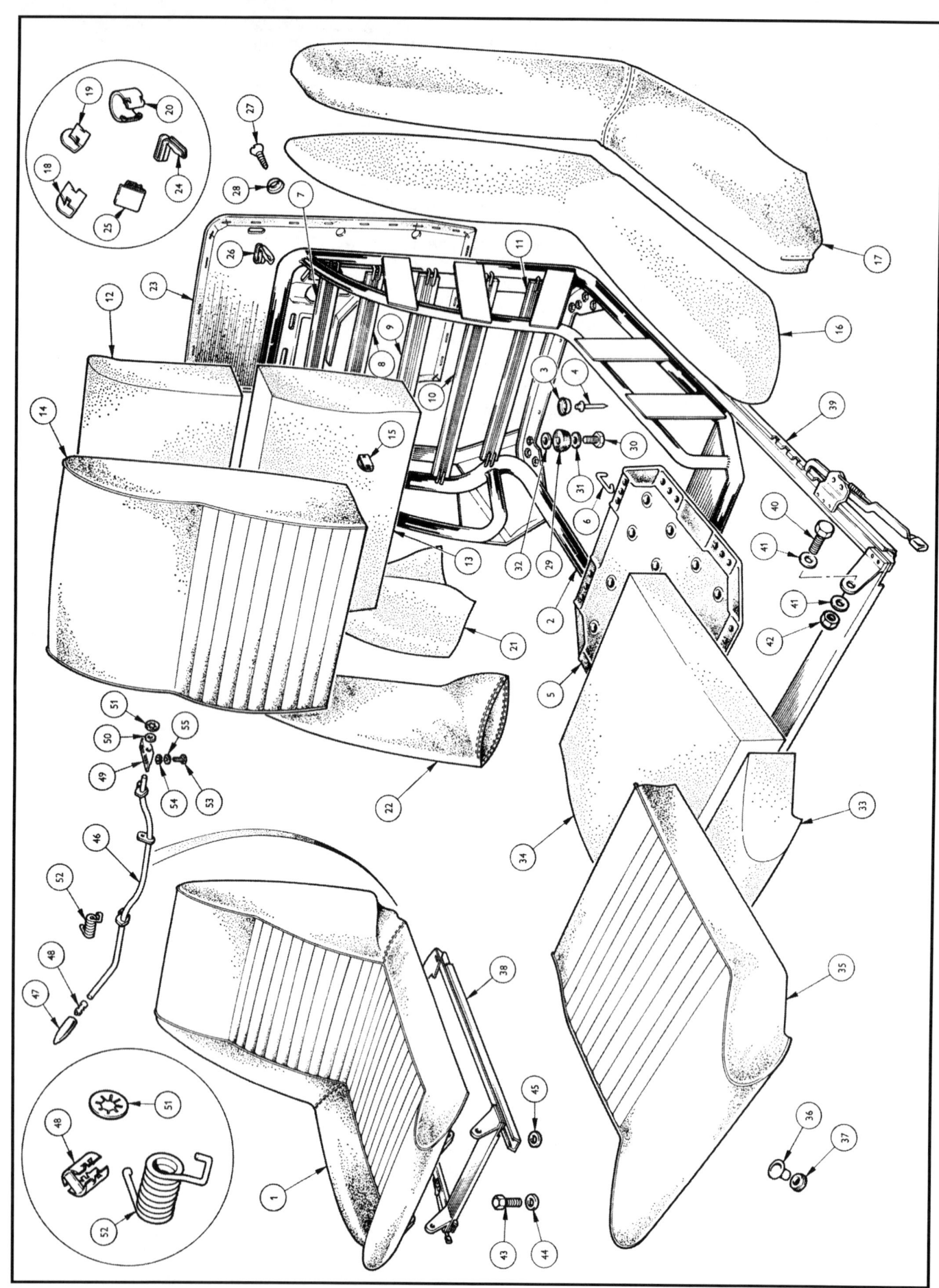

PLATE CP

BODY AND FITTINGS

Plate No.	Part No.	Description	No. per Unit	Remarks
CP1	909852	FRONT SEAT COMPLETE ASSEMBLY, TRIMMED—LEATHERCLOTH (Red)—R.H.	1	
	909842	FRONT SEAT COMPLETE ASSEMBLY, TRIMMED—LEATHERCLOTH (Red)—L.H.	1	
CP1	909853	FRONT SEAT COMPLETE ASSEMBLY, TRIMMED—LEATHERCLOTH (Light Tan)—R.H.	1	
	909843	FRONT SEAT COMPLETE ASSEMBLY, TRIMMED—LEATHERCLOTH (Light Tan)—L.H.	1	
CP1	909857	FRONT SEAT COMPLETE ASSEMBLY, TRIMMED—LEATHERCLOTH (Shadow Blue)—R.H.	1	
	909847	FRONT SEAT COMPLETE ASSEMBLY, TRIMMED—LEATHERCLOTH (Shadow Blue)—L.H.	1	Mark II cars only. Fitted from Commission No. KC50001 and future (All markets except U.S.A.) For U.S.A. see pages 180 to 187 inclusive
CP1	909851	FRONT SEAT COMPLETE ASSEMBLY, TRIMMED—LEATHERCLOTH (Black)—R.H.	1	
	909841	FRONT SEAT COMPLETE ASSEMBLY, TRIMMED—LEATHERCLOTH (Black)—L.H.	1	
CP1	909872	FRONT SEAT COMPLETE ASSEMBLY, TRIMMED—LEATHER (Red)—R.H.	1	
	909862	FRONT SEAT COMPLETE ASSEMBLY, TRIMMED—LEATHER (Red)—L.H.	1	
CP1	909873	FRONT SEAT COMPLETE ASSEMBLY, TRIMMED—LEATHER (Light Tan)—R.H.	1	
	909863	FRONT SEAT COMPLETE ASSEMBLY, TRIMMED—LEATHER (Light Tan)—L.H.	1	
CP1	909877	FRONT SEAT COMPLETE ASSEMBLY, TRIMMED—LEATHER (Shadow Blue)—R.H.	1	

Note:—Items marked thus † are available on our Factory Exchange Unit Scheme

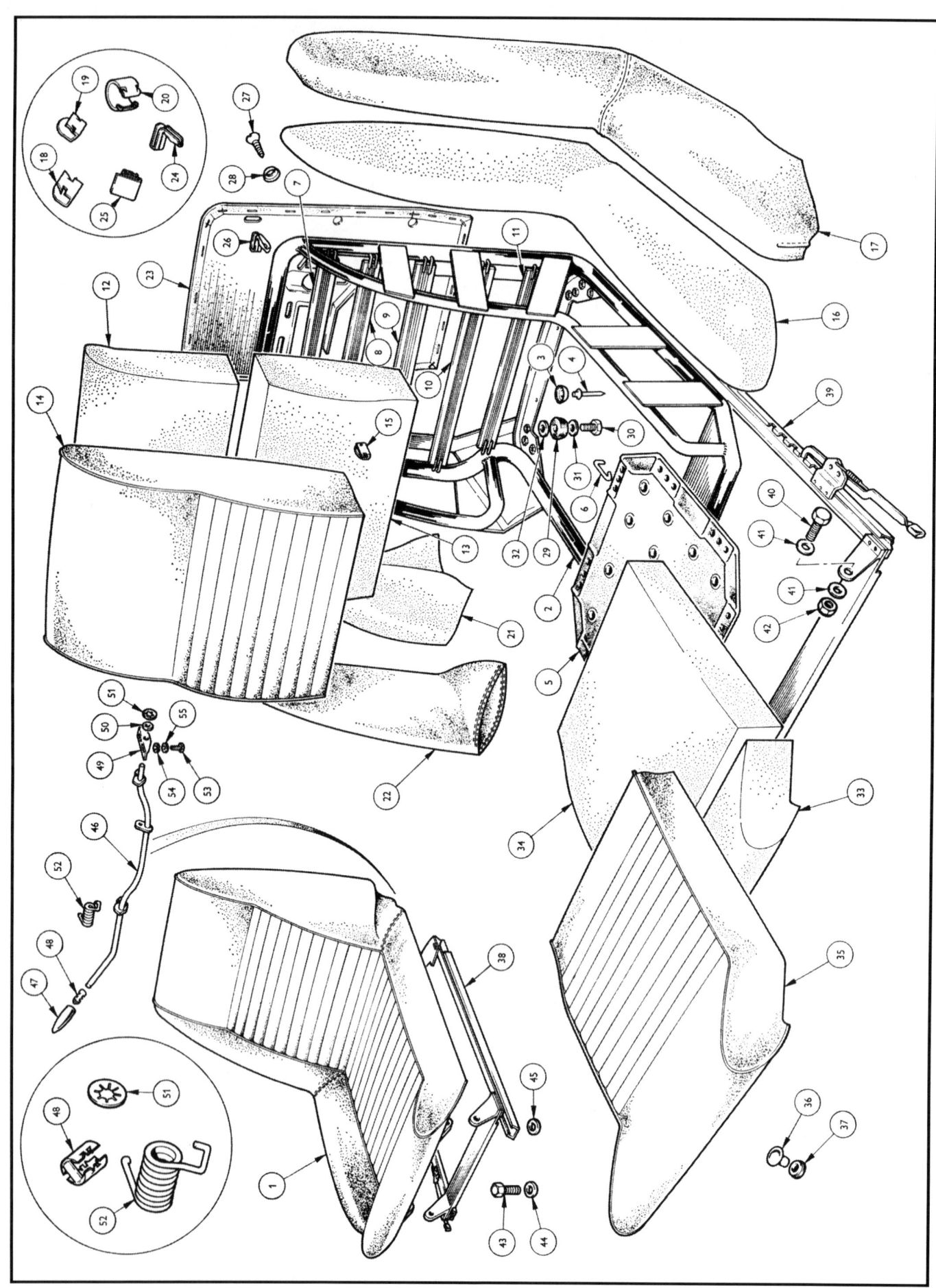

PLATE CP

BODY AND FITTINGS

Plate No.	Part No.	Description	No. per Unit	Remarks
	909867	FRONT SEAT COMPLETE ASSEMBLY, TRIMMED—LEATHER (Shadow Blue)—L.H.	1	
CP1	909871	FRONT SEAT COMPLETE ASSEMBLY, TRIMMED—LEATHER (Black)—R.H.	1	
	909861	FRONT SEAT COMPLETE ASSEMBLY, TRIMMED—LEATHER (Black)—L.H.	1	
	909892	FRONT SEAT FRAME AND SQUAB ASSEMBLY, TRIMMED—LEATHERCLOTH (RED)—R.H.	1	
	909882	FRONT SEAT FRAME AND SQUAB ASSEMBLY, TRIMMED—LEATHERCLOTH (RED)—L.H.	1	
	909893	FRONT SEAT FRAME AND SQUAB ASSEMBLY, TRIMMED—LEATHERCLOTH (LIGHT TAN)—R.H.	1	
	909883	FRONT SEAT FRAME AND SQUAB ASSEMBLY, TRIMMED—LEATHERCLOTH (LIGHT TAN)—L.H.	1	Mark II cars only Fitted from Commission No. KC50001 and future (All markets except U.S.A.) For U.S.A. see pages 180 to 187 inclusive
	909897	FRONT SEAT FRAME AND SQUAB ASSEMBLY, TRIMMED—LEATHERCLOTH (SHADOW BLUE)—R.H.	1	
	909887	FRONT SEAT FRAME AND SQUAB ASSEMBLY, TRIMMED—LEATHERCLOTH (SHADOW BLUE)—L.H.	1	
	909891	FRONT SEAT FRAME AND SQUAB ASSEMBLY, TRIMMED—LEATHERCLOTH (BLACK)—R.H.	1	
	909881	FRONT SEAT FRAME AND SQUAB ASSEMBLY, TRIMMED—LEATHERCLOTH (BLACK)—L.H.	1	
	909912	FRONT SEAT FRAME AND SQUAB ASSEMBLY, TRIMMED—LEATHER (RED)—R.H.	1	
	909902	FRONT SEAT FRAME AND SQUAB ASSEMBLY, TRIMMED—LEATHER (RED)—L.H.	1	
	909913	FRONT SEAT FRAME AND SQUAB ASSEMBLY, TRIMMED—LEATHER (LIGHT TAN)—R.H.	1	
	909903	FRONT SEAT FRAME AND SQUAB ASSEMBLY, TRIMMED—LEATHER (LIGHT TAN)—L.H.	1	

Note:—Items marked thus † are available on our Factory Exchange Unit Scheme

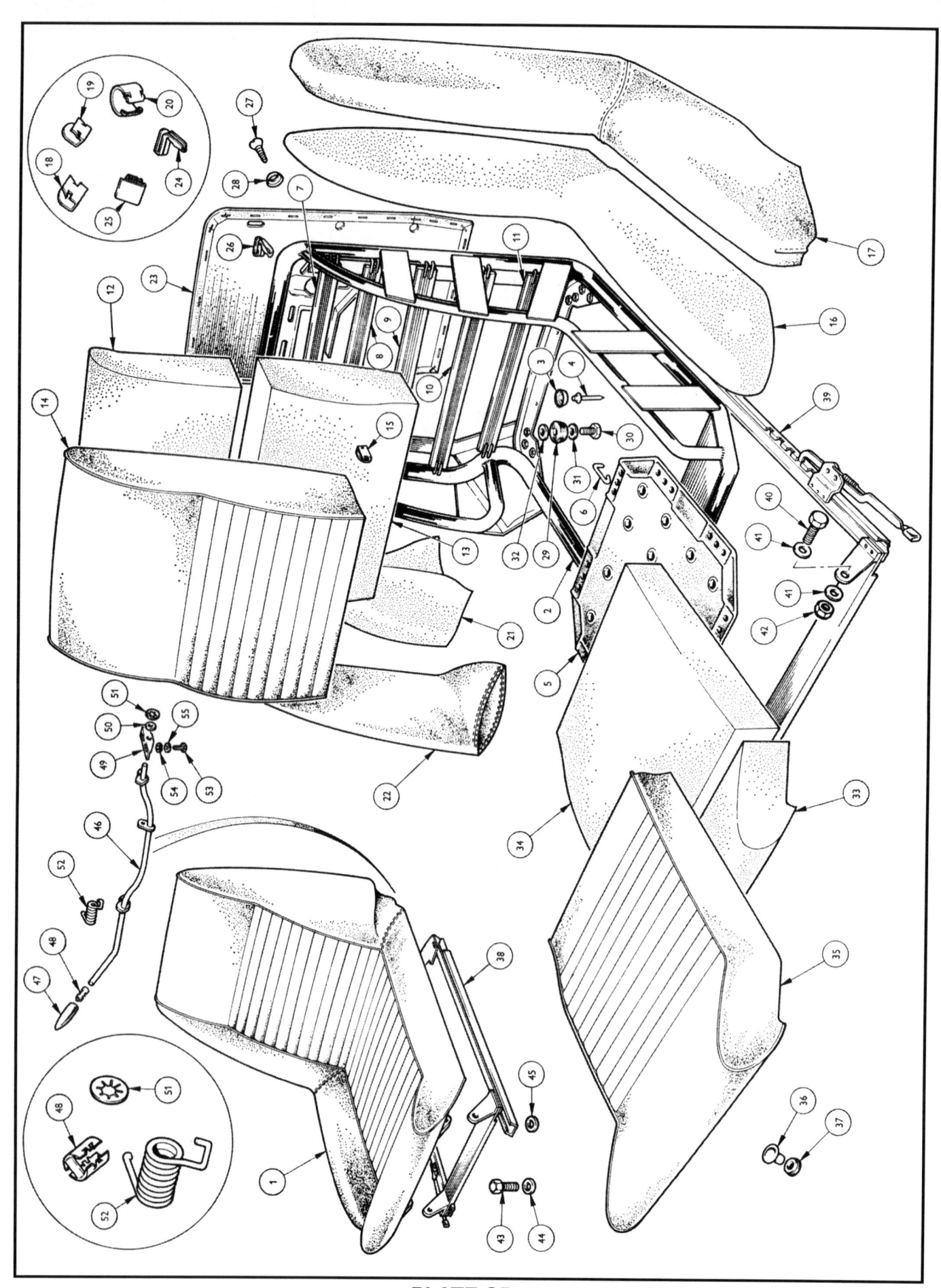

PLATE CP

BODY AND FITTINGS

Plate No.	Part No.	Description	No. per Unit	Remarks
		FRONT SEAT FRAME AND SQUAB ASSEMBLY, TRIMMED—continued		
	909917	**FRONT SEAT FRAME AND SQUAB ASSEMBLY, TRIMMED—LEATHER (SHADOW BLUE)—R.H.**	1	
	909907	**FRONT SEAT FRAME AND SQUAB ASSEMBLY, TRIMMED—LEATHER (SHADOW BLUE)—L.H.**	1	
	909911	**FRONT SEAT FRAME AND SQUAB ASSEMBLY, TRIMMED—LEATHER (BLACK)—R.H.**	1	
	909901	**FRONT SEAT FRAME AND SQUAB ASSEMBLY, TRIMMED—LEATHER (BLACK)—L.H.**	1	
	908396	**Frame** assembly, R.H. seat	1	
CP2	908395	**Frame** assembly, L.H. seat	1	
CP3	610624	**Stud,** cushion attachment	6	
CP4	561210	**Rivet,** stud to frame	6	
CP5	573900	**Diaphragm,** seat base	2	
CP6	613966	**Hook,** diaphragm	8	
	612261	**Hook,** diaphragm	4	
	623877	**Clip,** diaphragm	4	Mark II cars only
	623420	**Piece,** filler, squab side	4	Fitted from Commission No. KC50001 and future
CP7	619498	**Strap** assembly, squab, 11" long—Top	2	(All markets except U.S.A.)
CP8	619499	**Strap** assembly, squab, 12" long—Top intermediate	2	For U.S.A. see pages 180 to 187 inclusive
CP9	619500	**Strap** assembly, squab, 12·5" long—Centre	2	
CP10	619501	**Strap** assembly, squab, 13·75" long—Bottom intermediate	2	
CP11	619498	**Strap** assembly, squab, 11" long—Bottom	2	
CP12	810630	**Pad,** squab, upper	2	
	810632	**Pad,** squab, lower—R.H. seat	1	
CP13	810631	**Pad,** squab, lower—L.H. seat	1	
	714682	**Cover** assembly, squab, sewn—Leathercloth, Red—R.H. seat	1	
CP14	714672	**Cover** assembly, squab, sewn—Leathercloth, Red—L.H. seat	1	
	714683	**Cover** assembly, squab, sewn—Leathercloth, Light Tan—R.H. seat	1	
CP14	714673	**Cover** assembly, squab, sewn—Leathercloth, Light Tan—L.H. seat	1	
	714687	**Cover** assembly, squab, sewn—Leathercloth, Shadow Blue—R.H. seat	1	
CP14	714677	**Cover** assembly, squab, sewn—Leathercloth, Shadow Blue—L.H. seat	1	
	714681	**Cover** assembly, squab, sewn—Leathercloth, Black—R.H. seat	1	
CP14	714671	**Cover** assembly, squab, sewn—Leathercloth, Black—L.H. seat	1	
	714702	**Cover** assembly, squab, sewn—Leather, Red—R.H. seat	1	

Note:—Items marked thus † are available on our Factory Exchange Unit Scheme

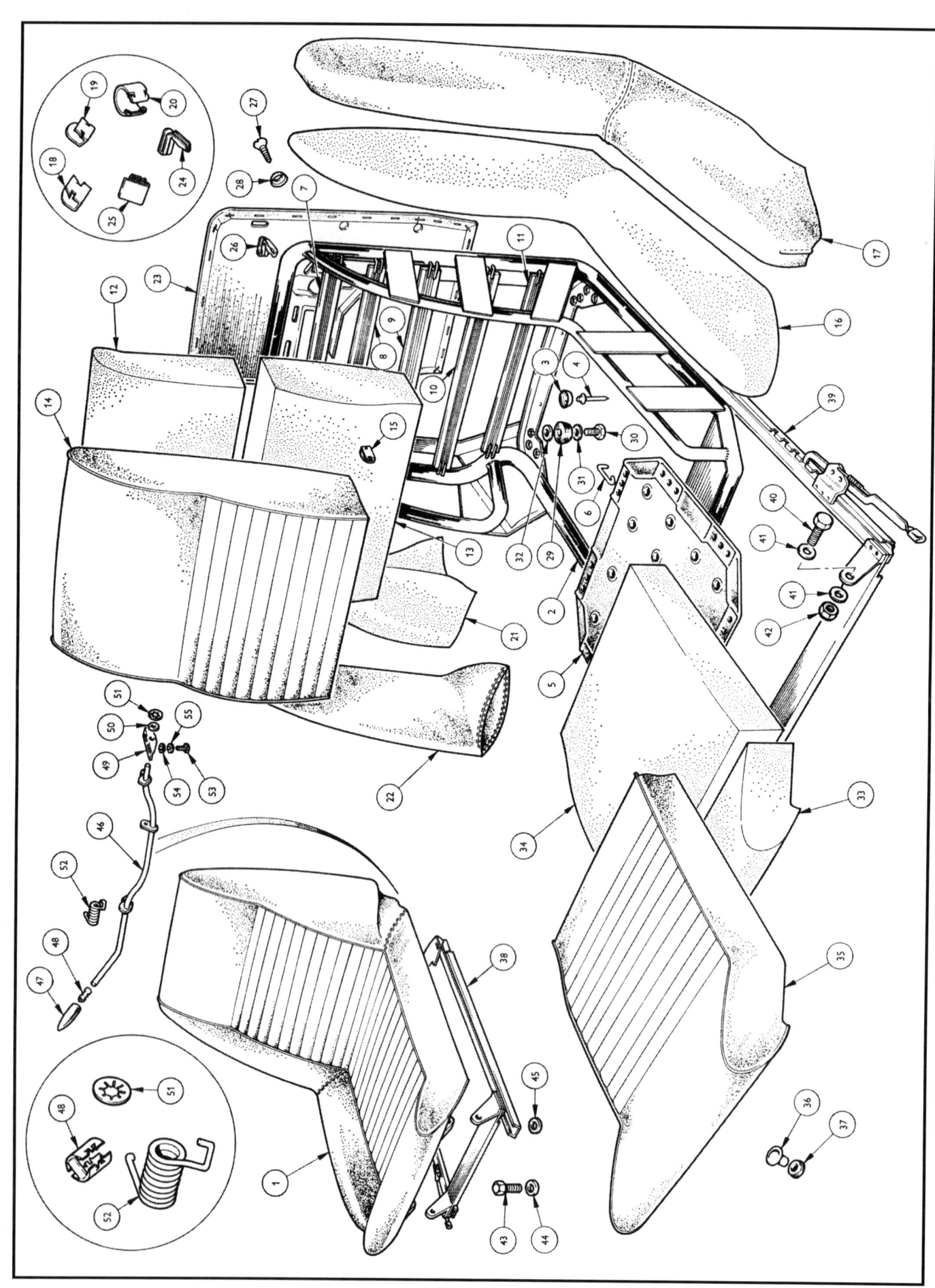

PLATE CP

BODY AND FITTINGS

Plate No.	Part No.	Description	No. per Unit	Remarks
		FRONT SEAT FRAME AND SQUAB ASSEMBLY, TRIMMED—continued		
CP14	714692	**Cover** assembly, squab, sewn—Leather, Red—L.H. seat	1	
	714703	**Cover** assembly, squab, sewn—Leather, Light Tan—R.H. seat	1	
CP14	714693	**Cover** assembly, squab, sewn—Leather, Light Tan—L.H. seat	1	
	714707	**Cover** assembly, squab, sewn—Leather, Shadow Blue—R.H. seat	1	
CP14	714697	**Cover** assembly, squab, sewn—Leather, Shadow Blue—L.H. seat	1	
	714701	**Cover** assembly, squab, sewn—Leather, Black—R.H. seat	1	
CP14	714691	**Cover** assembly, squab, sewn—Leather, Black—L.H. seat	1	
CP15	603811	**Clip**, trim, squab cover to frame	8	
	907242	**Padding**, seat side outer, R.H.—R.H. seat	1	
CP16	907241	**Padding**, seat side outer, L.H.—L.H. seat	1	
	623392	**Cover** assembly, sewn, side panel, outer—Leathercloth, Red, R.H.—R.H. seat	1	
CP17	623382	**Cover** assembly, sewn, side panel, outer—Leathercloth, Red, L.H.—L.H. seat	1	
	623393	**Cover** assembly, sewn, side panel, outer—Leathercloth, Light Tan, R.H.—R.H. seat	1	Mark II cars only Fitted from Commission No. KC50001 and future (All markets except U.S.A.) For U.S.A. see pages 180 to 187 inclusive
CP17	623383	**Cover** assembly, sewn, side panel, outer—Leathercloth, Light Tan, L.H.—L.H. seat	1	
	623397	**Cover** assembly, sewn, side panel, outer—Leathercloth, Shadow Blue, R.H.—R.H. seat	1	
CP17	623387	**Cover** assembly, sewn, side panel, outer—Leathercloth, Shadow Blue, L.H.—L.H. seat	1	
	623391	**Cover** assembly, sewn, side panel, outer—Leathercloth, Black, R.H.—R.H. seat	1	
CP17	623381	**Cover** assembly, sewn, side panel, outer—Leathercloth, Black, L.H.—L.H. seat	1	
	623412	**Cover** assembly, sewn, side panel, outer—Leather, Red, R.H.—R.H. seat	1	
CP17	623402	**Cover** assembly, sewn, side panel, outer—Leather, Red, L.H.—L.H. seat	1	
	623413	**Cover** assembly, sewn, side panel, outer—Leather, Light Tan, R.H.—R.H. seat	1	
CP17	623403	**Cover** assembly, sewn, side panel, outer—Leather, Light Tan, L.H.—L.H. seat	1	
	623417	**Cover** assembly, sewn, side panel, outer—Leather, Shadow Blue, R.H.—R.H. seat	1	
CP17	623407	**Cover** assembly, sewn, side panel, outer—Leather, Shadow Blue, L.H.—L.H. seat	1	
	623411	**Cover** assembly, sewn, side panel, outer—Leather, Black, R.H.—R.H. seat	1	
CP17	623401	**Cover** assembly, sewn, side panel, outer—Leather, Black, L.H.—L.H. seat	1	
CP18	608817	**Clip**, trim, side panel, outer cover to seat frame (Front trim plate)	4	

Note:—Items marked thus † are available on our Factory Exchange Unit Scheme

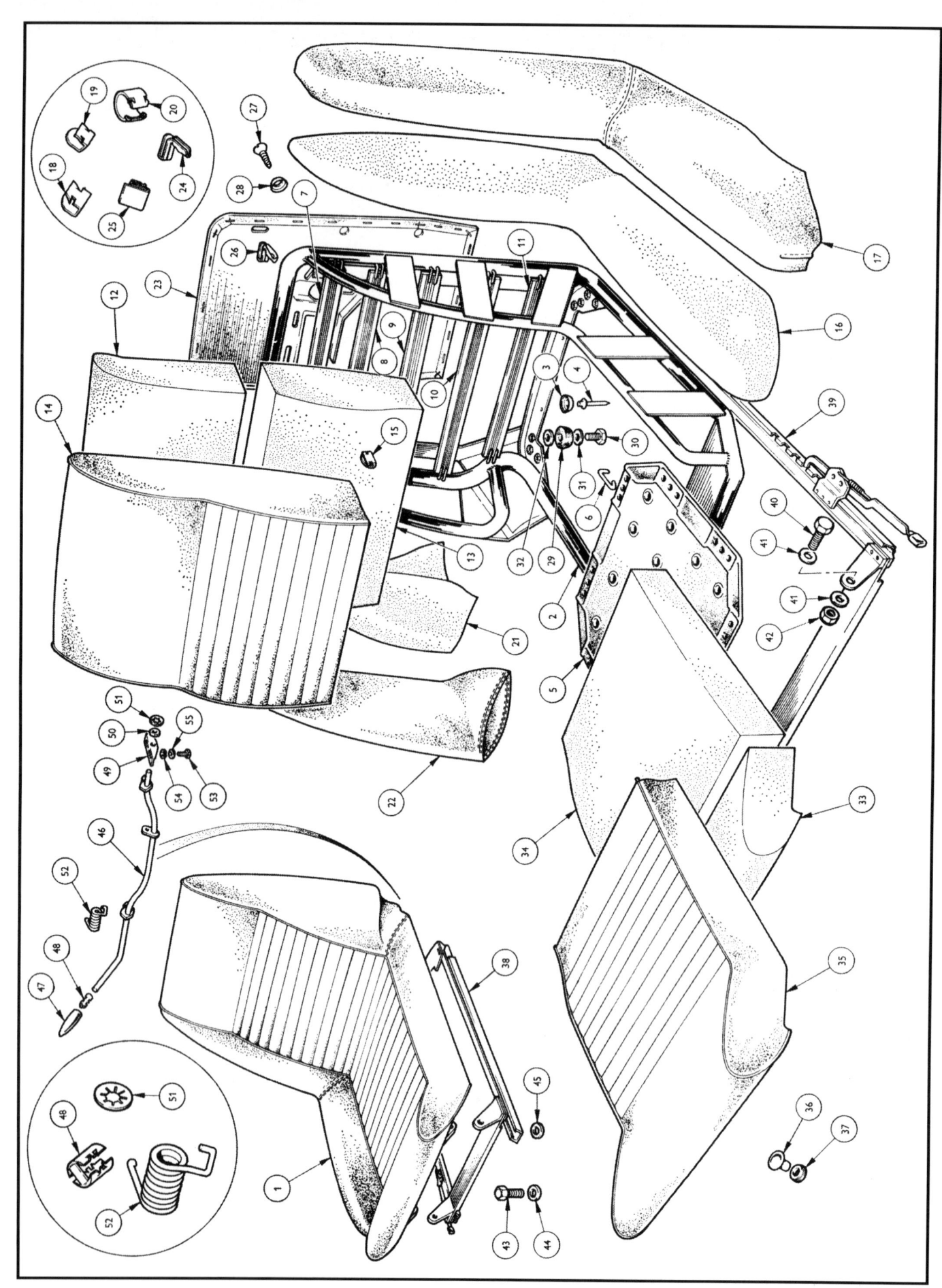

PLATE CP

BODY AND FITTINGS

Plate No.	Part No.	Description	No. per Unit	Remarks
		FRONT SEAT FRAME AND SQUAB ASSEMBLY, TRIMMED—continued		
CP18	608817	**Clip,** trim, side panel, outer cover to seat frame (Outer lower trim plate)	10	
CP18	608817	**Clip,** trim, side panel, outer cover to seat frame (Outer side trim plate)	6	
CP19	610520	**Clip,** trim, side panel, outer cover to seat frame, lower	4	
CP20	608862	**Clip,** tube, side panel, outer cover to seat frame	2	
	907244	**Padding,** seat side, inner, L.H.—R.H. seat	1	
CP21	907243	**Padding,** seat side, inner, R.H.—L.H. seat	1	
	623352	**Cover** assembly, sewn, side panel, inner—Leathercloth, Red, L.H.—R.H. seat	1	
CP22	623342	**Cover** assembly, sewn, side panel, inner—Leathercloth, Red, R.H.—L.H. seat	1	
	623353	**Cover** assembly, sewn, side panel, inner—Leathercloth, Light Tan, L.H.—R.H. seat	1	
CP22	623343	**Cover** assembly, sewn, side panel, inner—Leathercloth, Light Tan, R.H.—L.H. seat	1	
	623357	**Cover** assembly, sewn, side panel, inner—Leathercloth, Shadow Blue, L.H.—R.H. seat	1	
CP22	623347	**Cover** assembly, sewn, side panel, inner—Leathercloth, Shadow Blue, R.H.—L.H. seat	1	
	623351	**Cover** assembly, sewn, side panel, inner—Leathercloth, Black, L.H.—R.H. seat	1	Mark II cars only Fitted from Commission No. KC50001 and future (All markets except U.S.A.) For U.S.A. see pages 180 to 187 inclusive
CP22	623341	**Cover** assembly, sewn, side panel, inner—Leathercloth, Black, R.H.—L.H. seat	1	
	623372	**Cover** assembly, sewn, side panel, inner—Leather, Red, L.H.—R.H. seat	1	
CP22	623362	**Cover** assembly, sewn, side panel, inner—Leather, Red, R.H.—L.H. seat	1	
	623373	**Cover** assembly, sewn, side panel, inner—Leather, Light Tan, L.H.—R.H. seat	1	
CP22	623363	**Cover** assembly, sewn, side panel, inner—Leather, Light Tan, R.H.—L.H. seat	1	
	623377	**Cover** assembly, sewn, side panel, inner—Leather, Shadow Blue, L.H.—R.H. seat	1	
CP22	623367	**Cover** assembly, sewn, side panel, inner—Leather, Shadow Blue, R.H.—L.H. seat	1	
	623371	**Cover** assembly, sewn, side panel, inner—Leather, Black, L.H.—R.H. seat	1	
CP22	623361	**Cover** assembly, sewn, side panel, inner—Leather, Black, R.H.—L.H. seat	1	
CP18	608817	**Clip,** trim, side panel, inner cover to seat frame (Upper and lower, side, inner trim plates)	8	
CP19	610520	**Clip,** trim, side panel, inner cover to seat frame, lower	4	
CP20	608862	**Clip,** tube, side panel, inner cover to seat frame (Upper and lower)	4	
	811752	**Seat back** assembly, trimmed, Red—R.H. seat	1	
CP23	811742	**Seat back** assembly, trimmed, Red—L.H. seat	1	
	811753	**Seat back** assembly, trimmed, Light Tan—R.H. seat	1	
CP23	811743	**Seat back** assembly, trimmed, Light Tan—L.H. seat	1	
	811757	**Seat back** assembly, trimmed, Shadow Blue—R.H. seat	1	

Note:—Items marked thus † are available on our Factory Exchange Unit Scheme

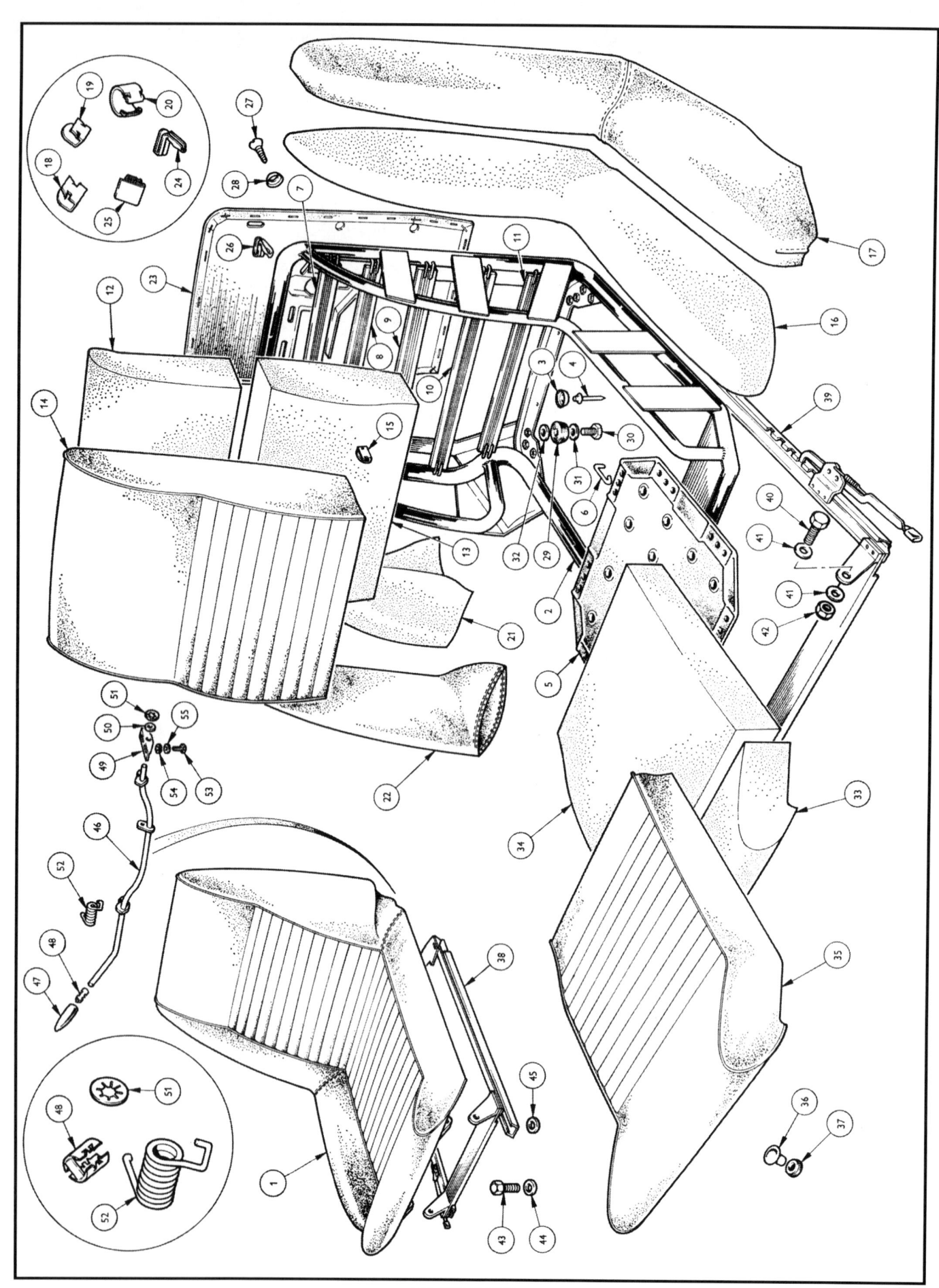

PLATE CP

BODY AND FITTINGS

Plate No.	Part No.	Description	No. per Unit	Remarks
		FRONT SEAT FRAME AND SQUAB ASSEMBLY, TRIMMED—continued		
CP23	811747	**Seat back** assembly, trimmed, Shadow Blue—L.H. seat	1	
	811751	**Seat back** assembly, trimmed, Black—R.H. seat	1	
CP23	811741	**Seat back** assembly, trimmed, Black—L.H. seat	1	
CP24	608516	**Clip**, trim, seat back to seat frame	4	
CP25	613770	**Clip**, trim, seat back to seat frame (Back, upper trim plate)	4	
CP26	613769	**Clip**, trim, seat back to seat frame	8	
CP27	512554	**Screw**, self-tapping, chrome ⎫ Seat back, lower	4	
CP28	619618	**Washer**, cup ⎭ attachment	4	
CP29	621515	**Buffer**, rubber	4	
CP30	509140	**Setscrew** ⎫ Rubber buffer	4	
CP31	516834	**Washer**, plain ⎬ to	4	
CP32	503923	**Washer**, plain ⎭ seat frame, lower	4	
	909932	**CUSHION ASSEMBLY, TRIMMED—LEATHER-CLOTH (RED)—R.H. SEAT**	1	
	909922	**CUSHION ASSEMBLY, TRIMMED—LEATHER-CLOTH (RED)—L.H. SEAT**	1	
	909933	**CUSHION ASSEMBLY, TRIMMED—LEATHER-CLOTH (LIGHT TAN)—R.H. SEAT**	1	Mark II cars only Fitted from Commission No. KC50001 and future (All markets except U.S.A.) For U.S.A. see pages 180 to 187 inclusive
	909923	**CUSHION ASSEMBLY, TRIMMED—LEATHER-CLOTH (LIGHT TAN)—L.H. SEAT**	1	
	909937	**CUSHION ASSEMBLY, TRIMMED—LEATHER-CLOTH (SHADOW BLUE)—R.H. SEAT**	1	
	909927	**CUSHION ASSEMBLY, TRIMMED—LEATHER-CLOTH (SHADOW BLUE)—L.H. SEAT**	1	
	909931	**CUSHION ASSEMBLY, TRIMMED—LEATHER-CLOTH (BLACK)—R.H. SEAT**	1	
	909921	**CUSHION ASSEMBLY, TRIMMED—LEATHER-CLOTH (BLACK)—L.H. SEAT**	1	
	909952	**CUSHION ASSEMBLY, TRIMMED—LEATHER (RED)—R.H. SEAT**	1	
	909942	**CUSHION ASSEMBLY, TRIMMED—LEATHER (RED)—L.H. SEAT**	1	
	909953	**CUSHION ASSEMBLY, TRIMMED—LEATHER (LIGHT TAN)—R.H. SEAT**	1	
	909943	**CUSHION ASSEMBLY, TRIMMED—LEATHER (LIGHT TAN)—L.H. SEAT**	1	

Note:—Items marked thus † are available on our Factory Exchange Unit Scheme

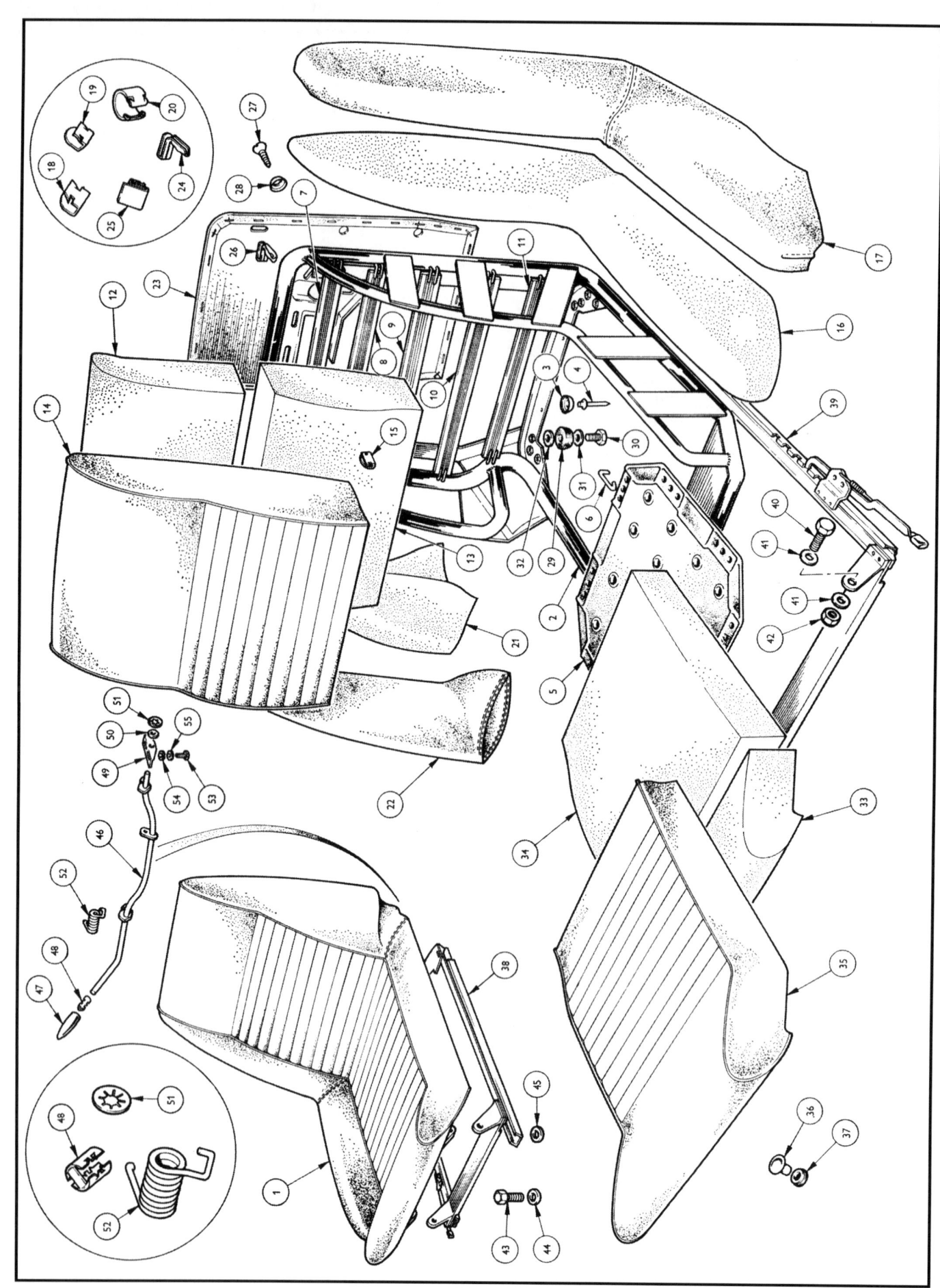

PLATE CP

BODY AND FITTINGS

Plate No.	Part No.	Description	No. per Unit	Remarks
		CUSHION ASSEMBLY, TRIMMED—continued		
	909957	**CUSHION ASSEMBLY, TRIMMED—LEATHER (SHADOW BLUE)—R.H. SEAT**	1	
	909947	**CUSHION ASSEMBLY, TRIMMED—LEATHER (SHADOW BLUE)—L.H. SEAT**	1	
	909951	**CUSHION ASSEMBLY, TRIMMED—LEATHER (BLACK)—R.H. SEAT**	1	
	909941	**CUSHION ASSEMBLY, TRIMMED—LEATHER (BLACK)—L.H. SEAT**	1	
	810241	**Pad,** cushion, front—R.H. seat	1	
CP33	810240	**Pad,** cushion, front—L.H. seat	1	
	813937	**Pad,** cushion, rear—R.H. seat	1	
CP34	813936	**Pad,** cushion, rear—L.H. seat	1	
	711142	**Cover** assembly, cushion—Leathercloth, Red—R.H. seat	1	
CP35	711132	**Cover** assembly, cushion—Leathercloth, Red—L.H. seat	1	
	711143	**Cover** assembly, cushion—Leathercloth, Light Tan—R.H. seat	1	Mark II cars only
CP35	711133	**Cover** assembly, cushion—Leathercloth, Light Tan—L.H. seat	1	Fitted from Commission No. KC50001 and future
	711147	**Cover** assembly, cushion—Leathercloth, Shadow Blue—R.H. seat	1	(All markets except U.S.A.) For U.S.A. see pages 180 to 187 inclusive
CP35	711137	**Cover** assembly, cushion—Leathercloth, Shadow Blue—L.H. seat	1	
	711141	**Cover** assembly, cushion—Leathercloth, Black—R.H. seat	1	
CP35	711131	**Cover** assembly, cushion—Leathercloth, Black—L.H. seat	1	
	711162	**Cover** assembly, cushion—Leather, Red—R.H. seat	1	
CP35	711152	**Cover** assembly, cushion—Leather, Red—L.H. seat	1	
	711163	**Cover** assembly, cushion—Leather, Light Tan—R.H. seat	1	
CP35	711153	**Cover** assembly, cushion—Leather, Light Tan—L.H. seat	1	
	711167	**Cover** assembly, cushion—Leather, Shadow Blue—R.H. seat	1	
CP35	711157	**Cover** assembly, cushion—Leather, Shadow Blue—L.H. seat	1	
	711161	**Cover** assembly, cushion—Leather, Black—R.H. seat	1	
CP35	711151	**Cover** assembly, cushion—Leather, Black—L.H. seat	1	
CP36	565747	**Button** ⎫ Cushion cover	6	
CP37	567642	**Socket** ⎭ to frame	6	

SEAT SLIDES—For details see page 187

Note:—Items marked thus † are available on our Factory Exchange Unit Scheme

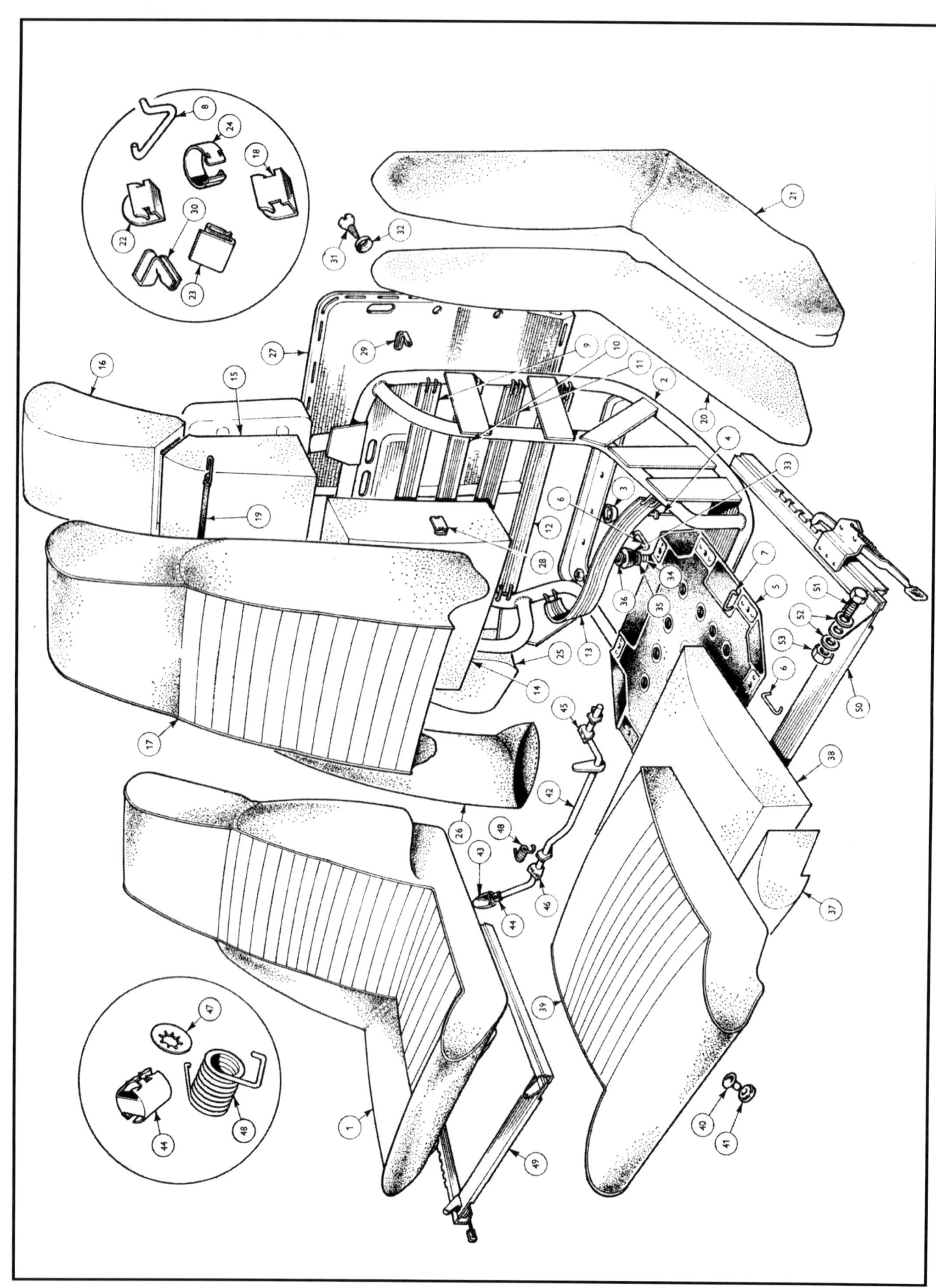

PLATE CQ

BODY AND FITTINGS

Plate No.	Part No.	Description	No. per Unit	Remarks
CQ1	910182	FRONT SEAT COMPLETE ASSEMBLY (WITH HEADREST)—TRIMMED —LEATHERCLOTH (Red)—R.H.	1	Mark II cars (G.T.6†) U.S.A. only Fitted from Commission No. KC50001 and future
	910172	FRONT SEAT COMPLETE ASSEMBLY (WITH HEADREST)—TRIMMED —LEATHERCLOTH (Red)—L.H.	1	
CQ1	910183	FRONT SEAT COMPLETE ASSEMBLY (WITH HEADREST)—TRIMMED —LEATHERCLOTH (Light Tan)—R.H.	1	
	910173	FRONT SEAT COMPLETE ASSEMBLY (WITH HEADREST)—TRIMMED —LEATHERCLOTH (Light Tan)—L.H.	1	
CQ1	910187	FRONT SEAT COMPLETE ASSEMBLY (WITH HEADREST)—TRIMMED —LEATHERCLOTH (Shadow Blue)—R.H.	1	
	910177	FRONT SEAT COMPLETE ASSEMBLY (WITH HEADREST)—TRIMMED —LEATHERCLOTH (Shadow Blue)—L.H.	1	
CQ1	910181	FRONT SEAT COMPLETE ASSEMBLY (WITH HEADREST)—TRIMMED —LEATHERCLOTH (Black)—R.H.	1	
	910171	FRONT SEAT COMPLETE ASSEMBLY (WITH HEADREST)—TRIMMED —LEATHERCLOTH (Black)—L.H.	1	
CQ1	910202	FRONT SEAT COMPLETE ASSEMBLY (WITH HEADREST)—TRIMMED —LEATHER (Red)—R.H.	1	
	910192	FRONT SEAT COMPLETE ASSEMBLY (WITH HEADREST)—TRIMMED —LEATHER (Red)—L.H.	1	
CQ1	910203	FRONT SEAT COMPLETE ASSEMBLY (WITH HEADREST)—TRIMMED —LEATHER (Light Tan)—R.H.	1	
	910193	FRONT SEAT COMPLETE ASSEMBLY (WITH HEADREST)—TRIMMED —LEATHER (Light Tan)—L.H.	1	
CQ1	910207	FRONT SEAT COMPLETE ASSEMBLY (WITH HEADREST)—TRIMMED —LEATHER (Shadow Blue)—R.H.	1	

Note:—Items marked thus † are available on our Factory Exchange Unit Scheme

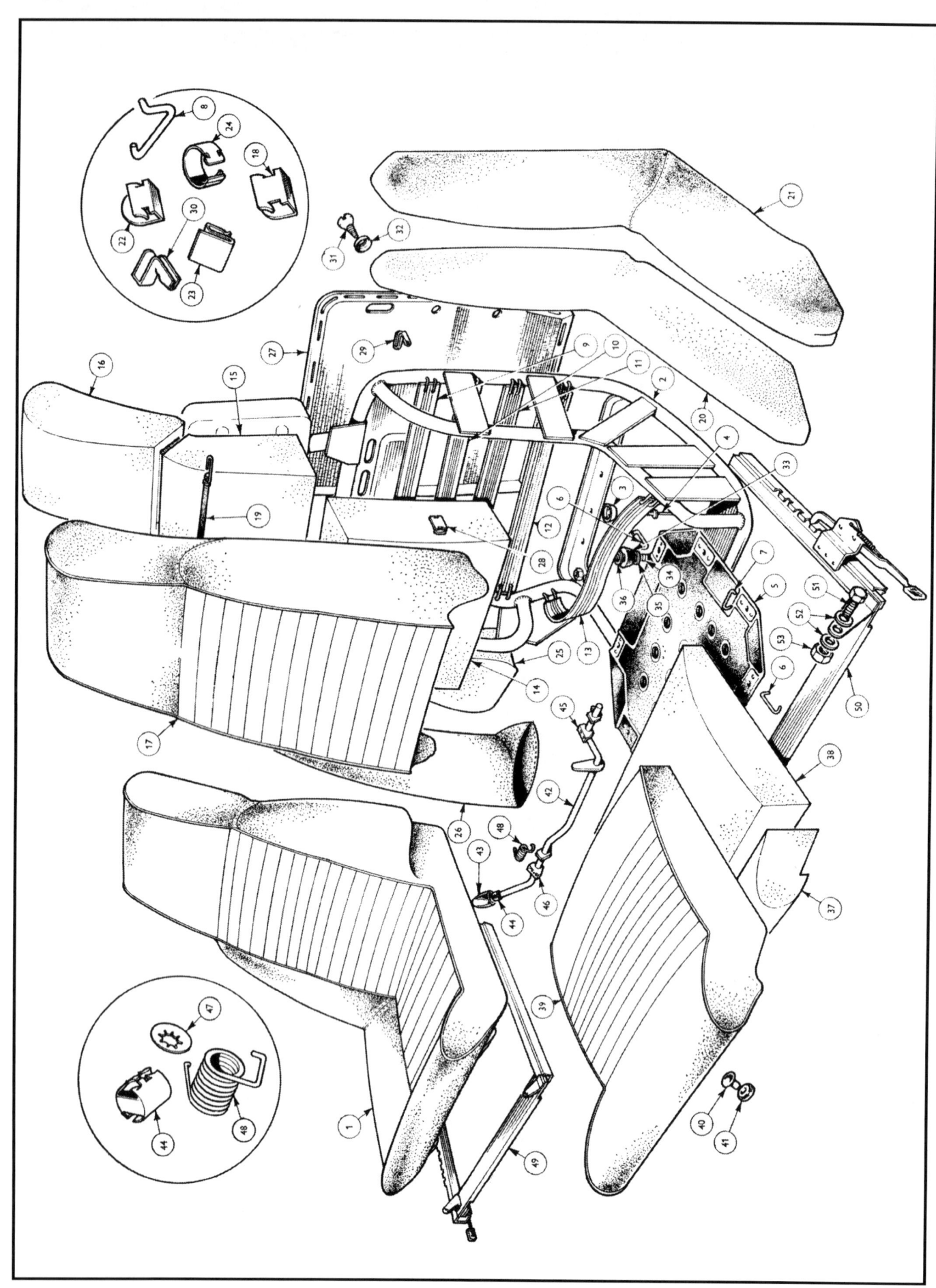

PLATE CQ

BODY AND FITTINGS

Plate No.	Part No.	Description	No. per Unit	Remarks
	910197	FRONT SEAT COMPLETE ASSEMBLY (WITH HEADREST)—TRIMMED—LEATHER (Shadow Blue)—L.H.	1	
CQ1	910201	FRONT SEAT COMPLETE ASSEMBLY (WITH HEADREST)—TRIMMED—LEATHER (Black)—R.H.	1	
	910191	FRONT SEAT COMPLETE ASSEMBLY (WITH HEADREST)—TRIMMED—LEATHER (Black)—L.H.	1	
	910222	FRONT SEAT FRAME, SQUAB AND HEADREST ASSEMBLY, TRIMMED—LEATHERCLOTH, RED—R.H.	1	
	910212	FRONT SEAT FRAME, SQUAB AND HEADREST ASSEMBLY, TRIMMED—LEATHERCLOTH, RED—L.H.	1	
	910223	FRONT SEAT FRAME, SQUAB AND HEADREST ASSEMBLY, TRIMMED—LEATHERCLOTH, LIGHT TAN—R.H.	1	
	910213	FRONT SEAT FRAME, SQUAB AND HEADREST ASSEMBLY, TRIMMED—LEATHERCLOTH, LIGHT TAN—L.H.	1	Mark II cars (G.T.6+) U.S.A. only Fitted from Commission No. KC50001 and future
	910227	FRONT SEAT FRAME, SQUAB AND HEADREST ASSEMBLY, TRIMMED—LEATHERCLOTH, SHADOW BLUE—R.H.	1	
	910217	FRONT SEAT FRAME, SQUAB AND HEADREST ASSEMBLY, TRIMMED—LEATHERCLOTH, SHADOW BLUE—L.H.	1	
	910221	FRONT SEAT FRAME, SQUAB AND HEADREST ASSEMBLY, TRIMMED—LEATHERCLOTH, BLACK—R.H.	1	
	910211	FRONT SEAT FRAME, SQUAB AND HEADREST ASSEMBLY, TRIMMED—LEATHERCLOTH, BLACK—L.H.	1	
	910242	FRONT SEAT FRAME, SQUAB AND HEADREST ASSEMBLY, TRIMMED—LEATHER, RED—R.H.	1	
	910232	FRONT SEAT FRAME, SQUAB AND HEADREST ASSEMBLY, TRIMMED—LEATHER, RED—L.H.	1	
	910243	FRONT SEAT FRAME, SQUAB AND HEADREST ASSEMBLY, TRIMMED—LEATHER, LIGHT TAN—R.H.	1	

Note:—Items marked thus † are available on our Factory Exchange Unit Scheme

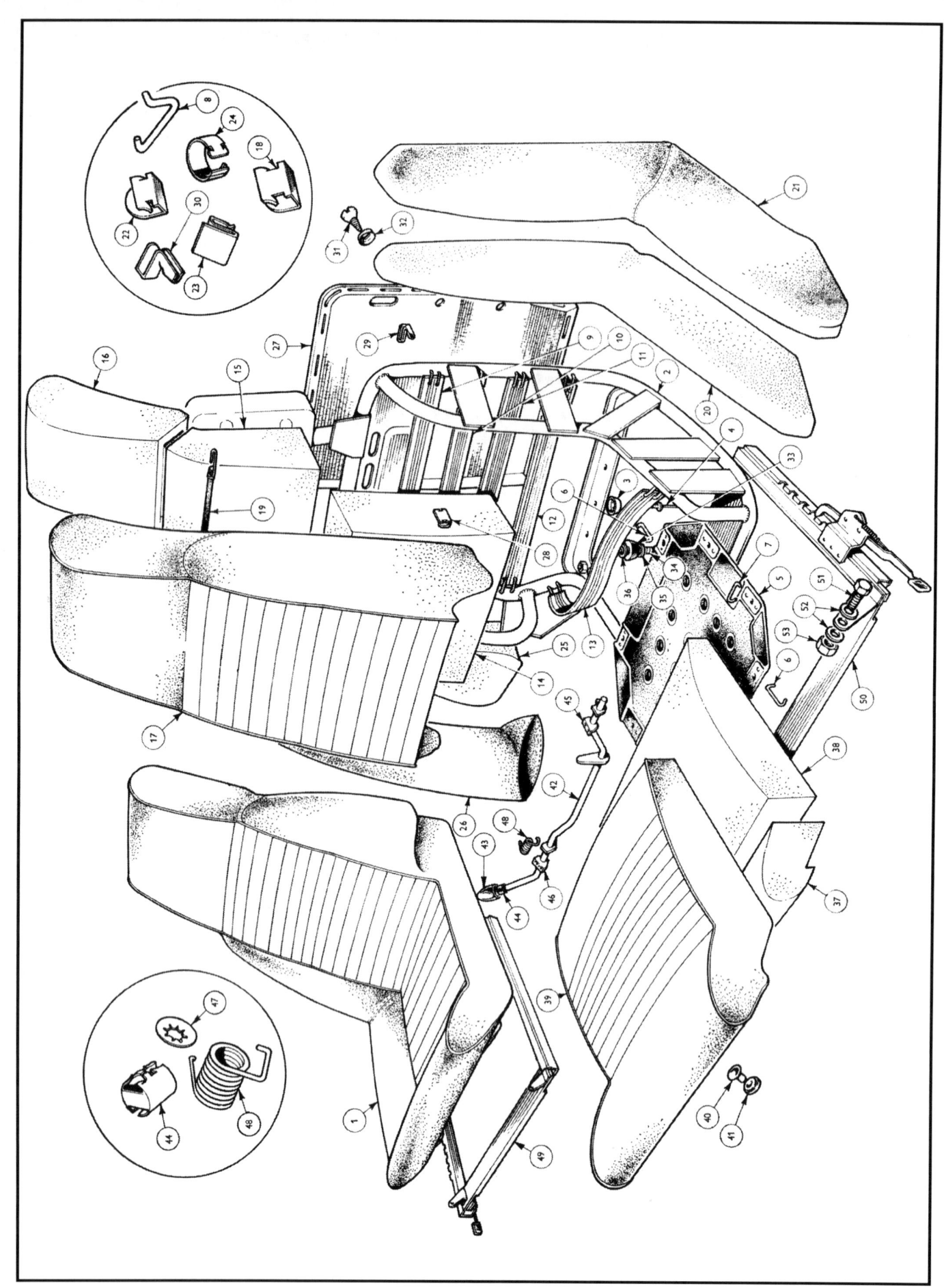

PLATE CQ

BODY AND FITTINGS

Plate No.	Part No.	Description	No. per Unit	Remarks
	910233	**FRONT SEAT FRAME, SQUAB AND HEADREST ASSEMBLY, TRIMMED—LEATHER, LIGHT TAN—L.H.**	1	
	910247	**FRONT SEAT FRAME SQUAB AND HEADREST ASSEMBLY, TRIMMED—LEATHER, SHADOW BLUE—R.H.**	1	
	910237	**FRONT SEAT FRAME SQUAB AND HEADREST ASSEMBLY, TRIMMED—LEATHER, SHADOW BLUE—L.H.**	1	
	910241	**FRONT SEAT FRAME, SQUAB AND HEADREST ASSEMBLY, TRIMMED—LEATHER, BLACK—R.H.**	1	
	910231	**FRONT SEAT FRAME, SQUAB AND HEADREST ASSEMBLY, TRIMMED—LEATHER, BLACK—L.H.**	1	
	908394	**Frame** assembly—R.H. seat	1	
CQ2	908393	**Frame** assembly—L.H. seat	1	
CQ3	610624	**Stud**, cushion attachment	6	
CQ4	561210	**Rivet**, stud to frame	6	Mark II cars (G.T.6+) U.S.A. only
CQ5	573900	**Diaphragm**, seat base	2	Fitted from Commission No. KC50001 and future
CQ6	613966	**Hook**, diaphragm	8	
CQ7	612261	**Hook**, diaphragm	4	
CQ8	623877	**Clip**, diaphragm	4	
	623420	**Piece**, filler, squab side	4	
CQ9	619498	**Strap** assembly, squab, 11" long—Top	2	
CQ10	619499	**Strap** assembly, squab, 12" long—Top intermediate	2	
CQ11	619500	**Strap** assembly, squab, 12·5" long—Centre	2	
CQ12	619501	**Strap** assembly, squab, 13·75" long—Bottom intermediate	2	
CQ13	619498	**Strap** assembly, squab, 11" long—Bottom	2	
	810632	**Pad**, squab, lower—R.H. seat	1	
CQ14	810631	**Pad**, squab, lower—L.H. seat	1	
CQ15	716633	**Pad**, squab, upper	2	
CQ16	815560	**Pad** assembly, headrest	2	
	716862	**Cover** assembly, squab and headrest, sewn—Leathercloth, Red—R.H. seat	1	
CQ17	716852	**Cover** assembly, squab and headrest, sewn—Leathercloth, Red—L.H. seat	1	
	716863	**Cover** assembly, squab and headrest, sewn—Leathercloth, Light Tan—R.H. seat	1	
CQ17	716853	**Cover** assembly, squab and headrest, sewn—Leathercloth, Light Tan—L.H. seat	1	
	716867	**Cover** assembly, squab and headrest, sewn—Leathercloth, Shadow Blue—R.H. seat	1	
CQ17	716857	**Cover** assembly, squab and headrest, sewn—Leathercloth, Shadow Blue—L.H. seat	1	
	716861	**Cover** assembly, squab and headrest, sewn—Leathercloth, Black—R.H. seat	1	

Note:—Items marked thus † are available on our Factory Exchange Unit Scheme

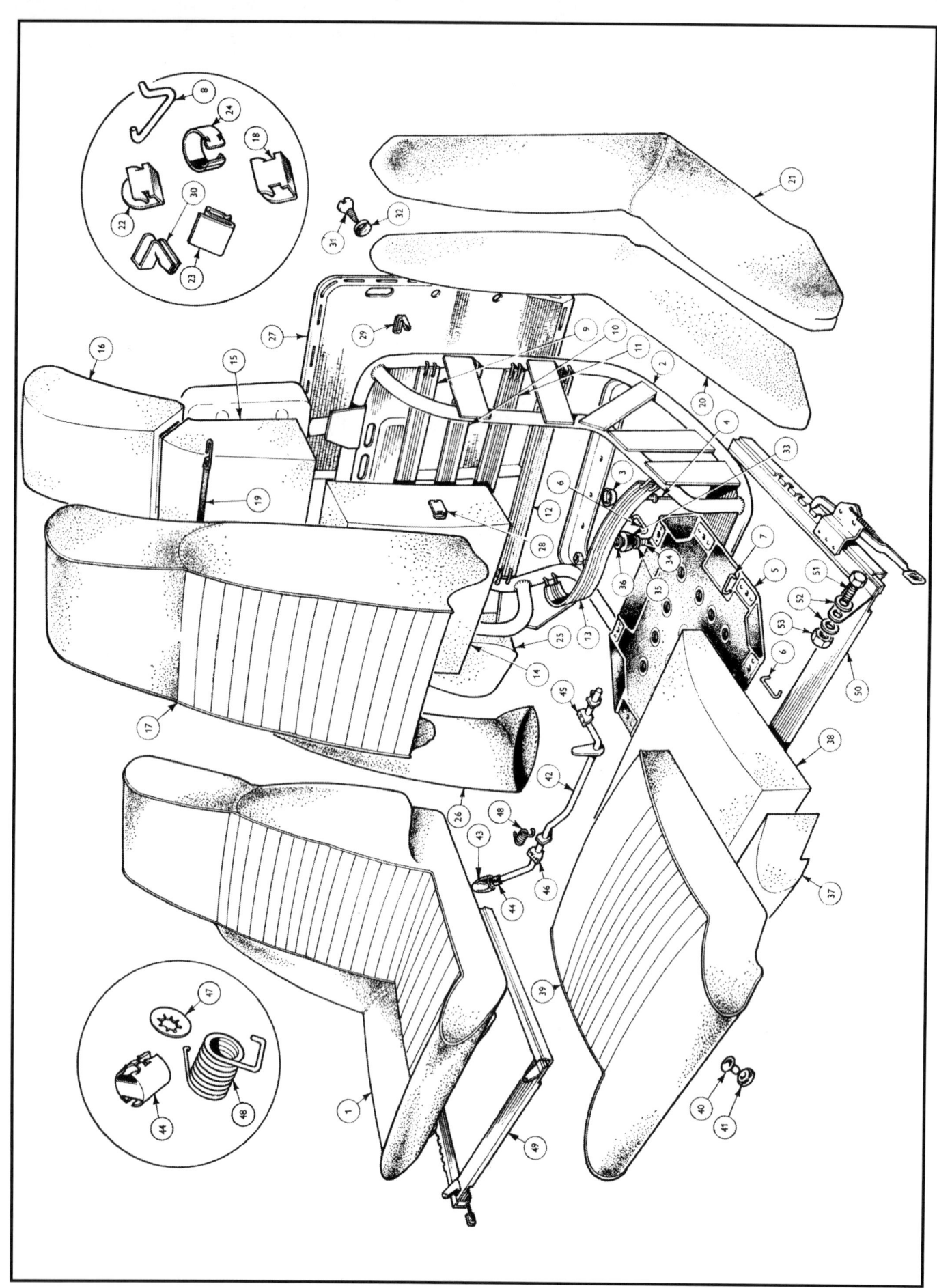

PLATE CQ

BODY AND FITTINGS

Plate No.	Part No.	Description	No. per Unit	Remarks
		FRONT SEAT FRAME, SQUAB AND HEADREST ASSEMBLY, TRIMMED—continued		
CQ17	716851	**Cover** assembly, squab and headrest, sewn—Leathercloth, Black—L.H. seat	1	
	716882	**Cover** assembly, squab and headrest, sewn—Leather, Red—R.H. seat	1	
CQ17	716872	**Cover** assembly, squab and headrest, sewn—Leather, Red—L.H. seat	1	
	716883	**Cover** assembly, squab and headrest, sewn—Leather, Light Tan—R.H. seat	1	
CQ17	716873	**Cover** assembly, squab and headrest, sewn—Leather, Light Tan—L.H. seat	1	
	716887	**Cover** assembly, squab and headrest, sewn—Leather, Shadow Blue—R.H. seat	1	
CQ17	716877	**Cover** assembly, squab and headrest, sewn—Leather, Shadow Blue—L.H. seat	1	
	716881	**Cover** assembly, squab and headrest, sewn—Leather, Black—R.H. seat	1	
CQ17	716871	**Cover** assembly, squab and headrest, sewn—Leather, Black—L.H. seat	1	
CQ18	603811	**Clip**, trim, headrest cover to back trim plate (Seat frame)	4	
CQ18	603811	**Clip**, trim, headrest cover piping to side trim plate (Seat frame)	4	Mark II cars (G.T.6+) U.S.A. only Fitted from Commission No. KC50001 and future
CQ19	625511	**Tensioner**, fly, headrest cover to frame	2	
	907242	**Padding**, seat side, outer, R.H.—R.H. seat	1	
CQ20	907241	**Padding**, seat side, outer, L.H.—L.H. seat	1	
	623392	**Cover** assembly, sewn, side panel, outer—Leathercloth, Red, R.H.—R.H. seat	1	
CQ21	623382	**Cover** assembly, sewn, side panel, outer—Leathercloth, Red, L.H.—L.H. seat	1	
	623393	**Cover** assembly, sewn, side panel, outer—Leathercloth, Light Tan, R.H.—R.H. seat	1	
CQ21	623383	**Cover** assembly, sewn, side panel, outer—Leathercloth, Light Tan, L.H.—L.H. seat	1	
	623397	**Cover** assembly, sewn, side panel, outer—Leathercloth, Shadow Blue, R.H.—R.H. seat	1	
CQ21	623387	**Cover** assembly, sewn, side panel, outer—Leathercloth, Shadow Blue, L.H.—L.H. seat	1	
	623391	**Cover** assembly, sewn, side panel, outer—Leathercloth, Black, R.H.—R.H. seat	1	
CQ21	623381	**Cover** assembly, sewn, side panel, outer—Leathercloth, Black, L.H.—L.H. seat	1	
	623412	**Cover** assembly, sewn, side panel, outer—Leather, Red, R.H.—R.H. seat	1	
CQ21	623402	**Cover** assembly, sewn, side panel, outer—Leather, Red, L.H.—L.H. seat	1	
	623413	**Cover** assembly, sewn, side panel, outer—Leather, Light Tan, R.H.—R.H. seat	1	
CQ21	623403	**Cover** assembly, sewn, side panel, outer—Leather, Light Tan, L.H.—L.H. seat	1	

Note:—Items marked thus † are available on our Factory Exchange Unit Scheme

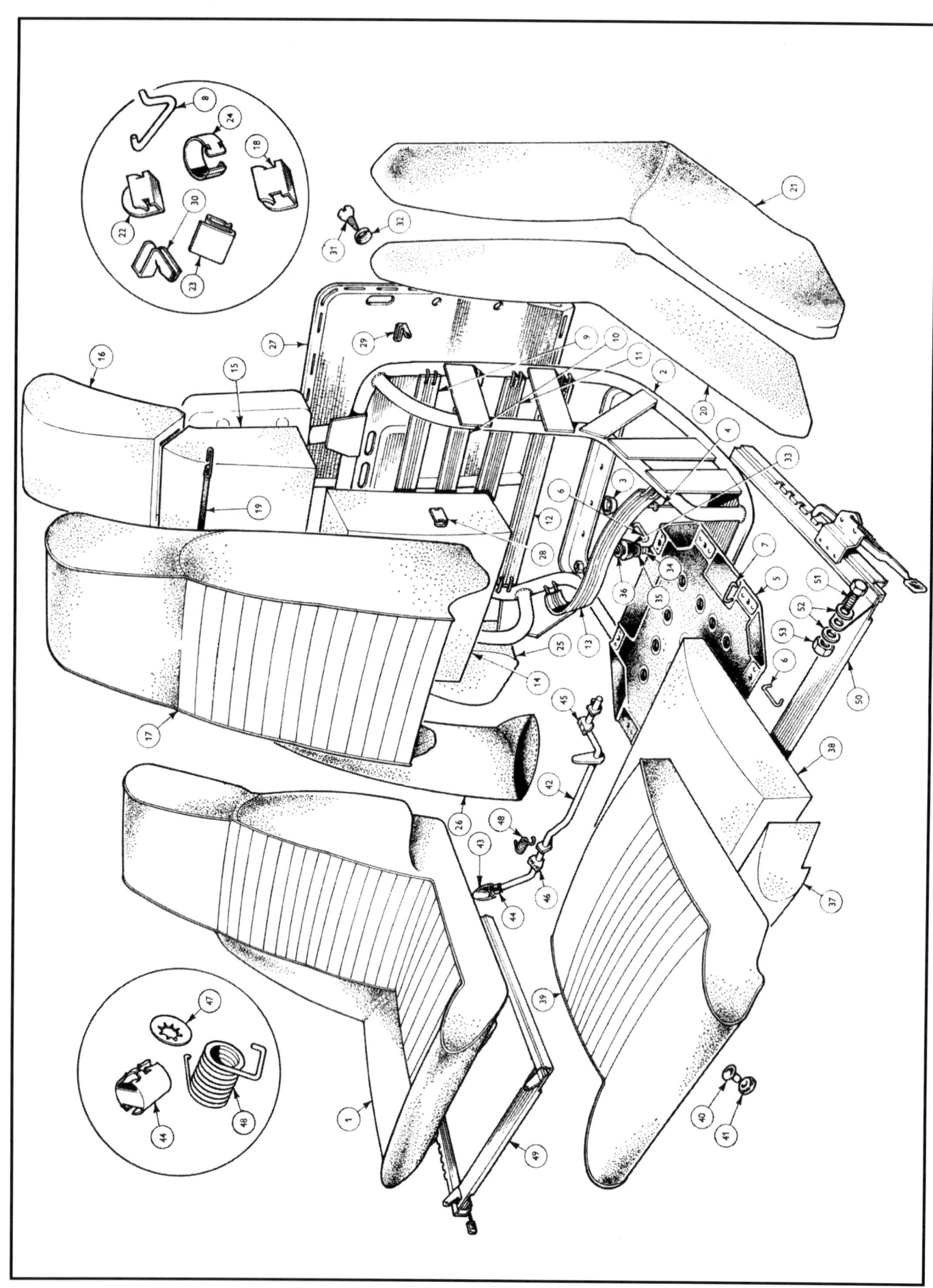

PLATE CQ

BODY AND FITTINGS

Plate No.	Part No.	Description	No. per Unit	Remarks
		FRONT SEAT FRAME, SQUAB AND HEADREST ASSEMBLY, TRIMMED—continued		
	623417	**Cover** assembly, sewn, side panel, outer—Leather, Shadow Blue, R.H.—R.H. seat	1	
CQ21	623407	**Cover** assembly, sewn, side panel, outer—Leather, Shadow Blue, L.H.—L.H. seat	1	
	623411	**Cover** assembly, sewn, side panel, outer—Leather, Black, R.H.—R.H. seat	1	
CQ21	623401	**Cover** assembly, sewn, side panel, outer—Leather, Black, L.H.—L.H. seat	1	
CQ22	608817	**Clip**, trim, side panel, outer cover to trim plate, bottom rail, seat frame	10	
CQ22	608817	**Clip**, trim, side panel, outer cover to trim plate, lower outer side, seat frame back	4	
CQ22	608817	**Clip**, trim, side panel, outer cover to seat frame, upper	2	
CQ23	610520	**Clip**, trim, side panel, outer cover to seat frame, lower	4	
CQ24	608862	**Clip**, tube, side panel, outer cover to seat frame, upper	2	
	907244	**Padding**, seat side, inner, L.H.—R.H. seat	1	
CQ25	907243	**Padding**, seat side, inner, R.H.—L.H. seat	1	
	623352	**Cover** assembly, sewn, side panel, inner—Leathercloth, Red, L.H.—R.H. seat	1	
CQ26	623342	**Cover** assembly, sewn, side panel, inner—Leathercloth, Red, R.H.—L.H. seat	1	
	623353	**Cover** assembly, sewn, side panel, inner—Leathercloth, Light Tan, L.H.—R.H. seat	1	Mark II cars (G.T.6+) U.S.A. only Fitted from Commission No. KC50001 and future
CQ26	623343	**Cover** assembly, sewn, side panel, inner—Leathercloth, Light Tan, R.H.—L.H. seat	1	
	623357	**Cover** assembly, sewn, side panel, inner—Leathercloth, Shadow Blue, L.H.—R.H. seat	1	
CQ26	623347	**Cover** assembly, sewn, side panel, inner—Leathercloth, Shadow Blue, R.H.—L.H. seat	1	
	623351	**Cover** assembly, sewn, side panel, inner—Leathercloth, Black, L.H.—R.H. seat	1	
CQ26	623341	**Cover** assembly, sewn, side panel, inner—Leathercloth, Black, R.H.—L.H. seat	1	
	623372	**Cover** assembly, sewn, side panel, inner—Leather, Red, L.H.—R.H. seat	1	
CQ26	623362	**Cover** assembly, sewn, side panel, inner—Leather, Red, R.H.—L.H. seat	1	
	623373	**Cover** assembly, sewn, side panel, inner—Leather, Light Tan, L.H.—R.H. seat	1	
CQ26	623363	**Cover** assembly, sewn, side panel, inner—Leather, Light Tan, R.H.—L.H. seat	1	
	623377	**Cover** assembly, sewn, side panel, inner—Leather, Shadow Blue, L.H.—R.H. seat	1	
CQ26	623367	**Cover** assembly, sewn, side panel, inner—Leather, Shadow Blue, R.H.—L.H. seat	1	
	623371	**Cover** assembly, sewn, side panel, inner—Leather, Black, L.H.—R.H. seat	1	
CQ26	623361	**Cover** assembly, sewn, side panel, inner—Leather, Black, R.H.—L.H. seat	1	

Note:—Items marked thus † are available on our Factory Exchange Unit Scheme

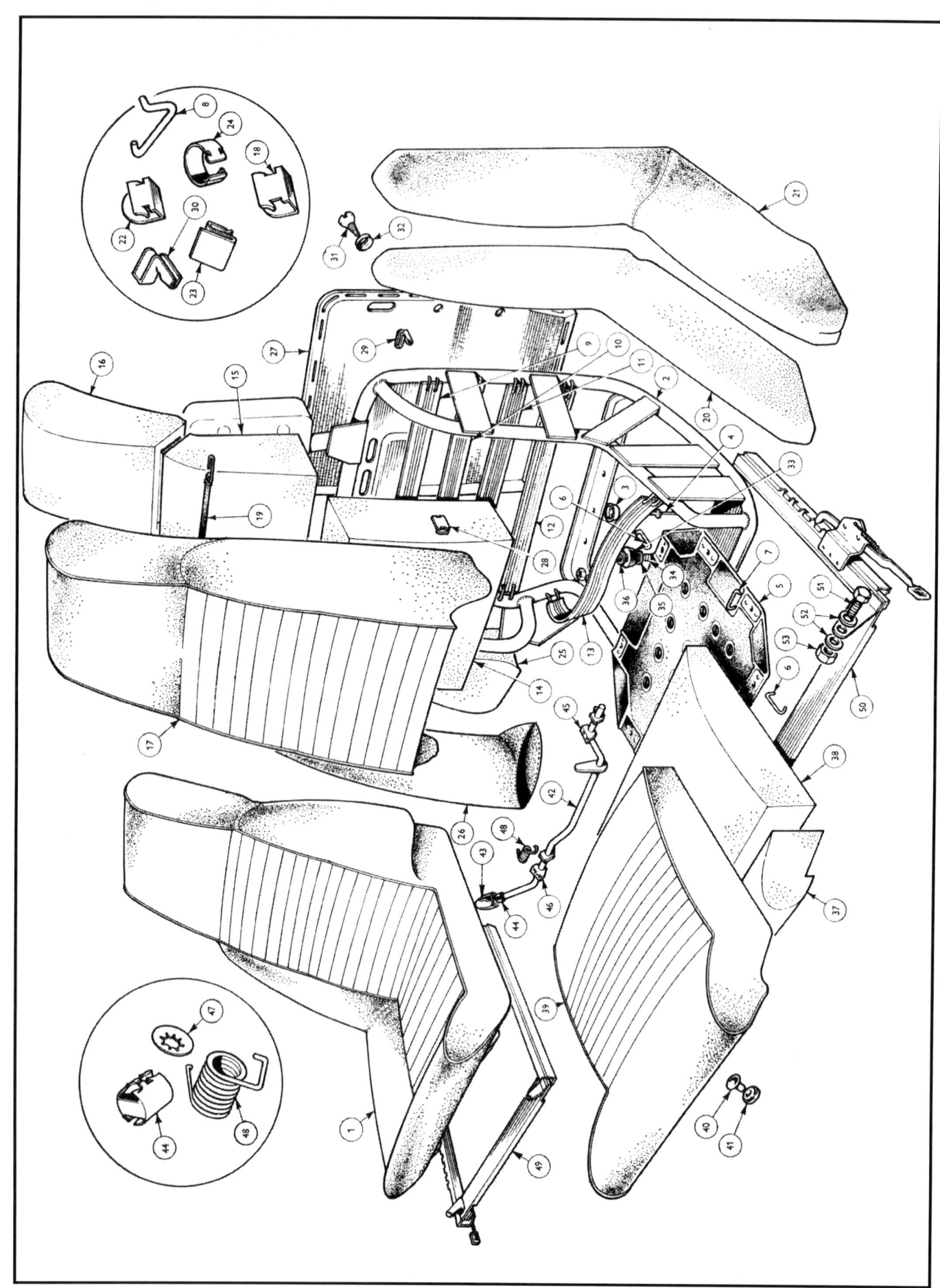

PLATE CQ

BODY AND FITTINGS

Plate No.	Part No.	Description	No. per Unit	Remarks
		FRONT SEAT FRAME, SQUAB AND HEADREST ASSEMBLY, TRIMMED—continued		
CQ22	608817	**Clip,** trim, side panel, inner cover to seat frame (Upper and lower, side, inner trim plates)	8	
CQ23	610520	**Clip,** trim, side panel, inner cover to seat frame, lower	4	
CQ24	608862	**Clip,** tube, side panel, inner cover to seat frame (Upper and lower)	4	
	811752	**Seat back** assembly, trimmed, Red—R.H. seat	1	
CQ27	811742	**Seat back** assembly, trimmed, Red—L.H. seat	1	
	811753	**Seat back** assembly, trimmed, Light Tan—R.H. seat	1	
CQ27	811743	**Seat back** assembly, trimmed, Light Tan—L.H. seat	1	
	811757	**Seat back** assembly, trimmed, Shadow Blue—R.H. seat	1	
CQ27	811747	**Seat back** assembly, trimmed, Shadow Blue—L.H. seat	1	
	811751	**Seat back** assembly, trimmed, Black—R.H. seat	1	
CQ27	811741	**Seat back** assembly, trimmed, Black—L.H. seat	1	
CQ28	608516	**Clip,** trim, seat back to seat frame	4	
CQ29	613770	**Clip,** trim, seat back to seat frame (Back, upper trim plate)	4	
CQ30	613769	**Clip,** trim, seat back to seat frame	8	
CQ31	512554	**Screw,** self-tapping, chrome ⎫ Seat back, lower	4	
CQ32	619618	**Washer,** cup ⎭ attachment	4	
CQ33	621515	**Buffer,** rubber	4	Mark II cars (G.T.6+) U.S.A. only
CQ34	509140	**Setscrew** ⎫ Rubber buffer	4	Fitted from Commission No.
CQ35	516834	**Washer,** plain ⎬ to	4	KC50001 and future
CQ36	503923	**Washer,** plain ⎭ seat frame, lower	4	
	910262	**CUSHION ASSEMBLY, TRIMMED—LEATHER-CLOTH (RED)—R.H. SEAT**	1	
	910252	**CUSHION ASSEMBLY, TRIMMED—LEATHER-CLOTH (RED)—L.H. SEAT**	1	
	910263	**CUSHION ASSEMBLY, TRIMMED—LEATHER-CLOTH (LIGHT TAN)—R.H. SEAT**	1	
	910253	**CUSHION ASSEMBLY, TRIMMED—LEATHER-CLOTH (LIGHT TAN)—L.H. SEAT**	1	
	910267	**CUSHION ASSEMBLY, TRIMMED—LEATHER-CLOTH (SHADOW BLUE)—R.H. SEAT**	1	
	910257	**CUSHION ASSEMBLY, TRIMMED—LEATHER-CLOTH (SHADOW BLUE)—L.H. SEAT**	1	
	910261	**CUSHION ASSEMBLY, TRIMMED—LEATHER-CLOTH (BLACK)—R.H. SEAT**	1	
	910251	**CUSHION ASSEMBLY, TRIMMED—LEATHER-CLOTH (BLACK)—L.H. SEAT**	1	
	910282	**CUSHION ASSEMBLY, TRIMMED—LEATHER (RED)—R.H. SEAT**	1	

Note:—Items marked thus † are available on our Factory Exchange Unit Scheme

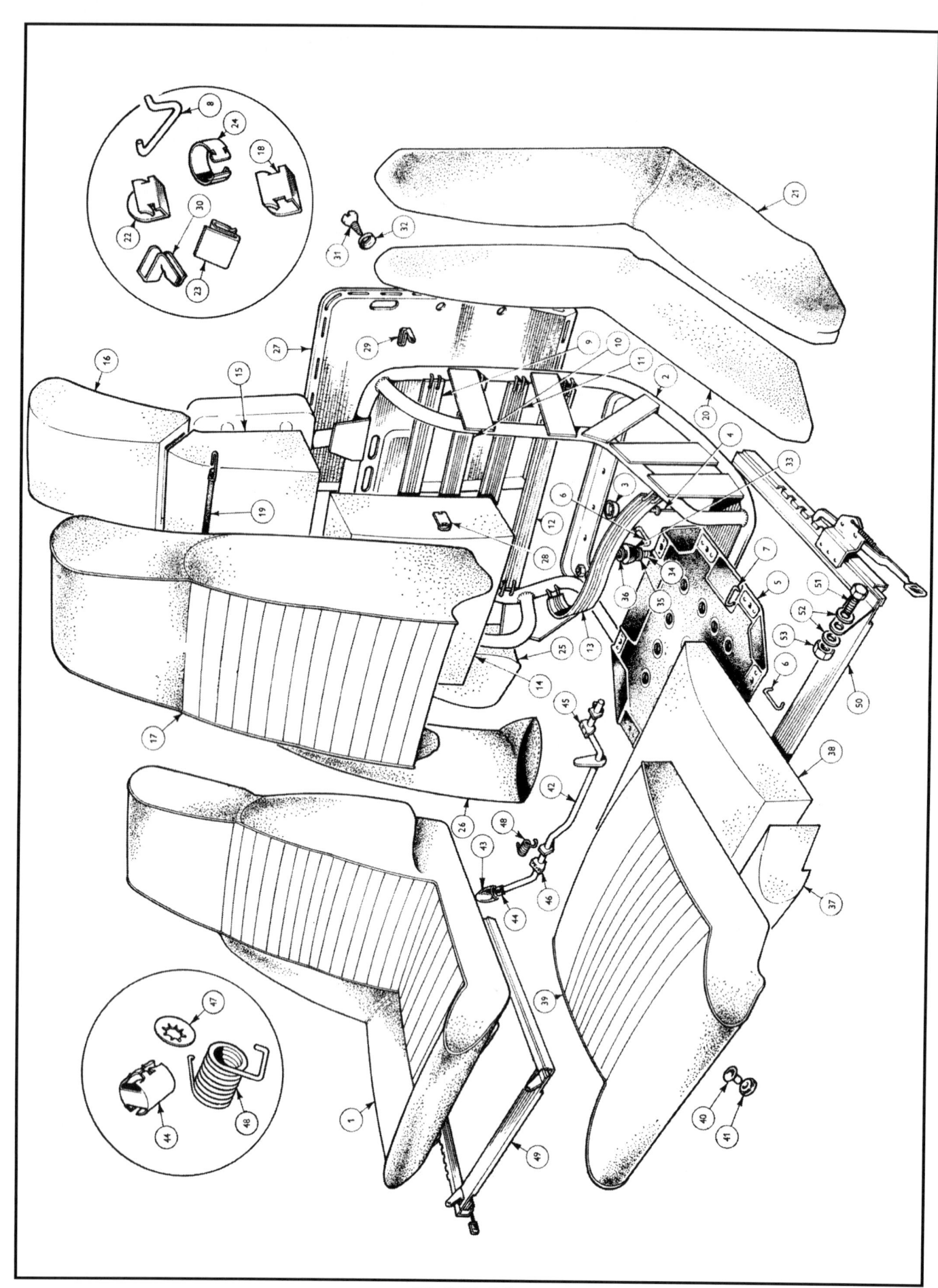

PLATE CQ

BODY AND FITTINGS

Plate No.	Part No.	Description	No. per Unit	Remarks
	910272	CUSHION ASSEMBLY, TRIMMED—LEATHER (RED)—L.H. SEAT	1	
	910283	CUSHION ASSEMBLY, TRIMMED—LEATHER (LIGHT TAN)—R.H. SEAT	1	
	910273	CUSHION ASSEMBLY, TRIMMED—LEATHER (LIGHT TAN)—L.H. SEAT	1	
	910287	CUSHION ASSEMBLY, TRIMMED—LEATHER (SHADOW BLUE)—R.H. SEAT	1	
	910277	CUSHION ASSEMBLY, TRIMMED—LEATHER (SHADOW BLUE)—L.H. SEAT	1	
	910281	CUSHION ASSEMBLY, TRIMMED—LEATHER (BLACK)—R.H. SEAT	1	
	910271	CUSHION ASSEMBLY, TRIMMED—LEATHER (BLACK)—L.H. SEAT	1	
	810241	Pad, cushion, front—R.H. seat	1	
CQ37	810240	Pad, cushion, front—L.H. seat	1	
	813937	Pad, cushion, rear—R.H. seat	1	
CQ38	813936	Pad, cushion, rear—L.H. seat	1	
	716902	Cover assembly, cushion—Leathercloth, Red—R.H. seat	1	Mark II cars (G.T.6+) U.S.A. only Fitted from Commission No. KC50001 and future
CQ39	716892	Cover assembly, cushion—Leathercloth, Red—L.H. seat	1	
	716903	Cover assembly, cushion—Leathercloth, Light Tan—R.H. seat	1	
CQ39	716893	Cover assembly, cushion—Leathercloth, Light Tan—L.H. seat	1	
	716907	Cover assembly, cushion—Leathercloth, Shadow Blue—R.H. seat	1	
CQ39	716897	Cover assembly, cushion—Leathercloth, Shadow Blue—L.H. seat	1	
	716901	Cover assembly, cushion—Leathercloth, Black—R.H. seat	1	
CQ39	716891	Cover assembly, cushion—Leathercloth, Black—L.H. seat	1	
	716922	Cover assembly, cushion—Leather, Red—R.H. seat	1	
CQ39	716912	Cover assembly, cushion—Leather, Red—L.H. seat	1	
	716923	Cover assembly, cushion—Leather, Light Tan—R.H. seat	1	
CQ39	716913	Cover assembly, cushion—Leather, Light Tan—L.H. seat	1	
	716927	Cover assembly, cushion—Leather, Shadow Blue—R.H. seat	1	
CQ39	716917	Cover assembly, cushion—Leather, Shadow Blue—L.H. seat	1	
	716921	Cover assembly, cushion—Leather, Black—R.H. seat	1	
CQ39	716911	Cover assembly, cushion—Leather, Black—L.H. seat	1	

Note:—Items marked thus † are available on our Factory Exchange Unit Scheme

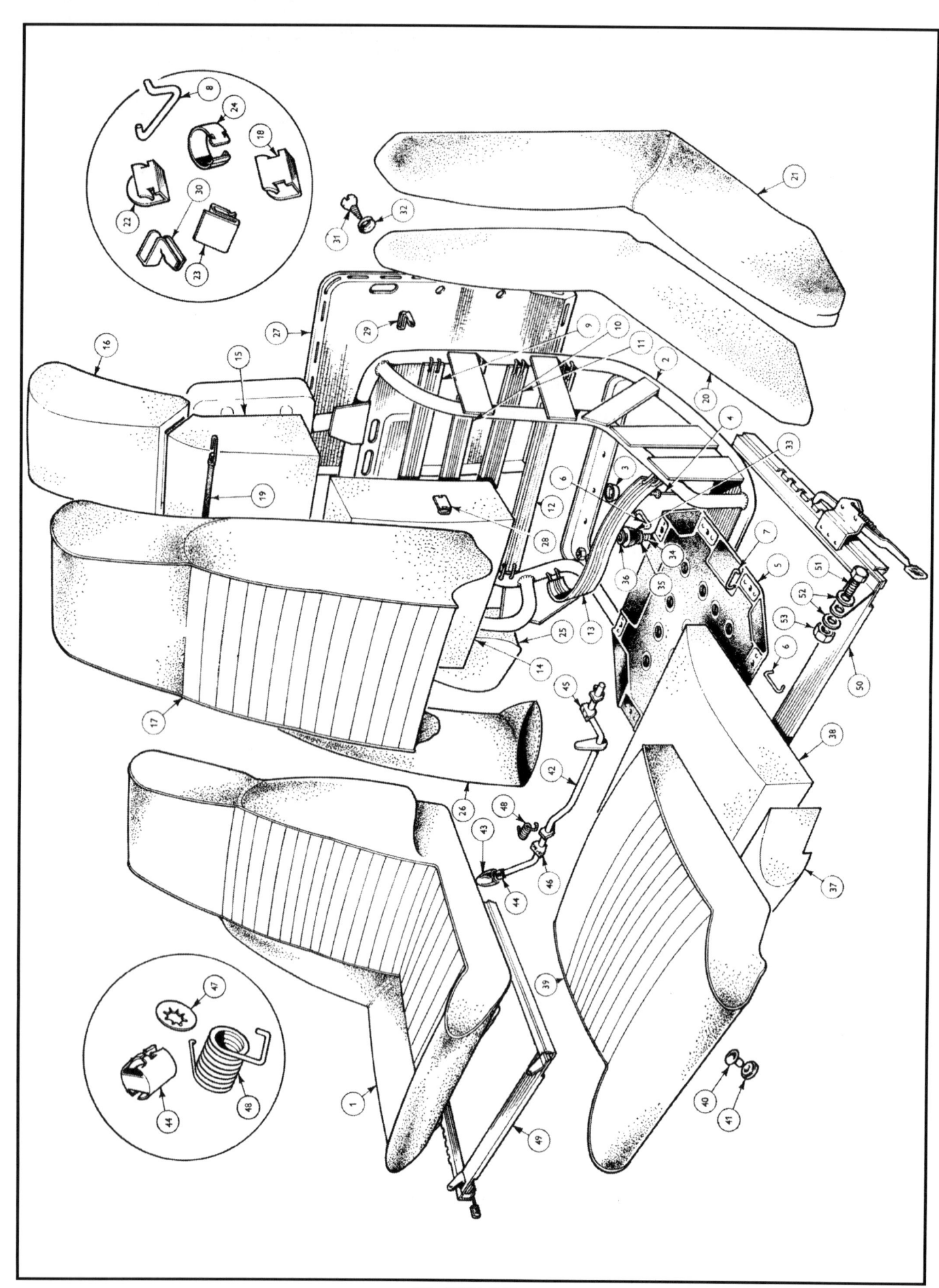

PLATE CQ

BODY AND FITTINGS

Plate No.	Part No.	Description	No. per Unit	Remarks
		CUSHION ASSEMBLY, TRIMMED—continued		
CQ40	565747	**Button** ⎱ Cushion cover	6	
CQ41	567642	**Socket** ⎰ to frame	6	
	714784	**SEAT SAFETY CATCH AND CONTROL LEVER ASSEMBLY—R.H.**	1	
CQ42	714783	**SEAT SAFETY CATCH AND CONTROL LEVER ASSEMBLY—L.H.**	1	Mark II cars (G.T.6+) U.S.A. only Fitted from Commission No. KC50001 and future
CQ43	621458	**Knob**, control lever	2	
CQ44	621776	**Clip**, knob fixing	2	
CQ45	621266	**Bracket**, attachment, safety catch and lever	2	
CQ46	623803	**Bracket**, attachment, outer	2	
	503661	**Washer**, plain, spacing	4	
CQ47	574841	**Fix**, multi-prong, securing bracket	2	
	623486	**Spring**, tension, between link and frame—R.H.	1	
CQ48	623485	**Spring**, tension, between link and frame—L.H.	1	
	506731	**Setscrew** ⎱ Safety catch	8	
	508875	**Washer**, plain ⎰ and control lever	8	
	505307	**Washer**, lock ⎰ to seat	8	
CQ49	813679	**SEAT SLIDE ASSEMBLY—R.H. SEAT**	1	
CQ50	813678	**SEAT SLIDE ASSEMBLY—L.H. SEAT**	1	Mark II cars (G.T.6+) Fitted to all markets from Commission No. KC50001 and future
CQ51	HU0807	**Screw**, set ⎱	4	
CQ52	WP0150	**Washer**, plain ⎰ Seat slide to seat	8	
CQ53	YN2908	**Nut**, nyloc	4	
	HU0706	**Screw**, set ⎱ Seat slide	8	
	WP0023	**Washer**, plain ⎰ to floor	8	
	WP0048	**Washer**, plain, between seat slide and carpet	8	

Note:—Items marked thus † are available on our Factory Exchange Unit Scheme

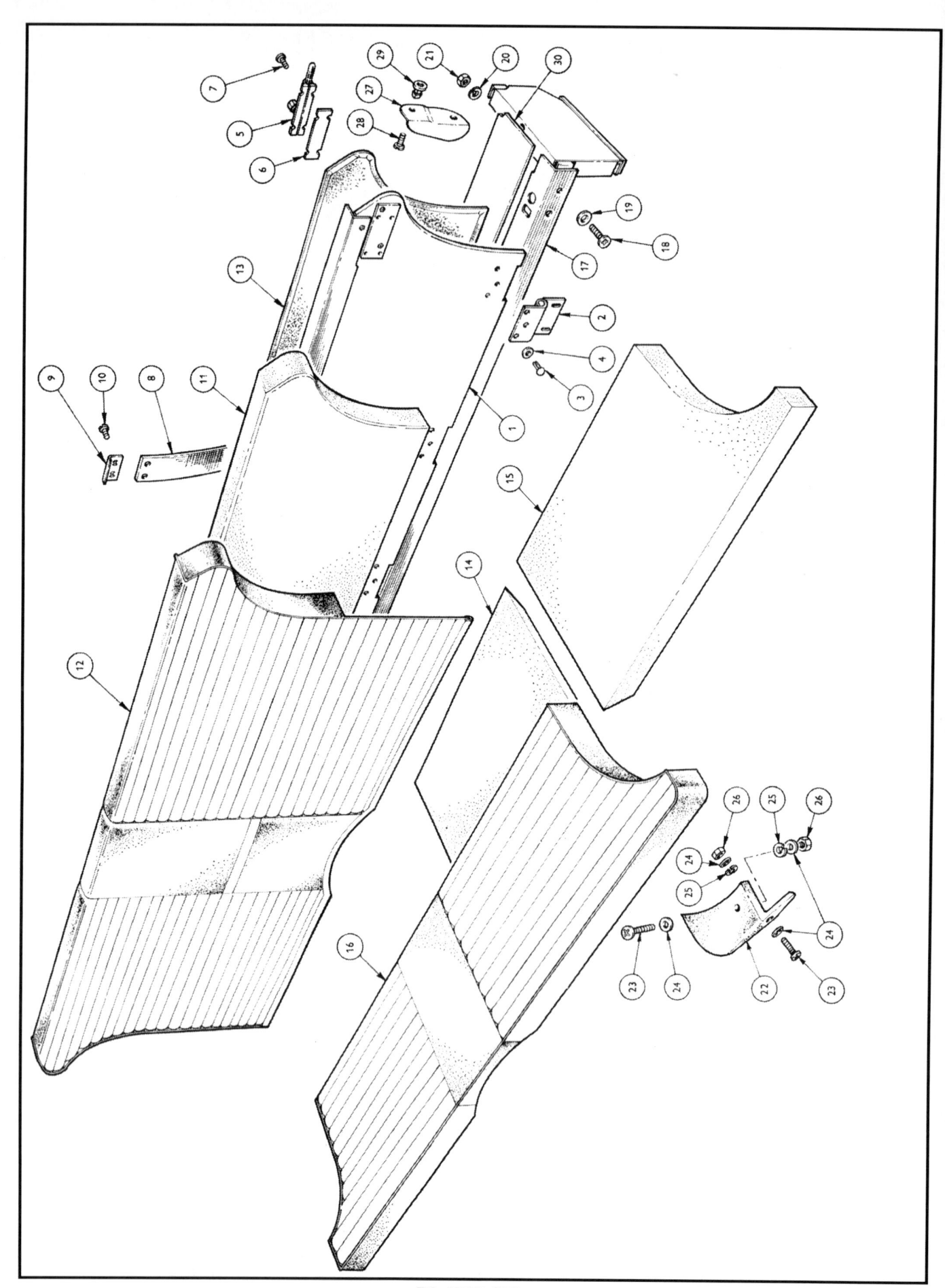

PLATE CR

BODY AND FITTINGS

Plate No.	Part No.	Description	No. per Unit	Remarks
		OCCASIONAL SEAT DETAILS (FITTED TO SPECIAL ORDER FROM COMMISSION No. KC50001—ALL MARKETS EXCEPT U.S.A.)		
	575294	**OCCASIONAL SEAT KIT**—LEATHERCLOTH (Red)	1	
	575295	**OCCASIONAL SEAT KIT**—LEATHERCLOTH (Light Tan)	1	
	575293	**OCCASIONAL SEAT KIT**—LEATHERCLOTH (Shadow Blue)	1	
	575292	**OCCASIONAL SEAT KIT**—LEATHERCLOTH (Black)	1	
	575298	**OCCASIONAL SEAT KIT**—LEATHER (Red)	1	
	575299	**OCCASIONAL SEAT KIT**—LEATHER (Light Tan)	1	
	575297	**OCCASIONAL SEAT KIT**—LEATHER (Shadow Blue)	1	
	575296	**OCCASIONAL SEAT KIT**—LEATHER (Black)	1	
	908722	**Squab** assembly, complete, occasional seat—Leathercloth, Red	1	
	908723	**Squab** assembly, complete, occasional seat—Leathercloth, Light Tan	1	
	908727	**Squab** assembly, complete, occasional seat—Leathercloth, Shadow Blue	1	
	908721	**Squab** assembly, complete, occasional seat—Leathercloth, Black	1	
	908732	**Squab** assembly, complete, occasional seat—Leather, Red	1	
	908733	**Squab** assembly, complete, occasional seat—Leather, Light Tan	1	
	908737	**Squab** assembly, complete, occasional seat—Leather, Shadow Blue	1	
	908731	**Squab** assembly, complete, occasional seat—Leather, Black	1	
CR1	714780	**Board**, hinged assembly, squab	1	
CR2	623067	**Hinge**, squab board—Luggage floor	4	
CR3	RB5508	**Rivet**, bifurcated ⎱ Hinge	12	
CR4	500381	**Washer**, plain ⎰ attachment	12	
CR5	613663	**Bolt**, shoot	2	
CR6	623070	**Plate**, packing ⎱ Shoot bolt	2	
CR7	517478	**Setscrew**, chrome ⎰ attachment	8	
CR8	623881	**Strap**, squab retaining	1	
	565747	**Button** ⎱ Squab retaining	1	
	565748	**Socket** ⎰ strap	1	
CR9	619216	**Retainer**, strap ⎱ Squab strap	1	
CR10	515170	**Setscrew** ⎰ attachment	2	
CR11	814089	**Pad**, foam, squab	1	
CR12	715172	**Cover** assembly, sewn, squab—Leathercloth, Red	1	

Note:—Items marked thus † are available on our Factory Exchange Unit Scheme

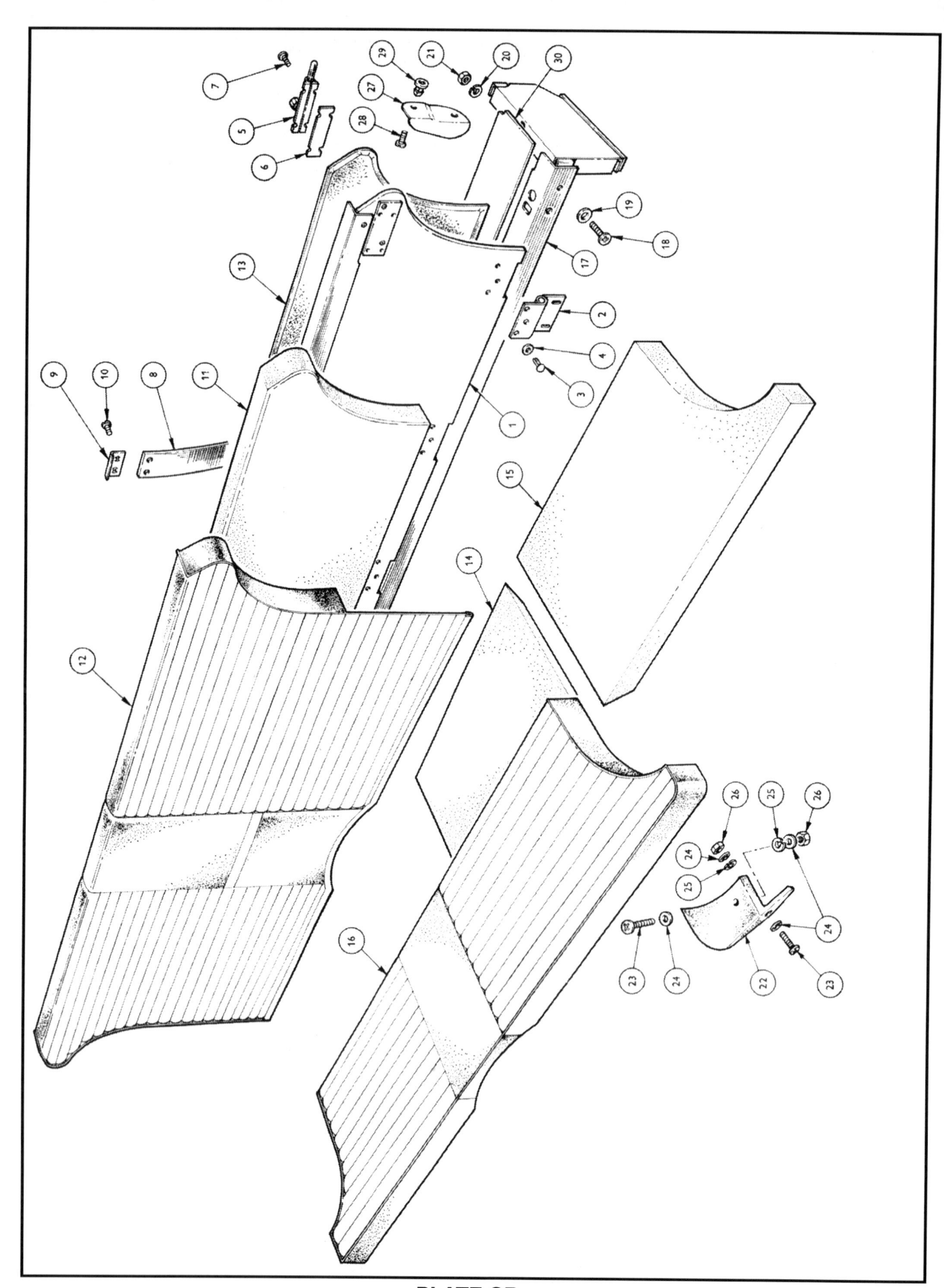

PLATE CR

BODY AND FITTINGS

Plate No.	Part No.	Description	No. per Unit	Remarks
		OCCASIONAL SEAT DETAILS—continued		
CR12	715173	**Cover** assembly, sewn, squab—Leathercloth, Light Tan	1	
CR12	715177	**Cover** assembly, sewn, squab—Leathercloth, Shadow Blue	1	
CR12	715171	**Cover** assembly, sewn, squab—Leathercloth, Black	1	
CR12	715182	**Cover** assembly, sewn, squab—Leather, Red	1	
CR12	715183	**Cover** assembly, sewn, squab—Leather, Light Tan	1	
CR12	715187	**Cover** assembly, sewn, squab—Leather, Shadow Blue	1	
CR12	715181	**Cover** assembly, sewn, squab—Leather, Black	1	
CR13	623911	**Carpet** assembly, squab board	1	
	815602	**Cushion** assembly, complete, occasional seat—Leathercloth, Red	1	
	815603	**Cushion** assembly, complete, occasional seat—Leathercloth, Light Tan	1	
	815607	**Cushion** assembly, complete, occasional seat—Leathercloth, Shadow Blue	1	
	815601	**Cushion** assembly, complete, occasional seat—Leathercloth, Black	1	
	815612	**Cushion** assembly, complete, occasional seat—Leather, Red	1	
	815613	**Cushion** assembly, complete, occasional seat—Leather, Light Tan	1	
	815617	**Cushion** assembly, complete, occasional seat—Leather, Shadow Blue	1	
	815611	**Cushion** assembly, complete, occasional seat—Leather, Black	1	
CR14	715152	**Pad,** foam, cushion, R.H.	1	
CR15	715151	**Pad,** foam, cushion, L.H.	1	
CR16	715212	**Cover,** sewn, assembly, occasional seat cushion—Leathercloth, Red	1	
CR16	715213	**Cover,** sewn, assembly, occasional seat cushion—Leathercloth, Light Tan	1	
CR16	715217	**Cover,** sewn, assembly, occasional seat cushion—Leathercloth, Shadow Blue	1	
CR16	715211	**Cover,** sewn, assembly, occasional seat cushion—Leathercloth, Black	1	
CR16	715222	**Cover,** sewn, assembly, occasional seat cushion—Leather, Red	1	
CR16	715223	**Cover,** sewn, assembly, occasional seat cushion—Leather, Light Tan	1	
CR16	715227	**Cover,** sewn, assembly, occasional seat cushion—Leather, Shadow Blue	1	
CR16	715221	**Cover,** sewn, assembly, occasional seat cushion—Leather, Black	1	
CR17		**Rail,** support, assembly, occasional seat (For details see Luggage Floor Section)		
CR18	508790	**Setscrew** ⎫	8	
CR19	508875	**Washer,** plain ⎪ Squab hinges to	8	
CR20	505307	**Washer,** lock ⎬ support rail	8	
CR21	505771	**Nut** ⎭	8	
	625501	**Bracket** assembly, trimmed, squab support, R.H.	1	
CR22	625491	**Bracket** assembly, trimmed, squab support, L.H.	1	

Note:—Items marked thus † are available on our Factory Exchange Unit Scheme

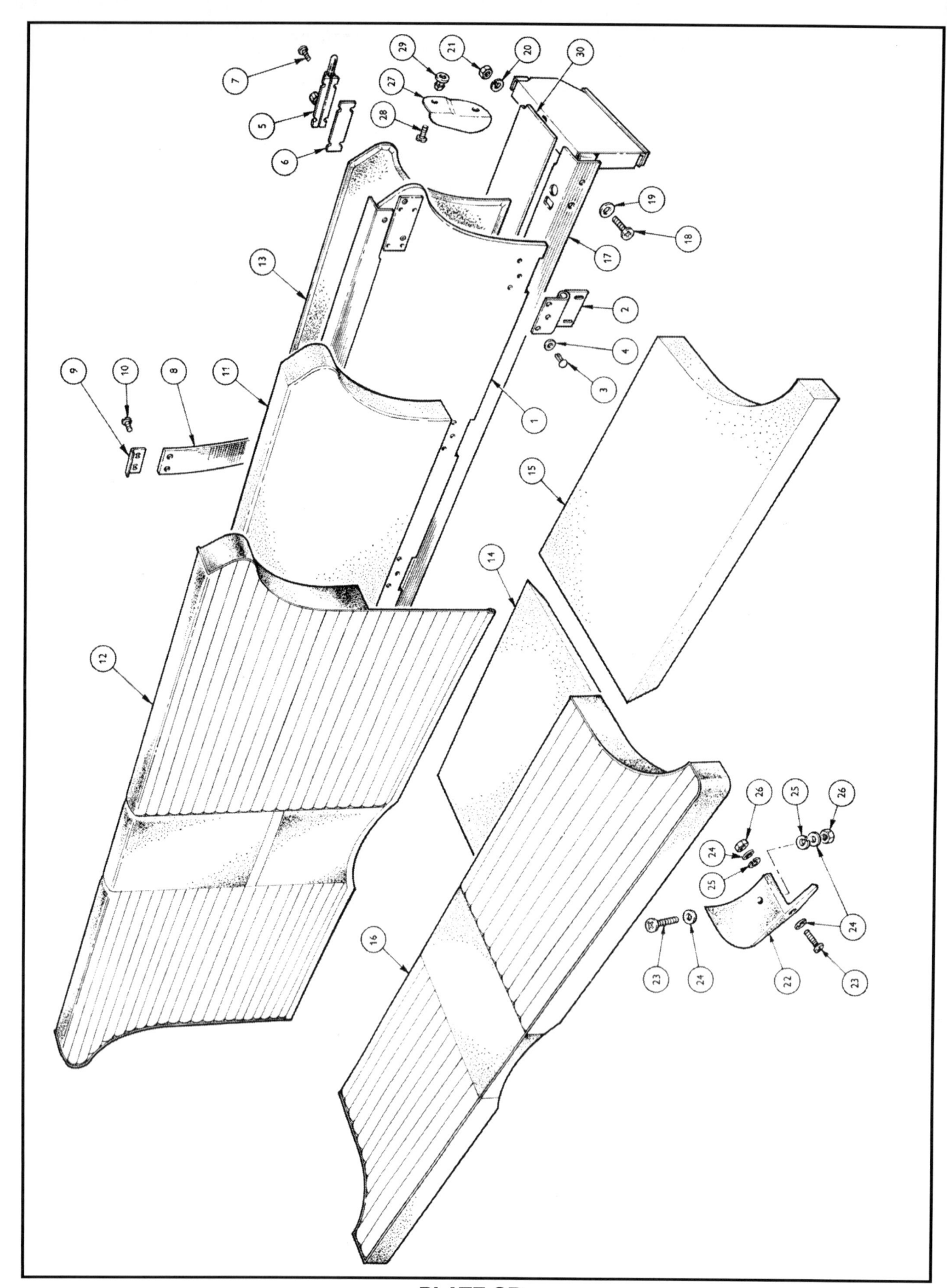

PLATE CR

BODY AND FITTINGS

Plate No.	Part No.	Description	No. per Unit	Remarks
		OCCASIONAL SEAT DETAILS—continued		
CR23	508194	**Setscrew**, chrome ⎫	4	
CR24	508875	**Washer**, plain ⎬ Support brackets	8	
CR25	505307	**Washer**, lock ⎬ to wheelarches	4	
CR26	505771	**Nut** ⎭	4	
	623854	**Bracket**, squab support and shoot bolt locating, R.H.	1	
CR27	623853	**Bracket**, squab support and shoot bolt locating, L.H.	1	
CR28	510996	**Setscrew** ⎫ Support brackets	4	
CR29	621535	**Nut**, 'Lokut' ⎭ to body	4	
CR30		**Board** assembly, centre luggage floor (For details see Luggage Floor Details)	1	
		Carpet, luggage floor (For details see Body Trim Section)		
	610624	**Stud** ⎫ Squab retaining strap	1	
	511198	**Screw**, set ⎭ to heelboard	1	

MISCELLANEOUS BODY DETAILS

Plate No.	Part No.	Description	No. per Unit	Remarks
		GROMMETS, BLANKING PLUGS, ETC.		
	61917	**Grommet**, choke control through bulkhead	1	
	131155	**Grommet**, windscreen wiper—Bulkhead	1	
	61917	**Grommet**, windscreen washer tubing through dash	1	
	600396	**Grommet**, rear wing, for tail lamp leads	2	
	600396	**Grommet**, speedometer cable	1	
	600396	**Grommet**, rev. counter cable	1	
	600398	**Plug**, rubber, heater fixing holes	4	⎫
	600399	**Plug**, rubber, water pipe holes	2	⎬ Not required
	600398	**Plug**, rubber, blower switch hole (Facia)	1	⎬ when heater
	600398	**Plug**, rubber ⎫ Heat control	1	⎬ is fitted
	CD25672	**Plug**, rubber ⎭ holes	1	⎭
	61917	**Grommet**, heater water control valve, fitted in dash	1	
	602037	**Grommet**, rubber, rear overrider spring bar	2	
	600421	**Plug**, blanking, back door (Front and rear face)	2	
	CD27769	**Plug**, rubber, paint drainage holes, back door	2	
	600421	**Plug**, rubber, battery drain tube	1	
	611953	**Plug**, rubber, blanking facia switch hole	1	Only required when locking steering column is fitted
	600399	**Plug**, 1" hole, main floor	4	
	600399	**Plug**, 1" hole, trunk floor	2	
	600399	**Plug**, 1" hole ⎫ Seat ⎫	3	
	612301	**Plug**, 1⅛" hole ⎭ pan ⎬ Paint	2	
	CD25672	**Plug**, ⅝" hole, heelboard crossmember ⎬ drainage	2	
	600398	**Plug**, ½" hole, sill panel ⎬ holes	4	
	600399	**Plug**, 1" hole, heelboard crossmember ⎭	2	
	CD27769	**Plug**, rubber, ⅜" hole, heelboard panel	4	
	HU0803	**Screw**, set ⎫ Build skid hole	2	
	WP0008	**Washer**, plain ⎭ blanking	2	
	PX0703	**Setscrew** ⎫ Dash shelf blanking, L.H.S.	1	⎫ Fitted from Commission No.
	WP0007	**Washer**, plain ⎭ if dual brakes not fitted	1	⎭ KC7051 and future
	612306	**WING MIRROR**	1	Switzerland and Special Order

Note:—Items marked thus † are available on our Factory Exchange Unit Scheme

190 and 191

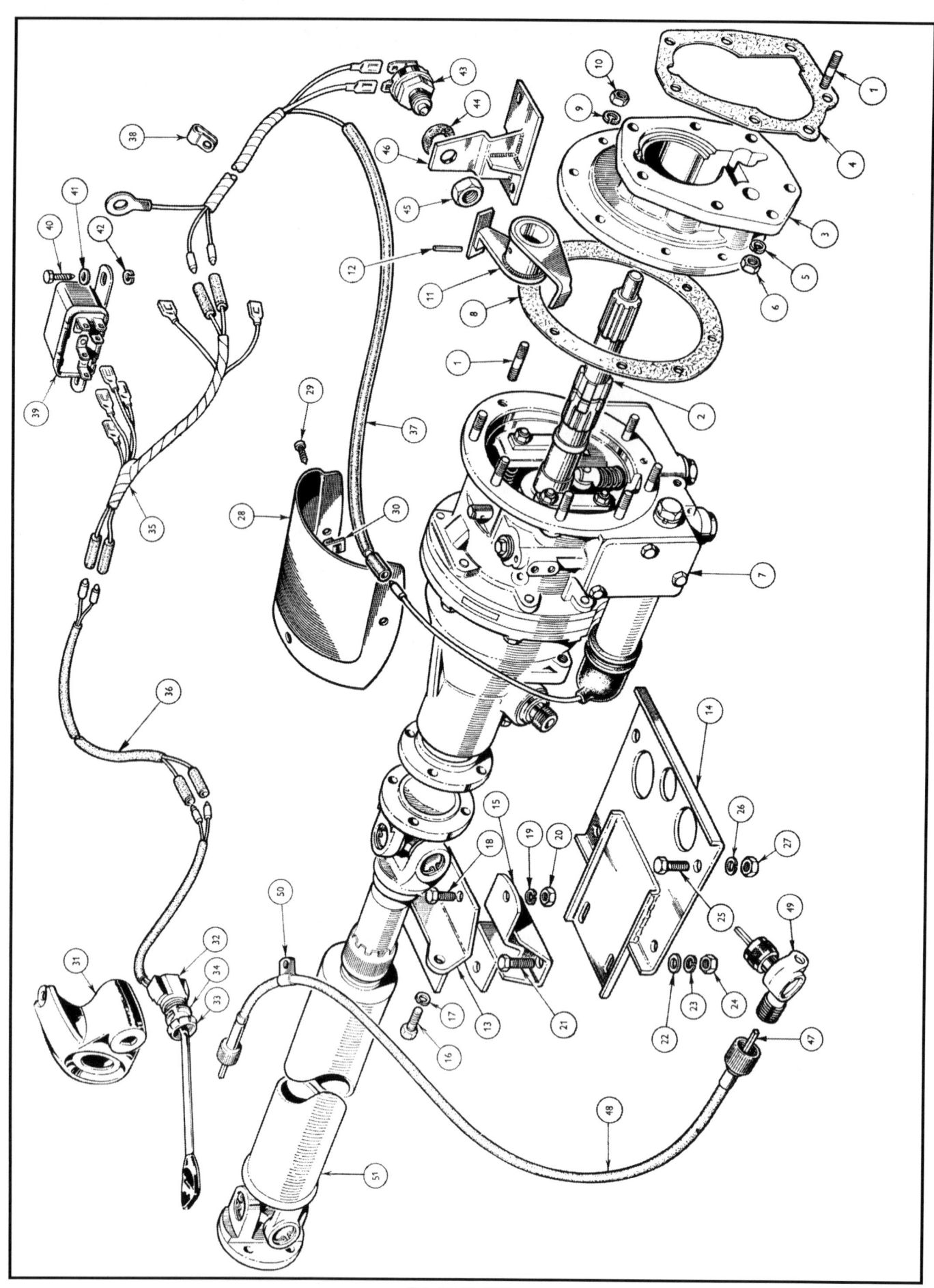

PLATE CS

462

OVERDRIVE

Plate No.	Part No.	Description	No. per Unit	Remarks
	515616	**OVERDRIVE KIT—R.H.S.**	1	
	515617	**OVERDRIVE KIT—L.H.S.**	1	
CS1	132115	**Stud,** adaptor to gearbox case	7	
CS2	213561	**Mainshaft**	1	
CS3	305137	**Adaptor,** gearbox	1	
CS4	106437	**Gasket** ⎫	1	
CS5	WL0208	**Washer** ⎬ Adaptor to	7	
CS6	HN2008	**Nut** ⎬ gearbox case	6	
	JN2108	**Nut,** jam ⎭	1	
CS7	307862	**Overdrive unit** (For details see pages 194 to 196)	1	
CS8	112626	**Gasket** ⎫ Overdrive unit	1	
CS9	WL0207	**Washer,** lock ⎬ to	8	
CS10	HN2007	**Nut** ⎭ gearbox adaptor	8	
CS11	133771	**Arm** assembly, overdrive switch and reverse light switch operating	1	
CS12	52413	**Pin,** mills, securing arm to actuator shaft	1	
CS13	144866	**Bracket** assembly, overdrive support	1	⎫ Fitted up to Comm. No. KC12495
CS14	144868	**Platform** assembly, overdrive mounting	1	⎬ only except on KC12423,
CS15	134229	**Mounting,** flexible	1	⎭ KC12439, KC12440, KC12446
	147630	**Plate,** support, overdrive	1	⎫ Fitted from Comm. No. KC12496
	147629	**Platform,** overdrive mounting	1	⎬ and future and on KC12423,
	147632	**Mounting,** rear engine	1	⎭ KC12439, KC12440 and KC12446
CS16	HU0807	**Screw,** set ⎱ Support bracket	2	
CS17	WL0208	**Washer,** lock ⎰ to overdrive	2	
CS18	HU0805	**Screw,** set ⎫ Flexible mounting	2	
CS19	WL0208	**Washer,** lock ⎬ to	2	
CS20	HN2008	**Nut** ⎭ support bracket	2	
CS21	HU0806	**Screw,** set ⎫	2	
CS22	WP0008	**Washer,** plain ⎬ Flexible mounting to	2	
CS23	WL0208	**Washer,** lock ⎬ mounting platform	2	
CS24	HN2008	**Nut** ⎭	2	
CS25	HU0806	**Screw,** set ⎫	4	
CS26	WL0208	**Washer,** lock ⎬ Mounting platform	4	
	WP0008	**Washer,** plain ⎬ to chassis frame	4	
CS27	HN2008	**Nut** ⎭	4	
CS28	611938	**Plate,** cover, main floor, providing access to overdrive	1	
CS29	YZ3403	**Screw** ⎱ Securing cover	3	
CS30	FJ2444/4	**Nut,** fix ⎰ plate	3	
CS31	611974	**Escutcheon,** flasher, and overdrive switch	1	
CS32	145909	**Switch,** overdrive, R.H.S.	1	
	145910	**Switch,** overdrive, L.H.S.	1	
CS33	609792	**Bezel,** overdrive switch	1	
CS34	WN0712	**Washer,** shakeproof, overdrive switch	1	
CS35	145908	**Harness,** overdrive	1	Fitted up to Comm. No. only
CS36	138323	**Extension,** overdrive harness—R.H.S. only	1	
CS37	134330	**Harness,** gearbox	1	Fitted up to Comm. No. only
	147668	**Harness,** overdrive	1	⎱ Fitted from Comm. No.
	138322	**Harness,** gearbox	1	⎰ and future
CS38	511345	**Clip,** harness attachment	1	
CS39	126792	**Relay,** overdrive	1	
CS40	YZ3504	**Screw,** self-tapping ⎫	2	
CS41	508875	**Washer,** plain ⎬ Relay to dash	2	
CS42	WL0205	**Washer,** lock ⎭	2	

Note:—Items marked thus † are available on our Factory Exchange Unit Scheme

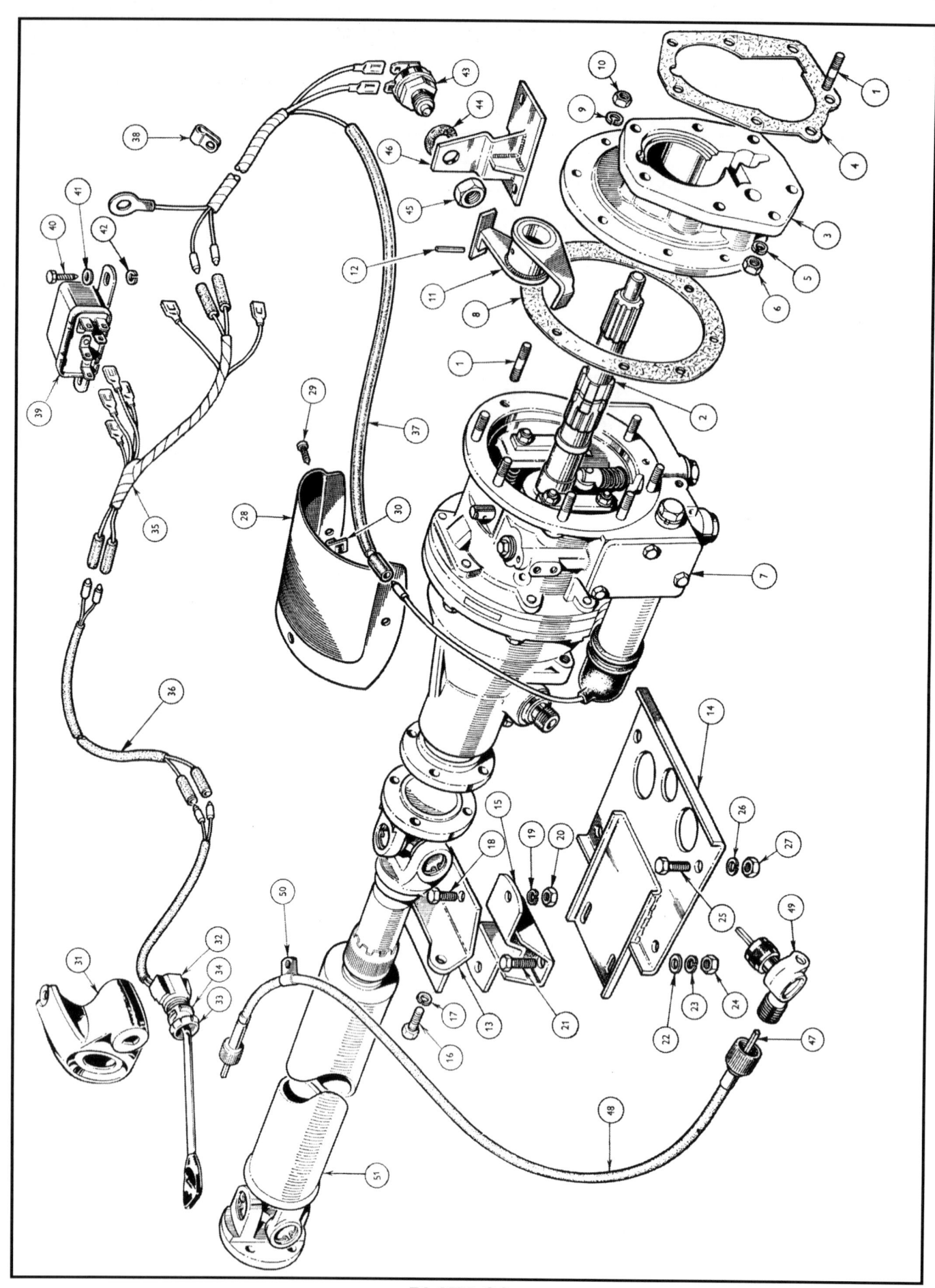

PLATE CS

OVERDRIVE

Plate No.	Part No.	Description	No. per Unit	Remarks
		OVERDRIVE KIT—continued		
CS43	127380	**Switch**, inhibitor	1	
CS44	502146	**Washer**, packing ⎫ Inhibitor switch	1	
CS45	59474	**Nut** ⎬ to bracket	1	
CS46	133770	**Bracket** assembly, inhibitor switch mounting	1	
	HU0708	**Screw**, set, top cover, reverse light switch bracket and inhibitor switch bracket to gearbox	4	⎫ Fitted up to Gearbox No.
	HU0707	**Screw**, set, top cover to gearbox	3	⎬ KC3761 only
	HU0708	**Screw**, set, top cover, inhibitor switch bracket to gearbox	2	⎫ Fitted from Gearbox No.
	HU0707	**Screw**, set, top cover to gearbox	5	⎭ KC3762 and future
	127740	**Shaft**, gear lever	1	Fitted from Gearbox No. KC3762 and future. For previous see Gear Shift Mechanism details
CS47	504621/I	**Cable**, speedometer, inner, R.H.S.	1	
CS48	504621/O	**Cable**, speedometer, outer, R.H.S.	1	
	504603/I	**Cable**, speedometer, inner, L.H.S.	1	
	504603/O	**Cable**, speedometer, outer, L.H.S.	1	
CS49	120694	**Angle-drive**, speedometer	1	
	510969	**Clip**, speedo cable to valance—R.H.S.	1	
CS50	100148	**Clip**, speedo cable to gearbox	1	
CS51	213151	**Propellor shaft**	1	
	147374	**Rivet**, blanking breather hole in gearbox top cover	1	

GEARBOX ASSEMBLY
(Less top cover, extension and handlever)
For details see Gearbox Section

REAR AXLE CENTRE ASSEMBLY
(Less road spring studs)
For details see Rear Axle Section

SPEEDOMETER
For details see Electrical Section

Note:—Items marked thus † are available on our Factory Exchange Unit Scheme

193

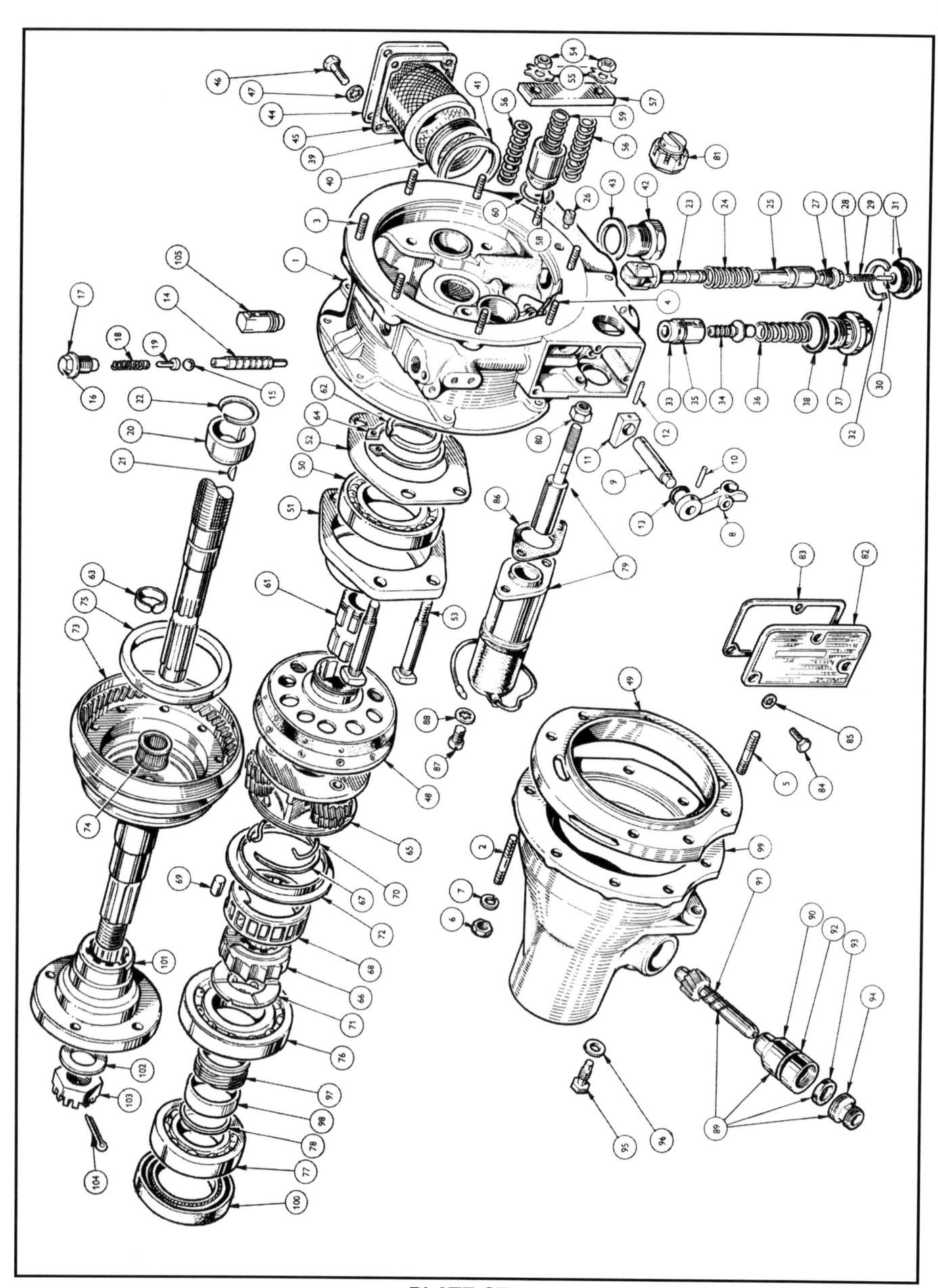

PLATE CT

OVERDRIVE

Plate No.	Part No.	Description	No. per Unit	Remarks
	307862	**OVERDRIVE UNIT**	1	
CT1	515814	**FRONT CASING ASSEMBLY**	1	
CT2	506082	**Stud**, $\frac{1}{4}''$, rear casing to main casing	6	
CT3	506083	**Stud**, $\frac{1}{4}''$ ⎫ Main casing	7	
CT4	506105	**Stud**, $\frac{1}{4}''$ ⎭ to gearbox	1	
CT5	506103	**Stud**, $\frac{1}{4}''$, rear casing to main casing	2	
CT6	HN2007	**Nut**, $\frac{1}{4}''$	16	
CT7	WL0207	**Washer**, spring, $\frac{1}{4}''$	16	
	506101	**Joint**, paper	1	
CT8	515813	**OPERATING VALVE LEVER**	1	
CT9	515811	**Shaft**, valve operating	1	
CT10	500412	**Pin**, lever to shaft	1	
CT11	515812	**Lever**, cam	1	
CT12	513888	**Dowel**, spring, cam lever to shaft	1	
CT13	500594	**'O' ring**	1	
CT14	138926	**Operating valve**	1	
CT15	BL0020	**Ball**, $\frac{5}{16}''$	1	
CT16	506117	**Plug**, valve	1	
CT17	500568	**Washer**, valve plug	1	
CT18	506070	**Spring**, valve	1	
CT19	500591	**Plunger**, ball valve	1	
CT20	513216	**Cam**, oil pump operating	1	
CT21	KW0316	**Woodruff key** ⎫ Securing cam	1	
CT22	137308	**Spring**, ring ⎭	1	
CT23	513196	**OIL PUMP PLUNGER ASSEMBLY**	1	
CT24	500633	**Spring**, for plunger	1	
CT25	513222	**Body**, pump	1	
CT26	506076	**Screw**, retaining pump body	1	
CT27	515810	**Body**, non-return valve	1	
CT28	BL0014	**Ball**, $\frac{7}{32}''$, in valve body	1	
CT29	513207	**Spring**, valve	1	⎫ Alternative fitment
CT30	514889	**Pin**, spring support	1	⎭ to 517294
	517294	**Spring**, valve	1	Alternative fitment to 513207 and 514889
CT31	513206	**Plug**, valve	1	
CT32	506118	**Washer**, for plug	1	
	515816	**RELIEF VALVE KIT**	1	
CT33	Not Serviced	**Body**, valve	1	
CT34	Not Serviced	**Plunger**	1	
CT35	506129	**'O' ring**	1	
CT36	Not Serviced	**Spring**	1	
CT37	Not Serviced	**Plug**	1	
CT38	506118	**Washer**, plain, on plug	1	
CT39	513202	**Oil filter**	1	
CT40	513205	**Magnet**, filter	1	
CT41	506097	**Plate**, sealing, oil filter to casing	1	
CT42	506114	**Plug**, drain	1	
CT43	506118	**Washer**, drain plug	1	
CT44	506097	**Plate**, side cover	1	
CT45	506098	**Joint**, for plate	1	
CT46	HU0706	**Screw**, set, $\frac{1}{4}''$ ⎫ Side cover plate	4	
CT47	WN0707	**Washer**, shakeproof ⎭ to casing	4	

Note:—Items marked thus † are available on our Factory Exchange Unit Scheme

PLATE CT

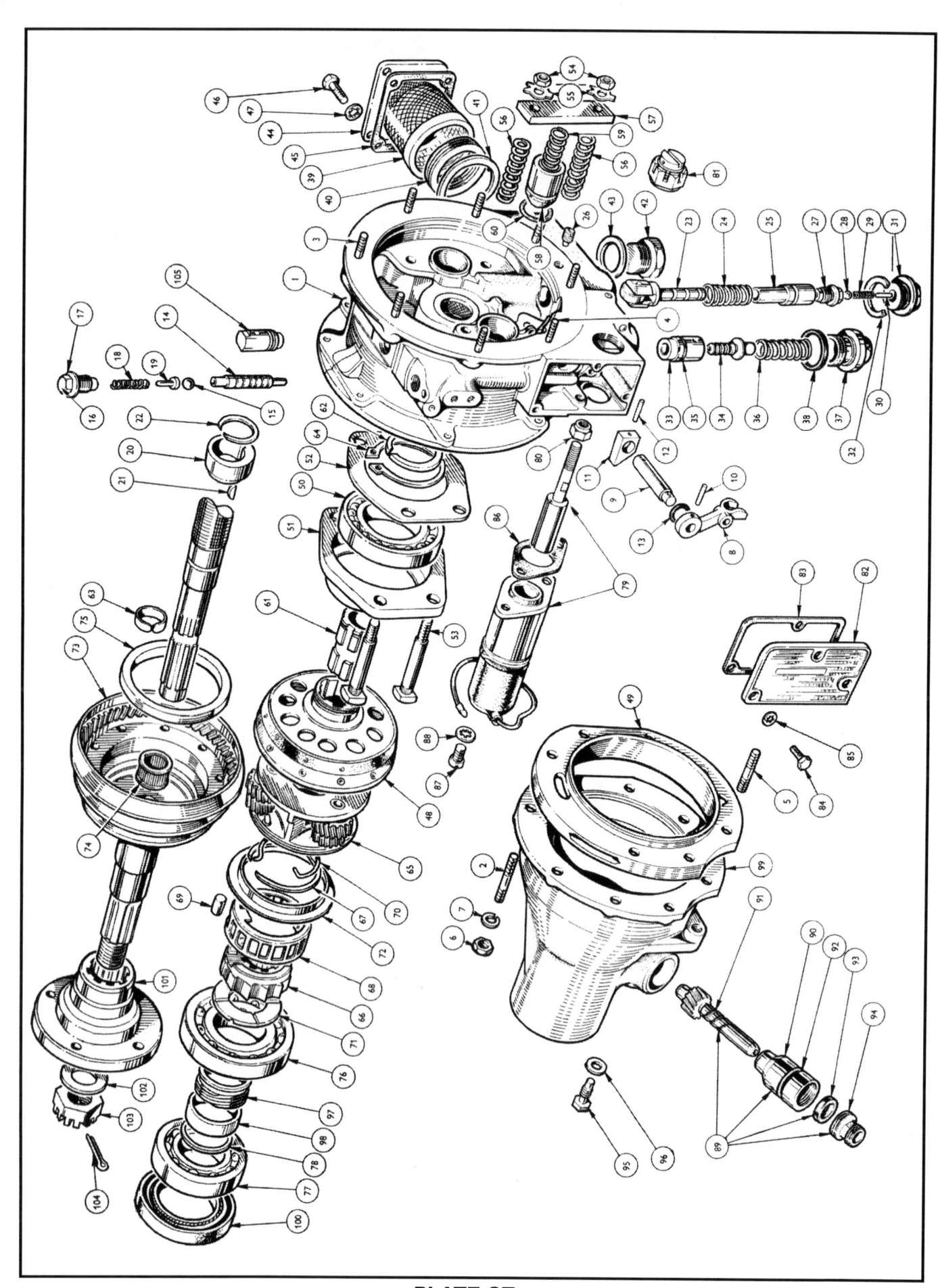

OVERDRIVE

Plate No.	Part No.	Description	No. per Unit	Remarks

OVERDRIVE UNIT—continued

Plate No.	Part No.	Description	No. per Unit	Remarks
CT48	513200	**CLUTCH SLIDING MEMBER ASSEMBLY** (with Linings)	1	
CT49	513228	Ring, clutch brake	1	
CT50	506112	Bearing, ball, clutch thrust	1	
CT51	506081	Housing, clutch thrust bearing	1	
CT52	506104	Plate, retainer, clutch thrust bearing	1	
CT53	513203	Bolt	4	Securing thrust bearing housing
CT54	513227	Nut	4	
CT55	500642	Washer, tab	5	
CT56	513199	Spring, clutch	4	
CT57	506084	Bridge piece, clutch	2	
CT58	513220	Piston	2	Operating clutch
CT59	513219	Spring, piston	2	
CT60	506130	'O' ring, on piston	2	
CT61	506044	**SUNWHEEL ASSEMBLY**	1	
CT62	506091	Snap ring	1	
CT63	513223	Spring, ring	1	
CT64	137308	Circlip	1	
CT65	515815	**PLANET CARRIER ASSEMBLY**	1	
	513224	Bearing, needle roller	6	
	500412	Pin, Mills, securing bearings	3	
CT66	513209	Freewheel Inner Member	1	
CT67	513210	Spring, ring	1	
CT68	502559	Cage, roller	1	
CT69	502550	Rollers, steel, in cage	Set	
CT70	513208	Spring, for cage	1	
CT71	500613	Washer, thrust	1	
CT72	513215	Plate, retaining	1	
CT73	513195	**ANNULUS ASSEMBLY**	1	
CT74	506113	Bearing, needle roller	1	
CT75	Not Serviced	Member, outer, freewheel	1	
CT76	506111	Bearing, ball, front	1	Annulus support to rear casing
CT77	513229	Bearing, ball, rear	1	
CT78	513214/1	Adjustment washer, correcting end float, ·105″	A/R	
CT78	513214/2	Adjustment washer, correcting end float, ·100″	A/R	
CT78	513214/3	Adjustment washer, correcting end float, ·095″	A/R	
CT78	513214/4	Adjustment washer, correcting end float, ·090″	A/R	
CT79	512114	**SOLENOID ASSEMBLY**	1	
CT80	TN3207	Nut, nyloc, solenoid adjusting	1	
CT81	514200	Adjusting screw assembly	1	
CT82	506109	Plate, side cover	1	
CT83	513204	Washer, joint, side cover plate	1	
CT84	513226	Screw, hex.	3	Securing side cover plate
CT85	WN0705	Washer, shakeproof	3	
CT86	513201	Washer, joint, solenoid to casing	1	
CT87	513225	Screw, set, securing solenoid	2	
CT88	WN0705	Washer, shakeproof, under setscrew	2	

Note:—Items marked thus † are available on our Factory Exchange Unit Scheme

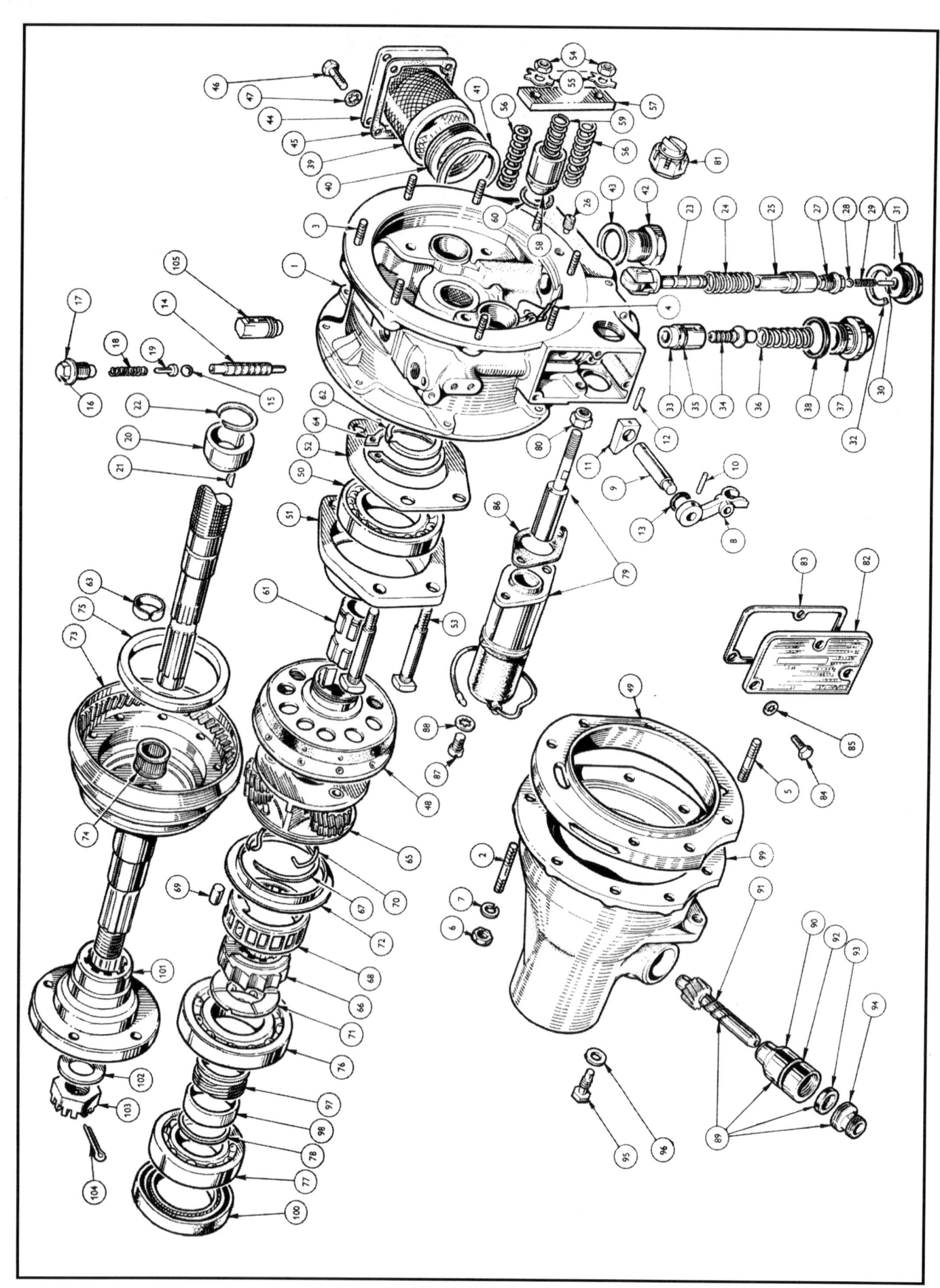

PLATE CT

OVERDRIVE

Plate No.	Part No.	Description	No. per Unit	Remarks

OVERDRIVE UNIT—continued

Plate No.	Part No.	Description	No. per Unit
CT89	506067	**SPEEDOMETER DRIVE ASSEMBLY**	1
CT90	506066	**Bearing** assembly, speedometer	1
CT91	506119	**Gear**, driven	1
CT92	506115	**'O' ring**	1
CT93	Not Serviced	**Seal**, oil	1
CT94	Not Serviced	**End**, screwed	1
	501606	**Pin**, Mills, $\tfrac{1}{16}''$	1
CT95	506071	**Screw**, locking	1
CT96	506108	**Washer**, on locking screw	1
CT97	506099	**Gear**, speedometer driving, on mainshaft	1
CT98	513211	**Tube**, spacing, on mainshaft	1
CT99	513198	**REAR CASING ASSEMBLY**	1
CT100	513231	**Oil seal**	1
CT101	146102	**Coupling flange**	1
CT102	515818	**Washer**, plain ⎫ Securing coupling flange to annulus	1
CT103	515817	**Nut**, slotted ⎬	1
CT104	PC0012	**Pin**, cotter ⎭	1
CT105	502560	**Breather**	1

Note:—Items marked thus † are available on our Factory Exchange Unit Scheme

196

ACCESSORIES

Plate No.	Part No.	Description	No. per Unit	Remarks
	572759	**ANTI-FROST SHIELD (WINDSCREEN)**	1	
	562116	**BONNET LOCK KIT (2 LOCKS)**	1	
	514600	**"POWER STOP" VACUUM SERVO KIT**	1	
	138737	**CIGARETTE LIGHTER (PULL OUT TYPE)**	1	
	514106	Element, for cigarette lighter	1	
	514940	**BRACKET FOR CIGARETTE LIGHTER**	1	
	569116	**CIGARETTE LIGHTER (PUSH DOWN TYPE)**	1	
	554449	**FIRE EXTINGUISHER**	1	
	515448	**FUEL LINK FILTER**	1	
		HEATER KIT For details see page 136	1	
		BULBS For details see Electrical Equipment Section		
	517632	**BRAKE FLUID** (Girling) — 8 fluid oz.	1	
	517633	**BRAKE FLUID** (Girling) — 16 fluid oz.	1	
	517634	**BRAKE FLUID** (Girling) — 32 fluid oz.	1	
	710587	**LUGGAGE STRAP (REAR FLOOR)**	2	
	573677	**WING MIRROR, RACING TYPE, SILVER ANODISED, LIGHTWEIGHT**	2	
	573461	**WING MIRROR—DESMO 168 (LONG ARM)—FLAT GLASS**	2	
	574863	**WING MIRROR—DESMO 168 (LONG ARM)—CONVEX GLASS**	2	
	573349	**WING MIRROR—DESMO 166 (SHORT ARM)—FLAT GLASS**	2	
	574862	**WING MIRROR—DESMO 166 (SHORT ARM)—CONVEX GLASS**	2	
	574579	Extension kit, for converting Desmo mirrors to trailer towing length	2	
	574580	**REPLACEMENT FLAT GLASS LENS FOR 573461 and 573349** — Card of 12 Glasses		

Note:—Items marked thus † are available on our Factory Exchange Unit Scheme

ACCESSORIES

Plate No.	Part No.	Description	No. per Unit	Remarks
	574586	**WING MIRROR—MAGNATEX 09 —CONVEX**	2	
	560632	**WING MIRROR—D TYPE—MAGNATEX S6 (FLY BACK—CONVEX GLASS)**	2	
	570409	**WING MIRROR—WINGARD FLYBACK —TURINA (FLAT GLASS)**	2	
	502459	**WING MIRROR—MAGNATEX R7 —ROUND (FLYBACK—CONVEX GLASS)**	2	
	608467WL	**WING MIRROR—WINGARD—CURVED ARM—ROUND—RIGID**	2	
	608467M	**WING MIRROR—MORGAN—STRAIGHT ARM—ROUND—RIGID**	2	
	612306	**WING MIRROR—WINGARD—SWING ARM—ROUND**	2	
	505825	**WING MIRROR BASE PLINTH —MAGNATEX**	2	
	557493	**WING MIRROR—DESMO 169—ROUND —BOOMERANG—FLAT GLASS**	2	
	573096	**MUD FLAPS (TRIUMPH MOTIF)**	1 pair	
	568511	**SAFETY BELT—2 POINT FIXING**	2	Suitable for vehicles up to Body No. 1040KC only, and on 1047KC, 1052KC, 1065KC and 1217KC
	568496	**SAFETY BELT—3 POINT FIXING**	2	
	712600	**SAFETY HARNESS**	2	Suitable for fitment to vehicles from Body No. 1041KC and future except 1047KC, 1052KC, 1065KC and 1217KC
	808271	**SILL PROTECTOR (Black Plastic)—R.H.**	1	
	808270	**SILL PROTECTOR (Black Plastic)—L.H.**	1	
	616196	Plasti-rivets, sill protector attachment	12	
		WIRE WHEELS For details see Propellor Shaft and Road Wheels Section		
	515852	**CONTINENTAL TOURING KIT**	1	
	113256	**MEDALLION (WHEEL NAVE PLATE)**	4	
	128348	**Bolt** } Medallion attachment	4	
	WL0208	**Washer,** lock	4	

Note:—Items marked thus † are available on our Factory Exchange Unit Scheme

ACCESSORIES

Plate No.	Part No.	Description	No. per Unit	Remarks
	516375	**OIL COOLER KIT**	1	
		Suitable for Engine No. KC5001E and future only		
	214572	Oil cooler	1	
	148124	Bracket, mounting, R.H.	1	
	148125	Bracket, mounting, L.H.	1	
	HU0705	Setscrew ⎫	4	
	WP0007	Washer, plain ⎬ Mounting brackets	4	
	WL0207	Washer, lock ⎨ to chassis frame	4	
	HN2007	Nut ⎭	4	
	HU0705	Setscrew ⎫ Oil cooler	4	
	WL0207	Washer, lock ⎬ to	4	
	HN2007	Nut ⎭ mounting brackets	4	
	505155	Clip, 'P' wiring harness	1	
	HN2005	Nut ⎫ 'P' clip to grille	1	
	WP0005	Washer, plain ⎭ mounting screw	1	
	148504	Hose assembly, oil cooler to filter	1	
	148505	Hose assembly, oil cooler to cylinder block	1	
	146285	Adaptor, oil cooler hose to cylinder block	1	
	148514	Bracket, hoses to front engine mounting bolts	1	
	148513	Clip, hoses to bracket	1	
	PT0353	Setscrew ⎫	1	
	WL0203	Washer, lock ⎬ Hose clip to bracket	1	
	HN2053	Nut ⎭	1	
	516657	Shell, oil filter, and adaptor assembly	1	
	146273	Plate, deflector, oil flow	1	
	146275	Seal, plate to cylinder block	1	
	621421	Finisher, P.V.C., engine valance and radiator cowl	2	
	516543	**TOW ROPE AND LUGGAGE RACK STRAP**	1	
	210953	**TOWING ATTACHMENT KIT—REAR**	1	Fitted up to Commission No. KC50000 only
	214521	**TOWING ATTACHMENT KIT—REAR**	1	Fitted from Commission No. KC50001 and future
	574704	**ROOF RACK**	1	
	574722	**EMERGENCY WINDSCREEN**	1	
	148957	**SPARKING PLUG—CHAMPION TYPE UN-12Y**	6	
	137531	**WHEEL BALANCE WEIGHT** ½ oz	A/R	
	140073	1 oz	A/R	
	140074	1½ oz	A/R	
	140075	2 oz	A/R	
	516279	**FOG LAMP**—Iodine Quartz, back mounting	1	
	516278	**SPOT LAMP**—Iodine Quartz, back mounting	1	
	59844	**DEFROSTER-ELECTRIC**	1	

Note:—Items marked thus † are available on our Factory Exchange Unit Scheme

ACCESSORIES

Plate No.	Part No.	Description	No. per Unit	Remarks
	569521	**TOUCH-IN PAINT** (¼ pint Tins) — White	A/R	
	575194	Damson		
	569527	Wedgwood Blue		
	571276	Conifer (Acrylic)		
	554264	Signal Red		
	571228	Royal Blue		
	569286	Conifer		
	574626	Valencia Blue		
	574885	Jasmine		
	574592	**HEATED BACK LIGHT**	1	
	515396	**Switch,** for heated back light	1	
	148533	**STEERING COLUMN LOCKING DEVICE AND IGNITION SWITCH KIT**	1	Fitted up to Commission No. KC50000 only
	152330	**STEERING COLUMN LOCKING DEVICE AND IGNITION SWITCH KIT**	1	Fitted from Commission No. KC50001 and future
	611953	**Plug,** blanking ignition switch hole	1	
	132135	**Lock** and ignition switch	1	
	150064	**Steering column** upper assembly	1	Fitted up to Commission No. KC50000 only
	151496	**Steering column** upper assembly	1	Fitted from Commission No. KC50001 and future
	140549	**Clip,** trafficator cancelling	1	
	148461	**Strap,** anti-torque	1	Fitted up to Commission No. KC50000 only
	151190	**Strap,** anti-torque	1	Fitted from Commission No. KC50001 and future
	147951	**Bolt,** locking device to strap	1	
	147621	**Lead** set, extension, ignition switch	1	
	HB0720	**Bolt,** upper and lower clamps to mounting bracket	2	
	HU0706	**Setscrew,** support bracket to channel	2	
	516770	**GLOVE—STEERING WHEEL—BROWN LEATHER**	1	
	516771	**GLOVE—STEERING WHEEL—SIMULATED BROWN LEATHER**	1	
	574761	**SINGLE GAUGE INSTRUMENT MOUNTING PANEL**	1	
	574762	**DOUBLE GAUGE INSTRUMENT MOUNTING PANEL**	1	
	574890	**SAFETY WARNING TRIANGLE**	1	
	516675	**"PLUGMASTER" SPARKING PLUG SPANNER**	1	
	516676	**"LEVERMASTER" WHEEL BRACE**	1	
	575246	**HEADREST—BLACK** (Mark I Cars only)	2	

Note:—Items marked thus † are available on our Factory Exchange Unit Scheme

200

© Copyright British Leyland Motors Corporation 1970
and Brooklands Books Limited 2015

This book is published by Brooklands Books Limited and based upon text
and illustrations protected by copyright and first published in 1970 by
British Leyland Motors Corporation and may not be
reproduced transmitted or copied by any means without the
prior written permission of Rover Group Limited and
Brooklands Books Limited.

Published by Brooklands Books Ltd., PO Box 146, Cobham,
Surrey KT11 1LG, England Phone: 01932 865051 Fax: 01932 868803
E-mail: sales@brooklands-books.com www.brooklands-books.com

Part Number: 515754/2

ISBN 9781783180448   Ref: TGT6PH   2341/1T5

OFFICIAL TECHNICAL BOOKS

Brooklands Technical Books has been formed to supply owners, restorers and professional repairers with official factory literature.

Workshop Manuals

TR2 & TR3	502602	9780948207693
TR4 & TR4A	510322	9780948207952
TR5, TR250 & TR6 (Glove Box Autobooks Man.)		9781855201835
TR5-PI Supplement	545053	9781869826024
TR250 Supplement	545047	9781783181759
TR6 inc. TC & PI	545277/E2	9781869826130
TR7	AKM3079B	9781855202726
TR7	Autobooks Manual	9781783181506
TR8	AKM3981A	9781783180615
Spitfire Mk 1, 2 & 3 & Herald 1200, 12/50, 13/60 & Vitesse 6	511243	9780946489992
Herald 948, 1200, 12/50, 13/60 Autobooks Man.		9781783181513
Spitfire Mk 4	545254H	9781869826758
Spitfire 1500	AKM4329	9781869826666
Spitfire Mk 3, 4, 1500 (Glove Box Autobooks Man.)		9781855201248
2000 & 2500	AKM3974	9781869826086
GT6 Mk 1, 2, 3 & Vitesse 2 Litre	512947	9780907073901
GT6 Mk 2, GT6+ & Mk 3 & Vitesse 2 Litre - Mk 2 1969-1973	Autobooks Manual	9781783181322
Stag	AKM3966	9781855200135
Stag	Autobooks Manual	9781783181490
Dolomite Sprint	AKM3629	9781855202825

Parts Catalogues

TR2 & TR3	501653	9780907073994
TR4	510978	9780907073949
TR4A	514837	9780907073956
TR250 US	516914	9781869826819
TR6 Sports Car 1969-1973	517785A	9780948207426
TR6 1974-1976	RTC9093A	9780907073932
TR7 (1975-1978)	RTC9814CA	9781855207943
TR7 1979+	RTC9828CC	9781870642231
TR7 & TR8	RTC9020B	9781870642651
Herald 13/60	517056	9781869826154
Vitesse 2 Litre Mk 2	517786	9781869826147
Stag	519579	9781870642996
GT6 Mk 1 and Mk 2 /GT6+	515754/2	9781783180448
GT6 Mk 3	520949/A	9780948207938
Spitfire Mk 3	516282	9781870642873
Spitfire Mk 4 & Spitfire 1500 1973-1974	RTC 9008A	9781869826659
Spitfire 1500 1975-1980	RTC9819CB	9781870642187
Dolomite Range 1976 on	RTC9822CB	9781855202764

Owners Handbooks

Triumph Competition Preparation Manual TR250, TR5 and TR6		9781783180011
TR4	510326	9780948207662
TR4A	512916	9780948207679
TR5 PI	545034/2	9781855208544
TR250 (US)	545033	9780948207273
TR6	545078/1	9780948207402
TR6-PI	545078/2	9781855201750
TR6 (US 73)	545111/73	9781855204348
TR6 (US 75)	545111/75	9780948207150
TR7	AKM4332	9781870642736
TR8 (US)	AKM4779	9781855202832
Stag	545105	9781855206830
Spitfire Mk 3	545017	9780948207181
Spitfire Mk 4	545220	9781870642439
Spitfire Mk 4 (US)	545189	9781855207967
Spitfire 1500	RTC9221	9781870642453
Spitfire Competition Preparation Manual		9781870642606
GT6	512944	9781855201583
GT6 Mk 2 & GT6+	545057	9781855201422
GT6 Mk 3	545186	9780946489848
GT6, GT6+ & 2000 Competition Preparation Manual		9781855200678
2000, 2500 TC and 2500S	AKM3617/2	9781855202788
Herald 1200 12/50	512893/6	9781855200616
Herald 13/60	545037	9781855201415
Vitesse 2 Litre	545006	9781855200746
Vitesse Mk 2	545070/2	9781855200418
Vitesse 6	511236/5	9781855207974

Carburetters

SU Carburetters Tuning Tips & Techniques	9781855202559
Solex Carburetters Tuning Tips & Techniques	9781855209770
Weber Carburettors Tuning Tips and Techniques	9781855207592

Truimph - Road Test Books

Triumph Herald 1959-1971	9781855200517
Triumph Vitesse 1962-1971	9781855200500
Triumph 2000 / 2.5 / 2500 1963-1977	9780946489237
Triumph GT6 Gold Portfolio 1966-1974	9781855202443
Triumph TR6 Road Test Portfolio	9781855209268
Triumph Spitfire Road Test Portfolio	9781855209534
Triumph Stag Road Test Portfolio	9781855208933

From Triumph specialists, Amazon or all good motoring bookshops.

Brooklands Books Ltd., P.O. Box 146, Cobham, Surrey, KT11 1LG, England, UK
Phone: +44 (0) 1932 865051 info@brooklands-books.com
www.brooklands-books.com

www.brooklandsbooks.com

Printed in Great Britain
by Amazon